Understanding Music

Seventh Edition

Jeremy Yudkin

Boston University

PEARSON

Boston   Columbus   Indianapolis   New York   San Francisco   Upper Saddle River
Amsterdam   Cape Town   Dubai   London   Madrid   Milan   Munich   Paris   Montréal   Toronto
Delhi   Mexico City   São Paulo   Sydney   Hong Kong   Seoul   Singapore   Taipei   Tokyo

Editorial Director: Craig Campanella
Editor-in-Chief: Sarah Touborg
Senior Publisher, Music: Roth Wilkofsky
Editorial Project Manager: David Nitti
Editorial Assistant: Lily Norton
Executive Director of Marketing: Brandy Dawson
Senior Marketing Manager: Kate Stewart Mitchell
Marketing Assistant: Paige Patunas
Senior Managing Editor: Melissa Feimer
Production Liaison: Brian Mackey/Joseph Scordato
Full-Service Management: GEX Publishing Services
Media Director: Brian Hyland

Sr. Digital Media Editor: David Alick
Digital Media Project Manager: Rich Barnes
Senior Operations Specialist: Diane Peirano
Senior Manufacturing and Operations Manager for Arts & Sciences: Mary Fischer
Cover Photo: Maugli/Shutterstock; Pavel K/Shutterstock
Cover Illustration: Pat Smythe/Corin Skidds
Creative Director (Cover): Pat Smythe
Image Permissions Coordinator: Ben Ferrini
Composition: GEX Publishing Services
Printer/Binder: The Courier Companies
Cover Printer: Lehigh-Phoenix Color

Credits and acknowledgments borrowed from other sources and reproduced, with permission, in this textbook appear on appropriate page within text or on pages 317–318.

Library of Congress Cataloging-in-Publication Data
Yudkin, Jeremy.
 Understanding music / Jeremy Yudkin.—7th ed.
  p. cm.
 Includes index.
 ISBN 978-0-205-44101-3 (pbk.)
 1. Music appreciation. 2. Music—History and criticism. I. Title.
 MT6.Y86U53 2012
 780—dc23

                            2012003328

10 9 8 7 6 5 4 3 2

ISBN-10 (Student Edition): 0-205-44101-7
ISBN-13 (Student Edition): 978-0-205-44101-3
ISBN-10 (Examination Copy): 0-205-49323-8
ISBN-13 (Examination Copy): 978-0-205-49323-4
ISBN-10 (a la carte Edition): 0-205-88708-2
ISBN-13 (a la carte Edition): 978-0-205-88708-8

**For M and D,
and
K, d, and s.**

"Music is the expression of the deepest part of our souls. It expresses what words and paintings cannot. And for true understanding, music requires careful attention and the engagement of the intellect . . ."

J. Y.

FOREWORD

This book is as engaging as it is informative. I particularly like Jeremy Yudkin's lively presentation of an extraordinary amount of fascinating musical information within a broader historical and cultural context. Through this book Professor Yudkin conveys not only a wealth of knowledge, but also the message that music can be a uniquely rewarding medium of personal expression. It will surely encourage readers, students, and music lovers alike to become active participants in their musical experiences, whether as performers or listeners.

Yo-Yo Ma

CONTENTS

CHAPTER 12
The Twentieth Century and Beyond, Part II: Jazz, an American Original 260

CHAPTER 13
The Twentieth Century and Beyond, Part III:
Popular Music in the United States   278

Jeremy Yudkin was born in England and educated in England and the United States. He received his B.A. and M.A. in Classical and Modern Languages from Cambridge University and his Ph.D. in Historical Musicology from Stanford University. He has taught at San Francisco State University, the École Normale Supérieure in Paris, Harvard University, Oxford University, and (since 1982) at Boston University, where he is chair of the Department of Musicology and Ethnomusicology, professor of music, and associated faculty of the Department of Judaic Studies and the Center for African American Studies. From 2006 to 2010 he also served as visiting professor of music at Oxford University.

A recipient of fellowships from the National Endowment for the Humanities, Boston University's Society of Fellows, the Camargo Foundation, and the Marion and Jasper Whiting Foundation, he has written articles for the *Journal of the American Musicological Society*, the *Journal of Musicology*, the *Musical Quarterly*, *Musica Disciplina*, *American Music*, and *Music and Letters*, and contributed to several volumes of essays. His research specialties include the Middle Ages, early Beethoven, jazz, and the music of the Beatles. A noted lecturer, Professor Yudkin has given talks and presented papers across the United States and in Europe and Russia. He is the author of eight books on various aspects of music and music history, including *Music in Medieval Europe* (1989), *The Lenox School of Jazz* (2006), and *Miles Davis: Miles Smiles and the Invention of Post Bop* (2008).

Welcome, Students!

Welcome to *Understanding Music*, the Seventh Edition of my book about listening to music. Everyone listens to music, but this book will help you listen with more depth, more focus, and more knowledge. You will start to enjoy music you have never heard before, and you will even listen to music you know in a completely new way. This book invites you to improve your understanding of all kinds of music with a lively text, clear and interesting Listening Guides, recordings, videos, and many Web-based activities. Here is a list of some of the special features of this book.

The Art of Listening

This book approaches listening as an active and engaging experience. Throughout the book, the text invites you to listen carefully and helps you with ideas and vocabulary to deepen your listening experience.

Listening Guides

The Listening Guides are clear and easy to follow. They guide you step-by-step through all kinds of different pieces, explaining details of what is going on. Special moments are highlighted, so that you can read about the things that are happening *as they happen and as you hear them*. With the Listening Guides you learn as you listen! *On the Web site (www.MySearchLab.com), you can even follow automated versions of the Listening Guides, which highlight the descriptions as the music plays.*

Three Ways to Listen

Understanding Music offers students access to a variety of exciting performances with world-renowned artists:

- A three-CD set of recordings
- A downloadable set, which will allow you to load each track directly to your computer
- Free streaming audio on *MySearchLab* through the all-new automated Listening Guides

"Need to Know" Lists

These little summary lists appear every so often in each chapter, just to remind you of the main points that have been covered and that you will need to remember.

New *MySearchLab* Web Site

You can now visit www.MySearchLab.com, a site with all of the Web-based resources you'll need. MySearchLab includes the following:

- Access to the interactive eText
- Streaming audio with the Listening Guides
- Chapter-by-chapter quizzes to help you assess your understanding of the material
- Access to the *Inside the Orchestra* and "Quick Listen" videos, as well as the audio "MusicNotes" found throughout the book
- Writing and Research Tools to help you hone your skills and produce more effective papers

At the end of each chapter a "Study and Review" prompt will remind you to visit the Web site while the material is still fresh in your mind.

Inside the Orchestra Video

On the MySearchLab Web site is an interactive video that you will find very helpful. It shows you what most classical instruments look like, how they work, and especially how they sound. It also shows you the workings of an orchestra and the various instrumental sections, as well as the changing makeup of the orchestra throughout history. Several live performances are filmed and analyzed in detail. This unique feature beautifully illustrates how the classical orchestra works from the inside out.

Audio "MusicNotes"

These short passages, demonstrating basic musical concepts and styles, are also on the Web site. Each one is designed to help you learn directly about specific aspects of music: melody, harmony, etc., with simple tunes and short musical examples.

"Quick Listen" Links in the Margins

These are all links to really interesting YouTube videos. Just go to the Web site and type in the quoted title (e.g., "South Indian Violin" or "Didjeridoo"), or visit MySearchLab for links to bring up the searches.

Three Ways to Remember!

At the end of each chapter, I have added three features to help you remember the principal points made during the chapter:

1. **Style Summaries:** Each Style Summary encapsulates the musical style of each historical period and summarizes the musical elements central to each style.
2. **Fundamentals:** This is a brief chart that lists the basic elements of each historical style.
3. **For Further Discussion and Study:** The chapter ends with a list of questions to think about and discuss with your friends. These will engage you directly in the material under discussion.

Enjoy This Book, and Enjoy "Understanding Music"!

Welcome, Professors and Instructors!

This new Seventh Edition of *Understanding Music* is the result of a great deal of consultation with teachers just like you who have taught music appreciation and have used earlier editions of this book to help them with the task of teaching students how to listen. I have made some changes in this new edition, while keeping those features that professors and instructors have found so helpful over the years. There are also a significant number of new ways of intriguing students through technology-based listening and learning techniques.

Features of the Seventh Edition

Revised Text

The text for this Seventh Edition of *Understanding Music* has been revised from beginning to end, making the text more focused and more accessible, the explanations clearer, and the Listening Guides even more helpful and easier to follow.

A New Elements Chapter (Chapter 2)

As we all know, teaching the elements of music is crucial to the teaching of music appreciation. I have tightened and reorganized the Elements chapter for this edition. It is based on very careful listening, and it divides listening tasks into separate units. The idea is to focus distinctly on a few very basic elements each time the student listens to a single, simple piece. This helps the student concentrate carefully on each new element, while the music stays the same.

Diversity in the Listening Chapter (Chapter 3)

The three pieces chosen for the Listening Chapter are extremely varied. The quality, attractiveness, and diversity of these pieces will engage students immediately, and the selections will illustrate the basic elements of music in a clear and accessible way.

Updated Chapters on Twentieth-Century Music: Classical, Jazz, and Popular (Chapters 11, 12, and 13)

I have rewritten the last three chapters to make sure that they are as up to date as possible. The classical chapter includes consideration of what is called the "downtown" music scene. The jazz chapter includes discussion of contemporary groups in Sweden, England, and the United States. And the chapter on popular music has been updated to include the latest artists and recording techniques and a discussion of the impact of the availability of music online.

New Listening Guides

The highly praised Listening Guides for the central repertoire have been tightened and clarified, and new Listening Guides have been created for the new repertoire. The Listening Guides are clear and easy to follow. They guide students step by step through all kinds of different pieces, explaining details of what is going on—including form, melody, harmony, instrumentation, and musical phrases. Special moments such as surprising gestures, unexpected key changes, or departures from conventional form are highlighted, so that students can read about the things that are happening *as they happen and as they hear them.* With the Listening Guides they learn as they listen! *On the Web site (www.MySearchLab.com), they can even follow automated versions of the Listening Guides, which highlight the descriptions as the music plays.*

New "Performance in Context" Feature

Each historical chapter now contains a special feature highlighting particular buildings in which music has been made over the centuries. These include 10 iconic venues, from churches to theaters to sports stadiums. For example, some venues featured are St. Mark's in Venice, Versailles, Wagner's Festspielhaus in Bayreuth, and the Savoy Ballroom. Each of these venues is discussed in terms of its importance in the history of music performance.

New "Quick Listen" Links in the Margins

Students are now, more than ever, visual learners. These new "Quick Listen" links scattered throughout the book are keyed to interesting YouTube videos of performances, performers, and instruments. All students have to do is go to the Web site and type in the quoted title (e.g., "South Indian Violin" or "Gregorian Chant.")

Three Ways to Listen

Understanding Music offers students access to a variety of exciting performances with world-renowned artists:

- A three-CD set of recordings
- A downloadable set, which will allow students to load each track directly to their computers
- Free streaming audio on *MySearchLab* through the all-new automated Listening Guides

New *MySearchLab* Web Site

You and your students can now go to www.MySearchLab.com, a site with all of the Web-based resources you and they will need. MySearchLab includes the following:

- Access to the interactive eText
- Streaming audio with automated Listening Guides
- Chapter-by-chapter quizzes to help students assess their understanding of the material
- Access to the *Inside the Orchestra* and "Quick Listen" videos, as well as the audio "MusicNotes" found throughout the book
- Writing and Research Tools to help students hone their skills and produce more effective papers

At the end of each chapter a "Study and Review" prompt will remind students to visit the Web site while the material is still fresh in their minds.

Online Instructor's Manual

On the Web site you will find a newly revised version of the extensive instructor's manual, containing sample syllabi, suggested lecture topics, hundreds of teaching tips, suggested classroom activities, viola jokes, additional listening and reading materials to recommend or use in class, listings of the available *MySearchLab* materials, and dozens of other ways of really engaging your students in the classroom.

Online Test Item File

Also available online is the updated and expanded test item file, available for download through the interactive *MyTest* platform, which allows you to create and save customized exams almost effortlessly.

PowerPoint Slides

A set of PowerPoint slides, complete with links to the resources found in *MySearchLab*, is available to highlight the key points brought up in the text. These slides can be easily edited and customized for your own lectures.

The Features That Have Proven the Worth, Accessibility, and Pedagogical Value of *Understanding Music* over the Years

Focus on Listening

Understanding Music is focused throughout on the importance of active listening. It has a complete and independent chapter on the Art of Listening, which guides students moment by moment through three short works, each of which illuminates different musical elements, techniques, and vocabulary for the listening experience. These activities lay a solid foundation for the students' listening work throughout the remainder of the book. *The Elements chapter is carefully coordinated with the Listening chapter.*

The first three chapters work together. From the beginning students will hear music from around the world, which will open their ears to new sounds. The second chapter gives them the vocabulary to think and talk about the building blocks of music, with audio examples they can hear and download at the book's Web site. Then a unique and independent chapter on listening leads them moment by moment through three short and very diverse works, each one of which illuminates different musical elements, techniques, and vocabulary. These activities lay a solid foundation for careful and knowledgeable listening throughout the remainder of the book.

Clear and Informative Listening Guides

The Listening Guides are clear, easy to follow, and illuminating. Form and structure, texture, instrumentation, and musical motives are explained, and special moments, such as surprising gestures, unexpected key changes, or departures from conventional form are highlighted. On the Web site, students can follow the automated Listening Guides as the music plays.

Cultural and Social Context

Music does not occur in a vacuum. Throughout the book, music is presented in the context of its social and historical milieu. In addition, each chapter contains a special box that discusses the changing role of patrons and audiences in the history of music.

Serious Consideration of Music as a Worldwide Phenomenon

The book opens with a short chapter entitled *Music Around the World*. The main focus of the book is music of the European tradition, but this focus is both rationalized and put into context by a look at music as a global phenomenon.

Proper Consideration of Popular Music

Popular music is treated not just as a token but as a cultural phenomenon in its own right. The history of popular music is surveyed from its beginning until the present, and due weight is given to musical, cultural, and commercial considerations.

Unique *Inside the Orchestra* Interactive Video

Also on the Web site is an interactive video program called *Inside the Orchestra*. You can screen this to the whole class in short sections over the course of the semester, or you can give portions of it as assignments for the students to view by themselves. The first segment introduces students to the sections of the orchestra and then features young people of their own age playing orchestral instruments one at a time with an explanatory voice-over and with demonstrations of how each instrument is played and what it sounds like. The second segment displays a chart of the seating arrangement of a classical orchestra, and then swoops over the orchestra with a bird's-eye view of that arrangement with a real (student) orchestra, explaining how the various sections work, what they play, and how they interact. Finally, the video features a student orchestra performing five different orchestral works that progress through the history of the orchestra from Handel's time to the twentieth century. (The first piece performed is the same one used throughout Chapter 2, "The Elements of Music.") These video performances are very carefully edited so that each instrument or orchestral section is in close-up as they play. On-screen information guides the viewer through each work. This unique video was produced especially for *Understanding Music*.

Details of the *Inside the Orchestra* Interactive Video

SEGMENT 1: Instruments of the Orchestra.

  I. Introduction to the Instrument Families: String, Woodwind, Brass, Percussion, and Keyboard.
 II. Introduction to the Instruments within the Instrument Families.

SEGMENT 2: How an Orchestra Works.

  I. A Tour of an Orchestra. How Instruments Sound Performing in Unison.
 II. Video of the Mozart Clarinet Concerto and the Classical Orchestra. Video of Various Combinations of Instruments.

SEGMENT 3: The Orchestra through History.

  I. Examine the Orchestra through Various Periods in History: The Baroque Era. The Classical Era. Beethoven. The Nineteenth Century. The Twentieth Century.
 II. Watch the Orchestra Playing Pieces from Five Different Periods in Music History.
    Handel, *Water Music*, Suite No. 2
    Mozart, Clarinet Concerto in A Major, Second Movement
    Beethoven, Symphony No. 6 in F Major, Op. 68, "*Pastoral*," First Movement
    Smetana, *The Moldau* (opening)
    Foss, Renaissance Concerto for Flute and Orchestra, Third Movement

Audio "MusicNotes"

These short passages, demonstrating basic musical concepts and styles, are also on the Web site. Each one is a short musical example or well-known tune that helps students learn easily about specific aspects of music.

Three Ways to Remember!

Each chapter concludes with three features that help students remember the principal points made during the chapter:

  1. **Style Summaries:** These summarize the key elements of a particular style period. Each Style Summary describes the essence of the musical style of each historical period.
  2. **Fundamentals:** This is a brief chart that lists the basic elements of each historical style.
  3. **For Further Discussion and Study:** Each chapter ends with a list of questions for students to think about or write short papers about.

"Need to Know" Lists

These little summary lists appear every so often in each chapter, just to remind the students of the main points that have been covered and that they will need to remember.

Flexibility

This book lends itself to great flexibility. It has been used very effectively in courses of one quarter, one semester, and two semesters. Sample syllabi for all these applications are given in the online instructor's manual.

A Note from the Author

Nowadays there is more music in our lives than at any previous time in history. Music surrounds us as we buy food or clothes, drive our cars, sit in the park, or jog down the street. Much of this is our own choice: we have radios in our cars and portable mp3 players in our pockets. Some of it may be unwanted: our neighbor's stereo, for example, or a "boom box" on the beach. Some of it we actually do not notice. There is so much noise in our daily environment that the music playing in elevators or stores sometimes simply merges with the surroundings.

In addition to the sheer *quantity* of music around us, there is a wider range of music available than ever before. We can listen to jazz, reggae, Vivaldi, alternative rock, or country ballads. Twenty-first-century technology has presented us with an unparalleled wealth of musical possibilities. The very idea that a symphony orchestra can be heard in our ears as we walk down the street would have startled most of the composers in this book.

The consequences of this situation are (like the consequences of most technological advances) both good and bad. It is a wonderful thing to be able to go online and buy a recording of a piece of music composed hundreds of years ago or thousands of miles away. But the ubiquitous nature of music today has also had negative consequences on the role that music plays in our society. For most of our history, music was rare; it therefore had more importance in people's lives. The composition and performance of music required deliberation and effort. Whether it was the commissioning of a symphony by an aristocratic patron or the playing of a country dance by peasants, music was performed with care and listened to with attention—it was never without significance.

The result of all this is that we have lost the art of listening.

Music is the only one of the three great arts—literature, the visual arts, and music—that can be absorbed without attention, passively. Music can surround us while we concentrate on other things; it can even be there in the background, entirely unnoticed.

This is not true of painting. To appreciate a painting we have to give it some of our attention. We have to study the forms and colors, the balance and proportions of its overall design. We may admire its style and technique—its humor, vigor, or despair. A good painting shows us objects or people or *life* in a new light. A great painting affects us profoundly and leaves us changed. Few people have seen Picasso's *Guernica* and not been deeply moved.

Literature has the same demands and the same rewards. We must pay attention to a book or a play. They cannot merely fill the room while we vacuum or accompany us while we jog or shop. And the effort of attention is repaid. A good book resonates in our own lives; a great book changes us forever.

Music, too, is the expression of the deepest part of our souls. It expresses what words and paintings cannot. And for true understanding, music requires careful attention and the engagement of the intellect, just as painting and literature do.

But even careful listening is not enough. Music is the expression of people in society. And, like the other arts, music is formed in a historical and social context. In the eighteenth century, for example, European music was the reflection of a hierarchical and orderly society, influenced by the ideals of the Enlightenment. Much eighteenth-century music, therefore, is carefully ordered and balanced, organized in a framework of fixed and widely accepted formal patterns. How can we truly understand this music if we do not know the forms used by composers of the time? It would be like reading Hawthorne's *The Scarlet Letter* without understanding the attitude of seventeenth-century New England Puritans toward adultery, or reading Shakespeare without knowing the meaning of blank verse.

Like literature, music has its rules of grammar and its rhetorical effects. Without understanding the grammar and rhetoric of music, we experience it as a sensation and little else. By learning about the social context and the structural language of music, we can experience it to its fullest. We can hear the passion of Beethoven, the brilliance of Bach, the wit and genius of Mozart. We can understand how a jazz musician can weave compelling improvisations, seemingly out of thin air. We can engage with music at its deepest level. And like a great painting or a great book, it will change us forever. It will fill our lives with beauty and joy. It will deepen our understanding of what it means to be human.

It is with this philosophy in mind that I have come to write *Understanding Music*. I believe that today's college students taking music appreciation courses want to learn how to listen to music more deeply. To this end, I have written a book that will be sensitive to the needs of today's students, a book that will guide them carefully and methodically through the art of listening itself, as well as one that will teach them the power of music as a form of human communication, and in doing so will transform them from passive recipients to active participants. Unique in its design, approach, and content, *Understanding Music* offers students a global approach, an explanation of the richness and diversity of the European tradition, a focus on listening, a thoughtful selection of works for study, a discussion of patrons and audiences, careful consideration of the role of women in creating music, and an enlightening treatment of the history of popular music. Listening to music is one of the great pleasures of human existence. I believe strongly that it is our vital task to demonstrate to our students that with a little effort, knowledge, and concentration, that pleasure can be immeasurably enriched.

Reviewers for the Seventh Edition

Carlos Abril, Northwestern University
Amy Black, Clayton State University
Charles Carson, University of Texas at Austin
Shannah Cummings, University of Arkansas Community College at Morrilton
L. H. Dickert, Winthrop University
Jane Florine, Chicago State University
Randall Hooper, Texas A&M University-Commerce
Jean Hutchinson, University of Louisville
Yugo Ikach, California University of Pennsylvania
Timothy Justus, Dickinson State University
Zachary Kreuz, Owens Community College
Douglas Mead, Owens Community College
Jeff Morris, Texas A&M University
Donald Olah, Clarion University
Alex Powell, Nashville State Community College
Charles Sharer, California University of Pennsylvania
Cecilia Smith, South Texas College
Diane Temme, Doane College

Acknowledgments

I would like to take this opportunity to remember longtime Prentice Hall editor Bud Therien, who talked me into taking on this project in the first place, and who since that time demonstrated a commitment to the subject and its importance far beyond professional necessity. He was for decades a zealous promoter of the arts at Prentice Hall, and the company and I shall miss him. The music editor for the last two editions was Richard Carlin, who is an author and music expert himself. He was a pleasure to work with. His assistant was Lily Norton, who has always gone out of her way to be helpful. Joe Scordato is the hardworking, extraordinarily efficient, and responsive production editor. I have worked with him for many, many years, and he is never less than completely thorough, professional, and deeply human. Joe is a *mensch*.

A group of scholars and teachers provided invaluable guidance at the outset of the project. Their ideas formed the initial impetus to think clearly and consistently about the challenges that lay ahead. Since that time, many experts in the field have given of their time and knowledge to review all the elements of the book and its accompanying materials. They come from all across

North America, and their comments, criticisms, and suggestions have been invaluable. Special thanks go to Dr. Evan Scooler, who prepared the extremely rich Web resources for the Fifth Edition of this book and to Terry Miller, professor emeritus at Kent State University, Ohio, who gave great insights into the music of the Middle East and provided the recording for the Turkish Call to Prayer featured in this new edition. Others who have contributed over the years include Courtney Adams, Franklin and Marshall College; Hugh Albee, Palm Beach Community College; Marci Alegant, McGill University; James Anthony, Towson State University; Graeme Boone, Ohio State University; Gregory D. Carroll, University of North Carolina at Greensboro; Donald L. Collins, University of Central Arkansas; Liane Curtis, Cambridge, Massachusetts; Barbara Harbach, Washington State University; John M. Heard, Louisiana Technical University; James Henry, Duke University; H. Wiley Hitchcock, Brooklyn College (Emeritus); Edward Hotaling, University of Central Florida; Douglas A. Lee, Vanderbilt University; Dale Monson, Brigham Young University; Claire Nanis, University of Delaware; Charles Postlewate, The University of Texas at Arlington; Julia Ehlers Quick, South Carolina State University; Jane Reeder, Chattanooga State Technical Community College; Andrea Ridilla, Miami University; Thomas Riis, University of Colorado; Michael E. Scott, Shelby State Community College; Barry M. Shank, East Carolina University; Gary Sudano, Purdue University; Jewel T. Thompson, Hunter College–City of New York; Stephen Valdez, University of Oregon; Bertil H. van Boer, Western Washington University; Paul Verrette, University of New Hampshire; Michael Votta, Duke University; Rodney Waschka, North Carolina State University; and Steven Moore Whiting, University of Michigan at Ann Arbor.

Professor Liane Curtis helped with comments and timings for several Listening Guides. Professor Graeme Boone of Ohio State University read the chapter on jazz and offered helpful criticism. Professor Jennifer Wolfe wrote the instructor's manual for earlier editions.

I have relied on many books by other scholars in the preparation of this text. They include Mark C. Gridley's *Jazz Styles: History and Analysis*; Charles Hamm's *Yesterdays: Popular Song in America*; William Malm's *Music Cultures of the Pacific, the Near East, and Asia*; Bruno Nettl's *Folk and Traditional Music of the Western Continents*; Bruno Nettl, et al.'s *Excursions in World Music*; Lewis Porter and Michael Ullman's *Jazz: From Its Origins to the Present*; Leonard G. Ratner's *Classic Music: Expression, Form, and Style*; Maynard Solomon's *Beethoven*; David P. Szatmary's *Rockin' in Time: A Social History of Rock-and-Roll*; and Piero Weiss and Richard Taruskin's *Music in the Western World: A History in Documents*.

My thoughts on music and insights into musical works have benefited through the years from discussions with many friends and colleagues: Kofi Agawu, Rebecca Baltzer, Jonathan Berger, Tom Binkley, Evan Bonds, Patrick Botti, Richard Bunbury, Larry Chud, Victor Coelho, Steven Cornelius, Bill Crofut, John Daverio, Robert Dodson, Gene Drucker, Joe Dyer, Margot Fassler, Joshua Fineberg, Cathy Fuller, Sean Gallagher, Brita Heimarck, Jan Herlinger, H. Wiley Hitchcock, Bill Hopkins, George Houle, Andrew Hughes, David Hughes, Michel Huglo, Peter Jeffrey, James Johnson, Lewis Lockwood, Yo-Yo Ma, William Mahrt, Tim McGee, William McManus, Holly Mockovak, Sandi Nicolucci, Roger Norrington, Edward Nowacki, Thomas Peattie, Leonard Ratner, Joshua Rifkin, Edward Roesner, Emilio Ros-Fabregas, Lee Rothfarb, Andrew Shenton, Joel Sheveloff, Norman Smith, Arnold Steinhardt, Peter Swing, Judith Tick, Michael Tree, Roye Wates, Christoph Wolff, Craig Wright, Neal Zaslaw, and many others.

Several graduate students (some of whom are now professors in their own right) provided considerable assistance along the way. They include Jim Davis, Todd Scott, Simon Keefe, and John Howland. My assistant in the production of the Second Edition was Zbigniew Granat, for the third, Lisa Scoggin, and for the sixth, Andrew Shryock. For this most recent edition my assistant has been Basil Considine. I am grateful to all of them.

It would be impossible to mention here all those professors, instructors, students, reviewers, authors, performers, and critics who have taken the time and trouble to comment on the first six editions of this book in the sincere desire to see it improved in the seventh. Those friends and colleagues from universities, four-year colleges, two-year colleges, and community colleges throughout North America whose contributions have substantially aided in the revision of this book include Carlos Abril, Northwestern University; Joseph Akins, Chattanooga State Technical Community College; Alexandra Amati-Camperi, University of San Francisco; Robert Amchin, University of Louisville; Laura Artesani, University of Maine; Jack Ashworth, University of Louisville; Robert Aubrey, University of Mississippi; Amy Black, Clayton State University; Mark Evan Bonds, University of North Carolina; Pierre Bouchard, University of La Valle, Quebec; Jean

Bynum, Enterprise State Junior College; Charles Carson, University of Texas at Austin; John Chiego, University of Memphis; Donald L. Collins, University of Central Arkansas; Steve Cooper, NorthWest Arkansas Community College; Shannah Cummings, University of Arkansas Community College at Morrilton; L. H. Dickert, Winthrop University; James Douthit, Bloomsburg University; Suzann Rhodes Draayer, Winona State University; Jane Florine, Chicago State University; Sean Gallagher, Harvard University; David Green, Southeast Missouri State University; A. C. "Buddy" Himes, University Louisiana; Randall Hooper, Texas A&M University–Commerce; Jean Hutchinson, University of Louisville; Yugo Ikach, California University of Pennsylvania; Timothy Justus, Dickinson State University; Shelly M. Klassen, Kutztown University; Keith Kramer, Harford Community College; Zachary Kreuz, Owens Community College; Jonathan Kulp, University of Louisiana at Lafayette; Douglas A. Lee, Vanderbilt University; Kevin J. McCarthy, University of Colorado; Douglas Mead, Owens Community College; Julie Moffitt, Harrisburg Area Community College; Jeff Morris, Texas A&M University; Sterling E. Murray, West Chester University; Sheri Neill, Texas Christian University; Donald Olah, Clarion University; James Parsons, Southwest Missouri State University; Ron Penn, University of Kentucky; Heather Platt, Ball State University; Alex Powell, Nashville State Community College; June Reeder, Chattanooga State Technical Community College; Andrea Ridilla, Miami University; Dennis Ritz, Shippensburg University; Patty Roy, Chattanooga State Technical Community College; Harris Saunders, University of Illinois at Chicago; Paul Schultz, University of Puget Sound; Charles Sharer, California University of Pennsylvania; William Shepherd, University of Northern Iowa; Elaine Sisman, Columbia University; Ed Smaldone, Queens College; Cecilia Smith, South Texas College; Gary Sudano, Purdue University; Diane Temme, Doane College; Richard Thorell, Indiana University; Phillip Todd, University of Kentucky; Thomas Trimborn, Truman State University; Paul Verrette, University of New Hampshire at Durham; Paul Vogler, Chattanooga State Technical Community College; Albin Zak, University of Michigan; and Katrina Zook, University of Wyoming. I thank them all.

I would also like to thank all my students—both graduate and undergraduate, music majors and other majors, young and not so young—at Boston University, Oxford University, the Summer Music Seminars, Harvard University, the Tanglewood Music Center, the Moscow and St. Petersburg Conservatories, and the École Normale Supérieure in Paris, who seemed to enjoy listening to my ideas and who offered many of their own.

J. Y.

CHAPTER 1

Music Around the World

Introduction to the Study of Music

Although much of this book focuses on American and European music, music is an art that appears in all cultures around the world. Each nation or ethnic group develops its own music and preserves its *own* musical traditions. Our study of the rich and ancient store of European music is made possible by the existence of written records that stretch back over a thousand years. Other classical traditions around the world—such as Indian raga and some forms of Chinese music—have similarly lengthy traditions that can be studied through documentary evidence and performances. But in much of the world music is not written down; it is transferred from one person to another, and from one generation to the next simply by ear. One person learns the music by hearing someone else perform it; an older person teaches it to a younger person.

In most cases, in cultures around the world, it is very difficult to determine how old a musical tradition may be. And there is no way of knowing how the music may have changed over the generations. Some cultures regard their musical heritage as sacrosanct and

The market in the Old City of Jerusalem.

try to keep the music of the past more or less intact. Others continuously adapt their music to modern tastes: this kind of music will be in a constant state of change.

It would be a mistake to assume that the music of an unfamiliar small group is "purer" or more "natural" than our own. The music of the European tradition was also kept alive for centuries without being written down.

Nor should we imagine that music of other cultures is nothing but a pristine representation of the soul of that people since "time began." Representative it may be, because music reflects the society that performs it, but certainly not since "time began." There is very little music in the world that has not undergone change and influence from outside forces. Native American music continues to bear traces of its people's origin across the Bering Strait in East Asia, and since the arrival of Europeans in North America, this music has interacted with many other traditions. Music in Africa has for centuries been affected by outside influences from Indonesia, India, and Europe. In Brazil, one hears a mixture of music from West Africa and Portugal. In the Philippines, traditional dance is accompanied by music of Spanish origin. And in western Nigeria, the Yoruba people have mingled a native singing style with guitar music borrowed from Ghana. We may wish that the situation were simpler and more "authentic," but life—and the history of the world—is not like that. People adapt their music to their own ideas of what they like, not to other people's views of what they "should" like.

Decorated manuscript of written music from medieval Europe.

Elsner, Jacob. Ascension. At the bottom animals singing. Page from a Gradual ("Geese Book"), Nuremberg, 1507. M.905, Vol. I, f. 186. The Pierpont Morgan Library, New York, N.Y., U.S.A. The Pierpont Morgan Library/Art Resource, NY.

Today, the greatest influence on music around the world is that exerted by Western classical and popular music. Throughout Asia, orchestras play symphonic music of the European tradition, and young Asian musicians are trained in the styles and techniques of Western classical music. In West Africa, the music is influenced by American country music, soul, reggae, and disco. In France, cafés and restaurants in the smallest villages are filled with the recorded sounds of English and American rock. In the Middle East, modern popular songs merge the sounds of Western pop with local rhythms and singing styles.

One of the richest tapestries of musical culture is found in Israel, where the music of native-born Jews and Arabs mingles with that of Jews from Iraq, Latvia, Romania, Holland, Ethiopia, and Yemen, as well as with the music of Christian Arabs and Christians from Armenia and Russia. In addition to this colorful tangle of music from all over the world, Israeli Arabs and Jews have created a modern Israeli music: dance songs or pop songs with a Western beat and melodies sung in an ornamented, intense, Middle Eastern style.

It has often been said that music is a universal language: that it transcends boundaries of nation and race. This is true, but only in a very specific sense. The fact that there is music seems to be universal: every known human group has music. But for each culture, music has a different meaning. It takes different forms in different cultural groups. Even the definition of music differs from culture to culture. Some cultures don't even have a word for "music," because it is integral to their experience of the world, whereas others use different words to distinguish among several types of music.

Music reflects the society that creates it, and each society creates the music that it wants. This statement sounds obvious, yet it is important, because it reminds us that in order to understand a culture's music, we need to understand the culture itself.

Perhaps we could say that even if music is *not* a universal language, it is universal *like* language. Music, like language, is an accomplishment that distinguishes us as humans. Linguists tell us that there are more than 5,000 languages spoken in our world. It would not be surprising to discover that there are just as many types of music. And learning to understand the music of another culture is not very different from learning to understand the language of another culture.

Mariachi band.

Young girl in North America learning to play the violin.

NEED TO KNOW

- Music is a reflection of the society that makes it.

- Music is not a universal language; it is universal *like* language, in that it distinguishes us as humans.

Music as a Reflection of Society

Each culture possesses its own musical language that reflects its own traditions, concerns, and activities; and to begin to understand the music of another culture, we need to understand something of the nature of that culture's systems and the role that music plays in them.

African musical instruments.

because he alone is familiar with the intricacies of genealogy.

This brief description, though by no means complete, gives us a deeper appreciation of Mandinka music. It explains the central role of solo singing in the society, the declamatory nature of the texts, the repetitive but highly flexible style of accompaniment (to accommodate the varying texts), and the formal nature of the performances. A full analysis of the music would go into far more detail than this, but it could not even legitimately begin without a basic understanding of the social context in which the music is made. In turn, understanding the music can provide significant insights into the culture of which it is a part.

The United States: A Test Case

Let's take a look at music in the United States today as a reflection of American culture. We'll describe the situation as though we were anthropologists looking at an unfamiliar people. This will help us focus on the kinds of questions we might ask about music in the rest of this book.

Let's start with classical music. In the United States, we note that classical music is treated as an elitist activity. Performances are very formal: members of the audience sit listening very quietly until the end of each piece. Most of the music that is performed in classical-music concerts was composed in past centuries. The society treats the music of the past with great reverence. There is a written musical tradition stretching back over a thousand years, although most of the music that is performed is between 100 and 250 years old. Concerts often feature the same pieces by a relatively small roster of composers, from one concert to another and from one year to the next.

In addition to classical music, people in the United States listen to many other types of music. There seems to be a distinction by class and age among these different types. Listeners of different age groups and social classes prefer different styles of music. Most young people listen to popular music, although some may also be interested in classical music. Popular music is mostly heard on recordings, though there are also public performances in small clubs, in outdoor locations, and sometimes in concert halls. Our anthropological survey would also note that there is another type of music making that often occurs in cafés, bars, and nightclubs, as well as in outdoor venues. This music is called jazz. Like classical music,

This is just as true of Western culture. To begin to understand the music of the Middle Ages, or eighteenth-century opera, we will need to understand something of the cultural background of the West.

In other cultures, music plays many different roles. Among the Mandinka of Gambia and Senegal, for instance, there is a highly specialized type of professional musician known as the *jali*. The *jali* is both the historian of the tribe and the official singer of praises. The significance of these two roles will not become clear to us until we understand how Mandinka society operates.

Mandinka society is based upon a rigid class system in which class is determined by lineage (or family history). A person from the "right" family background enjoys considerable social status and may choose among a variety of professional jobs. However, someone from a working-class family is obliged to take a job as an artisan, a carpenter, or a metalworker. Members of the working class are looked down upon by other members of the tribe.

Because family background is so important in determining people's lives, family history is entrusted to the male *jali*, who specializes in historical knowledge. (Women are not allowed to be *jalis*). The *jali*'s job as historian and singer of praises, therefore, is of paramount importance. When hired to perform, the *jali* can evoke the noble ancestry of a patron, thereby enhancing that person's standing in society. Or he can turn praise into insult and innuendo, thus damaging a person's social status. The *jali* is even called upon to determine questions of inheritance, jazz attracts attentive listeners who attend concerts, study certain musicians and their compositions, and follow closely the development of the music. Like popular music, jazz is experienced through recordings as much as through live performance.

Women are becoming more and more accepted by society as music makers. For many years—apart from roles as singers—women were rarely seen performing music in public, but today there are many female performers. In popular music and jazz, women used to have restricted roles. Today, however, female instrumentalists, entrepreneurs, songwriters, producers, and recording executives are much more common.

Many other types of music occur in the United States. Each ethnic group has a distinctive traditional music that helps to foster its separate identity (polkas, square dancing, the blues). Religious groups are often distinguished by the kind of music they perform (gospel, Orthodox chant). Some large public events are marked by the singing of nationally known songs ("Take Me Out to the Ball Game").

What does this "anthropological" description tell us about the society? It tells us that American culture is extremely diverse, divided as it is by age, class, and ethnicity. Divisions by gender role are gradually being erased. We learn that a very ancient musical tradition has been carefully preserved, and that new music is constantly being produced. It is clear that the society is undergoing rapid change: popular artists can change from year to year or week to week! And popular music has become a highly lucrative and competitive branch of the country's commerce. Change is also evident in the way each of the many different subgroups of the society—defined by ethnicity, age, social class, and the like—uses a very small segment of the total musical culture to reinforce its own identity. This seems to suggest a sense of anxiety within the society as a whole and a fragmentation of the society into a multiplicity of separate groups. There are, however, some national songs that help all the people feel unified, at least for brief moments.

Woman playing the cello.

The accepted notions about music in American society—the use of music primarily for entertainment, the separation of popular and classical music, the existence of a fixed repertory of ancient masterworks, and the use of music to divide groups as well as to reinforce the sense of membership within a group—are not necessarily found in other cultures. Even such a deeply ingrained concept as the idea that music should be enjoyable to hear may not form a part of another culture's views. *We must realize that every society views music in its own way—and that way may be very different from our own.*

World Music: A View from a Satellite

For the purposes of our discussion, it is possible to divide the world into five large areas, each encompassing a large array of different musical cultures, yet each containing certain unifying features. These areas are (1) North America and Europe, (2) Latin America and the Caribbean, (3) sub-Saharan Africa, (4) the Middle East and North Africa, and (5) Asia and the Pacific Islands. These five large areas have some things in common. They all contain cultures that have developed a sophisticated, *classical* repertory of music, played primarily by professional musicians. And they also contain non-literate cultures whose music is not written down or regulated by theory but is generally performed by most of the members of the society. We can call this music *traditional*.

There are also two types of music that lie somewhere between these two extremes. These we may call *folk* and *popular* music. Folk music exists in sophisticated societies alongside classical music and continues to be performed in rural areas away from the educated, usually urban, élite. It is often several generations old. Examples occur from China to Peru to Wales. In addition to folk music, most cultures that have a classical system of music also have a flourishing popular-music industry. This music tends to be short-lived (a hit may last only a few weeks), commercial (designed to sell), and aimed at a broad, generally urban, audience. This is as true in India, for example, as it is in Finland or Argentina or in any number of other countries.

NEED TO KNOW

- Much traditional music around the world is part of an oral tradition; it is not written down, but is passed along the generations by memory.

- Most cultures use both voices and instruments in musical performance.

- Music is a reflection of a culture. To understand the music, we need to understand the role it plays in that culture.

What to Listen for in World Music

There are some more detailed observations we can make about music that lies outside the European-American classical tradition. These concern the nature of the music itself, its various melodic and rhythmic structures as well as the various sounds produced by the different singing styles and instruments in use around the world. We will also consider the context in which music appears in different cultures, the participants involved, and the length of musical events. But let us first look at attitudes toward music of the past. In the following pages, we will take the music of the

European-American tradition as a point of comparison, not to make value judgments but simply because for many of us it is the most familiar.

Attitude Toward Music of the Past   We have already noted that in the United States, much of the music played in concerts dates from hundreds of years ago. In those cultures around the world where music is not written down, a different attitude exists with regard to music of the past. In some cultures, there are a number of works from the past that serve as a basis for improvisation. In India and Japan, for instance, although there is a repertory of classical music that is fairly fixed, there are also some traditional pieces that serve as the framework for learned improvisations by highly trained master musicians. In other countries, music is regarded as a living, flexible artifact, constantly open to change. In these cultures, the music is constantly being reinvented, so that, in a sense, music of the past doesn't really exist: it is constantly turning into music of the present.

Texture   The sound of most of the world's music is very different from that of European classical music. Starting in the twelfth century, European music became more and more focused on **polyphony**—music that contains two or more musical lines performed at the same time. As a result, harmony—the chords formed by these lines—also became a central concern. Polyphony and harmony have become the underlying principles for most European and American concert music.

In other cultures music has focused on different musical elements. With significant exceptions, particularly in Africa, most other music has only one tune sounding at a time (**monophony**), often supported by a rhythmic accompaniment of considerable interest. The essence of monophonic music is very different from that of polyphonic music, and our way of listening to it must therefore be consciously modified. In some cultures, several different performers play the same melody, but each in his own way. The result is simultaneous, slightly varying, interweaving strands of a single tune.

Melody   Although a great deal of European-American classical music contains beautiful melodies, melody is not the only focus of the music. During the Middle Ages, European music was primarily text and melody. However

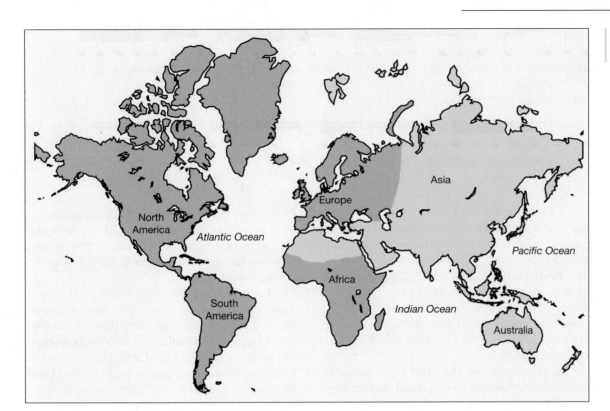

The two broad musical areas of the world.

for most of Western classical music since the Middle Ages, melody has become a secondary concern to harmony.

In many musical styles around the world, melody is of paramount interest. In Iran, a trained singer will improvise on a melodic pattern, exploring all of its possible aspects in high and low notes, varying the quality of her voice, and using a wide range of ornamental flourishes. An Indian player of the sitar—a long-necked, resonant lute—weaves sinuous melodic lines above and around a constant, fixed drone, exploring different scales. A Japanese master of the *shakuhachi* (an end-blown, bamboo flute) bends pitches, plays notes "between the notes," and generally utilizes every melodic possibility available to him.

Rhythm Rhythmically, Western music—classical and popular alike—is rather simple. Most pieces use the same beat or meter throughout. It is only fairly recently that classical composers have begun to explore more intricate approaches to rhythm in their music.

By contrast, many musical styles around the world are extremely intricate in their rhythm. African drummers frequently produce several complex rhythms simultaneously. In the dance musics of Mexico, Venezuela, and Argentina, three-beat and two-beat meters alternate in catchy, irregular patterns. In India, rhythm is raised to the level of a special art, and rhythmic patterns are explored in Indian music theory. There are hundreds of these patterns; an Indian drummer has to study for years to learn them all.

An Indian master of the *tabla* or drums.

Excerpt from a *majara*, a type of North Indian drumming pattern that often occurs at the close of a phrase or entire work. The syllables below the notes refer to specific drum strokes.

na ga dhet ta   ka ra dha ti ra ki ta   dha ti ra ki ta ta ka ta   ti ra ki ta ta ka

ti ra ki ta ta ka dha tit   dha ta ka ta dha tit   dha ta ka ta dha tit dha

Tone Color: Voices and Instruments

European-American classical music encompasses a wide range of instrumental and vocal sounds. A symphony orchestra boasts dozens of different instruments, which can play singly or in large numbers of different combinations. Music of other cultures, however, often displays tone colors, vocal and instrumental, that are very different from anything heard in a symphony orchestra.

In many cultures, the ideal vocal sound is not smooth, flowing, and relaxed, as it is in the cultivated European tradition. Singers often use a very tense, strained technique. This is true of many Native American tribes. Or they may be able to produce two tones at once (in Tibet, Mongolia, Siberia), or sing in an extremely florid manner, with incredibly fast, clean runs, trills, and ornaments (in Morocco, Saudi Arabia, Pakistan). The singers of some areas practice a yodeling technique, in which the voice moves rapidly between a regular singing voice and a high falsetto. This technique is practiced by the Swiss, the Pygmies of central Africa, and the Berbers of the Sahara. And voice ranges can defy gender expectations. Brazilian cowboys sing in harmony at the very top of their range, whereas female folk singers in Turkey sing in a low, throaty voice.

Instruments around the world produce a wide variety of tone colors. The type of instruments a culture develops often depends on the raw materials available. In Africa, instruments are made of wood, animal skins, and animal horns, sometimes even of ivory. In China, Laos, Cambodia, Vietnam, and Indonesia—where metalworking has been a part of the culture for thousands of years—bronze instruments, such as gongs and chimes, are favored.

NEED TO KNOW
TYPES OF MUSICAL INSTRUMENTS

Chordophones (strings)

Aerophones (winds)

Membranophones (drums)

Idiophones (scrapers, gongs, etc.)

Alphorn players in a Swiss village.

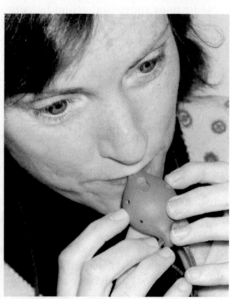

Tiny clay ocarina.

Musical instruments around the world can be classified into four groups: stringed instruments, including those that are plucked and those that are bowed; wind instruments, which are blown; and two types of percussion instruments, those whose sound is produced by hitting some material stretched over a hollow object (drums) and those whose sound is made by hitting, shaking, or waving a solid object (gongs, chimes, rattles, scrapers, etc.). Ethnomusicologists—specialists who study music around the world—have developed special names for each of these categories: chordophones (strings); aerophones (winds); membranophones (drums); and idiophones (scrapers, gongs, etc.).

Each of these categories includes an enormous variety of instruments. Stringed instruments can be long or short, have one or many strings, and range in sound from very loud to exceedingly soft and delicate. Wind instruments range from the gigantic alphorn, designed to be heard over mountain ranges, to the small clay ocarina, which produces gentle dovelike tones. Percussion instruments represent the largest class of instruments in the world. Some can be pitched—that is, they can produce a definite note rather than just a "bonk" or a "clunk" (un-pitched). Drums occur in pitched and un-pitched varieties. Many percussion instruments are pitched: xylophones, chimes, bells, and gongs can all produce specific pitches.

In many cultures, percussion is produced without instruments. Rhythmic sounds and complex rhythmic patterns are made by hands clapping, slapping thighs, and foot stamping.

Some Western instruments, such as the violin, have been adapted to local use by various cultural traditions. The violin, sometimes with modifications, is a central instrument in the traditional musics of India, Iran, and the Apache and Navajo tribes of the southwestern United States.

Indian street musician.

And even when the instrument is familiar, the sounds produced in different cultures are unusual to Western ears. In South India, a violinist plays on an instrument that is indistinguishable from that used in a symphony orchestra, but the sound he or she produces is totally unlike that of symphonic music. The player sits cross-legged on the floor, and the violin is supported between the chest and the ankle. This allows the fingers of the left hand complete freedom to slide up and down the strings. Pitches are not clean and distinct but flexible, loose, and joined by slides. The *hardingfele*, or Norwegian fiddle, is a violin that has been adapted to folk culture. It has extra strings that are not bowed, but vibrate when the fiddle is played. (They are placed under the fingerboard, parallel to and below the four melody strings.) The sound is highly resonant and penetrating.

Many instruments are completely independent of any Western equivalent, and their tone colors are distinctive. An instrument in widespread use in Africa is the *mbira* (pronounced "em-beera"), often translated as "thumb piano." The mbira has thin metal strips or tongues fastened to a small wooden box or gourd. The box is held in both hands while the thumbs pluck the strips. The sound is soft, buzzy, watery, and plunky. Players often enhance the buzz by attaching metal bottle-tops to the wood or by wrapping small pieces of metal around the tongues. In Eastern Europe, a short woodwind instrument known as a *shawm* is played in

Find the **Quick Listen** on **MySearchLab** "South Indian Violin"

Xylophone.
Musser, a Division of The Selmer Co.

Dancers in Zaire.

Find the **Quick Listen** on **MySearchLab** "Didjeridoo"

public places such as the marketplace or the town square. It is extremely loud and piercing and can be heard at a considerable distance.

The most dramatic illustration of the importance of tone color in instrumental playing is given by the *didjeridoo* of the Australian aboriginal people. This is a long hollowed-out eucalyptus branch, played like a trumpet. It can produce only a small number of notes, but the subtlety of the instrument lies in its tonal qualities. A skilled player can produce upwards of nine or ten different tone colors on his instrument. For the didjeridoo player, a wide range of tone color is more important than a wide pitch range.

Social Context   In many regions of the world, music is an integral part of a ceremony or a group activity. Studying the music without considering its context can provide only half the picture, if that. The most common context for music around the world is dance. Think, for example, of the ubiquity of the samba and

the tango both as dance and as musical genres in the Caribbean and South America. In some African cultures, music is regarded as primarily an accompaniment to dance.

But there are many other contexts in which music plays a role. In Africa, rhythmic group singing is widely used to facilitate work. In Japan, music is a central part of traditional theater, and a vital component of spiritual rituals known as *Shinto*. Japanese girls perform music to demonstrate a refined upbringing. Native American tribes use music to accompany gambling games, contact guardian spirits, conduct the medicine-bundle ceremony, cure illnesses, and distinguish among age and gender groups.

Attitudes Toward the Participation of Women   The place of women is closely defined, and often severely restricted, in most cultures around the globe. In particular, the role of women in music making is often carefully delineated. In a great many traditional societies, women do not take part in musical activities, these being reserved for men. In Japanese *Kabuki* theater and Chinese traditional opera, for example, female roles are sung by men.

In other communities, singing and dancing are considered to be appropriate for women but playing instruments is not. South Indian classical dances are danced by women, but only men play in the accompanying instrumental group. In Islamic countries, where women's roles are strictly defined, women traditionally sing only wedding songs. In Korea, however, both women and men sing the *japka* narrative songs, and among the Pwo Karen people of northern Thailand, both women and men sing the funeral songs.

A unique form of matriarchy is practiced by the Tuaregs of the Sahara. The men wear veils, and only the women know how to read and write. Women are the instrumentalists in this culture and do most of the singing. Men, however, are permitted to sing love songs at special communal gatherings.

Time   One final facet of music that differs greatly among cultures is time. In twentieth-century European and American society, the length of a musical performance is highly conventionalized. A classical music concert is designed to take almost exactly two hours, including a 15- or 20-minute intermission. The concert often starts at 8:00 p.m., so that members of the audience can have a meal beforehand, and it ends at 10:00 p.m., so that people do not get to bed too late.

Scene from a Chinese opera.

Mbira in the shape of a human figure.

Australian aboriginal playing a didjeridoo.

Even in Western society, these conventions change from one era to the next. In the late eighteenth and early nineteenth centuries, for example, concerts could last much longer. When Beethoven presented his Fifth and Sixth Symphonies in 1808, they were on the same program with his Fourth Piano Concerto; his Mass in C; a solo vocal piece; and a work for piano, chorus, and orchestra. The concert lasted more than four hours. Not only concerts but church services, too, lasted longer in the past than they do now: a typical Sunday service at Bach's Lutheran church would have gone on for four hours, including half an hour of music and an hour-long sermon.

But in other cultures, ideas about the length of a musical event can be very different. The Peyote ceremony of many Native American tribes consists of an entire night of singing. The religious Hako ceremony of the Pawnee lasts for several days. And the Navajo curing ceremony continues over a period of nine days and nights and includes hundreds of different songs. Even this does not exhaust the possible durations of musical ceremonies among certain peoples. The Pygmies, for example, who enjoy a deep and spiritual relationship with the forest in which they live, have developed a ceremony in which they sing to the forest every night over a period of several months.

In almost every facet of its existence, then, music is regarded in different ways among the various peoples of the world: in the melody, rhythm, tone color, and texture of the music itself; in the context in which music is performed; and in attitudes toward music of the past, the participation of women, and the duration of a musical event. As we have seen, even the definition of what music *is* can differ from one culture to the next. As human beings, we vary widely in our understanding of the meaning of music and the role it plays in our lives. Yet music is one of the great human accomplishments that we all share.

Korean women's chorus, playing traditional plucked instruments.

Listening to Music from Around the World

By now, you have some basis for listening to some examples of music from around the world. These will be chosen primarily to illustrate the enormous variety of kinds of music and attitudes toward music that exist on our planet. In all cases, we shall consider cultural context to help us understand the music itself. We shall listen first to solo music for the Japanese *shakuhachi*, then to a Turkish call to prayer, next to the sounds of the Indonesian gamelan orchestra, and finally to mbira music from Africa.

Japanese *Shakuhachi* Music

Japanese music dates back at least to the early Middle Ages. In this feudal period (ca. 1200–1600), rival warlords established their own courts and fought for power, and Buddhism, imported (together with the system of writing) from China, joined the local rituals of Shinto. The music of this period includes religious chants for the Buddhist liturgy, choral singing for Shinto observances, medieval courtly orchestral music known as *gagaku* ("elegant music"), and music for the Noh theater, which combines singing, dancing, and the playing of instruments. The Noh theater, a genre derived from the medieval samurai period, is highly stylized, elegant, and formal. It reflects the samurai's philosophy of simplicity, submission to Buddha, and personal enlightenment.

In addition to this ancient repertoire, there is a body of "classical" music from Japan's Edo period, which lasted from 1615 to 1868. It is called "Edo" because the ruling clan at that time established the capital of the country in Edo (modern-day Tokyo). This was a period of relative peace and prosperity after the military strife of the samurai era, and a prosperous middle class developed in the cities. The colorful music of this period is a reflection of this prosperous, urban audience.

Music from the Edo period is both theatrical and instrumental; and of Japan's classical music, it is Edo music that is performed most today. Two types of theatrical music developed in the Edo period: music for the Bunraku puppet theater and music for Kabuki theater. *Bunraku* is akin to Western opera, except that there is only one (very versatile) performer, who manipulates all the puppets and performs all the voices. Kabuki theater is performed by an all-male cast, includes dancing as well as lively traditional drama, and is accompanied by three different instrumental ensembles.

The purely instrumental music of the Edo period includes both small-group music and solo music. The traditional small ensemble is made up of a singer and three instruments: a *shamisen*, which is a three-stringed, long-necked lute; a *koto*, which is a delicate, 13-stringed plucked zither; and the *shakuhachi*, a bamboo flute. The repertories of exquisite solo music for koto and shakuhachi have been passed down the generations by means of oral tradition. Many, many years of dedicated learning, careful listening, and self-discipline are required to become a master of the koto or the shakuhachi. (**See the Listening Guide.**)

Japanese folk music consists mostly of songs, sung unaccompanied in a high, tense voice, but there are also folk dances. The folk music of Japan reflects the culture's strong, early influences from China. Popular music in Japan is highly varied, ranging from folk-inspired melodies to Western pop and rock styles. Indeed, much popular music played now in Japan is imported from the United States and England, reflecting the current Japanese fascination with the West. Many young musicians are also trained in Western classical music, and Japanese composers write symphonic music that is a blend of the Western style and traditional Japanese elements.

To summarize, Japanese music has responded to the changing nature of its society over time as follows:

1. **The feudal period:** Japanese culture produces Buddhist chants and Shinto songs and prayers, together with courtly instrumental music and Noh theater.

Male actor in a Japanese *Kabuki* performance. Two *shamisen* players are visible behind.

LISTENING GUIDE

((•—Listen on MySearchLab

LISTENING SKETCH FOR *SHAKUHACHI* MUSIC

"Koku Reibo"
("A Bell Ringing in the Empty Sky")

Duration: 4:31

The shakuhachi is a bamboo flute with five finger holes. It is blown from one end. Its name means "one and eight-tenths," because in Japanese measurement the shakuhachi has the length of one and eight-tenths *shaku* (a shaku is roughly a foot).

Music for the shakuhachi has a profound, mystical quality. The instrument was used in religious ceremony by Zen Buddhist monks in the seventeenth century, and it has been said that a single note of the shakuhachi can bring one to the state of *nirvana* (perfect blessedness).

"Koku-Reibo" is one of the oldest pieces in the repertory, dating back to the seventeenth century. The title refers to the death of Zen monk Fuke-Zenji, who used to walk around ringing a small handbell. When he died, the sound of his bell could be heard getting fainter and fainter as it ascended into the clear blue sky. "Koku-Reibo" and other ancient shakuhachi compositions are regarded as sacred and to be played only by great masters.

Playing the shakuhachi requires an enormous amount of control and subtlety of expression. The musician performing here, Nyogetsu Seldin, has studied the traditional art of the shakuhachi for 30 years. He studied with Kurahashi Yodo Sensei in Kyoto and is now a Grand Master of the instrument.

The music is riveting. It demands all of your attention, because it involves such minute details. There are only a few notes, but the variety of sounds is amazing. The player uses slides between notes, shadings of color and sound, variations of intensity, and carefully controlled gradations of volume to produce an atmosphere that is truly mystical. Our excerpt ends after only a few minutes, but the entire composition lasts more than 15 minutes. Listen to the excerpt very carefully, and listen to it several times. Each time you will hear something new. The music will capture your imagination in an entirely new way.

CD I, 1

2. **The Edo period:** Musical performance is geared toward the new urban and middle-class populations. It includes entertaining stage works as well as instrumental compositions for master musicians.

3. **The modern period:** Music becomes more focused on popular songs and begins to show Western popular and classical influences.

Music and Islam

The extent to which listening to music is permissible is highly controversial in Islam. There is no explicit condemnation of music in the Qur'an. Accounts of the prophet Mohammed's life describe him as either participating in musical activities or condemning them, so there is still debate as to whether certain kinds of music are acceptable or not. What is clear is that the call to prayer—which occurs in Muslim societies five times a day—and the recitation of the Qur'an, although they sound like singing, are not considered to be musical entertainment.

We shall listen to a Turkish call to prayer, which sounds musical to us, but is more thought of by Muslims as a heightened recitation. Sharia law provides detailed instructions on which types of musical entertainment are acceptable in strict Muslim societies. Acceptable types are work songs, family or celebratory music (such as lullabies and wedding music), and the singing of noble poetry. Unacceptable is sensuous music.

In Islamic countries of the Middle East, music has always been regarded with ambivalence. For centuries the scholarly study of music was assiduously pursued. Nearly 2,000 medieval treatises on music were written in Arabic, Turkish, and Persian. But during this time no tradition of religious instrumental music grew up, and the performance of music was usually handed over to non-Muslim minorities. Other aesthetic interests were pursued, however, such as visual art, architecture, and literature, and the Muslim world is filled with remarkable examples of these.

The Turkish musical tradition is very rich and has many and varied roots, including the Islamic tradition but also folk music from Asia and the cultures of Persia and Byzantium. As in other Muslim countries, the call to prayer is heard five times a day echoing from the top of a minaret, or tall tower of a mosque. Because of its ubiquity, its sound has influenced many other kinds of music in Turkey.

LISTENING GUIDE

((•─Listen on MySearchLab)

LISTENING SKETCH FOR A TURKISH CALL TO PRAYER

Duration: 3:16

Singing in the East is often strained (as opposed to the more relaxed vocal style of the West) and highly ornate. It often involves very rapid articulation of notes and sometimes a tremolo back and forth between two notes or an ornamental vibrato on final notes. The call to prayer is declaimed in classical Arabic, in free rhythm, and each phrase is repeated several times. We shall listen to the first three phrases of this Turkish call to prayer. The full version includes five or six additional phrases of text.

CD I, 2

Allahu akbar, Allahu akbar.	God is great, God is great.
Ash-hadu anna alla ilaha ill'Allah.	I testify that there is no god but God.
Ash-hadu anna Muhammadan rasul Allah.	I testify that Muhammad is the prophet of God.

African Drumming and Mbira Music

Americans and Europeans tend to think of Africa as a single entity. This is, of course, an enormous oversimplification. The continent contains several hundred distinct ethnic groups. Today's "countries" were created by European colonizers of the African continent, and often represent artificial divisions. Some ethnic groups are spread among several countries, while many countries contain groups that historically had no association.

The African diversity of social organization, language, ethnicity, race, and religion is mirrored in a great diversity of musical practices. Yet it is possible to make some generalizations about African music:

1. There is a broad cultural division between North Africa and sub-Saharan Africa, which is mirrored in their musics. Music in North Africa (primarily Morocco, Algeria, Tunisia, Libya, and Egypt) is very similar in style to that of the Middle East, whereas music in the rest of the continent is more like what we think of as "African" music.
2. There are certain general characteristics within the music of sub-Saharan Africa, despite its enormous size and diversity. These include elements of context, style, aesthetics, and practice.

Briefly, these are the musical elements that seem to bind together the peoples of sub-Saharan Africa, from the northwestern savanna region to the central rain forest to the cattle country of the southeast:

1. Music is strongly associated with dance.
2. Instruments are numerous and widespread.
3. Sounds of percussion are heavily favored; these include drums as well as other percussion instruments.
4. Polyphonic (multiple) sounds predominate. These may involve several rhythms produced simultaneously or two or more interwoven melodies.
5. Melodies are made up of repetition, variation, and improvisation on short melodic fragments.

The two most widespread instruments in sub-Saharan Africa are the drum and the mbira. Drums come in many different sizes and forms. They include tall, single-headed drums, closed at the lower end; large, open-ended

African drummers.

drums; small drums in an hourglass shape; two-headed drums with even-sized heads or with one small and one large head; and even a two-headed drum whose pitches can be changed by tightening or loosening the tension on the heads while the drum is being played.

African drumming is often extremely complex. A single drummer can produce a broad array of rhythms, as well as a variety of notes and tone colors. Drumming ensembles are common: several players of different-sized drums produce a dense, interlocking texture of multiple, simultaneous rhythms and notes.

Mbira music is no less complex. An mbira ("em-beera") is an instrument that consists of a small wooden box or gourd with a row of thin metal strips attached to it. The strips are plucked by the thumbs of both hands. The mbira also comes in many different types, depending on the material of the resonating body, the size and number of the strips, and the objects (beads, shells, bottle tops) that are sometimes attached to the instrument to enrich the sound. The mbira is regarded as sacred by certain tribes. The Shona of Zimbabwe, for example, use it to summon the spirits of their ancestors.

Mbira music, like drum music, illustrates a very African view of music, which itself derives from a special sense of time. Mbira music and drum music are not frozen into "pieces" that can be reproduced more or less identically on any given occasion. Each performance involves a lengthy combination of repetition and very gradual variation, so that the music may be heard as a process rather than as a piece.

Mbira instrumentalists play a short melodic pattern over and over again. As time passes, they

The Zimbabwean musician Forward Kwenda with his mbira.

gradually weave slight changes into the melodic pattern, creating variation. Each slightly different variation is also played over and over again before a new change is introduced. Change thus takes place over a long period of time.

This special conception of time may derive from observations of the natural world, in which the world of the plains, the forests, and the jungle unfolds at its own pace. Perhaps the music of African peoples is a reflection of this natural unfolding.

LISTENING GUIDE

(((•─[Listen on **MySearchLab**

LISTENING SKETCH FOR MBIRA MUSIC

"Mandarendare" (*"A Place Full of Energy"*)

Duration: 5:34

CD I, 3

For the Shona, a people who make up most of the population of Zimbabwe and extend also into Mozambique, mbira music is mystical music that is used to communicate with the spirits of ancestors and guardians of the tribe. "Mandarendare" ("a place full of energy") is usually played at a dawn ceremony. The performer on this recording, Forward Kwenda, has been involved in keeping alive the musical traditions of the Shona people since he was a young boy. He says, "When I pick up my mbira, I don't know what is going to happen. The music goes by itself. It is so much greater than a human being can understand."

Although it sounds as though two or more people are playing this piece, there is only one performer. Three distinct layers of sound can be detected: a deep, regular pattern in the bass and two interlocking lines above it. Although at first there seems to be constant repetition, careful listening will reveal slow, but constant, change. The tone quality is unusual; the notes are surrounded with a hiss or buzz that sounds to our ears like a sonic distortion. This hiss, which adds depth and complexity to the sound, is considered an essential element in mbira playing.

Like drum music, mbira music displays the African fascination with complex, multiple sounds. Because of the resonance of the instrument, each note continues to sound for a while during the next few notes. Also, the attachment to the body of the instrument of beads or bottle tops—which vibrate or buzz slightly when the instrument is played—gives each note a rich, slightly hazy quality, like the moon on a misty night. An mbira melody, even on one instrument, is made up of the interlocking of two parts, one played by the right thumb, the other by the left. Often, however, mbiras are played in pairs or in groups, producing an even more complex web of sound. Finally, in some ceremonies, mbiras are accompanied by gourd rattles, handclaps, and the sounds of several people singing.

Conclusion

In this chapter, we have taken a glance at several different cultures around the world and seen how very different the music is in each of them. And yet we can make a few general observations. The first is that music is a reflection of the society that creates it. In order to understand the music of a given society, we need to understand something about that society. The second thing we have learned is that understanding the music can help us to understand the culture that produced it. The culture forms the music, and the music represents the culture.

Looking at the Japanese, Turkish, and African cultures as briefly as we have, we begin to see how daunting a task it is to get a full picture of the meaning and significance of music in a particular cultural context. To understand even one type of music, in one corner of the world, requires knowledge of a society's historical and cultural background, specific listening skills, and a method for putting musical observations into words. Each type of music could fill a book on its own.

For most of *this* book, we will be examining music of the Western tradition, which has such a rich and lengthy written history that a thousand years of it can be explored in great detail. To do this, we will need a working vocabulary for talking about this music. We will need to examine just what skills are necessary for hearing a piece of music both as a whole and as a combination of elements. And we will need to work on a greater understanding of the culture surrounding the different historical periods of Western music.

FOR FURTHER DISCUSSION AND STUDY

1. Learn a brief tune. Before the next class, teach the tune to another student, who should then teach it to yet another. Continue this process through four or five students, and have the last one repeat the tune at the next class. Compare it with the original. How has the tune changed? What does this tell us about oral tradition?

2. Describe your ethnic and musical background. How have you been influenced by the customs and music of this heritage?

3. Discuss the way in which American popular culture has infiltrated other societies: Mickey Mouse, Coke, and McDonald's, for example, can be found nearly the world over. The world is quickly becoming homogenized. Are we in North America to blame? What could or should be done to preserve ethnic uniqueness?

4. Many symphony orchestras are wooing younger audiences by offering lighter fare, pops concerts in large arenas, casual dress, and special student subscriptions. What, if anything, would inspire you to attend a symphony concert? While attending a concert, take note of the type of people who are in the audience. What are your findings?

5. Not so long ago, European women were forbidden to perform onstage, and the female characters in operas were played by men. Discuss why so many different cultures might independently have decided that the theater was an inappropriate place for women.

6. Explain how music is used in religious ceremonies or services that you attend. Focus on the type of music played, who participates in singing or music making, and the instruments used (if any).

7. Compare Japanese music to another Japanese art form: for example, cooking, clothing, or calligraphy/graphic arts. What similarities or differences do you see between these cultural expressions?

8. Working with three other students, simulate the cross-rhythms of African drumming. As you provide a slow, steady main pulse (perhaps by tapping on a desk), have each of the others divide it into three, five, and seven beats respectively. Each student should use a different form of percussion (perhaps clapping, stomping, and counting).

9. Think of one of the world music traditions discussed in this chapter. What are the similarities and differences between this musical style and Western music? How do these reflect the similarities and differences between the two cultures or societies? Now, answer these same questions for a musical culture that is *not* described in this book.

CHAPTER 2

The Elements of Music

What Is Music?

What exactly is music?

This sounds like an easy question. We all know music when we hear it. And yet, if you think about it, perhaps it's not so easy to define.

Here are various thoughts about music from writers through the ages, from 400 BCE up to today.

"Music gives soul to the universe."
—Plato
"The food of love."
—Shakespeare
"Heaven is music."
—Thomas Campion
"Without music, life would be a mistake."
—Friedrich Nietzsche
"Music is a decoration of time."
—Frank Zappa
"Music washes away from the soul the dust of everyday life."
—Red Auerbach
"An explosive expression of humanity."
—Billy Joel
"Ah music...a magic far beyond anything done here."
—Albus Dumbledore

There is a difference between music and sound. Not many of us would consider the unpleasant sounds of a jackhammer to be music. But we cannot simply say that unpleasant sounds are noise and pleasant sounds are music. Many of us enjoy listening to the pleasant sounds of nature, such as rain falling or the rustle of leaves, yet we would not call these sounds "music."

We need to sense an element of human organization before we can call something music. In general, we define music as the deliberate organization of sounds by people for other people to hear.

The Elements of Music

Composers rely on certain basic organizing principles to express their ideas in music. Indeed, each art form has its own organizing principles. In literature, for example, we learn about vocabulary, grammar, and rhetoric. In music, the three basic elements are **melody**, **rhythm**, and **harmony**.

Melody

Memorable melodies are an integral part of our lives. Many people sing to themselves as they are walking around, sitting at their desks, or showering. We hear melodies every day: on the radio, on television, at school, and at work. Melodies can be smooth or jagged, short or long, simple or complex. Some melodies, like those in television ads or video games, stick in our heads even if we want to forget them. Popular melodies are an important element of all cultures.

A melody typically consists of different types of **melodic motion**. Melodic motion describes the way the melody moves from note to note. Most melodies contain a mixture of *steps* (movement to adjacent notes), *leaps* (movement to notes more than a step away), and *repeated notes*.

The distinctive quality of a melody is determined by the combination of steps, leaps, and repeated notes.

The melody of "Happy Birthday to You" contains a mixture of steps, leaps, and repeated notes. It is very simple in construction and can be divided into four sections: 1, 2, 3, and 4. Each of these sections is called a **phrase**. A musical phrase is marked by a small pause at its end, like a comma in a sentence. If you sing "Happy Birthday," you will notice that you naturally take a breath at the end of each phrase.

MusicNote 1

Listen to the **Music Notes** on **MySearchLab**

The first phrase starts out with repeated notes and steps on the words "happy birthday." Then there is a leap between "-day" and "to," and then another step between "to" and "you." The second phrase is similar. The third phrase has a much bigger leap (on the words "happy birth-"). That leap is the most memorable part of the melody.

In other ways, the four phrases are very similar. Each is the same length. Each features almost the same rhythm. The difference between the phrases is in their melodic motion and shape.

MusicNote 2

"America," also known as "My Country 'Tis of Thee," has a longer melody than "Happy Birthday," but it too contains phrases of equal length featuring similar rhythm. This melody, however, is made up almost entirely of steps. In fact, if you don't count the leaps that occur *between* phrases, there are only three leaps in the whole song. The first is a downward leap right at the beginning on "-try 'tis." The second, ascending, comes toward the end on "-'ry moun-." And the third, descending again, comes on the single word "let." These are all very small leaps, but they sound big since the rest of the melody is in stepwise motion. The word "let" also has the highest note. These two factors together create a strong climax for the words "let freedom ring!"

"Twinkle, Twinkle, Little Star" is an example of a melody that ends the same way as it begins. Again, all the phrases are the same length, and all the phrases have exactly the same rhythm. You will notice that the last two phrases (5 and 6) are identical to the first two (1 and 2). The middle two (3 and 4) provide contrast. The organizing structure of a composition, whether it is very simple (like this one) or very complex, is known as musical **form**.

The melody of "Twinkle, Twinkle, Little Star" is made up primarily of repeated notes and descending steps, though there is an upward leap at the beginning of the first phrase (and phrase 5). The simple form, the repetitive rhythm, and the pattern of its melodic motion make this a favorite early song for children.

MusicNote 3

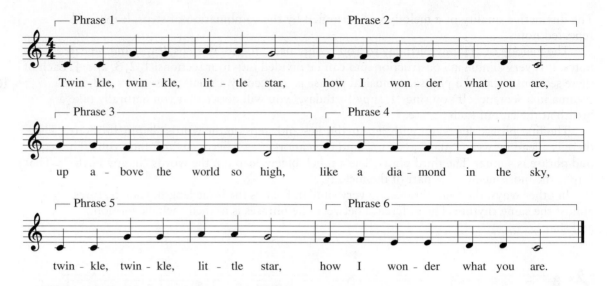

"Happy Birthday," "America," and "Twinkle, Twinkle, Little Star" are very simple melodies. Yet they all exhibit the most important aspects of melody: the mixture of steps, leaps, and repeated notes known as **melodic motion,** and the division into **phrases.** They also demonstrate the idea of organizational **form.**

Pitch

In any melody some notes are higher or lower than others. Pitch is the term used to describe the exact highness or lowness of a note. If you sing the first two words of "Twinkle, Twinkle, Little Star," you will hear that the notes on the second "twinkle" are higher in pitch than those on the first.

Sound is created through vibrations. When an object vibrates, the vibrations are picked up by the ear and transmitted to the brain as sound. The rate (or "frequency") at which the object vibrates determines the pitch that we hear. The faster the vibrations, the higher the pitch. For example, the high note at the top end of a piano has a frequency of 4,186 (that is, it vibrates 4,186 times per second), whereas the low note at the bottom end has a frequency of 27.5.

Most differences in pitch are not so extreme. Two adjacent notes on the piano may have a difference of only about 10 vibrations, but there is still a clear difference in pitch between them. Most of us can hear differences in pitch much smaller than this (for example, on an out-of-tune guitar), and some trained musicians can detect a difference in pitch of only one vibration per second.

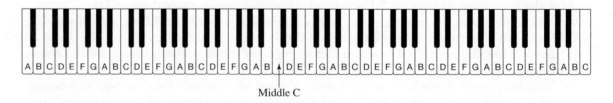

Middle C

Note Names

We use the first seven letters of the alphabet to indicate notes: A, B, C, D, E, F, and G. The seven letter names are repeated again and again for notes of different frequencies. For example, find "middle C" on the piano keyboard. There are lots of other Cs on the piano, both higher and lower. Similarly there are lots of other Ds and Es and so on. All notes with the same name are closely related. The C above middle C, for example, has exactly twice the number of vibrations as middle C. The C below middle C has half the number of vibrations. So these notes are very closely related in pitch. That is why they have the same name.

Intervals

The distance between any two pitches is called an **interval**. The closest possible interval is a **unison**. A unison is made up of two notes on the same pitch. You hear a unison when two different people sing the same note at the same time. But most intervals are made up of combinations of half steps and whole steps. A **half step** is the distance between a white note on the piano and the adjacent black note. A **whole step** is the distance between one white note and the next, if there is a black note in between. (Some of the white notes do not have black notes between them. That is because they are only a half step apart.) In the first phrase of "Happy Birthday," the two notes on the syllables "-py" and "birth-" are a whole step apart.

MusicNote 4

After the unison, the other intervals are the *second*, *third*, *fourth*, *fifth*, *sixth*, *seventh*, and *octave*. You determine the name by counting the distance from one note to the next. (In music, you always count the first note as 1.) The interval from C to F, for example, is a fourth: count C as one, D as two, E as three, and F as four. The interval from C to A is a sixth. If you count up to eight, you'll get to another note of the same name (C up to C, for example). The name for this interval is an **octave**. In "Happy Birthday," the interval between "-py" and "birth-" in the third phrase is an octave.

We use the word *sharp* to indicate a note that is just a half step up from a particular note. For example, the black note just above C on the piano is called "C-sharp (C♯)." We use the word *flat* to indicate a note that is just a half step *down* from a particular note. For example, the black note just below E is called "E-flat (E♭)."

The clever ones among you (and that's all of you, right?) will have noticed something interesting. Look at the C-sharp again. Now find D-flat. Yes, *it's the same note!* Every black key on the piano has two names: D-sharp is the same as E-flat; G-sharp is the same as A-flat; F-sharp is the same as G-flat; and so on.

Here's just one more thing to notice: look again at those white notes that don't have black notes between them. There is no black note between E and F, and there is no black note between B and C. So, for example, E-sharp is the same as F, and C-flat is the same as B.

The quality of sound of each of the intervals can be described in terms of *consonance* and *dissonance*. Generally speaking, an interval is **consonant** when the two notes played together sound pleasing or stable. The most stable or consonant intervals are the unison, the fourth, the fifth, and the octave; somewhat consonant are the third and the sixth.

The intervals of a second, from C to D, and a seventh, from C to the B above it, sound harsh. These intervals are **dissonant**. To our ears, dissonances sound unstable or "unfinished." The harsh dissonances of the second and the seventh seem to require *resolution* to a consonance. We can "resolve" the dissonance of the seventh made by playing C and B together by playing the octave C and C after it. And the interval of the second can be resolved by either moving up to a third or down to a unison. (Unisons are rather hard to play on one piano!)

Dynamics

Loudness and softness, or **dynamics**, are an intrinsic part of the character of most music. A melody can surge and ebb in volume—and there is no quicker way to get an audience's attention than with a sudden change in dynamics.

Dynamics are indicated by a simple system of three letters: *p*, *m*, and *f*, which represent the Italian words *piano* (soft), *mezzo* (medium), and *forte* (loud). The letters are combined to create a wide variety of dynamic markings.

p	piano	soft
mp	mezzo piano	medium soft
pp	pianissimo	very soft
f	forte	loud
mf	mezzo forte	medium loud
ff	fortissimo	very loud

When composers want to indicate a *gradual* change in volume, they use the term **crescendo** for a gradual increase in volume and **decrescendo** or **diminuendo** for a gradual decrease.

LISTENING GUIDE

((•─[Listen on MySearchLab

GEORGE FRIDERIC HANDEL (1685–1759)

From the Water Music

Date of composition: 1717
Orchestration: two trumpets, two horns, oboes, bassoons, and strings
Tempo: *Allegro*
Key: D major
Meter: 4/4
Duration: 1:58

CD I, 4

Let's take a break from this discussion to listen to a wonderful piece of music. It is from Handel's *Water Music*. In the summer of 1717, an English newspaper reported the following about a trip taken by King George I along the river Thames in London:

> On Wednesday evening, at about 8, the King went up the river in an open barge. Many other barges with persons of quality attended. A barge was employed for the orchestra, wherein were fifty instruments of all sorts, which played the whole way the finest music, composed expressly for this occasion by Mr. Handel, which His Majesty liked so much that he caused it to be played over three times.

Listen to some of the music the king heard. Listen first without thinking too much. Just concentrate on the sound and the energy. Now listen again, and think about this music in the context of what you have learned. It presents lots of melodies, which have motion, are divided into phrases, and add up to a larger form. Listen also for pitch, intervals, consonance and dissonance, and dynamics. Listen to just one section at a time. Read what to listen for in each short section first, and then play it.

Time	Listen for
0:00	The piece starts with a single chord. Then we hear two trumpets ringing out. The accompaniment to the trumpets (played on oboes and stringed instruments) has descending runs, which add to the excitement. The **melodic motion** is of repeated notes that go ever higher and then are rounded off. The melody is divided into short **phrases**, the first three of which are very similar to each other, but comprise different **pitches**.
0:09	The music is repeated, but there are significant differences the second time. Can you hear what they are? This time, (1) the instruments playing the melody are two horns instead of two trumpets, and (2) the accompanying runs are played an octave lower (actually one **octave** lower on the first repeat and two octaves lower on the second repeat). These differences are very effective, because they make the whole passage sound like an echo of the trumpet music.
0:18	Very short two-note phrases (down–up), with trumpets and horns alternating. A change of **dynamics** occurs here: the second alternation is played more quietly.
0:22	Short repeated notes in small descending waves. Notice that the accompaniment is in the same rhythm. Again, the melody is echoed in the horns. You might notice that the accompaniment to the horns has a tinkling instrument playing along; this is a harpsichord.
0:30	More military phrases here, like a fanfare. The accompaniment is in a different rhythm. The phrases are again echoed by the horns, and again the accompaniment is an octave lower, in the bass. Throughout the piece, the trumpets and the horns play in pairs. Different intervals are used between them, but the most common interval is a third.
0:45	Short phrases staying around the same pitch.
0:49	Now this is clever: the last part of the short phrases is repeated a couple of times to make a new phrase. But this is played by only one of the instruments (trumpet/horn). The other holds a high note, which then gets louder (**crescendo**) and rounds off the section.
0:58	Now Handel intensifies the music by introducing much shorter notes that go back and forth and reach a long, high note before rounding off.

1:13	Handel saves his most brilliant idea for the last section of the piece. All along, as we have seen, every phrase has been played first by the trumpets and then echoed by the horns. Now the composer *combines* the trumpets and horns to get the fullest possible sound. He also brings back the accompanying descending runs from the very beginning of the piece. The melody is played in longer notes that gradually descend. Since every phrase in the whole piece so far has been repeated, this time Handel also repeats this phrase; but just to get a little variety and final intensity, he divides each of the longer notes into two (*de-de de-de* **daa** instead of *da da* **daa**).
1:30	Four short chords end the whole piece.

This is wonderful music. No wonder the king wanted to hear it three times! Later in this chapter we'll analyze it again. Here, we have seen how the music can be analyzed in terms of melodic motion, how it is divided very clearly into phrases, and how these phrases give the piece its form. We have also heard differences in pitch and noticed some intervals. We can hear that the music is almost entirely consonant throughout. We should also note that the dynamics are mostly *forte* (loud) with occasional crescendos to *fortissimo* (very loud). Remember, the sound had to carry across water!

Rhythm

When we analyzed simple melodies ("Happy Birthday," "America," and "Twinkle, Twinkle, Little Star") and when we listened to Handel's *Water Music*, I had to sneak in an occasional reference to the second main organizing principle of music: rhythm. Rhythm is a fundamental component of all music.

If a melody is sung without its rhythm, it immediately loses much of its essence. Rhythm is as fundamental to music as pitch, possibly even more so. Rhythm is built into our bodies: there is rhythm in the beating of our hearts and in the motion of our limbs when we walk. Rhythm is one of the most important distinguishing features in music.

Beat If you are listening to music and find yourself tapping your finger on the table or your foot on the floor, then you are following the **beat**. You are responding to the *regular pulse* of the music. If you tap a steady, even rhythm while singing "Happy Birthday," the rhythm that you tap is the beat. Try it a couple of times.

MusicNote 5

You will notice that on the syllable "-py" of "happy," you are singing a note, but there is no accompanying beat. This is because the two notes of "happy" are contained in the same beat. On the other hand, when you sing "you," the note is held for two beats. All the other syllables receive one beat each.

In the case of "Happy Birthday," the beat corresponds to one **quarter note**. It's called a quarter note because *usually* there are four of them in a unit, and the unit is called a whole note. We'll get into this more in a minute. In a lot of music, the quarter note is the basic "unit" for measuring the beat.

If a quarter note equals one "beat," then a half note equals "two beats," and a whole note "four beats." Moving down in value, an eighth note (written like a quarter note with a single flag on the stem) is a half-beat; a sixteenth note (two flags) is a quarter-beat; and a thirty-second note (three flags) is an eighth-beat. Corresponding to all these note values are **rests**, which indicate units of pause or silence.

When the beat is steady, each row of this chart will take the same amount of time to play. You can see just how fast thirty-second notes might be!

Notes	Rests	Name
		whole
		half
		quarter
		eighth
		sixteenth
		thirty-second

Measure and Meter   When musicians say that a certain melody or theme is in two-four or six-eight "time," they are referring to the number of beats in a measure. A measure is a grouping of beats. In most music, every measure in the piece has the same number of beats. The measures are marked off by **bar lines** (small vertical lines). **Meter** describes the *number* and the *length* of the beats in each measure. The **time signature**, one number placed above another, is a symbol that gives the player this information. The upper number tells the number of beats in the measure, the lower note the value of each beat (see accompanying chart).

MusicNote 6   For example, if the measures each contain three quarter-note beats, then we say that the meter is $\frac{3}{4}$. The upper number (3) indicates that there are three beats in a measure; the lower number (4) indicates that the value of each beat is a quarter note.

TIME SIGNATURE	EXPLANATION	EXAMPLE
Duple Meters		
$\frac{2}{4}$	Two beats per measure; quarter note = one beat	"Yankee Doodle"
$\frac{4}{4}$	Four beats per measure; quarter note = one beat	"When the Saints Go Marching In"
Triple Meters		
$\frac{3}{8}$	Three beats per measure, eighth note = one beat	"I Feel Pretty"
$\frac{3}{4}$	Three beats per measure, quarter note = one beat	"Happy Birthday to You"

Duple meters are those whose upper number (the number of beats) is divisible by two. Duple meters sound firm and solid. Marches, for example, are always in duple meter. **Triple** meters tend to be graceful or flowing. Waltzes are in $\frac{3}{4}$ meter.

There is one other meter you are likely to come across fairly frequently, and that is $\frac{6}{8}$ (six eighth notes to a measure). The eighth notes are divided into two groups of three, and here each *group* gets the beat. $\frac{6}{8}$ meter has a very special feel to it. Melodies in $\frac{6}{8}$, such as "Row, Row, Row Your Boat" and "Greensleeves," often have a gentle, lilting, slightly swinging quality. Other well-known melodies in $\frac{6}{8}$ include the lullaby "Rock-A-Bye Baby" and "Take Me Out to the Ball Game."

Syncopation   Sometimes a melody contains notes that seem to come ahead of the beat. When this happens, the rhythm is said to be **syncopated**. Tap your foot or your finger lightly as you sing through the first lines of Stephen Foster's "Camptown Races," paying special attention to the rhythm on the words "doo-dah, doo-dah."

MusicNote 7

These measures are syncopated. Instead of placing "dah" directly on the beat, the composer placed it ahead of the beat, making for a much livelier rhythm. Try it again, and see how the syncopation pushes the melody along. Now try singing "dah" a little later, right on the beat. See how dull and plodding it sounds?

Syncopation makes you "feel" the rhythm physically, so it's often used in dance music and jazz. It gives the music a special rhythmic drive.

Tempo

A composer usually indicates the speed, or **tempo,** at which a piece should be played. This can be done in two different ways. Sometimes composers use both methods in the same piece.

The first way is to use a general indication in words at the beginning of a piece. These indications often appear in Italian; the most common are listed here. You'll notice that some of them indicate the character or *spirit* in which the piece is to be played, as well as the speed.

Largo	Broad
Adagio	Easy
Andante	At a walking pace
Moderato	Moderate
Allegro	Fast
Vivace	Lively
Presto	Very fast

The second way to indicate tempo is by means of a **metronome marking.** A metronome is a machine that can be set to click regularly at a specified tempo. The composer might indicate, for example, ♩ = 60 or ♩ = 96. This means that the quarter notes should be played at the rate of 60 per minute (one every second) or 96 per minute. Performers often check their metronomes before practicing a piece, to get a clearer idea of what tempo the composer intended.

Musicians realize, however, that music is a living, breathing thing and not a machine. A metronome speed is rarely maintained exactly throughout a piece. It is usually used only as a guide.

LISTENING GUIDE

((•⸱ **Listen** on **MySearchLab**

GEORGE FRIDERIC HANDEL (1685–1759)   *From the* Water Music

Date of composition: 1717
Orchestration: two trumpets, two horns, oboes, bassoons, and strings
Tempo: *Allegro*
Meter: ⁴⁄₄
Key: D major
Duration: 1:58

CD I, 4

Let's listen again to Handel's *Water Music* and think of it this time in terms of its rhythm. We will consider the **beat, measures and meter, syncopation,** and **tempo.**

Time	Listen for
0:00	In this section, the **beat** is firmly established. It's the beat that you tap your foot to. You'll find yourself tapping to the first chord and to the three repeated notes of each trumpet phrase. These are all **quarter notes.** The **tempo** is quite fast (*Allegro*).
0:09	Keep tapping your foot as the horns play.
0:18	In this section each note is on the beat.
0:22	Two notes to a beat here (*de-de, de-de…*). These are **eighth notes.**
0:30	This is the military, bouncy, fanfare-like rhythm. The accompaniment, however, has even eighth notes.
0:45	Short phrases staying around the same pitch, mostly eighth notes.

0:49	The very short notes in these phrases are **sixteenth notes**.
0:58	Most of the notes now are sixteenth notes (four to a beat: *diddlediddle*).
1:13	Now let's start concentrating on **measure and meter**. You have probably noticed that there is a heavier accent every four beats of the music. If you tap your foot and count **one** on the heavier accent and *two, three, four* on the lighter ones, you'll see that there are four beats to every measure. This means that the meter is ⁴⁄₄: four beats (each a quarter note) to every measure.
1:30	Four quarter-note chords end the whole piece. These chords have quarter-note rests between them, which make them particularly effective. Rests are used before this point, of course, when some of the instruments aren't playing, but here, when all the instruments are silent, we can really *hear* the rests.

We've figured out that the **meter** in this piece is ⁴⁄₄, that the **beat** is very steady, and that the **tempo** is *Allegro*. The piece doesn't seem to have any **syncopation** (off-beat accents), so the rhythm is very straightforward. To make sure that this is all clear to you, listen to the music again and follow the outline. Remember, I said at the beginning of the chapter that the two most important things about listening to music are concentrating carefully and listening several times.

Harmony

The third basic element of music is harmony.

Keynote The melodies we have studied ("Happy Birthday," "America," and "Twinkle, Twinkle, Little Star") have one feature in common, one that is shared by almost every memorable tune: each is dominated by a **keynote**. If you sing "Twinkle, Twinkle, Little Star" and stop at the end of phrase 4 ("like a diamond in the sky"), the melody will sound incomplete. This happens because phrase 4 does not end on the keynote of the melody. The keynote of "Twinkle, Twinkle" comes at the end of the last phrase. Only when you reach that note does the melody sound finished. In "Twinkle, Twinkle" the last note is C. We call the last note the keynote (or **tonic**) of the piece.

Because C is the keynote, "Twinkle, Twinkle, Little Star" can be said to be *in the key* of C.

Keys and Scales Most musical compositions begin and end in the same key, and this provides a sense of stability to the music. A key is a bit like gravity: it keeps everything in place.

Because the keynote of "Twinkle, Twinkle" is C, the song uses notes from the *scale* of C to form its melody. A **scale** is a group of notes arranged in an ascending or descending order. If you play all the white notes on the piano going up from middle C to the C an octave above it, you've just played a scale—the scale of C major.

MusicNote 8

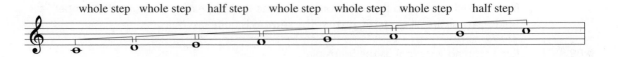

The C-major scale is made up of a series of half steps and whole steps. Play the scale of C major again, or look at it on the diagram. Between C and D there is a whole step. Between D and E there is a whole step. Between E and F there is a *half* step. F to G is a whole step. G to A is a whole step. A to B is a whole step. B to C is another half step. So the pattern of intervals in this scale is whole, whole, half, whole, whole, whole, half. *All major scales use this same pattern: whole, whole, half, whole, whole, whole, half.* You can create any major scale by starting on any note and reproducing this pattern of intervals.

Try the scale of G major. Start on G and go up, keeping the same pattern of intervals. The pattern again is whole, whole, half, whole, whole, whole, half. Start on G. Then go to A (a whole step from G), then B (a whole step from A), then C (a half step from B), then D (a whole step from C), then E (a whole step from D), then F-sharp (a whole step from E), and finally G (a half step from F-sharp). You'll see that to keep the pattern, you have to use an F-sharp instead of a plain F. So the scale of G major looks like this:

MusicNote 9

The same pattern applies to any major scale: just start on the keynote and keep the interval pattern exact. You'll see that some major scales need quite a few sharps or flats.

When a composer writes a piece *in the key of C*, he or she uses notes from the C-major scale. Now let's look back at the melody of "Happy Birthday." The melody ends on G, so the keynote is probably G. (Most melodies end on their keynote.) The notes used for this melody are from the G-major scale (G, A, B, C, D, E, F-sharp, G), so "Happy Birthday" is in the key of G.

Major and Minor Scales   There are two main types of scales: major and minor. Pieces that use a **major scale** are said to be in the major *mode*; pieces using a **minor scale** are said to be in the minor mode. As we will see, there is a difference in sound between the two modes. Many people say that pieces written in major keys sound positive or optimistic and that pieces written in minor keys sound a little sad or thoughtful. That difference is created by *differences in the pattern of the intervals.*

The minor scale uses whole and half steps, but the arrangement is different from that of the major scale. The pattern in the minor scale is this: whole step, half step, whole step, whole step, half step, whole step, whole step. The easiest minor scale is A minor, because it has no sharps or flats. So if you play the white notes on the piano starting on A, you get the minor-mode pattern. But a minor scale can be built on any note, just as a major scale can. Start on D and keep the pattern: *whole step, half step, whole step, whole step, half step, whole step, whole step*. Here's D minor, with the same pattern of intervals: D, E, F, G, A, B-flat, C, D.

MusicNote 10

MusicNote 11

As you can see, D minor needs one flat. Try building other minor scales. For example, try building C minor. You'll see that C minor needs *three* flats: B-flat, E-flat, and A-flat.

Major-key pieces *sound* different from minor-key pieces. Pieces in a major key usually sound bright, positive, or cheerful, whereas pieces in a minor key sound more serious—even a little sad. Notice the difference in the sound of "Twinkle, Twinkle, Little Star" if we change it from C major to C minor.

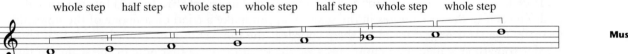

Twin - kle, twin - kle, lit - tle star, how I won - der what you are.

MusicNote 12

A well-known song in the minor mode is "All the Pretty Little Horses." This beautiful song is in D minor. And the Beatles' "While My Guitar Gently Weeps" is in the key of A minor.

There are many other kinds of scales. For example, a scale that is made up entirely of half steps (all the adjacent black and white notes on the piano) is called the **chromatic scale**. There is also a scale called the **pentatonic scale**, which has only five notes in it. Some Asian music uses the pentatonic scale.

MusicNote 13

MusicNotes 14–16

Related Keys When we constructed the G-major scale, we needed an F-sharp to keep to the pattern. But there is another key that always has an F-sharp, and that is the key of E minor. If you construct the minor scale on E following the correct interval pattern, you get the following: E, F-sharp, G, A, B, C, D, E. Because they use the same notes, E minor and G major are said to be *related* keys, or *relatives*. (They have different keynotes, though.) Each major key has a relative minor and vice versa. The relative minor of C major, for example, is A minor. (Both have no sharps or flats.) And the relative major of D minor is F major. (Each has one flat.)

When a composition is in a particular key, most of the notes in it are taken from the scale of that key, both in the melody and in the accompaniment. If a piece is quite long, then it is likely to wander into other keys before returning to the home key at the end. The process of moving from one key to another in music is called **modulation**. Modulation adds interest to music. It is another technique that composers use to vary the mood, like changes in tempo or dynamics.

Chords Although melodies can be sung unaccompanied, most of them have accompaniment. Accompaniment adds depth and richness to a melody. **Harmony** is the combination of a melody and its accompaniment. A composer can create different moods and feelings by changing the harmony in a piece of music.

MusicNote 17

A **chord** is formed when three or more different notes are played together. The intervals among these notes determine whether the chord is consonant or dissonant. The most common consonant chord is the **triad**, which consists of one primary note (called the "root") and two other notes, one a third above it and the other a fifth above it. This is the most frequently used of all chords. Let's build a triad on the root C. A third above C is E, and a fifth above C is G. So a triad on C would consist of the chord C–E–G.

MusicNote 18

Both of the notes above the root are consonant with it, creating a very stable overall sound. If the notes are played one after another, rather than all at once, the result is called an **arpeggio**. An arpeggio contains the notes of a chord played consecutively rather than simultaneously.

Sometimes composers write a triad with the notes rearranged, so that the third or the fifth, or both, lie *below* the root. The C chord can be spelled E–C–G, or E–G–C, or G–E–C, or G–C–E. All these chords sound slightly different, but the root in each case remains C, because that is the primary note of the triad.

MusicNote 19

Triads can be built on any root. Let's build a triad on F. A third above F is A; a fifth above F is C. So a triad on F is F–A–C.

Like scales, triads can be either major or minor. The difference depends on whether you count up the major or minor scale to find your chord notes.

Each key has a series of chords associated with it. The chords are formed by constructing triads on each of the seven notes in the scale. You can make a triad on any one of the notes in the scale. The most important of all these chords is the **tonic** chord, built on the keynote. This chord is sometimes called the I chord, because the keynote is the first note of the scale. (In music we use Roman numerals to designate chords.) More often than not, a piece will begin and end with the tonic chord, thereby establishing the key at the beginning of the piece and reaffirming it at the end.

MusicNote 20

The **dominant** chord (chord V) in a key is second in importance to the tonic chord. It is built on the fifth note of the scale; so, for example, the dominant chord in C major is built on G. This chord has the notes G–B–D (root–third–fifth). The dominant chord in any key always sounds as though it requires resolution back to the tonic chord.

The effect of the chord progression I–V–I is the same whether it is played in C major or in any other key.

There are dozens of other possible chords, of course. And many of them have more than three notes in them. Some chords imply movement to another chord; this implication provides a sense of direction to the music. The movement from one chord to the next is called a **chord progression**.

Cadences Cadences in music are like punctuation in grammar. They provide stopping points in the flow of the discourse. Stopping points in grammar have varying degrees of strength. A period marks the end of a sentence. A comma sets off a phrase. A semicolon provides both closure and continuity.

There are three main types of musical cadences: the authentic (or full) cadence, the plagal cadence, and the half cadence. Each consists of a different progression of two chords.

An **authentic** or **full cadence** consists of a V chord followed by a I chord. It is used to mark the ends of phrases or sections in a composition and to mark the end of the entire piece. You heard several authentic cadences in the *Water Music*.

MusicNote 21

The **plagal cadence**, on the other hand, consists of a IV chord (known as the **subdominant** chord) followed by a I chord. If you play these two chords consecutively, you will notice that the cadence is not as definitive or forthright as the authentic cadence. The plagal cadence is often called the "Amen" cadence, because it is frequently used to close hymns or liturgical pieces.

MusicNote 22

Both the authentic and plagal cadences end on a tonic chord (I). The **half cadence** ends on the dominant (V) chord, so it lacks the finality of the authentic and plagal cadences. It may be preceded by a IV chord or a I chord; in either case, it provides a pause at the end of a musical phrase, but not an actual ending. It leaves the listener with the sense that there is more music to come.

MusicNote 23

Texture   An important aspect of harmony is what is known as the **texture** of music. Texture describes the way in which different musical sounds are combined. One kind of texture, for example, is known as **monophony**. Monophony is a texture that involves melody with *no* accompaniment. Monophony can be produced by one or more people. A single person singing in the shower or a family singing in a car is usually singing monophony. Monophonic texture means solo singing or singing in unison.

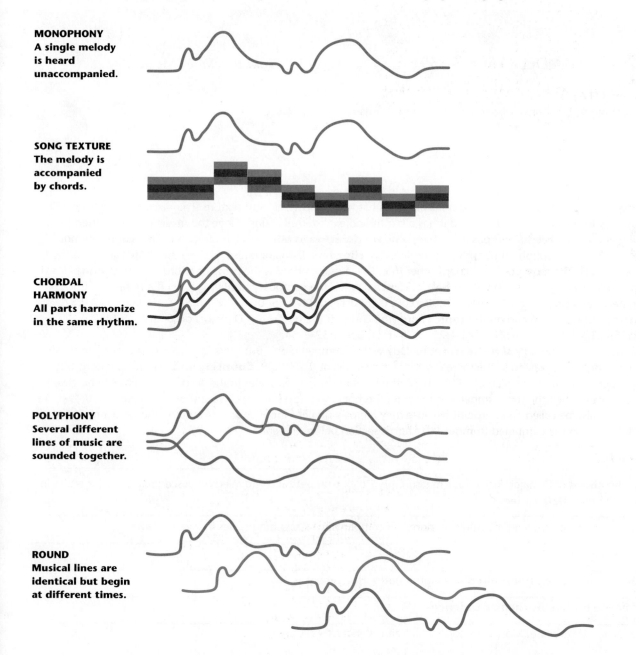

MONOPHONY
A single melody is heard unaccompanied.

SONG TEXTURE
The melody is accompanied by chords.

CHORDAL HARMONY
All parts harmonize in the same rhythm.

POLYPHONY
Several different lines of music are sounded together.

ROUND
Musical lines are identical but begin at different times.

MusicNote 24   Homophony is music that moves by chords. The most common form of homophony, sometimes called **song texture**, involves a solo voice with chordal accompaniment, such as a folk singer accompanying him- or herself on the guitar. Song texture can also be used to describe instrumental music—for example, a solo instrument playing a melody with an accompaniment.

MusicNote 25   Polyphony, on the other hand, is music in which you can hear two or more distinct musical lines at once. This kind of texture is obviously more complex. Much Western classical music—a Beethoven symphony, for example—is at least partly polyphonic. If you listen carefully, you can hear several different musical lines at the same time.

The musical texture in which the separate musical lines are particularly clear and stay inde-
MusicNote 26   pendent more or less throughout a piece is called **counterpoint**. A special kind of counterpoint is
MusicNote 27   the **round** (for example, "Row, Row, Row Your Boat"), in which one musical line is sung at stag-
gered intervals to produce interweaving lines.

These textures may be easier to remember if you consider them visually. Look carefully at the accompanying diagram.

LISTENING GUIDE   ((•─Listen on **MySearchLab**

GEORGE FRIDERIC HANDEL (1685–1759)   *From the* Water Music

Date of composition: 1717
Orchestration: two trumpets, two horns, oboes, bassoons, and strings
Tempo: *Allegro*
Key: D major
Meter: $\frac{4}{4}$
Duration: 1:58

CD I, 4

Let's listen once more to Handel's *Water Music*, and think about its harmony, cadences, and texture. The piece is in the **key** of D major. This is a good key for trumpets to play in, and it has a bright and extroverted sound. Since the music was composed for the outdoors, everything about it is cheerful and positive. There is no **modulation** to other keys; it remains in D major throughout. Because the piece is in D major throughout doesn't mean that every **chord** is a D-major chord. Rather, the chords are all formed on notes from the *scale* of D. The most common chord other than the D-major chord is the A-major chord, the **dominant** chord of the key of D major. It is used most prominently in **half cadences**, when the composer wants to close off a phrase, but not halt the music. You can hear half cadences on A major at 0:08–0:09, 0:15–0:17, 0:24–0:25, 0:28–0:29, 0:52–0:53, and 0:56–0:57. **Authentic cadences**, cadences that end on the **tonic** chord (the chord of the home key, D major) occur at 0:35–0:37, 0:44–0:45, 1:04–1:05, 1:12–1:13, 1:20–1:21, 1:28–1:29, 1:30–1:31, and 1:32–1:34.

The **texture** of the music is primarily **song texture**: melody with accompaniment. But there are some passages of homophony, when all the instruments are playing in the same rhythm, for example at 0:18–0:29. **Counterpoint** is used sparingly, but to telling effect. In the opening section, for example, 0:00–0:17, the rushing downward scales in the accompaniment can be clearly heard as independent lines. When the top trumpet and the top horn hold long notes and then round off the phrase (at 0:49–0:53 and 0:53–0:57), this can also be called counterpoint because they are playing lines independent from the other instruments. And the downward scales return in the combined trumpets-and-horns section before the end (1:14–1:29).

Time	Listen for
0:00	Opening **chord** of D major. Rising four-measure phrase by trumpets accompanied by descending D-major scales in sixteenth notes. **Half cadence**.
0:09	Repeat ("echo") of opening measures on horns. Accompanying descending scales in lower octaves.
0:18	Half-measure phrases.
0:22	Two-measure phrases, **homophonic** in eighth notes. Half cadences.
0:30	Fanfare-like rhythm. **Authentic cadences**.
0:45	Phrases of one measure. Mostly homophonic. Half cadences.

0:49	Continuing closing gesture of previous phrases. Two-measure phrases. Solo instruments in **counterpoint**. Half cadences.
0:58	Four-measure phrases using sixteenth notes. Authentic cadences.
1:13	Trumpets *and* horns and whole orchestra combine for closing passages. Four-measure phrases in descending pattern match the opening. Descending scales return as accompaniment. "Echo" repetition breaks quarter notes into eighths. Authentic cadences.
1:30	Four quarter-note chords separated by rests. Authentic cadences. End of movement.

We have discussed melody, rhythm, and harmony, the main elements of music. Now let's complete the picture by looking at aspects of form, sound, performance, and musical style.

Musical Form

All art needs form. A book is written in words that are made up of letters and arranged into sentences; sentences are organized into paragraphs; and the whole book is divided into sections or chapters. Similarly, musical flow is carefully organized into notes, melodies, chords, phrases, sections, **movements** (long, self-contained units of a larger work), and entire works. Structure is vital to music. It enables us to make sense of what we hear.

The organizing structure of a piece of music is known as its **form**. We can look at form in music in short pieces. Let's look again at "Twinkle, Twinkle, Little Star." We already noticed that the first four measures are repeated in measures 9–12 (see pages 19–20). We can label both of these sections A. (Using letters makes musical analysis much simpler.) Measures 5–8, however, are different from measures 1–4, so we can label that section B.

This melody may therefore be described as being in ABA form, otherwise known as **ternary form**. This is the most frequent form in small units such as melodies and themes. But ternary form is also quite common on a far larger scale in music. It is one of the forms that can be used for a whole movement. Occasionally, composers even use a type of ABA form for an entire composition. People seem to find the idea of departure-and-return musically very satisfying. Sometimes the A section returns slightly modified; the form is then indicated as ABA'.

Binary form focuses on the idea of contrast. There are two sections, A and B, each of which is usually repeated to make the pattern AABB.

Sonata form, employed as the structure for many large movements, uses both the idea of contrast and the idea of departure-and-return. A movement in sonata form begins with a large opening section, which contains two contrasting smaller units. This is followed by a middle section that contrasts with the opening in harmony, tonality, atmosphere, and presentation of thematic material. After this contrasting section, the opening section recurs, modified.

Theme and variations form also involves the idea of contrast. A theme is presented and then played several more times, but each time it recurs it is varied in some way: in melody, rhythm, dynamics, tempo, or harmony. In each variation, the theme is recognizably changed and yet recognizably the same.

MusicNote 28

Jazz and Rock Forms

Two forms basic to jazz and rock are the **12-bar blues** and **32-bar AABA form**. Both of these forms depend on repeated patterns of chord progressions. The 12-bar blues has three lines of verse, with the second line being a repeat of the first. For example, let's make up a blues song. The first line might go something like this:

I'm bored to death with all this music stuff.

Then the second line is an almost exact repetition of the first:

Yeah, I'm just bored to death with all this music stuff.

And the third line would rhyme with the first two:

Gotta tell my teacher that I've really had enough.

So now you have the three lines of verse, and each line gets four measures of music.

MusicNote 29

I'm bored to death with all this music stuff. (4 measures)
Yeah, I'm just bored to death with all this music stuff. (4 measures)
Gotta tell my teacher that I've really had enough. (4 measures)

That gives you twelve measures, or bars, of music—hence, the 12-bar blues form.

The harmony of the 12-bar blues is fairly simple. The first four measures are accompanied by the I chord. Measures 5 and 6 use the IV chord, then back to I for measures 7 and 8. Measure 9 uses V, measure 10 uses IV, and then measures 11 and 12 go back to I. So the whole pattern looks like this:

I	I	I	I	(measures 1–4)
IV	IV	I	I	(measures 5–8)
V	IV	I	I	(measures 9–12)

If you can play three notes on the piano, you can play the blues. Let's try it in C. The I chord is C–E–G. The IV chord is F–A–C. And the V chord is G–B–D. Go for it!

Now make up your own blues lyrics. All you need are two lines (preferably with five accented syllables) that rhyme. Then sing them with those three chords. Voilà! You're singing the blues.

The **32-bar AABA form** sounds complicated, but it's not. Many, many songs use this form, especially older ones. Here the uppercase letters stand for eight measures of music. So you start with an eight-measure phrase. Let's sing:

Deck the **halls** with **boughs** of **holly**, Fa-la-la-la-la, la-la-la la.

That's the first A. And it's set to eight measures of music. Now the second A is next. It has different words, of course, but exactly the same music:

'**Tis** the **season** to be **jolly**, Fa-la-la-la-la, la-la-la la.

Now the B section starts. It is made up of another eight bars, but it has different music, to provide contrast:

Don we **now** our **gay** apparel [higher] Fa-la-la, fa-la-la, la-la-la.

And the final eight bars of the A music starts again:

Troll the **ancient Yule**-tide **carol** Fa-la-la-la-la, la-la-la la.

That's 32-bar form. Do you know how many thousands of songs use this form? Neither do I.

Sound

The first thing that strikes you when you first hear a piece of music is the **sound**. Who or what is making the music? Is it a rock band? A church choir? A symphony orchestra? The kind of sound you hear will greatly influence the way you experience the music.

Making Music: Voices

Singing is one of the most widespread ways of making music. Almost all people sing, whether they can carry a tune or not. Some people sing in the shower, walking along the street, driving their car, or just lying in bed. Others whistle or hum all the time.

Singing can be done alone or in groups. Workers around the world have devised ways of singing together that help them work, lighten their loads, and create a sense of togetherness. Songs can also create a sense of national identity. Every country has its own national anthem. On a smaller level, songs can confirm a sense of belonging to a recognizable group, such as when people sing their school song or the latest pop hit.

Find the **Quick Listen** on **MySearchLab**

"National Anthem Marvin Gaye"

Songs can also evoke a strong sense of nostalgia. People often have only to hear a tune to recapture the entire atmosphere of an event or period in their lives.

Some music allows quite informal standards of singing. Family sing-alongs, folk songs, and most rock songs are like this. Jazz singing, however, is quite specialized. Jazz singers use their voices in very special ways, with "slides" between notes and with "bent" or "blue" notes. They also perfect a kind of singing that uses nonverbal syllables like "boo-dee-ba-doo-bah" (this is called "scat" singing), in which the voice is used as a kind of very flexible instrument.

Singing classical music also takes a great deal of training. The voice must be carefully controlled for pitch and dynamics. Breathing has to be developed so that long phrases can be sung. And singers have to learn how to sing clearly in several different languages.

An outdoor "sing" in Sweden.

In folk, rock, and jazz, singers are simply divided into men's and women's voices. In classical music, however, there are several voice classifications, depending on the range of the voice. The high women's range is known as *soprano*; the low women's range is called *alto* or *contralto*. The high men's range is called *tenor*, the low men's range *bass*. There are two intermediate voice ranges as well. A voice between soprano and alto is known as *mezzo-soprano*; a voice between tenor and bass is known as *baritone*.

	WOMEN	MEN
High:	Soprano	Tenor
Medium:	Mezzo-Soprano	Baritone
Low:	Alto	Bass

Find the **Quick Listen** on **MySearchLab**

"High Soprano Notes/Low Bass Notes"

MusicNote 30

It is possible for men and women to make their voices go higher artificially. This type of singing, called *falsetto*, is hard to control precisely, but it can be perfected with practice.

Making Music: Instruments

Playing instruments also has a very long history. Some of the oldest surviving instruments are thousands of years old.

Around the world, people have devised many ways of creating musical instruments. In the Caribbean, instruments called steel drums are made from used oil barrels. In Africa, a musical bow is made from a stick, a string, and a gourd. In the Middle East, a type of double-reed pipe is made from unequal lengths of narrow bamboo cane.

Apart from the way they are made, what most distinguishes one instrument from another is the **tone color**, or **timbre**, of the sound it makes. A flute playing a certain pitch sounds very different from a guitar playing exactly the same pitch. [MusicNote 31]

Instruments can play alone or together in small or large groups. Examples of small groups include a rock band, a jazz combo, or a chamber group. In classic rock, the group is usually made up of lead guitar, rhythm guitar, bass guitar, and drums. A common jazz combo is one or two "horns" (trumpet or saxophone) plus a "rhythm section," made up of piano, bass, and drums. **Chamber music** is classical music played by a small group of instruments. A chamber ensemble can range from a single violin and a piano to a **string quartet** (two violins, one viola, and one cello) to a group of up to eight or ten instruments. Examples of large groups include a marching band and a classical orchestra.

A steel-drum band.

The Orchestra

The term *orchestra* is used loosely to describe any large group of instrumental musicians playing together at one time. It generally refers to a classical group, though some jazz bands call themselves orchestras. The size of a classical orchestra can vary considerably depending on the work being played. The instruments of the modern classical orchestra are divided into four groups: strings, woodwinds, brass, and percussion.

Watch the **Inside the Orchestra** video on **MySearchLab**

Musical bow from Africa.

Strings

Four stringed instruments are permanent members of the classical orchestra: violin, viola, violoncello (cello), and double bass. The violin is the smallest and the highest in pitch; the viola is slightly larger than the violin and consequently lower in pitch; the cello plays in the tenor and baritone ranges; and the double bass is the largest and the lowest in pitch of all the stringed instruments. These four instruments are all related, and their appearance and construction are similar.

MusicNote 32

The **violin** is small enough to be held under the chin by the performer as it is played. It is one of the most versatile instruments of the orchestra. It has a wide range and is very expressive. For these reasons, a great deal of music is written for solo violin. But the most recognizable violin sound is that of many violins playing together in an orchestra. An orchestra usually has two groups of violins that play different notes. The instruments are the same in each group.

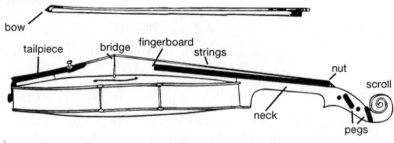

The main parts of a string instrument.

The **viola** is played in the same manner as the violin, but it is slightly larger, deeper in pitch, and mellower in sound. The viola does not usually play as many solo melodies as the violin does, yet its dark tone quality is an essential component of the string section of an orchestra. The viola usually plays in the middle range, filling in harmonies and enriching the sound. **[MusicNote 33]**

The rich, romantic sound of the **cello** is very special. The cello is quite large, so it is held between the knees rather than under the chin. A spike protruding from the bottom of the instrument helps to support the weight. **[MusicNote 34]**

The largest and deepest member of the string family is the **double bass**. Whereas a cellist always plays sitting down, the double bass player either stands in place or sits on a high stool. Although the double bass cannot be played with as much agility as the cello, it provides a firm harmonic bass for the string section and for the entire orchestra. When many double basses play together, the sound is strong, deep, and rich. In jazz, the bass is played mostly by plucking the strings, though sometimes the bow is used. **[MusicNote 35]**

All four stringed instruments are usually played with a bow made of horsehairs stretched on a stick. The hairs are drawn across the strings, producing the sustained, intense sound that is characteristic of stringed instruments. The player's right hand holds the bow, and the way he or she draws the bow across the strings determines the character of the sound. The fingers of the left hand control the pitch of the sound. There are four strings, each tuned to a different note, and the player can change the pitch on any of the strings by pressing it down on the fingerboard at a certain point. It is extremely difficult to find the exact position on the string for each note while at the same time controlling the speed and the pressure of the bow. Stringed instruments are among the hardest to learn.

Cello.

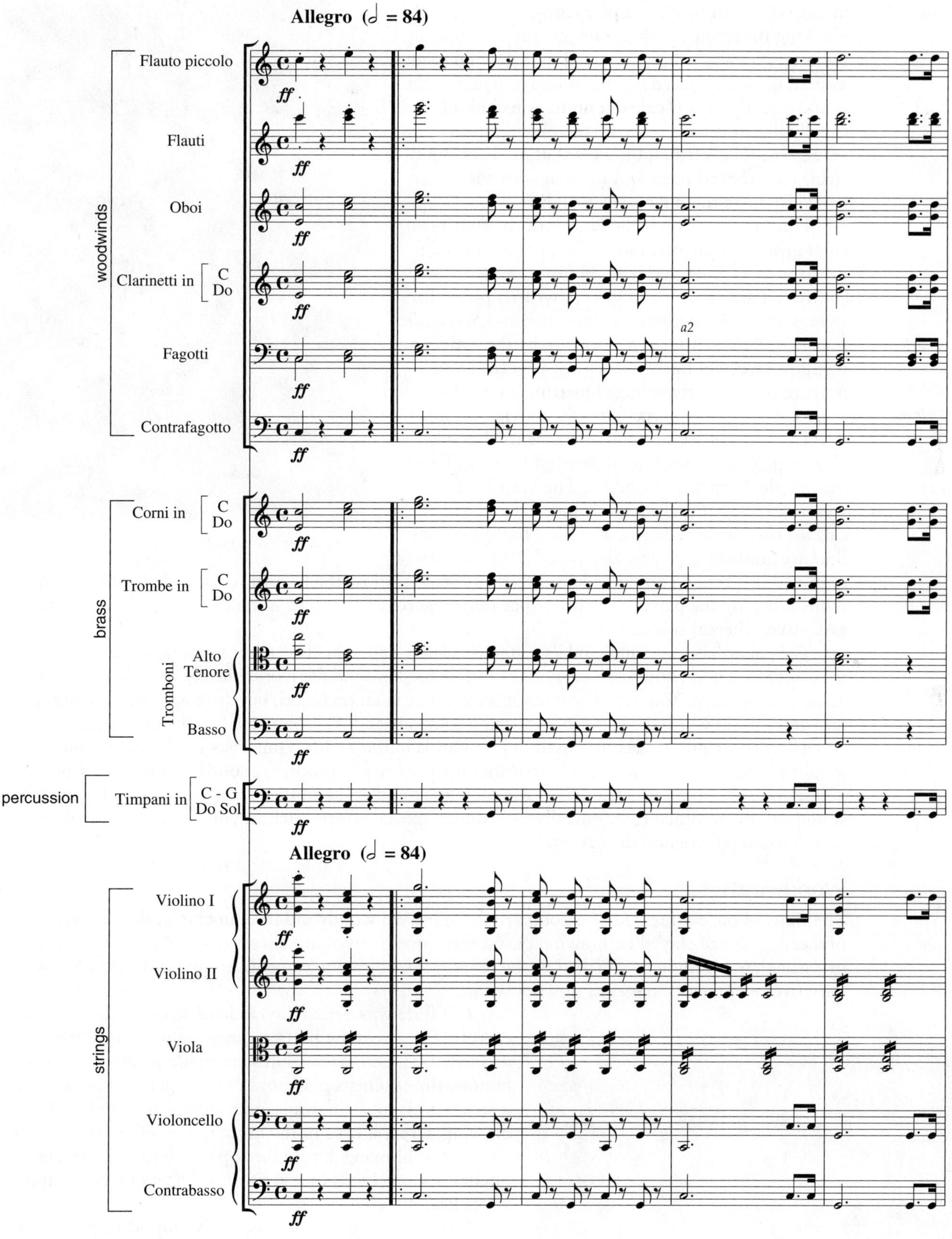

A printed musical score.

MusicNote 36

A variety of techniques have been developed to increase the sound possibilities of stringed instruments. They can be played **pizzicato**—that is, by plucking the strings with the fingers instead of using the bow (the way a bass is played in jazz). Sometimes a small device is placed on the bridge to dampen the sound slightly: this is called a **mute**. A technique called **vibrato** is used to make the playing more expressive. The left-hand fingers that are pressing the strings are rocked back and forth against the fingerboard to make the pitch waver slightly.

The string section is the largest of the four principal groups of the orchestra. The instruments complement each other perfectly. Many composers, such as Mozart and Tchaikovsky, have written pieces for strings alone (*Eine kleine Nachtmusik* and *Serenade for Strings*). The *Adagio for Strings*, by the American composer Samuel Barber, is a most beautiful and moving piece just for stringed instruments. (This piece is the famous music from the movie *Platoon*.)

Find the **Quick Listen** on **MySearchLab** *"Adagio for Strings"*

There are other stringed instruments that are always played by plucking instead of bowing. These include the harp and the guitar. The **harp** is often seen in expanded orchestras. Some very big pieces call for two or more harps. The harp has 42 strings that are graduated in size. Sharp and flat notes are obtained by pressing down pedals. The many strings allow the harpist to play **glissando**, a technique whereby the player runs his or her fingers across the strings in quick succession, creating an evocative, ethereal sound.

MusicNote 37

Legendary cellist Pablo Casals.

The **guitar** has six strings, and its sound is delicate and light. The guitar is strongly associated with music of Spain and Latin America, but it is widely used around the world, mostly for solo playing or to accompany singing. You will almost never see a guitar in an orchestra, but there are some classical guitar **concertos**, in which the guitar has the main solo part and is accompanied by the orchestra.

The **electric guitar** was first used in jazz bands in the 1930s. Guitarists used pickups and amplifiers on their hollow-bodied (acoustic) instruments to produce a louder sound. Solid-bodied guitars became popular in the 1950s for early rock and roll and then later for rock and pop. The sound can be modified electronically to produce special effects such as vibrato (wavering of pitch), *reverb* (echo effect), and *distortion*.

Woodwinds

The flute, oboe, clarinet, and bassoon are the standard **woodwind** instruments in the modern orchestra. All are played by blowing past a reed (one or two thin slivers of bamboo that vibrate) or through a mouthpiece attached to the main body of the instrument. An orchestra usually has only two or three of each kind of woodwind.

Left to right: Contrabassoon, bassoon, English horn, oboe, bass clarinet, clarinet, flute, piccolo, tenor saxophone, baritone saxophone.

The **flute** was originally made of wood and is therefore classified as a woodwind instrument. Nowadays, however, it is usually metal. Most flutes are made of silver, but some famous flute soloists play gold or even platinum flutes. The instrument is held sideways, and sounds are produced by blowing across a hole in the mouthpiece—the same principle used in blowing across the top of a bottle. Different pitches are produced by moving the fingers on holes and keys. **[MusicNote 38]**

The flute is famous for its bright, liquid upper notes and its haunting lower notes. It has a wide range and can be played very fast. The **piccolo**, a small version of the flute played in exactly the same way, is an octave higher than the flute and sounds very brilliant, even shrill.

The **oboe** and the **bassoon** are played by blowing through a double reed made of cane. Two small pieces of cane are tied together, and when air is forced through them, they vibrate against each other. The suave, yet edgy quality of the oboe made it a favorite among eighteenth- and nineteenth-century composers. Because the oboe varies little in pitch, the other instruments usually tune to it. Just at the beginning of a classical concert, you can listen carefully and hear the pitch being given first by an oboe. **[MusicNote 39]**

Far Left: Oboe player.
Left: Bassonist.

Whereas the oboe and the flute are among the highest-sounding instruments of the orchestra, the bassoon is one of the lowest. It is a large instrument and uses much larger double reeds than the oboe. Its length is disguised, because it is made of a tube doubled back on itself. If it were straight, it would be more than nine feet long! The bassoon has a full, rounded, vibrant sound in its low **register** (area of sound) and a strange, rather haunting sound in its high register. The most famous example of a bassoon playing high is at the opening of Stravinsky's *The Rite of Spring*, which is the music that accompanies the creation-of-the-world sequence in the movie *Fantasia*.

MusicNote 40

The **English horn** is neither English nor a horn. It is really a low oboe, pitched a fifth lower than the standard oboe. The English horn has a rich, evocative sound. It is one of the most distinctive instruments of the orchestra. Perhaps for that reason, it is used quite rarely. Its most well-known appearance is in the slow movement of Dvořák's *New World* Symphony.

MusicNote 41

The **contrabassoon** is the lowest woodwind instrument of all. It plays an octave lower than the bassoon and is a very large instrument. It is made of a tube doubled back on itself twice. Unwound, it would stretch to eighteen feet!

The **clarinet** is the most versatile of all the woodwinds. For this reason, perhaps, it is the only orchestral woodwind instrument that has been successfully used in jazz. It is played with a single cane reed that is attached to the mouthpiece. The clarinet has a very wide range (nearly four octaves) and three distinct registers. In the low register, it sounds rich and melancholy; in the middle register, it is singing and warm; in the high register, it is piercing and shrill. Mozart was said to have adored the sound of the clarinet.

MusicNote 42

Far Left: Piccolo player in a marching band.
Left: Clarinet player.

MusicNote 43

The **bass clarinet** plays an octave lower than the standard clarinet; it has a wonderfully rich, buttery sound. You can hear it in the famous "Dance of the Sugar-Plum Fairy" in Tchaikovsky's *Nutcracker* ballet. The **E-flat clarinet** is smaller and higher than the standard clarinet. It is bright and piercing and is often used in marching bands.

MusicNote 44

Other woodwind instruments that are used mostly outside the orchestra are the saxophone and the recorder. Like the flute, the **saxophone** is made of metal, and, like the clarinet, it has a single reed. Saxophones come in many sizes. The most common are the alto and tenor, though soprano, baritone, and bass saxophones have also had their proponents. The saxophone was invented in the mid-nineteenth century; it is used mostly in jazz, where its smooth, flexible, melodious quality works particularly well.

MusicNote 45

The **recorder** also comes in different sizes, the most common being the soprano and alto. Recorders are fine instruments for children, because they are fairly easy to play at a basic level. Advanced recorder playing, however, is not at all easy.

Brass Instruments

MusicNotes 46–49

The French horn, trumpet, trombone, and tuba are brass instruments. All four require the player to blow through a mouthpiece that can be detached from the main body of the instrument. There is no vibrating reed here; what sets up the sound in brass instruments is the vibration of the player's lips. Composers tend to use brass instruments sparingly, because they produce considerable volume and can overwhelm all the other instruments in the orchestra. Yet the strident, extroverted character of brass instruments is balanced by a warm, mellow quality when they are played softly.

Left to Right: Clockwise from Top Left: French horn, tuba, trombone, trumpet. Right: Tuba player.

Different notes are obtained on brass instruments by tightening or slackening the lips in the mouthpiece and also by changing the length of the tube that has air going through it. On the French horn, trumpet, and tuba, this is done by using the fingers to press down valves. On the trombone, however, the length of the tube is changed by means of a slide: sliding one length of tubing over another varies the length of the column of air.

Each of the brass instruments has its own distinctive sound. The **French horn**, often known simply as the horn, is often associated with "outdoor" sounds like hunting calls, though it also has a warm, rich quality. The **trumpet** is the highest-pitched brass instrument. Composers often take advantage of its bold, strident quality in fanfare-like passages. The **trombone** sounds very powerful and grand, sometimes even frightening. As with the horn, however, it has the potential to produce a rich, smooth, and mellow sound. Both the trumpet and the trombone are favored in jazz ensembles. The **tuba** is to the brass section what the double bass is to the string section—the lowest-pitched instrument and the supporting bass. Its sound is deep and round.

When a whole choir of brass instruments is playing together, the sound is unparalleled. It can range from introspective and religious to overwhelming. **[MusicNote 50]**

In jazz, trumpets and trombones are common, French horns are quite rare, and the tuba is usually only found in bands that play early jazz, from the 1920s and '30s.

Percussion Instruments

Percussion instruments are those that involve hitting or shaking. They can be divided into two categories: those that produce pitched (tuned) sounds and those that produce unpitched sounds. Pitched percussion includes timpani, xylophone, glockenspiel, and celesta.

The **timpani** have been an important feature of the symphony orchestra since the late eighteenth century. Two, three, or sometimes four of these large drums are arranged in a semicircle around the player. Timpani have a skin stretched across the top (this used to be animal skin but is now usually made of plastic), and each drum is tuned to a different (low) pitch. The drums are played either with soft padded sticks or with hard wooden ones. Timpani can sound like distant thunder, or they can sound powerful and stirring (as in the main theme of the movie *2001: A Space Odyssey*). Often, however, they are used simply to reinforce the beat and the bass.

The **xylophone** and the **glockenspiel** are very similar to each other. Each has two sets of bars—like the black and white keys of a piano—played with two hard sticks. The glockenspiel bars are made of metal and therefore produce a bright, luminous sound. The xylophone's bars are made of wood, so their sound is mellower.

The **celesta** is based on the same principle as the previous two instruments, but it looks like a tiny upright piano. The hammers that strike the metal bars are controlled from a small keyboard. The sound of the celesta is tinkling, delicate, and sweet. You can hear it used most effectively (together with the bass clarinet) in the "Dance of the Sugar-Plum Fairy" in Tchaikovsky's *Nutcracker* ballet.

Untuned percussion instruments include the snare drum, bass drum, triangle, and cymbals. The **snare drum** has strings, attached to its underside, which sizzle or rattle when the drum is struck. The sound is dry and crisp. The **bass drum** is large and is suspended on its side. It gives a deep thump. The snare drum and the bass drum are prominently featured in marching bands, and occasionally in classical music, as well. The snare drum is the most conspicuous instrument in Ravel's *Bolero*.

The **triangle** is made of metal and is played with a metal beater. Its high, hard noise can be heard above the sound of a full symphony orchestra.

Cymbals come in many different sizes. Orchestral cymbals are usually a pair about fifteen inches in diameter. When they are struck together, the crashing sound can last for several seconds.

In a jazz combo, the **drum set** is the heartbeat of the music. A jazz drum set (or **kit**) is made up of many instruments grouped together so that they can be played by one person. There is usually a snare drum, a bass drum, two tom-tom drums (cylindrical drums without snares, usually just called "toms") of different sizes, a hi-hat, a ride cymbal, and crash cymbals. The hi-hat is a pair of small cymbals operated by a foot pedal, the ride cymbal is the one that keeps the jazz rhythm going, and the crash is used for special effect. Drum kits can be expanded to include many more drums, cymbals, shakers, suspended metal strips, cowbells, and so on.

MusicNote 51

MusicNotes 52–53

MusicNote 54

MusicNote 55

MusicNote 56

MusicNote 57

MusicNote 58

Keyboard Instruments

The most important keyboard instruments are the piano, the harpsichord, the organ, and the synthesizer. The **piano** is best known as a solo instrument, but it can also appear with an orchestra. This happens in one of two ways. In a *piano concerto*, the piano takes a starring role in front of the orchestra. But occasionally the piano appears as just another orchestral instrument.

The piano can claim to be both a stringed instrument and a percussion instrument. Each key on the keyboard activates its own hammer. The hammer strikes the piano's strings inside the body of the instrument, and a note is sounded. The harder the pianist strikes a key, the louder the sound. This ability to control dynamics so directly gave the piano its original name, *piano e forte*, which is Italian for "soft and loud."

The most important predecessor of the piano was the **harpsichord**. The harpsichord was the fundamental keyboard instrument of the seventeenth and eighteenth centuries. Although the harpsichord may look quite similar to the piano from the outside, its internal mechanism is quite different. Pressing a key causes the string to be *plucked*. Regardless of how hard the key is pressed, the string is plucked in the same manner and produces the same dynamics. The sound of the harpsichord is delicate and dry, though full chords can be quite loud. (The sound was once colorfully, though unfairly, described as "like two skeletons copulating on a tin roof.")

The workings of a modern piano.

A magnificent church organ.

MusicNote 59

An organ console, showing the multiple keyboards, the "stops," and the pedals.

The **organ** is sometimes called the "king of instruments." Organs range in size from tiny, portable models to the enormous instruments found in large halls or churches. Air is propelled through pipes, and the route the air takes is controlled from a keyboard. Large organs can have hundreds of pipes and even two or three keyboards ("manuals"). They usually have a pedal keyboard operated by the player's feet for the lowest notes. To play the pedals, the organist wears special shoes.

The pipes of an organ may be made of a variety of materials, in a variety of shapes, and with or without reeds. Big organs have many different sets of pipes. Each set has a different quality of sound and is made accessible from the keyboard by special control buttons known as stops. This is where we get the expression "pulling out all the stops." As a result of this array of stops, the sound of the organ is very rich.

An instrument that can imitate the sounds of other instruments is the **synthesizer**. This is an electronic instrument, usually with a keyboard, that can be programmed to imitate the sound of almost any other instrument. The synthesizer can also modify sounds or create completely new ones. It is widely used in popular music. The synthesizer has also revolutionized the recording, film, and musical theater industries. It can be made to sound like a full orchestra or like a single electric guitar. Synthesized film soundtracks are very common, and musical shows often use synthesizers. It is far less expensive to use one synthesizer than to hire a conductor and an orchestra for several days!

Musical Performance
Rehearsal

The amount of rehearsal time that goes into music depends greatly on the type of music involved. Jazz, for example, depends a great deal on **improvisation**—people making up the music as they go along. Nonetheless, creative improvisation takes a great deal of practice. You have to know your instrument very well, and you have to be able to hear harmonies and listen carefully to what the other members of the group are doing.

Pop and rock music are mostly made in the studio, and much of the work in making a recording is done by the engineers or producers. Most recorded pop music is "manufactured" in the studio by engineers mixing different tape tracks, adding synthesized sounds, and manipulating the overall result.

Classical concert music takes an enormous amount of rehearsal. Much more time is spent rehearsing for a concert than actually presenting it. A typical orchestral musician will work for 25 or 30 hours a week, of which two-thirds are devoted to rehearsals. In addition, of course, the musician is expected to practice his or her instrument and learn new music.

During rehearsals, the conductor and orchestra will rehearse the pieces to be featured on that week's program, deciding questions of tempo, tuning, dynamics, balance among the instrumental groups, and interpretation. This last factor is what distinguishes one performance of a piece of music from another: whether to slow down a little here, speed up a little there, pause for a moment between sections, allow the brass section to let it rip in the last movement, and thousands of other tiny details. There is much more to a conductor's job than just "beating time!"

Attending a rehearsal is one of the most fascinating ways to learn about orchestral music. You hear the music several times, you see which ways the conductor decides to shape the music, and you learn what these changes can do to the overall effect. Most orchestra rehearsals are private, but many orchestras have taken to offering inexpensive seats for occasional "open rehearsals."

Leonard Bernstein as a young man.

Attending a Concert

When you go to a concert, there are certain conventions that everyone follows. First, most people get dressed a little more formally than usual. Tee shirts and jeans aren't really appropriate for a concert.

It's a good idea to get to the concert hall 15 or 20 minutes early. There is a lot to see and do during that time. In fact, some people start preparing to hear a concert a day or two beforehand. They find out exactly what pieces are on the program. They might listen to recordings of the pieces and read a bit about them. If there are vocal works on the program, they might look at the texts (and, if necessary, translations of the texts) beforehand.

Different types of concerts generally have different kinds of programs. Again, there are conventions about this. An orchestral concert usually has three works in the program, usually by three different composers. The first piece is usually fairly short and somewhat lighter than the others. This piece is often an overture (a short introductory orchestral work). The second piece is sometimes a concerto: a work for an orchestra that features a soloist. This is usually followed by an intermission. The second half of the concert is often taken up by one longer and more serious work, like a full-length symphony.

In the 15 minutes before the concert begins, take a careful look at the program. In addition to the name of the orchestra and the conductor, it will tell you the titles and the order of the pieces, the titles of the movements, and the names and dates of the composers. Take a look at the accompanying sample program.

The first piece, by Rossini, is an overture that he wrote for one of his operas, *La Gazza Ladra*. That is why it says overture "to" *La Gazza Ladra*. You don't need to know the opera. You just need to know that an overture is a short, generally quite light, orchestral work. The second piece is in three movements (remember: a movement is a self-contained section of a larger work), and each of them has a tempo marking. You learned some of these terms already (see page 25). But there are still some words you may not know. You learned that *Allegro* means fast. *Maestoso* means "majestic," so the first movement is marked "fast and majestic." *Andante* means "at a walking pace" (see your list). And the last movement is an *Allegretto*, which means "a little allegro," therefore, a rather light fast movement. The name of the solo pianist is also given, because she will have a starring role in this concerto.

In the second half of the program, the orchestra will be playing a Brahms symphony. *Non troppo* means "not too much," so the first movement is marked "not too fast." The second movement will be at a moderate walking pace. *Giocoso* means "light-hearted" or "joky," so the third movement will be fast and light-hearted. The last movement is marked "fast, energetic, and passionate."

By the time you have absorbed all this, most of the players will have arrived and taken their places on the stage. Most of them will be warming up or practicing difficult passages, so there will be

Find the
Quick Listen on
MySearchLab
"Mozart Piano Concerto K. 503"

Find the
Quick Listen on
MySearchLab
"La Gazza Ladra Overture Rossini"

Find the
Quick Listen on
MySearchLab
"Brahms's Fourth Symphony"

The Greater Kakofony Orchestra

Heffing von Fogeza

Conductor

Overture to **La Gazza Ladra**	**Gioacchino Rossini** (1792-1868)
Concerto in C Major for Piano and Orchestra, K. 503	**Wolfgang Amadeus Mozart** (1756-1791)

Allegro maestoso
Andante
Allegretto

Ticklin Dee Iories
Piano

Intermission

Symphony No. 4 in E minor	**Johannes Brahms** (1833-1897)

Allegro non troppo
Andante moderato
Allegro giocoso
Allegro energico e passionato

a general hubbub. This is a good time to see where all the instrumentalists sit and see if you can recognize some of the instruments you have learned about. About five minutes before the concert starts is the perfect time to make sure that your cell phone is turned OFF. (You will get very nasty looks from your neighbors if you forget to do this!) You should also know that you cannot get up during the concert to go to the bathroom, that you shouldn't talk during the concert, unwrap candies, rustle your program, or do anything that might spoil other people's enjoyment of the music.

Now the musicians are starting to settle down, and a single long pitch is sounded. This is called "concert A," the pitch to which all the instruments tune. Sometimes it is sounded by a single oboe; sometimes it is just an electronic pitch. The instrumental groups tune to it in turn, and then everyone falls silent. There is an expectant hush, and then the conductor comes in from the wings, takes a bow, and the music starts. (Some orchestras also give a separate bow to the concertmaster or concertmistress, the person who plays at the head of the violins and sits immediately to the conductor's left.) For the second work on the program, the piano concerto, the solo pianist will also get a separate entrance and special applause after the piece. (If there is a piano concerto, there will be some moving of furniture on the stage!)

Most concerts last about two hours. This includes a 20-minute intermission, during which time you can go to the bathroom, get a drink of water or a soda, and get ready for the second half of the concert.

Watch the **Inside the Orchestra** video on **MySearchLab**

This description has followed the order of events at an orchestral concert. Things are a little different for chamber-music (small-group) concerts or for recitals. At voice recitals, there are usually shorter pieces, even though the concert as a whole may still be one and a half or two hours long.

Emotion in Music

Music involves communication and the expression of feelings. The composer communicates by means of the written notes, and the performer communicates by interpreting those written notes for an audience. Performers often get deeply involved with the feelings they are trying to convey.

Conductors grunt and moan, violinists often close their eyes and sway, and rock guitarists thrash at their guitars. Sometimes these emotions can seem theatrical, but a great performer can seem genuinely in touch with the deepest impulses of the soul and convey those feelings directly to the audience.

Live Performances

A live performance has an air of excitement about it that can never be matched by a recording. Whether it is a rock concert, a jazz performance, or a full-dress classical concert, there is something special about hearing people create music on the spot. Music *needs* performance to bring it to life.

Yo Yo Ma immersed in his music.

Many rock concerts are as much stage shows as they are musical performances. Makeup, clothes, dancing, and often elaborate stage machinery help create the special atmosphere. Orchestra concerts are more formal affairs. Opera performances are even more formal. Members of the audience sometimes wear full evening dress. Opera fans can be as passionate about their favorite singers as rock fans are. At the end of a performance, some opera stars are showered with roses or presented with bouquets of flowers. Jazz concerts are usually much less formal. Often they are held in a club, where the audience may be eating and drinking during the performance, and where music is a *part* of the experience, rather than the *focus* of the experience. Since the '40s, though, jazz has also sometimes been presented in concert halls and at festivals, where audiences are more likely to give the artists their undivided attention.

Itzhak Perlman playing the violin.

In many countries around the world, music is integrated into the life of society, and the concept of a concert is quite alien. Music just appears in many aspects of life. But in every culture of the world, in whatever format or environment it is performed, music is regarded as special magic.

Historical Periods and Individual Style

History is a strange affair. If we contemplate the present, we don't really consider it history. And yet after a while, of course, it turns into history. Similarly, people 100 years ago didn't think of themselves as living in a historical period. They were just living.

Time simply continues. Years, centuries, and historical periods are artificial constructs—but they are useful ones. It gives us a sense of clarity and perspective to know when Shakespeare, Jesus, or John F. Kennedy lived, or to be able to discuss "The Middle Ages" or "Romanticism."

Of course, people in the eleventh century didn't think they were living in the Middle Ages. And in the nineteenth century, nobody said, "Okay, time for Romanticism to begin!" It's only in retrospect that we can distinguish different historical periods because certain characteristics set them apart. When we study literature or the arts, these period labels are useful because we feel that a book or a painting actually *reflects* the historical period in which it was created. A painting of the Virgin Mary from the Middle Ages has very different aims and expresses very different things from a painting of a nude made in 1830.

Jean-Pierre Rampal playing the flute.

The history of Western music is much shorter than the history of art or literature. The great epics of Homer, the *Iliad* and the *Odyssey*, date from nearly 3,000 years ago. Cave paintings have been discovered in France and Spain that are more than 20,000 years old. We can imagine that people must have sung and played music that long ago, but unfortunately we have absolutely no trace of it. If music is not written down, it tends to disappear, for it is a *sounding* art.

We have a few fragments of written music from ancient Greece and Rome, but not enough to be able to reconstruct whole pieces. The earliest manuscripts of whole pieces date from the Middle Ages, starting about the ninth century, though they contain music that seems to have been already a few hundred years old.

The main historical periods in music of the European tradition are given here, with approximate dates for each.

Middle Ages	400–1400
Renaissance	1400–1600
Baroque	1600–1750
Classic	1750–1800
Romantic	1800–1900
Twentieth Century	1900–2000

The word *style* in music is used in two senses. First, it is used to describe those characteristics that set apart the music of one historical period from another. We speak about the style of Baroque music or the style of Classic music. It is also used to describe the individual style of one particular composer. No composer works in a vacuum: his or her music reflects the period in which he or she lives. And yet the music of a great composer also has some special features that set it apart from the music of other composers of the time. Mozart, for instance, used the language of mid- to late-eighteenth-century Classicism. And yet there are things about the works of Mozart that mark them as unmistakably his. And, try as they might, nobody else sounds like Louis Armstrong. Throughout this book, I will try to balance very carefully these two aspects of style: the historical and the individual.

To end this chapter, I return to the point I made at the very beginning. The only way to understand great music is to listen to it *very* carefully. Finally, let us listen once more to Handel's *Water Music*.

LISTENING GUIDE

((•—Listen on **MySearchLab**

GEORGE FRIDERIC HANDEL (1685–1759)   *From the* Water Music

Date of composition: 1717
Orchestration: two trumpets, two horns, oboes, bassoons, and strings
Tempo: *Allegro*
Key: D major
Meter: $\frac{4}{4}$
Duration: 1:58

CD I, 4

Let's listen one last time to Handel's *Water Music*, and think about it in terms of **form**, **instruments**, **historical period**, and its composer's individual **style**.

In terms of **form**, the piece is quite simple. The form is provided by the simple device of the "echo." Every phrase of the melody is played twice, usually first by the trumpets and then by the horns. This tight organization provides so much structure for the short piece that Handel did not seem to feel the need for any more.

The choice of **instruments** adds to the bright and extroverted effect of the music. **Trumpets** and **horns** are designed for outdoor use. There is also a full complement of **stringed instruments** (two groups of violins, and violas, cellos, and double basses). A **harpsichord** plays along with the cellos and basses, as was traditional in the eighteenth century. And, although they are hard to hear, a pair of **oboes** plays along with the violins. If you listen very carefully, you might hear the extra edge they give to the violin timbre. Even harder to hear are a pair of **bassoons** that play along with the basses. Again, the difference is one of tone color or timbre more than anything else.

As already mentioned, the style of a piece of music can be thought about in two ways: historical and individual. The *Water Music* of Handel was composed in the first part of the eighteenth century and therefore belongs in the **Baroque period** (1600–1750). This was a period of clearcut music, in which the mood of a piece stays constant from beginning to end, the harmonic structure is strong, and the bass line is firm and direct. All these things are true of our piece.

What makes the music typical of Handel, however, is a different and more subtle matter. Handel's music is always clear and accessible. Even when he writes counterpoint, it is easy to follow. But there is always something interesting and subtly unconventional about his music, even if it sounds extremely simple and straightforward.

The special features to notice in this piece include the following:

1. The variable phrase lengths: In the first section the opening trumpet melody and the answering horn melody are exactly four measures long. But this is followed by two-note phrases (half a measure each!). Then the homophonic section has two-measure phrases. This variety of phrase length is typical of Handel and makes his music much more intriguing than it would otherwise be.
2. Very careful planning of ideas: For example, listen again to the very first chord. You might think this chord is unnecessary. (In fact, I thought so for a while.) The piece could just start with the trumpets. So why did Handel put in this first chord? Well, one can never really *know* the answer to a question like that, but a couple of ideas come to mind. First, it makes the trumpets sound more ringing when they enter right after it, since the chord uses neither the trumpets nor the horns. In fact, it's the only moment in the whole piece in which both the trumpets and the horns are silent. Second, that opening chord balances the four chords at the end of the piece and makes them sound more "correct."

As another example, think of the way Handel *combines* the trumpets and horns at the end, after having alternated them throughout. He must have planned this from the beginning. Think, too, of how the downward scales come back at the end, rounding off the piece perfectly with a subtle reference to the opening. Even more subtle is the fact that the *rhythm* of the trumpets' and horns' melody in this combined ending section is the same as the rhythm at the opening of the piece, but the instruments move down instead of up. (Down feels more right for an ending, and up for a beginning.)

Handel may have thought of all these things consciously or unconsciously. It doesn't really matter. What matters is that they are there, that they are strokes of genius, and that you have already learned enough to be able to hear them!

Here is a final Listening Guide that summarizes these points about form, instruments, historical period, and the composer's individual style.

Time	Listen for
0:00	Opening chord on **strings**, **oboes**, and **bassoons**. Rising four-measure phrase on trumpets accompanied by descending scales on strings and oboes.
0:09	Repeat ("echo") of opening measures on **horns**. Accompanying descending scales in lower octaves.
0:18	Half-measure phrases.
0:22	Two-measure phrases.
0:30	Fanfare-like rhythm.
0:45	One-measure phrases.
0:49	Continuing closing gesture of previous phrases. Two-measure phrases.
0:58	Four-measure phrases.
1:13	Trumpets *and* horns and whole orchestra combine for closing passages. Four-measure phrases in descending pattern match the opening. Descending scales from opening return as accompaniment. "Echo" repetition breaks quarter notes into eighths.
1:30	Four final chords also remind us of opening. End of movement.

FOR FURTHER DISCUSSION AND STUDY

1. What distinguishes music from other sounds that we hear? Can you think of a definition of music that is better than the one in this book?

2. What are the three basic elements of music? Are they found in *all* types of music? (Think of some actual examples.)

   To answer problems 3–6, go to Classical.com or your library and listen to these five examples:

   i) "On the Beautiful Blue Danube" by Johann Strauss II (theme stated by the horns after the introduction)

   ii) "Maple Leaf Rag" by Scott Joplin (first theme)

   iii) "Farewell to Tarwithie" (folk)

   iv) "Nobody Knows You When You're Down and Out" (chorus)

   v) *Moonlight Sonata* by Ludwig van Beethoven, (first movement, first theme)

3. Graph the melodic motion for each example.

4. Identify whether the piece is written in a major or a minor key.

5. Identify the basic texture of each piece.

6. Describe the main instrumentation for each piece.

The Art of Listening

When all is said and done, the most important part of the musical experience is *listening*. There are many ways of listening to music. One of the most common is a passive kind of listening, the kind we do when music is playing as we are doing something else: eating at a restaurant, talking at a party, reading a book. There is even a kind of unconscious listening—to some movie soundtracks, for example, or in stores when the music creates a particular mood without our focusing on how or why. The kind of listening this book encourages is a conscious, active, *committed* kind of listening, in which we really concentrate on everything that is happening, just as we would when reading a great work of literature. This kind of listening takes a great deal of concentration. It also offers very special rewards.

NEED TO KNOW
THREE TYPES OF LISTENING

Passive: Hearing music playing in the background while we perform other tasks

Unconcious: Hearing "Muzak™," such as music played in a store, and hardly noticing it

Active: Listening to music in a fully engaged, committed manner in order to experience it fully

Chapter 2, on the fundamentals of music, presented some of the building blocks of the art of music; it also introduced you to some of the vocabulary that musicians and educated listeners use to talk and *think* about music. I will be using some of this vocabulary throughout the book because it provides the most accurate way of describing the music. However, much of what we experience in listening to great music cannot be described in words, and this is the magic of music. It expresses things that cannot be expressed any other way.

The first and most important thing to know about listening to music is that you have to listen to a work several times to appreciate what is in it. Imagine reading a serious poem. The first time you read it, some of the meaning comes across, but you miss a great deal. Further readings provide you with greater insight into the thoughts and feelings expressed, the rhythm and sound of the words, and the interplay of

form and meaning. The words remain the same, but your understanding of them changes. The same is true of music. A great composition repays repeated hearings, and some of the greatest works reveal something new every time you listen to them.

This type of *active listening* is not easy at first. It takes practice. The secret of enjoying music, especially complicated and unfamiliar music, lies in your willingness to listen to a work more than once, and in the quality of your concentration as you listen.

In this chapter, you will be introduced to three very different pieces of music. Each one has something special about it, and the way we talk about each piece will differ according to the type of music under discussion. In each case, however, I will try to explain something of the essence of the work: what makes it special, what sorts of feelings it expresses, and how it expresses those feelings.

These questions call for a variety of approaches, including direct musical description, historical information, and social and cultural background.

The clearest way to present some of the material is by means of a *Listening Guide*. This is a kind of road map. You can follow it as you listen, and it will point out significant features in the journey. These "landmarks" are indicated by the point in the recording at which they occur, measured in minutes and seconds. Using the timer on your MP3 player or computer, you can easily locate them. Each listening guide will begin with some basic information about the piece—title, instruments, tempo, meter, and the like—to which you can refer at any time. It will then give some general observations about the piece, including historical and biographical context, and some of the important features to recognize as you listen. Throughout this chapter, the technical terms are highlighted. If you come across a word or a concept you have forgotten, just turn back a few pages to Chapter 2, or look it up in the Glossary at the back of the book. The main musical terms in this chapter are printed in **bold**.

Sound, Rhythm, and Dynamics

We shall first listen to a wonderful piece by Aaron Copland, an American composer. The main elements to notice are the **sound**, the **rhythm**, and the **dynamics**.

LISTENING GUIDE

((•—Listen on MySearchLab

AARON COPLAND (1900–1990)

Fanfare for the Common Man

Date of composition: 1942
Orchestration: three trumpets, four horns, three trombones,
    tuba, timpani, bass drum, gong
Duration: 3:39

CD I, 5

The first thing you will notice when you listen to this piece is the **sound**. There is nothing quite like the sound of many brass instruments playing together. What is special, too, is the contrast between the bright assertive sound they make when they play loud and the slightly mysterious sound when they play soft.

Aaron Copland wrote this piece during the Second World War. He wanted it to be stirring and patriotic. *Fanfare for the Common Man* has become one of the best-known pieces of classical music in America. Much of its triumphant mood comes from its instrumentation, as it is scored entirely for brass instruments and percussion. The percussion group includes timpani, a bass drum, and an uncommon instrument: a gong (a circular metal sheet with a rim that is struck by a stick with a large felt head). The gong gives a kind of whooshing sound; you can hear it right away on the first and fourth notes at the beginning of the piece. The simplicity of the fanfare, with its strong rhythms and simple melodies, make the piece instantly appealing. The dynamics increase from quiet (*piano*) to very loud (*fortissimo*). The melodies are based on the simplest **intervals—triads**, **fifths**, and **octaves**—which give an open, spacious, particularly American quality to this wonderful fanfare.

Time	Listen for
0:00	Somber strokes on the bass drum, timpani, and gong (*piano*).
0:25	Fanfare on trumpets alone.
0:54	Bass drum and timpani.
0:59	Fanfare, louder (*mezzo forte*), slightly modified, on trumpets with horns.
1:39	Bass drum, timpani, and gong.
1:50	Trombones and tuba are added, and the opening phrase of the fanfare is echoed, surprisingly, by the tuned timpani; richer harmonies.
2:38	Fanfare developed, even louder (*forte*), with all instruments, followed by stepwise descents.
3:27	The work ends with a massive climax (*fortissimo*) with a rolling crescendo on the timpani.

The two other elements to notice in this piece are the **texture**, and the overall **form**. The prevailing texture is **homophonic**—mostly the instruments play in the same rhythm at the same time. (Only occasionally is there some **counterpoint**, with the trumpets playing the melody and the other instruments playing a contrasting line.) The form is a simple alternation of phrases.

Words, "Blue Notes," Rhythm, Swing, Improvisation

One of the most important musicians in the history of jazz was Duke Ellington. Ellington was a pianist, a composer, and a bandleader.

He wrote the music for the song "It Don't Mean a Thing (If It Ain't Got That Swing)," and his band manager Irving Mills wrote the lyrics. The song was recorded in 1932, a few years before the period known as the Swing Era, and was the first song to use the word "swing" in its title.

Swing is the rhythm you feel in a jazz piece that makes you want to move in some way—from dancing with your whole body to just tapping your foot. The song suggests that a jazz piece is no good if it doesn't have that special feel.

LISTENING GUIDE

((•— Listen on MySearchLab

DUKE ELLINGTON (1899–1974)

"It Don't Mean a Thing (If It Ain't Got That Swing)"

Date of performance: 1932
Orchestration: voice, three trumpets, two trombones, three saxophones,
    piano, banjo, bass, drums
Duration: 3:11

CD I, 6

Well, this piece certainly swings! The driving bass is contrasted with the lively melody, the **trumpets** and **trombones** are juxtaposed with the **saxophones**, and the improvised solos on muted trombone and alto saxophone are sensational. The word "ain't" in the lyrics is sung to a "blue note," a note that is half a step lower than you expect. (Try singing the word "ain't" to the *same* note as the word "thing"—it sounds so "proper" and boring!)

The performance begins with some **improvisation** (making the music up as you go along) by the vocalist. (A singer making up sounds, such as "wa-da doo," is said to be "scatting.") Then there is an improvised trombone solo based on the tune of the song. After the first chorus of the song, the alto saxophone improvises on the tune. Then there's a bit more scatting before the final fade-out. It's amazing how catchy the music is and how much variety Ellington manages to get into a three-minute song.

Time	Listen for
0:00	Introduction with scat improvisation and driving bass and drum.
0:11	Improvised trombone solo atop the subdued saxophones and trumpets who also respond (blare?) to the phrases of the trombone's solo.
0:46	First chorus of song. Blue note on "ain't." Responses from band.
1:23	Transitional section of contrasting character, including saxophone solo.
2:17	Saxophone and the band play variants on the tune.
2:43	Scat improvisation.
2:52	Return to first line of lyrics and fade-out by muted trumpets on the music of their response.

Form, Tempo, Meter, Keys, and Cadences

The next piece can help you appreciate how several musical elements can be combined to create a musical work. It is a **movement** from a symphony by Wolfgang Amadeus Mozart, one of the most brilliant composers of eighteenth-century Europe. The symphony was written in 1772, when Mozart was only 16 years old!

Mozart as a teenager.

Anonymous, 18th century. Wolfgang Amadeus Mozart as a child. Mozart House, Salzburg, Austria. Photo credit: Scala/Art Resource, NY.

LISTENING GUIDE

((•─Listen on MySearchLab

WOLFGANG AMADEUS MOZART (1756–1791)

Minuet and Trio from Symphony No. 18 in F Major, K. 130

Date of composition: 1772
Orchestration: two flutes, four horns, Violins I and II (this designates the two groups
   of violins in the orchestra), violas, cellos, double basses
Meter: $\frac{3}{4}$
Key: F major
Duration: 2:09

CD I, 7

The first thing to note about this piece is that it is a minuet; that is, it conforms to the spirit and form of a favorite eighteenth-century ballroom *dance*. Minuets were graceful and elegant dances, and music in the minuet style often appeared as one of the movements in **symphonies** (orchestral works) of the Classic Era.

Form: Every minuet is in **binary form**. There are always two sections, A and B, and each is repeated, making the pattern AABB. Usually in a symphony the first minuet is followed immediately by a second minuet (called the trio), which is also in binary form (CCDD). Then the first minuet is played again, sometimes without repeats.

Therefore the overall pattern of the symphonic minuet is AABB/CCDD/AABB (or AABB/CCDD/AB). It is easy to see that across the binary (two-part) scheme there is actually a ternary (three-part) pattern, with a large-scale ABA form:

Minuet	Trio	Minuet
A	B	A
AABB	CCDD	AABB (or AB)

This pattern is quite clear in most minuet movements. There is a **cadence** (closing sound) at the end of each section. The sections are usually quite short.

The challenge for the composer in writing a minuet and trio is to find the right balance between contrast (difference) and continuity (similarity). The trio is sandwiched between appearances of the minuet. The composer has to give the trio a little contrast, to make it interesting, and yet still make it sound as though it belongs in the sandwich!

I have provided three listening guides for this piece, each of which focuses on different elements. The first explains the **form** of the piece, with its repeated sections. The second shows you how to notice **tempo** and **meter**. The third concentrates on **cadences** and **keys**. Remember, the piece is only two minutes long.

Listening Guide 1: FORM

Listen for the repeated sections.

Time	Listen for
	Minuet
0:00	First section of minuet (A). Begins with a graceful melody played softly by the strings; flutes and horns join in for loud ending.
0:09	Repeat of the first section of the minuet (A).
0:18	The second section of the minuet (B). Full orchestra, continuing loud.
0:27	Repeat of the second section (B).
	Trio
0:37	First section of trio (C). Contrast of rhythm and texture, soft strings; answered by loud phrase including the flutes.
0:51	Repeat (C).
1:04	Second section of trio (D). Whole orchestra, loud; answered by a quiet phrase that gets louder at the end.
1:17	Repeat (D).

Minuet [The minuet is played again, exactly as before.]

1:29	First section (A).
1:38	Repeat (A).
1:47	Second section (B).
1:56	Repeat (B).

Now let's go on to the second Listening Guide and listen for the **tempo** and the **meter**. The tempo is moderate and regular enough that you can practice counting three **beats** per **measure** while you listen: 1-2-3, 2-2-3, and so on. This means that the piece is in triple *meter*, designated as $\frac{3}{4}$ or three quarter notes in a measure.

If you tap your foot on each strong beat in this piece, you'll be tapping your foot about once every second. Try doing that for a while as you listen. Once you are secure about that, try tapping three times as fast. It's not hard. Just keep tapping along until you are coordinated with the music. With a little practice, you can get good at both kinds of tap and even switch between them in the middle of the piece.

The slower tap counts each measure; the faster taps are the beats within each measure. The *number* of beats in each measure is called the meter; the *speed* at which the beats occur is called the tempo. We have three beats per measure, which means that the piece is in triple meter, and we have about three beats per second, which is medium-fast.

> *NEED TO KNOW*
>
> Beat: Basic pulse
>
> Measure: Group of beats
>
> Meter: Number of beats per measure
>
> Tempo: Speed at which the beats occur

Listening Guide 2: TEMPO AND METER

Time	Listen for
	Minuet
0:00	A. First section. (Try tapping.)
0:09	Repeat. (The slower taps are the measures. The faster taps are the beats within each measure.)
0:18	B. Second section. (Keep going.)
0:27	Repeat.
	Trio
0:37	C. Trio first section. (The *notes* are longer here, but the tempo and the meter stay exactly the same.)
0:51	C. Repeat.
1:04	D. Second section.
1:17	D. Repeat.
	Minuet [whole minuet repeated]
1:29	First section (A).
1:38	Repeat.
1:47	Second section (B).
1:56	Repeat.

Notice as you are tapping that the tempo and the meter remain constant all the way through the piece from beginning to end. This is extremely common in many kinds of music.

Keys and Cadences

One of the things that non-specialists think is difficult to listen for in music is **key**. But it's not really that difficult. Key is a bit like color in a painting: the color gives a painting a particular quality. Most paintings do not use only one color. Similarly, a piece of music does not usually stay in the same key the whole time, though most pieces end in the key in which they began. Often, they move to a different key in the middle and return to the original key at the end. Both the minuet and the trio in Mozart's movement do that. The minuet begins in F major and moves to C major (the **dominant** of F major) in the middle before returning to F at the end. The trio begins and ends in C major and moves to G major (*its* dominant) in the middle. The best way to hear this is to listen especially hard at the cadences where the musical sections end. Remember, a cadence is an ending sound, like punctuation in a written text.

Listening Guide 3: KEYS AND CADENCES

Time	Listen for
	Minuet
0:00	First section. Begins in F major, ends with a cadence in C major.
0:09	Repeat.
0:18	Second section. Returns to F major, ends with a cadence in F.
0:27	Repeat.
	Trio
0:37	First section. Begins in C major, ends with a cadence in G major.
0:51	Repeat.
1:04	Second section. Starts in G major, returns to C for the cadence.
1:17	Repeat.
	Minuet [whole minuet repeated]
1:29	First section. F, cadences in C.
1:38	Repeat.
1:47	Second section. Returns to F and ends with a final cadence in F.
1:56	Repeat.

Listen to this a few times, and notice how the **keynote** is different at the end of the different sections.

By now you should have listened to this little piece several times. If you have, you've probably learned a great deal about how classical music works. Don't worry if you didn't get it all. These things take time. You need to listen to a piece many, many times to appreciate all its subtleties. Take a break from this one. Then listen to it again a few more times tomorrow with the three listening guides. And a few more times the day after that. . . .

The three pieces we have studied in this chapter—the Copland fanfare, the Ellington song, and the Mozart minuet—are all very different. They are different in date, style, type of musical composition, rhythm, instrumentation, and emotional content. Their composers, too, are diverse: a twentieth-century American classical composer, one of the most famous African American jazz musicians, and an Austrian teenager from the eighteenth century. Yet the works all have one thing in common: they all use the language of music to communicate. In addition, they all reveal greater and greater depth as the result of active and committed listening.

FOR FURTHER DISCUSSION AND STUDY

1. The "soundscape" of our world is constantly changing as old sounds disappear and are replaced by new ones. Identify different sounds that you hear on a daily basis. What is the loudest sound you hear? The most annoying? The rarest? The highest? The most beautiful?

2. Using some type of recording device, record a "soundscape." Swap your recording with another student and see if you can each identify where the recording was made.

3. "Muzak" is the registered trade name for a type of music developed to be played in the "background" in public places like malls and doctor's offices. In some cases, background music is used to increase worker productivity or to encourage consumers to buy more products. Is this ethical?

4. Listen to a favorite piece of music at least four times. After each time, jot down a log of what you hear and feel when you listen to the music. After the last time, compare your notes and see how your perceptions and feelings changed as you continued to listen to the piece.

5. Compare the three examples in this chapter, specifically focusing on how each composer has achieved variety and held the attention of the listener in the composition.

✓●[**Study** and **Review** on **MySearchLab**

The Middle Ages:
400–1400

For the sake of convenience, historians today usually divide the Middle Ages into two periods: an early period, from 400 to 1000, and a later period, from 1000 to 1400. In the early Middle Ages, most of Europe was covered with forests. Most of the countries we know today did not exist: the land was divided into small areas ruled by kings or queens, counts, duchesses, lords, and ladies. Society was highly organized by a rigid class system known as *feudalism*. Most of the population worked in near servitude.

As time went on, the land was gradually cleared and small villages were established. By the later Middle Ages, some of these villages had grown into towns, and a more centralized economic system had evolved. The towns were magnets for trade and commerce and for many of the people from the countryside. The streets were filled with peddlers and beggars, children playing, and wagons carrying goods to market. Shopkeepers set up tables to display their wares and tried to attract the attention of wealthy merchants as they passed. The rise of a middle class—represented by bankers and traders, merchants, and shippers—helped to break down the feudal system. Gradually the boundaries of many of the European countries were established more or less as we know them today.

For many people, life in the Middle Ages was not pleasant. They were serfs—virtually slaves—and spent their lives working in miserable conditions. Wars were frequent, and whenever one occurred, all the serfs controlled by the local lords were forced to take part. There were no vaccines or antibiotics, so many diseases and infections that we regard today as minor inconveniences were fatal.

But the image that people have nowadays of the Middle Ages as the "Dark Ages" is incomplete. The spread of Christianity resulted in the spread of learning. Literature and scholarship were kept alive by monks in their isolated monasteries all over Europe. Gradually, education became more widespread, and universities were established in towns from England to Hungary. In addition to being centers of trade and commerce, the new towns were centers of cultural exchange. The arts—music, painting, poetry, sculpture, and architecture—all flourished.

In the Middle Ages, most artistic endeavors were inspired, encouraged, and paid for by the Church. And in each important town, the place where all the medieval arts

MEDIEVAL TECHNOLOGY

We tend to think of technology as belonging exclusively to our modern world. And yet medieval technological innovations were at least as inventive and influential as those of today.

In the sixth century, the invention of a heavy wheeled plow enabled millions of acres of Europe to be cultivated, leading to increased food production and a significant growth in population. In the eighth century, the development of safer oceangoing ships encouraged the Viking raids from Scandinavia and changed the racial, cultural, and linguistic makeup of Europe. The invention of the stirrup in the tenth century enabled soldiers to fight from horseback and led to the formation of the powerful class of knights.

In the later Middle Ages, the rate of technological innovation increased dramatically. From the twelfth century come the spinning wheel, the wheelbarrow, and the mechanical clock; from the thirteenth century, compasses, windmills, and eyeglasses; and from the fourteenth century, plate armor and gunpowder for war, and paper and fixed-type printing for peace.

The technological brilliance of medieval times is most spectacularly displayed by cathedrals. They are triumphs of engineering; many of them are still standing, centuries after much more recent buildings have collapsed.

were concentrated was the cathedral. Medieval cathedrals are marvels of architecture. Superb sculptures graced their doorways and outer walls, paintings and tapestries adorned their inner walls, and every day the cathedrals were filled with music.

General Characteristics of Medieval Music

A huge quantity of music has survived from the Middle Ages. The earliest written examples come from the eighth or ninth century, but much of the music dates from even earlier. This earlier music must have passed from generation to generation simply by ear.

One generation taught it to the next. By the year 1000, an enormous amount of music had been composed and was being performed throughout Europe.

Because one of the unifying characteristics of the Middle Ages is the influence of Christianity, it is not surprising that the Church dominated medieval music. Most of the surviving music from the medieval period was designed for use in the Christian (Roman Catholic) liturgy. This music is known as **liturgical music**. In addition, music was composed for events of a semireligious character, such as weddings, funerals, and coronations. Most of the liturgical and ceremonial music is vocal music. The melodies are very smooth and flowing.

Besides religious vocal music, there were many other kinds of music as well: folk songs, work songs, dances, and instrumental pieces. We know this from visual evidence in illustrated manuscripts and from poems and books written at the time. Very little of this music, however, has survived in notation. The few pieces we do have are fascinating, with irregular phrase lengths and lively rhythms.

By the later medieval period, two innovations were emerging. One was the rise of written **secular song** ("secular" means "nonreligious"), and the other was the rise of polyphony—music with more than one line sounding at a time. Both of these innovations had vital consequences for the entire

Find the
Quick Listen on
MySearchLab
"Medieval Dance Music"

later history of Western music. The idea that composers could devote their attention to topics outside of religion—such as love or politics—broadened the scope of music immensely. And polyphony gave rise to harmony, which is one of the main features of Western music.

NEED TO KNOW

Early medieval music was written primarily to accompany religious services.

The oldest surviving written music from the Middle Ages dates from about 800, but the music may be older.

Later in the period, secular songs—songs with nonreligious topics—became popular. Also, polyphony—music containing more than one line at a time—started to appear.

Our survey of medieval music is divided into two parts. Part I discusses liturgical chant, and Part II looks at the music of the later Middle Ages: secular song and polyphony.

The Music of the Middle Ages

I: Plainchant

The vocal music for church services from the early Middle Ages is known as **plainchant**. Many people call it "Gregorian chant" after the famous Pope Gregory I, who lived from about 540 to 604. During the early Middle Ages, from about 400 to 1000, thousands of chants were composed. (**See Listening Guide.**)

Plainchant is monophonic: only one line of music is performed at a time. Several people may sing that one line in unison, but still only one note is sounded at a time. It may seem very limiting to have music restricted to one line, but in fact, plainchant is extremely varied. It ranges from very simple melodies, centered primarily on a single pitch, to highly elaborate ones, with long, flowing lines.

There are also other ways in which plainchant is varied. The number of singers can change, with shifts among a solo singer, a small group of singers, and a whole choir. Or the text can be set in different ways. The text setting may be **syllabic**, with one note for every syllable of the text; it may be **melismatic**, with a large number of notes sung to a single syllable; or it may be something in between. The middle style, with a small number of notes per syllable of the text, is known as **neumatic**. Most

A medieval depiction of Pope Gregory. The Holy Spirit, in the form of a dove, is whispering chants in his ear; in turn Gregory is dictating the chants to scribes.

Pope Gregory VII (1073–1085), previously Hildebrand; ca. 1021–Salerno 25.5.1085. Gregory VII and a scribe. Book illustration, contemporary. Leipzig, University Library. Photo: AKG London.

well-known songs today are syllabic ("On Top of Old Smoky," for example). But the Beatles' song "Not a Second Time" starts out quite neumatically. You may be familiar with the Christmas carol "Angels We Have Heard on High," which includes a long melisma on the first syllable of the word "Gloria."

Finally, the most important element of variety in plainchant is given to it by the system of melodic **modes**. The modes are like colors used in painting; they give richness and variety to the music. There are four main modes in the medieval system, which

end, respectively, on D, E, F, and G. All D-mode chants have a similar sound because of the characteristic series of intervals that occur in that mode. The D mode (usually called the Dorian), has, from top to bottom, a whole step, a half step, three whole steps, a half step, and a whole step. None of the other modes has exactly that pattern, so no other mode has the same sound. Many modern folk songs are in Dorian mode. You can hear the special evocative quality of the Dorian mode in a song such as "Scarborough Fair."

Find the **Quick Listen** on **MySearchLab** "Scarborough Fair"

Syllabic.

Partly neumatic.

Melismatic.

LISTENING GUIDE

((• Listen on MySearchLab

KYRIE (PLAINCHANT)

Men's choir
Duration: 2:09

CD 1, 8

This is a chant from a medieval Roman Catholic Mass. It is one of many settings of this text. Although most of the Mass was in Latin, the words to the Kyrie are in Greek. The text consists of three phrases: "Kyrie eleison—Christe eleison—Kyrie eleison" ("Lord, have mercy—Christ, have mercy—Lord, have mercy"). Each of these three statements is sung three times. There is great symbolism in this repetition scheme: in medieval Christianity, the number three represented the Trinity, and three times three was considered absolute perfection.

Corresponding to the three statements of the text, there are three phrases of music. The whole piece begins and ends on G, so it is in the G mode (usually called Mixolydian). As in painting, however, a composition may have a mixture of colors, and there are hints of the Phrygian mode in the first phrase, which ends on E. The shape of the melody is very carefully designed. The first phrase is the shortest and moves in waves. The second phrase starts high, and the motion is mostly descending. The last phrase is in the form of an arch and starts and ends on the same note (G). At the top of the arch, the music reaches the highest note in the whole piece. The last time the third statement of the text is sung, the music changes slightly, with the addition of three notes to the beginning of the phrase.

I

1., 2., 3. Ky - - ri - e _____ e - - le - i - son.

II

1., 2., 3. Chri - ste _____ e - - - le - i - son.

III

          1., 2. Ky - - ri - e _____ e - - le - i - son.
3. Ky - ri - e _____ e - - le - i - son.

Kyrie eleison.	*Lord have mercy.*
Kyrie eleison.	*Lord have mercy.*
Kyrie eleison.	*Lord have mercy.*
Christe eleison.	*Christ have mercy.*
Christe eleison.	*Christ have mercy.*
Christe eleison.	*Christ have mercy.*
Kyrie eleison.	*Lord have mercy.*
Kyrie eleison.	*Lord have mercy.*
Kyrie eleison.	*Lord have mercy.*

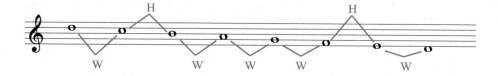

The Dorian mode.

Find the **Quick Listen** on **MySearchLab** "Phrygian Gregorian Chant"

The pattern of intervals in E-mode (Phrygian) pieces is different. So chants composed in that mode sound different from those composed in the D mode. And the same is true for F-mode and G-mode pieces, because of their characteristic pattern of intervals.

The accompanying chart gives the names and the patterns of these four main medieval modes. You will notice that the modes are given with their notes descending, whereas the scales we have looked at were shown in ascending form. This is because most medieval melodies descend to their keynote, giving the music a feeling of relaxation at the end, whereas many later melodies end with a more intense rise to the top of the scale.

This system of modes is very important. It is the basis upon which the music of the Middle Ages is built, and it is this system that makes the world of medieval plainchant so colorful, rich, and appealing.

Why does plainchant sound the way it does, with its serene, otherworldly character? The first reason has to do with rhythm. The music flows along without a clearly defined rhythm and with no regular pattern of strong or weak beats. The second reason for the sound of plainchant is the nature of the modes. The modes are very subtle. The colors they impart to the music are not stark or strong: they are gentle pastels. They lack the intense drive of modern scales or keys. Finally, because there is only one musical line, the listener can concentrate entirely on the shape and direction of the melody. Indeed, plainchant is the greatest collection of pure melody in the history of Western music and has been called "one of the great treasures of Western civilization."

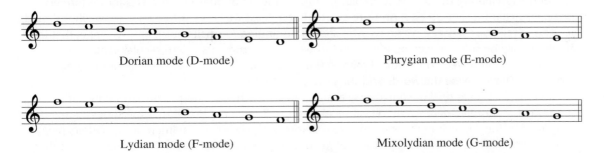

Dorian mode (D-mode)

Phrygian mode (E-mode)

Lydian mode (F-mode)

Mixolydian mode (G-mode)

II: Secular Song and Polyphony

Secular Song   The rise of secular song can be dated to the twelfth century, when the troubadours were active. Troubadours were poet-musicians who composed songs for performance in the many small aristocratic courts of southern France. (In northern France, such musicians were called *trouvères*.) Troubadours and trouvères wrote their own poetry and music, and the subjects they favored were love, duty, friendship, ceremony, and poetry itself. Their primary topic was love. For the most part, the poems address an ideal-ized vision of a woman, who is remote and usually unattainable. (Most of the troubadours were men.) The lover pines away and pleads for some sign of favor, however slight. There are also a few songs by women troubadours about men, written in the same manner.

This topic is sometimes called "courtly love," because it derived from a conventional code of manners that flourished in the aristo-cratic courts of the Middle Ages. But it had enormous influence on the entire history of Western love poetry. Eight centuries of love songs, up to and including those of the present day, have been influenced by the conventions and vocabulary of courtly love.

As an example of troubadour music, we will listen to a song, "A chantar," by Beatriz de Dia. (**See Listening Guide.**)

A medieval manuscript from the fifteenth century, showing the music for a Kyrie, with an illumination of monks and a choirboy singing.

Monks singing from a choir book, in an initial "K" ("Kyrie eleison"). Kyriale, Italy (Cremona), third quarter 15th ca. M.685, f.1. The Pierpont Morgan Library, New York, NY. Art Resource, NY.

PERFORMANCE OF MEDIEVAL MUSIC

One of the fascinating things about medieval music is the set of questions it poses for performers today. Plainchant is difficult enough to re-create. But at least we know the context in which it should be sung (a religious service); we know who should be singing (a small choir); and we know that it should usually be sung unaccompanied (that is, without instruments). With secular song, many questions are unresolved. The original manuscripts of the music tell us very little about how to perform it. They provide the words and the notes, but that is all.

There is still a great deal of controversy among modern scholars and performers about the question of accompaniment for medieval secular songs. Some people feel that the songs should be performed as they appear in the manuscripts—that is, with no accompaniment at all. Others point to the elaborate descriptions and pictures of instruments in medieval manuscripts and suggest that musicians must have improvised instrumental accompaniments for so sophisticated a repertory.

LISTENING GUIDE

((•●[Listen on **MySearchLab**

BEATRIZ DE DIA (LATE TWELFTH CENTURY)

Song, "A chantar"

Date of composition: ca. 1175
Duration: 5:22

CD 1, 9

Most of the troubadours of the Middle Ages were men, but a few were women. Contrary to popular belief, women in the early Middle Ages enjoyed considerable freedom and political equality. Women of all social classes were involved in music, either as patrons, composers, or performers. The powerful and charismatic Eleanor of Aquitaine (1122–1204, Duchess of Aquitaine and Countess of Poitiers, Queen of France, and later Queen of England) was a great patron of the arts.

Beatriz de Dia, also known as the Comtessa de Dia (Countess of Dia), lived in the late twelfth century. She was the wife of the Count of Poitiers and the lover of a well-known nobleman, who was himself a troubadour, and a composer. Only a small number of her poems survive, and only this one has survived with music.

Like almost all the secular songs of the Middle Ages, this song is **strophic**: the same music is repeated for all the stanzas of the poem. The language is that of the south of France; it is known as Occitan, sometimes called Provençal. The poem has five stanzas and a brief two-line ending known as a *tornada*.

In this song, Beatriz de Dia addresses her lover, who has scorned her, and she expresses her pain at his treating her so badly. It is difficult to gauge the depth of true feeling, because the topic of unrequited love was a highly conventional one in troubadour poetry. Yet beneath the convention, the blending of words and music produces a song of great beauty.

Each line of poetry has its own musical phrase. The first phrase ends with an ornamented half cadence (a cadence that leaves more to be said) on E; the second with a full cadence on D. These two musical phrases are repeated for the third and fourth lines of the poetry. The next two lines are joined and are set higher in the range; they end with the E cadence. The last line, on the other hand, uses the whole musical phrase of lines 2 and 4 with its D ending. The pattern is as follows:

Line 1	Phrase A
Line 2	Phrase B
Line 3	Phrase A
Line 4	Phrase B
Lines 5 and 6	New higher phrase, with A ending
Line 7	Phrase B

Each stanza uses the same arrangement. This pattern gives a rounded feeling to the melody as a whole and a sense of increased intensity before the close. We will listen to only two stanzas.

In this performance, the singer is accompanied by a **vielle** (a bowed instrument—you can see one in the medallion at the top of this listening guide) and a low wooden flute, which provide an introduction and a close to the song as well as some interludes between stanzas. They are joined by lute and drum for the *tornada*.

Time	Listen for
0:00	Vielle prelude: The vielle establishes the musical mode and character of the song.
	Stanza 1 [vielle accompaniment]
0:25	The voice establishes a lovely melodic contour, with ornamental flourishes at the end of each line.

A chantar m'er de so q'ieu no voldria.   I must sing, whether I want to or not.
Tant me rancur de lui cui sui amia,   I feel so much pain from him whose friend I am,

[repetition of melody]

Car eu l'am mais que nuilla ren que sia.   For I love him more than anything.
Vas lui nom val merces ni cortesia,   But neither grace nor courtesy has any effect on him,

[voice goes higher]

Ni ma beltatz, ni mos pretz, ni mos sens.   Nor my beauty, my decency, or my intelligence.
C'atressim sui enganad'e trahia,   I am despised and betrayed,
Cum degr'esser, s'ieu fos desavinens.   As though I were worthless.

1:50	Wooden flute plays interlude based on melody.
	Stanza 5 [vielle accompaniment]
3:01	Return of music from first stanza with more elaborate accompaniment and flourishes.

Valer mi deu mos pretz e mos paratges,   My decency and my ancestry have their value,
E ma beutatz e plus mos fis coratges.   As do my beauty and the depth of my heart.
Per q'ieu vos mand lai on es vostr'estatges.   So I send to your noble home
Esta chansson que me sia messatges.   This song: let it be my messenger!
E voill saber, lo mieus bels amics gens,   And I want to know, my fair friend,
Per que vos m'etz tant fers ni tant salvatges.   Why you are so savage and cruel to me.
Non sai si s'es orguoills o mals talens.   I don't know: is it pride or ill will?

	Tornada [flute and drum join in softly]
4:18	*Mas aitan plus vuoill li digas, messatges,* But I want even more for you to tell him, messenger,
	Q'en trop d'orguoill ant gran dan maintas gens. That pride has been the downfall of many people!
5:01	Florid ending with voice and instruments

Polyphony   It took some time before medieval composers began to be interested in polyphony. The plainchant and secular song repertories were entirely monophonic, and the subtleties of melodic construction and the text/music relationship in these genres satisfied the musical aims of medieval composers for centuries. Only gradually did the idea of polyphony gain popularity.

The idea of composing music with two or more independent musical lines first arose in the tenth century and really took hold about 1200, when there was a sudden explosion of polyphonic liturgical composition. The polyphony of this time is striking in its power and grandeur. Compositions of two, three, and even four voices were composed to celebrate the major feasts of the church year. At a time when the cycle of life revolved around the church calendar, feasts such as Christmas and Easter must have been spectacular and vivid occasions. People spent days or even weeks preparing for the special celebrations that surrounded the feast days themselves.

An Italian manuscript from the fourteenth century showing many different kinds of instruments

The original medieval manuscript of *Viderunt Omnes*.

Because of the clothes that were worn, the meals that were prepared, and the brief escape from the constant burden of work, these days must have had special significance for the majority of medieval society. It is not surprising, therefore, that such days were marked by very special music.

Paris was the city where the most significant amount of polyphony was composed in the twelfth and thirteenth centuries. It was one of the primary centers of the late medieval world. The kings of France had their palaces in Paris, and the first medieval university was established there. Paris was also a hub of commercial activity for the whole of Europe.

In the center of Paris—on an island in the middle of the river Seine—stood a huge cathedral, which was built about 1200. It was a magnificent sight. Indeed, it still is. Visitors

to Paris still visit Notre Dame Cathedral, because it remains one of the great architectural marvels of Europe.

To match the splendor and beauty of this cathedral, and to celebrate the main feasts of the church year, two composers created the first great collection of polyphony in the history of Western music. Their names were Leoninus and Perotinus, and we know little about either of them. They probably were officials at the cathedral in some capacity. Leoninus was the elder of the two and started the collection; Perotinus added to it and extended the range and scope of the music.

The collection of compositions by these two men is known as the *Magnus Liber Organi* (*Great Book of Polyphony*). This book contains a series of elaborate polyphonic compositions for the main feasts of the church year. These compositions are based directly on the ancient plainchants for those feasts. A piece may contain several independent musical lines, but one of them is always the original chant melody. Sometimes the chant is heard by itself. Among the most famous of the pieces written for the Cathedral of Notre Dame is the four-voice *Viderunt Omnes* by Perotinus, based on the plainchant of the same name. This chant was sung right in the middle of the Mass for Christmas Day. **(See Listening Guide.)**

Perotinus set some portions of the chant polyphonically for solo singers. The rest of the chant, sung by the choir, is monophonic. So the piece alternates both its performing forces (soloists–choir) and its textures (polyphonic–monophonic).

But there is more to it than that. First, the textural contrast is reinforced by a rhythmic contrast. The monophonic (choir) sections are sung in the traditional way, in a free, smooth, essentially rhythmless style, whereas the polyphonic (soloist) sections are marked by very clear-cut rhythms. In addition, there are contrasts within the polyphonic sections themselves. Parts of these sections have extremely long, sustained notes underpinning them; other parts have faster notes in the lower voice that move almost as quickly as those in the upper voices.

Find the **Quick Listen** on **MySearchLab** "*Viderunt Omnes* (Christmas, Gradual)"

LISTENING GUIDE

((•—Listen on **MySearchLab**

PEROTINUS (CA. 1170–CA. 1236)

Viderunt Omnes (four voice polyphony for the Cathedral of Notre Dame)

Date of composition: 1199
Solo singers and choir
Duration: 4:47

CD 1, 10

In this Listening Guide, the text is given with indications specifying whether it is sung in chant or in polyphony. In the polyphonic section, the contrast between sustained-tone and rhythmic accompaniment is marked. Note also the intricate intertwining of the three upper voices over the two different styles of the lower voice. The rich harmonies, the unrelenting rhythmic drive, and the sheer scope of the piece show how magnificent and awe-inspiring a piece of music from 800 years ago can be. (Here only a portion of the overall work is given; the entire piece lasts for nearly 12 minutes.)

Time	Listen for		
	Polyphony		
0:00	(soloists)	*Vi-* (sustained-tone)	[rhythmic upper voices throughout]
0:57	(soloists)	*de-* (sustained-tone)	
1:25	(soloists)	*-runt* (sustained-tone)	[dissonant opening; brief cadence for end of word]
2:29	(soloists)	*om-* (rhythmic/sustained-tone)	
3:40	(soloists)	*-nes* (sustained-tone)	[strong dissonance just before cadence]
	[cadence]		
	Monophony		
3:46	(choir)	*fines terrae salutare Dei nostri.* *Jubilate Deo omnis terra.*	[smooth plainchant]
	[cadence]		
		Viderunt omnes fines terrae salutare Dei nostri.	All the ends of the earth have seen the salvation of our God.
		Jubilate Deo omnis terra.	Praise God all the earth.

Notre Dame Cathedral from the east end, showing the choir and flying buttresses.

PERFORMANCE IN CONTEXT
An Icon of Paris

The growth of modern Paris obscures how completely the Cathedral of Notre Dame dominated the skyline of Paris. The cathedral towers, 226 feet tall and completed around 1250, reigned unchallenged over the city skyline for hundreds of years. Today, the only taller buildings in the city of Paris are the great dome of the Hôtel des Invalides (added 1706–1708) and modern skyscrapers, which are kept well away from the old part of town. The cathedral is an iconic part of the Parisian landscape, and has inspired music ranging from the thirteenth-century Great Book of Polyphony of Leoninus and Perotinus to organ works and musicals in the present day. Victor Hugo's novel *The Hunchback of Notre Dame* prominently features the cathedral and its bells, which even today are used to mark festivals, funerals, and occasions of state.

Artist Unknown. *Bishop's Palace and the Cloister, Notre Dame, Paris,* ca. 1595. © Stock Montage/ Superstock, Jacksonville, FL.

The accompanying figure is a sample of this kind of polyphony, showing some of these elements: a bottom voice starting with a sustained tone but turning more rhythmic, a somewhat more complex middle voice, and an extremely elaborate upper voice.

The remarkable thing about this music is the fact that, despite its variety and density, it retains all of the original plainchant embedded in it.

All the words are still there, and all the original notes are retained in the lower voice. The composition is a complex and sophisticated edifice, but it is built entirely on the foundation of an ancient structure. This is entirely appropriate, because the music was designed for a cathedral that was one of the glories of the new Gothic age but that was erected on the site of a Paris church many centuries old.

Di ___ xit Do- mi- nus

Late Medieval Polyphonic Song By the 1300s, the two main developments of the later Middle Ages—the growth of secular song and the introduction of polyphony—came together, often in delicate settings of great sophistication. France and Italy were at the forefront of the art of polyphonic song; in France, the master composer was Guillaume de Machaut (ca. 1300–1377).

Machaut is one of the first composers about whom we know a few biographical details. He was educated at Rheims, an important town in northeastern France. Soon he became quite well-known as an administrator, poet, and composer. He held positions at the courts of some of the most prominent members of the French ruling aristocracy, including Charles, Duke of Normandy, who later became King Charles V of France. Machaut also was an administrator of

the cathedral at Rheims. He died in his late 70s after a busy and productive life.

A great deal of Machaut's work survives. He wrote many long poems and was probably the author of the lyrics for his own songs. He wrote some sacred music, but most of Machaut's pieces are polyphonic secular songs.

Machaut's musical style is both subtle and intense. His music is full of small rhythmic and melodic motives that tie the composition together and form beautiful melodies. The rhythm is very fluid and depends upon a constant interplay between duple and triple meters. Machaut often uses chromatic notes (unexpected sharps and flats) to make the sound more colorful. (**See Listening Guide.**)

> "Music is a science that would have us laugh and sing and dance."
>
> —Guillaume de Machaut

LISTENING GUIDE

((•—Listen on **MySearchLab**

GUILLAUME DE MACHAUT (CA. 1300–1377)

Secular song (rondeau) Doulz Viaire Gracieus

Date of composition: mid-fourteenth century
Voice, lute, and recorder
Duration: 2:02

CD 1, 11

This short piece is a good example of Machaut's style. It is a setting of a poem that has a two-line refrain or chorus (printed in italics). The refrain comes at the beginning and the end, and its first line comes in the middle of the poem, too. This kind of poem is known as a **rondeau**.

The music sounds very simple but is actually quite complex. There are only two sections of music, which alternate in setting each line of the poetry. The first section is five measures long, the second section seven. This contrasts with later music, where the number of measures in each phrase or section tends to be much more regular. A short descending passage on the lute joins the sections together.

There are other aspects of this music that seem unusual to a listener of today. Although the prevailing **meter** of the piece is triple, there are several places where the music moves in duple meter. **Bar lines** were not used in medieval music (although we print them today for the sake of clarity), so the meter could be much more flexible. Also, many of the notes are **chromatic**: even the opening chord contains two sharps. And although the first section ends on G, which leads you to expect that the whole piece will end on G, the final cadence is on B♭.

The voice is accompanied by two instruments: a recorder below the voice and a **lute** above. (A lute is a plucked instrument similar to a guitar.) Although the accompanying parts are quite independent, all three lines together create interesting harmonies, and there is a brief echo among them at the beginning of the B section.

This kind of carefully constructed polyphony, as well as the overall gentle beauty of the piece, is typical of Machaut's music and of fourteenth-century French music in general.

Time	Listen for	
0:00	[voice is accompanied by delicate lute and soft recorder]	
	Doulz viaire gracieus,	Sweet, gracious countenance,
0:12	[voice goes higher, echoed by recorder]	
	De fin cuer vous ay servy.	I have served you with a faithful heart.
0:30	*Weillies moy estre piteus,*	Take pity on me,
0:42	*Doulz viaire gracieus;*	Sweet, gracious countenance;
0:55	*Se je sui un po honteus,*	If I am a little shy,
1:07	*Ne me mettes en oubli.*	Do not forget me.
1:25	*Doulz viaire gracieus,*	Sweet, gracious countenance,
1:38	*De fin cuer vous ay servy.*	I have served you with a faithful heart.

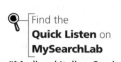

Find the
Quick Listen on
MySearchLab
"Medieval Italian Caccia"

Find the
Quick Listen on
MySearchLab
"Medieval Music
at Avignon"

In Italy, the musical style was rather different from that in France. Italian music was more lively, and often more down-to-earth. It tended to concentrate on florid vocal display. A favorite kind of Italian song was known as the *caccia*. The name is a play on words. *Caccia* means "hunt," and the songs often describe outdoor hunting scenes. But *caccia* also means a musical *round*, in which the voices sing the same music but begin at different times. This gives the impression of a melody "chasing" itself. Italian caccias are great fun. Usually two voices sing the text, with an instrumental third part for accompaniment. The lyrics describing the hunt are realistic and lively, and the voices usually indulge in some kind of dramatic dialogue, often with cries and shouts.

The End of the Middle Ages

At the end of the fourteenth century, the two distinct musical styles of France and Italy began to merge. There were many reasons for this. There was more commerce between the two areas, and political alliances were formed. In some of the Italian city-states, French was spoken at court, and French was also used for official documents and scholarly writings. But the most important reason for the merging of

the two musical styles was the split in the papacy that started in 1378.

For centuries, the popes had lived in Rome. But popes were not necessarily Italian by birth, just as they are not necessarily Italian by birth today. And when a Frenchman was elected pope at the beginning of the fourteenth century, he decided to set up his papal residence in Avignon in the south of France. Succeeding popes continued to live in the palace at Avignon, but political factions arose that insisted upon the election of an Italian pope. There were riots in Rome, and some of the cardinals engineered the election of a rival pope. From 1378 to 1417 (a period known as the Great Schism), there were two popes ruling simultaneously: one in Rome and the other in Avignon.

The papal court at Avignon was notoriously corrupt and immensely wealthy. A great deal of money was spent on bribes, banquets, clothes, furniture, paintings, and music. The court employed both French and Italian composers who lived at court and were able to learn from one another.

The result of this intermingling of composers in a place of such influence and prestige was a fusing of the French and Italian styles in music. This affected both sacred and secular music. The new international style was the basis for a new period of musical history—a period known as the Renaissance.

Palace of the Popes in Avignon.

COMPOSERS, PATRONS, AND AUDIENCES

THE MEDIEVAL AUDIENCE

At the beginning of this book, we defined music as sounds organized for people to hear. Without an audience, music has no meaning. And throughout the ages, music has changed as the audiences for it have changed.

In the Middle Ages, there were two main kinds of audience for serious music: human and divine. For plainchant and the elaborate polyphony woven around it, the clearly intended audience was God. Much sacred music was sung in monasteries, where there was no congregation at all. The monks were singing because it was their primary duty to sing to God.

The other main audience for medieval music was a small aristocratic élite. These were the queens and kings, dukes and duchesses, and lords and ladies of the numerous small courts scattered across Europe, who listened to music as a pastime. The secular songs of the Middle Ages were designed for their ears and reflected their interests: courtly love, noble exploits, and hunting expeditions.

For the remaining 90 percent of the population, we can only guess about their musical interests and experiences. The work songs, nursery rhymes, tavern music, and lullabies of the Middle Ages have disappeared from our collective memory along with the people who enjoyed them.

STYLE SUMMARY

The Middle Ages

Music in the Middle Ages was extremely varied. We have to remember that we are dealing with nearly a thousand years of history—from the year 400 to about 1400. Most of the music that survives from this period is plainchant—melodies ranging from very simple to very complex, but all designed to be sung by a group in unison, with no harmony and no accompaniment. This music is based on the modes, which are different from our modern scales. The modes give the melodies a sound that is fascinating and slightly exotic, as though we were listening in on another world.

From about 1100, a culture of secular love songs arose. These songs, which are mostly strophic, express an idealized vision of the beloved. The songs and the poems on which they are based started the whole tradition of writing and singing about love, a tradition that has carried through to Romantic poetry and even to many of the pop songs of today.

We have many pictures and descriptions of instruments from the Middle Ages, but we do not know exactly how or when they were used. We can only guess that instrumental music must have been very common and that instruments must often have been played to accompany vocal music.

In the last part of the Middle Ages, polyphony was developed, and polyphonic settings were made both of plainchant melodies and of secular songs. Some of the polyphonic chant settings are very grand, impressive works in three or four voices with detailed, complex upper parts and a lower part of almost architectural strength. The polyphonic secular songs, on the other hand, are fine, sophisticated pieces that are based on subtle poetry and displaying delicate, interweaving musical lines.

FUNDAMENTALS OF MEDIEVAL MUSIC

- ❑ The music is based on modes, not on modern scales
- ❑ Plainchant was sung in unison, with neither harmony nor accompaniment
- ❑ Stylized courtly love songs became popular
- ❑ Instruments were many and varied
- ❑ Polyphony was invented

FOR FURTHER DISCUSSION AND STUDY

1. Compare the feudal system with the modern corporate hierarchy. Be sure to note that a specific hierarchy exists in both, with the king and the CEO representing the highest points and the peasants and the factory workers representing the lowest.

2. Choose a work of medieval art or architecture. Compare it with one of the works discussed in this chapter in terms of its structure, details, and overall composition.

3. Listen to a few tracks from CDs that have featured medieval chant, such as *Chant* by the monks of Santo Domingo de Silos monastery, and *Vision*, on which monophonic chants of Hildegard of Bingen have been recorded with a drum track and instruments such as saxophones. Each has caused controversy among classical music scholars, performers, and religious people alike. What is your reaction? Do these modern reinterpretations have validity? Why or why not?

4. Compare several modern love songs to the example by Beatriz de Dia in this chapter. How has the concept of the ideal beloved changed or stayed the same?

5. Compare the religious and secular music of the Middle Ages. How are they similar and how are they different?

CHAPTER 5

The Renaissance: 1400–1600

Life and Times in the Renaissance

The dates historians assign to the European Renaissance vary greatly, depending on whether they are discussing art, music, or literature. For music, the Renaissance is generally regarded as beginning about 1400 and ending at 1600. As with the other historical periods, these dates are very approximate.

"Renaissance" means "rebirth." The term is used to indicate a revival of interest in the humanistic values of classical Greece and Rome. In fact, people in the Renaissance deliberately modeled themselves after the ancient Greeks and Romans—in their feeling of individual and collective responsibility; in their embracing of education; and, most important, in their sense of the enduring human value in the arts. The Renaissance was a time of remarkable artistic and scientific accomplishments.

There were three notable changes from the climate of the Middle Ages. First, there was more focus on individual achievement. Second, people began to show more interest in the real world than in spirituality. And third, the growing ease of travel and the spread of printed books led to a widespread mingling of European cultures.

St. Peter's Square in Rome.

NEED TO KNOW

THREE MAJOR CHANGES IN THE RENAISSANCE

1. New focus on individual achievement

2. Greater focus on the daily world than on the spiritual afterlife

3. Widespread mingling of cultures, facilitated by easier travel and spread of printed materials

These facets of life in the Renaissance are reflected in the artistic accomplishments of the time. Artists and sculptors concentrated on the dignity of the individual human figure: portraits of rulers exude self-confidence and splendor. Painters developed the techniques of perspective, three-dimensional representation, and working with oils—with which the most detailed effects of light and shade could be rendered naturally. The works of Renaissance painters such as Michelangelo and Leonardo da Vinci are still famous over 500 years later.

Renaissance architects throughout Europe used buildings from antiquity as models for their new buildings. Florence Cathedral, St. Peter's Basilica in Rome, Fontainebleau castle in France, and the palace of Charles V in Spain show how the Renaissance style became an international style. Columns and rounded roofs replaced the soaring, spiky look of medieval architecture.

Literary masters of the age included Petrarch of Italy, Cervantes of Spain, Rabelais of France, and Shakespeare of England. In the works of these writers, a new emphasis on self-expression and on the worth of the individual is clearly felt.

Leonardo da Vinci in a self-portrait.

Courtesy of the Library of Congress.

A Renaissance painting reveling in the newfound technique of perspective.
Piero della Francesca (ca. 1420–1492). Italian (Pierodella Francesca?). View of an Ideal City. Galleria Nazionale delle Marche, Urbino, Italy. Photo credit: Scala/Art Resource, NY.

The world of science, largely ignored by Europe in the Middle Ages, became a major focus of the European Renaissance. Inventions and scientific discoveries were impressive in quantity and scope. The most important of these was the invention, in 1450, of printing—a development as revolutionary in its time as the computer has been in ours. The rapid increase in the number of available books had an incalculable effect on education, as well as on the fame of individuals, the spread of scientific knowledge, and the growth of internationalism. Toward the end of the Renaissance, the invention of the telescope and the microscope changed forever the way people looked at the world.

People began to feel more in control of their own destinies than they had in the Middle Ages. Scholars pursued both literary and scientific studies. Many of the great figures of the Renaissance were highly educated and knowledgeable in all known fields—hence our modern phrase "Renaissance man (or woman)." The perfect example of the true Renaissance man was Leonardo da Vinci, who was a brilliant painter, sculptor, musician, engineer, and scientist.

New branches of Christianity were founded in this era. The Protestant movement known as the Reformation was begun by the German theologian Martin Luther (1517), and the Anglican movement was founded when King Henry VIII of England refused to accept the supremacy of the pope in Rome (1538).

In many ways, the Renaissance must have been an exciting time in which to live. New lands were discovered and explored, including much of the Far East, the coast of Africa, and North and South America. By the sixteenth century, there was enormous economic and commercial expansion throughout Europe, and a larger middle class was formed. Members of the middle class were also interested in learning and culture, and the growth of education and the new availability of books helped them achieve their goals.

Renaissance Music

Music played an important role in Renaissance society. Most educated people could either play an instrument or sing written music. People were not considered socially accomplished if they did not have musical training. An evening's entertainment usually included some kind of musical performance. Music printing, which became widespread in the sixteenth century, greatly increased the amount of available music. Amateur music making became more and more common.

The professional musicians included composers and performers. Many more individual musicians found jobs at aristocratic courts, and many towns supported musicians as public employees. Although very few women achieved careers as composers, some women began to be included in the ranks of performing musicians. Some of them were highly paid and became internationally known.

As with the other cultural achievements of the Renaissance, music reached great heights. Some of the most beautiful compositions in the history of Western music were composed during this period; in their depth and beauty, the greatest musical works of the Renaissance match the finest works of Renaissance literature, painting, and architecture.

General Characteristics of Renaissance Music

Renaissance music is distinguished from late medieval music in one important way: the overall sound is much smoother and more

Find the **Quick Listen** on **MySearchLab** "Renaissance Music Instrumental"

"Next to the Word of God, music deserves the highest praise."
—Martin Luther

homogeneous, with less contrast. This change in sound is the result of a change in the way music was composed. The highly contrasting and independent lines of late medieval polyphony were replaced by a new style based on **imitation**.

In medieval polyphony, *different* melody lines are performed at the same time. Imitation is a form of polyphony in which all the musical lines present part of the *same* musical phrase one after the other. As each line enters, the previous ones continue, so there is a constant sense of overlapping. The strictest kind of imitation is a **round**, in which all the voices sing exactly the same thing in turn. But often, imitation is much freer than that. In free imitation, *only the first few notes* of a melodic phrase are sung by each entering voice; the voices then continue freely.

Strict imitation (round):

Free imitation:

Even though the *style* of music in the Renaissance was very different from that in the Middle Ages, the predominant types of composition were the same. They were (1) liturgical music (music for church services, usually Mass settings), (2) motets (settings of Latin texts that are sacred but not liturgical), and (3) secular songs.

	MEDIEVAL MUSIC	**RENAISSANCE MUSIC**
Structure of compositions:	*Early:* Plainchant: monophony (one melody sung by many voices) *Later:* Polyphony: several musical lines sung or played at once	Imitation: the opening of the same melody is performed by different voices, entering one at a time
Tonality:	Compositions based on modes, rather than on modern scales	Still primarily modal, although some more modern harmony
Types of compositions:	1. Liturgical music (for church services) 2. Motets: songs that have religious texts but are not part of the actual service 3. Secular (nonreligious) songs	

Music in the Early Renaissance

The early Renaissance saw a merging of the individual musical characteristics of the different European countries into an international style. Composers throughout Europe began to write similar music—polyphonic, often imitative, and concentrated primarily in the three main types: Mass, motet, and secular song. The foremost composers of the time were John Dunstable of England and Guillaume DuFay of France. Their careers show how the musical style of the Renaissance crossed national boundaries. Dunstable was born in England in 1390 and died there in 1453, but he spent nearly 15 years in France at the height of his career. DuFay (ca. 1400–1474) was born in northern France but traveled extensively throughout Europe and spent many years in Italy. He was therefore exposed to the very different musical styles of northern and southern Europe and played an important role in bringing about a fusion of the two in his own music.

Both Dunstable and DuFay, and the many other composers who flourished in the early Renaissance, wrote music of great beauty and sophistication. Their polyphonic Masses often use musical phrases that recur in different movements; their motets are based on Latin texts often taken from the Bible or designed to celebrate an important civic event; and their secular songs are usually three-part gentle love songs in French or Italian.

The Renaissance Mass

A Roman Catholic Mass as it was celebrated in the 1400s was a long service, with many different readings and prayers, ceremonies and processions, and a large amount of music. Some of the service changed from day to day, and some of it stayed the same. Through most of the Middle Ages, all of this music had been sung in plainchant. It was only with the advent of polyphony in the twelfth and thirteenth centuries that some parts of the Mass began to be sung polyphonically. Gradually, composers began to concentrate on those sections of the Mass that remained the same, regardless of the day, feast, or season. There are five of these sections—the Kyrie, Gloria, Credo, Sanctus, and Agnus Dei—known collectively as the Ordinary of the Mass. The tradition of setting these five sections to music began in the fourteenth century and has continued through the Renaissance to the present day.

The musical setting of a Renaissance Mass is based on the most important musical texture in Renaissance music, as previously mentioned. This texture is imitation, or music that features melody lines performed by several different voices in succession, creating an overlapping effect. The flexibility and variety of approach displayed by composers in the fifteenth and sixteenth centuries in using this one compositional technique is remarkable.

The Mid-Renaissance

During the middle part of the Renaissance, imitation was fully established as the major technique used by composers to create coherent musical works. Composers also experimented with ways to link the five different sections of the Ordinary so they would all sound related. One common solution was to use a single melody—drawn from a piece of plainchant or even a popular song of the day—woven into all the movements. The source melody usually appears in the tenor voice (the second musical line from the bottom in a four-voice piece), but the other voices are often derived from it as well.

Find the **Quick Listen** on **MySearchLab** "Dufay"

THE STANDARD FOUR VOICE PARTS IN RENAISSANCE MUSIC			
Soprano	Alto	Tenor	Bass

Josquin Desprez (ca. 1440–1521)

Josquin Desprez was the most versatile and gifted composer of the mid-Renaissance. He was from northern France and spent much of his career there, as well as at some of the cathedrals and courts of Italy. During his lifetime he became quite famous, and rich nobles were eager to hire him for their households.

Josquin Desprez in a sixteenth-century woodcut.

Josquin composed prolifically in the three main genres of Renaissance music: Masses, motets, and secular songs. He brought the Renaissance technique of musical imitation to new heights of clarity and flexibility.

As an example of Josquin's style, we will study one of his Mass settings: the *Pange Lingua* Mass, composed toward the end of his life. (**See Listening Guides.**) This composition is known as the *Pange Lingua* Mass because all of its five movements are based on the plainchant hymn *Pange Lingua Gloriosi*. Before examining Josquin's polyphonic Mass setting, let's look at the plainchant that provided the basis for it.

"Josquin is master of the notes; others are mastered by them."

—Martin Luther

Josquin's *Pange Lingua* Mass In his Mass based on the *Pange Lingua* hymn, Josquin took almost all of his musical ideas from a centuries-old plainchant. Remarkably, each vocal line in every section of the Mass is derived from the chant in some way or another. But it is the way in which Josquin uses the source material that demonstrates his talent as a composer.

In the first place, of course, Josquin's Mass is polyphonic. It is written for four voice lines: sopranos, altos, tenors, and basses. Second, the Mass—unlike the chant—has rhythm (plainchant is usually sung with all the notes equal in length). Josquin designs the rhythm of every musical phrase to fit the words of the Mass. Josquin also molds and varies his phrases by adding notes or modifying notes from the chant melody. His composition is in five movements, setting all five sections of the Ordinary.

The Mass is by no means a lesser piece because of its dependence on earlier melodic material. Indeed, it is precisely in the molding of a well-known original that Josquin shows his ingenuity. The *Pange Lingua* Mass is colored throughout with the presence of a sacred tradition, not only in the words of the Mass itself, but also in the music and the text of the plainchant hymn that stands behind the Mass—a hymn that would have been very familiar to Josquin's audience. The words of the original hymn are not sung in Josquin's Mass, but they would have been called to mind when his audience heard the strands of the hymn's melody woven into the polyphony.

Three characteristics of Josquin's special musical style can be heard clearly in this work:

1. Josquin has given each short segment of the music its own **point of imitation**, a musical passage presenting a single tiny musical phrase that is copied in the other voices. For each new segment of the music, he presents a new phrase. Each voice states the phrase in turn, and then a cadence follows. The number of statements, the voices that present them, the number of measures between them—all these things may vary.
2. The music features **overlapping cadences**: the next group of voices begins its statements just as the first group comes to a cadence. This provides shape and structure for the music while allowing the forward motion to continue.
3. The imitation is usually *paired imitation*: one pair of voices begins and another pair answers.

LISTENING GUIDE

((•┤Listen on **MySearchLab**

THOMAS AQUINAS (1225–1274)   *Plainchant hymn,* Pange Lingua

Date of composition: thirteenth century
Choir Duration: 2:25

CD 1, 12

The *Pange Lingua* hymn was written by Thomas Aquinas, one of the foremost scholars and theologians of the late Middle Ages. The hymn is *strophic*, which means that all four stanzas are sung to the same music. Each stanza has six lines, and they seem to fall into pairs. The chant is in the E (Phrygian) mode, but the only line that ends on E is the last one. This gives the music a sense of continuity until the end. The chant is almost entirely syllabic, and the text urges praise for the miracle of Christ's birth and death.

We shall listen to all four stanzas, but what is important here is the *music*; therefore, the entire text is not given. Remember: all four stanzas have exactly the same music. Listen carefully and more than once. If you do, you will understand the next piece much more clearly.

Time	Listen for
0:00	Stanza 1 (*"Pange lingua ..."*)
0:33	Stanza 2 (*"Nobis datus ..."*)
1:04	Stanza 3 (*"In supremae ..."*)
1:39	Stanza 4 (*"Verbum caro ..."*)
2:12	"Amen"

LISTENING GUIDE

((•— Listen on MySearchLab

JOSQUIN DESPREZ (c. 1440–1521)

Kyrie from the Pange Lingua *Mass*

Date of composition: ca. 1520
Sopranos, altos, tenors, basses
Duration: 2:54

CD 1, 13

All of the three basic characteristics of Josquin's style that we have discussed may be heard in the opening Kyrie of Josquin's *Pange Lingua* Mass:

1. Simple imitation: a point of imitation introduces each short melodic phrase.
2. Overlapping cadences: just as the first group is completing its phrase and moving into a cadence, a second group enters, and so on.
3. Paired imitation: one pair of voices sings a phrase of imitation, then another pair enters.

Let us first look at the phrase that provides the material for the first point of imitation. It is derived from the first phrase of the plainchant hymn. Notice, however, that Josquin adds a short turning passage between the last two notes to provide intensity and drive to the cadence. Notice, too, the rhythm that Josquin has applied to the notes. It starts out with long notes (which stress the characteristic E-F half step of the Phrygian mode) and increases in motion until just before the end. The *meter* of this music is also very flexible. Composers of this era did not use measures or bar lines (as you can see from the facsimile of the original score). This creates a very fluid sound without the regularly recurring accents that occur in later music.

The movement as a whole has three main sections:

1. Kyrie eleison
2. Christe eleison
3. Kyrie eleison

Each section begins with a new point of imitation, and all are derived from the original hymn. The "Christe" section is based on the third and fourth lines of the melody, the final "Kyrie" section on the fifth and sixth lines. Toward the end of the last section, Josquin adds new rhythmic material to create a strong drive to the final cadence.

Time	Listen for	
0:00	*Kyrie eleison*	(Based on opening of hymn melody.) Tenors and basses; cadence overlaps with entry of altos. Sopranos enter before final cadence.
0:45	*Christe eleison*	(Based on lines 3 and 4 of hymn melody.) Paired imitation, overlapping entries.
2:02	*Kyrie eleison*	(Based on lines 5 and 6 of hymn melody.) Sopranos, altos, tenors, and basses enter in turn; increase in activity before final cadence.

The Late Renaissance

The sixteenth century was a time of remarkable musical achievements. The balance, beauty, and exquisite sound of imitative polyphony were fully explored by composers throughout Europe. In addition, composers began to use more **homophony**—chordal texture—in their compositions. There are few greater contrasts in music than that between imitative polyphony, with its emphasis on the overlapping of individual musical lines, and homophony, with its emphasis on block chords; and Renaissance composers from Josquin onward took full advantage of this contrast. They alternated and interwove the two styles in their compositions to achieve ever greater variety of texture and to underscore the meaning of their texts.

In fact, the development of music during the Renaissance is marked by this increasing focus on expressing the text. During the sixteenth century, the combination of a high degree of technical accomplishment and a new interest in text expression led to the creation of some of the most beautiful works in the history of music. Masses, motets, and secular songs were created by composers throughout Europe—in France and Germany, the Netherlands, Spain, Poland, and England. But probably the main center of musical activity was Italy.

Italy was the focal point of the Roman Catholic movement known as the Counter-Reformation, which began partly in reaction to the Protestant Reformation and partly as the result of a genuine desire to reform the Catholic Church from within. The Counter-Reformation had important consequences for music, as we will see.

One technical change that may be noticed in late Renaissance music is the sound of the last chord at the end of sections. Until this time, final chords contained only the "perfect" intervals (**octaves** and **fifths**). But in the late Renaissance, composers began to think that final chords should present the fullest sound possible and therefore should include the **third**, as well as the **root**, the fifth, and the octave of the chord. You can clearly hear the difference between a piece that ends with the open sound of an octave and a fifth and a piece that ends with a full chord. Compare the ending sound of the Machaut song in the previous chapter (p. 65) with the sound at the end of the following Palestrina motet (p. 78).

COMPOSERS, PATRONS, AND AUDIENCES

Patronage

Music costs money. Composers have to make a living, and so do performers. In the days before public concerts, ticket sales, and commercial recordings, music had to be financed by patrons (supporters). During the Renaissance, most patrons were wealthy aristocrats who could afford to employ musicians at their courts or palaces. Musicians were on the staff at these courts just like doormen, dressmakers, cooks, and other servants.

Some wealthy aristocrats employed several composers at once. In the later part of the fifteenth century, the duke of Milan appointed the great composer Josquin Desprez to his staff, although he already had four other composers on the payroll.

Sometimes patrons had to pay handsomely to hire the most famous musicians. When Josquin left Milan, he moved to the court of the duke of Ferrara. He was hired in 1503, against the advice of the duke's private secretary, who urged the duke to hire a composer named Heinrich Isaac instead. "Isaac gets on better with his colleagues and composes more quickly," he wrote. "It is true that Josquin is a better composer, but he composes only when he feels like it and not when he is asked. Moreover, Josquin is demanding 200 ducats, while Isaac will take 120." The duke decided to go first-class, and Josquin got his 200 ducats.

The Counter-Reformation and the Music of Palestrina

The Counter-Reformation was not primarily concerned with music, but music played a role in the deliberations of the church reformers. In 1534, the reformer Paul III was elected pope, and in 1545, he convened the Council of Trent, a council of cardinals that met from time to time over a period of about 20 years to discuss needed reforms in church administration and liturgy.

Music was discussed only during the last two years of the council. Many complaints were heard:

- ❏ Secular songs were being used as the basis for sacred compositions.
- ❏ Singers had become too theatrical and were distracting people from the liturgy.
- ❏ Polyphony had become too complicated and florid, obscuring the sacred words.

The council considered banning polyphony altogether, thinking that a return to plainchant was the best solution. In the end, however, the cardinals agreed that polyphonic music could be used in church, in addition to the traditional chants, provided that the words could be heard clearly and the style was not too elaborate.

The composer whose music most clearly represents these ideals is Giovanni Pierluigi da Palestrina (ca. 1525–1594). Like many people during the Middle Ages and the Renaissance, this man took his name from his hometown. He was born in Palestrina, 40 miles from Rome, and was sent to Rome as a choirboy to study and sing. He spent most of his life at some of that city's greatest musical institutions, including the Sistine Chapel (the private chapel of the pope).

The purity, serenity, and perfection of Palestrina's music have made him the most highly regarded composer of late Renaissance choral music. The principal characteristics of his style are balance, control, evenness, clarity, and perfect text setting. The overall effect conveyed by Palestrina's music is achieved by careful control of two primary elements: the structure of the individual melodic lines and the placement of dissonance.

In the structure of the individual melodic lines for his polyphonic pieces, Palestrina followed these strict guidelines:

a. The melody moves most of the time by steps with no gaps (leaps) between the notes.
b. If there is a leap, it is small and is immediately counterbalanced by stepwise motion in the opposite direction.
c. The rhythmic flow is not rigid or regularly accented, but is shifting, gentle, and alive.

Four hundred years after Palestrina, the composer Charles Gounod observed the following: "This severe, ascetic music is as calm and horizontal as the line of the ocean; monotonous by virtue of its serenity; anti-sensuous; and yet it is so intense in its contemplativeness that it verges sometimes on ecstasy."

Agnus Dei from *Pope Marcellus* Mass

A — gnus De — i

Contemporary accounts of Palestrina's music include the following: "Chaste and correct style ... confined with sweet harmony." "His music is extraordinarily acclaimed, and by virtue of its entirely novel character, astonishes even the performers themselves."

The second primary element in Palestrina's style is his careful control of dissonance (notes that fall outside of the basic harmony of the composition). His music has some dissonances (for without them, the music would be very bland indeed), but they appear only in particular circumstances. Usually, they are short passing notes or are off the beat. When dissonances do occur on the beat, they are always prepared and immediately resolved.

It might be thought that such a highly disciplined approach to composition would lead to dull, constricted music. On the contrary, Palestrina's music is so inspiring that it has been taken as a model of perfection for all those wishing to imitate the grace and beauty of Renaissance polyphony. In this case, as so often in artistic endeavors, strict formal rules produced masterpieces of great and lasting value.

Palestrina was a superbly gifted and resourceful composer, and despite the rigor of his approach, he found many ways to introduce variety into his music. In the first place, there is a constant interplay between **counterpoint** (two or more musical lines interweaving) and **homophony** (block chords). And within the sections of counterpoint, Palestrina draws on an almost limitless variety of methods. The imitative entries among the voices can vary in distance, number of entries, voice pairings, and even pitch. Different points of imitation can even be introduced at the same time—something that never happened in Josquin's music. And through it all, the text sounds clearly, with its natural rhythm perfectly conveyed.

Find the **Quick Listen** on **MySearchLab** "Palestrina"

Palestrina wrote more than 100 settings of the Mass and several volumes of secular songs, but perhaps his most impressive achievement is the composition of 250 motets. Motets could be written on almost any sacred text: biblical stories, passages from the Psalms, and so on. Almost always, composers chose expressive texts with elements of drama or mystery, and they matched the words with music of remarkable intensity or poignancy. (**See Listening Guide.**)

The Renaissance Motet

The Renaissance motet usually has four voice parts. It is entirely vocal and is usually sung by a small choir rather than by soloists. All the voices sing the same text—a sacred text—in the same language, almost always Latin. The music may be imitative or homophonic and is usually a mixture of the two.

Motets often have very expressive words. Renaissance composers tended to write richer and more unusual music for motets than they did for the fixed liturgical texts of the Mass. As a result, the music of Renaissance motets is often highly expressive, with a sensitive and compelling approach to the meaning of the text.

The Renaissance Secular Song

The Renaissance secular song evolved in two phases. In the fifteenth century, secular songs (songs with nonreligious texts) were not very different from those of the late Middle Ages (those of Machaut, for example). And an international musical style had been adopted in most countries, resulting in a lack of variety from place to place. But in the late Renaissance, several European countries developed their own distinct national styles for secular songs.

The most influential of all these countries was Italy, and the distinctive type of secular song that developed there was the **madrigal**. Madrigals are secular vocal pieces for a small group of singers, usually unaccompanied. The favorite topics were love, descriptions of nature, and sometimes war or battles. The music for madrigals mingles chordal and imitative textures and sensitively reflects the meaning of the text. The Italian madrigal became so influential in the course of the sixteenth century that composers of many other nationalities wrote madrigals in Italian, and some composers in England copied the style and wrote madrigals in English.

LISTENING GUIDE

((•▪ **Listen** on **MySearchLab**

GIOVANNI PIERLUIGI DA PALESTRINA (ca. 1525–1594)   *Motet*, Exsultate Deo

Date of composition: 1584
Sopranos, altos I, altos II, tenors, basses
Duration: 2:28

The motet *Exsultate Deo* was first published in Palestrina's fifth book of motets in 1584. This book contains 21 motets written for five voice lines instead of the usual four. (There are two groups of altos.) The text is from Psalm 81. Palestrina uses only the first three lines of the psalm.

CD I, 14

Exsultate Deo adiutori nostro, iubilate Deo Iacob.
Sumite psalmum et date tympanum, psalterium iucundum
   cum cithara.
Buccinate in neomenia tuba, insigni die solemnitatis vestrae.

Sing out in praise of God our refuge, acclaim the God of Jacob.
Raise a melody; beat the drum, play the tuneful lyre and harp.

Blow the trumpet at the new moon, and blow it at the full
   moon on the day of your solemn feast.

In his setting, Palestrina concentrates only on these exuberant opening verses of the psalm. The music is bright and joyful, filled with march rhythms and running eighth-note patterns, which help to enliven the work. In addition, the composer uses some **word-painting** (echoing the meaning of words in music), such as on the opening word "Exsultate," where the musical line rises triumphantly.

With five independent musical lines, the number of possible combinations is large, and Palestrina constantly varies the texture of his music. The clearest examples of this variation are when the sopranos drop out briefly, leaving only the lower voices, or (on the words "psalterium iucundum"—"tuneful lyre") when only three voices are sounding. *Exsultate Deo* is full of imitation, but Palestrina emphasizes the entrance of new lines of text by having them sung homophonically by a pair of voices, which adds an underlying structure to the work as a whole. Cleverly, he departs from this technique toward the end of the motet on the words "Buccinate" ("blow") and "tuba" ("trumpet"), where there is very close imitation, suggesting the echoing of trumpet blasts.

This performance is by the choir of Christ Church Cathedral, Oxford, England. This choir, which has been in continuous existence since the early sixteenth century, is made up of the same distribution of voices as it was originally: 16 boys and 12 men. So all the high voices you hear are those of boys.

Time	Listen for		
0:00	*Exsultate Deo adiutori nostro,*	Sing out in praise of God our refuge,	[Imitation in pair of upper voices alone; rising line on "Exsultate."]
0:11			[Pair of lower voices. Cadence in all five voices; overlaps with:]
0:28	*iubilate Deo Iacob.*	acclaim the God of Jacob.	[Many entries, suggesting a crowd "acclaiming."]
0:37			[Lower voices.]
0:49	*Sumite psalmum et date tympanum,*	Raise a melody; beat the drum,	[Quite homophonic, becoming more imitative. Note dotted rhythm on "tympanum."]
1:04	*psalterium iucundum cum cithara.*	play the tuneful lyre and harp.	[Elaborate flowering of the voices on "iucundum" ("tuneful").]
0:00	*Buccinate in neomenia tuba,*	Blow the trumpet at the new moon,	[Multiple echoes on "Buccinate;" homophonic climax on "neomenia."]
0:13			[Running echoes on "tuba."]
0:23	*insigni die solemnitatis vestrae.*	and blow it at the full moon on the day of your solemn feast.	[Slower, lower, more "solemn."]

The Madrigal

As we have seen, matching the words of the text with music that expresses their meaning was a primary concern of late-Renaissance composers. The madrigal is the musical genre that demonstrates this desire most colorfully.

The madrigal flourished in the courtly atmosphere of Italian aristocratic families. The poetry is serious and elegant, with a sonorous beauty of its own. And the music is carefully designed to reflect the text.

Composers used a variety of techniques to bring out the meaning of the words they set.

The title page to Thomas Morley's *A Plaine and Easie Introduction to Practicall Musicke*, printed in 1597.

In his book, Morley provides a detailed description of the way to write a madrigal. He then concludes, "Keeping these rules, you shall have a perfect agreement and, as it were, an harmonical consent betwixt the matter and the music."

In general, the same mixture of chordal textures and imitative polyphony was used in madrigals as in motets, but composers went much further in their search for direct expression. If the text had words such as "rising," "flying," or "soaring," then the music would have fast upward scales. "Peace" and "happiness" might be set to sweet major chords, "agony" and "despair" to wrenching dissonances. In fact, contrasts of this kind—between happiness and despair, for example—often appeared in madrigal texts within the same poem. In poetry this contrast is known as *antithesis*, and it presented ideal musical opportunities for madrigal composers. A sigh might be represented by a sudden, short pause—to be followed by a long flowing line evoking the elation of love.

The madrigal became immensely popular during the sixteenth century and survived well into the seventeenth. Composers strove for ever-greater intensity of expression, and the late madrigalists managed to wring every ounce of feeling from each nuance of the text. They often used **word-painting** to do this.

Toward the end of the sixteenth century, a fascination with madrigals had taken hold in England. Italian madrigals sometimes appeared in English translation. But English composers also wrote their own madrigals with English texts. These were often lighter in tone and more cheerful than their Italian counterparts.

The guiding force for the development of English madrigals was Thomas Morley (1557–1602), a gifted composer and the author of an important textbook on music. Morley is important for more than his own composing and writing, however. During his lifetime, music publishing was controlled by the government; Morley was granted sole permission to print music for the whole of England. Morley published more madrigals than any other English composer and established a style that was followed by most other English madrigalists.

We will listen to a pair of extremely short madrigals by Thomas Morley from a collection he published in 1595. Both are for two voices rather than the conventional four. The first (*Sweet Nymph Come to Thy Lover*) is for two women; the second (*Fire and Lightning*) is sung by two men. They make a wonderfully pleasing and contrasting pair. (**See Listening Guide.**)

MUSICAL BORROWING

The idea that originality is the most important characteristic of a composer is a very modern one. For most of music history, composers borrowed freely from one another. Borrowing from another composer was considered a mark of respect.

During the Renaissance, composers made widespread use of previously existing material for their works. This included plainchant, popular songs, other people's compositions, and sometimes earlier pieces of their own. Palestrina, one of the greatest composers of the Renaissance era, was a frequent borrower from the works of other composers. Scholars have traced compositions by at least 10 other composers among the building materials of Palestrina's works.

Occasionally, you can trace the metamorphosis of the same piece from a chant to a motet to a Mass. For example, Palestrina wrote a motet based on the plainchant *Assumpta Est Maria*. The motet weaves the original notes of the chant into a beautiful polyphonic whole. Later, Palestrina wrote an entire Mass based on his motet using the musical fabric of the motet as the basis for an impressive, new, large-scale composition.

LISTENING GUIDE

((•—**Listen** on **MySearchLab**

THOMAS MORLEY (1557–1602)

Two English Madrigals

Date of composition: 1595
Two sopranos (*Sweet Nymph Come to Thy Lover*)
Duration: 1:34

CD I, 15

The texts for these short pieces were probably written by Morley himself. Each one contains picturesque images, which the music captures beautifully. The first madrigal, *Sweet Nymph*, compares the lover to a nightingale, a favorite image for composers. The second, *Fire and Lightning*, uses the imagery of thunder and storms to describe the "stormy" nature of love. It is lively and frenetic, with a kicker at the end. Both are primarily imitative, with very close imitation in some sections to liven up the proceedings or to intensify the sound. The very last line of *Fire and Lightning* is suddenly homophonic to draw attention to the sting at the end. This last line also exploits antithesis ("fair"/"spiteful") to make its effect.

Both madrigals have such short texts that there are many repetitions of each phrase, and you will hear many instances of word-painting. The fine performances here are by Sarah Pelletier and Suzanne Ehly—sopranos—and William Sharp and Mark Aliapoulios—baritones.

Time	Listen for	
0:00	Sweet nymph come to thy lover,	Imitation.
0:12	Lo here alone our loves we may discover,	Touches of homophony on "Lo here alone."
0:20	(*Repeat of first two lines*)	
0:39	Where the sweet nightingale with wanton gloses,	Imitation; high notes and close harmony on "gloses" [trills].
0:49	Hark, her love too discloses.	High notes, very close imitation, especially last time through.
1:03	(*Repeat of last two lines*)	

Date of composition: 1595
Two baritones (*Fire and Lightning*)
Duration: 1:13

CD I, 16

Time	Listen for	
0:00	Fire and lightning from heaven fall	Lively; very close imitation.
0:08	And sweetly enflame that heart with love arightful,	Smooth descending scales on "sweetly."
0:16	(*Repeat of first two lines*)	
0:31	Of Flora my delightful,	Scales in opposite direction on "delightful."
0:45	So fair but yet so spiteful.	Last time through: homophonic, close pungent harmony, dissonance on "spite-," incomplete sound on "ful."
0:47	(*Repeat of last two lines*)	

After the work of the late Italian and English madrigalists, the Renaissance polyphonic style had run its course. It had produced works of great beauty and variety, but new composers had new ideas. Their interest in text expression remained paramount, but they felt that new ways had to be found to allow the words to dominate the music. These new ways were the foundation of a new musical style in the seventeenth century, the Baroque style, in which single voices were accompanied by instruments, and instrumental music became more and more prominent. Let's examine the origins of this style in the rise of instrumental music in the late Renaissance.

The Rise of Instrumental Music

During the Renaissance, instrumental music became more and more popular. A wide range of instruments was in use, from loud, extroverted trumpets to soft, delicate strings and recorders. Compositions ranged from serious contrapuntal works to lighthearted dances.

One of the former types was the *canzona*, a serious contrapuntal instrumental piece based on the style of secular songs. The master of the canzona was Giovanni Gabrieli (ca. 1555–1612), an organist and composer at St. Mark's Church in Venice. St. Mark's had two choir lofts facing each other, and Gabrieli took advantage of this to place contrasting groups of instruments in the two lofts, creating an early version of stereo sound. (**See Listening Guide.**)

The largest category of instrumental music during the Renaissance was dance music, since dancing was one of the most popular forms of entertainment. Dance music was usually binary in form (AABB) and followed the characteristic tempos and rhythms of each type of dance (fast or slow, two-in-a-bar, three-in-a-bar, etc.). Dances were frequently performed in pairs, contrasting slow with fast, or duple meter with triple meter. (**See Listening Guide.**)

Find the **Quick Listen** on **MySearchLab**

"Renaissance Dance Music"

PERFORMANCE IN CONTEXT

St. Mark's in Venice: The Church of Gold

Often called the *Chiesa d'Oro* ("Church of Gold") from its Byzantine mosaics, St. Mark's Church in Venice has been an important site for music making since its foundation in the eleventh century. The spectacular domes and double choir lofts create an imposing echo, which was exploited by composers particularly in the Renaissance and Baroque periods. Adrian Willaert, a Flemish composer appointed in 1527, was the first to show Venetians the possibilities of fine music making in St. Mark's. He stayed in the post for 35 years. Composers came from all over Europe to study with him. He was followed by three great Italian masters of music: Andrea Gabrieli, his nephew Giovanni Gabrieli, and Claudio Monteverdi. St. Mark's is situated at the east end of the famous St. Mark's Square in Venice and was originally the private chapel of the Doge, the Venetian head of state. Since 1807 it has been the city's cathedral. The extraordinary mosaics are covered in gold leaf and made up of millions of tiny stones. They depict Jesus and the saints as well as scenes from the Bible.

San Marco, Venice, Interior.

LISTENING GUIDE

((•— **Listen** on **MySearchLab**

GIOVANNI GABRIELI (ca. 1555–1612)

Canzona Duodecimi Toni

Date of composition: 1597
Two brass choirs
Duration: 3:55

CD I, 17

This work by Giovanni Gabrieli is divided into several sections and contrasts two brass groups or "choirs," which are heard in dialogue. As in Josquin's *Pange Lingua* Mass, the music is pushed forward by overlapping cadences, one choir beginning as the previous choir ends. Sometimes the two choirs play together. The piece features dynamic contrasts of loud and soft, which are characteristic of late Renaissance and early Baroque music. A special effect involving dynamic contrast is "echo," in which the exact repetition of a phrase at a lower volume suggests distance.

The canzona is full of varied rhythmic patterns, but the most pervasive is the "canzona rhythm," LONG-short-short (♩ ♪♪), which you will hear throughout the piece, in fast and slow tempos.

Time	Listen for
	Introduction
0:00	Both brass choirs. Fairly slow, medium loud; canzona rhythm is prominent.
	Section 1
0:15	Choir I. Faster tempo, same musical motive and rhythm, faster tempo, homophonic.
0:20	Choir II, growing louder.
0:27	Both choirs, loud, featuring flourishes by trumpets in imitation; cadence.
	Section 2
0:43	Second idea, quieter, mostly homophonic, echoes, passages of imitation between choirs, lively rhythms; cadence.
	Section 3
1:26	Third idea, loud, mostly homophonic, echoes, both choirs.
1:43	Trumpet flourishes, cadence.
1:49	Canzona rhythm; close imitation, cadence.
	Section 4
2:10	Fourth idea, quiet, canzona rhythm, lots of imitation between choirs, cadence.
2:35	Multiple echoes, from loud to soft, between choirs; crescendo . . .
3:02	Final idea, both choirs loud, leading to big climax.

THE IMPORTANCE OF DANCING

This text comes from a dance treatise published in 1589. The treatise is cast as a dialogue between student and teacher.

Student: Without knowledge of dancing, I could not please the damsels, upon whom, it seems to me, the entire reputation of an eligible young man depends.

Teacher: You are quite right, as naturally the male and female seek one another, and nothing does more to stimulate a man to acts of courtesy, honor, and generosity than love. And if you desire to marry, you must realize that a mistress is won by the good temper and grace displayed while dancing. And there is more to it than this, for dancing is practiced to reveal whether lovers are in good health and sound of limb, after which they are permitted to kiss and touch and savor one another, thus to ascertain if they are shapely or emit an unpleasant odor as of bad meat. Therefore, apart from the many other advantages to be derived from dancing, it becomes essential to a well-ordered society.

LISTENING GUIDE

((•—Listen on **MySearchLab**

TIELMAN SUSATO (fl. 1543–1570)   *Ronde and Saltarello*

Date of composition: 1551
Recorders and percussion
Duration: 1:55

CD I, 18

This example is a dance pair written by the Flemish composer and publisher Tielman Susato. The *ronde* and *saltarello* are both Renaissance dances in binary form. On the repeats, the melodies are occasionally ornamented with trills and decorative figures.

The two dances use the same melody, but the ronde is in duple meter, whereas the saltarello is in triple meter; the effect of the meter change is dramatic.

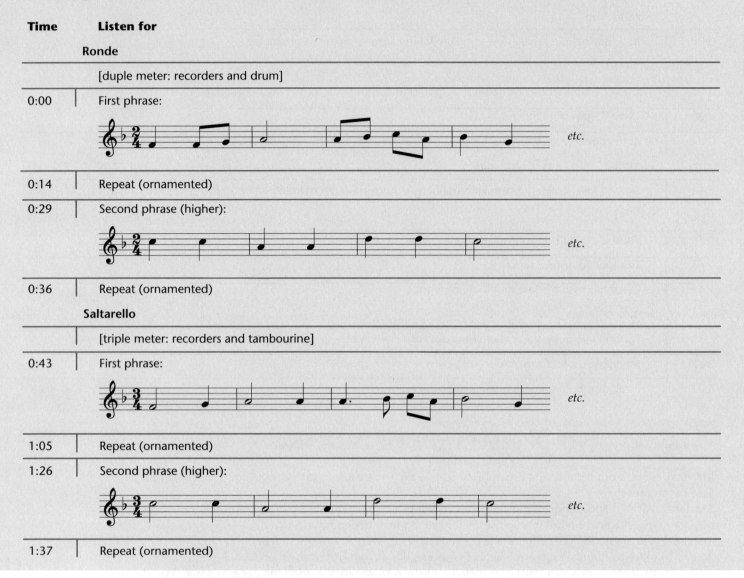

Time	Listen for
	Ronde
	[duple meter: recorders and drum]
0:00	First phrase:
0:14	Repeat (ornamented)
0:29	Second phrase (higher):
0:36	Repeat (ornamented)
	Saltarello
	[triple meter: recorders and tambourine]
0:43	First phrase:
1:05	Repeat (ornamented)
1:26	Second phrase (higher):
1:37	Repeat (ornamented)

STYLE SUMMARY

The Renaissance

Renaissance musical style was very different from that of the Middle Ages. In place of the stark or subtle sounds of medieval music, Renaissance compositions offer smoothly contoured and carefully woven textures. Renaissance music encompasses three main musical genres: Mass movements, other Latin texts (motets), and secular songs. All of these genres are vocal.

The principal ways of combining voices in the Renaissance were through homophony (harmonizing voices singing in the same rhythms) and imitation (voices copying each other a few measures apart). Sometimes these

styles were adopted uniformly throughout a piece, but more often they were juxtaposed or subtly blended. The typical sound of Renaissance music, therefore, resembles a tapestry, in which the separate strands can be recognized and traced, and yet the combination presents a complete and integrated picture.

Many Renaissance works are based on sacred texts, and the resulting music is dignified, beautiful, and spiritually uplifting. Renaissance secular songs such as madrigals, however, are more down-to-earth. And although word-painting (the depiction of the meaning of individual words in music) can be

A page from a Renaissance manuscript. The chant is for the beginning of the Mass on Easter Sunday. The illustration depicts the Resurrection.

found in Latin motets, it was widely used in madrigals, whose subject matter was usually love and its ramifications.

Word-painting led to all kinds of clever musical effects: running scales to depict a chase, dissonant chords for the pain of love, and low notes for death. We can hear these in some of the English madrigals of the later sixteenth century as well as in the more frequent Italian ones.

The last noteworthy component of Renaissance music is the rise in popularity of works for instruments. Even though vocal music still predominated, more and more instrumental music was being composed, and musicians sometimes played instrumental arrangements of vocal pieces. The main types of instrumental music were serious polyphonic pieces that involved imitation (canzonas) and lighthearted, rhythmic dances. The latter were usually in binary (AABB) form.

It was the instrumental music of the Renaissance that had the most influence on music of the following style period. In the Baroque era, instruments became central to the sound of the new style.

FUNDAMENTALS OF RENAISSANCE MUSIC

- ❏ Sound is smooth and homogenous
- ❏ Harmony is still primarily based on modes
- ❏ Most prominent feature is imitation
- ❏ Vocal genres include Mass movements, motets, and secular songs
- ❏ Motets and madrigals often use word-painting, which can involve dissonance
- ❏ Instrumental music is either serious and imitative or light and dancelike

FOR FURTHER DISCUSSION AND STUDY

1. Compare medieval and Renaissance musical styles. What are the principal similarities and differences?

2. How did the Renaissance and Counter-Reformation movements in European society affect musical composition?

3. Describe the basic structure of the Mass. How was music used in the Mass during the Renaissance?

4. What are the differences between the texts of a motet and a madrigal? How does the music for these forms reflect these differences?

5. Go to Classical.com or to your library and listen to a Renaissance madrigal that is not discussed in this chapter. Write your own Listening Guide for it, pointing out the use of chord harmony, word-painting, and antithesis.

The Baroque Era:
1600–1750

Often, innovations in music are greeted with skepticism and disapproval. New musical styles are often described as ugly, disagreeable, or even offensive, and critics use unflattering names for them. The word "baroque" began as a term of disapproval. In the seventeenth century, it was used by philosophers to describe tortuous forms of argument, and by jewelers to describe oddly colored or misshapen pearls. The word was first applied to music in the eighteenth century. In 1768, the French philosopher Rousseau defined Baroque music as that in which

> the harmony is confused, full of modulations and dissonances; the melody is harsh and unnatural; the intonation is remote; and the motion is constrained.

Today, the word "baroque" is no longer a negative term. The creative works of the seventeenth and early eighteenth centuries are recognized for their grandeur, depth, and technical mastery. The Baroque period, after all, is the age of the poet Milton and the playwrights Racine and Molière; the artists Rembrandt and Velázquez; and the composers Bach, Handel, and Vivaldi.

Life in the Baroque Era

The Baroque era was a period of absolute monarchs. These monarchs had total control over every aspect of their realms: the economy, the content of books, the style of art, and even life and death. The model for absolute monarchy was set by Louis XIV, who raised the power of the king to unparalleled heights. He regarded himself as synonymous with the whole nation of France. "I *am* the state," he said.

In many parts of Europe, life was characterized by a strict social hierarchy, rigid laws, and elaborate codes of dress and manners. The political instability and wars that had dominated Europe for so many years gave way to a period of international peace and economic expansion. There may have been political repression, punitive taxation, and gross social inequities, but there were no major wars, and rulers supported the arts as a way of expressing their cultivation and learning.

During the seventeenth and eighteenth centuries, a radical change took place in philosophical and scientific thinking. Aided by new technological developments, scientists began to test their ideas by measurement and mathematical analysis rather than by relying on traditional ideas. The foremost scientist of the age

A Baroque painting of the palace and gardens at Versailles.

Jean-Baptiste Martin, "Bassin du Dragon et de Neptune." Photo: Amaudet/Lewandowski. Chateaux de Versailles et de Trianon, Versailles, France. Reunion des Musées Nationaux/Art Resource, NY.

was Sir Isaac Newton, who discovered the principle of gravity, developed calculus, and determined that white light is made up of all the colors of the spectrum.

The discoveries of Newton and other scientists had a profound effect on philosophers, who began to search for comparable principles to apply to human life and society. They began to apply the techniques of mathematical analysis to human thought.

Order and organization were valued above all else in society and in the arts. Baroque artists thought that the emotions could be objectively classified and that art could be designed to arouse these emotions in its audience. Indeed, Baroque art displays a fascination with states of emotion: grief, religious ecstasy, joy, passion, despair. Baroque artists studied these emotional states and strove to represent them. Baroque works of art involve the viewer immediately. Portraits stress the grandeur and personality of their subjects; sculptures depict fleeting moments of emotional intensity; buildings radiate opulence, strength, and rhythmic order.

The most impressive building of the Baroque period is surely the palace of Versailles, built by Louis XIV in the mid-1600s. It is breathtakingly grand and symmetrical, with more than a thousand rooms, including one hall lined entirely with mirrors. The effect of grandeur continues outside, where the geometrically organized landscape—with its long rows of trees, pools, and elegant gardens—extends for miles.

> There are only six simple and primitive passions, that is, wonder, love, hatred, desire, joy, and sadness. All the others are composed of some of these six.
> —René Descartes (1646)

PERFORMANCE IN CONTEXT
Versailles

The grand Palace of Versailles was the center of French musical life and patronage in the century before the Revolution. Louis XIV built this expansive palace as his "golden cage" to keep the nobles of France close at hand and under closer watch. Musicians followed the royal court and nobility to Versailles, forming a great concentration of talent. One of these musicians was the Italian-born dancer–composer Jean-Baptiste Lully, who arrived in 1652 or 1653 and spent most of his life at the palace. Lully's ballets attracted the attention of Louis XIV, who appeared in several as a dancer, and the composer soon became famous for operas and theatre music as well. Through Versailles, Lully's music became the basis of a new French style, one that musicians traveled across Europe to hear in the palace's salons, concert hall, and theatre. The Palace of Versailles was looted during the French Revolution but was gradually restored following its conversion into a museum in 1833. Today, Versailles retains its old duality of politics and art. Heads of state are greeted in the famous Hall of Mirrors, while visitors from Paris and beyond attend concerts on the lawn and in the lavishly restored opera house.

Jean-Léon Gérôme (1824–1904). *The Reception for the Prince of Condé at Versailles*, 1878. Oil on canvas.

Self-portrait by Rembrandt as an old man.

Rembrandt Harmensz van Rijn (1606–1669). Rembrandt, self-portrait at old age. Oil on canvas. National Gallery, London, Great Britain. © Photograph by Erich Lessing. Erich Lessing/Art Resource, NY.

In all Baroque art, contrast and illusion are the dominant forces. Painters discovered the dramatic possibilities of strong contrasts between light and shade. In Rembrandt's portraits, light falls generously on the subject's face, while the background falls away in the gloom.

Illusion was a favorite device: paper was decorated to resemble dense marble; doors and windows were painted onto walls; scenes creating the effect of outdoor vistas were drawn inside false window frames. Painted ceilings offered special opportunities for spectacular effects: the ceilings seem to open up to the heavens, with whirling clouds and cherubs leaping out of the sky.

Comparable characteristics are found in Baroque music. Baroque composers set out to portray specific states of emotion, and they created contrast and illusion through the use of dynamics and contrasting performing groups.

The emphasis on contrast can be heard most clearly in the concerto. **Concertos** are built on the idea of contrast: between the entire orchestra and a small group, or between the orchestra and a single instrument.

NEED TO KNOW
NEW DEVELOPMENTS OF THE BAROQUE

1. Emphasis on scientific understanding and measurement

2. Interest in balance, order, and organization

3. Artists highlighted contrasting emotions

4. Illusion was highly prized

COMPOSERS, PATRONS, AND AUDIENCES

Audiences in the Baroque Era

The Baroque era was an important period of transition from the time of small, elite, aristocratic audiences to that of a wider concert-going public. The trend began in Italy with a new musical invention: opera. Public opera houses were built in Venice and Rome about the middle of the seventeenth century. In the 1670s the first public concert series was organized in London. Toward the end of the Baroque period, similar public concerts began to be held in France (in 1725) and Germany (in the 1740s).

These concerts were funded by subscription. People would sign up for the series, and the organizer could then use the money to hire the performers, rent the hall, print programs, and the like. Instead of an individual patron—a king or member of the nobility—underwriting a performance, the audience itself provided the funds through ticket sales.

Some Baroque composers arranged subscription concerts for their own benefit. Handel gave many concerts of his own music and made a considerable amount of money during his lifetime. He was also very generous: he inaugurated the idea of giving annual performances of his *Messiah* for charity. A contemporary wrote that *Messiah* "fed the hungry, clothed the naked, fostered the orphan, and enriched succeeding managers of oratorios, more than any single musical production in this or any other country." Handel's *Messiah* performances were very popular. At the 1750 performance, there wasn't enough room for the large audience, despite the request in the announcement that "Gentlemen are desired to come without swords, and the Ladies without hoops." (Swords worn on men's waists and the hoops used to fill out women's skirts took up enormous amounts of room.)

Dynamic contrasts can also achieve illusion. In Baroque instrumental music, the same phrase is often played first loud and then soft. This echo effect gives the illusion of space and distance. Instruments sometimes give the illusion of being other instruments: a flute may play a trumpet fanfare.

General Characteristics of Baroque Music

The Baroque era lasted only 150 years; it was somewhat shorter than the Renaissance and a fraction of the length of the Middle Ages. In spite of its brevity, it is the first period of our musical history that is featured with any frequency in today's concert halls or on radio programs. Even then, only the last half century of the Baroque era, the period of Bach and Handel and Vivaldi, is generally represented. It is logical, then, to divide our examination of Baroque music into two parts: the early Baroque (1600–1700) and the late Baroque (1700–1750). In fact, this division corresponds to actual musical events, because the early Baroque was the period in which stylistic trends were established, while the late Baroque was the time of the well-known masters and of fixed musical forms.

The early Baroque was a period of excitement and experimentation. The composers of the early 1600s combined expressiveness with great originality. The greatest invention of the age was opera, which displayed the best of all contemporary arts. It featured elaborate stage machinery, gorgeous costumes, and beautiful stage sets. All this was combined with moving stories, expressive acting, and dramatic music.

Early Baroque music was designed to be emotional. Both vocal and instrumental works were written to evoke specific states of mind. Certain melodic and harmonic patterns came to be associated with particular feelings. Composers experimented with ways to make music imitate the irregularity, the rise and fall, of impassioned speech.

However, there were opposing forces that balanced these trends in early Baroque music. There was a tendency toward more rigid formal design. The uninterrupted, flowing meters of earlier music were giving way to more regular metric organization. Composers began to use bar lines to organize their music into regular metric groupings. The earlier modes with their varied colors were yielding to the more straightforward major and minor keys.

As the Baroque period progressed, organization and control began to replace experimentation. The forms used in opera and in instrumental music became standardized. The rigid hierarchy of society was reflected in opera plots, which often revolved around the effect on people of a powerful ruler's whims. The growth of tonality, with its carefully organized sequence of keys and harmonic patterns, may also be seen as a mirror of the Baroque social order.

With the Baroque fascination with structure and organization came the development of fixed musical forms. The chief vocal forms of the early Baroque were the opera and the cantata. **Operas** were large-scale productions, expressive and elaborate. They immediately became extremely popular. Great rulers and aristocratic

Find the **Quick Listen** on **MySearchLab** "French Baroque Opera"

Find the **Quick Listen** on **MySearchLab**
"Baroque Trio Sonata"

Find the **Quick Listen** on **MySearchLab**
"Chamber Cantata"

Find the **Quick Listen** on **MySearchLab**
"Protestant Chorale"

Find the **Quick Listen** on **MySearchLab**
"Christmas Oratorio"

Find the **Quick Listen** on **MySearchLab**
"Concerto Grosso"

Find the **Quick Listen** on **MySearchLab**
"Baroque Music Passion"

families built their own private theaters for the performance of opera, and opera houses sprang up across Europe.

Cantatas were, in effect, very short unstaged operas: they were written for instruments and one or two voices and portrayed a single scene or situation. Some of the later **church cantatas** (notably those of Bach) were based on liturgical themes and were performed in church on Sundays, but the earlier **chamber cantatas** were secular in nature, telling stories of love lost and found, of nymphs and shepherds. They were perfect for performance in a salon or a small music room.

During the Baroque period, instrumental music gained great importance. Instruments began to take on the shape and sound of their modern counterparts, and instrumental technique began to rival the brilliant speed, expressiveness, and control of the famous opera singers of the day. The most important instrumental forms of the Baroque era were the concerto, the sonata, and the dance suite.

Concertos are based on contrast. Their texture is formed by the interplay between a small group (or soloist) called *solo* and a large group called *ripieno*. The resulting instrumental dialogue allowed Baroque composers to create considerable drama within a purely instrumental form.

Sonatas are chamber works, smaller in scale than concertos and less dependent on contrast. Numbers could range from two or three instruments to a small handful, but a sonata was always designed for a group smaller than an orchestra.

Dance suites were originally designed exclusively to accompany dancing. An evening's entertainment often consisted of a series, or "suite," of contrasting dances, usually in binary form. Later, the dance suite became one of the most popular independent instrumental genres of the late Baroque.

The spread of the Protestant movement had an important influence on music. The most distinctive musical feature of a Protestant service was the **chorale**, a hymn with a steady rhythm and simple tune, usually sung in unison by the whole congregation. Chorale tunes, often dating from the Renaissance or even earlier, found their way into many forms of Baroque music, including organ pieces and church cantatas. Another form of sacred music was the **oratorio**. This is a large-scale work like an opera, but it is based on a sacred story, and it is not staged. Instead, a narrator sings the story, and other singers sing the words of people in the story. Similar to the oratorio is the **Passion**, a composition based on the gospel account of the last days of Jesus.

Baroque Vocal and Instrumental Forms

I. *Vocal Forms*

1. **Opera:** large-scale stage productions featuring music, dance, costumes, and elaborate plots and settings

2. **Cantata:** short, unstaged operas portraying a single scene
   a. Church Cantata: based on a religious subject
   b. Chamber Cantata: based on a secular subject

3. **Oratorio:** Opera-like work on religious theme, but not staged. The **Passion** is similar to an oratorio, but describes the final days of Jesus's life

4. **Chorale:** Protestant hymn sung in unison by the entire congregation, with a simple melody and regular rhythm

II. *Instrumental Forms*

1. **Concerto:** instrumental work based on opposition of two groups
   a. **Concerto grosso** ("large concerto"): full orchestra and small group of soloists
   b. **Solo concerto:** full orchestra and a single soloist

2. **Sonata:** chamber work for a small group
   a. **Sonata da camera** ("chamber sonata"): movements based on dance rhythms
   b. **Sonata da chiesa** ("church sonata"): more serious movements alternating slow and fast

3. **Dance suite:** series of short, contrasting dance movements

Late Baroque music is characterized by rhythmic vitality. The driving rhythmic pulse of a Vivaldi concerto and the brilliantly organized harmonic motion of a Bach fugue are manifestations of the late style. Again, the vitality is given strength through order and control. But it would be a mistake to think that the emotions that were present in early Baroque music were suppressed in the late period. They were more organized and more formally presented, but they still constituted an essential part of the musical experience.

Stylistically, all Baroque music has one very notable characteristic: a strong bass line. This line not only forms the harmonic underpinning for Baroque music but also provides a strong foundation for its rhythmic momentum. But whether the upper parts of a Baroque composition have strong rhythmic drive or extended expressive melodies, the bass part is always the driving force, both harmonically and rhythmically. Since the bass line is almost never silent in a Baroque composition, it is known as the **basso continuo** ("continuous bass"), or sometimes just **continuo**. The basso continuo part is usually played by a harpsichord and low strings. Whatever the genre, you can recognize a Baroque piece by the strength and powerful sense of direction of its bass line.

The Early Baroque (1600–1700)

The beginning of the Baroque period was a time of experimentation and excitement. Composers were trying out new ideas, and there was a great deal of discussion about music and the way it should be written. Some clung to the Renaissance ideal of many-voiced polyphony, with its careful shaping of melodic lines and strict control of dissonance. Others felt that music should serve the text, and that the rules of counterpoint and dissonance should be disregarded if they did not serve this primary aim. The latter composers favored a new song style known as **monody**, a type of music written for solo voice and basso continuo that imitated the natural rhythms of speech. Monody was composed for both sacred and secular texts; in all cases, the single voice part ranges freely and flexibly above the bass. In the end, both types of music—monody and traditional Renaissance-style polyphony—existed side by side.

One of the early composers of monody was Francesca Caccini (1587–ca. 1640). She was the principal composer at the court of Tuscany, in northern Italy. She was multitalented: she could sing brilliantly, write poetry in both Latin and Italian, and play three different instruments, all equally well.

The most daring experiments in the new compositional style were carried out by a group of composers in Italy and led to the development of a completely new musical genre: opera. Among these composers was a man who was clearly the greatest composer of his age. His name was Claudio Monteverdi. Monteverdi made important contributions in two distinct historical periods. He lived a long life—from 1567 to 1643—and his life cut across the convenient boundaries that historians like to create. Monteverdi wrote many pieces in Renaissance style, especially madrigals, but he was also the first great opera composer of the Baroque era.

Monteverdi and the First Great Opera

The first great opera in the history of Western music was Monteverdi's *Orfeo*, written in 1607. The opera is based on the ancient Greek myth of Orpheus and Eurydice.

The Story of the Opera   Orpheus ("Orfeo" in Italian) and Eurydice are in love. Shepherds and nymphs sing and dance together. Suddenly the revelries are interrupted by a messenger who announces that Eurydice has been bitten by a snake and is dead. Orpheus, a musician, is grief-stricken and decides to travel to the underworld to bring Eurydice back to life. The king of the underworld is moved by Orpheus's plea and allows Eurydice to return, but on one condition: that Orpheus not turn back and look at her. On their journey home, Orpheus becomes anxious and steals a glance at his beloved. She disappears forever.

Monteverdi sets this story with a wide variety of music. There are madrigal-like choruses, dances, and instrumental interludes. But the most striking style of all is called **recitative**, which developed out of the early experiments with monody. Recitative is designed to imitate as closely as possible the freedom and expressiveness of speech.

Recitative is always sung by one singer with accompanying **basso continuo**. It is very flexible, because it follows the changing meanings of the text, with the bass line supporting the voice and providing punctuation. It can be very simple or quite elaborate and songlike. It is designed to mirror, moment by moment, the emotional state of the singer. In all of his music, but especially in his recitatives, Monteverdi displays the talent that all great opera composers share: the ability to capture and reflect the feelings of the human soul. "The modern composer," he said, "builds his works on the basis of truth." (**See Listening Guide.**)

Find the **Quick Listen** on **MySearchLab** "Monteverdi's *Orfeo*"

Francesca Caccini, *Maria dolce Maria*

Voice

Ma – ria, dol – ce Ma-ri – a, no – me so-a – ve tan-to

Basso continuo

che a pro-nun-ci-ar ti in pa-ra-di – s'il co – re. No – me

Find the **Quick Listen** on **MySearchLab** "Francesca Caccini"

sa – cra – t'e san – to che'l cor m'in-fiam – mi di ce –

"Mary, sweet Mary, a name so sweet that in saying it my heart is in paradise. A name so sacred and holy that my heart is aflame with heavenly love."

le – ste a – mo – re.

LISTENING GUIDE

((•—[Listen on MySearchLab

CLAUDIO MONTEVERDI (1567–1643)

Orfeo's recitative, Euridice's recitative, chorus of nymphs and shepherds, and instrumental ritornello from the opera Orfeo

Date of composition: 1607
Tenor and soprano solo, chorus, instrumental
  ensemble and basso continuo
Duration: 3:59

CD I, 19

This scene comes from the first act of the opera, in which the love of Orfeo and Euridice is celebrated. In his lyrical recitative "Rosa del Ciel . . ." ("Rose of Heaven . . ."), Orfeo expresses his passion for Euridice and his happiness that she returns his feelings. Euridice, responding to Orfeo's proclamation of love, affectionately pledges her heart to him in a declamatory passage ("Io non dirò . . ."—"I shall not say . . ."). A chorus of nymphs and shepherds follows with a celebratory dance ("Lasciate i monti . . ."—"Leave the hills . . ."), and the scene is closed by an instrumental **ritornello** (a short passage that appears in several places in a musical work).

Monteverdi uses a variety of musical means to depict this pastoral setting. Both Orfeo and Euridice sing in a free, expressive recitative. The melody imitates the rhythms and the inflections of speech and mirrors the meaning of the text. In Orfeo's part, for instance, Monteverdi accentuates significant words such as "fortunato amante" ("happy lover") or "Mio ben" ("My love") by means of rising phrases and matches the musical rhythm with the rhythm of the words:

"fe-li-cís-si-mo" ("happiest") [♪♪♪ ♪♪]

"sos-pi-rá-i" ("I sighed"); "sos-pi-rás-ti" ("you sighed") [♪♪♪♩♩]

In Euridice's recitative, the composer uses similar lively motives for the words "gioir," "gioia," and "gioisca" ("rejoicing," "rejoice," "enjoys"); employs wide leaps to represent "Quanto" ("How much"); and provides the words "core" ("heart") and "Amore" ("Love") with soothing cadences.

The choral dance consists of two sections: the first, in duple meter, is based on imitative phrases that evoke the movement of dancers; the second provides a distinct contrast, because it is set in triple meter and its texture is completely homophonic. The instrumental ritornello that ensues is a faster dance, which adds variety and brings closure to this short and happy scene.

Time	Listen for	
	Orfeo	
0:00	[soft arpeggiated chords in continuo] *Rosa del Ciel, vita del mondo, e degna* *Prole di lui che l'Universo affrena,*	O Rose of Heaven, life of the world, And worthy offspring of him who rules the universe,
0:25	[voice becoming more animated] *Sol, ch'il tutto circondi e'l tutto miri* *Da gli stellanti giri,* [rising melody]	Sun, you who surround and watch everything From the starry skies,
0:34	*Dimmi, vedesti mai* *Di me più lieto e fortunato* *amante?* [gentle cadence]	Tell me, have you ever seen A happier or more fortunate lover than I?
0:45	*Fu ben felice il giorno,* *Mio ben,* [loving phrase] *che pria ti vidi,*	Blessed was the day, My love, when first I saw you,
0:56	*E più felice l'ora* *Che per te sospirai* *Poich'al mio sospirar tu sospirasti.* [sighing phrases]	And more blessed yet the hour When first I sighed for you, Since you returned my sighs.
1:15	*Felicissimo il punto* *Che la candida mano,* *Pegno di pura fede, a me porgesti.* [many notes]	Most blessed of all the moment When you offered me your white hand, As pledge of your pure love.
1:34	*Se tanti cori avessi* *Quant'occh'il Ciel eterno, e quante chiome* *Han questi colli ameni il verde maggio,*	If I had as many hearts As the eternal sky has eyes, and as many as these hills Have leaves in the verdant month of May,
1:45	[one "full" note] *Tutti colmi sarieno e traboccanti* *Di quel piacer ch'oggi mi fa contento.* [soft cadence]	They would all be full and overflowing With the joy that now makes me happy.

Euridice

Time	Italian	English
	[soft lute chords]	
2:09	*Io non dirò qual sia*	I shall not say how much
2:15	[happy phrases]	
	Nel tuo gioir, Orfeo, la gioia mia,	I rejoice, Orfeo, in your rejoicing,
2:21	*Che non ho meco il core,*	For my heart is no longer my own
2:27	*Ma teco stassi in compagnia d'Amore;*	But stands with you in the company of Love;
2:35	["lui" emphasized]	
	Chiedilo dunque a lui, s'intender brami,	Ask of *it* then, if you wish to know,
2:42	*Quanto lieto gioisca, e quanto t'ami.*	How much happiness it enjoys, and how much
	[soft cadence]	it loves you.

Chorus

Time	Italian	English
	[happy imitation, duple meter]	
2:59	*Lasciate i monti,*	Leave the hills,
	Lasciate i fonti	Leave the streams,
	Ninfe vezzose e liete,	You charming and happy nymphs,
3:09	[same music]	
	E in questi prati	Practiced in dancing,
	Ai balli usati	And in these meadows
	Vago il bel pie rendete.	Move your pretty legs.
3:18	[change of key, homophony, triple meter]	
	Qui miri il Sole	Here the Sun
	Vostre carole	Sees your dances,
	Più vaghe assai di quelle	More beautiful yet than those
	[same music]	
3:26	*Ond'a la Luna*	Which the stars dance
	La notte bruna	To the light of the moon
	Danzano in Ciel le stelle.	In dusky night.

Instrumental Ritornello

Time		
3:33	Faster; recorders, strings, basso continuo.	

Opera in the Seventeenth Century

In Baroque opera, a distinction gradually arose between those portions of the recitative that were lyrical and songlike and those portions that were more straightforward and conversational. The lyrical part came to be known as **aria,** and the conversational part kept the old name of recitative. Arias were usually written in set forms, with a fixed pattern of repetition, whereas recitatives were freer in form and quite short. The sparse accompaniment and flexible style of recitative made it ideal for setting dialogue and quick interchanges between people in the drama, while arias were reserved for contemplative or passionate moments when the composer wanted to explore the full emotional content of a situation. Recitative usually had simple basso continuo accompaniment; the arias were usually accompanied by full orchestra. The most common melodic forms for arias were **ABA form** (the B section providing a contrast) and **ground bass form,** in which a single phrase in the bass is repeated over and over again while the voice sings an extended melody above it.

AN ARGUMENT OVER THE FUTURE OF MUSIC

About 1600, composers and music theorists engaged in a furious debate over the direction that music should take. The most important figures were Giovanni Artusi, a prominent Italian music theorist, and the illustrious composer Claudio Monteverdi. They were on opposite sides of the debate. Artusi believed in the conservative *prima prattica* ("first practice"), whereas Monteverdi was an adherent of the more progressive *seconda pratica* ("second practice"). Supporters of the *prima prattica* believed that all composers should adhere to the strict rules of composition adopted by the great composers of the late sixteenth century, (most notably Palestrina), regardless of the text they were setting. The slogan "Harmony is the ruler of the text" therefore became Artusi's battle cry.

Monteverdi, however, believed that in passages with very expressive text, the rules could be broken to make the music more intense. He reversed Artusi's slogan to claim that "Text is the ruler of the harmony." In return, Artusi said that Monteverdi and other modern composers had "smoke in their heads" and that their compositions were "the product of ignorance."

Henry Purcell and English Opera

While music flourished in Italy, the state of music in England was highly fragmented because of its unstable political situation. The royal family was under attack by those who wished to abolish its excesses and return British society to a purer, less materialistic state. The result of the conflict between the Puritans (Protestants who believed in focusing on religious truth rather than on "frivolous" things like music and art) and the Roundheads (royalists) was the English Civil War, which raged from 1642 to 1649. It ended with the beheading of the constitutional monarch, Charles I, and the rise to power of the Puritan Oliver Cromwell. Under Cromwell, most musical positions were abolished, and theaters and opera houses were closed. In 1660, the son of Charles I returned from exile in France and assumed the throne as Charles II. His return, known as the Restoration, brought with it a rebirth of musical life in England.

The most talented English composer of the late seventeenth century was Henry Purcell, who lived from 1659 to 1695. He held the important position of organist at Westminster Abbey in London and was one of the most prolific composers of his day. In his short life,

Purcell wrote a large amount of vocal and instrumental music, including sacred music for the Anglican church, secular songs and cantatas, and chamber music for various combinations of instruments, as well as solo harpsichord music. His best-known work is a short opera called *Dido and Aeneas*, written in 1689.

Dido and Aeneas is a miniature masterpiece. It is based on a portion of the epic Roman poem, the *Aeneid* of Virgil. It tells the story of the love affair between Dido, Queen of Carthage, and Aeneas, a mythological Trojan warrior. Their affair ends tragically, however; Aeneas abandons Dido, and she commits suicide. There are three acts—with arias, recitatives, choruses, dances, and instrumental interludes—but the whole opera takes only an hour to perform. It requires only four principal singers and a very small orchestra of strings and harpsichord.

The most famous aria from *Dido and Aeneas* is Dido's lament. Dido has been abandoned by Aeneas and has decided to kill herself. She expresses her determination, her grief, and the pathos of her situation in a deeply moving musical framework. The lament is a **ground bass** aria—that is, the entire melody is set over a repeated pattern in the bass.

Gustav Holst, the twentieth-century English composer, called Purcell's *Dido and Aeneas* "the only perfect English opera ever written."

Find the **Quick Listen** on **MySearchLab** "Purcell's *Dido and Aeneas*"

LISTENING GUIDE

((•• Listen on MySearchLab

HENRY PURCELL (1659–1695)

Dido's lament from the opera Dido and Aeneas

Date of composition: 1689
Voice, strings, and harpsichord
Duration: 4:09

A short recitative ("Thy hand, Belinda . . .") sets the stage for the emotional intensity of Dido's aria. The recitative has a sparse accompaniment that moves steadily downward, reflecting Dido's grief.

CD I, 20

Immediately after this recitative, the ground bass for the aria is heard alone. It is worth looking closely at this phrase, not only because it occurs so many times in the aria (11 times in all), but also because it is very carefully constructed, and the overall effect of the aria depends upon it.

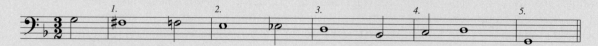

The first important element of this phrase is its descent down the scale by half steps. This is called a **chromatic descent**. This falling line immediately establishes a sad mood, which continues throughout the piece.

The next thing to notice is the rhythmic shift in the fourth measure of the phrase. This is a very subtle shift, but it is very important: it gives the bass line extra interest.

Finally, the ground-bass pattern that Purcell establishes for this aria is five measures long, which is quite unusual. Most musical phrases are made up of four or eight measures. But Purcell chose this irregular length deliberately. It sets up a tension in the music, which contributes to the overall sense of strain and grief. It also enables Purcell to allow the vocal line more freedom as it floats over the ground bass. Throughout the aria, the endings of the ground-bass pattern and the vocal phrases sometimes coincide and sometimes do not. As the intensity increases, the vocal line becomes freer and freer from the constraint of the bass pattern. At the end of the aria, the voice and the ground bass come to a cadence together, and the orchestra provides a short conclusion that is in keeping with the overall mood of the piece.

There are few words in this aria, but, as in most opera arias, they are repeated for dramatic effect. Arias are designed not to convey information or to further the plot but to explore an emotional state. The aria lasts much longer than the opening recitative. It is worth listening to this piece several times to appreciate the skill with which Purcell created it.

Time	Listen for	
	Recitative	
0:00	Thy hand, Belinda, darkness shades me,	[slowly descending voice throughout the recitative]
0:19	On thy bosom let me rest.	
0:29	More I would, but Death invades me:	
0:40	Death is now a welcome guest.	[minor chord on "Death;" dissonance on "welcome guest"]
0:54	[beginning of ground bass: quiet, slow, descending chromatic line heard throughout aria; note rhythmic shift at 1:06]	
	Aria	
1:08 (1:43)	When I am laid in earth,	[ground bass pattern begins again on "am"]
1:20 (1:55)	May my wrongs create	[no pause between these two lines]
1:27	No trouble in thy breast.	[voice falls on the word "trouble"]
(2:02)	[repeat]	
2:17	Remember me, but ah! forget my fate.	[much repetition; highly expressive rising lines; last "ah" is particularly lyrical]
2:42	[several repeats]	
3:30	[cadences of voice and ground bass coincide]	
3:32	[quiet orchestral closing; conclusion of chromatic descent]	
4:02	[final cadence with trill]	

Sonata and Concerto

Along with the invention of opera, the other major development in the early Baroque was the rise of instrumental music. And the most important instruments were those of the violin family.

Some Italian towns specialized in the making of violins, violas, and cellos, and some makers became very famous. The instruments of Antonio Stradivari and Giuseppe Guarneri are considered to be the finest ever produced. A genuine "Strad" can be worth millions of dollars.

The favorite genres of violin music in the last part of the seventeenth century were the sonata and the concerto. A sonata is a chamber piece written for a small number of instruments, with several contrasting movements. It can be a **solo sonata** for a single instrument with basso continuo, or a **trio sonata** for two instruments and basso continuo. The basso continuo was usually made up of a harpsichord and a low stringed instrument, such as a cello. The cello would play the bass line and the harpsichord would double the bass line in the left hand and play chords or melodic figures in the right. A strong bass line was a characteristic feature of Baroque chamber music, as it was of other Baroque musical genres.

Both the solo sonata and the trio sonata had several contrasting movements. If the movements were based on dance rhythms, the sonata was known as a **sonata da camera** ("chamber sonata"). The movements of a **sonata da chiesa** ("church sonata") were more serious in character and alternated between slow and fast.

Apart from the sonata, the favorite form of instrumental music in the Baroque era was the concerto. This was a larger composition, meant for performance in bigger spaces such as public halls, and it involved solo players and an orchestra.

The Italian word *concertare* has two meanings. It means to struggle or fight; it also means to cooperate. Both of these contrary meanings are present in a concerto, in which a solo player or a group of solo players is contrasted with an entire orchestra. Sometimes soloists and orchestra play together, sometimes separately. Sometimes they play contrasting music, sometimes the same music. This dramatic balance and contrast of opposing forces is the essence of the concerto.

The concerto emerged about the end of the seventeenth century. In the earliest concertos, a small group of soloists was contrasted with the whole orchestra. This type of concerto is known as a **concerto grosso** ("large concerto").

The usual solo group was made up of two violins with basso continuo, but other instrumental groups were possible. The orchestra consisted of violins, violas, cellos, and basso continuo.

The **solo concerto** developed later. In a solo concerto, a single soloist is highlighted against the whole orchestra, and the element of drama becomes particularly striking. It was the rise of the solo concerto that led to an increase in technically demanding playing and the **virtuoso** or "show-off" element that has been a characteristic of concertos ever since.

The composer who first brought Italian violin music to international prominence was Arcangelo Corelli (1653–1713). In his compositions, Corelli expanded the technique of violin playing, using repeated notes, fast scales, and **double stops** (playing more than one string at a time). He once wrote that the aim of his compositions was to "show off the violin." He concentrated entirely on violin music, writing only sonatas and concertos. Corelli was one of the first composers to become famous for writing exclusively instrumental music.

French Music

During the seventeenth century, while England was still racked by civil war, France was ruled by one of the most powerful monarchs in European history. Louis XIV reigned for 72 years, from 1643 to 1715, and his tastes

The beauties and graces that are practised on the violin are so great in number that they force listeners to declare the violin to be the king of instruments.

—From a book of instruments published in 1673

Louis XIV.

Hyacinthe Rigaud (1659–1743). Louis XIV, King of France (1638–1715). Portrait in royal costume (the head was painted on a separate canvas and later added). Oil on canvas, 277 × 194 cm. Louvre, Dpt. des Peintures, Paris, France. © Photograph by Erich Lessing. Erich Lessing/Art Resource, NY.

The Main French Baroque Dances

DANCE	METER	TEMPO	DESCRIPTION
Allemande	Duple	Moderate	Continuous motion
Bourrée	Duple	Moderate to fast	Short, distinct phrases
Courante	Triple	Moderate to fast	Motion often in running scales
Gavotte	Duple	Moderate to fast	"Bouncy" sound
Gigue	Usually $\frac{6}{8}$	Fast	Lively, often imitative
Minuet	Triple	Moderate	Elegant
Sarabande	Triple	Slow	Stately; accent often on second beat

Find the **Quick Listen** on **MySearchLab** "Louis XIV Dancing"

All Europe knows what a Capacity and Genius the French have for dancing and how universally it is admired and followed.

—Luigi Riccoboni

governed French life for the entire second half of the seventeenth century and well into the eighteenth. Fortunately, Louis XIV was an avid supporter of the arts, and French music flourished under his patronage.

Louis XIV loved to dance, and one of the most important influences on French music was dance. Dance was featured prominently in French opera and French instrumental music throughout the seventeenth century. By the 1700s, French dances, which were elegant and dignified in their steps, had influenced instrumental music across Europe. One of the most popular French dances, the minuet, even became established as one of the standard movements of the eighteenth-century Classic symphony.

A Baroque instrumental concert. Notice the central position of the basso continuo players.

"Court concert at Prince Bishop of Luettich at Seraing Palace" (with violoncello of Prince Bishop Cardinal Johann Theodor of Bavaria). Painting, 1753, by Paul Joseph Delcloche (1716–1759). Oil on canvas, 186 × 240.5 cm. Munich, Bayerisches Nationalmuseum. Photo: AKG London.

Dance influenced music in France in two ways. First, French opera included a great deal of ballet. Seventeenth-century French operas were splendid affairs, with elaborate scenery, large choruses, and frequent interludes for dancing. The most important composer of French opera was Jean-Baptiste Lully (1632–1687), the king's music director. Lully's ballet scenes were so popular that the dances from his operas were often played as independent suites. This popularity gave impetus to the second trend, which had begun late in the Renaissance: the use of dance forms as independent instrumental music.

There were many different kinds of French dance in the seventeenth century, each with its own meter, rhythm, and characteristic melodic style. The most important was the minuet, a triple-time dance in moderate tempo, but there were many more. Each had its own special character.

A series of dances is known as a dance *suite*. Usually, all the dances in the suite are in the same key. Composers of instrumental suites included François Couperin (1668–1733), known as *le grand* ("the great"), and Elisabeth-Claude Jacquet de la Guerre (1667–1729), who enjoyed the patronage of Louis XIV himself and was one of the first women to publish widely in French music and to be recognized for her musical achievements during her own lifetime.

The Late Baroque (1700–1750)

In the early Baroque period (1600–1700), the main styles and genres were established; in the late Baroque (1700–1750), the fixed musical forms flourished in the hands of the Baroque masters who have become so popular today: Vivaldi, Bach, and Handel.

Late Baroque Opera

Opera continued to flourish in the late Baroque period. Other countries developed their own operatic traditions as well, but the favorite type of opera throughout Europe was Italian opera, and the main form of Italian opera was **opera seria** ("serious opera"). This had become quite stylized by the late Baroque period. The plots were often standard. Usually they were based on some story from ancient history and involved dramatic situations, two pairs of lovers, and a prince or king who resolves the situation in the end. There were always three acts, and the music was built around a constant alternation between recitatives and arias.

Recitatives were still used for carrying forward the plot. They were simple, fast, speech-like, and accompanied only by the basso continuo. However, the main reason people went to the opera was to hear arias. Arias provided the opportunity for the great singers of the time to display their talents. During an aria, the action would stop, and the singer would sing about the emotion created by the story: grief, rage, love, or despair. Every opera contained three or four arias for each of the main characters.

The standard form for arias was ABA. The mood was established in the first A section. The B section was sung as a contrast, usually in a different key or tempo. After the B section, the A section was repeated, with the same words and the same music but considerably ornamented with improvised figures, runs and scales, high notes, dramatic pauses, and the like. It was here that a singer could really show off his or her talent, vocal agility, and taste (or lack thereof!).

The Late Baroque Concerto

By the beginning of the eighteenth century, the concerto had also become fixed in form. Composers continued to write both concerti grossi (for small group and orchestra) and solo concertos, but the solo concerto became more and more popular. Instruments such as the flute, the oboe, and the trumpet began to be featured in solo concertos. Composers even began to write concertos for keyboard instruments. This was quite revolutionary, because the role of keyboard instruments in concertos had previously been restricted to the basso continuo.

There were many concerto composers active at this time, but the undisputed master of the concerto in the late Baroque period was Antonio Vivaldi.

Antonio Vivaldi (1678–1741)

Vivaldi's father was a violinist at St. Mark's Cathedral in Venice, where Gabrieli and Monteverdi had made their careers, and Antonio learned music at an early age. Like many young men in the Baroque era, Vivaldi trained for the priesthood. Because of his red hair, he earned the nickname "The Red Priest." Illness prevented him from continuing his priestly duties, however, and he soon began the job that would carry him through the remainder of his career: he was appointed director of music at the Ospedale della Pietà in Venice. This was a residential school for orphaned girls and young women, which combined basic education with religious training and placed a strong emphasis on music.

Vivaldi wrote a large amount of music for the Ospedale. The girls gave frequent concerts, and people traveled from all over Europe to hear them play. Among the composer's works are solo and trio sonatas, oratorios, sacred music, and nearly 600 concertos! Vivaldi wrote so much music that some of it has still not been published, and many of his pieces have not been heard since he first wrote them.

Vivaldi must have been inspired by the special talents of the young women in his school, because several of his concertos are for instruments that were then not normally thought of as solo instruments: small recorder, clarinet, bassoon, viola, and even mandolin. But most of his concertos are for one or more violins.

By the time of Vivaldi and the late Baroque period, concerto form had become clearly established. There are usually three movements,

Find the **Quick Listen** on **MySearchLab** "Vivaldi"

Antonio Vivaldi.

| COMPLETE RITORNELLO | EPISODE 1 | PARTIAL RITORNELLO | EPISODE 2 | PARTIAL RITORNELLO | EPISODE 3 | COMPLETE RITORNELLO |

TONIC → OTHER KEYS → TONIC

Find the **Quick Listen** on **MySearchLab** "Johann Sebastian Bach Life"

Vivaldi was himself an accomplished violinist. A young German law student saw him playing in 1715 and recorded the following in his diary: "Vivaldi played an improvisation that really frightened me. I doubt anything like it was ever done before, or ever will be again."

in the pattern fast–slow–fast. The first movement is usually an Allegro (a movement in moderately fast tempo). The second movement usually has an expressive, slow melody that sounds like an opera aria. The third movement is a little faster and livelier than the first.

The first and third movements of a Baroque concerto are in **ritornello form**, which exploits the contrast between the solo instrument(s) and the orchestra in a highly organized way. The ritornello in a concerto is an orchestral passage that constantly returns. Between appearances of the ritornello, the solo instrument plays passages of contrasting material, which are known as **episodes**.

At the beginning of a movement in ritornello form, the orchestra plays the entire ritornello in the **tonic**, or "home," key. During the body of the movement, the ritornello will recur in partial form and in different keys, but at the end it will return in its entirety in the tonic key. The solo episodes occur between these occurrences.

Perhaps the most famous of Vivaldi's concertos today are a group of four concertos known as *The Four Seasons*. They were published in 1725, when Vivaldi was 47 years old. They show Vivaldi's wonderful sense of invention in the concerto medium and his extraordinary flexibility within this seemingly rigid form.

These are solo violin concertos; but in several of the solo episodes, other instruments from the orchestra join in, so that the sound sometimes approaches that of a concerto grosso. There is also constant variety in the handling of the ritornello form, both in the keys employed for the partial returns and in the choice of which part of the ritornello is used. (**See Listening Guide.**)

The *Four Seasons* concertos are an early instance of **program music**: music that is designed to tell a story. Each of the four concertos represents one season of the year. At the head of each concerto, Vivaldi printed a poem describing the season. In addition, Vivaldi actually wrote lines from the poem directly into the musical score, so that each musical phrase for the instrumental players is directly tied to its poetic description. For example, there are passages for thunder and lightning, a dog barking, and birds singing. But even apart from the poetic texts, the concertos are wonderful examples of the late Baroque violin concerto in their own right.

The Baroque concerto may seem rather rigid, with its set pattern of movements and its strict ritornello form, but, as pieces such as Vivaldi's *Four Seasons* show, it could be handled with great flexibility to produce music of variety, color, and contrast.

Vivaldi's music was heard and its influence felt not only in his native Italy but throughout Europe. Vivaldi's concertos were studied in great detail and closely imitated by another of the great masters of the late Baroque era: Johann Sebastian Bach.

LISTENING GUIDE

((•● **Listen** on **MySearchLab**

ANTONIO VIVALDI (1678–1741)

First Movement from Violin Concerto, Op. 8, No. 1, La Primavera ("Spring"), from The Four Seasons

Date of composition: 1725
Solo violin, strings, and harpsichord
Duration: 3:35

CD I, 21

Like most late Baroque concertos, Vivaldi's *La Primavera* ("Spring") has three movements: fast–slow–fast. Both of the fast movements are in ritornello form and are in a major key (E major). The slow movement has a long, lyrical melody and is in E minor. In both of the outer movements, instruments from the orchestra join the soloist in some of the solo episodes, giving the impression of a concerto grosso. Both movements are also full of echo effects. The orchestra is made up of first and second violins, violas, cellos, basses, and a harpsichord. Like all the *Seasons*, the "Spring" concerto is headed by a poem in the form of a sonnet. A sonnet has fourteen lines of poetry—eight lines followed by six lines that are divided into two groups of three. Vivaldi uses the first eight lines for the first movement and the two groups of three for the next two movements.

First movement
(First eight lines of the poem):

Spring has arrived, and, full of joy,
The birds greet it with their happy song.
The streams, swept by gentle breezes,
Flow along with a sweet murmur.
Covering the sky with a black cloak,
Thunder and lightning come to announce the season.
When all is quiet again, the little birds
Return to their lovely song.

The first movement is written in the bright and extroverted key of E major. The ritornello, which is made up of two phrases, is played in its entirety only at the beginning of the movement; in all its other appearances, only the second half of the ritornello is played. Between these appearances, the solo violin plays brilliant passages, imitating birdsong and flashes of lightning. Sometimes it plays alone, and sometimes it is joined by two violins from the orchestra.

Time	Listen for	
	Allegro ["Fast"]	
0:00	"Spring has arrived, and full of joy,"	[ritornello in tonic, first half, loud and then soft]
0:15		[ritornello in tonic, second half, loud and then soft]
0:32	"The birds greet it with their happy song."	[trills; three solo violins alone, no basso continuo]
1:08		[ritornello in tonic, second half, once only, loud]
1:16	"The streams, swept by gentle breezes, Flow along with a sweet murmur."	[quiet and murmuring]
1:41		[ritornello in dominant key, second half, once only, loud]
1:49	"Covering the sky with a black cloak, Thunder and lightning come to announce the season."	[fast repeated notes; flashing runs and darting passages]
2:17		[ritornello in C♯ minor, second half, once only, loud]
2:25	"When all is quiet again, the little birds return to their lovely song."	[long, sustained, single note in bass; rising solo phrases, trills again]
2:43		[buildup to:
3:10		ritornello in tonic, second half twice, first loud and then soft]

Johann Sebastian Bach (1685–1750)

One of the most influential musicians of all time, and certainly one of the greatest composers in the history of music, was Johann Sebastian Bach. His mastery of musical composition is so universally acknowledged that the date of his death is used to mark the end of the entire Baroque era.

Bach's entire career was spent in one region of Germany. He moved from one small town to another as job opportunities arose. The last part of his life was spent in the somewhat larger town of Leipzig.

Bach did not see himself as an artistic genius, but rather as a hard-working craftsman. He wrote most of his music to order, or to fulfill the requirements of a job. During his life, he was not widely known outside the relatively small circle of his family and acquaintances, and he traveled very little. He never wrote an opera, although that was the most popular musical genre of the time, because his jobs never required it.

The first job Bach held was church organist in the small towns of Arnstadt and Mühlhausen, near his birthplace. At the age of 23, he married and found a better position at the court of the Duke of Weimar, first as

Other composers on Johann Sebastian Bach: Beethoven called him "the immortal god of harmony." Charles Gounod wrote that "Mozart is the most beautiful, Rossini the most brilliant, but Bach is the most comprehensive: he has said all there is to say." Debussy called him "a benevolent god, to whom all composers should offer a prayer before setting to work."

organist and later as leader of the orchestra. He stayed there for nine years (until 1717), leaving finally when he was turned down for the position of music director. The Duke of Weimar was so angry at Bach's decision to leave that he had him put in jail for a month!

But Bach got the position he wanted at the court of a nearby prince. The Prince of Cöthen was young, unmarried, and an enthusiastic amateur musician. He kept a small orchestra of his own and made Bach music director. Here, Bach was very happy. He was well paid, he could write a range of varied music, and he was highly regarded by the prince.

In 1720, when Bach was 35, his wife Barbara died. The following year he married again. His new wife was a young singer, Anna Magdalena, who, like Bach, was employed at the court of the Prince of Cöthen. With his two wives, Bach had 20 children. Eleven of them died in childhood, as was common in those days, but nine grew to adulthood, four of whom became famous composers in their own right.

Bach might have stayed at Cöthen for the rest of his life, but the prince also married at

The sole surviving portrait of Johann Sebastian Bach. Stadtgeschichtliches Museum Leipzig.

1. Die St Thomas Kirche. 2. Die Thomas Schule. 3. Der Steinerne Wasser-Kasten.

A contemporary engraving of St. Thomas's Church and its school (left), where Bach worked for the last 27 years of his life.

this time, and his new wife did not like music. The prince's support for Bach and his activities diminished, the orchestra was dismissed, and Bach started looking for a new job.

At this time, the town of Leipzig—a relatively large town with a university, two theaters, and a population of 30,000—was looking for a music director for its St. Thomas's Church. This position involved responsibility for all of the town's church music, including that of St. Thomas's and three other churches. The town council interviewed several musicians and finally settled on Bach as its third choice. (The first choice, composer Georg Philipp Telemann, turned them down, and the second man on the list was not permitted to leave his post.) But third choice or not, Bach happily accepted the position and moved with his growing family to Leipzig in 1723, when he was 38 years old. He remained there for the rest of his life.

Bach was extremely busy in Leipzig. There were several aspects to his job, all of which he fulfilled cheerfully and efficiently. He was required to compose, rehearse, and direct a new church cantata for every Sunday and feast day of the year. He was also head of the music school attached to St. Thomas's and was responsible for composing, teaching Latin, playing the organ, maintaining all the instruments, and preparing the choirs for the services at the three other main churches in Leipzig.

In 1747, Bach was invited to visit Frederick the Great, the powerful and autocratic king of Prussia. Like Louis XIV of France, Frederick loved music and employed several well-known musicians at his court. Frederick also played the flute and composed some flute music. One of Johann Sebastian Bach's sons, C. P. E. Bach, was the harpsichordist at Frederick's court. It was the younger Bach who was considered the more up-to-date composer. Johann Sebastian was known affectionately, but not very respectfully, as "Old Bach." By the middle of the eighteenth century, his music was regarded as old-fashioned and too complicated.

Bach died in 1750, leaving an unparalleled legacy to the musical world. Audiences have been attracted to Bach's music for its careful organization, clear tonal direction, expressive nature, and intellectual brilliance. Bach himself saw his music as a means of supporting his family, instructing his fellow human beings, and glorifying God. For his sons and for his second wife, Anna Magdalena, he wrote books of short keyboard pieces. One book of organ pieces was written "for the instruction of my fellow men." And at the end of many of his compositions, he wrote the letters "S. D. G.," which stand for "Soli Deo Gloria" ("For the Glory of God Alone").

Bach was also exceedingly modest. Toward the end of his life, he said, "I was obliged to work hard. But anyone who is equally industrious will succeed just as well." Family man, teacher, good citizen, humble and pious spirit, Johann Sebastian Bach was also one of the musicians in history on whom we can unhesitatingly bestow the title "genius."

NEED TO KNOW

- Bach composed in all Baroque instrumental and vocal styles, except opera.

- Bach was a master of counterpoint and his works have served as models for composers and students ever since.

- Bach wrote different types of music depending on the job that he held at the time:

  - Early years (working as an organist): primarily organ music

  - Middle years (leading the orchestra at Cöthen): keyboard and instrumental music

  - Final years (working in a church school in Leipzig): primarily religious choral music, as well as some final instrumental works

Find the **Quick Listen** on **MySearchLab** "Frederick the Great"

Bach's Organ Music   Bach's organ music is extremely varied. It includes settings of Lutheran chorales, organ trio sonatas, and preludes and fugues. The chorales are either set in harmony for organ or used as the basis for a series of variations. In the organ trio sonatas, the right hand plays one line, the left hand plays another, and the pedals of the organ are used for the basso continuo.

The preludes and fugues combine a free type of music with a very strict type. The **prelude** is a rambling, improvisatory piece of the kind that organists play to fill in time before, during, or after a church service. The **fugue** is a carefully worked out polyphonic composition that uses a theme

Find the **Quick Listen** on **MySearchLab** "Bach Toccata and Fugue in D Minor"

MUSICAL BORROWINGS

Bach's roles as teacher and performer during his years at Leipzig were extremely time-consuming. In addition, he was required to compose regularly. To save time, Bach sometimes reworked existing compositions (both his own and those of other composers) into new pieces.

Borrowings can be found both in Bach's instrumental and in his vocal compositions. One of Bach's crowning achievements, written near the end of his life, is the Mass in B Minor, much of which consists of movements from his own earlier cantatas. Bach welds a diverse range of compositions into a magnificent whole. One scholar has said that the B-Minor Mass demonstrates that Bach's technique of borrowing, compilation, and adaptation must itself be accepted as "a creative act almost on a par with what we normally think of as 'original composition.'"

In 1729, in addition to all his other activities, Bach was appointed director of the Collegium Musicum in Leipzig. During his years directing the Collegium, Bach produced fourteen harpsichord concertos. Only one of these, however, was an original work. Most of them are brilliant reworkings of violin concertos by another great eighteenth-century composer: Antonio Vivaldi.

(or "subject") that occurs in all the voices, or musical lines, in turn. It begins with a single voice playing the subject unaccompanied. As the second voice brings in the fugue subject, the first one continues playing—and so on, until all the voices are sounding independently. A fugue may have two, three, or four voices. After visiting Frederick the Great, Bach wrote one fugue that had six voices.

Bach was a master of counterpoint, and the fugue is the most demanding type of counterpoint to write.

Bach's Keyboard, Instrumental, and Orchestral Music
During his years at the Cöthen court, Bach produced a large amount of music for solo keyboard, other solo instruments, and small orchestra. In this music particularly, Bach melded the characteristics of Italian, French, and German styles. Italian music had rhythmic drive and brilliance. French music favored dance forms and ornamentation. German music was serious and contrapuntal. Bach drew on all these elements to produce an individual style that was the high point of the Baroque era.

Bach wrote much solo music, perhaps inspired by the fine players at the prince's court. There are suites and sonatas for solo violin and solo harpsichord, suites for solo cello, and a suite for solo flute. He also composed several sonatas and trio sonatas.

From the Cöthen years come a large number of orchestral compositions. These include some suites for orchestra, as well as several concertos, including the famous *Brandenburg* Concertos.

Bach's Vocal Church Music
During Bach's stay in Leipzig, he wrote hundreds of cantatas for church services, as well as some important sacred vocal pieces. These include motets, Passions, and the Mass in B Minor, which is regarded as one of the greatest traditional Mass settings that has ever been composed.

Bach wrote two Passions for the Lutheran churches of Leipzig. (A third is rumored to exist but has never been found.) A **Passion** is a musical setting of the story from the Gospels of the death and resurrection of Jesus. Bach based one setting on the account in the Gospel of St. John, and the other setting on the account in the Gospel of St. Matthew. Although Bach's musical legacy is full of masterpieces, the *St. Matthew Passion* is universally regarded as one of the monumental musical masterpieces of all time. It is a huge composition, lasting some three hours, for solo singers, two choruses, one boys' choir, two orchestras, and two organs. It runs the gamut of human emotion, from grief to awe to despair to spiritual transcendence. With this work alone, Bach shows us how music can reflect and deepen the meaning of human existence.

Find the **Quick Listen** on **MySearchLab** "Bach Solo Cello"

LISTENING GUIDE

((•—Listen on **MySearchLab**

JOHANN SEBASTIAN BACH (1685–1750)

St. Matthew Passion (excerpt)

Date of composition: ca. 1727
Soprano, tenor, and bass voices, chorus, orchestra, and basso continuo
Duration: 8:09

CD I, 22

This excerpt from Bach's *St. Matthew Passion* shows the composer's mastery at achieving a fusion of seriousness and expressiveness suitable to the biblical text. The role of narrator for the Gospel story is performed by the "Evangelist" (tenor), who sings in recitative with a simple continuo accompaniment. The words of Jesus (bass) are "haloed" by lush string accompaniment. The chorus portrays the responses of the twelve disciples. This happens most effectively when Jesus predicts that one of them will betray him, and they ask, "Lord, is it I?" (If you listen very carefully, you will hear eleven questions. The voice of the twelfth disciple—Judas—is missing.)

A soprano soloist begins this excerpt in an aria that beautifully reflects the theme (Jesus as the sacrifice for all) that is ultimately the focus of the entire work. The section is rounded off in peace and contemplation by the plain but moving harmonies of the final chorale.

Time	Listen for	
	Soprano	
	[orchestral introduction]	
	[aria]	
0:31	*Blute nur, blute nur*	Only bleed, only bleed,
	Blute nur, du liebes Herz,	only bleed, you dearest heart.
	[text repeated four times; answering phrases on flutes	and violins; motion throughout in orchestra]
1:19	[orchestral interlude]	
1:51	[change of key, similar accompanying figures as A section]	
	Ach! ein Kind das du erzogen,	Ah! a child that you raised
	das an deiner Brust gesogen,	and nursed at your breast
	droht den Pfleger zu ermorden,	has become a snake
	denn es ist zur Schlange worden;	and bites the one who cared for it;
2:21	[repeat, varied]	
3:00	[orchestral passage from beginning]	
3:32	*Blute nur, du liebes Herz . . .* [repeated exactly as beginning]	
4:20	[orchestral closing passage]	
	Evangelist	
	[simple basso continuo accompaniment]	
5:00	*Aber am ersten Tage der süssen Brot traten*	Now on the first day of the feast of unleavened bread
	die Jünger zu Jesu und sprachen zu ihm:	the disciples came to Jesus and said to him:
	Chorus	
	[noble, serious tone]	
5:10	*Wo, wo, wo willst du, dass wir dir bereiten,*	Where, where, where will you have us prepare
	das Osterlamm zu essen?	for you to eat the Passover?
	Wo willst du, dass wir dir bereiten das	Where will you have us prepare for you to
	Osterlamm zu essen?	eat the Passover?

0:00 [orchestral introduction]

Evangelist

	[recitative]	
5:36	*Er sprach:*	He said:

Jesus

	[accompanied recitative—violins form a "halo" around the words of Jesus]	
5:39	*Gehet hin in die Stadt zu einem* *und sprecht zu ihm:* *Der Meister lŠsst dir sagen:* *Meine Zeit is hier,* *ich will bei dir die Ostern halten* *mit meinen Jüngern.*	Go to the city to a certain man and say to him: The Master says to you: My time is here, I will keep the Passover at your house with my disciples.

Evangelist

	[recitative—simple basso continuo accompaniment]	
6:08	*Und die Jüngern täten, wie ihnen Jesus befohlen hatte,* *und bereiteten das Osterlamm.* *Und am Abend satzte er sich zu Tische* *mit den Zwölfen, Und da sie assen, sprach er:*	And the disciples did as Jesus had commanded, and prepared the Passover. And at evening he sat at the table with the twelve, and as they ate, he said:

Jesus

	[accompanied recitative]	
6:32	*Warlich, ich sage euch:* *Eines unter euch wird mich verraten.* ["halo;" dissonance and intensity on "betray"]	Truly, I say to you: One of you will betray me.

Evangelist

	[recitative]	
6:50	*Und sie wurden sehr betrübt* *Und huben an, ein jeglicher* *unter ihnen, und sagten zu ihm:*	And they became very troubled and they spoke, each one of them, and said to Him:

Chorus

	[fast, panicky music]	
6:59	*Herr, bin ichs? bin ichs?* *bin ichs? bin ichs?* *Herr, bin ichs? bin ichs?* *bin ichs? bin ichs?* *Herr, bin ichs?* *bin ichs? bin ichs?*	Lord, is it I? Is it I? Is it I? Is it I? Lord, is it I? Is it I? Is it I? Is it I? Lord, is it I? Is it I? Is it I?

Chorale

	[calm setting of final chorale]	
7:11	*Ich bins, ich sollte büssen,* *an Händen und an Füssen* *gebunden in her Höll;* *Die Geiseln und die Banden* *und was du ausgestanden,* *das hat verdienet meine Seel'.*	I should bear all of it, my hands and feet tethered in the bonds of Hell; the scourges and shackles that You endured so that my soul might be delivered.

A MUSICAL OFFERING

In May 1747, Bach traveled to Potsdam, near Berlin, to visit Frederick the Great of Prussia. He displayed his extraordinary skills of improvisation in the presence of the king, and as a result Frederick presented him with a theme to be used as the basis for a composition. When heard alone, the theme seems extremely unpromising.

It is a testimony to Bach's brilliance as a composer that on his return home, he managed to work this theme into an extended and impressive series of pieces, which he entitled *A Musical Offering* and sent with a florid dedication to Frederick the Great.

A Musical Offering consists of two fugues, ten **canons** (rounds), and a trio sonata. Each of the 13 pieces uses Frederick's theme. The unity that this provides is complemented by the wide variety of canonic procedures employed. These include conventional canons, a canonic fugue, a canon in contrary motion, puzzle canons, and a "crab" canon, in which one player starts at the beginning of the piece and works forward, while the other starts at the end and works backward! Bach's skill and ingenuity in *A Musical Offering* confirm his status as among the greatest composers of counterpoint in the history of music.

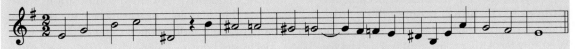

George Frideric Handel (1685–1759)

Although Handel's life overlapped Bach's almost exactly, their careers were remarkably different. As we have seen, Bach lived a quiet, busy life in one small region of Germany. By contrast, Handel traveled extensively and became an international celebrity. Although the central musical genre of the Baroque era was opera, Bach wrote no operas. Handel's career was built on the nearly 40 operas he wrote, mostly for the London stage. Bach was a family man; Handel never married. He may have been gay or a confirmed bachelor.

Handel was born in Halle, a small town in Germany. His family was not musical, and his father wanted him to study law. He was so obviously gifted in music, however, that he was allowed to study with the music director and organist of the local church. He learned to play the organ, the harpsichord, and the violin, and he studied counterpoint and composition. Handel studied law at the University of Halle for only a year and then left for Hamburg, which was the main center of opera in Germany. He joined the opera orchestra there as a violinist and harpsichordist. At the age of 19, Handel composed his first opera, which was performed at the Hamburg opera house.

Because most operas at this time were Italian operas, Handel decided to travel to Italy, to the center of operatic activity. At 21, he was still only a young man, but he scored a phenomenal success there.

After three years in Italy, Handel was appointed music director to the Elector of

George Frideric Handel.

Hanover, back in Germany. This was a well-paid position, but Handel was restless. He kept requesting leaves of absence to travel to London, which was fast becoming one of the most important musical centers in the world. In 1712, Handel was granted a short leave to London, which he greatly overstayed and ultimately turned into a lifelong residency.

He made important contacts in London and soon became the favorite of the queen. An embarrassing situation arose two years later when the queen died and the Elector of Hanover, Handel's former employer whose generosity he had exploited, became George I of England. It is said that Handel won his way back into favor by composing his famous *Water Music* suite for a party King George was having on the river Thames. (We listened to one section of this suite in Chapter 2 of this book.) Whether or not this story is true, the king employed Handel again, as he had in Hanover; Handel was given a sizable salary and was soon composing, conducting at court, and teaching the king's granddaughters. Certainly the king and

An English writer in the eighteenth century complained that the opera house was more of a social than a musical event: "There are some who contend that the singers might be very well heard if the audience was more silent, but it is so much the fashion to consider the Opera as a place of rendezvous and visiting that they do not seem in the least to attend to the music."

Find the **Quick Listen** on **MySearchLab** "Handel"

Handel had much in common. They were both foreigners in England, and they both spoke English with a strong German accent. A contemporary writer made fun of Handel's accent by reporting that one day when there was only a small turnout for one of his concerts, Handel said to the musicians, "Nevre moind; de moosic vil sound de petter."

Handel spent the remainder of his career in London. He was an amazingly prolific composer, a clever politician, and a tough businessman. He made and lost a great deal of money, loved food and drink, and had a quick temper and a broad sense of humor. A contemporary said that "no man ever told a story with more humor than Handel." He was at the center of English musical developments (and rivalries) for 40 years. And in the end, he became an institution. The British people still regard Handel as an English composer. He is buried in Westminster Abbey—an honor reserved for great English notables such as Chaucer, Queen Elizabeth I, and Charles Dickens.

Watch the **Inside the Orchestra** video on **MySearchLab**

The monument to Handel in Westminster Abbey in London.

During his London years (from 1712 until his death in 1759), Handel composed mainly operas and oratorios, though he wrote a great deal of other music as well.

Italian opera was very fashionable in London until the 1730s, when public taste began to change. It was at this time that Handel turned his attention to **oratorio**. The idea of a musical Bible story sung in English appealed to the English audience. Oratorio was also much less expensive to produce than opera. It was sung on the concert stage and required no costumes, no complicated stage sets or lights, and no scenery. Handel's first oratorio was *Saul*, produced in 1739. But his first real success came with *Messiah* in 1741. This soon became his most popular work and remains one of his most frequently performed compositions today. After this, Handel's oratorios became the mainstay of the London concert scene. They were performed during Lent, when opera was not allowed anyway, and they attracted large audiences, especially from the prosperous middle class, which had always regarded Italian opera with suspicion or disdain. A special feature of Handel's oratorio performances was the appearance of the composer himself playing organ concertos during the intermission.

Toward the end of his life, Handel became blind, but he continued to perform on the organ and to compose by dictation. When he died, 3,000 people turned out for his funeral. He had become a British citizen many years earlier, and the British people had taken him completely into their hearts.

Handel's Music   Handel's music is attractive and easy to listen to. It appeals to a wide range of people because it sounds simple and tuneful. Handel's is the "art that hides art": the skill and brilliant craftsmanship of his music are hidden under the attractive exterior.

Curiously, most people today do not know the compositions on which Handel spent most of his time and for which he was best known in his own day: his Italian operas. These portray events of dramatic and emotional intensity. The main musical forms are the standard ones of opera seria: recitative and aria.

As you read earlier, Baroque arias are usually built in ABA form, with ornaments on the return of the A section. This kind of aria is known as a **da capo** ("from the beginning") aria, because after the B section, the composer has simply to write the words "da capo" in the score to indicate the return to A. The singer is expected to improvise embellishments for the repeat of the A section.

Today, Handel's popularity rests mainly on his oratorios. Even in Handel's time, the oratorios appealed to a very wide public. Why have they always been so popular? First, and most important, the words are in English. Even in the eighteenth century, much of the audience for Italian operas couldn't understand Italian. Second, oratorios are based on stories from the Bible (mostly the Old Testament), which were familiar to everyone in those days. Behind the stories, there were political implications as well: references, for example, to the military triumphs and prosperity of Georgian England. Finally, oratorio performances were less aristocratic social events than opera performances were and thus had wider appeal.

The music of Handel's oratorios is vigorous and appealing. It is not so different from the music of his operas. There are recitatives and arias, just as there are in operas. But the main difference is in the choral writing.

Choruses are very rare in late Baroque opera, but they are central to Handel's oratorios. Some of the greatest moments in the oratorios come in the choral pieces, when the chorus comments on the action or summarizes the feelings of the characters. Perhaps the best known of Handel's choruses is the "Halleluyah" chorus from *Messiah*.

Messiah was composed in 1741 and soon became the composer's most famous work. It was written in the unbelievably short time of just over three weeks. Subsequently, Handel reworked it several times for different performances, omitting sections to make it fit a specific time, rearranging the sequence, and using more or fewer singers and instrumentalists as available. As he was composing it, Handel said, "I did think I did see all Heaven before me and the great God himself."

Messiah is in three parts, which last some two and a half hours altogether. The music is made up throughout of recitatives, arias, and choruses. The famous "Halleluyah" chorus closes Part II. (**See Listening Guide.**)

Handel was also an accomplished composer of instrumental music. His two most famous instrumental suites are the *Water Music* and *Music for the Royal Fireworks*.

Handel's music is less complex than that of Bach, with more focus on melody than on counterpoint, and he deliberately appealed to a wider audience than had been traditional. Music was becoming less the preserve of the wealthy and more the delight of everyone who cared to listen.

Find the **Quick Listen** on **MySearchLab**
"Handel's *Messiah*"

A French visitor to London in 1750 described a performance she had attended: "The Oratorio pleases us highly. Handel is the soul of it: when he makes his appearance, two wax lights are carried before him, which are laid upon his organ. Amidst a loud clapping of hands, he seats himself, and the whole band of music strikes up at exactly the same moment."

CASTRATOS

Castrato singers were exceedingly popular in the Baroque period. These were men who had been surgically castrated before puberty, so that they would retain the high voices of childhood but grow to have the vocal power and agility of adults. Although this practice was regarded as abhorrent by most people at the time, it was widely performed, especially among poor families. Few of these men made important careers, but some became musical superstars and acquired great fame and fortune.

In the early eighteenth century, the most famous castrato was named Farinelli. A critic described his remarkable prowess: "The first note he sung [*sic*] was taken with such delicacy, swelled by minute degrees to such an amazing volume, and afterwards diminished in the same manner to a mere point, that it was applauded for a full five minutes. Indeed he possessed such powers as never met before, or since, in any one human being."

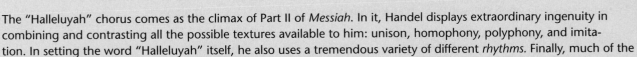

LISTENING GUIDE

((•• Listen on MySearchLab

GEORGE FRIDERIC HANDEL (1685–1759)　　　　　*"Halleluyah" Chorus from* Messiah

Date of composition: 1741
Chorus and orchestra
Duration: 3:51

CD I, 23

The "Halleluyah" chorus comes as the climax of Part II of *Messiah*. In it, Handel displays extraordinary ingenuity in combining and contrasting all the possible textures available to him: unison, homophony, polyphony, and imitation. In setting the word "Halleluyah" itself, he also uses a tremendous variety of different *rhythms*. Finally, much of the strength of the movement comes from its alternation of blocks of simple tonic and dominant harmonies, as well as its triumphant use of trumpets and drums. The jubilant feeling is immediately evident and is a direct reflection of the text: "Halleluyah" is a Hebrew word that means "Praise God."

The text itself is treated in two ways:

1. Declamatory statements (e.g., "For the Lord God omnipotent reigneth") characterized by long note values and occasional unison singing

2. Contrapuntal responses (e.g., "forever and ever, halleluyah, halleluyah"), characterized by faster notes, and offering musical and textual commentary on the declamatory statements

The "Halleluyah" chorus falls into nine relatively symmetrical sections, each featuring a single texture or combination of textures.

Time	Listen for
0:00	Instrumental opening ("pre-echo").
	Homophony
	[Two phrases, each with five statements of "Halleluyah." Notice the changing rhythms.]
0:07	First phrase, tonic.
0:16	Second phrase, dominant.
	Unison
	[With homophonic "halleluyah" responses: "For the Lord God omnipotent reigneth."]
0:25	First phrase, dominant.
0:37	Second phrase, tonic.
	Polyphony
0:49	Statement by sopranos, tonic.
0:56	Statement by tenors and basses, dominant.
1:05	Statement by tenors and altos, tonic.
1:14	Short instrumental interlude.
	Homophony
	[With noticeable change in dynamics: two phrases, one soft (*piano*), one loud (*forte*).]
1:16	*piano*: "The kingdom of this world is become . . ."
1:27	*forte*: ". . . the kingdom of our God and of His Christ."
	Imitation
	[Four entries, "And He shall reign forever and ever."]
1:38	Basses.
1:43	Tenors in counterpoint with basses.
1:49	Altos in counterpoint with basses and tenors.
1:55	Sopranos in counterpoint with all other voices.
	Unison
	[Three declamatory statements ("King of Kings and Lord of Lords") against homophonic responses ("forever and ever, halleluyah, halleluyah"), each at a different pitch, moving higher and higher.]
2:01	Sopranos and altos, answered by other voices.

Polyphony

	[Two statements of "And he shall reign forever and ever," against contrapuntal responses ("and he shall reign . . .").]
2:42	Basses, dominant.
2:48	Sopranos, tonic.

Unison/Homophony

	[Combination of unison and homophonic textures—"King of Kings" . . . ("forever and ever") "and Lord of Lords" . . . ("halleluyah, halleluyah").]
2:54	Tenors, answered by other voices.

Homophony

	[Statements by all voices.]
3:03	"And He shall reign forever and ever."
3:10	"King of Kings and Lord of Lords" (twice).
3:19	"And he shall reign forever and ever."
	[Final statement of "King of Kings and Lord of Lords."]
3:26	Tenors and sopranos, answered by other voices.
3:34	Pause; one final drawn-out homophonic statement: plagal cadence (IV–I).

STYLE SUMMARY

The Baroque Era

During the Baroque era, many elements of what we recognize today as "classical" music were formed. These include regular patterns of meter and a formalized hierarchy of keys and chord progressions. Instrumental music came to be regarded on a par with vocal forms, and two influential instrumental genres—the sonata and the concerto—were established.

The great new musical invention of the Baroque era was opera. Opera brought together all the arts, combining carpentry and painting (for the scenery), costume design, dramatic acting, instrumental music, and—of course—beautiful singing, into one superb spectacle. The main topics of Baroque opera were stories from Classical antiquity—from Greek and Roman myths or history. The principal vocal forms used in opera were recitative and aria.

Recitatives are relatively simple, with sparse accompaniment and with flexible and irregular rhythms designed to imitate speech. They are designed for dialogue and for moving the story along. Arias occur when the action stops and a character expresses his or her emotional reaction to the situation. Arias are lyrical and expressive; whether they are about love or rage or grief, they are the emotional high points of the opera.

The most common form for arias is ABA form. The central (B) section offers a contrast, and the return of the A section can provide an opportunity for the singer to ornament the melody. In the Baroque period, audiences liked to hear high voices on the great arias, so the male roles were usually sung by castratos, whose voices were as high as those of the female singers.

The development of instrumental music was helped along by the great skill of the Italian makers and players of stringed instruments, especially the violin. Sonatas and concertos for violins are the most important instrumental works of the Baroque era. Sonatas were composed for one violin and basso continuo (solo sonata) or for two violins and basso continuo (trio sonata). Since the basso continuo is usually played by both a keyboard and a low stringed instrument, the solo sonata is performed by three players and the trio sonata by four.

Concertos exploit the Baroque love of contrast. They employ contrasts between loud and soft, fast and slow, and fiery and lyrical; however, the most important contrast is between the sound of the solos (from one to four instruments) and that of the whole orchestra. In the outer (first and third) movements of a Baroque concerto, this contrast is created by using ritornello form.

In the Baroque period, clear national differences in musical style were evident. In Italy, instrumental music for strings and opera were particularly favored. France developed music influenced by the dance: French operas contained many ballet scenes, and instrumental suites were made up of a series of movements in different dance styles. German music incorporated two important elements: the Lutheran chorale and a tradition of counterpoint. Chorales are found in organ works, church cantatas, and Passions. The undisputed German master of counterpoint, whose skill was displayed throughout his enormously productive and varied career, was Johann Sebastian Bach.

Finally, in England, another German composer, George Frideric Handel, apart from composing many Italian operas, also established a very English genre, the English oratorio. Oratorios are based on biblical stories. Unlike operas, oratorios often include parts for a narrator and a chorus, in addition to the roles of the principals in the story. Oratorios, however, are not staged; they are sung in concert performances. The most famous English oratorio, *Messiah*, is unconventional in many respects: it has no narrator, the singers do not sing roles, and it doesn't tell a story. Rather, it is a series of descriptions and contemplations, set to exquisite arias, recitatives, and choruses.

From the earliest Italian opera—through instrumental suites, sonatas, and concertos; secular and sacred cantatas; organ works; and Passions—to the English oratorio, Baroque music is enormously expressive, colorful, and varied. Despite all of its variety, Baroque music has one unifying stylistic trait: the basso continuo. With a lute or keyboard instrument playing a constant chordal accompaniment and one or more low stringed instruments doubling the keyboard's lowest line, a Baroque piece is instantly recognizable from the power and momentum of its bass line. The Baroque era might easily be called the "Basso Continuo Era."

FUNDAMENTALS OF BAROQUE MUSIC

- ❏ Instrumental music is as important as vocal music
- ❏ Opera was invented, with vocal forms divided between recitative and aria
- ❏ Principal vocal genres are opera, cantata, and oratorio
- ❏ Principal instrumental genres are sonata, suite, and concerto
- ❏ Music is organized by a hierarchy of chords and keys (tonal harmony)
- ❏ Unifying feature of all Baroque music is the basso continuo

FOR FURTHER DISCUSSION AND STUDY

1. Select a representative artist of the Baroque period from the following list to study: the painters Rubens, Vermeer, Gainsborough, Rembrandt, and El Greco; the sculptor Bernini; and the architect Christopher Wren. How does this artist's work reflect the concerns and themes shown by Baroque composers?

2. Baroque keyboard instruments, such as harpsichords and organs, were not able to make dynamic changes gradually. To adjust the volume on the organ or the harpsichord, the player had to change the setting of the stops. How might have this affected Baroque composition?

3. The term *opera* came into use only during the 1630s; before that time stage works were known simply as dramas or intermezzos. Opera, meaning "works," was a far grander, even imposing word, when compared to these earlier descriptions.

Why do you think composers chose this more serious term for the new style?

4. Why do you think early opera composers were attracted to the Orpheus story?

5. Make up a simple, brief phrase such as "I'm very hungry" or "My dog bit me." Try saying this phrase in as many ways as you can imagine. Try singing it as a recitative and finally as a line from an aria.

6. Vivaldi's *La Primavera* is a difficult work to play, even by present-day standards. Compare a performance by a modern group with an original-instrument recording. What are the similarities and differences?

7. The organ has often been called "the king of instruments." Why might this be?

8. For a fascinating comparison of performance styles and a great example of how much a performer can affect the way a piece sounds, listen to Bach's Prelude and Fugue in E Minor as performed by Michael Murray (on *Bach Organ Blaster*, Telarc 80316), and compare it with any other version.

9. Create a chart showing the basic similarities and differences between the works of Vivaldi, Bach, and Handel. Include in your consideration the styles of the composers and the types of work they composed.

✓●—Study and Review on MySearchLab

The Classic Era: 1750–1800

The word "classic" is usually used to describe something with an appeal that is both very broad and very long-lasting. A novel may be described as a classic, and so may a movie or a car. This means that the novel, the movie, and the car continue to attract enthusiasts long after they first appeared. It also means that they appeal to a wide range of people.

Both of these things are true of Classic music. The music of the greatest composers of the Classic era has been popular with audiences ever since it was written. Indeed, the masterpieces of Classic music were the first works in musical history that have stayed in the concert repertoire ever since they were first composed. Before that time, a piece was usually performed once or twice and then set aside.

What is it about Classic music that has given it such enduring appeal? Before we can answer that question, we need to consider the social and political climate of Europe in the middle of the eighteenth century.

From Absolutism to Enlightenment to Revolution

The eighteenth century was a time of profound social and political change. It began with the death in 1715 of Louis XIV of

French Philosopher Jean-Jacques Rousseau.

France, the most powerful absolute ruler in Europe, and it ended with two of the most significant revolutions in modern history: the American War of Independence (1775–1783) and the French Revolution (1789–1794).

The whole period was colored by the philosophical movement known as the Enlightenment. This movement, led by the great French philosophers Voltaire and Rousseau who both died in 1778, attempted to apply the principles of scientific objectivity to issues of social justice. The Enlightenment favored the human over the divine, reason over religion, and clarity over complexity. Its adherents tried to improve education, eliminate superstition and prejudice, and break down the rigid class structure that separated people from one another.

The brilliant, witty French writer known as Voltaire.

NEED TO KNOW
THE ENLIGHTENMENT

- "The Age of Reason"—applied scientific methods to human society

- Elevated science/the rational over religion/faith—rejected superstition, prejudice, and long-held beliefs in favor of what could be measured scientifically

- "All men are created equal"—valued individual freedom and equality over the older class system

MORT DE LOUIS XVI, LE 21 JANVIER 1793
Place de la Concorde : on voit à gauche le socle de la statue de Louis XV déboulonnée

(Extrait des *Révolutions de Paris*)

King Louis XVI is led to the guillotine in 1793.

Although these changes were slow in coming, some of the rulers of the time were influenced by the ideas of the Enlightenment. Frederick the Great of Prussia and Emperor Joseph II of Austria, for example, were both regarded as "enlightened" monarchs (at least in comparison with their predecessors). Both men were also strong supporters of the arts. Frederick the Great, whom we have mentioned briefly already, played the flute and employed some of the most accomplished musicians of the day at his court. Joseph II, an amateur cellist, was a great patron of music and literature. In Vienna, which was the capital of the Holy Roman Empire and the place where Joseph held court, all the arts flourished. With names such as Haydn, Mozart, and Beethoven in the list of its citizens, Vienna was, by the end of the century, the musical center of Europe.

Enlightenment ideals reached their high point in Vienna in the 1780s and 1790s, but they exerted an influence on many other parts of the world as well. Throughout the century, England had a thriving economy and a rich and varied cultural life. Members of the middle class increasingly claimed free expression and leisure time as their own. In the New World, the ideals of the Enlightenment were realized in the growing resentment of the American colonists against the English government. The American Revolution culminated in the Declaration of Independence in 1776. The American experiment in democratic government had powerful implications for intellectuals and revolutionaries everywhere. In 1786, the French philosopher Condorcet wrote that the rights of humankind must be read "in the

example of a great nation. America has given us this example."

In France, the reign of Louis XIV was succeeded by those of Louis XV (1715–1774) and Louis XVI (1774–1789). The powerful central authority wielded by Louis XIV gradually eroded, and his successors became corrupt and increasingly out of touch with popular sentiment. The reign of Louis XVI ended in the turmoil of the French Revolution, which had as its slogan the rallying cry of the Enlightenment: "Liberty, Equality, Brotherhood!" Louis XVI was guillotined by his own people in the middle of Paris on January 21, 1793.

Brotherhood was the concept behind many new organizations founded in the eighteenth century. Chief among these was Freemasonry, founded in England in 1717. The Masons were—and are—an international secret society of mutual support and social charity. Freemasonry cut across the boundaries of class and profession. It spread quickly throughout Europe and America, and its ranks included kings, writers, composers, and politicians. Famous Freemasons of the eighteenth century were Joseph II, the great German poet Johann Wolfgang von Goethe, Mozart, and George Washington.

The idea of brotherhood did not include women, however. And because their roles were narrowly defined by society in this as in other eras, few women became monarchs, well-known writers, or famous composers. Important exceptions were Maria Theresa, ruler of Austria from 1740 to 1780, and Catherine II ("Catherine the Great") of Russia, who ruled from 1762 to 1796. One of the greatest novelists of the late eighteenth century was Jane Austen (1775–1817), whose masterpieces include *Pride and Prejudice* and *Emma*. But the author's name did not appear on the title pages of her books when they were published, and she received very little public recognition during her own lifetime. Similarly, there were women who composed music but did not have their works published. Anna Amalie, the Duchess of Saxe-Weimar, wrote German operas and chamber music and was highly influential in bringing together intellectuals, poets, and musicians at her court, but her own music was never published.

Nonetheless, women's influence in all other areas of musical life was great. Women were accomplished music teachers, singers, instrumentalists, authors of instruction manuals, patrons, and organizers of musical life. Marie Lieszcinska, who married Louis XV in 1725, inaugurated an important concert series at Versailles that attracted the leading

Rousseau, an "enlightened" philosopher, wrote in 1758: "Women, in general, possess no artistic sensibility. The celestial fire that ignites the soul ... the inspiration that consumes ... the sublime ecstasies that reside in the depths of the heart are always lacking in women's writings. Their creations are as cold and pretty as women themselves."

musicians of the day. This tradition was continued by Madame de Pompadour in mid-century and by Marie-Antoinette of Austria, the wife of Louis XVI, after 1770.

In the latter part of the century, society's attitudes toward women began to broaden, and women took a more public role in European musical life. Some became professional performers, others both performed and composed. Julie Candeille (1767–1834) was an opera singer, pianist, harpist, and composer. She made her performing debut at the age of 16 as piano soloist in a concerto; the following year, she played a concerto of her own composition. During her life, she published many of her own works and gave song recitals, accompanying herself on the piano in more than 150 performances. Her greatest success came in 1792–1793, when her comic opera *Catherine* became a hit in Paris. The opera received numerous revivals during the next 20 or 30 years. A great deal more research, publishing, and performance remains to be done to restore women's music from the Classic era to its rightful place.

The Musical Public

Changes in class structure in the eighteenth century had far-reaching effects on music. The flourishing economy created a large and prosperous middle class, whose members felt that they were entitled to the privileges and cultural diversions previously reserved for the aristocracy. The eighteenth century saw the rise of the public concert.

PERFORMANCE IN CONTEXT

A Provincial Theatre

The Estates Theatre today is a remarkably well-preserved example of an eighteenth-century neoclassical theatre. The oval hall is surrounded by five rows of private opera boxes, their edges sparkling with candelabras. Rows of chairs fill the ground floor, then—as now—the domain of the general public. The word "provincial" conjures up images of simplicity, plainness, and old-fashioned customs. This is not so with the city of Prague—the capital of the Austrian province of Bohemia and a vibrant center of literature, fashion, and the arts. Music and musicians thrived in Prague, and its large, musically-educated audiences lured performers and composers from the imperial capital in Vienna. A symphony or opera that failed to impress a conservative Viennese audience might find a receptive audience among Prague's progressive citizens. A difficult work that suffered from poor performances in the capital could be beautifully played in the province nicknamed "The Conservatory of Europe."

The early history of the Estates Theatre in Prague illustrates the progressive nature of Bohemian audiences. This opera house was built in 1783 by a theatre-loving Czech nobleman, and soon became home to the opera company of Pasquale Bondini, an Italian singer and impresario. In 1786, Mozart's opera *The Marriage of Figaro* opened to a cool reception in Vienna, closing after a disappointing nine performances; undeterred, Bondini decided to stage the opera in Prague. This second production was a critical and financial success, and Bondini soon commissioned Mozart to write a new opera—*Don Giovanni* (1787), which was also a great success in the city. Mozart's music returned to the Estates Theatre again in 1791 with the premiere of his opera *La clemenza di Tito*—performed to celebrate the coronation of Leopold II as King of Bohemia. You can see the Estates Theatre in the movie *Amadeus* (1984), where it is used for the staged productions of Mozart's operas.

Interior of the Estates Theater, Prague.

Beginning in France about 1725, the idea quickly spread across Europe. By the end of the century, public concerts were the primary musical forum in London, Paris, Vienna, Prague, and countless other cities and towns.

The vast increase in the number of musical consumers affected other areas of music, too. Music publishing became a profitable business, and music publishers sprang up in many cities, catering to a new class of amateur performers. Middle-class men and women wanted to learn to play music themselves. They arranged lessons for themselves and their children, and bought musical instruments to play at home, books to learn how to play, and sheet music to learn their favorite pieces.

The social changes of the eighteenth century also affected the status of performers and composers. Although many musicians were still supported by powerful rulers or wealthy aristocrats, some could begin to make a living on their own as the century progressed. One example of this gradual change is the life of the composer Joseph Haydn. He spent most of his career in the employ of a wealthy prince, but toward the end of his life he became independent, living off the sales of his music, traveling abroad, and taking charge of his own financial affairs.

Even the style of music composed in the Classic era was affected by the new audiences and consumers. The complex rhythms and counterpoint of Baroque music, with its heavy bass line and emotional intensity, were no longer in fashion. Music was now designed to appeal to a broader public. It had to be lighter, clearer, and more accessible. It had to be easier to listen to and easier to play. This was the era of several new genres, including the *divertimento*—a piece played as a "diversion"—and comic opera. A common musical language developed, one that could be understood by a broad range of society. In this language—the "classic" language of music—enormous amounts of music were composed. All of it is pleasant and accessible. A few geniuses used this language to produce masterpieces of enduring significance.

Find the **Quick Listen** on **MySearchLab**
"Papageno Papagena Duet"

Find the **Quick Listen** on **MySearchLab**
"Mozart Divertimento K. 136"

General Characteristics of Classic Music

Balance and proportion, clarity and accessibility—these are the primary features of Classic music. It is designed to be "easy on the ear." Yet that does not mean it cannot also be very beautiful, very moving, and very profound. Mozart once wrote to his father that his latest compositions would appeal to the most experienced listeners and to amateurs alike. The experts would appreciate all the subtleties, and the amateurs would be pleased "without knowing why."

Classic music was a reaction to the complexity of Baroque music. Classic music usually has just a melody and an accompaniment, and the accompaniment is light and simple. Imitative counterpoint is used only rarely, and then only for special effect. The melodies are pleasing and tuneful—the kind you can hum or whistle as you go through the day. Mozart was delighted when he was told that everyone on the streets of Prague was singing the tunes from his latest opera.

There are some technical aspects to the special sound of Classic music. The first has to do with the length of melodic phrases. Classic music is usually made up of two- or four-bar phrases, rather than the long lines common in Baroque music. This makes the music clear and balanced. These phrases are usually arranged into patterns of opening and closing phrases. A two- or four-bar opening phrase is immediately followed by a two- or four-bar closing phrase, creating a symmetrical pattern. This pattern makes the music easy to follow and establishes a sense of regularity in the mind of the listener.

Melody is the main thing.
—Joseph Haydn

Phrase 1 ⌐————————————⌐ Phrase 2 ⌐————————————

The second technical aspect of Classic music is its harmony. The harmony of Classic music is generally simple, logical, and clear. Classic composers do not usually go very far afield in their harmonies. They tend to stick to relatively straightforward keys, and they do not often use strange or dissonant chords.

Finally, the effect of Classic music depends a great deal on its accompaniment. Gone is the powerful basso continuo of the Baroque. In its place, we find a simple "walking bass" (in which the bass line moves mostly by step, in even notes and with a regular rhythm) or little bustling accompanying figures that keep the rhythm lively. A special development of the Classic era was the "Alberti bass," named after the composer Domenico Alberti (1710–1740). This is an accompaniment made up of a continuously moving pattern of short notes. The accompanying chords are broken up into separate notes played one after the other, not together, to keep the texture light and lively.

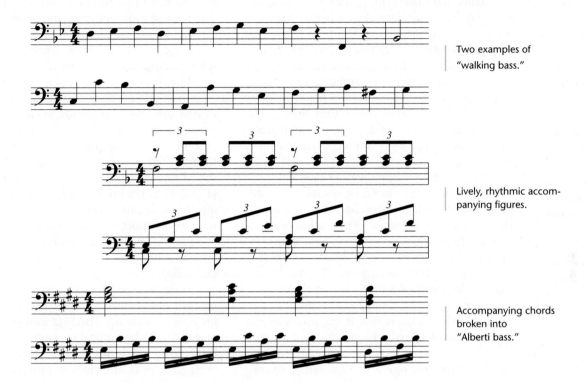

Two examples of "walking bass."

Lively, rhythmic accompanying figures.

Accompanying chords broken into "Alberti bass."

These three features—the balanced phrases, the simple harmony, and the light accompaniment—help to give Classic music its special sound and to provide a framework for its tuneful, pleasing melodies.

Genres of Classic Music

Several musical genres were popular in the Classic era. The most important genres were opera, symphony, string quartet, and sonata. Some composers wrote in other genres, too. Mozart, for example, composed many beautiful piano concertos and some string *quintets*. But on the whole, composers stayed within the conventional genres. Notice that these genres are all secular. Although composers still occasionally wrote sacred works such as Masses and oratorios, they were far less common in the Classic era, reflecting a shift in society's makeup and interests.

Operas were staged in the palaces of a few very wealthy aristocrats or in the public opera houses of big cities such as Prague, Paris, or Vienna. Symphonies also were performed in aristocratic courts or at the public concert venues springing up all over Europe. String quartets and sonatas, with their smaller ensembles and more intimate sound, were designed for private gatherings—in an aristocratic salon or in the living rooms of middle-class music lovers.

Let's look briefly at how the opera, the symphony, the string quartet, and the sonata developed in the Classic era.

Opera We have seen that opera was the Baroque art form *par excellence*. It combined a story with artwork, costumes, illusion, and best of all, superb singing. But during the late Baroque period, some people began to criticize Baroque opera as artificial. They complained that the plots were always about mythological or historical figures rather than about real people and actual situations; that

Find the **Quick Listen** on **MySearchLab**
"Stamitz Symphony in C"

Find the **Quick Listen** on **MySearchLab**
"*La Serva Padrona*"

the music was too heavy and complex; and that the stage sets, with their elaborate scenery and complicated machines for simulating battles and shipwrecks, were too involved. The arias, with their obligatory repeats (the *da capo* aria form, you remember, is ABA), were criticized for two reasons: (1) the repeat of the first part (the second A) interrupted the continuity of the story; and (2) singers abused the convention of embellishing the music on its repeat by showing off and drawing attention to themselves rather than to the plot. Finally, what could be more unnatural than a castrato (a man singing with a woman's voice!)?

This attack on Baroque opera was another sign of the changing social structure of the eighteenth century. Baroque opera was the province of the aristocracy; what was demanded was a style of opera that would appeal to everyone. It should be about real people in everyday situations. The result was the development of a new type of opera called *comic opera*. Comic opera became very popular in the Classic era. It featured simpler music, down-to-earth characters, and amusing plots.

In Italy comic opera was known as *opera buffa*, in France it was called *opéra comique*, and in Germany it was known as *Singspiel*. In French and German comic opera, the dialogue is spoken instead of being set to music, though there are still arias. In Italian opera the dialogue is in recitative. The most famous early example of Italian comic opera is Pergolesi's *La Serva Padrona* (1733). Even the title is meant to be comical: it means "The Servant Girl Who Became Mistress of the House." The opera is about a clever servant girl who tricks her master, a rich old bachelor, into marrying her. The story was designed to appeal to an age in which rigid class barriers were being called into question.

Symphony   The most important genre of instrumental music in the Classic era was the symphony. Indeed, the origins of the symphony date from the beginnings of the Classic era, about 1730, and it grew to maturity in the hands of the great Classic composers Haydn and Mozart.

The symphony began life as an introductory piece to Italian opera. At the beginning of the eighteenth century, Italian operas were usually preceded by an **overture**—an instrumental introduction in three short movements: fast–slow–fast. The Italian name for this type of

opera overture was *sinfonia*. The music of these overtures was unrelated to the music of the operas they introduced. Gradually these instrumental pieces achieved independent status and were played in concert performances. The idea of independent symphonies spread rapidly, and soon composers from Italy to Germany to England were writing symphonies with no connection to opera.

The most important center of symphonic composition and performance in the early Classic era was Mannheim, in Germany. Here was a wealthy court, which supported the largest and most accomplished orchestra in Europe. The concertmaster and conductor of the Mannheim orchestra was Johann Stamitz (1717–1757), who was famous for his rigorous discipline. Stamitz was also a prolific composer who wrote more than 60 symphonies. These symphonies established the norm for the Classic symphony for the remainder of the eighteenth century.

Stamitz expanded the fast–slow–fast pattern of the Italian *sinfonia* to a four-movement scheme. The first movement is fast and serious, the second movement slow and lyrical, the third movement graceful and moderate in tempo, and the last movement very fast and lively. This pattern of movements became standard for the symphony throughout the Classic period.

Stamitz also established the basic structure of the Classic orchestra, which had three main instrumental groups: strings, woodwinds, and (sometimes) trumpets and drums. The string section consisted of two groups of violins ("first violins" and "second violins"), as well as violas, cellos, and double basses. The woodwind section had two flutes or two oboes, plus two horns. Only bright, ceremonial symphonies used trumpets and timpani. In the later Classic period, the orchestra was augmented slightly, particularly in the woodwind section. Composers often used both flutes *and* oboes. Bassoons were employed to fill out the low sounds of the woodwind section, and in the late eighteenth century clarinets also became popular.

A composer could choose the number and types of instruments in a particular work to achieve different effects. If a composer wanted a delicate sound, he or she might write for strings, one flute, and two horns. A fuller, richer sound could be obtained with the strings plus all the woodwind instruments. And for a really festive piece, trumpets and drums were added.

In actual performance, the size of the string section varied according to the financial resources of the sponsor. In rich cities or aristocratic courts, there could be as many as twelve first violinists, twelve second violinists, six viola players, eight cellists, and four double bass players. In smaller orchestras, there were only three or four first violins, three or four second violins, two violas, two cellos, and one double bass.

Chamber Music   The increase during the eighteenth century in the number of middle-class householders who were interested in music created a demand for music that could be performed at home. Because this music was designed to be played in smaller rooms, it is usually known as **chamber music**. It includes duets, trios, and quintets for various instrumental combinations, but the most important types of chamber music during this period were the string quartet and the sonata.

The **string quartet** developed about the middle of the eighteenth century. It involves four stringed instruments: two violins, a viola, and a cello. This grouping had great appeal for Classic composers, and many of the finest works of the eighteenth century were written for string quartet. The string quartet provides an ideal balance between high and low instruments. The first violinist plays the principal melody while the second violinist plays the accompanying figures. Meanwhile, the violist fills in the harmony in the middle, and the cellist provides the bass line. The instruments cover a wide pitch band from high to low. The smooth, high, silvery sounds of the two violins are balanced by the drier, throatier quality of the viola and the strong, rich tones of the cello. Because all the instruments belong to the same family, they blend perfectly.

Works for string quartet closely followed the pattern of symphonic works. They usually had four movements: the first, fast and serious; the second, slow and lyrical; the third, graceful; and the fourth, lively.

Sonatas could be written either for a keyboard instrument alone or for a keyboard instrument with another instrument such as a violin or a flute. Until about 1775, the favorite keyboard instrument was the harpsichord. By the last part of the eighteenth century, the piano, invented early in the century, began to replace the harpsichord in this role. The piano was capable of

gradations of volume—that was why it was originally called the *piano-forte* ("soft-loud")—and it had a fine, delicate sound. Eighteenth-century pianos sounded very different from the large concert grand pianos of today. They were softer and lighter in the upper register, and more textured and less resonant in the bass.

Keyboard sonatas often contain some of the most interesting music of Classic composers, because it was (and still is) common for composers to compose while sitting at the keyboard—to experiment with ideas, play them through, and see how they sound. Some keyboard sonatas, therefore, have an improvisatory effect, as though we were actually hearing the composer at work.

Convention in Classic Music

The eighteenth century was a time of strict social conventions. In upper-class society, dress codes were carefully followed. People wore powdered wigs, brocaded coats, and silver shoe buckles. There was an elaborate pattern of rules that governed social behavior—when to curtsy, when to bow, what to talk about. Even written communication was highly formalized.

So it is not surprising to learn that strict conventions were established for music, too. The instruments used for particular types of works, the number of movements, and the approximate length of each movement were all fixed by convention. Yet the pattern of

Find the **Quick Listen** on **MySearchLab**
"Fortepiano"

I am issuing by subscription a work consisting of six quartets ... written in a new and special way [for] the great patrons of music and the amateur gentlemen.

—Joseph Haydn

Find the **Quick Listen** on **MySearchLab**
"Haydn String Quartet Op. 76 No. 5"

A group of eighteenth-century gentlemen playing a string quartet in a middle-class home. Notice the bust of Mozart on the wall.

String Quartet. Color engraving, 18th century, Austrian. Mozart Museum, Prague, Czech Republic. Giraudon/Art Resource, NY.

expectations in Classic music went further than that. Even the keys in which a composition might be written were governed by convention. Some keys were far more common than others, and each key was linked with a certain mood or atmosphere. D major, for example, is ceremonious and bright, whereas F minor is strained and melancholy. One reason is that major keys sound brighter than minor keys. Another has to do with the tuning system and instruments of the time. Trumpets and drums could play particularly well in D major, so that was the key often chosen for festive music. F minor, with four flats, was (and remains) a difficult key to play. In addition, more flat notes in a key tended to make the instruments of the time sound muffled and shadowy.

The most far-reaching convention in Classic music controlled the *form* in which a composer could write each individual movement of a composition. Only a few forms were used in Classic music. The most important of these are sonata form, aria form, minuet-and-trio form, and rondo form. We will look at each of these in turn, but before we do, let us consider the importance of convention in Classic music.

Today, nothing seems more important to us than originality. We look for it in our own work, in the books we read, the paintings we look at, and the music we listen to. The cult of originality, however, is a recent phenomenon. In the eighteenth century, writers, artists, and composers were respected not for the originality of their work but for its quality. Between about 1730 and 1800, hundreds of composers wrote tens of thousands of symphonies. From this enormous quantity of music, the works of Haydn and Mozart stand out, not because they are original, but because they demonstrate the most skill, the

greatest resourcefulness, and the widest range of expression. Haydn and Mozart were the greatest composers of the age, not because they ignored convention, but because they used it to better advantage than anyone else.

Forms of Classic Music

Sonata Form   The most important single-movement form in Classic music is **sonata form**. This form was used for almost all first movements of Classic instrumental music. Although it is called sonata form, it was used for the first movements not only of sonatas, but also of symphonies, string quartets, and many other genres. For that reason, it is sometimes known as "first-movement form." But sonata form became so popular in the Classic era that it was often used for other movements as well.

Sonata form is intellectually demanding, and composers used it for their most serious ideas. That doesn't mean it has to be difficult to listen to. As with any art form, however, it takes practice to become familiar with the ways in which it is organized. Once we understand sonata form, many of the secrets of Classic music are revealed to us.

Sonata form has three sections: **exposition**, **development**, and **recapitulation**. The exposition begins in the tonic key and presents the opening material of the piece. Then it moves to a second key (usually the dominant or the relative major) and presents new material in that key. The exposition ends with a clear cadence. In Classic sonata-form movements, the exposition is normally played twice.

The development section explores many different keys. It usually moves quickly from key to key, has a great deal of counterpoint, mixes up short phrases of the previous

SONATA FORM

	EXPOSITION		DEVELOPMENT	RECAPITULATION		CODA
MELODIC MATERIAL:	(a)	(b)	(bits and pieces of a & b)	(a)	(b)	(cadence)
KEY:	FIRST KEY	SECOND KEY	(VARIETY OF KEYS)	FIRST KEY	FIRST KEY	FIRST KEY
HARMONIC TRAJECTORY:						

material, and is generally quite turbulent. The development leads dramatically into the recapitulation, usually without an intervening cadence.

The recapitulation brings back all the music of the exposition, but with one crucial change: *the material that was previously presented in the second key is now played in the home key, so that the movement can end in the key in which it began.* Sometimes there is a short closing section added to the end of a sonata-form movement just to round it off. This short section is called the *coda* (literally "tail").

The most important place to listen carefully in a sonata-form movement is right at the beginning. If you remember the sound of the beginning of the exposition, you will be able to recognize the recapitulation when it comes, because it brings back the same music. Also, with practice, you will be able to recognize the development

section, partly because it changes key frequently and partly because it contains a great deal of turbulence—as though the material of the exposition had been thrown into a blender and was being cut up and tossed around.

Aria Form   Aria form is simple, and we have discussed it before in the context of opera. Classic composers often used it for the second, slow movement of a sonata, a symphony, or a string quartet. This movement is designed to be lyrical and songlike. Aria form is ABA, with a slow, lyrical opening section (A) that is often in triple meter. This is followed by a contrasting central section in a new key (B), which sometimes has slightly faster notes. Finally, the opening section (A) is repeated, often decorated or slightly modified. Slow movements are often in aria form, but they sometimes follow sonata form or theme-and-variations form.

ARIA FORM

| A (melody and first key) | B (new melody, new key) | A (repeated, often embellished) |

Minuet-and-Trio Form   Minuet-and-trio form is the standard form for third movements in sonatas, symphonies, and string quartets, although it is often omitted from piano sonatas. The minuet was originally a Baroque court dance in moderate triple meter. Gradually it became an instrumental form and made its way into Classic music. (We analyzed a Classic minuet and trio in Chapter 3 on page 50.) A minuet and trio simply means two minuets played in the pattern minuet–trio–minuet. The trio (second minuet) usually presents some kind of contrast to the first minuet—in instrumentation, texture, dynamics, or key.

The minuet itself is in two parts, each of which is repeated: AABB. The trio has the same pattern: CCDD. After the trio, the first minuet is played again (often without repeats). The whole scheme of a minuet-and-trio movement looks like this:

MINUET	TRIO	MINUET
AABB	CCDD	AABB (or AB)

The most important characteristics of a minuet-and-trio movement are as follows:

1. It is always in $\frac{3}{4}$ meter.
2. It has a moderate tempo.

3. It is always in ternary form (minuet–trio–minuet).
4. The trio always presents some kind of contrast to the minuet.

Rondo Form   Rondo form was often used for the last (fourth) movement of symphonies, string quartets, and sonatas. Rondos are usually fairly fast, with a lively or catchy tune that keeps on returning or coming round again (hence "rondo"). Between appearances of the tune (sometimes called the refrain or **main theme**) are **episodes** of contrasting material. Thus, if we designate the main theme as A and the contrasting episodes with other letters, we have the following:

ABACADA

Sometimes composers used the first episode again just before the last appearance of the refrain:

ABACABA

This makes a particularly symmetrical kind of rondo.

Four-Movement Structure

MOVEMENT	FORM	KEY
I	Sonata	Tonic
II	Aria or Sonata or Theme and Variations	Dominant or Subdominant or Relative minor
III	Minuet-and-Trio	Tonic (Trio is sometimes in a different key)
IV	Rondo or Sonata	Tonic

Summary

To summarize this overview of the main forms of Classic music, the most common and most serious form in classic music is sonata form. First movements are nearly always in sonata form. Second movements are often in aria form: ABA. Minuet-and-trio form ("ternary") is the usual form for third movements. Last movements are often in rondo form.

These are the main forms for the standard four movements of most Classic instrumental music. There are variants of this pattern, however. For example, Classic concertos had only three movements: sonata form, slow, and rondo. In the other genres, sonata form was sometimes used for movements in addition to the first. It is not uncommon for the slow movement of a Classic composition to be in sonata form, and sometimes composers used sonata form for the last movement also. Some compositions reverse the position of the slow movement and the minuet and trio, putting the minuet second and the slow movement third.

The Early Classic Period

Although the end of the Baroque era is generally given as 1750 (the date of Bach's death), the origins of the Classic style date from earlier than that. Starting about 1730, a new musical style began to appear that was lighter, more accessible, more varied, and less demanding. The name given to this musical style at the time was *galant*, which we might translate as "fashionable" or "up-to-date." Two of the composers involved in this stylistic change were Bach's sons: C. P. E. Bach, who was serving at the court of Frederick the Great in Berlin, and J. C. Bach, who made his career in London. Other important composers of this early Classic style were Johann Stamitz (1717–1757) in Mannheim and Giovanni Battista Sammartini (1701–1775) in Italy.

These composers rejected the dense contrapuntal style of the late Baroque era in favor of music that was lighter in texture, easier to listen to, and more varied. Early Classic music has far more variety than Baroque music. There are frequent changes of texture, dynamics, and instrumentation. The phrases are shorter, and each phrase may be quite different from the one that precedes it.

Many early Classic compositions have three movements instead of four, because the minuet did not become a standard feature of sonatas and symphonies until the second half of the eighteenth century.

The Classic Masters

The masters of the Classic style were Haydn and Mozart. Since their own time, these two composers have been regarded as the most accomplished among a large number of highly skilled musicians active in the second half of the eighteenth century. Both men were extraordinarily prolific, completing many hundreds of superb compositions during their lifetimes. Although the musical language and techniques they used were common throughout Europe at the time, their individual abilities were so remarkable; their grasp of harmony, form, and expression so assured; and their melodic invention so rich that they stand out from their contemporaries.

Franz Joseph Haydn (1732–1809)

> Anyone can see that I'm a good-natured fellow.
> —**Haydn**

Haydn was born in a small village in Austria. His father was a wheelmaker—an important trade in the eighteenth century—and Haydn was one of 12 children. There was much music making at home and in the village, and Haydn displayed an early talent for music.

Joseph Haydn.

At the age of eight, he was accepted as a choirboy at St. Stephen's Cathedral in Vienna, the biggest city in the Austrian empire. Here he stayed until he was 18, when his voice changed. (In those days, the onset of puberty for both boys and girls was much later than it is today.)

At the cathedral, Haydn had learned to play the harpsichord and the violin, so for the next 10 years (about 1750–1760), he made a living giving harpsichord lessons and playing in local orchestras. During this time, he lived in a small room in an apartment building in Vienna. Luckily for him, some of the grander apartments in the building were occupied by people who became very useful in furthering his career. One of his neighbors was Pietro Metastasio, the most famous poet and opera librettist (opera text writer) of his time; Metastasio introduced Haydn to many prominent figures in the musical world. Another was a woman who was the head of one of the most prominent aristocratic families of the time. Her name was Maria Esterházy, and the Esterházy family was to play a significant role in Haydn's life and career.

In 1761, Haydn was hired as assistant music director to the household of Prince Paul Anton Esterházy. The prince had a sizable retinue of servants, including a small orchestra of about 12 players. Haydn was responsible for composing music on demand, supervising and rehearsing the other musicians, and caring for the instruments.

Prince Paul Anton died in 1762 and was succeeded by his brother Nikolaus. Prince Nikolaus Esterházy was an avid music lover who spent a great deal of money on his court and entertainment. In the countryside, Prince Nikolaus built a magnificent palace that had two large music rooms and two small theaters for opera. He called this palace Esterháza after the family name.

In 1766 Haydn was promoted to music director at Esterháza. He was responsible for

Find the **Quick Listen** on **MySearchLab** "Esterhaza Orchestra"

COMPOSERS, PATRONS, AND AUDIENCES

The Classic Orchestra

By the time of the Classic period, the orchestra had inherited certain traits from the Baroque, but it also featured new ones. The main body of the orchestra was still formed by the strings: perhaps eight to twelve violins (divided into two groups), four violas, two or three cellos, and a double bass or two. (These numbers could be greater or lesser depending on the occasion for which the music was written or the financial resources of the sponsoring organization.) But now there was a clearer and more defined role for the wind instruments; no longer did they simply play along with the strings: they had more clearly defined music of their own. The wind section was formed of flutes, oboes, bassoons, and horns, usually in pairs. Toward the end of the eighteenth century clarinets were added.

A composer such as Mozart, with his subtle and refined sense of sound, would assign very distinctive roles to the winds. One flute might join the violins in a slow movement to add luster to their song. A pair of oboes and a bassoon might be featured in the trio section of a minuet. And often the winds would play passages of their own to contrast deliberately with the strings. In line with the Classic desire for symmetry and clarity, the balance of the strings and the winds was more clearly organized. Finally, for festive occasions, or for a symphony that the composer wanted to make stirring or more extroverted, the orchestra could feature trumpets and timpani. You can immediately hear the difference between an orchestra with trumpets and drums and one without.

Haydn in full dress.

Edouard Jean Conrad Hamman, Portrait of Joseph Haydn. Engraving. Bibliothèque Nationale, Paris, France. Giraudon/ Art Resource, NY.

I was never so devout as when I was at work on *The Creation.*

—Haydn

directing all the music at the palace. Two full operas, as well as two big concerts, were performed each week. Extra concerts were put on whenever an important visitor came to the palace. Music was performed at meals, and the prince had chamber music played in his own rooms almost every day. Haydn wrote much of this music himself.

Over the course of his lifetime, Haydn wrote about a dozen operas; more than 100 symphonies; nearly 70 string quartets; more than 50 keyboard sonatas; and a large amount of choral music, songs, and other chamber music. Haydn stayed in the service of the Esterházy family until 1790, when Prince Nikolaus died. The new prince, Nikolaus II, did not like music and disbanded the orchestra. Haydn, now nearly 60 years old, moved back to Vienna.

By this time, his work was internationally known, and he traveled twice to London—first from 1791 to 1792, and then from 1794 to 1795. For his visits to London, Haydn wrote his last 12 symphonies, which were performed there to wild public acclaim. These brilliant and fascinating works are known as the *London* Symphonies.

In his late years, back in Vienna, Haydn wrote mostly string quartets and vocal music. His quartets are varied and masterful, covering the entire range of expression from playfulness to profundity. The vocal works include six Mass settings for chorus and orchestra and the two great oratorios of his last years, *The Creation* (1798) and *The Seasons* (1801).

Haydn died in 1809 at the age of 77. His reputation transcended even national disputes. Vienna was under siege by the French army at the time, but Napoleon posted a guard of honor outside Haydn's house to pay homage to the greatest composer of the age.

The Esterhazy Palace in Austria.

Haydn's Music

For a long time, Haydn's music was regarded as genial and lively, and much of its depth, wit, and brilliance went unnoticed. This was because only a few of his compositions were performed regularly at concerts. Nowadays, however, more of Haydn's music is being performed, and the extraordinary range of his achievement is being recognized.

His operas are full of beautiful music: lyrical, inventive, and moving. His symphonies range from ceremonious public works with trumpets and drums to compositions of great delicacy, charm, and even tragedy. The string quartets explore an enormous range of expression, with a masterful handling of the intimate medium and brilliant writing for the four instruments. The early quartets give most of the melodic material to the first violin, but in the later quartets the other instruments are more fully integrated, with each of the four players contributing to the discourse. When the great German poet Goethe compared a string quartet to a conversation among four equally interesting individuals, he must have been thinking of the Haydn quartets.

HAYDN'S CONTRACT

When Haydn was appointed to the Esterházy court, his contract was very specific about his duties. He was required to dress "as befits an honest house officer in a princely court," that is, with powdered wig, brocaded coat, white stockings, and silver buckles on his shoes. He was to be in charge of all the musicians, serve as an example to them, and "avoid undue familiarity with them in eating and drinking or in other relations, lest he should lose the respect due to him." He was responsible for looking after all the music and the instruments. And he was required to compose music as the prince demanded, and was forbidden to give away or sell copies of his music or to compose for anyone else "without the knowledge and gracious permission of his Serene Princely Highness."

Haydn was quite content with this arrangement. He said later, "My Prince was happy with all my works; I received approval; I could, as head of an orchestra, make experiments in my music. I was cut off from the world: there was no one to confuse or annoy me, and I was forced to become original."

The Haydn Masses are noble, grand structures that combine a conservative choral style appropriate to the traditional texts with a brilliant orchestral and symphonic style. And Haydn's two oratorios, *The Creation* and *The Seasons*, display a wit and liveliness together with the kind of exquisite pictorial writing that never fails to captivate audiences. In *The Creation*, which describes the creation of the world, Haydn begins with a depiction of Chaos, in which darkness and void are represented by murky harmonies and unsettled rhythm. On the last word of the choral proclamation "And there was *light!*" there is a loud, radiant climax on a C-major chord. Both *The Creation* and *The Seasons* contain cleverly realistic musical descriptions of nature: a cooing dove, a flashing storm, a slithery worm.

In the middle of Haydn's career at Esterháza in the early 1770s, there was an interesting change of style that affected his string quartets, piano sonatas, and symphonies. Quite suddenly, some of Haydn's works began to display a mood of melancholy and longing that had not been there before. Haydn experimented with this style by writing several compositions in unusual minor keys, with sudden changes of dynamics, remote harmonic excursions, and intense expression. We will listen to a movement from one of Haydn's symphonies from this period. Possibly because the prince did not react favorably to the new style, Haydn abandoned it after a few years.

LISTENING GUIDE

((•● Listen on MySearchLab

FRANZ JOSEPH HAYDN (1732–1809)

Minuet and Trio from Symphony No. 45

Date of composition: 1772
Orchestration: two oboes, two horns,
    violins I and II, viola, cello, double bass
Tempo: *Allegretto* ("Moderately fast")
Meter: $\frac{3}{4}$
Key of movement: F♯ major
Duration: 4:55

CD II, 1

We studied a fairly simple minuet and trio in Chapter 3. This movement is more fascinating and complex. Understanding its many levels can take dozens of repeated hearings, and yet it is also graceful and lively, and a pleasure to listen to on any level.

Among the standard features of minuet form and style—a fixed pattern of repetition, triple meter, moderate tempo—Haydn has incorporated several others that make this particular minuet unique. The most striking is the amount of contrast he has written into this piece. There is contrast of dynamics, texture, instrumentation, and key.

The first—contrast of **dynamics**—is evident from the outset. In the first section of the movement, which takes only about 13 seconds to play, Haydn changes dynamics four times. These dynamic contrasts are reinforced by **textural** contrasts: Haydn tends to use monophony or very thin counterpoint for the quiet passages and thick polyphony for the loud ones. For this first section, the **instrumentation** follows suit. We hear violins alone in the quiet passages and the whole orchestra when the music is loud. All these contrasts continue throughout the piece. As for contrast of **key**, there is a move to the dominant key for sections B and C and a sudden and unexpected shift to F♯ *minor* in the middle of the D section.

In some ways it seems as though Haydn is deliberately trying to confuse his listeners. The form of a minuet movement is usually easy to hear. But in this movement, the form is deliberately obscured. Haydn tries every trick in the book to confuse us. He does this by (1) putting the strong cadences in the wrong place, (2) using linking phrases across the section divisions, (3) syncopating the rhythm, and (4) using internal repetitions. For example, he repeats some of the A section inside the B section and some of the C section inside the D section (this is known as *rounded binary* form).

There is more. In his internal repetitions (repeating A inside B, and C inside D), instead of repeating exactly, Haydn rewrites the music each time.

Let's look at the D section first because it is the easiest one to follow. The D section contains a shortened restatement of C. Haydn actually repeats only the first half of C (compare 1:41–1:56 with 2:33–2:40). But if you listen closely, you will hear that Haydn has actually rewritten the passage to make it sound fresh. In its first appearance, the instrumentation involves only the two horns, with a tiny touch of strings at the end. In its restatement, oboes, horns, and all the strings play the music.

The rewriting of the A section within the B section is even more subtle. Compare 0:00–0:14 with 0:49–1:05. Listening carefully, you'll find many differences involving dynamics, phrase lengths (including the length of the whole passage), and instrumentation. Haydn is really trying to keep his audience on its toes!

The best way to untangle all of this confusion is by means of the timed listening guide. If you glance frequently at your timer while you are listening, follow the listening guide carefully, and listen to the piece several times, you'll be able to get some sense of what a brilliant and sophisticated composer Haydn really was.

	Time	Listen for
		Minuet
A	0:00	The first section of the minuet, in F♯ major. Graceful dancelike character; full of contrasts; syncopation. Ends with quiet linking passage on violins alone.
A	0:14	Repeat of first section of the minuet.
B(+A')	0:30	The second section of the minuet, longer than the first. Dominant key (C♯ major). Short loud passage, longer quiet syncopated passage on strings alone. Then a crescendo into a restatement (A') of the first section of the minuet (**0:49**).
B(+A')	1:05	Repeat of entire second section, including its restatement of A.
		Trio
C	1:41	First section of trio. Rising phrase for horns, graceful answering phrase for violins.
C	1:56	Repeat.
D(+C')	2:11	Second section of trio, longer than the first. Back to tonic key (F♯ major). Divided into three parts: beginning, with descending phrases in horns; (2:21) oboes replace the horns, sudden shift to F♯ *minor*; (2:33) shortened restatement (C') of the first section of the trio.
D(+C')	2:40	Repeat of entire second section of trio, including its restatement of C.
		Minuet
		[The entire minuet is repeated exactly.]
A	3:10	A section.
A	3:24	Repeat of A section.
B(+A')	3:39	B section, including restatement of A.
B(+A')	4:14	Repeat of B section with restatement of A.

All of Haydn's pieces adhere to Classic formal procedures. Nevertheless, Haydn showed great ingenuity in exploiting the fixed forms of Classic music for his own expressive purposes. One device that he invented was the "false recapitulation." You remember that in sonata form, the opening music of the movement returns after the development section with the same melody and harmony that it had at the beginning. Haydn sometimes liked to play games with the expectations of his audience by *pretending* to start the recapitulation in the middle of the development section. The music of the opening of the movement is played, leading us to think that the recapitulation has started. But then the harmonies change, the development continues, and we realize we've been tricked. A little while later, the true recapitulation occurs.

Haydn liked to play other kinds of tricks on his listeners. In 1781 he published a set of six string quartets that have come to be called the "Joke Quartets." The quartets contain serious music and emotionally expressive passages, but there are many witty moments, too: cadences in the "wrong" places, oddly shaped melodies, and unexpected rhythms. At the end of the second quartet of the set (Opus 33, Number 2), there is a "false ending." The music seems to stop, suddenly moves on, stops again, and then seems to begin again. Then the movement ends. This kind of manipulation of audience expectations could occur only in a period in which formal procedures were strict. When there are no rules, breaking the rules is no fun!

Even today, there is still some of Haydn's music that is only rarely or never performed. But as time goes on, and more of his compositions become familiar, we realize that Haydn was one of the most versatile and gifted composers of his time.

LISTENING GUIDE

((●— Listen on MySearchLab

FRANZ JOSEPH HAYDN (1732–1809)

Fourth Movement from String Quartet, Op. 33, No. 2, in E♭ Major

Tempo: *Presto* ("Very fast")
Meter: $\frac{6}{8}$
Key: E♭ major
Duration: 3:07

CD II, 2

This movement is in the form of a rondo. There is a catchy main theme, which constantly returns in the course of the movement. Between appearances of the main theme are passages of contrasting material known as episodes. In this rondo, Haydn adopts the following form, with A as the main theme and B, C, and D as the three episodes:

A B A B A C A B A D A Coda

Haydn wrote this movement in the attractive and bouncy meter of $\frac{6}{8}$ and in a fast tempo, which makes the music particularly lively and fun. But the joke comes in the final measures, as the listener has no idea where the ending really is.

	Time	Listen for
A	0:00	Main theme.
	0:06	Repeat.
B	0:12	First episode.
A	0:28	Main theme.
B	0:34	Repeat of first episode.
A	0:50	Main theme.
C	0:57	Second episode, many key changes.
A	1:25	Main theme.
B	1:31	First episode again.
A	1:48	Main theme.
D	1:54	Third episode.
	2:13	Pace slows down, anticipation, then:
A	2:23	Main theme again.
CODA	2:30	Final cadence?
	2:32	Sudden change of texture and tempo.
	2:45	Final cadence?
	2:46	Main theme, broken up into four separate phrases.
	2:58	Ending?
	3:01	First phrase of main theme!

Wolfgang Amadeus Mozart (1756–1791)

Wolfgang Amadeus Mozart.

Find the **Quick Listen** on **MySearchLab**

"Mozart First Symphony"

For most listeners, Mozart's music is easier to appreciate than Haydn's. Compared with Haydn, Mozart wears his heart on his sleeve. His music is even more colorful, more intense.

Mozart was born into a musical family. His father, Leopold, was a distinguished violinist and composer who held the post of deputy music director at the court of the Prince-Archbishop of Salzburg in Austria. He was also the author of an important book on violin playing. Mozart's older sister was also a talented musician, though she did not pursue a life in music, as this was considered inappropriate for women at the time. Mozart's father decided to devote his career to promoting the abilities of young Wolfgang. Wolfgang was uniquely, breathtakingly gifted. His father piously referred to him as "this miracle God has caused to be born in Salzburg."

Mozart was born in 1756. By the age of four, he was already displaying amazing musical ability. At six, he had started to compose and was performing brilliantly on the harpsichord. For the next 10 years, his father took him on journeys to various courts, towns, and principalities around Europe where he played for noblemen, princes, and even the Empress of Austria Maria Theresa.

These constant travels in his formative years had a valuable effect on the young boy. Mozart's principal teacher at this time was his father, but he absorbed other musical influences like a sponge. Wherever he went, he picked up the musical style of the region and of the prominent local composers.

LEOPOLD MOZART

Leopold Mozart is often mentioned only in relation to his illustrious son, Wolfgang Amadeus Mozart. This is a little unfair, because he was a distinguished performer, composer, author, and music theorist in his own right.

In 1756, Leopold published a treatise entitled *Versuch einer grundlichen Violinschule* (*Essay on a Fundamental Violin Method*), designed partly as an aid for teaching the violin and partly as a discussion of musical performance and analysis. This treatise represents one of the most important contributions to music theory in the mid-eighteenth century.

Unfortunately, a large number of Leopold's compositions remain unresearched, uncatalogued, and unpublished. Those that are documented include Masses, symphonies, divertimenti, partitas, serenades, and a wide variety of chamber music. Much of Leopold's music exhibits a strong naturalistic tendency and employs instruments such as bugles, bagpipes, the hunting horn, the hurdy-gurdy, and the dulcimer. His scores sometimes call for dog noises, human cries, pistol shots, and whistles!

Leopold composed little after 1762. This sudden decrease in productivity can be attributed to the huge amount of time he devoted to teaching his son and to the numerous tours of Europe they undertook together in an attempt to promote Wolfgang's extraordinary talents. In short, Leopold sacrificed his own considerable career to further that of his son. No one was better qualified to recognize Wolfgang's gifts than his gifted father.

From all these sources and from his own teeming imagination, Mozart fashioned an individual style. By the time he was eight, Mozart had already had some music published. By 10, he was writing symphonies. At 14, he had produced his first full-length opera. By the time he was 17 years old, when he and his father returned home to Salzburg to try to find Wolfgang a job, he was a mature and fully formed creative artist.

Finding Mozart a job was not easy. The Prince-Archbishop of Salzburg was an autocratic ruler, and his patience had already been tried by the constant leaves of absence of his deputy music director (Mozart's father). The archbishop agreed to employ Mozart, but only in a junior position. Mozart wrote a fair amount of music in these years, but both he and his father felt that Salzburg was too stifling for him. After a few years, Mozart traveled again to try to find a position elsewhere. This time he traveled with his mother, because his father could not afford to leave his post for any more trips. He went to Munich, Mannheim (where Stamitz's great orchestra was centered), and Paris. But in none of these places was a job forthcoming. Most of Mozart's prospective employers thought he was too young and too talented ("overqualified" is the word we would use today) for a normal position. Indeed, any music director would have been threatened by this brash and brilliant youngster. In Paris he encountered not only disappointment but also tragedy: his mother died. He wrote to his father and sister:

I hope that you are prepared to hear with fortitude one of the saddest and most painful stories. . . . I can only judge from my own grief and sorrow what yours must be.

Although Mozart was given a promotion upon returning to Salzburg, he was still unsatisfied. In 1780 he accompanied the archbishop on a visit to Vienna. Mozart was outraged when he was forced to eat in the servants' quarters and infuriated when the archbishop refused to let him go to the houses of other aristocrats who had invited him to perform for them. Mozart angrily demanded his release from the archbishop's employ and received it, as he wrote to his father, "with a kick on my ass from our worthy Prince-Archbishop."

Thus began the freelance career of one of the most brilliant musicians in history. At first, Mozart supported himself by giving piano lessons. He also wrote several sonatas for the piano and some piano concertos. Piano music was very popular in Vienna. Mozart had some success with a German comic opera he wrote in 1782 called *The Abduction from the Seraglio* (so called because the action takes place in a Turkish *seraglio*, or harem). Also in 1782 he married his landlady's daughter, a young soprano named Constanze Weber. His father, to whom he continued to write regularly, disapproved strongly of the marriage.

For the next few years, Mozart was highly successful. He undertook a set of string quartets that were designed to emulate those of Haydn, and he dedicated them in a warm and heartfelt style to the older master. We know that the two composers met a few times at string quartet parties. Haydn played the violin, Mozart the viola.

In these years, Mozart won great fame—and made quite a lot of money—through his piano concertos. Between 1784 and 1786, he composed 12 piano concertos. He appeared before the Viennese public as both composer and pianist, because he played the solo parts in the concertos himself. The concertos were very successful and brought Mozart to the height of his career.

Gradually, however, Mozart's popularity began to wane. The Viennese were always eager for some new sensation, and Mozart had been around for a while. In addition, the city

Find the **Quick Listen** on **MySearchLab**
"Wolfgang Amadeus Mozart's Turkish Finale"

Watch the **Inside the Orchestra** video on **MySearchLab**

THE BOY GENIUS

The child Mozart caused such a sensation in London that he was examined and tested by a scientist. The scientist wrote a report attesting to Mozart's musical ability and age. The proof that he was indeed a boy and not a midget came at the end of a rigorous series of musical examinations.

While he was playing to me, a cat came in, upon which he immediately left his harpsichord, nor could we bring him back for a considerable time. He would also sometimes run about the room with a stick between his legs for a horse.

This boy will cause us all to be forgotten.

—composer Johann Adolf Hasse

COMPOSERS, PATRONS, AND AUDIENCES

Composers and Patrons in the Classic Era

Music patronage was at a turning point when Mozart went to Vienna in the last part of the eighteenth century. Many patrons of music continued to be wealthy aristocrats. Haydn's entire career was funded by a rich prince. Mozart's father and, for a time, Mozart himself were in the employ of another prince. But when Mozart went to Vienna in 1781, he contrived to make a living from a variety of sources. In addition to performances at aristocratic houses and commissions for particular works, Mozart gave piano and composition lessons, put on operas, and gave many public concerts of his own music.

The eighteenth century saw a considerable rise in the number and availability of public concerts. Three types were common: charity concerts to raise money for local poorhouses and orphanages; subscription concerts, for which tickets were sold in advance; and benefit concerts, at which composers played for their own profit. Music was becoming more and more the province of the general public, and composers less and less the servants of the rich.

Portrait of the Mozart family from about 1780. Mozart plays a duet with his sister, while his father listens, and his mother is remembered in a painting behind them.

Painting, Baroque, 18th Century. Johann Nepomuk Della Croce, *The Mozart Family* (1780–1781). Oil on canvas. 140 × 186 cm. Mozart House, Salzburg, Austria. Erich Lessing, Art Resource.

Find the **Quick Listen** on **MySearchLab**
"Mozart Symphony No. 39"

Find the **Quick Listen** on **MySearchLab**
Marriage of Figaro "Dove Sono"

Find the **Quick Listen** on **MySearchLab**
"Mozart Requiem"

was undergoing a recession, and concert dates and composing contracts were hard to come by. Mozart's correspondence from the late 1780s is full of letters requesting loans from friends. Despite his dislike of authority, he made attempts to find a secure position at the Viennese court.

Mozart did not write many new symphonies during this period, but in the summer of 1788, in the space of about eight weeks, he wrote three symphonies in a row. These last three symphonies, nos. 39, 40, and 41, are the culmination of his work in the genre. They are very different from each other, but all three are richly orchestrated, enormously inventive, and full of subtle details that repay frequent rehearings.

Perhaps the greatest achievement of Mozart's last years is represented by his operas. Mozart had been interested in opera since his boyhood travels to Italy. He had already written several youthful pieces and, since coming to Vienna, he had written both an opera seria (serious Italian opera) and a singspiel (German comic opera). Now, in what would be the last five years of his life, he completed five great operas. The best known of these are *The Marriage of Figaro* (1786), *Don Giovanni* (1787), and *The Magic Flute* (completed in the year of his death, 1791). These operas are all very different, but in each of them Mozart displays his remarkable understanding of human nature in all its richness. In *Figaro*, he depicts with the finest subtlety the urgent adolescent sexuality of a servant boy and the deeply moving despair of a neglected wife. In *Don Giovanni*, Mozart explores the richly human experiences of determination, pride, grief, comedy, and seduction. In *The Magic Flute*, the themes are noble ambition, marital harmony, and pure love. In Mozart's hands, these ideals and emotions are transformed from the conventions of the opera stage into the deepest expression of human feelings.

In November of 1791, while he was working on a Requiem Mass (Mass for the Dead), Mozart became ill. And on December 5, at the age of 35, with half a lifetime of masterpieces still uncomposed, Wolfgang Amadeus Mozart died.

Mozart's father Leopold—violinist, composer, and Mozart's first teacher.

Mozart's Music

Mozart's music is a remarkable combination of the accessible and the profound. As Mozart wrote to his father, his music appeals to experts and amateurs alike. Another reason so many people are so attached to Mozart's music is its extraordinary breadth. There is an incredibly wide range in his more than 800 compositions, from the lightest little comic pieces to works that explore the great themes of human existence: life and death, love, tragedy, romance, despair, and hope.

Mozart wrote in all the main genres of Classic music: opera, symphony, string quartet, and sonata. He wrote solo concertos for a wide variety of instruments: violin, flute, oboe, clarinet, bassoon, and horn. But for his own instrument, the piano, he composed more than 20 concertos, which are among his greatest masterpieces.

Mozart wrote dozens of sonatas, both for solo piano and for combinations of instruments, including piano, strings, and winds. He also composed many great string quartets. In addition to these works, Mozart wrote several string quintets, in which an extra viola is added to the two violins, viola, and cello of the string quartet. This makes the music richer and the counterpoint fuller.

Mozart also greatly enriched the expressive power of opera. *The Magic Flute, Don Giovanni,* and *The Marriage of Figaro*

transcend convention by portraying people in all their psychological complexity.

Even in his purely instrumental works, Mozart wrote music that flouted convention. He created works of great depth and seriousness for "background music" at garden parties. He wrote slow movements of heartbreaking simplicity for his piano concertos. Sometimes he used counterpoint to intensify his music in places where counterpoint was not usual. And his melodies often have passages that are chromatic (moving by half steps) at a time when most composers wrote melodies that are entirely diatonic (using only notes from the scale). Finally, Mozart's music sometimes passes briefly into the minor mode in the middle of major-mode passages, which creates added depth and emotional resonance. It is like the shadow of a small cloud passing over a sunny meadow.

Only a very small number of his works use a minor key as the tonic. Among these is the Symphony No. 40 in G minor, written in 1788. (See **Listening Guide.**)

Although Mozart's music is richer, more versatile, and more varied than most eighteenth-century music, it does use the same basic conventions as other music of the time. The instruments are the same, the forms are the same, and the primary genres that Mozart cultivated are the same. But Mozart's music speaks deeply to more people, covers a wider range of feeling, and resonates with more human significance than that of almost any other composer before or since. In that sense, Mozart's music is truly "classic."

O Mozart, immortal Mozart, how many, how infinitely many inspiring suggestions of a finer, better life have you left in our souls!
—Franz Schubert

Mozart's own manuscript of a song for voice and piano. Notice the speed and clarity of his handwriting.

MUSICAL FORGERIES

There is great excitement whenever a music manuscript purported to be by Haydn or Mozart turns up in an attic or an old desk drawer. Sometimes these documents are authentic. For example, in 2005 an authentic manuscript of an important work in Beethoven's handwriting was discovered in Philadelphia. It sold to a private collector for $2 million. But often the manuscripts are forgeries, and some of them are good enough to fool even the experts (for a while). In 1994, some "newly discovered" Haydn piano sonatas, authenticated by a world-renowned Haydn scholar and due for performance at Harvard University's Music Department, were declared to be fakes.

The name of one of the great composers on the title page virtually guarantees a favorable reception for a work. For nearly a hundred years, a well-known symphony was thought to be by Mozart (his "37th Symphony"). It was hailed by critics as "typical of the master." But when the symphony turned out to be not by Mozart at all but by a less famous contemporary of his, critics immediately described it as "obviously not on a par with the work of the master." The work hadn't changed; it was the same music! Only people's preconceptions had changed.

LISTENING GUIDE

((••[**Listen** on **MySearchLab**

WOLFGANG AMADEUS MOZART (1756–1791)

First Movement from Symphony No. 40 in G Minor, K. 550

Date of composition: 1788
Orchestration: flute, two oboes, two clarinets,
   two bassoons, two horns, and strings
Tempo: *Allegro molto* ("Very fast")
Meter: $\frac{2}{2}$
Key: G minor
Duration: 8:18

CD II, 3

In the space of eight weeks during the summer of 1788, Mozart completed three large-scale symphonies. Perhaps he intended them to be published and performed together. Though there was no reason for him to have known this, they were to be his last.

The G-minor Symphony, the middle one of the three, is one of Mozart's best-known works and represents one of his greatest achievements in the symphonic realm. It is marked by perfect balance and control, a wealth of harmonic and instrumental color, and a brilliant use of formal structure.

The first movement is a superb example of these characteristics. In it, Mozart takes advantage of the dramatic possibilities of sonata form, while also playing with its conventions for expressive purposes. The basic structure of sonata form is easy to hear, but we can also see how Mozart *manipulated* the form to surprise and delight his listeners. There are many examples, but the most obvious one is the way he leads us to expect the recapitulation at a certain point, only to pull the rug out from under us.

You should first listen to the piece a few times simply to enjoy the fine expressive writing: the brilliant balance between loud and soft, woodwinds and strings, descending and ascending phrases, and minor and major keys. Notice, too, how Mozart spices up the sound with chromatic passages and surprise notes. Next, listen for the structure, the basic template of sonata form, which is so clearly articulated in this movement. The next couple of times, listen for how Mozart plays with this structure (and with his audience's expectations) for expressive purposes. Finally, try putting all these things together and listen for them all at once.

Don't stop listening after that, however. You may find, as many of the most experienced listeners do, that you will hear something new in this movement every time you listen to it. And there are three other movements in this symphony, three other symphonies in the group, and dozens of other symphonies by Mozart.

Time	Listen for
	Exposition
0:00 (2:02)	[timings for the repeat are in parentheses] Opening theme: violins, quiet, G minor; closed by full orchestra, loud.

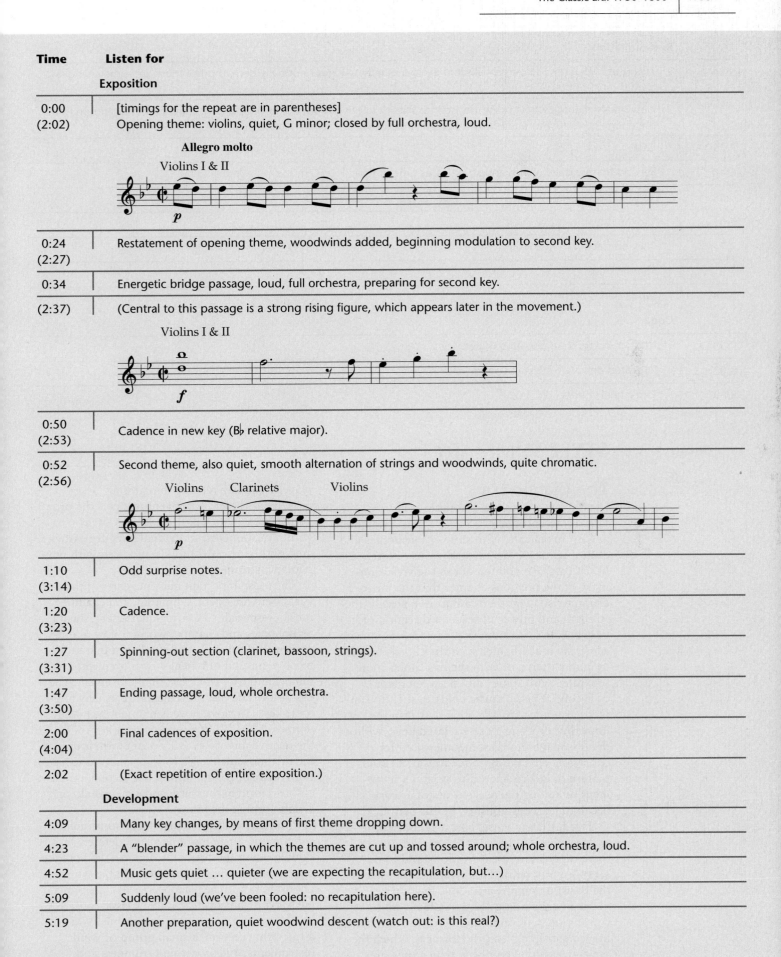

Allegro molto

Violins I & II

Time	Listen for
0:24 (2:27)	Restatement of opening theme, woodwinds added, beginning modulation to second key.
0:34 (2:37)	Energetic bridge passage, loud, full orchestra, preparing for second key. (Central to this passage is a strong rising figure, which appears later in the movement.)

Violins I & II

Time	Listen for
0:50 (2:53)	Cadence in new key (B♭ relative major).
0:52 (2:56)	Second theme, also quiet, smooth alternation of strings and woodwinds, quite chromatic.

Violins   Clarinets   Violins

Time	Listen for
1:10 (3:14)	Odd surprise notes.
1:20 (3:23)	Cadence.
1:27 (3:31)	Spinning-out section (clarinet, bassoon, strings).
1:47 (3:50)	Ending passage, loud, whole orchestra.
2:00 (4:04)	Final cadences of exposition.
2:02	(Exact repetition of entire exposition.)
	Development
4:09	Many key changes, by means of first theme dropping down.
4:23	A "blender" passage, in which the themes are cut up and tossed around; whole orchestra, loud.
4:52	Music gets quiet … quieter (we are expecting the recapitulation, but…)
5:09	Suddenly loud (we've been fooled: no recapitulation here).
5:19	Another preparation, quiet woodwind descent (watch out: is this real?)

Recapitulation

5:24	YES! (But notice how Mozart sneaks it in ever so quietly.) All goes normally here, though there are some changes from the exposition.
5:57	New material, loud, whole orchestra (sounds like it's left over from the development). It uses the rising figure from the opening bridge passage (shown previously at 0:34).
6:29	Back on track …
6:40	Second theme: quiet, winds and strings, this time in tonic key (G minor).
6:58	Surprise notes.
7:05	New material.
7:14	Back on track …
7:21	Spinning out.
7:44	Music opens out to:

Coda

7:53	Confirming tonic key, floating, quiet.
8:03	Repeated definitive cadences, loud.
8:09	Three final chords.

STYLE SUMMARY

The Classic Era

Classic music presents a notable contrast from that of the Baroque era. Classic music is lighter and more delicate, with simpler harmonies and clearer textures. The most obvious difference is in the bass. We pointed out in the style summary of the previous chapter that the most characteristic feature of a Baroque piece is the strength and powerful sense of direction of its bass line. In Classic music, the accompaniment is usually much lighter with the chords broken up into patterns or with the bass notes more separated with some "air" between them.

Second, Classic music tends to stick to simpler harmonies, usually staying within the home key or using closely related keys, without the dissonant chords sometimes used for expressive effect in Baroque music. A standard pattern of key relationships within a movement or among the movements of a work became clearly established in this period.

Third, Classic music uses a symmetrical arrangement of musical phrases. Phrases tend to be two or four measures long and to be arranged into pairs. This symmetry is used as the basis for simple, attractive melodies.

Finally, the ruling force in Classic music is convention. Convention governs the number of movements in a piece, the forms in which they are cast, and the tempos at which they are played. The key relationship among movements is set by convention, as is the order and approximate length of the key areas within movements. Individual keys are associated with particular moods and even with particular instruments.

The most important musical genres of the Classic era are opera, symphony, and chamber music—especially the string quartet and sonata. Symphonies and chamber works follow a four-movement format: a moderately fast first movement, a graceful or lyrical slow movement, a minuet and trio, and a fast final movement. The first, third, and last movements are usually in the tonic key. The slow movement might be in the dominant key (V), the subdominant key (IV), or the relative minor key (vi). Sonata form is used in the first movement; aria form, theme and variations form, or sonata form in the second; minuet-and-trio form in the third; and either rondo or sonata form in the fourth.

Convention dictated that concertos should contain only three movements: moderately fast, slow, and fast. (Historically, concertos did not take on the minuet-and-trio movement of the symphonic format.) The piano was one of the principal solo instruments featured in Classic concertos.

The instrumentation in symphonies was for a full string section, a small group of wind instruments, and sometimes trumpets and drums. The instrumentation in chamber music was either for piano alone or for one to four instruments (usually strings) and a piano. Sometimes a small group of wind or stringed instruments played together without piano. A favorite combination of the Classic period was the string quartet (two violins, viola, and cello).

Operas on serious subjects continued to be composed; however, a new, more down-to-earth, more realistic type of opera known as comic opera became popular. Mozart used to mingle types of opera. He introduced comic scenes into serious operas and generally broke out of the conventional mode, producing works of extraordinary variety and psychological insight.

The absence of the basso continuo in Classic music created the opportunity for a much lighter, more transparent texture, more freedom in instrumental writing, and a more accessible style. This was music for nonexperts as well as for connoisseurs.

FUNDAMENTALS OF CLASSIC MUSIC

- ❑ The music is more accessible, with shorter, symmetrical phrases, simpler harmony, and easier tunes
- ❑ No basso continuo
- ❑ Texture is more transparent
- ❑ Principal genres are opera, symphony, and chamber music, though concertos (especially for piano) are also popular
- ❑ New genres are piano concerto, comic opera, and string quartet
- ❑ The music is ruled largely by convention (number of movements, form and structure of movements, keys, harmony)

FOR FURTHER DISCUSSION AND STUDY

1. Listen to the "Sicilienne" by Maria Theresia von Paradis, the famous blind pianist and student of Mozart, on Classical.com. Identify the influences of Mozart on this piece. Can you tell that it was written by a woman and not by a man?

2. In today's society, where people of all classes can freely attend any public concert, the symphony nevertheless seems to attract predominantly middle- and upper-class patrons. Why do you think this is so? Is it a matter of money, attention span, or education? Or is there some other reason? Now that you are taking a music-appreciation course, are you more likely to go to a concert featuring classical music? Why, or why not?

3. Describe the evolution of the string quartet. How did it evolve out of the string section of the orchestra? Why did it become one of the most popular forms of chamber music?

4. Today's concert performances of eighteenth-century chamber music are often given in large halls on instruments created for nineteenth-century orchestras. Discuss the term *performance practice*, noting how different the instruments of that time would have sounded. Compare recordings of any classical piece on modern instruments and historical instruments.

5. Listen to the first movement of Mozart's *Eine kleine Nachtmusik*, K. 525, and count the themes aloud as they are heard. How is this work different from other, more typical sonatas?

6. Listen to a flute concerto by Johann Joachim Quantz (1697–1773) written for Frederick the Great during the 1740s. Make a list of the Baroque and Classic elements in this transitional piece.

7. Choose another movement from Haydn's String Quartet, Op. 33, No. 2, in Eb Major. Listen to it carefully and develop your own Listening Guide for it.

8. The world has always been in awe of the child prodigy. Think of modern prodigies in math, tennis, etc. Discuss the pros and cons of early celebrity. How did Mozart's early fame affect his life?

9. Watch the film *Amadeus*. From whose point of view is the story being told? How much of the movie corresponds with your knowledge of Mozart's life?

10. Discuss how composers and performers today make a living (university appointments, composer-in-residence programs, commissions, etc.), and relate these means to the patronage system of Mozart's time.

✓•⸺Study and Review on MySearchLab

Beethoven

Some composers simply do not fit conveniently into pigeonholes or into our conveniently constructed time periods. Most music historians place the end of the Classical era and the beginning of the Romantic era at about 1800. But there is one composer whose life spanned that boundary by about a quarter century in either direction and whose individuality was so strong that he simply cannot be labeled. That composer is Beethoven.

Beethoven was born in 1770 and grew up at a time when both Haydn and Mozart were still alive and actively composing. The music he heard and studied as a young man was strictly Classic in style. But he died in 1827, well into the nineteenth century, when Romanticism was in full flower.

Like all great artists who live at a time of change, Beethoven was both a beneficiary of that change and partly responsible for it. He took the forms, procedures, and ideals that he had inherited from the Classic era and developed them beyond their previously accepted limits. He brought Classic genres—symphony, concerto, sonata, string quartet—into the nineteenth century and transformed them into the vehicles of musical expression for a new age. He burst through the boundaries of Classic restraint to create works of unprecedented scope and depth. He enlarged the orchestra, changed musical structure, added a chorus to

Beethoven in his prime.

the symphony, and attached narratives to some of his purely instrumental works—all of which had wide-ranging repercussions for a century and more. Finally, he invested instrumental music with a personal subjectivity and with the stamp of his own extraordinary personality in such a way that music was never the same again. He was both the child of one era and the founding father of another. That is why Beethoven has a chapter of his own.

> The history of Beethoven is tantamount to an intellectual history of the nineteenth century.
> —Karl Dalhaus

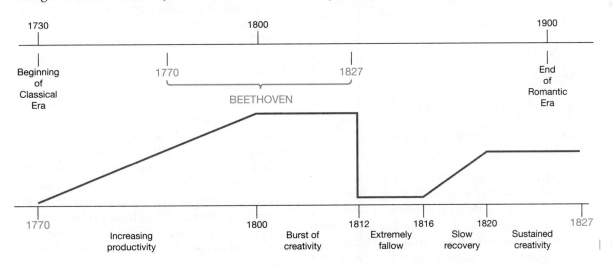

Beethoven's productivity.

Beethoven's Life

Beethoven is perhaps the most famous musician of all time. Ever since his death in 1827, he has been revered as the principal figure in the history of Western music. His influence on later composers was enormous, to the extent that many of them actually found his accomplishments intimidating.

Who was this man?

Beethoven's Early Life

Ludwig van Beethoven was born in 1770 into a family of musicians. Both his grandfather and his father were professional musicians at the court of the Elector (the local ruler) in the important German town of Bonn. His grandfather was highly respected, but his father became something of a problem at the court because he was an alcoholic. As a teenager,

Beethoven was put in charge of the family finances and started a job at the court. He studied organ and composition and helped look after the instruments. About the same time, he began to write music—mostly songs and chamber works.

NEED TO KNOW

BEETHOVEN TIMELINE

1770	Born in Bonn, Germany to a family of musicians
1792	Moves to Vienna to study with Franz Joseph Haydn
1792–1802	First performances and compositions (mostly keyboard and chamber works)
1802	First discovers that he is losing his hearing
1802–1812	Middle period of composing during which Beethoven writes six symphonies, four concertos, five string quartets, an opera, some orchestral overtures, and several important piano sonatas as well as other pieces of chamber music
1815	After the death of his brother, Beethoven fights with his sister-in-law for custody of his nephew Karl
1817	Fully deaf
1820–1822	Last piano sonatas
1824	Ninth Symphony
1825–1827	Last string quartets
1827	Beethoven dies at the age of 56

In 1790, an important visitor passed through Bonn: this was Franz Joseph Haydn, on his way to London for the first of his successful visits. He met the young Beethoven and agreed to take him on as a student when Haydn came back from London to Vienna. In 1792, Beethoven moved to Vienna to study with the great master. Beethoven was 22; Haydn was 60.

Apparently the lessons did not go well. Haydn was old-fashioned and a little pompous, Beethoven rebellious and headstrong. But Beethoven was a formidable pianist, and he soon found support among the rich patrons of the arts who lived in Vienna.

Though I had some instruction from Haydn, I never learned anything from him.
—Beethoven

Prince Lichnowsky gave him board and lodging at his palace, in return for which Beethoven was to compose music and play the piano at evening parties; at least that was the arrangement. In fact, Beethoven hated being dependent and often refused to play. But the prince was very tolerant; he finally gave Beethoven his own rooms in the palace so that he could work as he pleased.

In the early years, Beethoven wrote mostly keyboard and chamber-music pieces. As time went on, however, he decided to start composing in the larger musical forms of the day: string quartet, piano concerto, and symphony. By the time Beethoven was 32, he had written—among other works—piano sonatas, a great deal of chamber music, a set of six string quartets, three piano concertos, and two symphonies. The string quartets, concertos, and symphonies owe a great debt to Haydn and Mozart.

But Beethoven's music was already starting to show signs of considerable individuality. The First Symphony deliberately begins in the wrong key, before turning to the right one. The Third Piano Concerto features a powerful unifying rhythm. And the last movement of one of the early string quartets has a deeply expressive slow introduction entitled *La Malinconia (Melancholy)*.

Beethoven had every reason to feel melancholic at this time of his life. For it was in 1802 that he discovered the tragic truth that was to haunt him for the rest of his life: he was going deaf. He contemplated suicide but, overcoming his despair, decided that his first responsibility lay with his music. He had to produce the works that were in him.

His disease progressed gradually. It took some years for him to become totally deaf, and there were periods when normal hearing returned. But by 1817, Beethoven could not hear a single note, and his conversations were carried on by means of an ear trumpet and a notebook slung around his neck. His deafness eventually prevented him from performing and conducting, but he continued to compose until the end of his life. He could hear everything inside his head.

The Heroic Phase

The middle period of Beethoven's life was marked by a vigorous concentration on work and the sense of triumph over adversity. For these reasons, it is often called the "heroic" phase. He was determined to overcome all life's

BEETHOVEN'S PERSONALITY

Beethoven is often portrayed as a wild, aggressive individual, intolerant in the extreme, and prone to violent fits of rage. There is an element of truth to this image of the composer, though it hardly does justice to the complex nature of his personality.

He lived at a time when the established hierarchy of European society was in question, and he held ambivalent views toward authority. When he was asked to play in aristocratic homes, he insisted that no one be in the same room with him. He hated the idea of conforming to fixed social etiquette. His deafness, naturally enough, also made him more withdrawn and unsociable.

There were many contradictory strands to Beethoven's personality. At times he was warm and welcoming; on other occasions he could be cold and hostile. He was a loner, yet he enjoyed the company of a number of intimate friends. He appeared content to work in his cramped quarters in Vienna, yet he relished long walks in the countryside and often spent summers in country villages. He often expressed the desire for a tranquil home life, yet he never married. Perhaps we should expect such contradictions from a genius as extraordinary as Beethoven.

problems. In one of his letters he said, "I will seize Fate by the throat." This was a period of extraordinary productivity. In the 10 years between 1802 and 1812, Beethoven wrote six more symphonies, four concertos, five more string quartets, an entire opera, some orchestral overtures, and several important piano sonatas as well as other pieces of chamber music.

The music Beethoven wrote during this time is strong and muscular, with contrasting passages of great lyricism. This contrast exists *between* works (Symphonies nos. 4, 6, and 8—for example—are gentle, whereas Symphonies nos. 3, 5, and 7 are more powerful) and also *within* works. Some compositions build to aggressive climaxes and then move into moments of purest beauty and radiance. (The first movement of the Fifth Piano Concerto does this.) Like Mozart, Beethoven wrote his piano concertos to display his own virtuosity, but soon his deafness prevented him from playing in public, and he became increasingly introverted and antisocial. He was sometimes seen striding around the countryside without a coat or a hat, ignoring the weather and muttering to himself.

The most striking thing about the compositions from the heroic phase is their length. From the Third Symphony on, Beethoven was writing works much larger in scope than those of his predecessors. In the Third Symphony, the first movement alone is as long as many complete symphonies of Haydn and Mozart.

During this phase, Beethoven became very famous. His works were regarded as strong and patriotic at a time when his homeland was at war with France. He even wrote some overtly political pieces, such as a Battle

Symphony—complete with brass fanfares and cannon fire—to celebrate an early victory of the Duke of Wellington over Napoleon. He also became quite wealthy. His music was published and performed more than ever, and his income from these sources as well as from aristocratic and royal patrons was substantial.

Personal Crisis and Halt to Productivity

After the extraordinarily productive years of the heroic phase, Beethoven found himself embroiled in a family crisis that robbed him of his creativity for several years. In 1815, Beethoven's brother died and left his widow and Beethoven with joint custody of his son—Beethoven's nephew, Karl. This caused Beethoven great turmoil and distress. Having never married himself, he yearned often for a normal family life with a wife to comfort him and a child of his own. He once said to a friend that such intimacy was "not to be thought of—impossible—a dream. Yet . . . I cannot get it out of my mind."

To be thrust suddenly into a position of paternal responsibility for a child and into close contact with a young woman completely undermined Beethoven's equilibrium. He threw himself into a series of devastating legal battles with his brother's widow to obtain sole custody of Karl. The conflict dragged on for years, sapping Beethoven's energy and destroying his peace of mind (not to mention that of the boy and his poor mother). Ultimately, Beethoven won the legal battles (he had powerful friends), and Karl came to live with him. The relationship was a stormy one, however, because Beethoven was

Find the **Quick Listen** on **MySearchLab** "Beethoven Battle Symphony"

I must confess that I live a miserable life . . . I live entirely in my music.

—Beethoven, in a letter to a friend, 1801

BEETHOVEN'S WORK HABITS

As Beethoven grew older and withdrew more and more from society, he became wholly absorbed in his art. He would habitually miss meals, forget or ignore invitations, and work long into the night. He himself described his "ceaseless occupations." Beethoven felt the strongest urge to produce the music within him, and yet he suffered the same creative anxiety as lesser mortals: "For some time past I have been carrying about with me the idea of three great works. . . . These I must get rid of: two symphonies, each different from the other, and also different from all my other symphonies, and an oratorio. . . . I dread beginning works of such magnitude. Once I have begun, then all goes well."

We are fortunate in possessing many of the sketchbooks in which Beethoven worked out his musical ideas. They present a vivid picture of the composer at work.

Music manuscript in Beethoven's hand.

appallingly strict and possessive. At the age of 19, Karl pawned his watch, bought two pistols, and tried to kill himself. This action, from which Karl soon recovered, brought Beethoven to his senses. Karl was allowed to return to his mother's house, and he escaped from Beethoven's domination by joining the army.

Late Years

After the most intense period of the battle over Karl, Beethoven only gradually regained his productivity. The most important works of his late years are the last three piano sonatas, the Ninth Symphony, and a series of string quartets. The piano sonatas are remarkable pieces, unusual in form and design, and very moving in their juxtaposition of complexity and simplicity. The Ninth Symphony, finished in 1824, continued Beethoven's tradition of breaking barriers. It is an immense work with a revolutionary last movement that includes a choir and four vocal soloists. The use of singers in a symphony was unheard of at this time, although many later composers imitated the idea in one way or another. The text for the last movement of the Ninth Symphony is a poem by the great German poet Schiller: the *Ode to Joy*. It is a summation of Beethoven's philosophy of life: "Let Joy bring everyone together: all men will be brothers; let all kneel before God."

Beethoven's last three years were devoted entirely to string quartets. In this most intimate of genres, he found a medium for his most personal thoughts and ideas. Many people have found Beethoven's late string quartets to be

> In his final illness, Beethoven is reported to have said, "Strange—I feel as though up to now I have written only a few notes."

> I shall hear in Heaven.
>
> —Beethoven's last words

both his greatest and his most challenging music. Yet there are moments of tenderness and great beauty, as well as passages of dissonant harmonies and rhythmic complexity, and some of the most profound music in the Western tradition. Beethoven died on March 26, 1827, at the age of 56, leaving an indelible mark on music and the way it has been experienced by listeners ever since.

Beethoven's Music

Beethoven's music has always represented the essence of serious music. In the twentieth century, people who know of only one classical composer know of Beethoven. And his music is played, written about, and recorded more frequently than the music of any other composer in the world.

Beethoven's music is appealing, moving, and forceful. It reaches something inside us that is elemental. It has a unique combination of the simple and the complex, the emotional and the intellectual. We recognize, on hearing it, that it comes from the spiritual side of a man, but also from a man who was entirely, and sometimes painfully, human.

There are some stylistic traits in Beethoven's music that might be regarded as his "fingerprints"—traits that can be instantly recognized and that mark the music as unmistakably his. These include the following:

1. Long powerful crescendos that seem to carry the music inexorably forward
2. Themes that sound exactly right but very different played quietly and very loud

MUSIC CRITICS

During the latter part of Beethoven's life, music journalism began to appear. Daily newspapers started to carry articles and reviews of music, and journals devoted to music were established. Then, as now, critics were not always well disposed toward new music. Here are a few early reviews of Beethoven's compositions:

On the overture to Beethoven's opera *Fidelio*: "All impartial musicians and music lovers were in perfect agreement that never was anything as incoherent, shrill, chaotic, and ear-splitting produced in music."

On the Third Symphony: "It is infinitely too lengthy. . . . If this symphony is not by some means abridged, it will soon fall into disuse."

On the Fifth Symphony: ". . . a sort of odious meowing."

On the Ninth Symphony: ". . . crude, wild, and extraneous harmonies" ". . . ugly, in bad taste, cheap."

On the late music: "He does not write much now, but most of what he produces is so impenetrably obscure in design and so full of unaccountable and often repulsive harmonies that he puzzles the critic as much as he perplexes the performer."

On all his music: "Beethoven always sounds to me like the upsetting of bags of nails, with here and there also a dropped hammer."

---

3. Dramatic use of Classic structures such as sonata form
4. Sudden key changes that nonetheless fit into a powerful harmonic logic

The most famous of Beethoven's compositions come from the middle part of his life: the heroic phase. These include Symphonies nos. 3–8, the middle string quartets, Piano Concertos nos. 4 and 5, the Violin Concerto, and the opera *Fidelio*. Some of the pieces are actually about heroism: the Third Symphony is entitled the *Eroica* ("Heroic"), and *Fidelio* ("The Faithful One") displays the heroism of a woman who rescues her husband from unjust imprisonment. As a result, much of this music is strong, dramatic, and powerful.

But there is another side to Beethoven: the lyrical side. Some of the middle symphonies are very tuneful and smoothly contoured, like the Sixth Symphony, known as the Pastoral. Even in the more dramatic pieces, there are often passages of great tenderness. One of the secrets of Beethoven's style is the way he juxtaposes strong and tender passages within the same work.

Less well-known are the compositions from Beethoven's early period. These include pieces that he wrote before moving to Vienna and some compositions from his first years in that city. Some are deliberately modeled on the works of his great forebears, Haydn and Mozart; others already show signs of

remarkable originality. There are songs, piano pieces, and much chamber music.

Finally, there are the works from the last part of Beethoven's career. These are all very different, and there are fewer of them. They include the Ninth Symphony, the *Missa Solemnis*, the late piano sonatas, and the last five string quartets. Beethoven's late music is very rich. There is a sense of great depth juxtaposed with an extraordinary, almost heartbreaking, innocence and simplicity. In his last years, Beethoven was no longer concerned with drama and heroism but with pursuing the path of his own creativity, wherever it might lead. Some of the music from this period is demanding and challenging to listen to, but with repeated hearings it can provide listeners with a lifetime of enjoyment and reward.

Listening Examples

To get an idea of the range of Beethoven's achievement, we will listen to compositions from both the early and the middle periods of his life. The first is a set of variations on a theme, written by Beethoven in 1790 for solo piano. Next we will study the whole of the Fifth Symphony, perhaps the most famous of Beethoven's compositions; it was written in 1807–1808, right in the middle of the heroic phase.

Watch the **Inside the Orchestra** video on **MySearchLab**

Find the **Quick Listen** on **MySearchLab** "Beethoven Op. 135 Slow Movement"

A giant goblin crossing time and space.
—E. M. Forster in *Howard's End*, describing the Fifth Symphony

PERFORMANCE IN CONTEXT
The Theatre on the River Wien

The history of Beethoven's music is closely linked with the Theatre on the River Wien, a Viennese opera house where many of his most famous works were premiered. The theatre opened in 1801 and was constructed for Emanuel Schikaneder, a multitalented actor-impresario whose many accomplishments include writing the libretto for *The Magic Flute* and commissioning Mozart to write the music. Schikaneder later tried to repeat this success with a new opera by Beethoven, and appointed the latter as the resident composer of the new theatre. Beethoven moved into the building and began a program of composing and conducting concerts. Many of these concerts were all-Beethoven programs, although symphonies by Mozart and Haydn sometimes shared the stage. Between 1802 and 1812, the theatre hosted the world premieres of four Beethoven symphonies, his opera *Fidelio*, and numerous other works by the composer. In 1813, a change in ownership ended Beethoven's relationship with the theatre, which went on to become a center for operetta and (much later) musical theatre. Despite its name, the Theatre on the River Wien is located almost two miles from the river bank, and is just southwest of the center of Vienna. The theatre façade includes the famous Papageno gate, a set of statues depicting a scene from Mozart's *The Magic Flute*.

The Theater an der Wien (ca.1800), after an anonymous water-colored pen-and-ink drawing © Schloß Schönbrunn Kultur- und Betriebsges.m.b.H./Foto: Julia Teresa Friehs /Schloss Schönbrunn Kultur- und Betriebsges.m.b.H.

LISTENING GUIDE

((•‌ Listen on MySearchLab

LUDWIG VAN BEETHOVEN (1770–1827)

Six Easy Variations on a Swiss Tune in F Major for Piano, WoO 64

Date of composition: 1790
Tempo: *Andante con moto* ("Fairly slow but with motion")
Meter: $\frac{3}{4}$
Key: F major
Duration: 2:53

CD II, 4

This is one of many sets of variations that Beethoven wrote in his early years. Creating variations on melodies is an easy way for composers to learn their craft. The tune and the harmony already exist; all the composer has to do is think of ways to decorate or vary them.

The little Swiss tune that Beethoven uses as the basis for this composition is very simple and attractive. Underlying its simplicity, however, is an interesting quirk: it is made up of unusual phrase lengths. This is probably the feature that attracted Beethoven to the theme in the first place. Instead of the usual four-measure phrases, this tune is made up of two, three-measure phrases answered by a phrase of five measures.

This phrase structure, as well as the skeleton of the tune and its harmony, is maintained in all the six variations. Beethoven uses triplets, march rhythms, dynamic changes, eighth notes, sixteenth notes, and even the minor key to decorate and vary the music. If you listen to just the theme a few times before listening to the variations, you will be able to follow its outline throughout the piece.

Time	Listen for
	Theme [*Andante con moto*—"Fairly slow but with motion"]
0:00	The theme is simple and pleasant. Notice how it ends very much as it begins.
	Variation 1
0:23	Beethoven introduces triplets (three notes to a beat) in both the right and the left hand.
	Variation 2
0:40	The melody is mostly unchanged in the right hand, but the left hand has jerky, marchlike accompanying rhythms.
	Variation 3
1:02	This variation uses the minor key, and Beethoven indicates that it should be played "smoothly and quietly throughout."
1:28	The last part of this variation is repeated.
	Variation 4
1:48	Back to the major and loud again. Octaves in the right hand, triplets in the left.
	Variation 5
2:04	The fifth variation is mostly in eighth notes with a little syncopation and some small chromatic decorations.
	Variation 6
2:26	Dynamic contrasts, sixteenth-note runs, and trills mark the last variation, which ends with a two-measure coda to round off the piece.

BEETHOVEN'S PIANO PLAYING

Before he started going deaf, Beethoven was known as one of the foremost piano virtuosos of his age. When he was only 21, a newspaper article described him as "one of the greatest of pianists." Another contemporary described his brilliance as an improviser: "In whatever company he might chance to be, he knew how to produce such an effect upon every hearer that frequently not an eye remained dry, while many would break out into loud sobs; for there was something wonderful in his expression, in addition to the beauty and originality of his ideas and his spirited style of rendering them."

But by 1815, when Beethoven was almost totally deaf, the descriptions become heartrending: "On account of his deafness, there was scarcely anything left of the virtuosity of the artist which had formerly been so greatly admired. In loud passages the poor man pounded on the keys till the strings jangled, and in quiet passages he played so softly that whole groups of tones were omitted, so that the music was unintelligible."

CD II, 5

Two opinions of Beethoven's Fifth Symphony: "How big it is—quite wild! Enough to bring the house about one's ears!"
—Goethe

Ouf! Let me get out; I must have air. It's incredible!
—Jean François Le Sueur

Beethoven's Fifth Symphony Beethoven's Fifth Symphony was written in the middle of his heroic period when the composer was in his late 30s. It is his most famous piece and probably the most famous symphony ever written. The music is taut and expressive, and unified to an unusual degree. The opening four-note motive, with its short-short-short-LONG rhythm, pervades the whole symphony in one form or another. There is a cumulative sense of growth right from the beginning of the first movement to the end of the last movement, and many commentators have noted the feeling of personal triumph that this gives. Underlying this feeling is the motion from C minor to C major. Symphonies almost always end in the key in which they begin, but Beethoven's Fifth opens tense and strained in C minor and concludes triumphant and exuberant in C major. Beethoven also adds several instruments to the orchestra for the last movement, to increase the power and range of the music and add to the sense of triumph.

The feeling of unity in the symphony is reinforced by two further techniques. Instead of being separate, the last two movements are linked, with no pause between them. And Beethoven actually quotes the theme of the third movement in the last movement, thus further connecting them.

All of these elements—the progression from minor to major, the larger orchestra, the linking of movements, the reference back to earlier movements toward the end—were new to symphonic music at the time and had an enormous influence on later composers throughout the remainder of the nineteenth century.

In the Fifth Symphony, Beethoven set the stage for an entirely new view of music. Music was now seen as the expression of a personal and subjective point of view, no longer as the objective presentation of an artistic creation. This new view was the basis of Romanticism.

LISTENING GUIDE

((•⌐ **Listen** on **MySearchLab**

LUDWIG VAN BEETHOVEN (1770–1827)

Symphony No. 5 in C Minor

Date of composition: 1807–1808
Orchestration: two flutes, two oboes, two clarinets,
   two horns, two trumpets, timpani, strings
Duration: 32:19

FIRST MOVEMENT

Tempo: *Allegro con brio* ("Fast and vigorous")
Meter: $\frac{2}{4}$
Key: C minor
Form: Sonata-Allegro
Duration: 7:20

CD II, 5

The first movement of Beethoven's Fifth Symphony is dense and concentrated. There is not a superfluous note in the whole movement. The exposition begins with a short-short-short-LONG motive that colors almost every measure.

The second theme is announced by a horn call. The theme itself starts quietly and smoothly, but underneath it, on cellos and basses, the initial rhythmic motive quietly makes itself heard. Quickly another climax builds, and the exposition ends with the whole orchestra playing the original motive together.

During the development section, the horn call that introduced the second theme is gradually broken down into smaller and smaller elements until only a single chord is echoed quietly between the strings and the woodwinds. Then the recapitulation brings back the music of the movement's first part with crashing force. A short coda brings the movement to a powerful conclusion.

Throughout the movement, long crescendos (from *pianissimo*, **pp**, to *fortissimo*, **ff**) and short passages of quiet music (*piano*, **p**) serve to increase the intensity and drive. The overall effect is one of great power and compression.

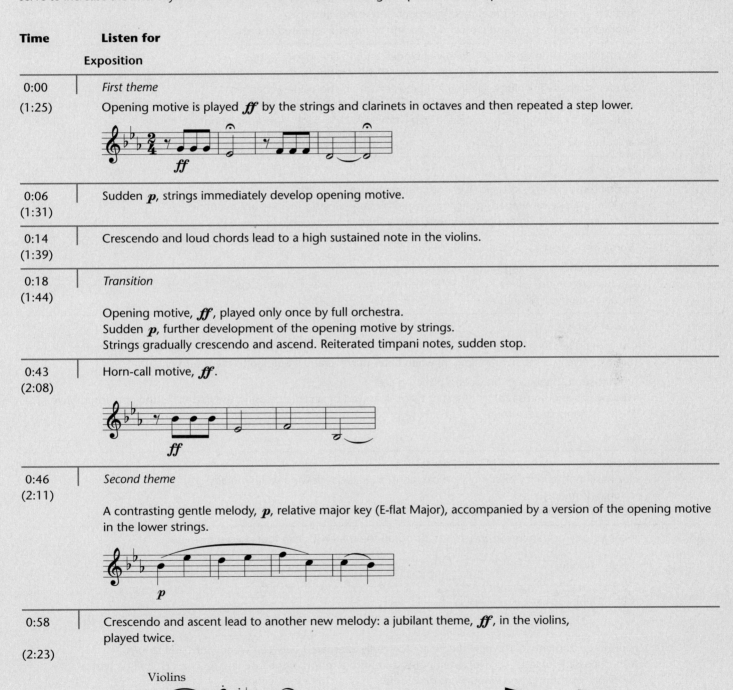

Time	Listen for
	Exposition
0:00 (1:25)	*First theme* Opening motive is played **ff** by the strings and clarinets in octaves and then repeated a step lower.
0:06 (1:31)	Sudden **p**, strings immediately develop opening motive.
0:14 (1:39)	Crescendo and loud chords lead to a high sustained note in the violins.
0:18 (1:44)	*Transition* Opening motive, **ff**, played only once by full orchestra. Sudden **p**, further development of the opening motive by strings. Strings gradually crescendo and ascend. Reiterated timpani notes, sudden stop.
0:43 (2:08)	Horn-call motive, **ff**.
0:46 (2:11)	*Second theme* A contrasting gentle melody, **p**, relative major key (E-flat Major), accompanied by a version of the opening motive in the lower strings.
0:58 (2:23)	Crescendo and ascent lead to another new melody: a jubilant theme, **ff**, in the violins, played twice.

| 1:15 | Woodwinds and horns rapidly descend, twice; then a cadence in E-flat minor, using the rhythm of the basic motive. Pause. |
| (2:40) | |

| 1:25 | (Entire exposition is repeated.) |

Development

2:50	Opening motive in horns, **ff**, in F minor, echoed by strings.
	Sudden **p**, basic motive developed by strings and woodwinds.
	Another gradual ascent and crescendo, leading to forceful repeated chords.

3:25	Horn-call motive in violins, **ff**, followed by descending line in low strings, twice.
	Pairs of high chords in woodwinds and brass, **ff**, alternating with lower chords in strings, **ff**.
	Sudden decrease in volume, alternation between single chords, key changes.
	Sudden **ff**, horn-call in full orchestra; return to alternation of wind and string chords, **ff**, with key changes.
	Sudden **ff**, opening motive repeated many times, leading back to recapitulation.

Recapitulation

4:08	*First theme*
	Opening motive, **ff**, in tonic (C minor), full orchestra.
	Opening motive developed, strings, **p**, joined by slow-moving melody on one oboe.
	Oboe unexpectedly interrupts the music with a short, plaintive solo.

4:39	*Transition*
	Development of opening motive resumes in strings, **p**.
	Gradual crescendo, full orchestra, **ff**, repeated timpani notes, sudden stop.
	Horn-call motive, **ff**, in horns.

5:02	*Second theme*
	Contrasting gentle melody, **p**, in C major (the major of the tonic!), played alternately by violins and flutes.
	(Basic motive accompanies in timpani when flutes play.) Gradual buildup to the return of:
	Jubilant string theme, **ff**, in violins, played twice.
	Woodwinds and horns rapidly descend, twice, followed by a cadence using the rhythm of the opening motive.
	Then, without pause, into:

Coda

5:52	Forceful repeated chords, **ff**, with pauses.
	Horn-call motive in lower strings and bassoons, along with flowing violin melody, **f**,
	in tonic (C minor).
	Descending pattern, violins, leads to:

| 6:17 | A completely new theme in the strings, rising up the minor scale in four-note sequences. |

Four-note fragments of the new theme are forcefully alternated between woodwinds and strings.
A short passage of fast, loud, repeated notes leads into a return of the opening motive, **ff**, full orchestra.
Suddenly **pp**; strings and woodwinds develop the motive for a few seconds.
A swift and dramatic return to full orchestra, ending with **ff** chords.

CD II, 6

SECOND MOVEMENT

Tempo: *Andante con moto* ("Fairly slow but with motion")
Meter: $\frac{3}{8}$
Key: A♭ major
Form: Modified Theme and Variations
Duration: 10:38

The second movement is lyrical and reposeful in contrast to the first movement, but there are passages of great strength and grandeur. The movement is cast as a theme and variations, but it is unusual because there are two themes instead of one. The first theme, which is very smooth and songlike, comes at the beginning on the low strings: violas and cellos, accompanied by pizzicato (plucked) basses.

The second theme is introduced softly on the clarinets and bassoons but is suddenly transformed into a blazing fanfare. Then come several variations on both of the themes, with changes of mood, instrumentation, and structure. Even the central section of the movement and the coda are based on the two themes.

The coda contains striking dynamic contrasts and ends with a big crescendo that leads to the short final cadence.

Time	Listen for
0:00	*Theme A*

Lyrical melody in tonic (A♭ major), first presented by violas and cellos, *p*. Accompaniment in basses, pizzicato.

Violas, Cellos

p dolce ... *f* *p*

0:26	Melody is continued by woodwinds, concludes with alternation between woodwinds and strings.
0:59	*Theme B (in two parts)*

(1) A gently rising theme in the clarinets, *p*, in the tonic.

Clarinets

1:15	Clarinet theme is taken over by violins, *pp*.

Sudden crescendo forms a transition to:

(2) A brass fanfare in C major, *ff*.

Violins continue this theme, *pp*. Slow sustained chords and a cadence in the tonic key form an ending to Theme B.

2:14	*Variation 1(A)*

Theme A, varied, in the tonic, again on the violas and cellos, *p*, enhanced by a smooth, continuously flowing rhythm, and with long notes from the clarinet.

Violas, Cellos

f ... *p*

(Note that Variation 1A contains all the notes of the original Theme A. These notes are printed in black in the example.) Again, a conclusion with an alternation between the violins and woodwinds.

3:05	**Variation 1(B)**
	The B theme—clarinet part as well as fanfare part—is presented with a more active accompaniment. The concluding sustained chords, ***pp***, are now accompanied by quick repeated notes in the cellos, and ended by a brighter cadence.
4:11	**Variation 2(A)**
	Theme A, varied, again enhanced by a smooth, flowing rhythm, but twice as fast as the first variation, and with long notes from the woodwinds. This embellished melody is repeated by the violins, ***pp***, in a higher register.
4:47	Then the embellished melody is played by the cellos and basses, accompanied by powerful repeated chords. The variation ends on two rising scales, leading to a high sustained note.
5:12	**Central Section**
	Sudden ***pp***, repeated string chords accompany a short, delicate phrase based on Theme A and played by the clarinet, bassoon, and flute in turn. This blossoms into a woodwind interlude, leading to a return of:
6:12	Brass fanfare from Theme B, ***ff***, with timpani rolls, in C major. A short repeated motive in the strings, ***pp***, leads to:
	Staccato passage in the woodwinds based on Theme A, but in A♭ minor. Ascending scales in the flute and strings, crescendo, into:
7:43	**Variation 3(A)**
	Climactic restatement of melody from Theme A by the full orchestra, ***ff***. (Violins play melody, while woodwinds work in imitation with violins.) The end of the first section of the melody is accompanied by rising scales in the strings and woodwinds. Once more, a conclusion with an alternation between the violins and the flute.
	Coda
8:36	Faster tempo, single bassoon, ***p***, plays a passage based on the beginning of Theme A, with comments from a single oboe. Rising melody in the strings, crescendo.
9:04	The original tempo resumes. Flute and strings, ***p***, again play the last section of Theme A, but the violins poignantly extend the final phrase. Cadence in tonic.
9:43	Another variation of the first phrase from Theme A, clarinets, ***p***. First three notes of Theme B (fanfare part), played repeatedly in the low strings, outlining the tonic chord. Gradually builds in intensity and leads to a cadence by the full orchestra, ***ff***.

THIRD MOVEMENT

Tempo: *Allegro* ("Fast")
Meter: $\frac{3}{4}$
Key: C minor
Form: Scherzo and trio, with transition
Duration: 4:53

CD II, 7

The third movement is quite remarkable. It is in the form of a scherzo and trio. Structurally, this is the same thing as a minuet and trio, but a scherzo is usually much faster and more vigorous than a minuet. In this case, there are also some striking changes in the traditional structure. The movement begins hesitantly, but suddenly the horns come blasting in with a repeated-note figure that is taken up by the whole orchestra:

The figure sounds familiar, and we recognize that it combines two features from the first movement: the short-short-short-LONG motive and the horn call in the middle of the exposition. In the trio section, a low, scurrying passage on cellos and basses is taken up in turns by other instruments in an imitative section that has the quality of an informal fugue.

At the return of the scherzo, the main surprises begin. Instead of repeating the scherzo music literally, Beethoven changes the atmosphere entirely. The music is played very quietly by plucked strings and soft woodwinds. The whole effect is mysterious, hushed, and a little ominous.

Also, instead of ending the movement after the return of the scherzo, Beethoven adds a transitional passage that continues the atmosphere of mystery, hesitancy, and questioning. Gradually the hesitant fragments take on more and more motion and get louder and louder until they build to a tremendous climax leading directly into the fourth movement.

Time	Listen for
	Scherzo [with several internal repetitions of phrases, but no overall repeats]
0:00	Short rising unison melody in cellos and basses, unaccompanied, **pp**, in the tonic (C minor).  Strings and woodwinds conclude the phrase. Pause.
0:08	Cellos and basses repeat and extend their melody. Same concluding phrase in the woodwinds and strings.
0:19	Sudden **ff**, horns state a powerful repeated-note melody based on the opening short-short-short-LONG pattern from the first movement.  This repeated-note melody is developed by the strings and winds, changing key, **f**.
0:37	The first melody is restated by the cellos and basses and answered by strings and woodwinds. Pause. This is resumed and developed. It intensifies, changing keys rapidly, and leads to:
0:59	The repeated-note melody in the tonic, played by the full orchestra, **f**. Volume decreases, dialogue between strings and woodwinds, **p**.
1:29	A sprightly, graceful theme in the violins, **p**, accompanied by offbeat chords in the woodwinds.
1:41	The scherzo concludes with cadence chords in the short-short-short-LONG rhythm.

Trio

1:47	*Trio Section A*

Scurrying melody, unaccompanied, in the cellos and basses; in C major, f.

Cellos, Basses

This develops in the style of a fugue and quickly comes to a cadence.

2:01	*Trio Section A* (exact repeat)

2:16	*Trio Section B*

After a couple of humorous false starts, the fuguelike theme continues, f, accompanied by a syncopated, leaping melody in the woodwinds. As the sound builds, a portion of the "fugue" theme is stated by the full orchestra, leading to a cadence.

2:42	*Trio Section B* (altered)

The section begins again, but now the music dwindles down from the winds to a pizzicato melody in the cellos and basses, leading to a return of the scherzo.

Return of Scherzo

3:11	The original minor melody returns, pp, but the answering phrase is stated by winds alone. Pause. The repeat of the melody is played by bassoons and pizzicato cellos and is answered by pizzicato strings. Pause.

3:30	The powerful horn melody appears, eerily and pp, on pizzicato strings with occasional wind comments. Both themes are again combined and developed (the pp continues). The sprightly theme returns, pp, and without its former bouncing character. Cadence chords, pp, in the short-short-short-LONG rhythm, end the scherzo but also begin the next surprising passage.

Transition to Last Movement

4:17	A low sustained string tone, ppp, accompanies ominous repeated notes in the timpani, pp.

4:27	A violin melody, pp, based on the opening of the scherzo, is added to this suspenseful moment. As the melody rises in pitch, it changes from minor to major. There is a rapid crescendo on a sustained chord, leading without pause into the fourth movement.

FOURTH MOVEMENT

Orchestration: three trombones, a piccolo, and a contrabassoon are added to the orchestra for this movement.
Tempo: *Allegro* ("Fast")
Meter: $\frac{4}{4}$
Key: C major
Form: Sonata
Duration: 10:11

CD II, 8

The fourth movement is the triumphant conclusion to the symphony. It is in the bright and forceful key of C major, and Beethoven now adds to the orchestra three powerful trombones, a deep, rich contrabassoon, and a high-flying piccolo. The overall atmosphere is one of triumph, glory, and exhilaration.

The movement is in sonata form. The exposition positively overflows with themes; there are four in all (two for each key area), each one bright and optimistic.

The development section concentrates on the third of these themes, which is tossed about in fragments among the instruments of the orchestra. We cannot help noticing that one pervasive fragment is very much like the opening short-short-short-LONG motive of the whole symphony.

Horns, Trumpets, Timpani

The development section builds up to a huge climax, and then suddenly Beethoven pulls off another amazing surprise. Between the end of the development section and the beginning of the recapitulation, Beethoven places a brief reminiscence of the music from the scherzo. This, too, is most unusual. It is as though Beethoven is remembering the past in the midst of his triumph. But the hesitancy and doubt are swept away by the blaze of the orchestra.

The movement ends with one of the longest codas Beethoven ever wrote. It is forceful and definitive. Often it seems as though the music will end, only to get faster and faster and come to a cadence yet again and again. It is as though Beethoven cannot stop emphasizing his feeling of triumph.

Time	Listen for
	Exposition
0:00	*Theme 1*
(1:54)	Electrifying marchlike melody, full orchestra, *ff*, with especially prominent trumpets. The first three notes spell out the tonic chord of C major.

Trumpets

0:14 (2:06)	The rising staccato notes of the end of the melody are developed at length, with full orchestration, *ff*.
0:29 (2:21)	A descending scalar melody with off-the-beat accents leads to the transition theme.
0:34 (2:26)	*Transition Theme (Theme 2)* A new, forceful theme, *ff*, begins in the horns.

0:45 (2:38)	Transition Theme is extended by the violins, leading to a quick dialogue between woodwinds, violins, and low strings, and then:
1:00 (2:52)	*Theme 3* A light, bouncing melody in the violins (dominant key, G major) with the short-short-short-LONG rhythm, incorporating triplets, contrasts of loud and soft, and a countermelody (colored notes in the example) that becomes important in the development section.

A frantic, *ff*, scalar passage in the strings, and two loud staccato chords, herald the entrance of:

1:25 (3:18)	*Closing Theme (Theme 4)* Theme 4, heard first in the strings and woodwinds: Immediate repeat by the full orchestra, *f*, leading to repeated chords by the full orchestra and an ascending motive in the strings, *ff*, and directly into:

(1:54)	(Repeat of Exposition)

Development   [wide mix of keys]

3:48	A long section concentrating on the recombination of the triplet motives of Theme 3, eventually accompanied by slowly ascending flute scales.
4:00	Theme 3's countermelody is now put in the spotlight, first by the lower strings and contrabassoon, then by the powerful new trombones, then by the strings and trombones in imitation, and finally by the full orchestra.

4:49	A long, gigantic climax leads to a real surprise: We hear the short-short-short-LONG horn melody of the scherzo, *pp*, but on strings, clarinets, and oboes. This reminiscence is swept away by a crescendo and the recapitulation.
	Recapitulation
5:52	*Theme 1* The marchlike melody is again stated in the full orchestra, *ff*. Once again, the staccato notes at the end of the melody are developed at length, and descending scales lead into the Transition Theme.
6:26	*Transition Theme (Theme 2)* Theme 2 is stated in the horns and continued at length by the violins, as in the exposition.
6:55	*Theme 3* The triplet-dominated Theme 3 is stated essentially the same way as in the exposition, but with a fuller accompaniment and in the tonic key.
7:21	*Closing Theme (Theme 4)* Theme 4 is presented but slightly reorchestrated, leading to a long coda.
	Coda
7:50	The coda begins with further development of Theme 3 and its countermelody.
8:13	After six staccato chords, the winds develop a variant of Theme 2 in imitation, *p*.
8:35	This is followed by rapid ascending piccolo scales.
8:45	The variant of Theme 2 returns, this time in the strings, with piccolo trills and scales. Then, an acceleration in tempo until:
9:12	A very fast return to the first part of Theme 4 in the violins. The motive gradually climbs higher, as the full orchestra joins in. There is a crescendo and fragmentation of the theme, leading to:
9:28	Theme 1, full orchestra, *ff*, but much faster. It is quickly developed and comes to an extremely long ending passage of incessantly pounded chords, finally coming to rest on the single note C, played *ff* by the full orchestra.

COMPOSERS, PATRONS, AND AUDIENCES

Beethoven's Orchestra

Beethoven grew up during the Classic period, so the orchestra he used in his early years was the one that he inherited from Haydn and Mozart: a string section made up of violins, violas, cellos, and basses; a wind section featuring pairs of flutes, oboes, clarinets, bassoons, and horns; and an occasional group of trumpets and drums. Beethoven enlarged this orchestra during his lifetime just as he expanded the boundaries of form and personal expression. For the last movement of his Fifth Symphony, Beethoven adds a piccolo, a contrabassoon, and three trombones. A piccolo and trombones appear also in the Sixth Symphony; and the Ninth Symphony of Beethoven's last years calls for the usual complement of strings and winds, plus piccolo, contrabassoon, two extra horns, three trombones, triangle, cymbals, and bass drum. After Beethoven, the orchestra, like almost everything else he touched, was expanded to encompass ever-greater areas of expression.

Beethoven's Late Music

Beethoven's late music presents great challenges to performers and listeners alike. Certainly, the music is technically difficult to play, yet the true challenge comes in the understanding. The performer has to understand the music in order to play it, and the listener has to concentrate on being receptive to its depth.

There is great variety in the late works of Beethoven, but they share some characteristics: a combination of inner depth and outward simplicity; new approaches to multi-movement design; and a return to some of the techniques of his youth, such as song forms and theme and variations form.

Among the compositions are piano sonatas, several profound string quartets, and the Ninth Symphony, whose last movement (*Ode to Joy*) is performed around the world as an international symbol of peace and understanding.

STYLE SUMMARY

Beethoven

Around the world, the music of Beethoven has come to symbolize one of the high points of Western artistic achievement, on a par with the plays and poetry of Shakespeare or the paintings of Rembrandt or Picasso. Beethoven stands as a giant in our cultural history.

This impression is reinforced both by the power of his music and by the impression it gives of conquering life's adversities. Beethoven was wholly devoted to his work and regarded it as sacred. In this way he changed the direction of music and society's attitude toward it for the next two hundred years.

Beethoven inherited the forms, genres, and conventions of the Classic era. He wrote symphonies, piano concertos, chamber music, piano sonatas, and other types of music just as Classic composers had done. And yet he invested these forms with greater scope and power and with a greater sense of personal expression than his predecessors had. His symphonies are longer and use more instruments than those of the Classic period. And for the last movement of his Ninth Symphony, Beethoven added four solo singers and a chorus.

In his loud music, Beethoven seems more urgent than his predecessors. In his soft music, he seems to reach for deeper emotion.

Special characteristics of Beethoven's music include insistent and driving rhythms, taut and muscular themes, and long crescendos and powerful climaxes. But his music also features themes of great beauty and lyricism, passages of extraordinary lightness and delicacy, and a gentleness and spiritual depth that are unprecedented.

He expanded the orchestra in terms of loudness (trombones), high notes (piccolos), and low notes (contrabassoon). In his first movements, he turned sonata form from an expression of wit and aesthetic beauty to one of narrative and drama. His slow movements can plumb the depths of human emotion. His third-movement scherzos range from sophisticated rhythmic play to grim humor. And his finales present moods of exuberance, triumphant exaltation, or spiritual transcendence. Beethoven also favored theme and variation form, which he used from his earliest learning days as a composer up to his very last works.

In a way, Beethoven single-handedly invented the idea of the personal in music and laid the groundwork for all our modern ideas of what a classical composer does and what his or her music means.

FUNDAMENTALS OF BEETHOVEN'S MUSIC

- ☐ Balance of forcefulness/strength and emotional depth/gentleness/lyricism

- ☐ Longer movements

- ☐ Expanded orchestra (contrabassoon, trombones, and piccolo)

- ☐ Expression of personal feeling

- ☐ Drama expressed through the sonata form

- ☐ Reaches unprecedented spiritual depth

- ☐ Beethoven wrote in all vocal and instrumental genres

- ☐ Leads the way to Romanticism

FOR FURTHER DISCUSSION AND STUDY

1. How did events during Beethoven's life—the breakdown of the patronage system, the rise of Napoleon, and the position of the artist in society—influence his music?

2. Children of alcoholics often display characteristic traits: (1) the "hero" who attempts to replace the dysfunctional parent by overachieving, or (2) the "jester" who compensates for a lack of parental guidance by being mischievous and unruly. Which role did Beethoven play in his family? What is the evidence for your choice?

3. Beethoven originally dedicated his Third Symphony to Napoleon, who led the revolution to free the French people from the tyranny of the King. However, soon after his victory over the royal forces, Napoleon crowned himself emperor. Beethoven angrily removed the dedication to his symphony with the remark, "Well, then, he's just like all the rest." Some have also suggested that the second movement, a funeral march, also comments on Beethoven's disappointment with Napoleon. How does this symphony reflect Beethoven's sympathy for human freedom?

4. How did Beethoven's treatment of his nephew, Karl, reflect his own experiences when he was young? Read the "Immortal Beloved" letters on MySearchLab. Why do you think Beethoven never married or had children of his own?

5. View the performance of the first movement of Beethoven's Symphony No. 6 in F Major, Op. 68, "Pastoral." How was Beethoven's orchestra different from earlier ensembles? What is uniquely "Beethovenish" in how he uses the different orchestral groups?

Watch the **Inside the Orchestra** video on **MySearchLab**

✓● Study and Review on MySearchLab

The Nineteenth Century I: Early Romantic Music

Romanticism as a musical style covers the period from the early nineteenth century to the beginning of the twentieth. It also encompasses a wide range of works by composers in all genres. For this reason, we will break our discussion of Romantic music into two distinct parts: early Romantic music and mid-to-late Romantic music. I shall set the scene by describing the Age of Romanticism and the social, cultural, and political developments that underpinned this revolutionary new music.

The Age of Romanticism

The nineteenth century was a time of great change in Western society. The foundations of modern industry were laid during this period, significant political and social changes were taking place, and the arts reflected a new concern with subjectivity and inner feeling. All three of these aspects of the new era—industrialization, changes in the structure of society, and a new artistic spirit—had powerful effects on nineteenth-century music.

NEED TO KNOW
KEY TRENDS IN THE NINETEENTH CENTURY

- Development of modern industry

- Growth of democratic governments and national pride

- Increased emphasis on individual thoughts and feelings in the creative arts

The Industrial Revolution

The Industrial Revolution began in England, where a long period of peace and prosperity encouraged expansion and innovation. Increased efficiency in agriculture led to a tripling of the population between 1750 and 1850. Advances in mechanical engineering made possible the invention of power machines, used initially in the textile industry and then in mining, iron and steel production, and railways. Communications were revolutionized first by the railways and the inauguration of a cheap postal system, and then by the American inventions of the telegraph and the telephone.

These technological advances spread rapidly throughout Western Europe and the United States. In many countries, especially Germany, new mining techniques led to the growth of the chemical industry. Minerals were used as the basis for new fertilizers that increased food production and hence population growth in industrialized societies. The French developed a process for bleaching cloth and a new loom for weaving patterns. And Americans were responsible for the sewing machine and a host of agricultural machines designed for the wide expanses of the continent. Toward the end of the century, the harnessing of electricity marked a new phase in the Industrial Revolution.

Political, Intellectual, and Social Changes

Politically, the most important event for the nineteenth century was the French Revolution, which began in 1789 but whose aftershocks continued to be felt throughout Europe until 1848. Originally a democratic movement, the Revolution unleashed brutal forces, first as the revolutionaries seized power and put their foes to death, and then as the movement itself evolved—in the hands of the dictator Napoleon—into a new form of repressive government. In 1814 the French monarchy was reestablished, and in 1815 the leaders of the last campaign against Napoleon restored the old European balance of power and the hierarchical systems of government. However, the struggle between monarchists and democrats continued in France—and the rest of Europe—through much of the century.

Romanticism was inspired by many developments. Writers, thinkers, and artists reacted against the rationalism and orderliness of the eighteenth century and yearned for a return to emotionalism, complexity, and traditional faith. God and nature were seen as more important than reason and science. Nature, with all its unpredictability and random profusion, became a central feature of the Romantic ideal.

The French Revolution and the ensuing Romantic movement had further consequences in the nineteenth century. One of these was the growth of **nationalism**. People throughout Europe began to foster their own national identities and to rebel against outside domination. Nationalism remained a potent force on the political landscape throughout the nineteenth century.

Changes in the structure of society were very dramatic in this era. The Industrial Revolution created great wealth and an increased standard of living for some, while

Come forth into the light of things,
Let Nature be your teacher.
One impulse from a vernal wood
May teach you more of man,
Of moral evil and of good,
Than all the sages can.
—William Wordsworth

The heroic Napoleon Bonaparte, painted in 1800.

> It was a town of machinery and tall chimneys, out of which interminable serpents of smoke trailed themselves forever and ever, and never got uncoiled. It had a black canal in it, and a river that ran purple with ill-smelling dye, and vast piles of buildings full of windows where there was a rattling and a trembling all day long . . .
>
> —Charles Dickens, *Hard Times*

> A work of art must always be a free creation of the spirit.
>
> —Arrey von Dommer, music theorist

condemning many others to work in appalling conditions in mines and factories.

Large numbers of women and children began to work outside the home. The hours were brutal. A factory worker testified to a committee of the English Parliament in 1832 that he and his entire family had to work from three o'clock in the morning until ten at night just to survive. Women and children were paid half the wages of a man. Children were often used for pulling heavy coal carts through low mining shafts, and half of the workers in the textile mills of England, France, Belgium, and Germany were children.

Towns and cities appeared throughout the newly industrialized Europe and United States. Many people left their rural environments for crowded city slums and polluted city air. Living conditions and the dreariness of life in London in the nineteenth century are dramatically described in some of the novels of Charles Dickens.

In spite of the hardships and inequities of the times, the nineteenth century also saw the rise of some of the benefits of modern civilization. Medical advances were dramatic. The prevention of infection by antiseptic measures was begun, and Louis Pasteur saved countless lives by developing a rabies vaccine and inventing the process for the sterilization of milk (still called pasteurization in his honor).

The plight of the new working class led to a vastly increased social consciousness. The nineteenth century saw the foundation of many charitable organizations, the birth of private philanthropy, the establishment of free public schools, and the development of the political ideals of socialism and communism. In those days, socialism meant putting the good of the general population ahead of the private interests of the few. An extreme form of socialist thinking found expression in the revolutionary ideas of Karl Marx (1818–1883). Marx predicted the 1917 Bolshevik Revolution, in which the workers would take over the government in a violent uprising. And in *Das Kapital* (1867) he argued that capitalism would eventually self-destruct.

The nineteenth century was also a time of colonial expansion, justified by the Darwin-inspired ideals of "helping" societies seen as poor, uneducated, and unenlightened. Africa, Asia, and the Pacific became networks of colonies ruled by different European countries; and the United States expanded westward, as well as to the south (Puerto Rico, 1898) and the north (Alaska, 1867). Colonialism played a role in the nineteenth-century obsession with the exotic, as foreign countries were explored and people began to get a sense of the diversity and richness of the world in which they lived.

The New Artistic Spirit

Romanticism was above all an artistic movement. It began in the last two decades of the eighteenth century with the literary works of the two great German writers Goethe (1749–1832) and Schiller (1759–1805).

Johann Wolfgang von Goethe was a poet, novelist, and dramatist—and the author of the single most influential literary work of the nineteenth century, his long dramatic poem *Faust*. Goethe's *Faust* tells the story of a man who flouts God and convention to follow his vision. The story served as inspiration to many composers throughout the nineteenth century.

Another element in literary Romanticism was a renewed fascination with the past. Friedrich von Schiller wrote a series of dramas based on historical and legendary figures, including Joan of Arc, Mary Queen of Scots, and William Tell. Of all historical periods, it was the Middle Ages that most captured the imagination of the Romantics. The best known early-Romantic novel in English was Walter Scott's *Ivanhoe* (1819), set in the days of the Crusades.

The mysterious, the supernatural, and even the macabre fascinated nineteenth-century readers.

A favorite American author of the nineteenth century was the ghoulish Edgar Allan Poe (1809–1849). And in 1818, Mary Shelley (second wife of the poet) published the perennially popular story *Frankenstein*.

Romantic poets like Keats and Longfellow exulted in a new freedom of style. The Romantics also developed a love affair with the works of Shakespeare, whose plays were freely structured and often based on medieval history or legend. Shakespeare's works underwent an enormous revival in the nineteenth century.

In architecture, medieval Gothic cathedrals, many of which had been gradually falling into ruin, suddenly became a Romantic inspiration. Great cathedrals such as Notre Dame in Paris underwent extensive restoration, and the latest "modern" architectural style in the nineteenth century was known as "Gothic Revival." Classical antiquity provided another inspiration from the past, and from Jefferson's Virginia to Napoleon's Paris, buildings were constructed in the "Greek Revival" manner, with columns, triumphal arches, and huge rounded domes.

In the second half of the century, the technological advances of the Industrial Revolution had a powerful impact on both sculpture and architecture. The new technology produced works of monumental size, the most famous of which are the Brooklyn Bridge (1883), the Statue of Liberty (1886), and the remarkable Eiffel Tower (1889).

In painting, Romantic artists attempted to capture their view of the exotic, the irrational, and the sublime. The paintings of the French artist Delacroix were often set in foreign lands with scenes of violence. He said that the aim of art was not to depict reality but to "strike the imagination."

Nature inspired the great artist William Turner, in whose paintings natural scenes such as a mountain range or a storm at sea take on a power and a significance that reflect the human emotions of fear, awe, and wonder. In Turner's paintings, we can see the foundations of the later Impressionist movement.

Of all the arts, however, music was the most quintessentially Romantic. With its embracing of nature and the exotic, its focus on national identity and individual consciousness, and its fascination with extremes of emotion, music was considered the perfect vehicle for the expression of Romanticism. The German author E. T. A. Hoffmann

The Supreme Court building in Washington, D.C., in "Greek Revival" style.

wrote in 1813 that music was "the most Romantic of all the arts, for its only subject is the infinite."

NEED TO KNOW
KEY THEMES OF ROMANTIC MUSIC

- Nature

- The "exotic" and foreign

- National themes

- Extremes of emotion and scale

- Individual feeling

> It is scarcely credible that a separate romantic school could be formed in music, which is in itself romantic.
> —Robert Schumann

Music for All

During the nineteenth century, music became more and more a public concern. Concert halls were built in every town, and many cities established their own symphony orchestras.

The astonishing Eiffel Tower in Paris.

Industrialization had made pianos cheaper and more plentiful, so by the last part of the century, most middle-class homes boasted a piano in the parlor. An evening of parlor songs or informal chamber music became commonplace in Victorian times.

The New Sound

If you listen to an orchestral piece from the Romantic era, you will notice that it is very different in *sound* from a piece of music from the Classic era. This, too, is partly a result of social and technological changes. As concerts moved from small halls to larger ones and audiences increased in size, orchestras became bigger, and instruments were adapted so that their sounds would be louder and carry farther. In contrast to the intense, focused sound of Baroque and Classic instruments, instruments in the nineteenth century were built for power. They were also built for speed. As a result of the new technology, nineteenth-century woodwind and brass instruments were equipped with complex key or valve systems whose primary aim was to facilitate fast finger work. New instruments were invented during the nineteenth century, especially instruments made of brass, such as the tuba and the saxophone.

A cozy domestic scene in a nineteenth-century home.

Pianos, too, changed enormously during the nineteenth century. The small, delicate, wooden instruments known to Haydn and Mozart were replaced by larger and louder pianos. A new mechanism was invented, allowing for much more rapid playing and faster repetition of notes, and the range was greatly extended. In Mozart's day, the piano had a range of five octaves. By 1830, the range was over seven octaves (the standard range today).

Orchestras also increased in size. Whereas a Mozart symphony requires perhaps 25 or 30 players, a Brahms symphony needs 50 or 60 people; some compositions, such as the Requiem Mass of Berlioz and Mahler's Second Symphony, call for an orchestra of more than 100 players.

Sound is also a matter of how an orchestra is used. Apart from creating huge volume, a large orchestra can be used to produce a very wide range of different combinations of instruments. Romantic composers often used their orchestras as Romantic painters used their palettes: to create an almost infinite variety of colors and textures. The technique of manipulating orchestral sounds is known as **orchestration**, and many Romantic composers were brilliant and sensitive orchestrators.

Finally, the sound of a Romantic work depends upon a number of other technical factors, such as dynamics, tempo, melody, harmony, and form, which we shall consider separately.

Dynamics   In most Classic music, the range of dynamics does not go beyond *piano* and *forte*. In Romantic music, this range is vastly extended. Dynamics up to triple or even quadruple *fortissimo* (***fff*** and ***ffff***) are common, and indications of quietness often go down to triple *pianissimo* (***ppp***). There is even a famous passage in a Tchaikovsky symphony in which the composer calls for sextuple *pianissimo* (***pppppp***). Changes of dynamics are much more frequent and less predictable in Romantic music than in music of earlier times.

Tempo and Expression   The range of tempo is also far wider in Romantic music. Long, languorous, slow movements are common in the nineteenth century, whereas the favorite slow tempo in the eighteenth century had been a graceful, moderate, walking pace (*Andante*). Changes of tempo within a movement are also much more frequent in the Romantic era. This creates a variety of moods within a single movement, not just a contrast between movements. A Romantic composition seems to ebb and flow as it goes along.

THE HISTORY OF THE PIANOFORTE, 1700–1860

About 1700, Bartolomeo Cristofori, an employee of the Medici Court in Florence, constructed the first working piano. The sound was similar to that of the harpsichord, and the instrument was called *gravicembalo col piano e forte* ("harpsichord with soft and loud"). The difference was that the strings of the new instrument were struck rather than plucked, so that gradations in volume could be achieved. If the pianist touched the keys lightly, the sound would be soft; if the pianist pushed them down hard, the sound would be loud.

Piano makers flourished all over Europe in the second half of the eighteenth century. Andreas Stein (Augsburg, Germany) and Anton Walter (Vienna, Austria) used a type of action called the "Prellmechanik." With this system, each key received an escapement lever instead of a stationary rail, allowing for reiterated notes. This system provided more control and accuracy of touch, though Stein's and Walter's pianos were very delicate in sound and unsuitable for any but the most intimate settings. Johannes Zumpe, a German maker who moved to England in 1760, produced instruments that provided a little more volume and dynamic variety.

The first English grand piano action was devised and developed by John Broadwood about 1770 and patented by Broadwood's apprentice, Robert Stodart, in 1777. Iron bracing, introduced to the piano about 1800, allowed for heavier hammers, thicker strings, and greater string tension. As a result, more volume and sustaining power could be achieved.

By the mid-nineteenth century, the five-octave range of the eighteenth-century piano had been expanded, and the modern pattern of white and black keys was adopted. In 1859, Steinway & Sons of New York took out a patent for an "overstrung" grand piano in which the strings were crossed inside the frame in a fanlike pattern. The huge frame of the Steinway grand piano could accommodate greatly increased string tension, which in turn resulted in the big, bright sound quality that characterizes the Steinway and other grand pianos to this day.

Beethoven's own piano, showing the shorter keyboard and wooden frame.

Find the **Quick Listen** on **MySearchLab**
"The Piano Beethoven Heard"

The way composers indicate tempo is also much more expressive. Before, simply the words *Allegro* or *Andante* had sufficed; now composers felt it necessary to indicate the emotional content of a piece by expressive descriptions. Markings such as *Allegro agitato* ("an agitated Allegro") or *Adagio dolente* ("a grieving Adagio") are often found, and the indication *espressivo* ("expressively") is scattered liberally throughout the pages of Romantic music.

Melody   Romantic melodies are very different from Classic ones. In the first place, they are usually much longer. Also, they often have a "surging" or "yearning" quality about them, which makes them highly emotional. They may speed up or slow down slightly in the middle, to make them sound more spontaneous, and the dynamics often change as well. Some of the most famous Romantic melodies are intense and strong, but others are wistful, dreamy, or deeply sad. The primary aim was always expression of feeling.

Harmony   One of the most important tools in the Romantic search for expression was harmony. In a sense, eighteenth-century harmony had been used mostly for its functionality (one chord leading to the next, which leads to the next, which moves toward the cadence); Romantic harmony, on the other hand, is often also an expressive device. Chords can create color and atmosphere, so more and more unusual chords are used, unexpected combinations appear, and **modulation** (movement among keys) is much more frequent. Toward the end of the century, composers even began to end their pieces in a different key from the one in which they had begun—a radical departure from centuries of convention. **Chromatic** melodies and harmonies become much more frequent, undermining the central,

Tempo and expression markings in a nineteenth-century piano piece.

Più moto ed espressivo *("More quickly and expressively")*
dolce ma espr. *("sweet but expressive")*

From Brahms's *Intermezzo,*
Op. 117, No. 3

A perfect example of Romantic melody—long (46 measures long!), emotionally charged, surging, ebbing and flowing, highly expressive.

Find the **Quick Listen** on **MySearchLab** "Rachmaninov Piano Concerto No. 2"

From Rachmaninov's *Piano Concerto No. 2, first movement*

static sense of key that had always governed music. It was only a few years after the end of the nineteenth century that the entire system of tonality was called into question. This would not have been possible without the adventurous experimentation of the Romantics.

Form   Along with the loosening of harmony came a loosening of form. Romantic pieces tend to blur the outlines of form rather than highlight them. It is often harder to "hear" the form in a Romantic composition than in a Classic piece. In part, this is because Romantic works are often much longer, making it more difficult to follow structural devices. But the blurring of formal outlines was often deliberate. It corresponded to the change in Romantic poetry from strict forms to freer, more exuberant writing. Romantic composers wanted their music to be as expressive as possible, to represent the spontaneous flow of feelings rather than to display a carefully organized structure.

Formal templates were still used, of course. Great art is never without form. In most Romantic pieces, one can still detect arrangements such as sonata form, scherzo and trio, aria form, or rondo. But these were used with great flexibility, and the exact points of articulation in them can often be a matter of debate.

Even formal organization on the phrase level is less clear-cut in Romantic music: phrases tend to flow into each other rather than to be separate and distinct. This fludity is achieved by avoiding or undermining cadences. As a phrase reaches its conclusion, it may turn away from the expected cadence in a completely new direction. Or the composer may make the end of one phrase overlap with the beginning of a new one.

Classic versus Romantic Music: Main Differences

	CLASSIC	ROMANTIC
Orchestra	25–30 players	60 or more players
Dynamic range	*Piano* (soft) to *forte* (loud)	Triple *piano* (***ppp***; very very soft) to triple *forte* (***fff***; very very loud)
Tempo	Slow or fast; few changes within a movement	Greater extremes of tempo, also more changeable within a movement
Expression	Rarely indicated	Often indicated
Melody	Short, balanced	Longer, more variety
Harmony	Functional: serves to support the melody and the form of the composition	Emotional: also serves to express the deepest feelings in the music
Form	Fixed	Flexible

Program Music

One of the most important differences between Classic and Romantic music lies in the distinction between "program" and "absolute" music. **Program music** is music that tells some kind of story. It may be a love story, a spiritual journey, scenes from nature, or a child's reverie. **Absolute music** is the term for music that has no meaning outside the meaning of the music itself and the feelings it produces in its listeners.

The nineteenth century did not invent the idea of program music. Vivaldi's *Four Seasons* is a famous example of Baroque program music. But never before had so many composers been so concerned with tying their music to ideas, stories, or events outside the actual notes they were writing. Sometimes composers even published lengthy written narratives to accompany performances of their works.

Massive and Miniature

We have noted before that many Romantic works are longer than their Classic counterparts. And some compositions are very long indeed. Some Romantic symphonies last nearly two hours. A Romantic opera can last four hours or more. And Wagner's cycle of operas, *The Ring of the Nibelungs*, is designed to be performed over four entire evenings!

This love of the massive, or monumental, also determined the size of orchestras, as we

I do not say that program music should not be written. But I do maintain that it is a lower form of art than absolute music.
—Edward Elgar, English composer

have seen. More and more instruments were added to orchestras, and larger numbers of the traditional instruments were used.

In contrast to the massive works of the Romantic era, there were some compositions that went to the opposite extreme, using delicate miniaturization. Most of these were works for solo piano, and lasted less than a minute. Some of these piano miniatures were not programmatic and were simply called "Prelude" or "Waltz" or "Intermezzo" (meaning "interlude"), but many of them had programmatic titles like "Dreaming," "Why?," and "Poet's Love." The piano miniature was the musical response to the Romantic interest in intimacy and individualism.

Favorite Romantic Genres

Many of the same genres that had been popular in the eighteenth century continued into the nineteenth. **Opera** and **symphony** were the most extensive genres, requiring large forces. After Beethoven's revolutionary Ninth Symphony, with its use of solo singers and choir in the last movement, other Romantic composers sometimes used voices in their symphonies, especially toward the end of the century.

Voice was the central component of two other Romantic genres: **song** and the **Requiem Mass**. These also display the contrast between intimacy and grandeur. Intimate solo song settings of Romantic poetry accompanied by piano were great favorites of the nineteenth century. And Requiem Mass settings often call for huge musical resources, including enormous orchestras, extra brass groups, solo singers, and large choruses. Their drama, subjectivity, and emotional appeal take the Romantic Requiems very close indeed to the style of Romantic opera.

Another favored orchestral genre was the **concerto**, which symbolized the highly Romantic notion of the individual against the group. Piano concertos were common, violin concertos even more so. But Romantic composers also chose other instruments to highlight in this way: cello, flute, clarinet, even viola.

Chamber music also was popular in the nineteenth century. After the string quartet, a particular favorite was the combination of piano and strings, as in a piano quintet (piano and string quartet). Composers also enjoyed writing chamber works for larger string groups—quintets, sextets, even octets—to obtain the rich sounds so typical of the Romantic ideal.

Solo piano works were very popular. Some composers continued to write piano sonatas in the usual three or four movements, but many composed more programmatic pieces, like the piano miniatures mentioned previously, or longer works with a series of short movements that tell a story or depict a series of scenes.

The link between program music and literature is particularly evident in a new genre: the **symphonic poem**. The symphonic poem is a relatively short orchestral work in one continuous movement, though it may fall into contrasting sections. Symphonic poems are always programmatic, though the source of the program need not be literary; it may be a painting or a scene from nature.

Finally, it is important to note that Romantic composers had a tendency to write music in what we might call "mixed genres." Romantic composers did not like to be constrained by conventions of genre, any more than they liked to be constrained by conventions of harmony, form, size, or duration. Many Romantic works do not fall conveniently into any one definition of genre, and some of them are fascinating precisely because they do not conform to expectations.

Favorite Romantic Instruments

The favorite Romantic instruments were probably the piano and the violin. The piano lends itself both to great intimacy and to great drama; the violin has a very wide range and possesses the potential for great lyricism. And yet there were other instruments that captured the Romantic imagination. Both the cello and the French horn—with their rich, expressive tenor range—were heavily favored by nineteenth-century composers. And for special effects, composers often turned to the English horn (tenor oboe) for its reedy, evocative sound.

The Individual and the Crowd

Romantic writers and thinkers were fascinated by the notion of the individual—a single person's thoughts and feelings. This focus on the individual is reflected in the Romantic concentration on dramatic musical genres such as the concerto, which contrasts the individual and the group, and in its love affair with great performing musicians.

During the nineteenth century, some performing musicians became very famous. The great Italian violinist Nicolò Paganini (1782–1840) used to travel around the world,

Find the **Quick Listen** on **MySearchLab** "Schumann Warum"

Nicolò Paganini.

Everyone is talking of Paganini and his violin. The man seems to be a miracle.

—Thomas Macauley, 1831

displaying his astounding virtuosity. Paganini's technical brilliance was the inspiration for several composers in the nineteenth century.

Another great virtuoso performer was the pianist and composer Franz Liszt. Audiences treated him the way modern audiences treat rock stars: women fainted and people mobbed the stage.

Women in Nineteenth-Century Music

The nineteenth century opened doors of opportunity to a wide range of people, and women were no exception. Music conservatories began to accept women for musical training, and although considerable prejudice remained, some women became famous as performers and composers during the nineteenth century. This is not to say that there was equal opportunity. Most orchestras were still composed entirely of men, and many people thought that it was "unseemly" for women to appear as professional musicians in public. Still, a large number of women played the piano or sang, and many performed in their own living rooms or at the homes of friends.

Some women played an important role behind the scenes in nineteenth-century musical life, either as hostesses of vibrant salons, where much music making took place, or as wealthy patrons of the arts. Tchaikovsky, one of the most famous composers of the Romantic era, was supported privately by a very rich woman. Other composers relied heavily on their personal relationships with women, as supporters and lovers or as colleagues and critics. Among the most important women in the history of nineteenth-century music were Fanny Mendelssohn and Clara Schumann; we shall look at their lives and contributions to music during the course of this chapter.

Romantic Song

Romantic songs are intimate miniatures. They are written for a single voice with piano accompaniment and are designed to be sung in private parlors rather than in large concert halls.

The setting of the song is always designed to mirror the meaning of the text, either with specific word painting or in general atmosphere. The greatest Romantic songs (and there are many great ones) add great richness and emotional depth to the poems that they set.

Romantic songs may be either strophic or through-composed. **Strophic songs** are those that use the same music for each stanza of the poetry. **Through-composed songs** are those in which the music is different for each stanza. Sometimes modifications or combinations of these forms may appear.

Although most Romantic songs stand on their own as self-contained works, composers sometimes linked together a group of songs to create what is known as a **song cycle**. A song cycle may present a series of songs that are woven together to make a narrative, or it may link several songs by presenting them as different facets of a single idea.

Early Romanticism

In addition to Beethoven, five great composers were active in the first half of the nineteenth century: Franz Schubert, Hector Berlioz, Felix Mendelssohn, Fryderyk Chopin, and Robert Schumann. Also important were Clara Schumann (1819–1896) and Fanny Mendelssohn Hensel (1805–1847), although their achievements are harder to assess, as we shall see.

Franz Schubert (1797–1828)

Schubert was the son of a Viennese schoolmaster and lived most of his life in Vienna. He sang as a choirboy when he was young and also played the violin, performing string quartets with his father and brothers at home and playing in the orchestra at the choir school, where he came to know the symphonies of Haydn, Mozart, and Beethoven. Schubert's gift for composition was already evident, and when his voice changed, he left the choir and was accepted as a composition student by the composer at the Imperial Court in Vienna, Antonio Salieri. His father wanted Schubert to become a schoolmaster like himself; Schubert tried briefly, but he was a poor teacher and soon gave it up. He then embarked on his quiet career as a composer, living in Vienna and working every morning. He seemed to be a limitless fountain of music. "When I finish one piece," he said, "I begin the next." In the afternoons, he spent time with his friends in the various cafés of Vienna.

It is extraordinary to think that Schubert and Beethoven lived at the same time and in the same city, but met only once. The two men could not have been more different. Whereas Beethoven was proud, assertive, and difficult to get along with, Schubert was shy, retiring, and exceedingly modest, with a large number of good friends. Their music, too, is very different: Beethoven's is dramatic and

Franz Schubert.

Find the **Quick Listen** on **MySearchLab**

"Schubert Trio in E-flat Op. 100"

Find the **Quick Listen** on **MySearchLab**

"Schubert Schoene Muellerin"

"My peace is gone, my heart is heavy, and I will never again find peace." I may well sing this every day now, for each night, on retiring to bed, I hope I may not wake again; and each morning but recalls yesterday's grief.

—Letter of Franz Schubert, 1824, quoting from one of his own songs

intellectually powerful, while Schubert's is gentle, relaxed, and lyrical, with a magical harmonic gift. Finally, whereas most of Beethoven's music was published during his own lifetime, only a small percentage of Schubert's enormous output was published while he was alive, much of it having to wait decades for publication. Schubert wrote more than 900 works in his very short life (he died at the age of 31), a level of productivity that surpasses even that of Mozart.

Schubert occasionally tried to win recognition by writing opera, the most popular (and lucrative) genre of his day; but although he composed many operas, they met with little success. He also applied for some important musical positions, with the same disappointing result. It seemed as though Vienna had room for only one brilliant composer, and the powerful figure of Beethoven cast a long shadow. In spite of these setbacks, Schubert's talent and modest personality won the affection of many people, who gave him moral and, occasionally, financial support. At one time, several of his friends banded together to pay for the publication of a group of his songs. Toward the end of his life, however, Schubert's essential loneliness often overcame him, and he despaired of achieving happiness. Some of Schubert's most profound works come from this period of his life.

In his last year, Schubert's productivity increased even further. Perhaps he knew that he did not have much time left. A month before he died, Schubert arranged to take lessons in counterpoint! "Now I see how much I still have

to learn," he said. He died of syphilis (a horrible, debilitating disease in the days before antibiotics) on November 19, 1828. According to his last wishes, he was buried near Beethoven in Vienna. His epitaph, written by a friend, reads, "Here the art of music has buried a rich possession but even more promising hopes."

Schubert's Music

"Everything he touched turned to song," said one of his Schubert's friends. Schubert's greatest gift was his genius for capturing the essence of a poem when he set it to music. In fact, his song settings often transcend the poetry that inspired them. The melodies he devised for the voice, the harmonies and figuration of the piano part—these turn mediocre poetry into superb songs and turn great poetry into some of the most expressive music ever written. During his pathetically short life, Schubert composed *more than 600* songs. These range from tiny poems on nature to dramatic dialogues to folklike tunes to songs of the deepest emotional intensity. In addition to this enormous number and variety of individual songs, Schubert also wrote two great song cycles, *Die schöne Müllerin* ("The Pretty Miller-Maid," 1824) and *Winterreise* ("Winter's Journey," 1827). The first tells the story of a love affair that turns from buoyant happiness to tragedy; the second is a sequence of reflections on nostalgia, old age, and resignation. Both contain music of the greatest simplicity as well as the greatest sophistication. Whether expressing the joys of youthful love or the resignation of old age, Schubert's music goes straight to the heart.

Schubert's gift for lyricism influenced everything he wrote, even his instrumental music. He composed a great variety of music for solo piano and some wonderful chamber music. Two of his chamber works are actually based on songs he wrote; one is called the "Death and the Maiden" String Quartet, the other, the "Trout" Quintet. Each has a movement that is a set of variations on a melody from one of those songs.

Among the larger compositions are several operas, a number of choral works, and eight symphonies. The best known of Schubert's symphonies are his last two, the so-called "Great" C-major Symphony (1828) and the "Unfinished" Symphony (1822; Schubert completed only two movements).

Schubert's music, from his tiny, moving, earliest songs to the expansiveness and grandeur of his late symphonies, is finally emerging from the enormous shadow cast by Beethoven. It is fascinating to contemplate how highly we would regard Schubert's music today if Beethoven hadn't been his contemporary.

Schubert chose the gentle theme from his song "The Trout" for a set of variations written for piano and strings. The original song was written in the key of D♭ major, but for the quintet he transposed it to D major, which is easier to play and more resonant on stringed instruments. Instead of the normal complement of strings (two violins, viola, and cello—the "string quartet" group), Schubert uses one each of violin, viola, cello, and double bass. This makes for a slightly more transparent texture and, of course, a deeper bass line.

Find the **Quick Listen** on **MySearchLab**
"Schubert Trout Quintet - 4. Theme and Variations"

LISTENING GUIDE

(((•—**Listen** on **MySearchLab**

FRANZ SCHUBERT (1797–1828)

Song, "Die Forelle" ("The Trout")

Date of composition: 1817
Voice and piano
Tempo: *Etwas lebhaft* ("Rather lively")
Meter: $\frac{2}{4}$
Key: D♭ major
Duration: 1:48

CD II, 9

"The Trout," written to the poem of a German poet, Christian Friedrich Schubart, has been a favorite among Schubert's songs since its composition. Part of the song's charm lies in the composer's remarkable ability to depict the atmosphere of the poem by blending the melody with its accompaniment, both of which have an equal share in the musical interpretation.

The song begins with a piano introduction based on a "rippling" figure that evokes the smooth flow of a stream. This figure becomes the dominant feature of the accompaniment, over which the voice sings an animated and lighthearted melody.

The song represents a modified strophic form with an unexpected change of mood in the last stanza. The first two stanzas are sung to the same music simply because the scene remains the same: as long as the water in the stream is clear, the fish is safe. In the third stanza, however, when the fisherman grows impatient and maliciously stirs up the water to outwit the trout, the music becomes more agitated and unsettled. After the fish is finally hooked, the smoothing of the water's surface is represented by the return of the gentle "rippling" figure, which gives a sense of artistic unity and makes the song a highly organic work.

The subtlety of expression, the perfect matching of feeling to music, and the gentle pictorial touches all combine to make this song a complete miniature masterpiece.

Time	Listen for
0:00	Piano introduction based on the rippling figure.
	Stanza 1 [rippling accompaniment continues]
0:08	*In einem Bächlein helle,* In a limpid brook, *Da schoss in froher Eil'* In joyous haste *Die launische Forelle* The whimsical trout *Vorüber wie ein Pfeil.* Darted about like an arrow.
0:20	*Ich stand an dem Gestade* I stood on the bank *Und sah in süsser Ruh'* In blissful peace, watching *Des muntern Fischleins Bade* The lively fish swim around *Im klaren Bächlein zu.* In the clear brook.
	[last two lines repeated]
0:39	Piano interlude
	Stanza 2
0:45	[same music] *Ein Fischer mit der Rute* An angler with his rod *Wohl an dem Ufer stand,* Stood on the bank, *Und sah's mit kaltem Blute,* Cold-bloodedly watching *Wie sich das Fischlein wand.* The fish's flicker.

0:57	*So lang' dem Wasser Helle,* *So dacht' ich, nicht gebricht,* *So fängt er die Forelle* *Mit seiner Angel nicht.* [last two lines repeated]	As long as the water is clear, I thought, and not disturbed, He'll never catch that trout With his rod.
1:17	Piano interlude	

Stanza 3 [sudden change of rhythm, harmony, and accompanying figures]

1:23	*Doch endlich ward dem Diebe* *Die Zeit zu lang. Er macht* *Das Bächlein tückisch trübe,* [diminished sevenths] *Und eh ich es gedacht,* [suspense gaps in piano]	But in the end the thief Grew impatient. Cunningly he made the brook cloudy, And in an instant
1:37	*So zuckte seine Rute,* *Das Fischlein zappelt dran,* [crescendo] *Und ich mit regem Blute* [earlier music returns] *Sah die Betrog'ne an.* [last two lines repeated]	His rod quivered, And the fish struggled on it. And I, my blood boiling, Looked at the poor tricked creature.
1:58	Piano postlude	

A pencil drawing of French composer Hector Berlioz (1803–1869), drawn by Ingres, signed and dated 'Ingres del Florence, 1824.'

Hector Berlioz (1803–1869)

In nineteenth-century France, Romanticism was a vital force, defined by writers such as Madame de Staël, Chateaubriand, and George Sand; poets such as Lamartine and Vigny; novelists and playwrights such as Stendhal, Balzac, and Victor Hugo; and painters such as Anne-Louis Girodet and Eugène Delacroix. No less important than these literary and artistic figures was the French composer Hector Berlioz, who established music as central to the Romantic ideal.

Berlioz was the oldest child of a distinguished French doctor and his strictly religious Catholic wife. As a child, Berlioz read widely; he also took music lessons and, on his own, studied music theory. He began to compose when he was a teenager.

His father wanted him to become a doctor, so Berlioz entered medical school in Paris. But he became more and more interested in music, and more and more horrified by what he saw as a medical student. He finally quit medical school against his father's wishes and supported himself by taking singing jobs and giving music lessons. Berlioz enrolled at the Paris Conservatory of Music as a composition student at the age of 23.

During the next few years, he wrote several compositions. He had several first-time experiences that were to affect him profoundly: hearing some of the great Beethoven symphonies, coming across a French translation of Goethe's *Faust*, and encountering Shakespeare's plays. He also fell in love with an Irish actress, Harriet Smithson, who was touring with a Shakespearean acting company.

During the 1830s, Berlioz composed two highly original symphonic works: *Harold in Italy*, which was inspired by a reading of the Romantic poet Byron's *Childe Harold*, and *Romeo and Juliet*, which was based on Shakespeare's play. He also wrote a powerful and expressive Requiem Mass, composed in memory of the national heroes of France.

In the 1840s, when Berlioz should have been approaching the peak of his career, he was generally spurned by the French establishment. His music was regarded as too innovative, his forms unconventional, his orchestration too demanding, and the emotionality of his music too direct. "They don't understand me," he said. But throughout the rest of Europe, Berlioz was more appreciated. The great Italian violin virtuoso Nicolò Paganini sent him 20,000 francs out of the blue, and Wagner described

Romeo and Juliet as a "revelation." He was often invited to conduct abroad, and other conductors, especially in Germany, scheduled performances of his music.

In the 1850s, despite his critics at home, Berlioz poured his energies into producing one of his greatest masterpieces, the five-act opera *Les Troyens* ("The Trojans"). Based on Virgil's *Aeneid*, it tells the story of the escape of Aeneas from Troy and his doomed love affair with Dido, the Queen of Carthage.

For the last part of his life, Berlioz was not in good health, and he felt bitter and depressed. He composed very little music but worked on his memoirs, which make fascinating reading today. Berlioz died in 1869, and his grave may be visited at Montmartre in Paris. In many ways, Hector Berlioz can be seen as the incarnation of the Romantic artist: brilliantly gifted, completely dedicated to his art, yet rejected by society and isolated during his lifetime.

Berlioz's Music

The most striking aspects of Berlioz's music are its color and atmosphere. He used the orchestra brilliantly, with great sensitivity to the different qualities of sound available from all the instruments. Some of his pieces call for very large performing groups: the Requiem Mass is written for an orchestra of 140 players, a huge chorus, and four groups of brass and timpani

> Find the **Quick Listen** on **MySearchLab** "Berlioz Les Troyens Love Duet"

> Berlioz on his prospects in medicine: "Become a doctor? Study anatomy? Dissect? Take part in horrible operations? Instead of giving myself body and soul to music?"

> Berlioz composes by splashing his pen all over the manuscript and leaving the result to chance.
> —Fryderyk Chopin

PERFORMANCE IN CONTEXT

The Paris Conservatory

The Paris Conservatory has been at the heart of French music since the founding of the school in 1795. It would be hard to find a famous French musician from the past 200 years who has not passed through its doors, either as a student, member of the faculty, or performer. The Conservatory Hall's acoustics were the best in Paris for orchestral music: rich and lush, but without the echo of an opera house or church hall. Berlioz, a graduate of the conservatory, naturally chose it for the premiere of his *Symphonie Fantastique*. Many of the orchestra members were also students at the school. A small sampling of the Conservatory's many famous graduates includes Georges Bizet, Claude Debussy, Olivier Messiaen, and Brigitte Bardot. The old conservatory building is located in Paris on the Right Bank, near the famous Palais Garnier opera house. The music program has moved to a new campus, but the old hall is still used by the Conservatory's theatre program.

Entrée du Conservatoire de musique et de déclamation.

placed at the four corners of the performing space; the *Te Deum* calls for a solo singer, a large orchestra, an organ, two choirs of 100 singers each, and a choir of 600 children!

But even more fascinating than these gigantic effects are those quiet places where Berlioz conjures up an unforgettable atmosphere with completely original orchestration. In the Requiem, for example, he uses violas, cellos, bassoons, and English horns in simple, long phrases for a passage of penitence and introspection. And his *Symphonie fantastique* is full of wonderful atmospheric moments: an echoing song between solo oboe and solo English horn; the quiet rumble of distant thunder on four timpani; and an eerie, menacing march on muted horns and plucked double basses.

The *Symphonie fantastique* ("Fantasy Symphony"), Berlioz's best-known work, is one of the earliest examples of Romantic program music. The piece, Berlioz said, describes various situations in the life of a young musician who falls desperately in love at first sight. The symphony depicts his dreams, despairs, and fantasies. Clearly the symphony is autobiographical.

Like many other composers, Berlioz felt ambivalent about tying a musical work to a specific verbal narrative. He wanted to explain the ideas behind his music to his audience, but he also felt that the music ought to be able to stand alone.

Felix Mendelssohn about 1829.

Felix Mendelssohn (1809–1847)

Mendelssohn is one of the two composers in this period (the other being Gustav Mahler) who illustrate the uncomfortable position occupied by Jews in nineteenth-century Europe. His grandfather had been the famous Jewish philosopher Moses Mendelssohn. His father was a banker, a prominent member of German middle-class society. His mother was also from a distinguished family; she was cultivated and very musical. In 1811 the Mendelssohn family was forced to flee from Hamburg to Berlin for political reasons, and when Felix was seven years old, his father had the children baptized; a few years later, his father converted to Christianity himself. Despite the increasing tolerance of nineteenth-century society, it was still easier to make your way in an "enlightened" age if you were not Jewish.

After their conversion, the family enjoyed increasing prosperity and social status. The Mendelssohn home was a focal point for writers, artists, musicians, and intellectuals in Berlin society. Chamber concerts were held every weekend, and under the tutelage of their mother, Felix and his older sister Fanny soon proved to be especially gifted in music. (About Fanny we shall say more later.)

Felix was precocious in everything he undertook. At the age of 10, he was reading Latin and studying arithmetic, geometry, history, and geography. He played the piano and the violin, and he started music theory and composition lessons. He began to compose, write poetry, and paint. Several of his early compositions were performed at the Sunday concerts in his parents' home.

As a youth, Mendelssohn was introduced to the most famous literary figure in Germany, Goethe, and a great friendship developed between the old man and the gifted teenager. Mendelssohn also traveled widely in Europe, either on holidays with his family or in the company of his father. Throughout this time, Mendelssohn was composing prolifically. By the time he was 20 he had written more than 100 pieces.

Mendelssohn was very interested in music of the past. At the age of 20, together with a family friend who was a professional actor, he arranged for a performance of one of the great masterpieces of Bach that had not been heard for nearly a century: the *St. Matthew Passion*. The performance, with Mendelssohn conducting, was a landmark in the revival and appreciation of Bach's music in the modern era. "To think," said Mendelssohn, "that it should be an actor and a Jew who give back to the people the greatest of all Christian works."

In his 20s, Mendelssohn continued to perform as a conductor and a pianist, to compose prolifically, and to travel a great deal, in Italy, Scotland, and England. In 1835, he was appointed conductor of the Leipzig Gewandhaus Orchestra, where he worked hard to improve the quality of performances and the working conditions of the musicians. He revived many important works of the past and also championed the music of his contemporaries. When the score of Schubert's "Great" C-major Symphony was discovered, the world premiere was given by Mendelssohn and his orchestra.

Mendelssohn was married in 1837, and the couple had five children. In 1843 he was appointed director of the Berlin Cathedral Choir and director of the Berlin Opera. He continued to divide his time between Berlin and Leipzig, and in the same year he was appointed director of the newly opened music conservatory in Leipzig. Despite all these activities, Mendelssohn continued to compose. Among the many works he wrote at this time were an opera, two large oratorios, symphonies, concertos, chamber music, and numerous pieces for solo piano.

In May of 1847, his closest friend and confidante, his sister Fanny, suddenly died. Felix was shattered. His last great work, the String Quartet in F Minor, Op. 80, was composed as a "Requiem for Fanny." He became ill and tired and could no longer conduct. A series of strokes in October led to his death on November 3, 1847, at the age of 38. He was buried in Berlin, near Fanny's grave.

Mendelssohn's Music

Mendelssohn was a composer who continued the Classic tradition in his works, while adopting some of the more moderate ideas of Romanticism. He wrote in most of the traditional genres of the Classic era, and the formal outlines of his works are clear and easy to follow. Mendelssohn maintained the greatest respect for the past—especially for the music of Bach, Handel, Mozart, and Beethoven—and his music shows the influence of these composers. His style is more transparent and lighter

than that of many early Romantic composers, certainly less extroverted and smaller in scale than that of Berlioz: it ranges from lively and brilliantly animated to lyrical and expressive.

Mendelssohn's main orchestral works include five symphonies and several overtures. Many of these are programmatic, though only in a general sense: they evoke scenes and landscapes rather than tell a detailed story. The best known of these are the "Scottish" Symphony (Symphony No. 3), the "Italian" Symphony (Symphony No. 4), and the "Hebrides" Overture. The "Hebrides" Overture was inspired by his trip to Scotland and evokes a rocky landscape and the swell of the sea. Like many early Romantics, Mendelssohn read and admired Shakespeare; his Overture to Shakespeare's *A Midsummer Night's Dream* is often performed today. It is hard to believe Mendelssohn composed it when he was only 17.

Mendelssohn also wrote several concertos, mostly for piano but also for violin. His Violin Concerto in E Minor is one of the most popular of his works because of its beauty and lyricism.

Mendelssohn's admiration for Bach and Handel led to his interest in choral writing. After the revival of Bach's *St. Matthew Passion*, Mendelssohn studied Handel's oratorios and composed two major oratorios of his own, *Elijah* and *St. Paul*. He also wrote a great deal of other choral music, and his sacred music includes works for Jewish, Catholic, Lutheran, and Anglican services.

His chamber music consists of songs, string quartets, sonatas, and piano trios. Perhaps the most popular of these works is the Piano Trio in D Minor. In addition, Mendelssohn wrote a large number of miniatures for solo piano; in the typical mold of early Romanticism, he called them *Songs Without Words*. They are gentle, delightful, and lyrical—expressive without being deeply profound. In these ways, they distill the essence of Felix Mendelssohn's music.

Find the **Quick Listen** on **MySearchLab** "Mendelssohn Op. 80"

Fanny Mendelssohn Hensel (1805–1847)

Fanny was four years older than Felix, and they were very close throughout their lives. Fanny was a talented pianist and also a gifted composer, but her career as a composer illustrates the distance women still had to travel to achieve equal opportunity in the nineteenth century.

Her father strongly disapproved of the idea of her pursuing a career in music. Like many people of his time, he felt that a professional career was unsuitable for a woman. Amateur music making was entirely acceptable—indeed, it was the province of a cultivated young woman—but making a living as a performer or a composer was out of the question. Even her brother Felix agreed with this view.

So Fanny led the conventional life of a well-educated middle-class woman. At 24, she married Wilhelm Hensel, a painter and artist at the court in Berlin. Fanny had a son and ran the family household. She continued to play the piano, and after her mother's death she took over the organization of the famous

Fanny Mendelssohn about 1830.

Sunday concerts at her parents' home. She often played the piano at the concerts and directed a choral group that performed there. One day, at the age of 41, while rehearsing the chorus for a performance of a cantata composed by Felix, she had a stroke. She died that same evening.

Despite discouragement from her father and her brother, Fanny had composed a great deal. She wrote many songs, some cantatas and oratorios, chamber music, and small piano works. Like Felix, she called the short pieces for piano *Songs Without Words*. (**See Listening Guide.**) Some of her early songs were published in collections with pieces by her brother, though they carried Felix's name. After the death of her father, she did arrange for the publication of one or two works under her own name.

All in all, Fanny composed about 400 works, though most of them have never been published. They remain in manuscript in American and European libraries. In the last few years, with increasing focus on the contributions of women to the history of music, more and more of her works are being published and recorded. It is impossible to assess her true contributions or to compare her achievement with Felix's until her compositions have received the same attention as those of her brother.

LISTENING GUIDE

(((•─Listen on **MySearchLab**

FANNY MENDELSSOHN HENSEL (1805–1847)

Lied *from* Songs Without Words, *Op. 8, No. 3*

Date of composition: 1840?
Tempo: *Larghetto* ("Fairly slow")
Meter: $\frac{4}{4}$
Key: D major
Duration: 3:07

CD II, 10

The *Lieder ohne Wörte* ("Songs Without Words") were not published until after Fanny's death. The third of this four-piece set, simply entitled *Lied* ("Song"), is also marked *Lenau*, the name of a German poet, suggesting that an actual poem may have inspired her to write this song. The tuneful, flowing phrases are indeed highly singable and memorable. The form is a typical one for a song: ABA. Throughout the piece, there is an accompaniment of gentle, repeated chords in the middle range, and slow, isolated bass notes. The atmosphere suggests a reflective inner dialogue.

Time	Listen for
	A
0:00	Melody repeats a gently curving motive, followed by an ascending leap, as a kind of questioning idea. This is followed by a balanced descending motive. The mood is one of contemplation.
0:30	Questioning idea in low range, response in higher range.

B

| 1:03 | Modulating, unstable B section—shorter, faster exchanges of questioning idea, answered by descending arpeggios. |
| 1:20 | Minor version of questioning idea in low range. Crescendo, then decrescendo, leads to: |

A′

| 1:39 | Clear return of the beginning, moving quickly to faster sequential phrases. |
| 2:15 | Closing section using questioning idea, including crescendo and leap to highest note of the piece. Ends with gentle decrescendo. |

COMPOSERS, PATRONS, AND AUDIENCES

Music for the Middle Classes

The nineteenth century witnessed the rise—across Europe—of a large, primarily urban, middle class. Members of this class not only formed the largest audience for music, but also became music "consumers," buying sheet music of songs or chamber music for performances at home. An evening was not complete without a song recital or an amateur piano performance after dinner. Nineteenth-century novels, such as those of Eliot or Thackeray, are full of references to such performances, mostly by women.

Composers, too, belonged mostly to the middle class. They were small entrepreneurs in their own right, negotiating fees with publishers and concert promoters. Many composers made a comfortable living from their music. They were also freer from the constraints of employers such as the church or aristocratic courts, which had often dictated terms of style or content to composers in previous eras. The artistic freedom of composers in the nineteenth century was therefore the result of economic as well as aesthetic conditions.

Fryderyk Chopin (1810–1849)

Chopin was the first of the great piano virtuosos in the Romantic era. Most composers before Chopin played the piano, and many of them actually composed at the keyboard, even if they weren't writing piano music. But after Beethoven, Chopin was the first important nineteenth-century composer to achieve fame as a performing pianist, and almost all of his compositions are written for solo piano.

Chopin was born in 1810 to a French father and a Polish mother. His father taught French, and his mother taught piano at a school in Warsaw. Chopin began formal piano lessons at the age of seven, and his first composition was published the same year. At the age of eight, he gave his first public concert, and at the age of 15, he was sufficiently accomplished to play before Tsar Alexander I of Russia, who presented him with a diamond ring.

When Chopin was 19, he heard the great violinist Paganini play and was inspired to become a touring virtuoso himself. Most of his compositions at this time were designed for his own use. Chopin would improvise for hours at the keyboard and only occasionally write down what he had played. His music was often based on traditional Polish dances such as the polonaise or the mazurka.

In 1830, Chopin completed two piano concertos, which he performed in public concerts, and toward the end of the year he left Poland, unaware that he would never see it again. From a distance he heard of the Warsaw uprising and the storming of the city by the Russian army. From this time on, the Polish quality of his music deepened, and his compositions became more intense and passionate. A review stated, "Chopin has listened to the song of the Polish villager; he has made it his own and united the tunes of his native land in skillful composition and elegant execution."

In 1831, at the age of 21, Chopin settled in Paris, an important center of European artistic activity. Soon he was caught up in the whirl of Parisian society, and his brilliant and poetic playing made him very much in demand in the city's fashionable salons. He had a wide circle of friends, including some of the great

Chopin as a young man.

Eugène Delacroix (1798–1863). *Portrait of Frederic Chopin* (1810–1860), 1838. Oil on canvas, 45.5 × 38 cm. Louvre, Dpt. des Peintures, France. © Photograph by Erich Lessing. Erich Lessing/Art Resource, NY.

cultural figures of the time, such as Berlioz, Liszt, and the artist Delacroix.

In his late 20s, Chopin was introduced by Franz Liszt to Aurore Dudevant, a well-known novelist who published under the male pseudonym George Sand. They soon started living together, and the years they spent together were among the most productive of Chopin's life. He was often ill, however, displaying the first signs of the tuberculosis that would later kill him. George Sand looked after him devotedly, although Chopin was a difficult patient. There is a rather unflattering portrait of him in one of her novels, *Lucrezia Floriani*, in the character of Prince Karol.

The relationship ended in 1847, after which Chopin's health rapidly deteriorated. He composed little but gave public recitals in London and Paris. It was reported that he was too weak to play louder than *mezzo-forte*. Chopin died in 1849 at the age of 39. At his request, Mozart's Requiem was played at his funeral.

Chopin's Music

The best way to think of Chopin's music is as poetry for the piano. His style is entirely a personal one, as might be expected from one who improvised so freely. Most of his pieces are fairly short, and they fall into several categories:

Dances: polonaises, mazurkas, and waltzes. The **waltz** was fast becoming the favorite ballroom dance of the nineteenth century. Chopin managed to create enormous variety of mood with the basic format of this one dance. **Mazurkas** and **polonaises** are both Polish dances, and Chopin invested them with the spirit of Polish nationalism. Mazurkas are in triple meter with a stress on the second or third beat of the bar. Polonaises are stately and proud.

Free forms without dance rhythms: preludes, études, nocturnes, and impromptus. The **preludes** follow the pattern established by Bach in his *Well-Tempered Clavier*: there is one in each of the major and minor keys. **Étude** literally means "study piece," and each of Chopin's études concentrates on one facet of musicianship or piano technique. The **nocturnes** are moody, introspective pieces, and the **impromptus** capture the essence of improvisation ("impromptu" means "off the cuff"). The formal structure of these pieces is fundamentally simple, relying upon the ABA pattern common to aria or song form. However, Chopin usually varied the return of the opening section quite considerably, creating instead an ABA' structure.

In all these genres, Chopin wrote highly individual pieces, each one with a nostalgic or singing quality, perfectly suited to the special sound and capabilities of the pianos of his time. The sound of the instrument was softer, less brilliant than it is today, but it allowed for rapid repetition of notes and sustained sounds. Chopin's melodies and chords exploited these qualities. Chopin's left-hand harmony is varied and expressive, and sometimes the main melody will appear in the left hand with the accompaniment above it in the right. There is often much delicate, rapid ornamentation in the right hand, with short free passages or runs or trills that add to the impression of improvisation. Finally, Chopin's written directions often call for a special expressive device called **rubato**. Literally, this Italian word means "robbed." Using this technique, the player keeps the tempo going in the accompaniment while the melody slows down slightly before catching up a moment later. Carefully applied, rubato can suggest the kind of expressive freedom that must have characterized the playing of Chopin himself.

> Compared with Berlioz, Chopin was a morbidly sentimental flea by the side of a roaring lion.
>
> —J. W. Davison

LISTENING GUIDE

((•— **Listen** on **MySearchLab**

FRYDERYK CHOPIN (1810–1849)

Prelude in E Minor, Op. 28, for Piano

Date of composition: 1836–39
Tempo: *Largo* ("Broad")
Meter: $\frac{2}{2}$
Duration: 1:47

CD II, 11

Chopin composed 24 preludes between 1836 and 1839. They follow the same idea as Bach's two sets of preludes and fugues, presenting all 24 major and minor keys of the scale system.

This prelude features an ABA' structure. In the A section, an almost static melodic line is accompanied by steady chords that constantly descend. Notice the use of "neighbor" tones in the right-hand melody: the melody goes to an adjacent pitch and then returns. The B section is marked by melodic arpeggios and has more rhythmic movement. The return of the A section is varied, and there is a wonderfully expressive silence before the end.

Time	Listen for
	A section
0:00	Opening melody. Focus is on descending left-hand accompanying chords. Upper neighbor tone is heard several times in right hand.
0:20	New note, melodic motion continues to descend.
	B section
0:46	More motion in melody and change in accompanying figures.
1:01	End of section, little flourish in melody, returning to:
	A' section
1:07	Variation of A.
1:22	More rhythmic activity in both hands.
1:25	Loudest part.
1:35	Feeling of stasis.
1:48	"Goal" reached.
2:01	Final chord?
2:04	Expressive silence.
2:09	Real final cadence (three chords).

Robert Schumann (1810–1856)

Of all the early Romantics, Robert Schumann was the most imbued with a literary imagination. He was born in 1810 in a small German town. His father was a bookseller, so the young boy had unlimited access to the popular Romantic writings of the day.

Schumann read voraciously and began to pour his feelings into poems and novels of his own, before finding a more congenial outlet in music. He played the piano well, though his exuberance outran his discipline. "I was always a fiery performer," he said, "but my technique was full of holes."

After his father died, Schumann went to the University of Leipzig as a law student, but he had no interest in the subject. He drank heavily and spent his money on having a good time. While in Leipzig, he met Friedrich Wieck, an eminent piano teacher, and Schumann took lessons from him.

A turning point in Schumann's career came (as it did for so many Romantic musicians) upon hearing the Italian virtuoso Paganini play a concert. He was entranced by the showmanship and hypnotic intensity of the great violinist and decided to become a piano virtuoso. He gave up his undisciplined life, enrolled as a full-time student with Wieck, and took a room in Wieck's house in order to devote himself to constant practice. Unfortunately, Schumann took this to extremes, as he tended to do with everything. He overdid the practicing and permanently damaged his hand.

There was, however, a bright side to this episode: Schumann turned from performing to composing music, and he met Clara, Wieck's daughter, who was to become the love of his life. When Schumann moved in with the Wiecks, Clara was only 10 years old. But she was a brilliant pianist, and Wieck had the highest hopes for her. Clara could outplay Schumann, even though he was twice her age.

By the time Clara was 15, she was already a great pianist, astounding audiences at home and abroad. But her father suddenly noticed a cloud on the horizon: Clara and

Wieck, in a letter to Schumann's mother: "Taking into account his talent and imagination, I promise to make him into one of the greatest living pianists."

Clara and Robert Schumann.

Photograph of Clara & Robert Schumann, Musée d'Orsay, Paris. Réunion des Musées Nationaux/ Art Resource, NY.

The laws of morality are also those of art.
—Robert Schumann

Find the **Quick Listen** on **MySearchLab**
"Schumann *Du Bist Wie Eine Blume*"

To me, Schumann's memory is holy.
—Johannes Brahms

Robert were falling in love. This was not at all in the plans. His daughter had a career ahead of her and didn't need to get involved with a neurotic, obsessive student, 10 years her senior, who barely made a living. So he opposed the relationship with all the means at his disposal. He took Clara away on long tours, refused to let the couple meet, and even threatened to shoot Schumann if he tried to see Clara. During this long period, the two wrote secret letters to each other, and Schumann poured his feelings into his music. He described his F♯-minor piano sonata as "a single cry of my heart for you," and Clara wrote to him that when she played, she played for him: "I had no other way of showing you what was in my heart."

In the end, the couple had no choice but to go to court to obtain the freedom to marry, and they were finally wed in 1840, when Clara was 20 and Robert was 30. In that year, Schumann turned his attention to compositions for piano and voice. He was on fire with inspiration and composed no fewer than 140 songs, including three song cycles. His texts were taken from the great Romantic poets: Byron, Goethe, Heinrich Heine, and others. Schumann's wedding gift to Clara was a setting of "Du bist wie eine Blume," Heine's poem comparing his beloved to the beauty of a flower.

If 1840 was Schumann's "year of song," 1841 was his "year of the symphony." Robert and Clara settled into their home in Leipzig, with a music room each, and Clara wrote, "We enjoy a happiness such as I have never known before." Schumann had recently encountered a symphony by Schubert. He was overwhelmed, and Clara encouraged him to work on a symphony of his own. His Symphony No. 1 (*Spring Symphony*) was sketched out in four days. The first performance was given by the Leipzig Gewandhaus Orchestra, with Felix Mendelssohn conducting.

In 1842, Clara went on tour and Schumann threw himself into a new passion: chamber music. He studied the string quartets of Haydn, Mozart, and Beethoven intensively. On Clara's return, he wrote three string quartets in five weeks, and by the end of the year had also completed a piano quintet, a piano quartet, and a piano trio.

About 1845, Schumann began to experience the fits of depression and illness that were to haunt him for the rest of his life. He composed only sporadically, and he had occasional nervous breakdowns.

In 1850, Schumann was appointed music director in Düsseldorf, but it soon became clear that his health and mental state were not sufficiently stable to allow him to perform his duties. Newspaper reviews became highly critical, singers refused to attend rehearsals, and Schumann's assistant conductor had to take over concerts at the last minute. Schumann began to suffer from hallucinations.

On a rainy day in February 1854, Schumann left his house in his slippers and walked to the bridge over the Rhine. He stepped over the railing and threw himself into the water. He was pulled out by some fishermen and carried home. A few days later, he was committed to a mental institution.

With eight children, Clara could not long maintain her household alone. She began touring again, but in 1856, she was summoned back urgently by the doctors. "I had to go to him," she wrote in her diary. "I saw him between 6 and 7 in the evening. He smiled and with great effort put his arms around me. I shall never forget it. All the treasures in the world could not equal this embrace." Two days later Schumann died; he was 46.

Schumann's Music

Schumann was a literary Romantic. Much of his music is inspired by literary references, and even when the inspiration is not literary, there is often some other programmatic reference to people or ideas.

His writing for piano, his own instrument, is masterly. The pieces for solo piano range from short works deliberately designed for children to **character pieces** (small programmatic movements) to large sonatas. Many of the character pieces are grouped together into cycles. One such cycle, *Carnaval*, contains musical portraits of Schumann himself, some of his friends, Chopin, Paganini, and the 15-year-old Clara Wieck. The piano parts for his songs are also very beautiful, playing an equal role with that of the voice. Many of the songs are also grouped into cycles, the most famous being *Dichterliebe* ("A Poet's Love") and *Frauen-Liebe und Leben* ("Women's Lives and Loves").

Schumann wrote only one piano concerto. It is the complete opposite of the typical Romantic concerto. Rather than flashy and brilliant, it is restrained and tender—perhaps because it was written for his beloved Clara to play.

LISTENING GUIDE

((•●•**Listen** on **MySearchLab**

ROBERT SCHUMANN (1810–1856)   *Träumerei (Dreaming), from Kinderszenen, Op. 15, for Piano*

Date of composition: 1838
Meter: $\frac{3}{4}$
Key: F major
Duration: 2:59

CD II, 12

This selection comes from Schumann's *Kinderszenen* (*Scenes from Childhood*). It is a simple accompanied melody, in an **ABA'** structure. You'll notice that the melody features an ascending shape, and this shape characterizes all three brief sections. The slow tempo and the reiteration of the theme create a wonderfully "dreamy" atmosphere.

Time	Listen for
	A section
0:00	Melody is presented: first phrase:
0:08	High point of the first phrase.
0:19	Ending of the first phrase overlaps with the beginning of the second.
0:27	Melody reaches even higher, to its highest pitch.
0:38	Cadence.
0:42	A section repeated.
	B section
1:23	Melody is presented, but varied melodically and harmonically.
	A' section
2:03	Melody is restated.
2:31	Large, rolled chord under the highest pitch of melody ("signal" that the piece will end soon).
2:45	Ending cadence.

Two of Schumann's four symphonies have programmatic titles. The First Symphony is called the "Spring" Symphony, and the Third Symphony is called the "Rhenish." (Rhenish means "about the river Rhine.") He composed the latter immediately after taking up his appointment in the city of Düsseldorf, on the Rhine River. Like Berlioz's *Symphonie fantastique*, it has five movements instead of the normal four.

Schumann's chamber music is more Classical in form. There are fewer apparent programmatic references, but the music flows with intensity and charm. With his chamber music, songs, and symphonies Schumann invested Classic genres with his own particular brand of Romantic imagination.

Clara Schumann (1819–1896)

The first part of Clara Schumann's life, from the age of 10 to the age of 36, was closely bound up with that of Robert Schumann and has already been partly described. There is no doubt that she both loved and admired her husband. He, in turn, was deeply in love with her and depended heavily on her for emotional support. Robert encouraged Clara's performing career, but in their relationship, his composing certainly took precedence over hers.

Her musical career was nonetheless a remarkable one. She benefited from her father's close attention to her musical education. At the age of nine, she first performed in public; two years later, she gave her first complete solo recital.

By the time she married, at the age of 20, Clara Schumann had an international reputation as a concert pianist. She had received many honors and was admired by Goethe, Mendelssohn, Paganini, and Chopin. Clara was renowned for playing everything from memory and for her musicality at the keyboard. She had also composed a considerable

Find the **Quick Listen** on **MySearchLab**

"Clara Schumann Piano Trio"

The only woman in Germany who can play my music.

—Chopin, speaking of Clara Schumann

number of works by this time, and several had been published.

During her married life, Clara continued to perform and compose, although we must remember that in 14 years she had eight children. She submitted all her compositions to her husband for his criticism, and she clearly regarded him as the greater talent. By the time of his death, she had published 20 or 30 compositions of her own; several others remained unpublished. Her works include character pieces for piano, songs, some chamber music, and a piano concerto, which was completed when she was 15 years old. Perhaps her best-known work is her Piano Trio in G Minor, Op. 17, written in 1846. Mendelssohn regarded the piece highly, and it was widely performed in the nineteenth century.

After Robert Schumann's death, Clara continued to perform and to teach, though she wrote no more music. She maintained a heavy schedule, doubtless to support her large family. Clara continued to appear in public into her 70s and promoted her husband's music by performing it as much as possible. She also helped prepare a complete edition of his works for publication.

Throughout this latter half of her life, Clara was the friend and confidante of Johannes Brahms, a composer 14 years her junior. Brahms had been a protégé of Robert Schumann's, and the three musicians had been close. Brahms was especially supportive during the last terrible years of Schumann's illness. Brahms and Clara remained good friends. He often sent her drafts of his work for her encouragement and criticism. Brahms, however, remained a bachelor, and Clara never remarried.

Clara Wieck Schumann is an important figure in the history of nineteenth-century music. The daughter of a famous teacher, she became the wife of one remarkable composer and the lifelong friend of another. She was the inspiration for some of the greatest music of

CLARA SCHUMANN

Clara Schumann's life reflects the changing attitudes toward women in nineteenth-century society. She made a successful career as a professional pianist, though she was one of only very few women to do so. She managed this despite running a household and raising a large number of children. Her own ability to compose was clearly compromised by her marriage to one of the foremost composers of the age as well as by society's views, which were changing only slowly. She wrote in her diary, "I once thought that I possessed creative talent, but now I have given up this idea. A woman must not desire to compose. Not one has been able to do it, so why should I?"

the century. In addition to all this, she had a brilliant career as a pianist and piano teacher and was herself a gifted composer.

Clara Schumann died on May 20, 1896, at the age of 77, while her grandson played Robert Schumann's music at the piano.

STYLE SUMMARY

The Nineteenth Century I: Early Romantic Music

Beethoven set the tone for music in the nineteenth century. Almost every composer who followed Beethoven attempted to match the force and depth of his music. Many copied his formal innovations. Others built on his style of molding music into personal revelation.

In this last aspect, music was the strongest representative of the new Romantic spirit. Composers wanted their works to express the inexpressible: the height of joy, the depths of despair, the transcendence of love. Compositions ranged from the tiniest miniatures for solo piano to works for the largest conglomeration of performing forces ever seen.

Instruments themselves changed. They became bigger and louder, and new instruments, such as the tuba and the saxophone, were invented. For solo performance, the piano and violin were still favored. Many people in the growing middle class played the piano or chamber music at home, and great performers of the piano and violin became international stars. The warm sound of instruments that play in the middle range, such as French horn and cello, was also favored by Romantic composers. The range of dynamics in all music was widened, as was the range of expression. Above all, composers wanted their music to be expressive.

This striving for expression led to other, more systemic changes. Melodies became longer and more flowing. Tempo, rather than being more or less fixed from the beginning to the end of each movement, became more fluid, allowing the music to ebb and flow as it went along. Harmony became more adventurous, with more and more unusual chords appearing and with more rapid changes of key.

FUNDAMENTALS OF EARLY ROMANTIC MUSIC

❐ The size of musical works ranges from miniature to enormous

❐ Tempos are fluid and variable

❐ Melodies are longer, more flowing, and seemingly more spontaneous

❐ Forms are less structured and their outlines deliberately disguised

❐ Harmony pushes at the outer limits of tonality

❐ New instruments were invented, and older instruments were redesigned to make them louder and faster

❐ Brilliant individual performers on instruments such as the piano and violin ruled the concert stages

FOR FURTHER DISCUSSION AND STUDY

1. Discuss the development of technology in the nineteenth century. Think of how the steam engine made the world "smaller." Note also that feats of engineering such as the Suez and Panama Canals allowed access to other parts of the world. Discuss the far-reaching effects of inventions such as the harnessing of electricity.

2. Discuss the status of minorities and women in the nineteenth century.

3. The rise of manufacturing and salon society created the need for an all-purpose, easily

playable instrument for the general populace. This was the piano. Discuss the tonal differences between performances of Beethoven's "Moonlight" Sonata on the fortepiano (A. Newman, Newport Classics NCD 60040), the 1824 Graf piano (J. van Immerseel, Accent 78332), and the modern grand piano (V. Horowitz, CBS MK 34509).

4. Discuss the changes in instruments from the eighteenth to the nineteenth centuries. The violin, for example, had the sound post and the F-holes repositioned, the angle of the neck and curvature of the bridge changed, the strings updated from gut to wound metal, and the bow design altered. Trace the history of new instruments developed during the nineteenth century—for example, the tuba.

5. To appreciate the concept of the song cycle, take a journey through the 20 songs of *Die schöne Müllerin* (*The Pretty Miller-Maid*), from our hero's early infatuation (No. 5) to the peace of a watery grave (No. 20).

6. Discuss the way travel might have affected composers (for example, Mendelssohn). If you have been to Europe, what effect did it have on you?

7. Listen to one of Felix Mendelssohn's *Songs Without Words* and compare it with the one by Fanny Mendelssohn in this chapter. Comment on the similarities and differences.

8. Listen to a Romance by Robert Schumann (perhaps Op. 21, No. 1, in A minor) and one by Clara (perhaps Op. 28, No. 1, in B♭ minor). Discuss the similarities and differences.

✓•⟨Study and Review on MySearchLab

CHAPTER 10

The Nineteenth Century II: Mid- to Late-Romantic Music

By the middle of the nineteenth century, the main aspects of musical Romanticism had become established: music should represent human emotions to the utmost, and it must tell a story or express an idea that is profound, resonant, or uplifting. A favorite term of the Romantics was "sublime," which means grand, beyond normal experience, awe-inspiring. Works ranged from tiny to huge, and the range of musical expression in form, harmony, tempo, and dynamics was enormous.

During the mid-Romantic period, from the 1850s to the 1870s, the most important musical genres were solo piano works, symphonic program music, and opera. The most important composers were Franz Liszt, Giuseppe Verdi, Richard Wagner, and Pyotr Ilyich Tchaikovsky.

> All nineteenth-century music wishes it were opera.
>
> —Alvah Felix

Works for Solo Piano   Solo piano music appealed to the Romantics because of its focus on the individual. Audiences could concentrate on both the expression of individual emotions and the technical prowess of a great performer. This was the period during which the idea of the performer-hero first took hold, an idea that is still current today (witness our fascination with stars of popular music and athletics). The great piano performer of the mid-Romantic period was Liszt.

Symphonic Program Music   Symphonic program music followed two paths during the 1850s and 1860s. The first was that of the **programmatic symphony**. This path had been made secure by the earlier success of Berlioz's *Symphonie fantastique*. The programmatic symphony is a full-length symphony, with each of its three to five movements depicting an episode in the narrative.

The second path was that of the **symphonic poem**, the successor to such works as Mendelssohn's *Hebrides* Overture. The symphonic poem is a *single-movement* self-contained work, also for orchestra and also programmatic. Liszt was the greatest composer of symphonic poems and programmatic symphonies in the mid-Romantic era, though several other composers followed his lead in later decades.

Opera   During the nineteenth century, there were three national schools of opera: the French, the Italian, and the German. All three had roots going back at least 150 years, and all three had distinct national identities by the time of the mid-Romantic period.

French opera had two very different genres, each with its own style and even its own opera house in Paris. The first was **grand opera**, which incorporated lofty subject matter and spectacular staging, including ballet, choruses, and crowd scenes. The second was **opéra comique** (comic opera), with a much smaller cast and orchestra, simpler musical style, and more down-to-earth plots with humorous or romantic (love) interest. Another important distinction between grand opera and comic opera is that in grand opera the dialogue is set in accompanied musical recitative, whereas in comic opera the dialogue is spoken.

By the 1850s and 1860s a new, highly popular operatic genre had evolved in France, one that stood between grand opera and comic opera. It was known as **lyric opera**. Lyric opera was melodious, as its name implies; its primary subject matter was tragic love; and its proportions lay somewhere between the spectacular and the skimpy. The greatest lyric opera is *Carmen*, written by Georges Bizet (1838–1875). *Carmen* represented a turning point in the history of opera. With its realistic plot, down-to-earth characters, and turbulent passion, it set the stage for a new, more pointed approach to opera (known as **verismo**, or "Realism") toward the end of the nineteenth century.

NEED TO KNOW

THREE TYPES OF OPERA: FROM GRAND TO SIMPLE

- *Grand Opera:* Lofty subjects, grand productions
- *Lyric Opera:* Stories of tragic love, full productions
- *Comic Opera:* Humorous or happy subjects, simple productions

---

Italian opera was dominated by the achievements of one man: Giuseppe Verdi. He was preceded, however, by three important composers: Rossini, Donizetti, and Bellini. Rossini's gifts were best suited to comic operas, and the most famous of these is his *The Barber of Seville* (1816). Donizetti wrote both comic and serious operas, whereas Bellini composed only serious operas. Bellini's best-known opera is *Norma* (1831).

The central figure in German opera was Wagner, who created some of the most significant masterpieces of the entire nineteenth century, and whose powerful personality made him a major artistic figure of his time. We will study Wagner's contributions, both positive and negative, to Romantic culture. Wagner was influenced by the operas of Carl Maria von Weber (1786–1826), especially *Der Freischütz* (*The Magic Marksman*, 1821), with its supernatural and heroic subject matter and heavy emphasis on the role of the orchestra.

Nationalism The existence of distinct national styles in Romantic opera was one facet of an important movement in nineteenth-century music. This movement was known as **nationalism**, and it coincided with important political events in Europe.

After the Napoleonic Wars ended in 1814, European countries began to assert their independence and to stress national identity. Italy, which had previously been organized into several city-states, republics, and provinces, was finally unified under a constitutional monarchy in 1870. A single German empire was created out of a collection of separate states in 1871. There were rebellions of the Polish people against the ruling Russians, and of the Czechs against their Austrian rulers. Norway gained independence from Sweden, and Finland struggled for independence from Russia. In Russia itself, a sense of national identity was fostered by writers such as Dostoevski and Tolstoi. In America, the Civil War (1861–1865), in which over *600,000* men died, was fought partly to preserve a single national identity.

The nationalist movement was reflected in the arts. In each country, the local language was fostered, books of national poetry were published, and intellectuals turned with increasing interest to the folk tales, dances, and songs of their native heritage. Operas were based on national legend or history and were written in the native language. Folk tunes appeared in symphonic music, and the rhythms of folk dances were used in chamber works. Some composers became famous national symbols. Verdi, who often wrote barely disguised political protests into his operas, was regarded as a national hero by his countrymen.

Franz Liszt (1811–1886)

Franz Liszt was born in 1811 in Hungary. His father was an administrator and court musician at the Esterházy palace, where Haydn had spent most of his career. Liszt first learned to play the piano with his father. When the family moved to Vienna, he studied composition with the eminent court composer Antonio Salieri, who had previously taught Schubert and Beethoven. At the age of 11, Liszt gave his first concert, and a year later he played in public again. Beethoven was in the audience and, after the concert, kissed the young boy on the forehead.

When Liszt was 13, the family moved to Paris, and he began to tour Europe as a piano virtuoso. His incredible technique amazed audiences everywhere, and by his late teens he had become famous as a showman. His striking looks, flamboyant manner, and reputation as a womanizer did not hurt his career a bit.

At the age of 20, he heard the great violinist Paganini for the first time. Liszt was enormously impressed and vowed to attain the same level of mastery on his own instrument. This he did, and he was soon known as the "Paganini of the piano." Liszt's fingers were unusually long and thin, and he could easily play consecutive tenths (a very wide stretch of an octave plus two notes) on one hand. He soon became the greatest pianist of his age and may well have been the greatest pianist of any age.

Over the next few years Liszt developed great friendships with Berlioz and Chopin. He also began living with the Countess Marie d'Agoult, a novelist who published under the name Daniel Stern. The Countess left her husband to live with Liszt, and together they had three children (one of whom, Cosima, later left *her* husband to live with Wagner). They traveled frequently around Europe, and he continued to perform to ever more enthusiastic crowds and to compose prolifically.

In 1842, Liszt settled in Weimar, Germany, where he had been appointed music director and could devote himself to conducting and composing. After his relationship with the Countess ended in 1844, Liszt began an affair with a Russian princess. Between 1848 and 1858, with her encouragement, he completed most of the compositions upon which his fame as a composer now rests. The most important of these are 12 symphonic poems and two programmatic symphonies, as well as a large number of works for solo piano.

In 1861, Liszt suddenly resigned from his position at Weimar and went to Rome to begin religious studies. After four years he became a member of the church hierarchy and was officially known as an *abbé*. He now undertook several religious compositions, writing psalm settings, Masses, and an oratorio.

Toward the end of his life, Liszt turned again to compositions for solo piano and completed some remarkable pieces that anticipate

A smasher of pianos.
—Clara Schumann on Liszt

He has an excessively tall and thin figure and a pale face with sea-green eyes that shine with quick flashes like waves in flame . . . He appears uneasy and distracted, like a ghost about to return to the underworld.
—Marie d'Agoult on Liszt

He collected princesses and countesses as other men collect rare butterflies.
—Ernest Newman on Liszt

In 1836 an English pianist heard Liszt play in Paris and wrote the following: "Such marvels of skill and power I could never have imagined. In comparison with Liszt, all other pianists are children. Chopin carries you into a dream world, in which you would like to dwell forever; Liszt is all sunshine and dazzling splendor, overcoming his listeners with a power that no one can withstand."

| Franz Liszt as an old man.

the shifting harmonies and impressionistic colors of the early twentieth century. Liszt died in 1886 while visiting the new opera house at Bayreuth for some performances of Wagner's operas.

With his extraordinary personality, Liszt stood at the center of Romanticism. He was a complex of contradictions: a diabolical figure who sought spiritual solace in the Church, a flamboyant and narcissistic performer who devoted himself to the music of others, and a composer whose works range from the flashy and brilliant to the quietly searching.

Find the **Quick Listen** on **MySearchLab**

"Liszt Transcription Beethoven Fifth"

Liszt's Music

Together with Wagner, Liszt is regarded as one of the most avant-garde composers of the mid-Romantic era. He experimented with unusual harmonies and chords, and in some cases he seemed to ignore the rules of traditional harmony altogether.

Liszt's piano music is quite varied. Much of it is extremely difficult to play. Schumann once said that there were only "ten or twelve people in the world" who had the technical ability to play Liszt's music. Berlioz said that the only person who could play it was Liszt himself. Runs and rippling octaves surround the melody; cascades of notes tumble from top to bottom of the keyboard; often it sounds as though there must be more than one person playing. Liszt's *Transcendental Études* contain some of the most difficult piano music ever written. We will hear one of these studies in a moment. (**See Listening Guide.**)

One of Liszt's masterpieces is the superb Piano Sonata in B Minor, written in one long movement. It has three themes, which are stated at the outset and reappear in different forms throughout the piece. This technique is known as **thematic transformation**. Liszt used it in many of his other compositions.

A number of Liszt's piano pieces are in dance forms, including waltzes, mazurkas, polonaises, and Hungarian dances. Liszt's contribution to the beginning of nationalism in music was a large body of Hungarian music, including the well-known *Hungarian Rhapsodies*.

Finally, a large proportion of Liszt's piano music is made up of **transcriptions**. A transcription is the "translation" of a piece of music from one medium to another. Liszt made hundreds of transcriptions of orchestral and operatic works, rewriting them for the piano. At a time when recording devices had not yet

CRITICAL VIEWS OF LISZT

During the twentieth century, the reputation of Liszt's music suffered a serious decline. The popularity of certain composers is partly a matter of fashion, and Liszt's reputation as a showman and his extroverted musical style did not fit with the cool rational climate of Modernism. Recently, however, musicians and audiences have begun to appreciate the seriousness behind the showmanship. Here are two views on Liszt's music: one from a nineteenth-century musical journal, and the other by the celebrated pianist Alfred Brendel.

"Composition indeed! Decomposition is the proper word for such hateful fungi, which choke up and poison the fertile plains of harmony, threatening the world with drought."—*Musical World*, 1855

"Liszt is the most underrated composer of the nineteenth century."—Alfred Brendel, 1991

been invented, this practice made available the music of Bach, Beethoven, Berlioz, Wagner, and other composers to people in their own homes.

Liszt's orchestral music dates mostly from the 1840s and 1850s, when he was a conductor in Weimar. During that time, he wrote 12 symphonic poems and two symphonies. The best known of the symphonic poems are *Les Préludes* and *Hamlet*.

Liszt's two symphonies are perfect examples of the power of the programmatic ideal in mid-Romantic music. His *Faust* Symphony represents the three main characters in Goethe's famous

play. And Liszt's *Dante* Symphony is in three movements, corresponding to the three main parts of Dante's *Divine Comedy*.

Liszt influenced several generations of pianists and composers. His phenomenal technique and demanding piano writing expanded the boundaries of what was considered possible on the piano. His symphonic poems inspired other composers to write works in the same form. His Hungarian music contributed to the nationalistic movement. And his novel approach to harmony foreshadowed the great harmonic revolution of the twentieth century.

LISTENING GUIDE

((•—Listen on **MySearchLab**

FRANZ LISZT (1811–1886)

Transcendental Étude No. 10 in F Minor

Date of composition: 1839
Tempo: *Allegro agitato molto* ("Fast and very agitated")
Meter: $\frac{2}{4}$
Duration: 4:49

CD II, 13

The *Transcendental Études* were first composed in 1826, when Liszt was 15 years old. But, as with much of Liszt's music, the works were revised and reissued later—in this case, 1839. Though the music was extremely difficult to perform in its earlier version, Liszt's revisions made it even more demanding. Number 10 in particular was described as being "ten times more difficult than before." Contemporaries of Liszt were amazed by this music and by Liszt's own performances of it. Berlioz said, "No one else in the world could even begin performing music of this kind."

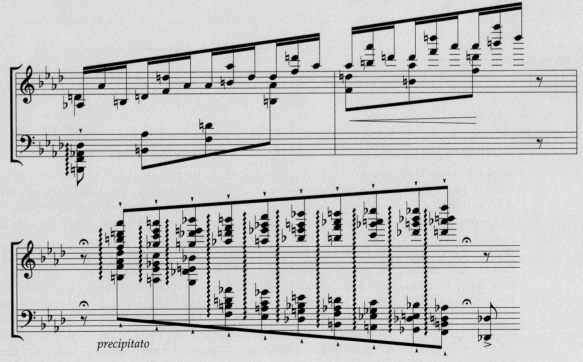

from Liszt *Transcendental Étude No. 10*

In this work, Liszt explores every possibility of demanding piano technique, including doubled octave passages, rapid skips, intricate bass tracery, fast runs, massive chords, and widely separated hands. It also has some unusual harmonies and a great sense of moving impetuously forward, with occasional slightly quieter passages serving only to heighten its overall intensity. The power and strength of the music are astounding. But the seeming randomness and uncontrollable energy are actually carefully organized.

Time	Listen for
0:00	Starts quietly with fast descending runs.
0:08	Crescendo, then quiet.
0:18	Loud and wild. Impetuous.
0:26	Descending runs again.
0:30	Surging melody in octaves in right hand, intricate passagework in left hand.
1:03	Agitated alternation of short phrases. Widely separated hands.
1:18	Heavy chordal melody in bass, fireworks in right hand.
1:30	Suddenly quiet, surging melody again, crescendo.
2:00	Descending runs again.
2:05	Slow down, quieter.
2:12	Crescendo and speed up.
2:20	Surging melody again, crescendo.
2:28	Moment of tenderness.
3:02	Huge crescendo, massive climax.
3:34	Alternating short phrases again.
3:50	Heavy bass chords again.
4:07	Contrary motion; stop.
4:12	Coda. Speed up; alternation of very high and very low.
4:37	Massive ending chords.

Verdi and Wagner

Both Giuseppe Verdi and Richard Wagner were born in 1813. Each transformed the operatic traditions he had received from the past to create new forms, and each became the musical symbol of his own country: Verdi for Italy, Wagner for Germany. In 1842 each composer had his first success. Wagner completed his first major masterpiece in 1850, Verdi in 1851. From then on, both composers turned out one great score after another, working fruitfully into old age. Wagner's last work was written when he was nearly 70, Verdi's as he approached 80. Together they made opera the central genre of mid-Romanticism.

Giuseppe Verdi (1813–1901)

In Italy today, Verdi symbolizes opera. His name inspires passionate declarations of affection, and many Italian shopkeepers, vineyard workers, professors, and politicians can sing Verdi arias by heart.

This adulation began when Verdi was still a relatively young man. He was born in a small village in northern Italy, where his father ran an inn. As a boy, he played the organ for services at the village church and conducted the town band in the small nearby town of Busseto. One of Busseto's wealthy merchants took him into his home and later sent him to Milan to study music.

Milan was the center of Italian opera and the home of the famous opera house called La Scala. Verdi resolved to become an opera composer. First he returned to Busseto and married his patron's daughter. He was 23, while his new wife was 16. Filled with hope, he returned to Milan and threw himself into composition. But tragedy struck. Within two years, the couple's two babies died; then Verdi's young wife, the girl with whom he had walked in the hills and fields of the Italian countryside, also died.

Verdi was overcome by depression and decided to compose no more. One night, however, the concert manager at La Scala made him take home a new libretto (opera text) called *Nabucco* (*Nebuchadnezzar*). According to Verdi's own account, the libretto first fell open on the chorus of the Jewish prisoners who mourn their native land by the waters of Babylon. "I was much moved," he said, "because the verses were almost a paraphrase from the Bible, the reading of which had always delighted me." He spent the whole night reading and rereading the libretto, and by the next day he was already working on his new opera. *Nabucco* was produced at La Scala in 1842 and was a great success. It brought Verdi fame throughout Italy, and by the end of the decade his name was known around the world.

Verdi followed *Nabucco* with a string of wonderful operas. During the next 11 years, he wrote 15 operas, including *Rigoletto* (1851), *Il trovatore* (1853), and *La traviata* (1853). By now Verdi was a wealthy man. He bought a country estate near his hometown and lived the life of a country gentleman. He married his second wife, a singer who had starred in his early operas, and their deep and devoted relationship lasted for nearly half a century.

Verdi's pace of composition relaxed, but the depth and richness of his music only increased. He became more and more involved in the details of the libretto and the staging of his works. In the 1860s and 1870s he wrote three fine operas, including the great *Aida* (1871), which was commissioned to celebrate the opening of the Suez Canal.

Although he spoke several times of retirement, Verdi was persuaded in his 70s to tackle two Shakespearean projects. The results of this final surge of creativity were two of his greatest masterpieces: *Otello* (1887) based on Shakespeare's tragedy *Othello*, and *Falstaff* (1893) based on Shakespeare's comedy *The Merry Wives of Windsor*.

Giuseppe Verdi.

During his life, Verdi became a national symbol. The chorus of Jewish prisoners in *Nabucco* lamenting the loss of their homeland was heard as a cry of the Italian people against their Austrian rulers. In other operas, a woman yearning for rescue or references to a free Italy were greeted with frenzy by audiences and provoked political demonstrations. Even Verdi's name became a rallying cry for the Italian nationalist movement. After independence in 1870, Verdi was named an honorary member of the new parliament. And when he died, at the age of 88, Italy declared a national day of mourning.

Verdi's Music

Verdi wrote in genres other than opera. His choral works include a magnificent Requiem Mass. He also wrote several songs and a fine string quartet. But it is on his remarkable operas that his reputation rests. During his long life, he completed 28 full-length operas, among which are some of the best-loved operas in the world.

What is the secret of Verdi's success? First and foremost, the secret lies in his melodies. His gift for vocal writing has never been exceeded, and singers and listeners alike love his soaring vocal lines. The second special element is rhythm. Verdi specialized in writing stirring rhythms that can set the heart pounding. But finally, the

Our music differs from German music. Their symphonies can live in halls, their chamber music in the home. Our music resides principally in the opera house.
—Giuseppe Verdi

Find the **Quick Listen** on **MySearchLab** "Verdi Chorus of the Hebrew Slaves"

I want subjects that are novel, big, beautiful, varied, and bold—as bold as can be.
—Giuseppe Verdi

true essence of a Verdi opera is in the human drama. Verdi constantly sought out dramatic situations, full of strong emotional resonance, violent contrasts, and quick action. He loved to explore the human emotional reaction to exciting or terrifying events.

As Verdi continued to compose, from the 1840s to the 1880s, his style became more fluid. In place of the set recitative-aria style of earlier Italian opera, Verdi created a continuing musical flow in which the drama could unfold naturally, held together by the orchestral accompaniment. Throughout the story, Verdi's orchestra binds the voices together in duets, trios, and ensembles; keeps the action moving; and supplies rich and colorful harmonies to underpin moments of climax or poignancy. Verdi also uses the orchestra to sound out musical motives that have symbolic content or to refer to people in the story as the drama progresses.

LISTENING GUIDE

((•—Listen on **MySearchLab**

GIUSEPPE VERDI (1813–1901)

Otello (*Excerpt*)

Date of composition: 1887
Duration: 6:47

CD II, 14

Otello was the last of Verdi's tragic operas. Inspired by Shakespeare's play *Othello*, it has a libretto by Arrigo Boïto (1842–1918).

Dramatic interest in this work lies not so much in the tragic plot as in the portrayal of human emotions. The story revolves around the evil cunning of Iago, a junior officer in the Venetian army. He is intensely jealous of the promotion of his friend Cassio to a high post. Iago is determined to destroy Cassio's career by deceiving Otello into thinking that Cassio is having an affair with Otello's new wife, Desdemona.

Much of the musical interest in *Otello* (and in many of Verdi's operas) lies in the use of accompanied recitative, which is a flexible form halfway between aria and recitative, and perfect for catching the changing feelings of the participants in the drama.

This excerpt begins toward the end of Act II, where Iago cleverly tries to convince his commander (Otello) that Cassio has romantic designs on Desdemona. The scene builds from the lightly accompanied opening and the representation of sleep-talk to a huge orchestral climax of sworn revenge.

Time	Listen for	
0:00	[horn, single note]	
	Iago [quiet string accompaniment]	
0:04	*Era la notte, Cassio dormia,* *gli stavo accanto.* *Con interrotte voci tradia* *l'intimo incanto.* *Le labbra lente, lente movea,* *nell'abbandono del sogno ardente;*	I watched Cassio the other night as he slept. All of a sudden he began to mutter what he was dreaming. Moving his lips slowly, very slowly, he betrayed his secret thoughts,
0:40	*e allor dicea, con flebil suono:* [separated wind chords]	saying in a passionate voice:
0:48	*"Desdemona soave!* *Il nostro amor s'asconda,* *cauti vegliamo* [back to strings]	"My sweetest Desdemona! let us be careful, cautiously hiding our love,
1:02	*l'estasi del ciel tutto m'innonda!"*	our heavenly rapture!"
1:14	[more agitated orchestral accompaniment]	

1:16	*Seguia più vago l'incubo blando;* *con molle angoscia l'interna imago,* *quasi baciando,* [menacing sounds]	Then he moved toward me and gently caressing the person in his dreams,
1:32	*ei disse poscia: "Il rio destino* *impreco che al Moro ti donò!"* [strings; high note in voice for "sogno" ("sleep")]	he said this: "Oh accursed fortune that gave you to the Moor!"
1:55	*E allora il sogno* *in cieco letargo si mutò.* **Otello** [louder]	And after his dream, he went calmly back to sleep.
2:17	*Oh, mostruosa colpa!* [brass] **Iago**	Oh, monstrous deed!
	Io non narrai che un sogno . . . **Otello** [timpani stroke on "fatto" ("truth")]	No, this was only his dreaming . . .
2:22	*Un sogno che rivela un fatto . . .* **Iago** [strings]	A dream that reveals the truth . . .
2:25	*Un sogno che può dar forma* *di prova ad altro indizio.* **Otello** [suspicious silence]	A dream that may support other evidence . . .
	E qual? **Iago** [a little slower; horn note]	What kind of evidence?
2:37	*Talor vedeste* *in mano di Desdemona* *un tessuto trapunto a fiore* *e più sottil d'un velo?* **Otello**	Have you ever seen in Desdemona's hand a handkerchief decorated with flowers and of the finest texture?
2:54	*È il fazzoletto ch'io le diedi,* *pegno primo d'amor.* **Iago** [quiet, with sudden ending]	That is the handkerchief I gave her, It was my first gift to her.
3:01	*Quel fazzoletto ieri, certo ne son* *lo vidi in man di Cassio.* **Otello** [agitated; furious; whole orchestra; fast strings]	That same handkerchief I'm sure I saw yesterday in Cassio's hand.
3:13	*Ah! Mille* *gli donasse Iddio!* *Una è povera preda al furor mio!* *Iago, ho il cuore di gelo.* *Lungi da me le pietose larve:* *Tutto il mio vano amor,* *esalo al cielo—Guardami, ei sparve!* *Nelle sue spire d'angue l'idra* *m'avvince!*	Ah! May God give the slave a thousand lives! One is all too little for my revenge! Iago, my heart is ice. Depart from me, you pitying tears. All my useless love I cast up to heaven— look, it's gone! Jealousy wraps me in its serpent's coils.
3:49	*Ah sangue! sangue! Sangue!*	Oh, blood! blood! blood!

[determined; low chords]

| 3:56 | *Si pel ciel marmoreo giuro!*
 Per le attorte folgori,
 per la Morte e per l'oscuro
 mar sterminator.
 D'ira e d'impeto tremendo,
 presto fia che
 sfolgori questa man
 ch'io levo e stendo! | I swear by yonder marble heaven <br> and the lightning above, <br> and by Death and the dark <br> destructive sea.
 Let it be soon that, <br> trembling with anger,
 I raise up this violent hand! |

Iago   [similar music]

| 4:28 | *Non v'alzate ancor!*
 Testimon è il Sol ch'io miro;
 che m'irradia e inanima,
 l'ampia terrae il vasto spiro,
 del Creato inter;
 che ad Otello io sacro ardenti,
 core, braccio ed anima s'anco
 ad opere cruenti | No, wait!
 Let the sun, on which I gaze, <br> which animates me and the wide earth <br> on which we live, you ambient air, <br> the Creator's breath: <br> witness that I eagerly dedicate to Othello <br> my heart, my hands, and my soul.
 Even if he should command me |

[whole orchestra]

| 5:01 | *s'armi suo voler!* | to bloody deeds. |

Otello & Iago   [duet, rising to a powerful climax]

| 5:07 | *Si pel ciel marmoreo giuro!*
 per le attorte folgori,
 per la Morte e per l'oscuro mar sterminator. | I swear by yonder marble heaven <br> and the lightning above, and by Death <br> and the dark destructive sea. |

[prominent brass]

| 5:25 | *D'ira e d'impeto tremendo*
 presto fia che sfolgori questa man,
 ch'io levo e stendo;
 presto fia che sfolgori questa man
 presto fia che sfolgori questa man, | Let it be soon that, <br> trembling with anger,
 I raise up this violent hand!
 Let it be soon that, <br> trembling with anger, |

| 5:46 | *ch'io levo e stendo.* | I raise up this violent hand! |

[unaccompanied]

| 5:53 | *Dio vendicator!* | God of vengeance! |

| 5:59 | [loud orchestral postlude; brass and timpani; whole orchestra] | |

| 6:13 | [End of Act II] | |

Richard Wagner (1813–1883)

Richard Wagner is a perfect example of the contradictions inherent in genius. His importance as a composer was enormous, and his writings on music, literature, and politics exerted a tremendous influence on artistic and intellectual thought throughout the second half of the nineteenth century. Yet he was an appalling egoist and an outspoken and virulent anti-Semite.

Wagner was born in Leipzig. His father died when Wagner was an infant, and when his mother married again, Wagner was educated under the influence of his stepfather, who was a writer and an artist. Wagner studied Shakespeare and Homer and was overwhelmed by hearing Beethoven for the first time. At Leipzig University he studied music, but, before completing his degree, he left to take a job in a

Wagner's art is diseased.
—Friedrich Nietzsche

Find the **Quick Listen** on **MySearchLab**
"Wagner Tannhauser Overture"

small opera house. For the next six years, Wagner learned about opera from the inside, as a chorus director and as a conductor. He married an actress, Minna Planer, and composed his own first operas. From the beginning, Wagner wrote his own librettos and was thus able to achieve remarkable unity between the drama and the music.

From the beginning, too, Wagner spent more than he earned. In 1839, he was forced to flee Germany to avoid ending up in debtor's prison. His passport and Minna's had been revoked, so they crossed the border at night and made a harrowing journey to Paris.

The two were extremely poor, and the Paris Opera would not accept Wagner's latest work, *Rienzi*, for production. He made a living by selling some music—and most of Minna's clothes! He also composed another opera, based on the folktale of *The Flying Dutchman*.

Discouraged by his reception in Paris, Wagner suddenly received news that both *Rienzi* and *The Flying Dutchman* had been accepted for production in Germany. He was overwhelmed with gratitude and swore never to leave his native land again. The operas were a great success. At the premiere of *Rienzi* at the Dresden opera house, Wagner "cried and laughed at the same time, and hugged everyone he met." At the age of 30, Wagner was appointed court conductor in Dresden.

The couple was financially comfortable for the first time, and Wagner was able to compose two more operas: *Tannhäuser* (1845) and *Lohengrin* (1848). In both operas, Wagner continued to base his librettos not on historical drama but on folk legend. *Tannhäuser* is the story of a medieval German troubadour; *Lohengrin* is based on Grimm's fairy tale of the Swan Knight of the Holy Grail.

After joining a failed coup against the monarchy in 1848, Wagner again had to leave the country. And despite his earlier vow, the next 12 years were years of exile. He and Minna settled in Zurich, and from this period date his most important writings: an essay called *The Art Work of the Future* (1849) and a book entitled *Opera and Drama* (1851). In these works, he called for a renewal of the artistic ideals of Greek antiquity, in which poetry, drama, philosophy, and music would be combined into a single work of art: the "complete art work," as Wagner called it. Music and words should be completely interwoven in a retelling of old myths, which could carry the resonance of profound human truth. This new type of opera was known as **music drama**.

Wagner spent the next 35 years fulfilling this vision. But before he did so, he revealed a far less attractive side of his personality by publishing a vicious anti-Semitic essay entitled *Jewishness in Music*. He attacked the music of Mendelssohn and other Jewish composers and called for the removal of the entire Jewish community ("this destructive foreign element") from Germany.

Wagner next started composing the poetry and the music for the largest musical project of the entire Romantic period: his cycle of music dramas entitled *The Ring of the Nibelungs*. This was to be a series of four long operas based on medieval German legend, involving

THE RING CYCLE

Wagner's *The Ring of the Nibelungs* is a cycle of four music dramas: *The Rhinegold, The Valkyries, Siegfried*, and *The Twilight of the Gods*. It represents one of the greatest achievements in the history of Western music. Its creation took Wagner more than 25 years. The four dramas together take more than 15 hours to perform.

Wagner wrote the music *and* the poetry for *The Ring*. Although the poetry is itself an impressive achievement, it is the manner in which the music describes and illuminates the poetry that is most extraordinary. Wagner's dense network of **leitmotivs**—musical phrases associated with objects, characters, events, thoughts, and feelings—adds meaning to the text and offers psychological insights into the characters and the reasons behind their actions.

The Ring explores universal and contradictory themes: love and hate, heroism and cowardice, good and evil, greed and selflessness, naïveté and unscrupulousness. Power, symbolized by the ring itself, is exposed as a corrupting force. The English playwright and critic George Bernard Shaw interpreted parts of *The Ring* as a political allegory of the oppressed masses in the nineteenth century. The German author Thomas Mann, a profound admirer of Wagner, considered the huge *Ring* cycle the equivalent of Émile Zola's cycle of novels or the epic Russian novels of Tolstoi and Dostoevski. Like those great literary masterpieces, *The Ring* is still powerfully relevant today.

gods and goddesses, dwarfs and giants, and human heroes. The central symbol of the cycle is a magic ring made of stolen gold that dooms all who possess it.

Wagner set about this enormous task with no hope of performance. Halfway through, he broke off work to write two other operas unconnected to the *Ring* cycle: *Tristan and Isolde* (1859) and *The Mastersingers of Nuremberg* (1867). Nonetheless, he was in the grip of an unstoppable creative urge. Speaking of these years later in life, he said, "The towering fires of life burned in me with such unutterable heat and brilliance that they almost consumed me."

He had affairs with other women: the wife of a French patron (her husband threatened to put a bullet through Wagner's head), the wife of a wealthy merchant who lent him money (she was the inspiration for *Tristan and Isolde*), and the new wife of a good friend (the conductor and enthusiastic Wagner supporter Hans von Bülow). Cosima von Bülow was the daughter of Franz Liszt, another loyal friend of Wagner's. The affair gradually deepened, and Wagner and Minna separated. But it was not until eight years later that Wagner and

Cosima could be married, after overcoming the objections of both Liszt and Hans von Bülow. By then the couple had already had two daughters and a son. Cosima was 32, Wagner 57.

During these last eight years, Wagner had despaired of having his new operas produced, but his hopes were suddenly realized beyond his wildest dreams. In 1864, an eighteen-year-old youth ascended the throne of Bavaria as King Ludwig II. King Ludwig was an ardent fan, having read Wagner's writings and admired his operas. He was also in love with Wagner. "An earthly being cannot match up to a divine spirit," the king wrote to Wagner. "But it can love; it can venerate. You are my first, my only love, and always will be."

For the rest of Wagner's life, his extravagant financial demands were met with unparalleled generosity by the young king. Wagner's work prospered. He was able to finish the gigantic *Ring* cycle, and he made plans for a new theater in which the four-evening event could be staged. These plans finally came to fruition in a new opera house in Bayreuth (pronounced "BYE-royt"), a small town in Bavaria.

Find the **Quick Listen** on **MySearchLab**

"Wagner Tristan and Isolde Prelude and Liebestod"

> To me *Tristan* is and remains a wonder! I shall never be able to understand how I could have written anything like it.
> —Richard Wagner

PERFORMANCE IN CONTEXT

The Home of Wagner Opera

The Bayreuth Festspielhaus, completed in 1876, is the final element in Wagner's concept of a "complete art work": the place of performance. This theater, designed by Wagner himself, is as unique in its interior as it is full of special devices to realize the composer's dream of an ideal performance space. To reach the Festspielhaus, one must first travel to Bayreuth, a modestly-sized town in the Bavarian region of Germany. Leaving the town, one proceeds north, where a massive theater looms suddenly amidst the trees. To actually enter and see an opera, one must also buy tickets years in advance, usually by joining an exclusive club or other group. None of this deters opera lovers, who speak reverently of the "pilgrimage" to Bayreuth! Once inside, the visitor enters and takes a seat in a curious, wedge-shaped hall. The stage appears unusually distant, the result of a clever design trick. There is no balcony or jutting opera box to block the stage; not even the orchestra is in sight. When the overture begins, clouds of sound roll out from the orchestra's hidden location beneath the stage. The theater seats almost 2,000, but the sound is clear and the seating tiered to allow a full view of the stage from any seat.

The interior of the Festival Theater (Festspeilhaus) in Bayreuth Germany, custom built for Richard Wagner.

Wagner's Music

Wagner's only important works are for the opera stage. His first two operas, *Rienzi* and *The Flying Dutchman*, are in the tradition of German Romantic opera, with grand scenes and with separate arias, duets, ensembles, and choruses. Already, however, Wagner was writing his own librettos and concentrating on human beings as symbols of grand ideas. (Verdi, by contrast, emphasized their basic humanity.) By the time of *Tannhäuser* and *Lohengrin*, Wagner had developed his poetic skill and found fertile ground in ancient legend. His poetry is terse and powerful. In both operas, the individual items (aria, recitative, chorus) are less distinct in musical style, and there is much more musical continuity.

The *Ring* cycle is made up of four music dramas: *The Rhinegold*, *The Valkyries*, *Siegfried*, and *The Twilight of the Gods*. In these works, Wagner developed his technique of continuity to the fullest. The music is absolutely continuous, and the orchestra carries the main musical content. The voices sing in an *arioso* style (that is, halfway between speech-like recitative and lyrical aria), blending into the instrumental fabric.

The orchestra is central to Wagner's music, and he wrote for a large one. He particularly enjoyed using brass instruments. He even invented a new musical instrument to cover the gap between the horns and the trombones. This instrument is known as a **Wagner tuba**.

The orchestra for the *Ring* uses four of them. Their sound is rounder, a little deeper, and more solemn than that of the horns.

Musical continuity in Wagner's music dramas is also achieved through harmonic means. In this, too, Wagner was a revolutionary. Instead of ending each phrase with a cadence, he tends to melt the end of one phrase into the beginning of the next. And whereas most music of the time is clearly in a specific key, Wagner's music is often so chromatic that it is hard to say which key is being used at any one point. This perfectly suits the sense of unfulfillment and longing that is the subject of the drama.

Finally, Wagner's music depends upon a technique that he invented (though it might be seen as the logical outcome of earlier musical developments). This technique is the use of **leitmotiv** (pronounced "LIGHT-moteef"). This is a German word that means "leading motive." A leitmotiv is a musical phrase or fragment that carries associations with a person, object, or idea in the drama.

You may remember that Berlioz used a recurrent theme (*idée fixe*) to refer to the beloved in his *Symphonie fantastique*. And other composers used themes associated with particular characters in their operas. Wagner's leitmotiv technique is different. First, leitmotivs can refer to many things other than a person. Leitmotivs in Wagner's music dramas are associated with a spear, longing, fate, and the

The French poet Baudelaire on Wagner's music: "I love Wagner, but the music I prefer is that of a cat hung up by its tail outside a window and trying to stick to the panes of glass with its claws."

Find the **Quick Listen** on **MySearchLab** "Wagner Ride of the Valkyries"

THE BAYREUTH FESTIVAL

Wagner laid the foundation stone for his own *Festspielhaus* ("Festival Theater") in Bayreuth on May 22, 1872. Initially, money for the project was hard to come by. However, King Ludwig's generous financial assistance enabled the theater to be completed. The first production—the entire *Ring* cycle—took place in August of 1876. The next Bayreuth Festival did not take place until 1882. The next year, on February 13, 1883, Wagner died of a heart attack.

Since Wagner's death the Bayreuth Festival has been run by members of Wagner's family. His widow and son, Cosima and Siegfried, were in charge until they both died in 1930, whereupon Winnifred, Siegfried's widow, took over. The ensuing years, 1930–1944, were clouded by Adolf Hitler's association with Winnifred and with Bayreuth.

The Bayreuth Festival closed in 1944 as a result of the Second World War. It reopened in 1951 with extraordinarily successful productions of *Parsifal* and *The Ring*, directed by Wieland Wagner, the composer's grandson. Under Wieland, Bayreuth attained a new acceptability, distancing itself from its Nazi association. Wolfgang Wagner, another of Wagner's grandsons, assumed responsibility for the Festival in 1966, following Wieland's death, and retired in 2008. Now his daughters have been named joint directors, continuing the tradition of having Wagner's descendants run the Festival. Wagner societies exist in countries around the world. Worshippers of the Wagner cult make the pilgrimage to Bayreuth for the annual Wagner Festival, though it is extremely difficult to get tickets. Music lovers may have to wait up to 10 years to obtain one.

Richard Wagner in his favorite velvet cap.

magic ring itself. Second, Wagner's leitmotivs are flexible, undergoing musical transformation as the ideas, objects, or people change in the course of the drama. Finally, Wagner uses his leitmotivs like threads in a tapestry. They can be combined, interwoven, contrasted, or blended to create an infinity of meanings.

Wagner, the political revolutionary, revolutionized music by his brilliant writing for orchestra, by making the orchestra the central "character" of his dramas, and by his development of the leitmotiv technique. In addition, Wagner's continuity of writing and tonally ambiguous harmonic style laid the foundation for the new language of twentieth-century music.

The Nationalist Composers

As explained in the previous chapter, one of the consequences of Romanticism was the growth of nationalism throughout Europe. We have seen how this affected some of the composers we have already discussed. Verdi's operas contain references to Italy's struggle for independence, and he became a national hero. Wagner's music focused on a mythic and heroic German past, and he became a symbol of German ethnic pride.

But there were other composers whose music more strongly reflects the nationalist

movements in their own countries. These composers deliberately rejected the German and Italian dominance in instrumental music and opera and fostered national pride in their own native traditions. They did this in several ways. First, they wrote operas in their own native languages—languages that had not previously been used for opera, such as Russian or Czech. Second, they based operas and symphonic poems on stories from national folklore and on descriptions of native scenes of natural beauty. Finally, composers often wove their own countries' folk tunes into their compositions to give their music a distinct national identity.

The main nineteenth-century nationalist composers were to be found in Russia, Czechoslovakia, Scandinavia, Spain, and France. In the early twentieth century, nationalism also affected Hungarian, Polish, English, and American composers.

Russia   The nationalist movement in music was first felt in Russia, where music had been dominated entirely by foreign influence. Starting in the middle of the nineteenth century, Russian composers began to write operas in their own language, on Russian themes, and they often based their librettos on literary works by the great Russian writers of the time. In the second half of the century, a group of composers known as "The Mighty Handful" set out consciously to forge a native musical tradition. Of these composers, the most stirring nationalist was Modest Mussorgsky (1839–1881), whose works include the opera *Boris Godunov*, based on a story by the Russian writer Alexander Pushkin; the series of pieces known as *Pictures at an Exhibition*, which describe paintings hanging in a gallery in St. Petersburg; and the symphonic poem *Night on Bald Mountain*, based on a short story by Nicolai Gogol, a Russian writer from the first half of the century. This last composition is vividly illustrated in the animated film *Fantasia*.

Bohemia   Bohemia had been an independent kingdom until it was taken over by Austria in the fifteenth century. (For most of the twentieth century, it formed part of Czechoslovakia but is now a region in the Czech Republic.) The two principal Bohemian composers of the nineteenth century were Bedřich Smetana (1824–1884) and Antonin Dvořák (1841–1904). Smetana based his most famous opera, *The Bartered Bride*, on Bohemian folklore.

Find the **Quick Listen** on **MySearchLab**

"Night on Bald Mountain Fantasia"

Another well-known piece by Smetana is the symphonic poem *The Moldau*, which describes the flow of a river across the Bohemian countryside. It cleverly combines depictions of nature with feelings of national pride. Dvořák wrote symphonies, concertos, operas, choral works, and chamber music. Chief among these are the Ninth (*New World*) Symphony (which he wrote in America), the Cello Concerto, and his *Slavonic Dances* for orchestra. The *New World* Symphony combines American themes with Bohemian folk melodies. Dvořák hoped it would inspire American composers to become nationalists. "America can have her own music," he said.

The United States America did have her own music, although a fully-developed American style did not flourish until the twentieth century. The history of classical music in America reaches back to Colonial times, during which period the most significant composer was William Billings (1746–1800), a composer of rough-hewn (he called himself a "carver") and highly original settings of psalms and songs for unaccompanied chorus. His publication in 1770 of *The New-England Psalm-Singer* marked the appearance of the very first published collection of American music.

In the nineteenth century, the American tradition was kept alive in the South and the Midwest by means of "shape-note" books, in which pitches are indicated (for people who cannot read music) by simple signs such as small triangles, circles, and squares. One of the best-known of these shape-note hymn collections is *The Sacred Harp*, published in 1844. African American spirituals were sung widely throughout the nineteenth century, although the first published collection of spirituals did not appear until 1867. And in the Midwest, one of the most original American composers, Anthony Heinrich (1781–1861, known as "the Beethoven of Kentucky") wrote elaborate and complex orchestral works descriptive of nature on the frontier.

But the rough-and-ready style of American music was soon overwhelmed by more "proper," European-trained composers. One of these was Lowell Mason (1792–1872), who wrote over a thousand hymn settings, some of which may still be found in Protestant hymnals.

Until the end of the nineteenth century, American music and music making were still strongly influenced by the European tradition. The United States did not participate in the nationalist wave that swept through many other countries from the 1860s to the 1890s. During this period, America was absorbed by its own inner turmoil: the Civil War, the assassination of President Lincoln, and Reconstruction. American composers, mostly trained in Europe, paid little attention to the enormously varied indigenous music around them: African American spirituals, New England hymn tunes, Native American songs and dances, the music of jazz bands, revival-meeting songs, and Irish-Scottish-English-American folk melodies. And the American public was interested almost entirely in imported music: Italian operas, Handel's English oratorios, and above all, German symphonies and chamber music.

Moravia Moravia—formerly independent, then a part of Czechoslovakia, and now a region of the Czech Republic—was the homeland of Leoš Janářek (1854–1928). Janářek collected authentic Moravian folk songs and was a great and innovative composer. His superb Czech operas and his two fine string quartets were written primarily in the 1920s.

Scandinavia Norway produced the most famous Scandinavian nationalist composer, Edvard Grieg (1843–1907). Grieg specialized in piano miniatures inspired by Norwegian tunes. His well-known orchestral *Peer Gynt* Suite was written for the play of the same name by the Norwegian writer Henrik Ibsen. The Danish composer Carl Nielsen (1865–1931) was an individualist whose main works (operas, symphonies, and string quartets) belong to the first two decades of the twentieth century. The leading composer of Finland was Jan Sibelius (1865–1957). He wrote seven superb symphonies and a deeply emotional string quartet, but his most famous work is the symphonic poem *Finlandia* (1899), whose intense national flavor caused it to be banned by the Russian rulers in Finland, though it was an immense success throughout the rest of Europe.

Spain The principal nationalist composers of Spain were Enrique Granados (1867–1916), Isaac Albéniz (1860–1909), and Manuel de Falla (1876–1946). Granados and Albéniz wrote piano suites in lively Spanish rhythms and with colorful melodies. De Falla is best known for his wonderful *Nights in the Gardens of Spain*, a series of three evocative and atmospheric pieces for piano and orchestra.

Watch the **Inside the Orchestra** video on **MySearchLab**

Find the **Quick Listen** on **MySearchLab** "Jean Sibelius – Finlandia"

Find the **Quick Listen** on **MySearchLab** "Nights in the Gardens of Spain"

Find the **Quick Listen** on **MySearchLab**

"Saint Saëns *Carnival of the Animals*"

France After the end of the Franco-Prussian War in 1871, a National Society for French Music was founded to encourage French composers. The most gifted of these were Camille Saint-Saëns (1835–1921) and Gabriel Fauré (1845–1924). Saint-Saëns' *Carnival of the Animals* for chamber orchestra is great fun; his Symphony No. 3 is a more serious work, but also very attractive. Fauré wrote exquisite French songs to poems by some of the leading French poets of his day.

Pyotr Ilyich Tchaikovsky (1840–1893)

The Russian composer Pyotr Ilyich Tchaikovsky wrote operas in Russian based on works of Russian literature and also made use of Russian folk songs—but he was not as committed a nationalist as some of his contemporaries. It may be partly for this reason that he achieved international success as a composer in the mid- to late-Romantic period. Therefore we shall consider him separately and in detail here.

Tchaikovsky's father was a Russian mining engineer. His mother, with whom he was very close, was of French extraction. He had piano lessons as a child and did some composing, but he turned to music as his main emotional outlet only after his mother died when he was 14. Tchaikovsky began to earn a living as a government clerk at the age of 19, but when the new St. Petersburg Music Conservatory was founded, he quit his job and entered the Conservatory as a full-time student. A family friend described him as "poor but profoundly happy" at having chosen music as a career. His talents were such that a year after graduating, he was appointed professor at the music conservatory in Moscow.

In Moscow he met many other composers and publishers and flourished in the lively atmosphere of the cosmopolitan city. He also traveled abroad. He wrote articles and a book on music and composed prolifically.

A portrait of Tchaikovsky.

> Repulsive and barbaric.
> —a Viennese newspaper on Tchaikovsky's Violin Concerto

> Where words fail, music speaks.
> —Tchaikovsky, quoting the German writer Heinrich Heine

All this time, however, Tchaikovsky lived with a secret: he was gay. He was tormented by self-hatred and the fear of being exposed. In 1877, at the age of 37, he suddenly decided to get married. Partly he may have felt that this step might "cure" him; partly he may have thought he needed the cover. The marriage was an instant disaster. Tchaikovsky fled, attempted suicide, and had a nervous breakdown.

After some months of convalescence, Tchaikovsky gradually recovered and turned once more to music. Both his Fourth Symphony and his opera *Eugene Onyegin* date from this time, and both contain powerful reflections of his emotional state.

COPYRIGHT

Before the first international convention on the issue of copyright, held in Berne, Switzerland, in 1886, composers' works were unprotected. There was little that famous composers could do to prevent "pirate" editions of their works from circulating. Unscrupulous publishers would simply get hold of a copy of the work and then print and sell copies of it. A fundamental principle was established at Berne, namely that a published work (including a musical one) is protected under copyright during the author's or composer's lifetime and for 50 years following his or her death; the principle has remained more or less intact to the present day. In addition, regarding musical works, a fee must be paid for each *performance* of a work, including the playing of a recorded performance.

A strange turn of events helped to provide emotional and financial support for Tchaikovsky. A wealthy widow named Madame von Meck decided to become his patron. She said she would commission some pieces and provide the composer with an annual income. There was only one condition: the two must never meet. This suited Tchaikovsky perfectly, and for the next 13 years Madame von Meck and Tchaikovsky carried on an intense personal relationship without ever seeing each other. They shared their innermost thoughts, but only by letter, and they wrote to each other every day.

Tchaikovsky was able to resign his teaching post, and he composed a great deal of music during those years. In 1890, Madame von Meck suddenly broke off the relationship and the patronage. No explanation was offered, although her family may have put pressure on her to direct her funds elsewhere. Tchaikovsky was deeply hurt, but by now he had a substantial income from his music, and the Russian czar had provided him with a life pension.

In his last years, Tchaikovsky wrote some of his best-known music, including a ballet entitled *The Nutcracker* and his Sixth Symphony, subtitled *Pathétique* ("Emotional"). Tchaikovsky died in 1893, apparently of cholera, though it has been suggested that, threatened with public exposure of his homosexuality, he committed suicide.

Tchaikovsky's Music

Tchaikovsky's music is highly emotional. It surges with passion and appeals directly to the senses. The range of expression is very great, from the depths of despair to the height of joy. There is sensuousness, delicacy, nobility, tenderness, and fire. *The Nutcracker* is one of the most popular ballet scores in the world, though it is followed closely by *Sleeping Beauty* and *Swan Lake* (both also by Tchaikovsky!). The Fourth and Sixth Symphonies are deeply emotional utterances, and his operas, such as *Eugene Onyegin* and *The Queen of Spades*, though less well-known, are powerfully dramatic works. Tchaikovsky also wrote three piano concertos, the first of which is very famous, as well as a violin concerto that enraptures audiences every time it is played.

Tchaikovsky used an orchestra of moderate size; he never went to the extremes of some other romantic composers, but he was very interested in orchestral color. There is little in music to match the stirring brass fanfare at the beginning of the Fourth Symphony or the

paired clarinets at the beginning of the Sixth. For "The Dance of the Sugar-Plum Fairy" in *The Nutcracker*, Tchaikovsky contrasts the delicate shimmery sound of the celesta with the deep richness of a bass clarinet.

Tchaikovsky was a master of melody. Many of his tunes have been featured in famous popular songs or as soundtracks to movies. He sometimes used folk tunes, but most of his melodies came from his own inexhaustible lyrical gift. Tchaikovsky was a Russian composer, as he always insisted, but his music speaks to millions of people who have never even been to Russia.

Late Romanticism

Toward the end of the nineteenth century, a new atmosphere reigned in Europe and the United States. Independence and unification brought more stability to many countries, and there were moves toward greater democracy, with monarchies being replaced by parliamentary governments, and slavery abolished in the United States, Latin America, and Russia. Free compulsory schooling led to a more educated public, and the early horrors of the sweatshops were gradually replaced by better working conditions. Commerce and industry were central preoccupations, and a more down-to-earth attitude replaced the dreamy fantasyland of high Romanticism. The movement known as Realism affected all culture, from the novels of Dickens, Flaubert, and Zola to the plays of Henrik Ibsen, the paintings of Gustave Courbet, and the philosophy of William James. Music was also affected, as we shall see. As the end of the century approached, a spirit of general dissatisfaction and uneasiness took hold.

The major composers of late Romanticism were Johannes Brahms, Giacomo Puccini, and Gustav Mahler. All these composers reflected the new atmosphere in different ways. Brahms found new force in the rigor of Classic and Baroque musical genres and forms. Puccini wrote dramatic realist operas of acute psychological insight. Mahler created a new synthesis of song and symphony in a mood tinged with resignation.

Johannes Brahms (1833–1897)

Johannes Brahms was born in Hamburg in 1833. His father was an orchestral and band musician; his mother came from a wealthy family and was 44 when Brahms was born, a fact that may have colored Brahms's later

Find the **Quick Listen** on **MySearchLab**
"Tchaikovsky Dance of the Swans"

Find the **Quick Listen** on **MySearchLab**
"Tchaikovsky Symphony 4, First Movement"

Johannes Brahms.

Find the **Quick Listen** on **MySearchLab**
"Four Serious Songs"

relationship with Clara Schumann, who was 14 years older than he was.

Brahms was a child prodigy. He gave his first piano recital at the age of 10, and an American entrepreneur tried to book him for a concert tour of the United States, but his piano teacher refused to let him go. Brahms spent much of his youth playing the piano at bars and coffee houses; he also wrote pieces for his father's band. While still a youth, he was exposed to Hungarian gypsy music as a result of the flight of many nationalist rebels from Hungary after the Hungarian uprising of 1848. This led to a fascination with gypsy tunes and rhythms. Brahms also met the great violinist Joseph Joachim, with whom he developed a lifelong friendship.

But the real turning point for Brahms came when he was 20 and he met Robert Schumann. Brahms played some of his own compositions for the great Romantic master in Schumann's study. After a few minutes, Schumann stopped him and went to fetch Clara. "Now you will hear music such as you have never heard before," he said to her. During the time of Schumann's illness, Brahms and Clara Schumann became very close. Their friendship lasted until Clara's death 43 years later, one year before Brahms's own.

Throughout his life, Brahms compared himself, mostly unfavorably, with other great composers of the past, especially Beethoven. He said that he felt the presence of Beethoven as "the step of a giant over my shoulder." It took him 20 years to summon the courage to publish his First Symphony.

Brahms settled in Vienna, the imperial capital, where he made a name for himself as a pianist. "He plays so brightly and clearly," wrote Joseph Joachim. "I have never met such talent." He also worked as a conductor. Brahms lived a quiet, reserved life, and although he enjoyed the company of many friends, he also needed a great deal of solitude. He usually hid his feelings. Clara Schumann, who knew him better than anyone else, called him "a riddle." In his musical life, he was not pleased to be seen as a symbol of conservatism and the leader of an "antimodern" movement in music. Wagner attacked him mercilessly in print, calling him a "street-musician," a "hypocrite," and a "eunuch."

Brahms deliberately avoided the innovative genres of modern music, such as the symphonic poem and music drama, preferring instead solo piano pieces, songs, choral works, chamber music, concertos, and symphonies. He continued to be conscious of the great achievements of the past. The last movement of his First Symphony makes a deliberate reference to Beethoven's Ninth, and the last movement of his Fourth Symphony uses a Baroque form and is based on a theme by Bach.

Throughout the years, Brahms continued to rely on Clara Schumann for advice and comments on his compositions. Her enormous enthusiasm undoubtedly bolstered his self-confidence. But in the spring of 1896 came terrible news: Clara had died of a stroke. Brahms traveled to Bonn to attend her funeral. On his return, he wrote one of his most beautiful works, the *Four Serious Songs* for piano and voice on texts that Brahms selected from the Bible. The fourth song, with a text from Corinthians, describes the immortality of love: "These three things endure: faith, hope, and love; but the greatest of these is love." A month after Clara's funeral, Brahms was diagnosed with cancer. He died on April 3, 1897, at the age of 64. Large crowds attended his funeral, and messages of sadness poured in from all over Europe. In the great port city of Hamburg, where Brahms had been born, all the ships lowered their flags to half-mast.

Brahms's Music

Brahms was a Romantic who expressed himself in Classic and sometimes even Baroque forms; within these forms, his music is highly original. Brahms avoided the fashionable genres of Romantic music, such as opera and symphonic poems. And he wrote no program music, though he liked to hide references to women he admired in his compositions. He adored the human voice, and his Romantic songs follow directly in the line of Schubert and Schumann. The main themes of his songs are love, nature, and (toward the end of his life) death. He also set many folk songs to music. The most famous of these is the exquisite "Lullaby," Op. 49, No. 4 (sometimes called "Brahms's Lullaby"), which is often used in music boxes or toys for babies.

His four symphonies are masterpieces—the first and the fourth powerful and intense, the second and the third more lyrical and serene. We shall study a movement from the Fourth Symphony. (See Listening Guide.) The Violin Concerto stands with those of Beethoven, Mendelssohn, and Tchaikovsky as one of the great violin concertos of the nineteenth century. It is technically impressive, powerful, and lively, but it also has passages of great calm and beauty. Brahms's two piano concertos are also masterpieces. In all his orchestral works, Brahms used an orchestra not much bigger than Beethoven's, avoiding the huge, showy sounds of Wagner and Liszt. One characteristic of Brahms's style is his thick orchestral textures. He liked to "fill in" the sound between treble and bass with many musical lines, and to double melodies in thirds or sixths. He especially favored instruments that play in the middle range, such as clarinet, viola, and French horn.

This warmth of sound may be found in his chamber music as well. Because he was a fine pianist, Brahms wrote several chamber works for piano and strings, but he also composed some excellent string quartets. His love of rich textures is shown in the two string *quintets* and two string *sextets*. Toward the end of his life, after he had decided to give up composition, Brahms met a fine clarinetist who inspired him to write several chamber works featuring the clarinet. In all these works there is passion, but the passion is mingled with resignation and an autumnal sense of peace. Brahms's solo piano music was written mostly for his own performance. The early pieces are strong and showy, but the later ones are much more delicate and profound.

Brahms composed several choral works. The most important of these is the *German Requiem*, for soprano and baritone soloists, chorus, and orchestra, for which Brahms chose his own texts from the German Bible. It was written not for a religious service but for concert performance. Nevertheless, the music is sincere and deeply felt. Brahms was a man who did not believe in organized religion, yet he was privately devout and read every day from the Bible he had owned since childhood.

Brahms has been called a conservative composer because of his adherence to models from the past. Yet he was an innovator in many ways. His rhythms are always complex and interesting, with syncopation and offbeat accents and with a very frequent use of mixed duple and triple meters. His phrases are often irregular—expanded or contracted from the usual four- or eight-bar format. And he was a master of variation, in which something familiar is constantly undergoing change. Indeed, in Brahms's music there is very little exact repetition or recapitulation: the music seems to grow organically from beginning to end. Brahms himself was both complex and fascinating, and the same can be said of his music.

Find the **Quick Listen** on **MySearchLab**
"Brahms "Lullaby" in German"

Find the **Quick Listen** on **MySearchLab**
"German Requiem Brahms"

LISTENING GUIDE

((•—Listen on MySearchLab

JOHANNES BRAHMS (1833–1897)   *Fourth Movement from Symphony No. 4 in E Minor*

Date of composition: 1885
Orchestration: two flutes, two oboes, two clarinets, two bassoons, contrabassoon, four French horns, two trumpets, three trombones, timpani, full string section
Tempo: *Allegro energico e passionato* ("Fast, energetic, and passionate")
Meter: ¾
Key: E minor
Duration: 10:37

CD III, 1

The fourth movement of Brahms's Symphony No. 4 is based on a regularly repeating eight-measure harmonic progression. This form is known as a *passacaglia*, a variation form that was popular with Baroque composers. Brahms's use of this form shows how he valued the musical past as a source of inspiration.

The repetitive harmonic element gives the movement a clear and accessible form, and the eight-measure patterns can be followed simply by counting. The harmonic progression is not repeated strictly each time but is used instead as a flexible point of departure. The variations range from pure harmonic chord progressions, as in the initial statement, to melodic ideas.

The initial presentation of the theme is bold, strong, and direct. Although this statement is primarily harmonic—a series of chords—it also has a powerful melodic element: a relentless ascending line that dramatically drops an octave just before the end. The theme begins in the tonic key and moves to the dominant in measure 6 before returning to the tonic. All these features—the eight-measure structure, the melodic line, and the harmonic trajectory—are drawn on for all the variations that ensue. This technique creates a movement of great strength.

Winds and Trombones

In addition to these basic elements, Brahms organizes the work by grouping the 30 variations into three large sections. The middle section contrasts with the outer sections; the last section includes some varied restatements of earlier material. Thus, the larger form of this movement is another manifestation of one that is by now very familiar: ABA', with a Coda.

A	**B**	**A'**	**CODA**
Theme, and Variations 1–11	Variations 12–15	Variations 16–30	

Within these large groups, Brahms focuses our attention by grouping similar variations together. Variations that share related ideas are bracketed in the timed description that follows.

Time	Listen for
	A section [minor key, $\frac{3}{4}$ meter]
0:00	Theme. Strong, measure-long chords, ascending melodic line, brass and woodwinds. (Count the eight measures.)
0:16	*Variation 1* Also chordal, with timpani rolls and string pizzicatos on the second beat of the measures.
0:30	*Variation 2* Smooth melody with regular rhythmic values and smooth motion. Flutes join clarinets and oboes in a crescendo.
0:46	*Variation 3* The regular rhythm of the melody is given a staccato articulation; brass is added.
1:01	*Variation 4* The ascending melody of the theme is used as a bass line in the lower strings, while the violins introduce a new melody, featuring leaping motion and jumpy rhythms.
1:18	*Variation 5* Violins elaborate this melody with faster rhythms; accompaniment thickens with arpeggios.
1:33	*Variation 6* Rhythms become even faster and more intense, building to the next variation.
1:48	*Variation 7* New melodic idea, with the violins strained in their upper register, and a new jumpy rhythm.
2:04	*Variation 8* Faster rhythms (sixteenth notes) used in violins, busy energetic feel; violins repeat a single high note while the flute plays a smoother melodic line.

2:19	*Variation 9* Suddenly loud; even faster rhythms (sixteenth-note triplets), violins swoop from high to low range; decrescendo with violins again on repeated note; descending chromatic scale in the winds.
2:35	*Variation 10* Calm exchanges of chords between winds and strings.
2:53	*Variation 11* More chord exchanges, but the violins elaborate theirs with faster, detached notes. Descending and slowing chromatic scale in the flute connects to solo of the next variation.
	B section [Here the new, slower tempo and meter ($\frac{3}{2}$) result in longer variations, although they are still eight measures. The descending chromatic scale that ended Variation 11 also ends Variations 13, 14, and 15.]
3:14	*Variation 12* Flute solo that restlessly ascends, gradually reaching into higher ranges, and then descends. Duple pattern in accompaniment emphasizes the new meter.
3:57	*Variation 13* Change to brighter E major. Much calmer mood. Clarinet and oboe alternate simple phrases. Duple pattern in accompaniment continues, supplemented by long rising arpeggios in the strings.
4:36	*Variation 14* Trombones enter with chordal, hymnlike sound. Short rising arpeggios in the strings are the only accompaniment.
5:17	*Variation 15* Brass and winds continue rich, chordal sound, with fuller string arpeggios, as in Variation 14. Descending line in flute slows to a halt.
	A' section [The return of the A material is bold and dramatic. The faster tempo has renewed drive and energy after the contemplative B section.]
6:03	*Variation 16* Repeat of the original statement of the theme, only joined in measure 4 by searingly high violins descending a scale. Back to E minor and $\frac{3}{4}$.
6:16	*Variation 17* String tremolos crescendo and decrescendo while winds emphasize beats 2 and 3 of the $\frac{3}{4}$ meter.
6:27	*Variation 18* String tremolos continue while winds and brass exchange a jumpy figure that builds in a rising melody.
6:40	*Variation 19* *f*; new staccato articulation as strings and winds alternate bold eighth-note gestures.
6:53	*Variation 20* Staccato figure builds in intensity, using faster triplet rhythm.
7:05	*Variation 21* Swift ascending scales in strings, ending with accented notes, alternate with brass unison attacks rising in pitch.

7:18	**Variation 22**
	p; syncopated quarter notes, creating a two-against-three feeling, are exchanged with staccato triplet figures.
7:30	**Variation 23**
	Suddenly *f*; theme in French horns, triplet figures build in strings and winds, ending in eighth notes moving by leaps.
7:44	**Variation 24**
	With its accents on beat 2, this variation recalls Variation 1 but is much more forceful, with heavy accents.
7:59	**Variation 25**
	Here the soft melody of Variation 2 returns, now frenzied in intensity through the loud volume and string tremolos. Emphasis on beat 2 continues with brass and timpani repeated notes.
8:12	**Variation 26**
	The staccato quarter notes of Variation 3 are smooth and rich here, in the French horns, then moving to the oboes.
8:25	**Variation 27**
	Sustained chords in the high winds, with smooth arpeggios rising and falling in the violas and cellos.
8:40	**Variation 28**
	Sustained melody in winds becomes more active; faster arpeggios rise to violins and violas.
8:53	**Variation 29**
	Rising two-note figures in flutes, accompanied by syncopated string offbeats; ends with stepwise violin melody.
9:07	**Variation 30**
	Suddenly *f*; accented quarter notes, with offbeats; slight slowing and ever wider leaps in the violins; four additional measures outside of the theme move us into the Coda.
	Coda
9:29	Based on melodic outline of theme; increasing tempo; high violin line accompanied by driving arpeggios and tremolos; two-note exchanges between high and low.
9:51	Trombones with two accented, compressed statements of the theme melody, punctuated by strings.
9:59	Violins crescendo; winds play theme statements answered by orchestra; strings and winds in a syncopated statement of the theme; vigorous descending arpeggios weight the concluding chords.

Giacomo Puccini (1858–1924)

The greatest opera composer of the late nineteenth century was Giacomo Puccini. He grew up in Lucca, a medieval town near the coast of Italy. Puccini came from a family of musicians: his father, grandfather, great-grandfather, and great-great-grandfather were all composers. At the age of 14, he became the organist at Lucca, and he surprised the congregation by working the tunes of opera arias into his organ playing during services. He was in love with opera, and after he saw a performance of Verdi's *Aida* at the age of 18, he decided to become an opera composer himself.

Puccini went to Milan, the opera capital of Italy, and spent many years there leading a typical student life, refining his composing skills, and soaking up opera. After graduation, he got his first break when he played and sang portions of one of his own works at a private party. An important promoter and the head of the largest publishing firm in Italy were at the party, and they were so impressed they decided to publish the opera and stage it. Puccini spent five years on his next opera, which was not a success.

For both of these early works, Puccini had relied on other people's choice of libretto. Now he decided to choose his own. At 35, he produced the first of his string of immortal Romantic operas: *Manon Lescaut*, based on a French love story. It came in the same year as the last opera of the grand old man of Italian opera, Verdi. Immediately, Puccini was hailed as "the heir of Verdi." He was an overnight success, his fortune was assured, and his name traveled around the world. *Manon Lescaut* was followed by *La Bohème* (1896), *Tosca* (1900), and *Madama Butterfly* (1904), three of the most popular operas in the entire repertory. They are all cast in the new *verismo* (realist) mode of opera. *La Bohème* tells the story of a group of poor students and artists living in Paris; *Tosca* contains scenes of attempted rape, murder, execution, and suicide; and *Madama Butterfly* describes the pathetic death of a devoted Japanese geisha girl. But all three are also full of life, love, and passion.

Puccini's next opera, *La fanciulla del West* (*The Girl of the Golden West*, 1910), was given its premiere at the Metropolitan Opera House in New York. This is Puccini's "American" opera, set in the "Wild West," with saloons, guns, and a manhunt. For the premiere, the great Arturo Toscanini was the conductor, and the legendary tenor Enrico Caruso took the leading male role.

Puccini's last opera was *Turandot*, set in China and based on a Chinese folk story. It was not quite finished when Puccini died in 1924. A colleague completed the last two scenes, and the first performance was given in 1926 at the great opera house of La Scala in Milan. Puccini's death was declared a national day of mourning in Italy.

Before he died, Puccini wrote, "When I was born, the Almighty touched me with his little finger and said: 'Write operas—mind you, only operas!' And I have obeyed the supreme command."

Puccini's Music

Puccini's music never fails to stir the strongest emotions. His senses of timing, drama, and poignancy are perfect, and he is able to

Giacomo Puccini.

Find the **Quick Listen** on **MySearchLab**
"*La Boheme* Si Mi Chiamano Mimi"

Find the **Quick Listen** on **MySearchLab**
"*Turandot* Nessun Dorma"

set a scene or a mood with just a few phrases of music. His melodies soar, and the vocal lines are buoyed up on waves of orchestral sound. A trademark of his style is the doubling or even tripling of the vocal lines by the orchestra, especially in the strings, so that the voices gain an almost luminous intensity. Puccini also wrote fresh and modern harmonies, with some strong dissonances and unexpected chord progressions, and these serve to heighten the drama. Sometimes he also employed unusual scales, such as the pentatonic scale, to suggest an exotic locale.

The action in Puccini operas is continuous, with short orchestral phrases woven together under the sung dialogue. For the most part, there is little distinction between recitative and aria, although in each of his operas there are some arias that are unforgettable. We will listen to one of them: the exquisite, passionate, heartbreaking melody of an aria from *Madama Butterfly*. "Without melody," said Puccini, "there can be no music."

LISTENING GUIDE

GIACOMO PUCCINI (1858–1924)

"Un bel dì" ("One Fine Day") from Madama Butterfly

Date of composition: 1904
Duration: 4:31

CD II, 15

Madama Butterfly, one of Puccini's most beloved operas, premiered in 1904, at a time when American naval vessels frequented Japanese seaports. Oriental customs and exotic scenery provide the background for this tragic plot, which involves Benjamin Franklin Pinkerton (an American lieutenant) and Cio-Cio-San ("Butterfly," a young Japanese girl). Pinkerton has rented a Japanese house for a period of 999 years. Also in the rental package is his "betrothal" to Cio-Cio-San.

Treating the marriage merely as a casual affair, Pinkerton returns to America after the wedding, and he marries an American woman shortly thereafter. When he returns to Japan three years later with his American wife, the deeply loyal Cio-Cio-San, in grief and humiliation, kills herself.

Butterfly's aria "Un bel dì" comes near the beginning of Act II, as she tries to convince herself and her servant that her husband will return to her. You will hear gorgeous soaring melodies and exotic "Oriental" sounds in this superb *da capo* (ABA) aria. Listen to the doubling and sometimes tripling of the vocal line in the orchestra, which gives great richness to Puccini's wonderful lyricism.

Time	Listen for	
	A section [voice doubled in orchestra]	
0:00	*Un bel dì, vedremo levarsi un fil di* *fuomo sull' estremo confin del mare.* *E poi la nave appare.* *Poi la nave bianca* *Entra nel porto,* [timpani; voice tripled in orchestra for second line]	One fine day, we'll notice a thread of smoke rising on the horizon of the sea. And then the ship will appear. Then the white vessel will glide into the harbor,
0:50	*romba il suo saluto.* *Vedi? È venuto!* *Io non gli scendo incontro,* *Io no...*	thundering forth her cannon. Do you see? He has come! I don't go to meet him, Not I...
	B section [delicate accompaniment]	
1:18	*Mi metto lá sul ciglio del colle,* *e aspetto, e aspetto gran tempo,* *e non mi pesa la lunga attesa.* [more movement]	I stay on the brow of the hill, and wait there, wait for a long time, but never weary of the long waiting.
1:44	*E...uscito dalla folla cittadina* *un uomo, un picciol punto,* [slowing down]	From the crowded city comes a man, a little speck in the distance,
2:00	*s'avia per la collina.* [very quiet]	climbing the hill.
2:15	*Chi sarà? chi sarà?* *E come sara giunto,* *che dirà? che dirà?* [slower, with solo violin, then clarinet]	Who is it? Who is it? And when he's reached the summit, what will he say? What will he say?
2:24	*Chiamerà "Butterfly"* *dalla lontana.* *Io senza dar riposta me* *ne star nascosta,*	He will call "Butterfly" from a distance. And I, without answering, will keep myself quietly concealed,

	un po' per celia, e un po' per non...	a bit to tease him, and a bit so as not to...

A section [return to original melody; voice tripled then doubled in orchestra]

2:52	morire al primo incontro, ed egli alquanto in pena, chiamerà, chiamerà, "Piccina mogliettina, olezzo di verbena!", i nomi che mi dava al suo venire. [crescendo]	die at our first meeting, and then, a little troubled, he will call, he will call, "Dearest, little wife of mine, dear little orange blossom!" the names he used to call me when he first came here.
3:28	Tutto questo avverrà, te lo prometto. [climax]	This will come to pass, I promise you.
3:34	Tienti la tua paura, io con sicura fede l'aspetto.	Banish your idle fears, I know for certain he will come.
3:48	[lush orchestral postlude]	
4:19	[final chords]	

Gustav Mahler (1860–1911)

Gustav Mahler was the last great Romantic composer. In his work, Romantic song and the Romantic symphony come together in a final (somewhat nostalgic) triumph of late Romanticism. Mahler was born in Bohemia of Jewish parents and made his career in Germany and Austria. His musical talent was evident at an early age, and he gave his first public piano recital at the age of 10. Mahler lived near a military base, and when he was small, he loved to listen to the marching bands. Band music and marches of all kinds show up constantly in Mahler's music. He also was attracted to folk poetry and songs.

As a student in Vienna, Mahler took many classes in history and philosophy as well as in composition. For the next 20 years, he made his living as a conductor. He had a large number of appointments in towns across Europe, most of them lasting for only a year or two. Mahler had tremendously high standards; he was autocratic and demanding of his musicians and uncompromising in his approach to the music. This did not endear him to administrators or to his players, but he gradually made a name for himself as a brilliant conductor, specializing in the works of Mozart, Beethoven, and Wagner. Mahler worked so hard that he had little time for composition, but gradually he developed a habit of composing during the summers, when the concert season was over. In this way, he managed to complete his first three symphonies, but people found them hard to understand.

The most important conducting position in Austria at that time was as music director of the Vienna Opera House. Mahler was by now the obvious choice for the job, but the fact that he was Jewish presented a formidable barrier in a city notorious for its anti-Semitism. He therefore had himself baptized as a Catholic and was appointed to the position in 1897. Mahler's tenure there had its problems: he was unpopular with the players because he was so strict; and there was considerable resentment over his appointment, despite his religious conversion. Mahler continued composing, and he completed several large-scale compositions during this time.

In 1902, when he was in his 40s, Mahler fell in love with Alma Schindler, a talented young woman of 23. Mahler was as autocratic in his marriage as he was in his work, and the couple had difficulties, but the depth of their relationship was never in doubt. Alma Mahler later published books of memoirs about her life with Mahler and with her two later husbands, one a famous architect and the other a novelist.

In 1907, Mahler suffered three profound setbacks. The campaign against him in Vienna finally led to his resignation from his job, his five-year-old daughter died of scarlet fever, and it was discovered that Mahler himself had a heart condition. In 1908, in an attempt to change entirely the circumstances of his life, Mahler accepted two positions in New York. He was appointed music director of the Metropolitan Opera and conductor of the New York Philharmonic. Mahler was superstitious and afraid to finish his Ninth Symphony, remembering that both Beethoven and Schubert had died after completing nine symphonies. Nonetheless, his Ninth was finished, and Mahler began working on his Tenth. But his worries turned out to be well founded. In 1911 he fell seriously ill. Mahler decided to return to Vienna, where he died at the age of 50, leaving the Tenth Symphony incomplete.

Mahler's Music

Find the **Quick Listen** on **MySearchLab** "Mahler Third Symphony"

Mahler's music represents the last great achievement of the Romantic ideal. In it, he tried to capture "the whole world": nature, God, love and death, exaltation and despair. To do this, Mahler had to invent new musical genres and forms. Most of his work is closely connected to song. Four of his symphonies use voices as well as instruments, and song melodies find their way into many of his instrumental works. Mahler wrote some important **orchestral song cycles**, in which the typical Romantic song takes on a completely new guise: in place of piano accompaniment, Mahler uses the orchestra, hugely expanding the range of expressive possibilities.

Find the **Quick Listen** on **MySearchLab** "Mahler *Adagietto*"

Mahler was a radical innovator in many other ways. He had the most precise idea of

what he wanted to express—and no fear of disregarding tradition to achieve this. "Tradition is a mess," he once said. His harmony is quite unorthodox, and he often ends a work in a key different from the one in which it began. We have seen that Beethoven was able to begin a symphony in a minor key and end it in the major, but actually changing the tonal center of a work was quite new. Some of Mahler's symphonies are longer than any that had come before, lasting 90 minutes or more.

Mahler was a brilliant and very subtle orchestrator. He had an exact idea of the sound he wanted to produce. He used enormous orchestras, and sometimes the effect is shattering; but the main reason he needed so many instruments was to achieve the widest possible range of tone colors. In the Third Symphony, he wrote a solo for a very rare instrument: the post horn, a small horn generally used on mail coaches. In the Second Symphony, he combined an English horn with a bass clarinet—an amazing and evocative sound. On the other hand, his Third Symphony begins with the awe-inspiring sound of *eight* horns blasting out a stirring fanfare *fortissimo*. He was extremely meticulous about how he wanted his works to be played. Because he was a professional conductor himself, his scores are covered with exact instructions for almost every phrase of the music.

Most of Mahler's music is programmatic in some way. The slow movement of the Fifth Symphony is a testament of love for his wife, Alma. And the scherzo of the same symphony is a portrait of his children playing. Some of

ALMA MAHLER

Gustav Mahler first met Alma Schindler at a dinner party in Vienna on November 7, 1901. Three weeks later he proposed to her, and on March 9, 1902, they were married in Vienna's Karlskirche. At Mahler's request and in spite of her considerable talent, Alma gave up composition after their marriage. She devoted herself entirely to her husband. Mahler's enormous productivity after their marriage can be attributed in no small measure to Alma's constant encouragement, but her diaries reveal that she resented the suppression of her own artistic abilities. Later, with Mahler's encouragement, she published five songs under her own name.

Alma's *Gustav Mahler: Memories and Letters* paints an interesting picture of her husband. He is portrayed as egocentric and incapable of profound love for anyone but himself. However, Mahler's letters to Alma and his adoration of his daughter Maria show us a different picture of his character. Although Alma knew Gustav better than anyone else did, scholars believe that much of her testimony is unreliable.

Before meeting Mahler, Alma had been in love with the artist Gustav Klimt and the composer Alexander Zemlinsky. After Mahler's death, she married the architect Walter Gropius in 1915 and the writer Franz Werfel in 1929. She was also the mistress of the painter Oskar Kokoschka. Alma outlived Gustav Mahler by 53 years and died in the United States in 1964, at the age of 85.

his programs are ambitious in the extreme, including representations of the creation of the world (Symphony No. 3) and the journey from life to death to resurrection (Symphony No. 2).

Throughout his music, there is a tinge of regret, of irony, even of deliberate distortion. A sense of yearning fills the pages of his work: a feeling of the impossible aims, the losses, the tragic undercurrent of human existence. If Mahler's musical impulse could be summed up in one musical phrase, it would look like this:

Try playing or singing these four notes. Notice how the phrase reaches up—only to fall back a little. Notice how the sense of striving overcomes the feeling of resolution. And notice (if you play the notes together as a chord) the slight dissonance, which sounds bittersweet and thoughtful. This is the essence of Mahler's music.

Mahler's music is full of quotations from Wagner, Brahms, Mendelssohn, and especially Beethoven. It is as though he were looking backward at the entire history of Romantic music. And this is appropriate, for he was its last and one of its greatest manifestations.

LISTENING GUIDE

((•─ Listen on MySearchLab

GUSTAV MAHLER (1860–1911)

*Fourth Movement, "Urlicht" ("Primeval Light")
from Symphony No. 2 in C Minor (Resurrection)*

Date of composition: 1888–94
Orchestration: alto voice; two piccolos, three flutes, two oboes,
   English horn, three clarinets, two bassoons, contrabassoon,
   four horns, three trumpets, glockenspiel, two harps, and strings
Tempo: *Sehr feierlich, aber schlicht* ("Very ceremonial, but straightforward")
Meter: $\frac{4}{4}$
Key of movement: Db major
Duration: 5:15

CD III, 2

The *Resurrection* Symphony is an enormous work, lasting nearly 90 minutes. It is in five movements, and it traces a spiritual journey from death to resurrection. In its sense of subjectivity and spiritual progression, it is reminiscent of Beethoven's Fifth Symphony. This parallel is made the more obvious by Mahler's choice of the same key, C minor, and by the move in the last movement to C major and triumph.

The fourth movement marks the beginning of Mahler's lifelong preoccupation with the blending of symphony and song. The movement is actually the setting of a song text, sung by a solo alto voice with the orchestra. It is entitled "Urlicht" ("Primeval Light"). The text's central message is contained in its eighth line: *"Ich bin von Gott und will wieder zu Gott"* ("I am made by God and will return to God"). Mahler said of this movement, "The stirring voice of simple faith sounds in our ears."

The melodic shape of the vocal line often follows the phrase shown above—an upward curve followed by a slight fall. In addition, Mahler has composed the most remarkable instrumental music for this movement: quiet, stately, and richly orchestrated, with striking changes of key. The music does far more than accompany the words: it gives them new and profound meaning beyond their own power of expression.

Song Text

O Röschen rot!	O red rose!
Der Mensch liegt in grösster Not!	Humanity lies in deepest need!
Der Mensch liegt in grösster Pein!	Humanity lies in greatest pain!
Je lieber möcht ich im Himmel sein!	I would rather be in Heaven!
Da kam ich auf einen breiten Weg;	Then I came upon a broad path;
Da kam ein Engelein und wollt mich abweisen.	Then came an angel that tried to turn me away.
Ach nein! Ich liess mich nicht abweisen!	But no! I will not be turned away!
Ich bin von Gott und will wieder zu Gott!	I am made by God and will return to God!
Der liebe Gott wird mir ein Lichten geben,	Dear God will give me a light,
Wird leuchten mir bis in das ewig, selig Leben!	Will light my way to eternal, blessed life!

Time	Listen for
0:00	Begins with words of alto ("*O Röschen rot!*"), accompanied by low strings.
0:22	Brass chorale: three trumpets, four horns, bassoons, contrabassoon.
1:07	"*Der Mensch liegt in grösster Not!*" (strings).
1:19	Change of key. "*Der Mensch liegt in grösster Pein!*" (strings).
1:32	Trumpets.
1:37	"*Je lieber möcht ich im Himmel sein!*" Note upward swoop on "*Himmel*" ("Heaven").
1:57	Repeat of previous line. Voice with oboe. Note curve of melodic line.
2:16	Oboe and strings.
2:49	Tempo marked: "somewhat faster." Clarinets, harp, and glockenspiel.
2:55	"*Da kam ich auf einen breiten Weg;*"
3:02	Solo violin, representing the "*ich*" ("I") of the poet (probably Mahler himself).
3:14	Miraculous key change, very quiet. "*Da kam ein Engelein und wollt mich abweisen.*" Fuller orchestration: piccolos, harps, strings.
3:32	Back to slow tempo: "*Ach nein! Ich liess mich nicht abweisen!*" (tremolo strings, oboes).
3:43	Higher: repeat of previous line.
3:55	Back to D♭: strings, horns, harp. "*Ich bin von Gott und will wieder zu Gott!*"
4:03	"*Der liebe Gott, der liebe Gott,*"
4:10	Very slow: "*wird mir ein Lichten geben,*"
4:21	"*Wird leuchten mir bis in das ewig, selig Leben!*" Note wondrous curve of melodic line and the muted violins shimmering *above* the voice on "*Leben*" ("Life").
4:50	Muted strings, harps; dying away.

STYLE SUMMARY

The Nineteenth Century II: Mid- to Late-Romantic Music

The second half of the century saw the widespread development of the symphonic poem, a one-movement symphonic work that tells a story. Indeed at that time all such narrative music, or program music, was popular. Another central genre was Romantic opera, which became far more fluid and continuous; much of the action unfolded in a style called *arioso* (singing between aria and recitative), and much of the feeling was portrayed in the orchestra.

The nationalist movement, which was primarily political and cultural, also strongly affected nineteenth-century music. Nationalist composers from Norway, Finland, Denmark, Russia, Bohemia, Moravia, Spain, France, and even the United States sought to portray national identity in their works. They incorporated folk themes and national dances in their music and set words for songs and operas in their own languages.

By the end of the century, the search for expression led to the final dissolution of the Romantic movement. Works could become no bigger, and the subject matter now ranged from murder, rape, and suicide to the creation of the world and life after death. Also, the system of tonality, with its ordered hierarchy of keys, had been stretched to the breaking point.

Romantic song, nineteenth-century symphony, and program music came together in the music of Gustav Mahler—music that has direct and strong links back to Beethoven but that also stands poised at the end of an era. Three years after Mahler's death, Europe was engulfed in the flames of the First World War.

FUNDAMENTALS OF MID- TO LATE-ROMANTIC MUSIC

- ❏ New genres, such as the programmatic symphonic poem, became popular, and other genres, such as the symphony, were used for program music

- ❏ Operas are more continuous in their music, with much of the action set in *arioso* style; the subject matter ranges from grandiose to gritty and realistic

FOR FURTHER DISCUSSION AND STUDY

1. Compare Liszt's *Transcendental Étude No. 10 in F Minor* with his D-flat Étude (*Un Sospiro*). In what sense is the latter piece "a sigh"?

2. Listen to one of Liszt's piano transcriptions of Beethoven's Fifth Symphony; compare this with the orchestral version.

3. Compare the extract from Verdi's *Otello* with the parallel passage from the Shakespeare play: Act III, Scene 3.

4. What are the elements that define a "music drama"?

5. Listen to the last movement from Mussorgsky's *Pictures at an Exhibition*, "The Great Gate at Kiev," as an example of a work for a large Romantic orchestra. Notice the many changes of tempo, the rubato, the dramatic crescendos, and the colorful use of percussion.

6. Make an iPod playlist featuring excerpts from several nationalist pieces. See if anyone can guess the nationality of each composer by just listening.

7. Note that the theme of the fourth movement of Brahms's Symphony No. 4 is taken from Bach's Cantata No. 150, to the words "My days of sorrow, God, will end in joy." Listen to this theme in the original Bach version, and then describe how Brahms has altered it.

✓•⌐ **Study** and **Review** on **MySearchLab**

The Twentieth Century and Beyond, Part I: The Classical Scene

An Overview

The twentieth century was a time of extraordinary contrasts. Technology reached dizzying heights of achievement. Radio, telephone, television, satellites, and computers radically altered both personal and worldwide communication. Travel was completely revolutionized. Medical science conquered many infectious diseases and invented complex surgical procedures for prolonging life.

But the twentieth century also displayed mankind's weaknesses, cruelty, and inhumanity at their worst. Two world wars decimated populations across Europe. World War II brought one of the most appalling instances of organized murder (the Holocaust) in human history and introduced a new word, "genocide," into the language. The destructive power of military technology was displayed by the explosion of two atomic bombs on civilian populations in Japan. In the Soviet Union, the Communist dictator Joseph Stalin—whose reign of repression, forcible resettlement, and prison camps was responsible for the murder, starvation, and terrorizing of countless millions of his countrymen—managed to wield his authority for over 30 years until the mid-1950s. The Vietnam War killed 3 to 4 million Vietnamese, 2 million Laotians and Cambodians, and 58,159 U.S. soldiers. In China from the mid-1960s to the mid-1970s, the so-called Cultural Revolution disguised a vicious power struggle within the country that led to the deaths of 3 million people and the permanent injury of a million more. In Cambodia from 1975 to 1979 nearly a third of the entire population of the country died from disease, starvation, or murder at the hands of the Communist ruling party. In 1994 in the small country of Rwanda, in east-central Africa, one ethnic group went on a killing spree, murdering between half a million and a million of their fellow countrymen, whose crime was belonging to a different ethnic group. In 2003 the United States invaded Afghanistan and Iraq, for reasons that much of the population thought were false or unnecessary. Although the United States deliberately does not keep statistics on casualties of the ordinary people of Iraq and Afghanistan, responsible groups have estimated a million soldiers and civilians killed on all sides in both wars, and perhaps as many as two million injured. Apart from the human cost, the massive financial cost of these wars threw the U.S. into economic turmoil, from which it may not recover. What has been gained from the invasions is not yet clear.

Although science made impressive gains in the last century, its limitations became more apparent as the century waned. AIDS swept through populations of Africa, the Caribbean, Europe, Asia, and North America, seeming to represent a return to the incurable plagues of the Middle Ages. Shortsighted economic policies and commercial greed caused widespread destruction to the world's environment. And most damning of all, the richest and most wasteful countries of the world were not able to find a way to save millions of people in other countries from starvation. By the end of the first decade of the twenty-first century the contrast between modern civilization's successes and its failures seemed particularly stark.

History and the Arts, 1900–1939

In 1900, Europe and the United States were in a period of unusual stability, peace, and prosperity. Economic growth was strong, the standard of living was improving rapidly, and scientific breakthroughs contributed to health and comfort.

At this time, the movement known as Modernism began to affect all the arts: literature, painting, sculpture, architecture, and music. Modernism was a movement of self-conscious innovation. Artists, writers, intellectuals, poets, and painters reacted strongly to the accepted rules of the nineteenth century and created works of striking experimentation and revolutionary force. Composers rejected tonality, the harmonic basis of music since the seventeenth century, and adopted radically new harmonic structures.

In this period of excitement, experimentation, and optimism, the greatest composers were Debussy, Schoenberg, and Stravinsky. The works they created during the period were innovative and daring. Their brilliance matched the extraordinary accomplishments of the greatest poets and painters of the age.

World War I (1914–1918) shattered this sense of optimism. In this long drawn-out conflict—ugly, brutal, and often senseless—40 million people died and 20 million were wounded. A sense of the devastation and despair caused by this war is given in the poems of Wilfred Owen, poems that were later used in the magnificent *War Requiem* of the English composer Benjamin Britten.

The period after the war was one of uncertainty and a gradual decline into new conflict. The Bolshevik revolution had given rise to the first Communist state, one of the most influential political developments of the whole twentieth century. The economic devastation

"Flapper" (fashionable young woman) on the cover of a magazine in the 1920s.
Courtesy of the Library of Congress.

instilled confidence in the nation and led to gradual economic recovery, the full impact of which was not felt until the new boom brought about by the outbreak of World War II.

In social terms, the period between the wars was one of turmoil and change. Women won the right to vote in 1920. Prohibition created an entire counterculture of bootleg liquor and organized crime. Many intellectuals were attracted by the social ideals of Marxism.

The greatest composers of the period between the wars were still Schoenberg and Stravinsky (Debussy had died in 1918) but also included two students of Schoenberg—Berg and Webern—as well as Bartók in Hungary, Shostakovich in the Soviet Union, Britten in England, and Ives and Copland in the United States.

1939–2000

World War II (1939–1945) broke out only 21 years after the end of the First World War. Thirty million people died; cities and towns in England, continental Europe, and the Far East suffered enormous and widespread damage; irreplaceable works of art and buildings, some of them dating back to the Middle Ages, were destroyed. The economy of Europe was in shambles, and the political map was highly uncertain. The Soviet Union and the United States emerged as the dominant powers of the postwar period, and Europe was divided by its allegiance to one or the other of these powers. Populations around Europe were uprooted, and many countries were flooded with refugees.

One of the magnets for refugees was the United States. Large numbers of people—including scholars, artists, writers, composers, and performing musicians—came from Europe to America. This influx made the United States the most prominent center of Western culture after the war.

From 1945 to the 1960s, two musical trends asserted themselves. The first was a tendency toward intellectualization. Music became so organized, so mathematical in its structure that many audiences turned away from classical music altogether. It seemed as though composers were writing only for other composers and were no longer interested in communicating to audiences.

The second trend in this period involved radical experimentation, parallel in some ways to the period of early Modernism at the beginning of the century. Composers experimented with music in every conceivable way, throwing out all the conventionally accepted norms of music making. They put the compositional process

of Germany led directly to Hitler's rise to power. In Italy in 1922, Mussolini founded the first Fascist state in Europe. A Fascist government was established in Spain after the Spanish Civil War of 1936–1939.

During the 1920s, the United States experienced a period of prosperity. The war had strongly stimulated America's economy. American products were sold all over the world, and President Calvin Coolidge made his famous statement that "the business of America is business." A break in this upward spiral came with the Great Depression of 1929–1933, which caused widespread unemployment and hunger. During the 1930s, President Franklin D. Roosevelt's policies

President Roosevelt (at head of table) is cheered by members of a crew of workers helping to bring the country back from the Depression in 1933.

into the hands of the performers. They challenged audiences and violated conventions of time, performing medium, and concert decorum. Most particularly, they experimented with *sound*. Conventional instruments were pushed to new limits, exotic instruments were introduced, and new instruments were invented. Most influential was the use of tape and then synthesizers and computers in the production of musical sounds. The foremost figures of this period were Pierre Boulez and John Cage.

Since the mid-1960s, a new movement was evident in Western culture, a movement called Postmodernism. (It is a troubling term. If "modern" means up-to-date, how can you have a historical period that is after that?) Indeed, literature, art, and music in the last few decades of the twentieth century were in a period of severe self-examination, which has continued into the twenty-first century. From the start of Postmodernism, everything was cast into doubt, including the worth and meaning of Western culture itself. Literary works struggled for identity. Paintings juxtaposed the old and the new in startling ways. Postmodern buildings became highly eclectic, combining an exaggerated variety of styles in a single unit. And music made a radical move away from the intellectualized compositions of the postwar period toward a new accessibility of style.

Composers began again to address their audiences. They borrowed ideas from rock music to appeal to a wider public. They expanded their frame of reference to include the rhythms, timbres, and harmonies of other countries. And many of them made a conscious return to traditional tonality, to provide an aural context and meaning that many Modernists had rejected.

General Characteristics of Twentieth-Century Music

Music of the twentieth century embodied more experimentation and diversity than in previous eras. Everything was called into question, including the tonal system upon which Western music had been based for centuries, and even the very idea of a concert itself. The length of

Arnold Schoenberg.

compositions changed a great deal: pieces could be very tiny or immensely long. All types of sound were used, and the distinction between sound and noise was often erased.

The Replacement of Tonality

As we have seen, the idea of **tonality**—the use of scales, chords, and harmonies—in music developed over many centuries, reaching its heights in the Classic and Romantic periods. However, by the late nineteenth century, composers were already experimenting with new ways of approaching tonality, including starting a piece in one key and ending in another, composing passages where it is difficult to determine what the key is, and other innovations.

This trend accelerated in the early twentieth century in the works of composers like Debussy, and reached its culmination in a musical revolution led by Arnold Schoenberg. Schoenberg and his students created a new theory that would become known as **atonality**—an attempt to "liberate" music from the traditional rules of composition. Schoenberg's work also led to the creation of new scales based on his new theory.

New scale patterns included the **pentatonic scale, the whole-tone scale**, and the **octatonic scale**.

The **pentatonic scale** has only five notes, usually in the following pattern:

Pentatonic Scale

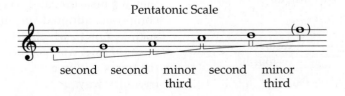

second   second   minor   second   minor
                     third   third

This pattern of intervals can be reproduced by playing only the black keys on the piano. (You can easily compose your own pentatonic melody this way. Just improvise on the black keys. The music will sound evocative and folk-like.) Pentatonic scales had been around for a long time in many Asian musics and Western folk musics, but they were new to Western classical music.

The **whole-tone scale** has a whole step between each pitch and the next, and the scale has only six notes:

Find the **Quick Listen** on **MySearchLab** "Whole-Tone Scale on the Piano"

Whole-tone Scale

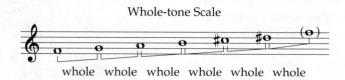

whole   whole   whole   whole   whole   whole

Because there are no half steps in this scale, the sense of "pull" given by the last half step in the traditional octave scale is missing, and tonality is bypassed.

The third new scale developed by composers in the twentieth century was the **octatonic scale**. This has eight pitches *within* the octave, in a pattern of alternating whole and half steps:

Find the **Quick Listen** on **MySearchLab** "Octatonic Scale"

Octatonic Scale

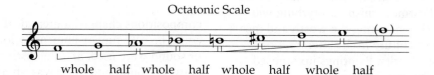

whole   half   whole   half   whole   half   whole   half

As well as inventing new scales, composers sometimes turned to a system that had been in use *before* the establishment of tonality. This was the **modal** system, the basis of music during the Middle Ages and the Renaissance. (See Chapter 4 for a discussion of the medieval modes.) The use of an old system made music sound new again and provided composers with a further alternative to tonality.

In addition to using new (or very old) scales, composers experimented with polytonality and nontriadic harmony. **Polytonality** means the simultaneous sounding of two or more keys at once. Both Igor Stravinsky and the American composer Charles Ives used polytonality. Ives once wrote a piece for two brass bands, each playing in a different key.

Nontriadic harmony means harmony that is not based on the triad, the standard basis for chords in conventional tonality. In the twentieth century, many composers experimented with alternative types of chord structure. The German composer Paul Hindemith, who emigrated to the United States in 1940 and was an extremely influential teacher, often used **quartal chords**, based on fourths instead of thirds:

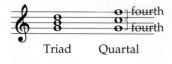

Triad   Quartal

Melody

Before the twentieth century, melody was generally smooth, balanced, and predictable. Pitches were usually closely connected, gaps were small, and phrases were balanced. In the twentieth century, melody often became erratic, with wide leaps, irregular rhythms, and unexpected notes. Phrase lengths changed constantly. It was impossible to anticipate where a melody would go next.

Rhythm

One of the greatest changes in twentieth-century music was in the use of rhythm. Compared with the music of other cultures, Western music had always used relatively simple rhythmic patterns. In the twentieth century, composers began to adopt far more complex rhythms in their music. Sometimes they achieved this goal by calling for constantly changing meters in the course of a composition. For example, instead of remaining in $\frac{4}{4}$ meter, a piece might have a measure in $\frac{3}{4}$ followed by a measure in $\frac{6}{8}$, then a $\frac{2}{4}$ measure, and so on. Sometimes composers adopted very unusual meters, such as $\frac{5}{4}$ or $\frac{7}{4}$, which give an irregular beat to the music. And sometimes they grouped the notes *within* a regular meter in an irregular way.

Irregular metrical groupings in twentieth-century music.

Find the **Quick Listen** on **MySearchLab**
"Bartók Quartet No. 5, 3rd Movement"

Another way in which rhythms became more complex was by the use of rhythmic *freedom*. Composers frequently directed each individual performer to play at his or her own speed, thus creating a series of overlapping rhythms in place of one steady pulse. Finally, the advent of the computer allowed composers to manipulate rhythm in an infinite variety of complex ways.

Length

Until the last part of the nineteenth century, the length of most musical compositions had been quite standardized. Audiences knew what to expect when they went to hear a symphony or a chamber work. But in the twentieth century, this changed radically. Some pieces were no more than a few measures in length, lasting only seconds, whereas others went on for hours. Some compositions were designed to last *ad infinitum* (or until people's patience wore out!).

Tone Color and Sound

One final element that distinguished twentieth-century music from music of earlier eras was a heightened awareness of tone color. This became a central focus in music, both to provide more variety and interest and to create a new structural element. Webern's *Six Pieces for Orchestra*, for example, written in 1909, calls for an enormous orchestra, including a wide range of brass and percussion—but these forces are rarely used all at once, and the instruments play mostly alone or in small combinations, creating an immense variety of sound. The piece *depends* upon the tone colors of specific instruments.

In addition, composers in the twentieth century called for greatly expanded playing techniques from instrumentalists. Wind players were asked to produce higher and higher pitches by means of special fingering and blowing techniques, and sometimes they were required to make squawking, squeaking, or chattering noises on their instruments. String players were asked to produce unusual glissandos (slides) on their strings, to bang their instruments with their bows, or to pluck the strings so hard that they hit the fingerboard. And both string and wind players were called upon to produce **quarter tones**—pitches *between* the half steps.

Instruments that had never or only rarely been used in traditional orchestras—such as bass clarinets, alto flutes, tenor tubas, and bass trombones—were now featured regularly. The greatest changes occurred in the percussion section. Previously, orchestral music had called for timpani, sometimes bass drum, and only very occasionally a snare drum, cymbals, or a triangle. Now, percussion sections were often large and varied, calling for a huge collection of instruments—including large and small cymbals, a whole array of drums of different sizes, bells, wooden blocks, whips, rattles, tambourines, bass drums, gongs, and melody percussion instruments, such as the xylophone, marimba, vibraphone, chimes, celesta, and glockenspiel.

Find the **Quick Listen** on **MySearchLab**
"Berio Sequenza III"

THE LONGEST PIECES IN THE WORLD

In the last hundred years or so, composers have experimented with creating really long pieces of music. Morton Feldman's Second String Quartet lasts for over six hours. Erik Satie's *Vexations* consists of one page of music that is to be played 840 times. A performance lasts 18 hours. There is an organ composition by John Cage that is currently being performed in Halberstadt, Germany. The tempo marking is "As Slowly as Possible," and at the current rate, the performance will take 639 years. Jem Finer, one of the founding members of the Irish band The Pogues, has composed a computer piece called *Longplayer*, which began on New Year's Day of the year 2000 and is designed to last for a thousand years. So far the record seems to be held by the English composer "Mel" (Ian Mellish), whose *Olitsky* is for four tape loops that are fractionally out of sync. The length of the piece is 1,648,171 years, 7 weeks, 6 days, 10 hours, 23 minutes, and 33 seconds.

Twentieth-Century Music: Summary of New Methods		
	TRADITIONAL	**TWENTIETH-CENTURY MUSIC**
HARMONY	Tonal (key centered)	Atonal
SCALES	Major and minor scales	New scale types: pentatonic (five-note), whole tone (six-note), and octatonic (eight-note) Revival of old modes
MELODY	Balanced, smooth, predictable	Erratic, with large gaps and unpredictable motions
RHYTHM	Rhythms are regular and largely predictable	Rhythm may change many times in a single piece
	All instruments perform a single rhythm together	Individual players may play slightly faster or slower than the group
LENGTH	Standardized by genre	Much shorter or much longer than traditional
TONE COLOR/ SOUND	Standardized around family of "classical" instruments	Expanded instrumentation and larger orchestras
	Ensemble size/types of instruments conventional for each genre	New ways of playing traditional instruments. New interest in electronic/computer-generated sound

Find the **Quick Listen** on **MySearchLab**
"Telharmonium"

Find the **Quick Listen** on **MySearchLab**
"Theremin Lesson One"

Modern technology strongly influenced the sounds of twentieth-century music. At the beginning of the century, new electronic instruments were invented, including the **telharmonium**, an instrument that produces sound by means of electronic generators; the **theremin**, an instrument that can make oscillating streams of sliding sounds, like ghost noises; and the first electronic organ. Later, in the 1940s and 1950s, the advent of magnetic tape brought many new experiments in sound production.

In the latter half of the century, the production and control of musical sounds were revolutionized by the computer and the synthesizer. On the computer, all the various parameters of sound—pitch, dynamics, duration, timbre, even spatial positioning—can be controlled digitally. Synthesizers can both generate and control sound. Almost any sound can be produced, changed, combined, and controlled on a single small keyboard. Synthesizers can imitate any instrument, including an entire orchestra, or produce a whole array of artificial sounds. Much music of the later twentieth century—including both classical and popular music, whether live or recorded or on a film soundtrack—would not have been possible without the synthesizer.

The Beginnings of Change

As we have seen, the Modernist movement at the beginning of the twentieth century had an effect on all the arts. Painting, poetry, architecture, and music were in the grip of a revolutionary fervor, a feeling that the rules of the past could now be challenged in favor of new forms of expression. In music, the chief figures of this movement were Debussy, Stravinsky, and Schoenberg. Although they were all striking innovators, each contributed to this movement in his own particular way: Debussy in orchestral color, Stravinsky in rhythm, and Schoenberg in the invention of a new system to replace tonality.

Impressionism and Symbolism

In the Modernist movement, which was centered in Paris, there were many parallels between music and the other arts. The most important movement in painting was known as Impressionism. Impressionist paintings are fresh, lively, and atmospheric. They revel in the play of light and color. Outlines are vague, and details are left to the viewer's imagination.

Parallel to the Impressionist movement in painting was the literary movement known as

Symbolism. Symbolists attempted to convey ideas by suggestion rather than by direct statement.

Impressionism in music refers to a style of composition in which the outlines are blurred and there is a great deal of harmonic ambiguity, often created by whole-tone, pentatonic, or chromatic scales. Indeed, it was sometimes felt that music, with its natural fluidity, could create an Impressionist atmosphere more successfully than the other arts.

Claude Debussy (1862–1918)

The composer whose music most closely paralleled these developments was Debussy, who was also French and lived in Paris. He attended many of the first exhibitions of Impressionist painting and was a friend of several of the Symbolist writers.

Claude Debussy was a talented pianist as a child and was accepted as a student at the Paris Conservatory of Music at the age of 10. When he was 18, he began to study composition, and in 1884 he won the prestigious Prix de Rome, the highest award for French composers. One of the influences on his music was the distinctive sound of the Indonesian gamelan (a small group of musicians playing metal instruments).

Debussy's most famous orchestral composition is the *Prelude to the Afternoon of a Faun* (1894), which is based on a poem by the Symbolist poet Stéphane Mallarmé. The music is dreamy and suggestive, using a large orchestra primarily for its variety of tone color. Other orchestral pieces by Debussy include *Trois Nocturnes* (*Three Nocturnes*) and *La Mer* (*The Sea*). *Trois Nocturnes* has three sections, entitled "Clouds," "Festivals," and "Sirens." *La Mer* also consists of three sections, evoking sun and sea, the play of waves, and the sound of the wind on the water. Later, Debussy wrote his only opera, *Pelléas et Mélisande*, to a Symbolist play by Maeterlinck. Debussy's piano music is highly varied and includes some of his greatest compositions. There are pieces of pure Impressionism, such as "Jardins sous la pluie" ("Gardens in the Rain") or "La Cathédrale engloutie" ("The Sunken Cathedral"), but also humorous pieces, technical studies, and music for children. The best-known piece for children is "Golliwog's Cake-Walk." Debussy also wrote some non-Impressionist chamber music, including a fine string quartet and sonatas for violin and piano; cello and piano; and flute, viola, and harp.

Debussy's music was little known until he was about forty. After the premiere of *Pelléas et Mélisande*, he became quite famous and

Monet's painting of Rouen Cathedral is vague, cloudy, and elusive.

Claude Monet (1840–1926), *The Cathedral of Rouen, façade,* circa 1892/94. Oil on canvas, 100.6 × 66 cm. Juliana Cheney Edwards Collection. Museum of Fine Arts, Boston/ Archiv für Kunst und Geschichte, Berlin.

Find the **Quick Listen** on **MySearchLab** "Debussy Prelude to the Afternoon of a Faun"

Find the **Quick Listen** on **MySearchLab** "Sunken Cathedral" Debussy

Claude Debussy in a portrait by Marcel Baschet, 1884.

Lauros-Giraudon/Marcel Baschet (1862–1941) © ARS, NY. Claude Debussy in Rome in 1884. Chateaux de Versailles, France. Photo credit: Bridgeman-Giraudon/Art Resource, NY.

traveled around Europe conducting performances of his work. He loved fine food and fancy clothes and, as a result, was often short of money. He had two wives and a mistress, though not all at the same time! Debussy died of cancer in his native Paris at the age of 56.

Primitivism

Primitivism is the name given to a movement in painting at the beginning of the twentieth century. Artists were attracted by what they saw as the directness, instinctiveness, and exoticism of nonurban cultures. This was a time during which writers such as Sigmund Freud were exploring the power of instinct and the unconscious.

Among the painters of Primitivism were Paul Gauguin, Henri Rousseau, and Pablo Picasso. Again, the center of this artistic movement was Paris. Paul Gauguin was fascinated by "primitive" cultures and eventually went to the South Sea Islands to live and work among the islanders. His paintings are bold and bright, and they use symbols of cultural primitivism. Henri Rousseau's paintings are deliberately naive but highly imaginative. Their vivid scenes are designed not as representations of nature but as evocations of a state of mind. Pablo Picasso was one of the greatest painters of the twentieth century, and he changed his style many times during his lifetime. But in the early

1900s, he, too, was interested in Primitivism, and his painting *Les Demoiselles d'Avignon* (*The Young Women of Avignon*) is an example of this style. It is also a landmark in twentieth-century art. The painting is raw, primitive, and deliberately shocking. Its flat planes, deconstruction of the bodies, angularity of form, and especially the use of African masks for some of the faces had a revolutionary impact on the development of modern painting.

Igor Stravinsky (1882–1971)

The musical equivalent of Picasso was Stravinsky. He, too, lived a long life, evolved several distinct styles during his career, and had a lasting impact on twentieth-century culture.

Igor Stravinsky was born in St. Petersburg, Russia. His father was an opera singer, but he insisted that Igor study law instead of music at the university. Stravinsky used to compose secretly. At the age of 21, he gave up law altogether and began formal music lessons with the great Russian nationalist composer Rimsky-Korsakov. From his mentor, Stravinsky learned how to obtain vivid colors and strong effects from an orchestra.

In 1910, Stravinsky moved to Paris, at that time the undisputed center of European culture. He was asked to produce some scores for the Ballets Russes, a famous and influential ballet troupe based in Paris and headed by the talented Russian producer Serge Diaghilev. Stravinsky wrote three of his most important ballet scores as commissions for the Ballets Russes: *The Firebird* (1910), *Petrushka* (1911), and *The Rite of Spring* (1913). All three were inspired by the prevailing style of Primitivism. The primitive atmosphere in Stravinsky's music is enhanced by his use of **polyrhythms** (different meters sounding at the same time), **bitonality** (two different keys sounding at the same time), and **ostinato** (constantly repeated phrases).

The Rite of Spring, a composition of tremendous power and boldness, is one of the most revolutionary works of the twentieth century. It depicts the rituals of ancient pagan tribes, and it caused a riot at its first performance in Paris in 1913. The audience was profoundly shocked by the violent and overtly sexual nature of the choreography on stage as well as by the pounding rhythms and clashing dissonances from the orchestra. Soon thereafter, the work was recognized as a masterpiece. **(See Listening Guide.)**

> Stravinsky's music used to be original. Now it is aboriginal.
> —Ernest Newman, 1921

Stravinsky in a pensive mood.

LISTENING GUIDE

((•─ **Listen** on **MySearchLab**

IGOR STRAVINSKY (1882–1971)   Le Sacre du Printemps (The Rite of Spring), *Opening Section*

Date of composition: 1913
Orchestration: piccolo, three flutes, alto flute, four oboes, English horn,
 E♭-clarinet, three clarinets, two bass clarinets, four bassoons, contrabassoon,
 eight horns, D trumpet, four trumpets, three trombones, two tubas,
 two timpani, bass drum, side drum, triangle, antique cymbals, strings
Duration: 5:02

CD III, 3

Le Sacre du Printemps is the third of the group of ballets that Stravinsky wrote for the Ballets Russes in Paris; it was completed in 1913. It features the largest orchestra ever used by Stravinsky. Stravinsky conceived the ballet as a series of tribal rituals. The music and the choreography present bold, daring, and often alarming moments that shocked the first audiences. *Le Sacre du Printemps* is one of the musical masterpieces that were visually realized in Walt Disney's animated feature *Fantasia* as musical background to the creation of the world. As you listen, see how your own imagination compares with Disney's or with Stravinsky's. Even without pictures, the music is brilliantly imaginative, colorful, and striking—maybe even more so!

We will listen only to the first several minutes of the ballet. It begins with a solo bassoon, playing in its eerie highest register.

Time	Listen for
0:00	Bassoon:
0:10	Horn enters.
0:20	Descending woodwinds; clarinet.
0:44	English horn enters. More bassoon.
0:58	Woodwinds gather momentum.
1:12	Trills, fuller texture; small high clarinet.
1:32	Bubbling bass clarinet.
1:45	Section comes to a close, trills in violins.
1:55	Small clarinet, interplay with English horn.
2:16	Flute response.
2:24	Oboe.
2:29	Small clarinet in high register.
2:47	Muted trumpet.
2:51	Begin orchestral crescendo.
3:01	Stop!
3:02	Bassoon reappears, high-register solo.
3:10	Clarinet trill, pizzicato strings, chords. Monotonous two-note figure starts and continues through the following:

| 3:34 | Pounding, steady orchestral chords, irregular accents. |

3:44	Movement in woodwinds, arpeggios.
3:53	Trumpet, triplet figures, quick runs on winds.
4:13	Orchestral pounding returns.
4:22	Bass melody: bassoons interspersed with orchestra rhythms.
4:32	Trombone, orchestral flashes of color: oboes and flutes.
4:53	Big brass chord; timpani; low brass.

PERFORMANCE IN CONTEXT
An Art-Deco Palace for the Avant-Garde

The opening of the Theatre of the Champs-Élysées in 1913 heralded a new direction in Parisian art. The theatre's appearance was impressively modern: made of concrete, and decorated in the new Art Deco style. (This same style can be seen in the Empire State Building, Rockefeller Center, and the Chrysler Building in New York City.) This progressive appearance was matched by the performances hosted by the theatre: from the beginning, it was devoted to new music, dance, and opera. It was a space well-suited for Diaghilev's Ballets Russes, and it hosted the company for the spring 1913 season. This season has become famous due to the riot at the premiere of Stravinksy's *The Rite of Spring*—an apt christening for a space devoted to the avant-garde. Today, the Theatre of the Champs-Élysées continues to be a vibrant part of the performing arts scene in Paris. It has hosted the premieres of hundreds of new works, but few have been able to approach the notoriety of its auspicious beginning. The theatre is located in Paris on the Right Bank, halfway between the Grand Palais and the Palais de Tokyo.

Theatre of the Champs-Élysées

Find the **Quick Listen** on **MySearchLab**

"Stravinsky *Pulcinella*"

Stravinsky lived in Switzerland during the First World War, and returned to Paris in 1920. His most important compositions from this period in Switzerland took a different direction entirely. Smaller and more transparent, they relied on small groups of varied instruments and sometimes were influenced by the new music emanating from America: jazz. The jazz-influenced pieces from this period include *Ragtime* for 11 instruments (1918) and *Piano-Rag-Music* (1919). Stravinsky was attracted to jazz because of its clear, clean textures and lively rhythms.

In 1920, Diaghilev invited Stravinsky to arrange some eighteenth-century music for a ballet called *Pulcinella*. Stravinsky orchestrated some chamber sonatas by Classic composers and also subtly reworked them, transforming the Classic style into a modern idiom. He organized the accompanying figures into ostinatos, rewrote some of the harmonies to make them a little more biting, and changed the phrase-lengths to make them slightly irregular. The result is a remarkable work and had an extraordinary influence on the development of twentieth-century music. Indeed, *Pulcinella* ushered in a completely new compositional style known as **Neo-Classicism**.

Stravinsky and Neo-Classicism Stravinsky's work on *Pulcinella* led him to a new consideration of Western musical traditions, and he used the past as a means of renewing the present. He said, "*Pulcinella* was my discovery of the past, the epiphany through which the whole of my late work became possible."

Neo-Classical composers adopted ideas not only from the Classic period, but also from the Baroque era. In place of the big, wild, expressive orchestral sounds of the 1910s (like those in *The Rite of Spring*), the focus now was on formal balance, clarity, and objectivity. Many Neo-Classical compositions use small ensembles, and some have titles that deliberately recall Classic and Baroque genres, such as "concerto" or "symphony."

As well as adopting the genres (concerto, concerto grosso, symphony) of eighteenth-century music, Stravinsky adopted their formal structures. In the music from his Neo-Classical period, you can find patterns that are like sonata form, theme-and-variations form, aria form, and rondo form. In no way, however, could one of Stravinsky's Neo-Classical compositions ever be mistaken for an original piece from the eighteenth century. Although the formal aesthetic is clearly influenced by the past, the style of the music has been updated and modernized. Harmonies are modern, accompanying figures are new, phrase-lengths are irregular, and the rhythm is lively, bouncy, even a little quirky.

In 1939, as Europe headed once again toward the catastrophe of a world war, Stravinsky moved to America. He settled in Los Angeles and was engaged by Hollywood to write some film scores. Unfortunately, none of these was ever completed. He did finish a Mass, as well as an opera called *The Rake's Progress* (1951). *The Rake's Progress* is the last composition of Stravinsky's Neo-Classical style and one of the finest.

After 1951, Stravinsky began to experiment with twelve-tone techniques and again radically changed his musical style. Many of his late compositions use twelve-tone methods of composition. These include an elegy for President John F. Kennedy (completed in 1964) and a Requiem written in anticipation of Stravinsky's own death. Stravinsky died in 1971, near the age of 90.

Stravinsky's Music

As we have seen, Stravinsky's personal style underwent several changes during the course of his career. He wrote in the splashy, colorful orchestral style of the Russian nationalists, composed music with the force and power of Primitivism, adopted jazz techniques, invented a new musical style known as Neo-Classicism, and turned finally to twelve-tone techniques.

Stravinsky took ideas from the medieval, Baroque, and Classic periods, as well as from contemporary music. He wrote for almost every known musical combination, both instrumental and vocal, choral and orchestral, chamber and stage. His genres included opera, ballet, oratorio, symphony, concerto, chamber music, sonata, piano solo, song, chorus, and Mass.

And yet some things remained common to all of Stravinsky's periods and compositional styles. First of all was his interest in rhythm. His rhythms are highly individual: catchy, unexpected, and fascinating. Stravinsky used syncopation with great effect, and often a short rest or silence appears to throw the rhythm off balance. He often used several different meters, one right after the other or even simultaneously.

Second, Stravinsky had an acute ear for tone color. He used unusual combinations of instruments to get exactly the effect he wanted, and he also used instruments in novel ways. *The Rite of Spring*, for example, begins with a bassoon, which is a low instrument, playing at the very top of its range, producing a strange, eerie sound.

Finally, Stravinsky's use of harmony was highly original. Much of his music is tonally based, and yet he often used *two* key centers instead of one. Another very characteristic harmonic effect is the use of an ostinato (repeated pattern) as an accompaniment. Above the ostinato, the harmonies may change, but the ostinato remains as a kind of tonal anchor.

Stravinsky used to compose carefully and consistently every day in his study, which was filled with the tools of his trade: paper, pencils, erasers, rulers, ink, scissors, and a large desk. He worked regular hours—"like a banker," he said. But the music produced in that study has produced an even more valuable legacy than banknotes.

Find the **Quick Listen** on **MySearchLab**
"Stravinsky *Ragtime* for 11 Instruments"

Expressionism

The links among the visual arts, literature, and music were particularly evident in one branch of Modernism that became popular during the years 1910–1939. This branch was known as Expressionism, and it evolved during a time of growing fascination with the unconscious and people's inner feelings. Although the Expressionist movement had its exponents in Germany, Norway, and other countries, the center of activity was Vienna. It was here that Sigmund Freud lived and worked, developing his groundbreaking theories on the human psyche. It was here that the writers Arthur Schnitzler and Hugo von Hofmannsthal, the political visionary Theodor Herzl, and the painters Gustav Klimt and Oskar Kokoschka revolutionized their own fields of endeavor. And it was in Vienna that the revolutionary musical world of Schoenberg and his students Berg and Webern was created.

The connections between painting and music at this time were particularly strong. In fact, Schoenberg himself was a talented painter. Both Expressionist painters and Expressionist composers attempted to focus on inner states of being and the evocation of extreme feelings. Today, their concentration on anguish, insanity, fear, hatred, and death may seem obsessive. But the movement was a reaction against what was perceived as the prettiness and superficiality of the Impressionists.

Arnold Schoenberg (1874–1951)

The most important Expressionist composer was Arnold Schoenberg. He was also one of the most radically innovative composers of the century, because he evolved a completely new approach to musical harmony that has had a profound influence on all music written up to the present day.

Schoenberg was born in 1874 in Vienna to a poor Orthodox Jewish family. He took violin lessons as a boy but had no other musical training. He studied the works of Mozart, Haydn, and Beethoven as well as those of Brahms and Mahler, who were still very active in Vienna as Schoenberg was growing up. Schoenberg began composing at about the age of eight. His early works, up to the age of about 25, continued in the Romantic tradition. But soon, Schoenberg started to take a different path.

He gradually came to feel that tonality—the centuries-old harmonic basis of music, with its carefully ordered hierarchy of keys and its focus on a single, central key for each movement or work—had outlived its usefulness. He began to develop a completely new system of musical organization. At first he called this system *atonality*—that is, a system *without* key. In Schoenberg's atonal works, the feeling of key is deliberately avoided. The music uses so many chromatic notes that no tonal center can be heard, as you can see in this line from his *Five Pieces for Orchestra*:

Schoenberg wrote many atonal pieces between 1908 and 1915. The most important of these are *Das Buch der hängenden Gärten* ("The Book of the Hanging Gardens"), 1908; *Five Pieces for Orchestra*, 1909; and *Pierrot Lunaire* ("Moonstruck Pierrot"), 1912. Schoenberg's atonal music was not well received. Yet he continued to struggle with the idea of writing music without tonality. "I feel that I have a mission," he said.

For the next several years, Schoenberg wrote no music at all. This period coincided with World War I and its immediate aftermath, and Schoenberg was facing a personal and intellectual crisis in addition to the national

and political one. The problem was in the direction his music should take. Atonality freed music from the "straitjacket" of tonality, but it had no organizing principle. How can you structure a piece with no keys? So far he had solved the problem in two ways: either the pieces were very short, or they were held together by a text.

Schoenberg gradually developed a solution to this problem, coming up with an idea that held composers in its grip for much of the remainder of the twentieth century. His idea was the **twelve-tone system.**

The twelve-tone system is an outgrowth of atonality, but it has a strict unifying principle.

Arnold Schoenberg.

The composer uses all the available notes, instead of just some of them (there are twelve notes in an octave, counting all the half steps). *But the notes are used in a strict order (established in advance by the composer), and this order must be followed throughout the piece.*

Schoenberg first used his twelve-tone system in his *Five Piano Pieces* of 1923. From then on, he used the system (more or less strictly) in almost all his compositions. The most important of these are the gigantic *Variations for Orchestra* (1928), the extraordinary opera *Moses and Aaron* (1932), the Violin Concerto (1936), the Fourth String Quartet (1937), and the Piano Concerto (1942). The twelve-tone system allowed Schoenberg to write far more extended compositions than had been possible before.

During the time of these developments, Schoenberg was fortunate enough to have two brilliant and like-minded students. They were Alban Berg and Anton Webern, only about 10 years younger than he was. The three shared a great many of their ideas and wrote similar kinds of pieces, yet each composer developed his own distinct musical personality.

This was a dangerous period for Jews in Germany, however: when the Nazis came to power in 1933, hundreds of thousands of Jews lost their jobs. Schoenberg was summarily dismissed from his teaching job at the Academy of Arts in Berlin. As a result, he embraced Judaism (from which he had lapsed at the age of 18) more firmly than ever before. Many of Schoenberg's works—including the oratorio *Jacob's Ladder* (1922), the opera *Moses and Aaron*, and a setting of the "Kol Nidrei" text from the Jewish liturgy (1938)—are based on Jewish themes. In addition, after World War II he wrote a cantata entitled *A Survivor from Warsaw* (1947), which relives the horror of the Warsaw Ghetto, in which more than 400,000 Jews were systematically murdered by the Nazis. The text is based on a personal account by one of the very few people who survived.

After Schoenberg was fired from his job in Berlin, he moved to the United States and settled in Los Angeles, where he taught composition at the University of California as well as teaching private students. This was the period of his large-scale twelve-tone works, but he also wrote two "old-fashioned" tonal pieces for student ensembles.

Schoenberg died in 1951. During his life, his music was not much performed—and even since then, most audiences have found it difficult and inaccessible. But Schoenberg was highly influential in two ways: directly, because he was the teacher of Berg and Webern, each of whom turned out to be a great composer in his own right; and indirectly, because his development of the twelve-tone system affected an entire generation of composers who came after him.

Find the **Quick Listen** on **MySearchLab**
"Schoenberg *Survivor from Warsaw*"

Schoenberg's Music

Schoenberg's music can be divided into three periods: the early period, the atonal period, and the much longer twelve-tone period. During the early period, from the 1890s to 1907, Schoenberg wrote music in a late-Romantic idiom. The pieces are passionate and intense; they range from the Piano Sonata (1894) to the programmatic string sextet *Verklärte Nacht* ("Transfigured Night") (1899) to the enormous cantata *Gurrelieder* (written in 1901 and orchestrated in 1911). In these pieces, we can see an increasing use of chromaticism and a gradual dissolving of a central tonality. The music wanders further and further afield through many keys other than the central one.

In Schoenberg's middle period, from 1908 to 1915, he developed his idea of atonality. His most important atonal compositions either

SCHOENBERG AND ATONALITY

By 1900, tonality had been a guiding feature in Western music for 300 years. It was the common denominator behind works by such diverse composers as Corelli, Bach, Mozart, Beethoven, Wagner, and Brahms. While musical forms, genres, styles, and idioms changed radically between 1600 and 1900, tonality remained a consistent musical element. Composers *assumed* that they would compose tonally.

By the late nineteenth century, the music of Wagner, for example, had become extremely unstable in its keys. Schoenberg was profoundly influenced by the rich harmonic style of Wagner. But he believed that Wagner had taken chromaticism and dissonance as far as it could go in the tonal system. Schoenberg's solution was to abandon tonality—in his words, "to emancipate the dissonance"—in favor of atonality.

An atonal piece contains none of the hierarchy among notes and chords always present in tonal music: each of the twelve notes of the chromatic scale is equally important. By 1924, Schoenberg had developed his twelve-tone system to reflect this fundamental principle of equality. A melody in Schoenberg's twelve-tone style would state each of the twelve tones before any are repeated. It is easy to make up your own twelve-tone series. For example,

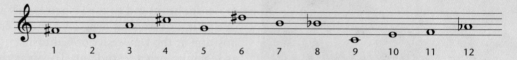

All you do is add rhythm and you have a melody. The art lies in finding a series and a rhythm that work together:

The twelve notes in their given order are referred to as a tone row. (The use of a tone row was fundamental to nearly every work by Schoenberg after 1924.)

Schoenberg believed that his system was a logical, evolutionary step. Nowadays, it seems as though composers are moving away from this system (and from atonality in general) and are reverting once more to tonality. Whatever the future holds, Schoenberg's initial forays into atonality will always be considered one of the most radical and audacious innovations in the history of Western music.

have a text (like *Das Buch der hängenden Gärten* and *Pierrot Lunaire*) or are quite short. (See Listening Guide.) The five movements of *Five Pieces for Orchestra*, although written for a huge orchestra, are dense and brief.

From 1923 until the end of his life, Schoenberg concentrated on twelve-tone composition. It is fascinating to notice how, at the beginning of his twelve-tone period, Schoenberg balanced his revolutionary ideas with very traditional forms. Many of the compositions from this time adopt the structures of eighteenth-century music, such as sonata form or minuet-and-trio form. It is as though Schoenberg felt the need to hang on to something familiar while he was striking off in such new directions! (See Listening Guide.) After the first few years, though, he was able to create works freer in form, such as the opera *Moses and*

Aaron and the Piano Concerto. By the middle of the twentieth century, there were large numbers of composers who modeled their careers and their own musical styles on the work of this remarkable man.

In fact, it would be accurate to say that almost no composer since Schoenberg has been able to ignore his accomplishments. The revolution he led—liberating music from the tonal system—affected musicians by creating a system so powerful that composers had to either adopt it or consciously avoid it. For an entire generation, composers were required to justify writing music that was *not* twelve tone. And even composers who avoided the twelve-tone system had available to them a vocabulary of sounds that could be called upon occasionally to enrich their overall language.

Find the **Quick Listen** on **MySearchLab** "Schoenberg *Moses and Aaron*"

LISTENING GUIDE

((•●─[Listen on MySearchLab

ARNOLD SCHOENBERG (1874–1951)

"Madonna" from Pierrot Lunaire

CD III, 4

Date of composition: 1912
Orchestration: voice; flute, bass clarinet, viola, cello, piano
Duration: 2:04

Schoenberg's *Pierrot Lunaire* sets 21 poems by Albert Giraud. The entire collection functions much in the same way as a song cycle, in that the individual movements share a single viewpoint—in this case, that of Pierrot, a deeply troubled clown who seems to have a fascination with the mysterious powers of the moon.

Pierrot Lunaire has been described as an Expressionist work because it reveals the darker side of human nature. Just as the visual creations of artists such as Edvard Munch, Maurice de Vlaminck, and Oskar Kokoschka abandon the familiar lines associated with beauty and form, *Pierrot Lunaire* similarly abandons tonality and normal singing style in favor of inner emotional expression.

A special feature of this work is the singing method of the soloist, who does not sing in the customary way. Instead, she *approximates* the written pitches, in an eerie effect that merges singing with speaking. This technique is called *Sprechstimme* ("speech-song").

The individual movements are accompanied by a small group of instrumentalists (who double on various woodwinds) and a pianist.

"Madonna" (No. 6) seems to be inspired by some of the more grotesque figures seen in large cathedrals. The lyrics speak of blood, wounds, redness of the eyes, and so on, which are effectively rendered in Schoenberg's setting. Notice particularly the instance of word-painting on the word "Rise" (*Steig*) in the second stanza. Here Schoenberg writes the widest interval between two notes in the whole song. Notice also how expressively the words "blood" (*Blut*) and "sorrows" (*Schmerzen*) are presented.

Time	Listen for	
0:00	[Flute, clarinet, cello (1 measure)]	
	Stanza 1	
0:03	*Steig, o Mutter aller Schmerzen,* *Auf den Altar meiner Verse!*	Rise, O Mother of all Sorrows, on the altar of my verses!
0:18	*Blut aus deinen magern Bruesten* *Hat den Schwerten Wut vergossen.*	Blood pours forth from your withered bosom where the cruel sword has pierced it.
	Stanza 2	
0:32	*Deine ewig frischen Wunden Gleichen Augen,* *rot und offen.*	And your ever-bleeding wounds seem like eyes, red and open.
0:42	*Steig, o Mutter aller Schmerzen,* *Auf den Altar meiner Verse!*	Rise, O Mother of all Sorrows, on the altar of my verses!
0:57	[Instrumental interlude; change in instrumental figures]	
1:09	*In den abgezehrten Haenden* *Haelst du deines Sohnes Leiche,* *Ihn zu zeigen aller Menschheit—*	In your torn and wasted hands holding thy Son's holy body, you reveal Him to all mankind—
1:23	*Doch der Blick der Menschen meidet*	but the eyes of men are turned away,
1:28	*Dich, o Mutter aller Schmerzen!* [Piano enters, loud and abrupt with cello]	O Mother of all Sorrows!
1:42	[Final chord, piano]	

LISTENING GUIDE

ARNOLD SCHOENBERG (1874–1951)

Theme and Sixth Variation from
Variations for Orchestra, *Op. 31*

Date of composition: 1928
Duration: 2:37

CD III, 5

The second piece we will study by Schoenberg, *Variations for Orchestra*, Op. 31, employs Schoenberg's twelve-tone method, and features a tone row, the basic building block for twelve-tone music. The row is

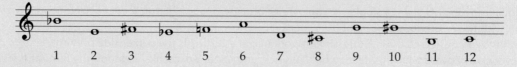

It is used four times to make up the theme. The theme itself is in ternary form, made up of the unusual and irregular phrases of five and seven measures. The main section is made up of twelve measures divided into five and seven. The middle section covers five measures, and the return of the main section is compressed into seven measures.

Even the accompaniment of the theme is numerically based. The first phrase, which consists of five notes, is accompanied by a five-note chord. The second phrase of four notes is heard against a four-note chord, and the following phrase of three notes is accompanied by a simple triad (three notes).

In this composition, Schoenberg uses a large orchestra. But the scoring is very sparse, so that the effect is like chamber music in its texture. We shall listen to the theme and the sixth variation.

(Read the Listening Guide first, and then reread while listening.)

Time	Listen for
	Theme [Molto moderato ("Very moderate")]
0:00	The first appearance of the row (cello melody, first twelve notes) presents the row in its ORIGINAL sequence (O):

0:12	The continuation of the cello melody (next twelve notes) presents the row in RETROGRADE INVERSION (RI: backwards and upside-down), beginning on the note G:

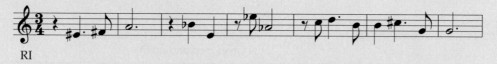

0:30	The middle section of the theme is played as RETROGRADE ORIGINAL (the row backwards):

0:42	Gentle cadence.
0:43	The melody travels to the violins, which present the row in INVERSION (upside-down), beginning on high G:

1:04	The movement ends very quietly. Conclusion.
	Variation VI [Andante ("Quite slow")]
	(This variation features several instruments playing the main theme, against varying combinations of instruments playing melodic figures derived from the row.)
1:06	Main theme, clarinets, answered by English horn and flute.
1:13	Continuation.
1:24	Main theme inverted, played by solo viola, answered by flute and horn.
1:32	Melodic fragments, all instruments.
1:37	Flute, short chromatic figure, followed by solo viola playing descending line in longer notes.
1:49	Main theme, clarinets.
1:57	More rhythmic movement, entire orchestra.
2:01	Muted trumpet chords.
2:13	Main theme, violins.
2:22	Faster motion.
2:34	Motion stops, movement ends.

Schoenberg's Students

The two most famous students of Schoenberg were Alban Berg and Anton Webern. Both men began studying with Schoenberg in their late teens, and both became deeply absorbed in his pursuit of atonality and finally of the twelve-tone system. Despite this close association, however, each composer managed to keep his own individual musical personality, and each one's work is clearly distinguishable.

Alban Berg (1885–1935)

Berg was, like Schoenberg, born in Vienna, and he also had no formal training before he began writing music. He played the piano and wrote some songs. Berg was 19 years old and working as a government clerk when he saw Schoenberg's newspaper advertisement for students and signed up for private lessons. He studied with Schoenberg for six years, and the two men became close friends. Berg's early compositions are in the late-Romantic style and include a piano sonata and several songs. His first atonal piece was the String Quartet, Op. 3, written in 1910. Just before the war, Berg completed his *Three Pieces for Orchestra*.

During World War I, Berg served three years in the army and worked in the Ministry

Alban Berg in his study.

of War, but he also managed to begin composing the first of his two great operas. *Wozzeck* was completed in 1922 and stands as the first atonal Expressionist opera. It is also one of the great operas of the twentieth century.

In 1925, Berg finished his *Kammerkonzert* (Chamber Concerto) for piano, violin, and 13 wind instruments. Hidden in the Chamber Concerto are musical references to the names of the three friends: Schoenberg, Berg, and Webern. The *Lyric Suite* was written in 1926. Originally for string quartet, it was later arranged for string orchestra by the composer.

In 1928, Berg began work on his second Expressionist opera, *Lulu*. The entire opera was complete, except for the orchestration of the third act, when Berg died in 1935 of an infected insect bite (this was before the use of antibiotics). Berg's widow refused to release his draft for the third act, and the opera was not performed in its entirety until 1979, after she had died.

Berg's last completed composition also comes from the year of his death. He broke off work on *Lulu* to write his Violin Concerto as a memorial to Manon Gropius, the daughter of Mahler's widow, Alma, with her second husband. Manon died at the age of 18 from polio. Berg dedicated the work "to the memory of an angel."

Berg's Music

Of the three colleagues, Berg retained the strongest links with the past. He adopted atonality and twelve-tone technique but much more flexibly than either Schoenberg or Webern. You can find passages of tonal music in many of his compositions, and he never abandoned the Romantic idea of lyricism. His music is more passionate and emotionally intense than that of the other two composers.

Wozzeck Berg's experience of war is reflected in his opera *Wozzeck*. The opera tells the story of a poor, working-class soldier (Franz Wozzeck) who is bullied by his superiors, betrayed by Marie (the woman he loves), and beaten up by his rival. Driven to madness, Wozzeck murders Marie and then commits suicide. The drama is intensely emotional, and the music, like much

of Berg's work, is both highly expressive and very succinct. Although the music is atonal, Berg uses tight, closed structures borrowed from the past: sonata form, rondo form, fugue, theme and variations, and many others. We shall listen carefully to one of the climactic scenes of *Wozzeck*. (See Listening Guide.)

The music that Berg crafted is brilliant, powerful, and enormously inventive; it is continuous within each of the three acts. Each act is divided into five scenes, but the scenes are connected by orchestral interludes. Stylistically, Berg borrowed from Wagner and Schoenberg. From Wagner he took the technique of the leitmotiv: each character is associated with a particular musical idea. The Expressionist quality of the music owes much to Schoenberg's *Pierrot Lunaire*. The music is jagged, distorted, careening wildly between extremes: between very loud and very soft, between very high and very low, between singing and talking. Perhaps the greatest variety comes in the vocal line: the singers use *Sprechstimme*, but they also use spoken words, flowing melody, screams, whispers, and folk tunes.

In Act I, we meet Wozzeck, a poor soldier who is tormented by nightmares. His captain persecutes him for no reason, and the army doctor uses him as a guinea pig in human experiments. In Act II, Wozzeck is driven mad by the woman he lives with, who sleeps with another man, and by his rival, who brutally beats him up. At the beginning of Act III, Wozzeck stabs Marie to death near a pond in the forest. We shall listen to Act III, Scene 4, in which Wozzeck returns to the pond to hide the knife. He tries to wash the blood off his hands, but it seems to him that the whole pond is turning to blood. He drowns. The captain and the army doctor hear him drowning but leave him to his fate. The music for this scene contains powerful pictorial descriptions in the orchestra: the moon rising, the forest at night, the water welling over Wozzeck's head, the gradual ebbing of life.

Find the **Quick Listen** on **MySearchLab**
"Berg Violin Concerto"

> Berg is the only one to have achieved large-scale development forms without a suggestion of "neoclassic" dissimulation.
> —Igor Stravinsky on Berg

> We must hail not only a great composer but a hero. Doomed to total failure, he still kept on cutting out his diamonds, his dazzling diamonds.
> —Igor Stravinsky on Webern

> Webern can say more in two minutes than most other composers in ten.
> —Humphrey Searle, English composer

LISTENING GUIDE

((•− Listen on **MySearchLab**

ALBAN BERG (1885–1935)   *Wozzeck, Act III, Scene 4*

Date of composition: 1924
Orchestration: piccolo, four flutes, four oboes, English horn, two E♭ clarinets, four clarinets, bass clarinet, three bassoons, contrabassoon, four horns, four trumpets, four trombones, bass trombone, tuba, two timpani, bass drum, side drum, tam-tams, two cymbals, triangle, xylophone, celesta, harp, strings
Duration: 4:50

CD III, 6

Time	Listen for	

Scene 4 [by the pond, scene of the crime, Wozzeck is looking for the knife he used to murder Marie]

Wozzeck

Time		
0:00	*Das Messer? Wo ist das Messer:* *Ich habs da gelassen. Näher, noch näher.* *Mir graut's. Da regt sich was. Still!* *Alles still und tot.* [Celesta]	Where is it? Where can the knife be? Somewhere here, I left it somewhere. I'm scared. There. Something moved. Quiet! All is quiet and dead.
0:31	[trumpets, low trombones] *Mörder! Mörder!!* *Ha! da ruft's?* *Nein. Ich selbst.* [discovering the corpse] *Marie! Marie! Was hast du für eine rote Schnur* *um den Hals? Hast Dir das rote Halsband* *verdient, wie die Ohr-Ringlein, mit Deiner* *Sünde?! Was hängen Dir die schwarzen* *Haare so wild?! Mörder! Mörder!! Sie werden* *nach mir suchen. Das Messer verrät mich!* [slide on strings]	Murder! Murder!! Ah, who cried? No. It was me. Marie! Marie! What is that like a crimson cord round your neck? And was that crimson necklace a gift, like the golden earrings, the price of sin?! Why is your fine black hair so wild on your face?! Murder! Murder!! They'll soon be coming for me. That knife will betray me.
	[discovering the knife] *Da, da ist's!* [throwing the knife into the pond] *So! da hinunter!* [bass tuba, trombones, contrabassoon] *Es taucht ins dunkle Wasser wie ein Stein.* [voice sinking]	Here it is! Down! To the bottom! It sinks through deep dark water like a stone.
	[looking up at the moon; harp] *Aber der Mond verrät mich.* *Der Mond is Blutig* [solo violins] *Will den die ganze Welt es ausplaudern?!* *Das Messer, es liegt zu weit vorn,* *sie findens beim Baden oder* *wenn sie nach Muscheln tauchen.*	See how the moon betrays me. The moon is bloody. Must the whole wide world be shouting it?! That knife is too near the shore. They will find it when bathing, or when they are gathering mussels.
	[wading into the pond] *Ich find's nicht.* *Aber ich muss mich waschen. Ich bin blutig.* *Da ein fleck und noch einer.*	I can't find it now. I should wash myself. I am bloody. Here's a spot and here another.
2:35	[lamenting] *Weh! Weh! Ich wasche mich mit Blut.* *Das Wasser ist Blut…Blut…* [slow rising strings, representing the water rising] [He begins to drown. The Captain and the Doctor enter.]	Woe! Woe! I wash myself with blood. The water is blood…blood…

Captain		
3:01	*Halt!*	Stop!
Doctor		
	Hören Sie? Dort!	Do you hear? There!
Captain		
	Jesus! Was war ein Ton.	Jesus! What a sound.
Doctor		
	Ja, dort!	Yes, over there!
Captain		
	Es ist das Wasser im Teich. Das Wasser ruft. Es ist schon lange niemand entrunken. Kommen Sie, Doktor! Es ist nicht gut zu hören.	It is the water. The water is calling out. No one has drowned here for a long time. Come, Doctor! It is not good to hear.
Doctor		
	Das stöhnt, [clarinets, horn] *als stürbe ein Mensch.*	Groaning like a man dying.
	Da ertrinkt Jemand!	Someone is drowning!
Captain		
	Unheimlich! [celesta and harp] *Der Mond rot, und die Nebel grau. Hören Sie? Jetzt wieder das Aechzen.*	Eerie! The moon is red, the mist gray. Do you hear? Again that sound.
Doctor		
	Stiller, jetzt ganz still. [silence]	Quieter now. Now completely quiet.
Captain		
	Kommen Sie! Kommen Sie schnell. [timpani, basses; low harp]	Come! Come quickly.
4:29	[End of scene]	

Anton Webern (1883–1945)

If Berg represented the link backward from Modernism to the past, Webern may be seen as the link forward from the first stage of Modernism to the second stage (after World War II). Whereas Berg's music is lush, intense, and emotionally committed, Webern's is spare, abstract, and restrained.

Webern was born in Vienna, like Schoenberg and Berg. He came from a middle-class family and as a teenager was immersed in music; he played the piano and the cello and studied music theory in addition to composing

many pieces. While he was at the university, Webern studied musicology and wrote a doctoral dissertation on the music of the Renaissance composer Heinrich Isaac. His close study of counterpoint had a strong influence on his own music. Like Berg, Webern took private composition lessons with Schoenberg.

Webern's death goes down in history as one of the many thousands of incongruous tragedies caused by war. In 1945, after the war had ended and American forces were occupying Austria, Webern went outside one night to

Anton Webern.

Webern had an exact ear for precisely the sounds he wanted to achieve. He wrote detailed instructions all over his scores, indicating exactly how he wanted each tiny phrase to sound. It is a measure of the refinement of his music that although there is a whole spectrum of dynamics in his works, almost all of it lies between medium loud and very, very soft.

Most of Webern's compositions are quite short. Many movements last less than a minute, and some are as short as 20 seconds. Even the biggest works are only 10 minutes long altogether.

Webern used a great deal of imitative counterpoint in his music, like the Renaissance masters he studied. But in Webern's style, the counterpoint is atonal and, from the 1920s on, twelve-tone. The intervals are often sevenths and ninths, and there are many dissonances, but the texture is so light and transparent that the dissonances sound colorful rather than harsh.

In addition to his finely honed ear for dynamics, Webern possessed a keen awareness of very fine distinctions in instrumental sound. He calls for a great variety of tones and timbres, especially from string instruments, which are asked to play *pizzicato* (plucked), *sul ponticello* (bowed near the bridge), *con sordino* (with a mute), or *tremolo* (very rapid bowing on a single note), as well as combinations of the four. And each one of these instructions may appear over a phrase of just two or three notes. We will listen to one of Webern's very short movements for string quartet. (**See Listening Guide.**)

In Webern's music, with its rarefied atmosphere and extreme concision, every note has meaning; every gesture is significant. The utmost attention is required from the listener. Nothing could be further removed from the soaring length of Romantic music.

smoke a cigarette and was shot by a jittery American soldier.

Webern's Music

Webern's music is extraordinarily concentrated and delicate. Everything is understated, and there is never an extra note. In this very finely sculpted atmosphere, the silences are as meaningful as the notes. In painting, a close parallel to Webern's music can be found in the *Constellations* series of Joan Miró, in which stars and tiny figures are carefully balanced with empty space throughout the canvas to create an overall effect.

LISTENING GUIDE

((•⁃[Listen on **MySearchLab**

ANTON WEBERN (1883–1945)   *Third Movement from* Five Movements for String Quartet, *Op. 5*

Date of composition: 1909
Orchestration: two violins, viola, cello
Duration: 0:43

CD III, 7

The third movement of Webern's *Five Movements for String Quartet* is so short that even the tiniest gesture is significant. Also, Webern uses a wide range of articulations and special string sounds that throw every note into relief. These include

1. *am steg,* "at the bridge." Bowing high on the strings produces very scratchy, high-pitched sounds.
2. *pizzicato,* "plucked."
3. *arco,* "bowed."
4. *staccato,* "short, detached notes."
5. *col legno,* "with the wood." The strings are struck with the wood of the bow.

Time	Listen for
0:00	*staccato,* cello, short notes.
0:01	*am steg,* violins and viola.
0:03	*pizzicato,* violins and viola.
0:04	*arco,* violins and viola.
0:08	*arco staccato,* first violin and cello.
0:10	*col legno,* violins and viola.
0:16	*arco,* first violin; *pizzicato,* second violin, viola, cello.
0:26	*arco,* cello; *pizzicato,* first violin and viola.
0:30	*arco,* first violin; *arco staccato,* second violin, viola, cello.
0:35	Loud finish, all instruments *staccato,* with two final *pizzicato* chords.

Other Composers Active Before World War II: Bartók, Shostakovich, Britten, Ives, Copland

We have examined the music of the most influential composers up to the middle of the twentieth century, but, as always in a survey of this kind, several important names have been omitted. Here we shall look briefly at the music of some of those figures. Although none of them founded a school or had brilliant and influential students, each one wrote compelling music of profound significance. Among the five composers—Bartók, Shostakovich, Britten, Ives, and Copland—four different nationalities are represented.

Béla Bartók (1881–1945)

Bartók at the age of 18.

One of the most independent and original composers of the first half of the century was Béla Bartók. His work grew out of the nationalist movement of the second half of the nineteenth century. Bartók was born in Hungary. As a student, he entered the Budapest Academy of Music, where he later became professor of piano. He toured extensively as a concert pianist. But he also spent a great deal of time in Eastern Europe, Turkey, and North Africa, recording and notating indigenous music, including songs and instrumental pieces. He ultimately published 2,000 tunes, notating as authentically as he could every inflection and detail of the performances he had heard.

In the 1930s, Bartók was able to spend more and more time on his own compositions. In 1940 he emigrated to the United States with his wife, who was also a concert pianist. The couple made a meager living playing concerts, and Bartók worked for the folk music collection at Columbia University. He was virtually unrecognized, however, and he wrote no new music.

In 1943, though very ill, Bartók was given an important commission by the music director of the Boston Symphony Orchestra, Serge Koussevitsky, whose patronage helped support many struggling artists. The composition, known as the Concerto for Orchestra, was first performed in 1944. The belated recognition and the stimulus of working on the piece helped to revive Bartók's health and his spirits. He began to compose once again and almost finished three more major works before he died on September 26, 1945.

Bartók's Music

Bartók had three simultaneous careers: as an ethnomusicologist (someone who studies indigenous musics), a concert pianist, and a composer. Each of the first two influenced the third. First, many of his compositions are colored by the rhythms and melodies of the indigenous music of Hungary (and Eastern Europe in general). Second, the piano is featured in many of his works.

Partly for his students at the Budapest Academy of Music and partly for his son Peter, Bartók wrote a long series of piano pieces. The early ones are easy, and they gradually get more difficult. The series is called *Mikrokosmos*. It is in six volumes, ranging from wonderful little pieces for beginners to extremely complicated works. Other Bartók piano compositions include three highly original piano concertos and a fascinating work, full of novel sounds, called *Sonata for Two Pianos and Percussion*, written in 1937.

Like Beethoven, Bartók reserved his most profound music for his string quartets. The six quartets span most of his career, the first dating from 1908, when he was 27, and the last from 1939, just before he left Hungary for the United States. Each quartet is a profound and brilliant example of his art.

The most famous of the works composed in America is the *Concerto for Orchestra* (1943). The title is a play on words, because concertos usually put the spotlight on a single instrument rather than on a whole orchestra. But the work was written to celebrate the brilliance of all the orchestra's players.

Bartók's musical style is very individual. It is also very profound. You always have the sense that Bartók was a man of great integrity and seriousness of purpose, although that doesn't mean his music is dull. On the contrary, his fast movements are often very exciting—both wild and passionate. And his slow movements range from pieces of delicate mystery to extremes of lyrical intensity.

In his harmony, too, Bartók was highly original. He mingled the modality that is present in much indigenous music with both chromaticism and tonality. You have the feeling that a key center is usually present, giving the work a gravitational center, but it may be lost or disguised for long passages. Bartók used strict structures, like sonata form or ABA form, but in novel ways. And he invented new forms. One of his favorites was the arch form. In a five-movement piece, movements 1 and 5 correspond, and so do movements 2 and 4.

Movement 3 is considered the apex of the arch. Bartók used this form with great effect in the Concerto for Orchestra and in his Fourth and Fifth String Quartets.

Dmitri Shostakovich (1906–1975)

Shostakovich was born just before the Russian Revolution and died 14 years before the collapse of Communism. He lived most of his life under the Soviet system, attempting to find a balance between creative freedom and the demands of a totalitarian state. His plight is movingly described in his memoirs, entitled *Testimony*, smuggled out of the Soviet Union and published in 1979. Because music in the Soviet Union was supposed to represent the policies of the state, Shostakovich often came in for official criticism. He had to withdraw several of his works from performance after they had been composed. Often he would write a piece and not even publish it. (And Shostakovich's terror was justified. Under Stalin, 20 million people were murdered, including many artists, writers, and musicians.)

After Stalin's death, Shostakovich wrote his Tenth Symphony in 1953. This is one of his greatest works. It is highly expressive and personal, with a voice of grieving introspection.

By the time of his death, Shostakovich had composed 15 symphonies. He also wrote 15 string quartets, some of which are also intensely personal. The Eighth String Quartet, written in 1960, is particularly moving.

Shostakovich often used a short musical motive in his works to put his signature on them. Bach had done this in the eighteenth century: the letters B-A-C-H are all names of notes in German (B is B♭, H is B♮). Shostakovich's signature is based on his monogram "D. Sch." S is E♭, so D-S-C-H in notes is D, E♭, C, and B♮. This musical signature is found in many works, especially the very personal Eighth String Quartet and the Tenth Symphony.

Shostakovich used traditional forms, such as the symphony and the string quartet, but he did so with great flexibility, expanding the number of movements, adding voices, and writing to a program. His language is intense, overlaying tonal areas with dense chromaticism or playing off highly dissonant chord structures with passages of great lyricism.

Like Bartók, Shostakovich was a composer who proved that tonality, updated, refreshed, and reinvented for the twentieth century, was still a highly viable means of expression.

Find the **Quick Listen** on **MySearchLab**
"Bartok Concerto for Orchestra Complete"

Find the **Quick Listen** on **MySearchLab**
"Shostakovich Eighth String Quartet"

I always try to make myself as widely understood as possible; and if I don't succeed, I consider it my fault.
—Dmitri Shostakovich

Shostakovich, pen in hand, always thinking.

Benjamin Britten (1913–1976)

Benjamin Britten was born in a small English country town in Suffolk. He was a child prodigy and began turning out compositions at the age of five. Later, he arranged some of these childhood pieces into the *Simple Symphony* (1934), which is one of his most attractive works. Britten's *The Young Person's Guide to the Orchestra* (1946) is designed to display all the different instruments of a symphony orchestra.

Britten was gay, and he lived with Peter Pears, a fine tenor singer, who remained his lifelong companion. During World War II, the couple was invited to America by the poet W. H. Auden, who was also gay and who had formed an artists' community in New York. But after only two years, Britten and Pears returned to England.

Then began the remarkable series of operas on which Britten concentrated for the next 10 years. The first was *Peter Grimes* (1945), then came *Billy Budd* (1951), *Gloriana* (1953) (written for the coronation of Queen Elizabeth II), and *The Turn of the Screw* (1954). In most of his vocal works, a central role is designed for tenor Peter Pears.

During the 1960s, Britten concentrated on two major projects. The first was the production of several cello works for the great Soviet cellist Mstislav Rostropovich, who had recently

Find the **Quick Listen** on **MySearchLab**

"Britten The Young Person's Guide to the Orchestra"

Benjamin Britten.

been allowed to travel from the Soviet Union and whose artistry Britten admired.

The other project of Britten's from this time was the *War Requiem* (1961). Britten's *War Requiem* was written for the dedication of the new cathedral in Coventry, England, which had been constructed to replace the great medieval church destroyed during World War II. For this event, Britten mingled lamentation for Britain's war dead with a powerful call for peace. He alternates settings of the age-old, timeless Latin Mass for the Dead with settings of poems by Wilfred Owen, who had been killed a week before the end of World War I at the age of 24. The *War Requiem* is richly varied and, with its expressive tension between the old and the new, both powerful and moving.

Britten's individual sound is based on many factors: the directness and lack of pretension in the melodic lines, the common use of high tenor voice (this range seems to affect even his instrumental compositions), and an almost constant tension between conflicting tonalities. This can extend sometimes to clear instances of bitonality.

The American Scene

As we saw in the last chapter, up until the twentieth century the United States was mostly absorbed in the creation and performance of European-style music. Americans looked down on their own musical traditions (New England hymns, African American spirituals, folk music, the blues) as unworthy.

Music was, however, becoming better established on the American scene. Conservatories of music were founded, concert halls were built, and music began to be taught as a serious discipline on university campuses. Most composers in the years around the turn of the century began or concentrated their careers in Boston. They included John Paine (1839–1906), who was the first professor of music ever to be appointed in the United States (at Harvard University); Edward MacDowell (1860–1908), a fine pianist as well as a composer; Horatio Parker (1863–1919), a choral composer on mostly religious texts; George Chadwick (1854–1931), a symphonist and American opera composer, who was for more than 30 years director of the newly founded New England Conservatory of Music in Boston; and Arthur Foote (1853–1937), whose best works are his beautiful solo songs and chamber music.

Boston was also the home of several women composers. They included Helen Hood, Mabel Daniels, Helen Hopekirk, and Margaret Lang, who died in 1972 at the age of 104.

Perhaps the best-known woman composer in Boston at the turn of the century was Amy Beach (1867–1944). She began her musical career as a concert pianist but also composed a wealth of important music, including a Mass, a piano concerto, an opera, a symphony, chamber music, piano works, and songs. She was the piano soloist in the first performance of her Piano Concerto (1899), which was premiered by the Boston Symphony Orchestra. Her symphony, entitled the *Gaelic Symphony* (1896) because it is based on Irish folk tunes, was also first performed by that orchestra and carries the distinction of being the first-known American symphony by a woman.

In the years after the Civil War, black Americans began slowly to enter the American mainstream. Among the important African American composers around the turn of the century were Scott Joplin (about whom we shall learn more in the next chapter); Henry Burleigh (1866–1949), who sang in churches and synagogues when he was young, and taught spirituals to Antonin Dvořák when he visited the United States (Burleigh was a pioneer in writing concert arrangements of spirituals for formal performance); Will Marion Cook (1869–1944), whose works include songs, an opera, and musical comedies; and William Grant Still (1895–1978), who wrote many large-scale works, including symphonies, operas, and ballets.

Today, although there are some attempts at revival, little of all this late nineteenth- and early twentieth-century American music receives regular concert performance. Perhaps the American inferiority complex vis-à-vis music from Europe has still not quite disappeared.

Charles Ives (1874–1954)

The first Modernist composer whose work was distinctively American was Charles Ives, who grew up in a small Connecticut town. He was the son of a bandmaster and music teacher whose approach to music was fun loving and unconventional. Ives's father used to play tunes in two different keys at once, and he sometimes asked Charles to sing a song while he played the accompaniment in the "wrong" key on the piano. This open-minded and experimental approach stayed with Ives all his life.

Ives went to Yale as an undergraduate and then went into the insurance business, devoting his spare time to music. Over the next 10 years, he wrote an enormous quantity of music, while his business prospered, too. Although he lived until 1954, most of his music dates from before World War I.

Ives's music is a remarkable, unique mixture. He was a radical experimentalist, who nonetheless believed in the values of small-town America. Most of his compositions are based on American cultural themes: baseball, Thanksgiving, marching bands, popular songs, the Fourth of July, fireworks, and American literature. Working alone, Ives developed some of the avant-garde innovations that would not take hold in the broader musical scene until the 1960s. He wrote music with wild dissonances. Once, Ives wrote a note to his music copyist, who had "corrected" some of the notes in his manuscript: "Please don't correct the wrong notes. The wrong notes are right." He wrote for pianos specially tuned in quarter tones; in his *Concord* Sonata he called for the pianist to use an elbow to press down notes and, in one place, a wooden board to play 16 notes at once. "Is it the composer's fault that a man has only ten fingers?" he asked. Ives's most famous composition is *The Unanswered Question* (1908), in which two different instrumental groups, sitting separately, play different music at the same time. And in his program piece called *Putnam's Camp*, the music depicts two marching bands passing each other, playing different tunes. (**See Listening Guide.**)

The music of Charles Ives was virtually unknown in its own time. It was only in the 1940s that Ives's work began to be performed, and only many years later that he began to be recognized as the first truly original American musical genius.

Find the **Quick Listen** on **MySearchLab**
"Amy Beach *Gaelic Symphony*"

Find the **Quick Listen** on **MySearchLab**
"William Grant Still Afro-American Symphony"

Find the **Quick Listen** on **MySearchLab**
"Ives *Unanswered Question*"

Charles Ives, composer and insurance agent.

LISTENING GUIDE

((•• **Listen** on **MySearchLab**

CHARLES IVES (1874–1954)

Second Movement from Three Places in New England (*"Putnam's Camp, Redding, Conn."*)

Date of composition: 1903–11
Orchestration: flute/piccolo, oboe/English horn, clarinet, bassoon, two or more horns, two or more trumpets, two trombones, tuba, piano, timpani, drums, cymbals, strings
Duration: 5:41

CD III, 8

"Putnam's Camp" captures a child's impression of a Fourth of July picnic with singing and marching bands. In the middle of the picnic, the boy falls asleep and dreams of songs and marches from the time of the American Revolution. When he awakes, he again hears the noise of the picnic celebration.

Ives's piece is a type of aural collage. Contrasting sounds and textures are overlaid and connected. Moments of simplicity provide the listener with points of repose and orientation before the vivacious tumult resumes. The moments of thinner texture—when one or a few instruments stand out with a clear and simple melodic idea—separate passages of fervent, strident, jumbled polyphony. Although Ives combines every melody and every rhythm very precisely, the effect is (and it is an effect he strove for) one of varying successions of vigorous, raucous noise. Audiences today delight in the energy of the work, and different impressions surface with every hearing.

Time	Listen for
0:00	*Introduction*: full orchestra with dissonant but rhythmically unified descending scales, leading to repeated notes; a vigorous march-like pulse.
0:10	*Allegro* ("quick-step time"): a bouncy, accessible melody accompanied by a regular thudding bass. The conventional harmonies contrast with the harsh introduction. Flutes and trumpets can be heard with competing melodies as Ives evokes the atmosphere of a chaotic festive event.
0:47	After a fanfare by a single trumpet, the confused fervor of the different simultaneous events continues even more energetically, with strong melodies in trombones and trumpets, and heavy use of cymbals and snare drum.
1:00	Thinner texture and softer dynamics lead to parodied quotations of "Rally Round the Flag" and "Yankee Doodle," with:
1:08	Disjunct melody in violins with conflicting piano and percussion, leading to:
1:50	Softly throbbing cellos and basses, gradually slowing down, illustrating the child gradually falling asleep.
1:55	Decrescendo, then quiet.
2:06	*Dream section*: Begins with an ethereal sustained high chord (the Goddess of Liberty), then continues with a legato but energetic melody (first flute, then oboe). But the regular pulse (percussion and piano) accompanying this melody accelerates and takes off on its own (the soldiers march off to pipe and drum). Different melodies in the violins, oboes, clarinets, and trumpets, in a number of different meters and keys, combine with a building tension. The conflicting pulse of the piano and snare drum against the slower pulse of the repetitive low strings can be clearly heard. This gradually dies down, and then:
3:10	A bold, new, brass melody emerges and leads to another section of conflicting melodies; simultaneously, "The British Grenadiers," a favorite revolutionary tune, is heard in the flutes.
3:36	A strongly accented and repetitive tune ascends in the brass and starts another dense passage.
3:57	*Awakening*: This comes to an abrupt halt (the boy suddenly awakens), and a lively tune is revealed in the violins (the boy hears children's songs in the background). This builds to another complex passage (different bands, songs, and games combine). Heavy, low rhythms and several meters combine. Fragments of lively string melody, "The British Grenadiers," and other tunes.
4:47	Repeated notes in trumpets and brass cut in suddenly.
4:54	Another swirl of melodies and rhythms, oscillating notes crescendo, frantic scales, as all the instruments push their dynamic limit, leading to the final jarring chord.

Aaron Copland (1900–1990)

If Ives represents the avant-garde in American music, Aaron Copland represents a more mainstream approach. Copland was born into a Jewish immigrant family in Brooklyn and decided to become a composer at the age of 15. When he was 20, he went to Europe—specifically to Paris, where he studied with Nadia Boulanger.

Boulanger was perhaps the most famous composition teacher of the twentieth century. She was also a composer, pianist, organist, and conductor. She was extremely strict in her teaching, insisting that her students learn all aspects of music, including careful and detailed analysis of musical scores. A large number of American composers of the twentieth century studied with Boulanger, forming in this way a thorough and rigorous background for their own work.

When Copland returned from Paris in 1924, he decided to write works that would be specifically American in style. To do this, he drew on the most recognizably American musical style: jazz. And many of his compositions are marked by the syncopated rhythms and chord combinations of American jazz. One of these is the Clarinet Concerto (1948), which he wrote for the famous jazz clarinetist Benny Goodman.

Another way Copland strove to put America into his music was by the use of purely American cultural topics. His ballet suites *Billy the Kid* (1938) and *Rodeo* (1942) are cowboy stories, and *Appalachian Spring* (1944) depicts a pioneer wedding in rural Pennsylvania.

Appalachian Spring also demonstrates a third technique used by Copland to make his music sound American: quoting from folk songs, hymns, and country tunes. The fourth scene of *Appalachian Spring* sounds like country fiddling, and the seventh scene is a series of variations on the exquisite Shaker melody "Simple Gifts." (**See the following example.**)

Finally, Copland made his music sound American by a rather more sophisticated technique. He used very widely spaced sonorities—deep basses and high, soaring violins—to evoke the wide-open spaces of the American landscape. In addition, he often used the intervals of a fifth and an octave in his music, very open-sounding intervals, and his chord changes are slow and static, suggesting the more gradual pace of nature's clock. Copland said that he wanted to write music "that would speak of universal things…music with a largeness of utterance wholly representative of our country."

Two of Copland's more accessible and popular works are *Lincoln Portrait* and

Aaron Copland.

Fanfare for the Common Man, both composed in 1942. For the *Lincoln Portrait*, Copland arranged extracts from Lincoln's speeches and letters to be recited with orchestral accompaniment. Both works were composed to provide patriotic encouragement at a time of national anxiety.

Copland wrote books on music, gave lectures, conducted around the world, composed film scores, and was the mentor of such luminaries as Leonard Bernstein. Copland's leading position in the world of twentieth-century American musical life led to his being called "the dean of American music."

Find the **Quick Listen** on **MySearchLab**

"'Simple Gifts' from *Appalachian Spring*"

'Tis the gift to be sim - ple, 'tis the gift to be free, 'tis the gift to come down where you ought to be. And when we find our-selves in the place just right, 'twill be in the val - ley of love and de - light.

The Shaker song "Simple Gifts."

We listened to Copland's *Fanfare for the Common Man* in Chapter 3, but let's listen to it again here in its historical context. (**See Listening Guide.**) Because it was written in 1942, in the middle of the Second World War, he wanted it to be stirring and patriotic. *Fanfare for the Common Man* has become one of the best-known pieces of classical music in America. By using the words "common man,"

Copland did not mean to exclude women; he meant that he had written the piece for everybody, especially for all ordinary people.

Much of its triumphant mood comes from its instrumentation, but there is also an American quality to the music. The melodies are based on the simplest intervals—triads, fifths, and octaves—which give an open, spacious, quality to this stirring piece.

LISTENING GUIDE

((∙●─ Listen on **MySearchLab**

AARON COPLAND (1900–1990)

Fanfare for the Common Man

Date of composition: 1942
Orchestration: three trumpets, four horns, three trombones, tuba, timpani, bass drum, gong
Duration: 3:39

CD I, 5

Time	Listen for
0:00	Somber strokes on the bass drum, timpani, and gong.
0:25	Fanfare on trumpets alone.
0:54	Bass drum and timpani.
0:59	Fanfare, louder, slightly modified, on trumpets with horns.
1:39	Bass drum, timpani, and gong.
1:50	Trombones and tuba are added, and the opening phrase of the fanfare is echoed by the tuned timpani. Richer harmonies.
2:38	Fanfare developed, even louder, with all instruments, followed by stepwise descents.
3:27	The work ends with a massive climax (*fortissimo* ***fff***) with a rolling crescendo on the timpani.

Building Bridges

Much of Copland's music is the result of an attempt to bridge the gap between "serious" music and its audience. Two other American composers did this in different ways: George Gershwin and Leonard Bernstein.

George Gershwin (1898–1937)

George Gershwin was primarily a composer of popular songs and a jazz pianist. But he was also attracted to the world of the concert hall, and he wrote four works that reach across the cultural divide between popular and classical music. The first was *Rhapsody in Blue* (1924), a highly attractive and successful mixture of the jazz idiom and concert music, scored for solo piano and

orchestra. Next came the jazzy *Piano Concerto in F* (1925). Both compositions were designed for Gershwin's own brilliant piano playing.

In 1928, Gershwin composed *An American in Paris*, a programmatic symphonic poem. The music is colorful, lively, and drawn from Gershwin's own experience in visiting Paris several times.

The last of Gershwin's works to bridge the gap between popular and classical music was by far the most ambitious: it was a full-length opera, in which Gershwin combined elements of jazz, church meetings, street cries, lullabies, and spirituals. The opera was *Porgy and Bess*, which contains some of Gershwin's best-known tunes, including "It Ain't Necessarily So" and "Summertime." Many people know these songs,

Find the **Quick Listen** on **MySearchLab**

"Porgy and Bess"

but not so many have heard the entire opera, which is one of Gershwin's greatest achievements. *Porgy and Bess* was completed in 1935. A year and a half later, the brilliant young composer was dead, cut off in the midst of his career by a brain tumor at the age of 38.

Leonard Bernstein (1918–1990)

The person who best represented American music and music making in the second half of the twentieth century was also one of the most famous musicians in the world. His name was Leonard Bernstein, and he continued the tradition, started by Copland and Gershwin, of blending popular and "serious" styles. Like Copland and Gershwin, Bernstein was Jewish and born of immigrant parents. Like them, he was a brilliant pianist and a prodigiously gifted all-around musician. Like Copland, Bernstein lectured and wrote books about music and loved to teach. Like Gershwin, Bernstein enjoyed fast cars, fancy clothes, and all-night parties.

Bernstein got his start in music at Tanglewood, where he became a protégé of the conductor and music patron Serge Koussevitsky. In 1943, Bernstein caused a sensation when he took over a New York Philharmonic concert as conductor on only a few hours' notice. From then on, his career was assured.

Bernstein was enormously versatile, and he had the energy of three men. He used to sleep only two or three hours a night. He could have been a great pianist, a great conductor, or a great composer. Instead, he was all three.

As a pianist, Bernstein enjoyed playing everything from Mozart to Gershwin. As a conductor, Bernstein's career was unparalleled. He was for 10 years the permanent conductor of the New York Philharmonic, but he was in demand by orchestras all over the world. His conducting was manically energetic: he would throw his arms around, shake his fists, twist, and cavort. Sometimes he would leap into the air to express his excitement. But underneath the showmanship, there was a profound musical intelligence.

As a composer, Bernstein was highly versatile. Like Stravinsky and Copland, he wrote ballet music. Bernstein also wrote musicals, including *On the Town* (1944), *Wonderful Town* (1953), and *Candide* (1956). His most successful musical, and his most famous composition, was *West Side Story*, written in 1957. An updating of Shakespeare's *Romeo and Juliet*, it tells the story of lovers separated by the gulf between rival gangs on Manhattan's West Side. The score is brilliant, combining jazz, snappy dances, and moving lyricism. Bernstein had an uncanny

Leonard Bernstein in 1947.
Photo © William P. Gottlieb; www. jazzphotos.com.

ability to write immensely moving music that seems simple and direct and completely hides the craft that went into it.

In addition to ballets and musicals, Bernstein wrote gentle songs and delicate piano pieces, as well as big choral works, three symphonies, two operas, and a Mass. Multiple reconciliations are attempted in his *Mass*, written in 1971. It is a rock setting of the Catholic Mass with singers and orchestra; it is a concert piece that is designed to be staged; and some of the text is in Hebrew.

However Bernstein's most popular work is the extraordinary *West Side Story*, which opened in New York in September of 1957. *West Side Story* has been called "a landmark in the cultural history of the United States." It was the result of a collaboration involving the playwright Arthur Laurents, choreographer Jerome Robbins, composer Leonard Bernstein, and the new young lyricist Stephen Sondheim.

Laurents based his story on a magisterial model: Shakespeare's *Romeo and Juliet*. The parallels are many, though Laurents modernized the context and themes in such a way that they resonated with 1950s American culture. Shakespeare's play is set in Verona, Laurents's story in New York's Upper West Side. Shakespeare's lovers are members of rival families; Maria and Tony are members of rival ethnic groups represented by street gangs. Romeo and Juliet meet at a ball; Tony and Maria meet at a

Find the **Quick Listen** on **MySearchLab** "*West Side Story* Prologue"

COMPOSERS, PATRONS, AND AUDIENCES

Audiences for Music in the Twentieth Century

Audiences for music expanded enormously in the twentieth century, largely as a result of new technology. The radio and the phonograph brought music to millions of people who would otherwise not have been able to hear it. The commercialization of popular music also brought with it an exponential increase in the number of people hearing music of all kinds, in dance halls and nightclubs as well as on radio and on recordings. From the earliest cylinders invented before the turn of the century to the compact discs and MP3 players of today, recording technology has turned music into a business worth billions of dollars.

In this atmosphere of popularization, classical music, with its greater subtlety and deeper intellectual challenges, had to struggle for survival. The audiences for live classical music are still dwindling. Many orchestras have had to disband. Others have had to rely more and more on a small repertoire of orchestral "standards" to ensure a viable level of attendance. This, in turn, has turned most orchestras (as well as most opera houses and chamber-music groups) into highly conservative organizations, rather than the places of excitement and experimentation they used to be. In Mozart's time, most performances were of new music; now most are of old music. The 2,000-year-old tradition of Western music, with its treasury of musical masterpieces and its proven ability to express the human soul in ways that words cannot reach, is at a turning point. Will it survive our new century?

high school dance. Shakespeare's balcony becomes a fire escape, Friar Laurence's church a drugstore. In Shakespeare's play Romeo's friend is killed, Romeo kills the killer, and finally, Romeo dies. In *West Side Story* Tony's friend is killed, Tony kills the killer, and finally, Tony dies. The principal difference and the one concession that Laurents made to Broadway sensibilities was that Maria does not die at the end of the show, as Juliet does in the original play.

The vigorous dancing in *West Side Story* vitally reflected the tension and liveliness of 1950s American streets. Robbins was highly praised for his choreography both on stage and in the film version, which he codirected in 1961 (and which won 10 Oscars). Sondheim's lyrics are snappy, colloquial, and glowingly tender, by turns.

But the real glory of the piece is the music. It is not only the songs that are enormously varied, creative, and deeply felt. The orchestral music that links scenes also provides brilliant atmosphere. Bernstein doesn't just import jazz to make his music; he creates a score that is highly original, expressive, and of the times. The whispered "Boy, Boy, Crazy Boy" employs dissonant rising tritones to suggest an atmosphere that is both taut and cool. The dance at the gym ends with the hushed and then passionate "Maria," which moves from B major to a warm and magical E flat. "I Feel Pretty" casts its spell with an orchestra that includes tambourine and castanets and a light, staccato $\frac{3}{8}$ meter. "Somewhere" is in a luminous E major, with a central section a third higher in G; its opening phrase ("There's a place for us"), which leaps up a minor seventh and then falls back to the sixth degree of the

scale, is hauntingly lovely. These are just some of the felicities of a score that is marked throughout by a sure touch and creative innovation. The portrayal of ethnic tension and gang violence—and the blend of symphonic richness with the idiomatic accents of American jazz and popular song—make *West Side Story* emblematic of the cultural and musical scene of the 1950s.

Bernstein lived his life to the hilt. It seemed that he didn't want to miss anything. He was bisexual, smoked and drank to excess, and loved to surround himself with people. His charisma was extraordinary. He managed to wring 72 years out of life, though he never stopped smoking, and suffered from severe emphysema. In the end, he simply dropped dead. In his passionate commitment and his manifold achievements, Leonard Bernstein personified American music for half a century.

After the War: Modernism, the Second Stage

Although the careers of many of the composers discussed earlier (e.g., Stravinsky, Shostakovich, Britten, Copland, Bernstein) continued well into the second half of the century, the ending of World War II marked a real turning point in the development of new music. It was a turning point for the Western world, of course. As societies struggled to recover from the enormous human loss and destruction of the war, economies boomed, and a new optimism reigned. In the 1950s, Americans enjoyed a higher standard of living than ever before, and in Europe, though recovery was much slower, gradual rebuilding

Pierre Boulez.

and long-term prospects for peace led to increased hopes for the future. The birthrate multiplied, resulting in what has been called the "baby boom," whose effects (and ripple effects) continue to have an enormous influence on our society.

After the war, and especially in the fortunate 1950s and the radical 1960s, the arts flourished, and music entered the second stage of Modernism. This was a period of radical experimentation, expanding upon ideas set forth in the first stage and marked by two opposing tendencies: extreme control and complete freedom. The controls were established by a technique known as total serialism, which we will discuss. The outer fringes of the "freedom movement" allowed performers to play what they liked when they liked.

Total Serialism

Before the war, the twelve-tone technique had been employed primarily by the Viennese trio Schoenberg, Berg, and Webern. After the war, many other composers in several different countries began to use the technique. But they felt that Schoenberg and his students had not gone far enough. If pitches can be organized into a strict sequence, then why not do the

same with all the elements of music: dynamics, rhythm, tone quality, and so on? The twelve-tone technique had sometimes been called **serialism**, because it arranged the notes into a series; this new idea was therefore called **total serialism**.

The first composition based on total serialism was *Structures I* (1952) by the French composer Pierre Boulez. Born in 1925, Boulez was one of the most influential musical figures in postwar Europe. He was 20 when the war ended. He possessed a formidable intelligence and a strong training in mathematics as well as in music.

> Just listen with the vastness of the world in mind. You can't fail to get the message.
>
> —Boulez on his own music

Order:	1	2	3	4	5	6	7	8	9	10	11	12
Pitch:	E♭	D	A	A♭	G	F♯	E	C♯	C	B♭	F	B
Dynamic:	*pppp*	*ppp*	*pp*	*p*	quasi *p*	*mp*	*mf*	quasi *f*	*f*	*ff*	*fff*	*ffff*

Boulez: Complete set of "series" for *Structures I*

For *Structures I*, which was written for two pianos, Boulez made series for four different musical elements: pitch, duration, attack (the way the pianist strikes the note), and dynamics. These elements are all arranged into series numbered from 1 to 12. If you look carefully for a minute or two at the chart, you will grasp this easily. The 12 available pitches are arranged in an order, starting E♭, D, A, A♭, and so on. Then durations (note lengths) are put in order, starting from the smallest duration (♪) and going all the way up to a dotted quarter note (♩.). These are also numbered from 1 to 12. Then Boulez lists 12 methods of attack, ranging from a very

aggressive striking of the note to a very smooth legato. Finally, 12 dynamic levels are arranged, from *pppp* to *fffff*. This chart is then used as the basis for composing the piece. (See Listening Guide.)

In practice, the method is used with some flexibility. Each series (pitch, duration, etc.) can be applied independently. And the entire series can be used backward or forward, even with the pitches transposed. The strange thing is that despite its strict and rigid compositional basis, the music sounds more or less random. The number of organizing elements is so large that it is very hard to *hear* the structure (let alone play it!).

WHO CARES IF YOU LISTEN?

The attitude conveyed by the title of the American composer Milton Babbitt's article "Who Cares If You Listen?" represents one extreme in a controversy that has raged for much of the twentieth century. On the one hand is the view that composers should write what people want to hear: audiences are consumers, and consumers can demand what they want. On the other hand, some of the greatest art has been created by people who were completely unappreciated during their own lifetime. Webern's music was almost never performed while he was alive; after his death, he became a catalyst for a whole generation of composers. Stravinsky's *Rite of Spring* caused outrage at its first performance; now it is considered one of the masterworks of the twentieth century.

Who decides if a work is great? Other composers? Contemporary audiences? Posterity?

During Bach's lifetime, he was considered an inferior composer to Telemann. Today, we hear Telemann's music as fluent but mostly not profound, and we regard Bach as an unmatched genius. Who's right? People in the eighteenth century or people today? Will people change their minds *again* about Bach in another 250 years? And will they necessarily be right because they have even more perspective?

Nowadays composers care quite a lot if you listen. They are reaching out to audiences in remarkable new ways. But how many people are listening?

LISTENING GUIDE

((•─ **Listen** on MySearchLab

PIERRE BOULEZ (b. 1925)

Structures I

Date of composition: 1952
Orchestration: two pianos
Duration: 3:27

CD III, 9

This piece demands a great deal of skill from the performers and considerable effort from the listeners. What at first might sound like a random, disjointed piano experiment is instead a precisely constructed work.

Numbers and mathematical principles have concerned composers for centuries, and Boulez has here extended the serial technique from a structured means of controlling pitches to a means of controlling every aspect of the music in a strictly rational way. What one hears in the piece, however, is a palette of shifting textures and contrasting panels of sound.

Time	Listen for
0:00	Sustained notes, use of extremes in range; although pitches overlap, few notes are struck simultaneously as chords.
0:11	Pause, then quick articulations, some fast repeated notes.
0:28	More sustained notes in low and middle range; a slight slowing.
0:39	This section begins with a surprise—a chord—and has more use of simultaneously sounded pitches and thus a richer harmonic feel. The pulse moves forward and seems to gain momentum. Scattered notes leap about in the high and middle ranges.
1:08	Low rumblings make a distinct line in that register.
1:18	A series of stark, accented notes, moving deliberately in different registers; ends with staccato note.
1:29	Another held chord; return to a sustained texture, much slower and smoother, gentle and atmospheric.
2:06	Sudden staccato chord moves into faster, more crisply articulated section.
2:16	Another chord; others follow, repeated notes, playful quality.
2:40	Pause; then sustained note in medium register leads to more sustained single notes; sustained notes contrast with staccato notes.
3:08	Pause; then fast chords, gentle flourish of notes, fading away in a faint high range.

Other composers who worked with total serialism in the 1950s were Karlheinz Stockhausen (b. 1928) in Germany, Luciano Berio (1925–2003) in Italy, and Milton Babbitt (b. 1916) in the United States. Audiences found the style difficult and unappealing and deserted concert halls in droves. But many composers felt that the music had its own validity, even if people didn't like it. And Milton Babbitt published a famous article that summarized this view. Its title was "Who Cares If You Listen?"

An important step for total serialism and for other experimental music was the development in the late 1950s of electronic music technology. The newly-invented music synthesizer could produce precisely defined sounds. All aspects of a sound could be controlled—pitch, length, tone color, intensity, attack, and decay (the ending of a note)—and the performance of a work no longer needed a human being!

The Radical 1960s: New Sounds, Freedom, and Chance

In the 1960s, the United States and Europe underwent profound change. The "baby boomers" grew to adulthood, and experimentation was in the air. It was a time of unprecedented freedom in the areas of sex, drugs, social mores, and individual lifestyles. This openness to radical experimentation was reflected in the music. This was the era in which popular music began to overwhelm the music of "serious" composers. And yet it was certainly in "serious" music that the most interesting musical experiments were being made.

New Sounds   Many of these experiments revolved around new sounds. The synthesizer, the tape recorder, and the computer made available to composers both new sounds and the ability to manipulate sounds in completely new ways. New sounds were also produced by an inventive and imaginative use of normal musical instruments. Composers began to call for a far more extended range of sounds from traditional instruments: squeaks, whines, and flutters from wind instruments, bonks and slides from string instruments. Modification of the piano became popular at this time, with nuts and bolts, plastic spoons, or pieces of paper inserted between the strings inside the piano or lying on top of the strings to create new sounds. And some of the more radical composers wrote fascinating pieces for large groups of instruments playing in quite novel ways.

The English conductor Sir Thomas Beecham was once asked if he had played any Stockhausen. "No," he replied, "but I have trodden in some."

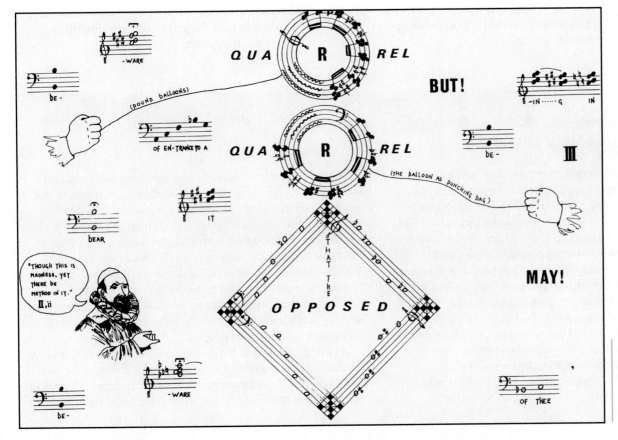

A "radical 1960s" musical score (actually 1971) by Edwin London.

From the *Polonius Platitudes,* copyright 1971 by Edwin London.

Find the **Quick Listen** on **MySearchLab**

"Threnody to the Victims of Hiroshima"

The two most interesting composers working with sound textures in the 1960s were the Hungarian composer György Ligeti (1923–2006, last name pronounced *Ligg*ety) and the Polish composer Krzysztof Penderecki (b. 1933, last name pronounced Pender*etz*ki).

Ligeti worked with large blocks of sound, created by having the singers or instrumentalists sing or play a whole mass of adjacent notes at once. A block created in this way can then expand or contract like a wedge, often over considerable amounts of time.

Other musical shapes—triangles, squares, and the like—can also be created in sound, though describing the shape doesn't begin to describe the musical effect, which is extraordinary. In Ligeti's 1961 orchestral piece *Atmospheres*, for example, there are sections in which the wide span of the block, sometimes covering as much as four octaves, remains fixed, but within the block the internal parts are constantly changing positions, creating a sense of continual motion within a static whole.

Find the **Quick Listen** on **MySearchLab**

"Ligeti *Atmospheres*"

In Poland, Penderecki was working with very similar techniques. One of his most ambitious works was his *St. Luke Passion* for solo singers, chorus, and orchestra, written in 1965. In scope and orchestration and spiritual commitment, the work pays homage to Bach, but the sounds are very new. Penderecki has the chorus shout, whisper, and moan; the solo singing is wild and dramatic; and the orchestra uses massive sound blocks, with special instrumental effects.

Penderecki's most famous composition dates from 1960. It is written for a string orchestra composed of 24 violins, 10 violas, 10 cellos, and 8 double basses, and it is entitled *Threnody* (which means a homage to the dead) *for the Victims of Hiroshima*. This is an incredibly powerful piece—lamenting, angry, and intense. Sometimes it seems even to assault the listener. Huge sound blocks are used, and the players produce a wide assortment of noises by knocking on the bodies of their instruments or by scraping the strings hard. Often the effects are strikingly similar to those produced by electronic means.

Freedom and Chance Both total serialism and the use of block sound textures require very careful control on the part of the composer. At the same time that these ideas were being explored, a completely opposite tendency was prevalent in music. This was a move *away from* control, in the direction of freedom for the performers—even to the point of leaving some musical matters to chance. Some scores have several pages of music for each of the performers, allowing them to choose which page they want to play and when. Others simply indicate time durations and give very general instructions: "As high as you can," or "Any sound repeated five times." And some scores simply give rough drawings or sketches on the page, abandoning musical notation altogether.

COMPOSERS, PATRONS, AND AUDIENCES

The Twentieth-Century Orchestra

In the first part of the twentieth century, large orchestras were still in vogue. Stravinsky uses an immense orchestra for his remarkable work *The Rite of Spring* (1913), and Schoenberg required enormous forces for his *Variations for Orchestra* (1928). But these orchestras are used in revolutionary ways: Stravinsky's to create the effect of frightening primitive power, and Schoenberg's to create very spare textures with a kaleidoscope of different colors. But there was also a reaction against the excesses of large performing groups and a return to the clarity and transparency of the smaller orchestras of the eighteenth century. In the second half of the twentieth century composers moved in two different but interrelated directions. They reconceived the ways in which traditional instruments could be played (in his *Threnody for the Victims of Hiroshima* Penderecki creates sounds both eerie and terrifying on 52 perfectly

ordinary stringed instruments), and they used newly invented technology (audio tape, electronic keyboards, computers, and synthesizers) to create new sounds (Olly Wilson's *Sometimes*). Often, however, the new technology is used to imitate the sounds of a traditional orchestra. This is much more common than you might think, especially on film soundtracks or at Broadway shows. So, after 300 years of development, the symphony orchestra—with its fascinating mixture of people and instruments, and its remarkable ideal of bringing together so many individuals to collaborate in an artistic endeavor—may finally have become obsolete.

A perfect example of the twentieth-century orchestra is Lukas Foss's third movement of the "Renaissance Concerto" for Flute and Orchestra. You can watch a live performance of this work in Segment 3 of the *Inside the Orchestra* video on MySearchLab.

The idea of leaving musical events to chance was the main focus of a musical revolutionary named John Cage (1912–1992). Cage was born in Los Angeles, the son of an inventor. At the age of 22, he studied with Schoenberg—who told him he had no ear for music and would never make it as a composer. But Cage decided that music was too narrowly defined. "Everything we do is music," he said.

Cage invented the idea of the "prepared piano," with objects placed on the strings inside the lid. He asked performers to throw dice and toss coins to determine which parts of a composition would be played. He wrote a piece called *Imaginary Landscape No. 4* (1951) for twelve radios, all playing on different stations. He stood on stage, smoking a cigarette and drinking a glass of water, with a microphone attached to his throat, the amplifier turned up as high as it would go. Once, when invited to give a lecture, he read for hours from various scraps of newspaper. "If my work is accepted," he once said, "I must move on to the point where it isn't."

Cage erased the boundaries between deliberate and random, between a performance and a "happening," between music and noise. His most famous composition was written in 1952 and is entitled 4'33". In it, the performer is instructed to sit at the piano for four minutes and 33 seconds and do *nothing*. The audience grows restless and finally starts listening to sounds inside and outside the hall: sounds of rustling, coughing, the buzz of the lights, police sirens—sounds that are not music. Or are they?

Cage was a leading member of the postwar avant-garde. He infuriated many critics, performers, and scholars, who thought he was destroying music, but his influence on other artists, ranging from the painter Robert Motherwell to the rock group the Grateful Dead, was vast. "One need not fear," he once said, "about the future of music."

We shall listen to one of the short pieces that make up the *Sonatas and Interludes* for prepared piano that Cage completed in 1948. (See Listening Guide.) This series of compositions includes sixteen "sonatas" and four "interludes"—all of them between two and five minutes long. The series has been regarded as one of Cage's greatest works: though it is made up of quiet pieces, they are all fascinating. "Preparing" a piano involves placing objects on or between the strings, thus necessarily muting the sound. The timbre of the strings can be clunky, dry, electronic, or wooden, but it is always quieter than that of a regular piano, so the music has an intimate, personal feel.

> He is not a composer but an inventor—with genius.
>
> —Schoenberg on Cage

LISTENING GUIDE

((•⎯ Listen on MySearchLab

JOHN CAGE (1912–1992)

Sonata III from Sonatas *and* Interludes *for Prepared Piano*

Date of Composition: 1946–1948
Scored for: prepared piano
Duration: 2:37

CD III, 10

Time	Listen for
0:00	A rhythmic motive in the middle range with a fuzzy electronic sound is constantly interrupted by a sudden quirky figure that comes both high (in a purer piano timbre) and low (in a hollow wooden timbre).
1:00	Louder, and then soft again.
1:12	A repetitive pattern in the bass sounds like African drums. Single high notes (piano sound).
1:26	Louder interruption.
1:35	Back to drums and piano.
1:49	Interruption.
1:53	Quiet ending.

CLASSICAL MUSIC TODAY

The first performances of new pieces are, and always have been, exciting events. People enjoy the prospect of experiencing newly created music. *Our* expectations of new music, however, are very different from those of people in the eighteenth century who listened to new works by Mozart or Haydn. The huge diversity of musical styles that now confronts us had no parallel in the eighteenth century. Classic composers were expected to conform to certain rules. Now there aren't any rules. A piece performed today in a concert hall by a trumpeter and a drummer, both with earphones, playing independently, with a recording of a baseball game heard in the background would be greeted with curiosity and interest rather than with disbelief or derision. We are used to aural and visual incongruity and radical experimentation. If art mirrors life, then the diverse and complex range of music in our new century may well reflect the splintered, multifaceted nature of modern culture.

Postmodernism

During the latter part of the twentieth century, artists began to question the continued viability of the Modernist movement. It had been unusually productive and long-lived: the feeling of innovation and experimentation had lasted from 1900 to the mid-1960s. Now some of its achievements were thrown into doubt. The meaning of art itself was no longer certain. Was a can of paint dropped on the floor "art"? How about graffiti on the subway?

During the century, people had become increasingly alienated from modern classical music. By the 1950s, audiences for new music were made up of tiny groups of specialists, mostly composers themselves. Concert organizations turned more and more to presenting the classics of the past. There was real validity to the claim that American symphony orchestras were turning into museums. The twelve-tone system and its later refinements produced music that was so arcane and "unfriendly" that few people enjoyed it. Young people turned increasingly to rock and other forms of popular music.

In the 1980s and 1990s, this profound debate affected public support for the arts. And as economies suffered, educational institutions and local and national governments cut deeply into their funding for the arts.

From the mid-1960s through today, a new movement has taken hold in music and the other arts. This new movement is known as Postmodernism. Postmodernism is a style that juxtaposes many varied elements, especially familiar ones, in new and interesting ways. It has attracted new audiences, while also stirring up controversy in today's highly reactionary political atmosphere.

Sydney Opera House.

ETHEL

The string quartet Ethel is made up of two men and two women who are all graduates of the Juilliard School of Music. They play traditional stringed instruments, but they use amplification and often include improvisation in their playing. They may stand or sit, and they wear colorful clothes. They perform original music as well as classical contemporary compositions. They have toured with rock guitarist Todd Rundgren and performed with David Byrne and Andrew Bird. They reflect both the eclecticism of modern classical music and the social responsibility of today's artists. They are affiliated with the Native American Composers Apprenticeship Project, which was founded to support Native American young people in composing classical music. They created their own Foundation for the Arts, which is a non-profit organization designed to promote contemporary classical music through collaboration, sponsorship, and outreach. A recent recording project (2010) is named *Oshtali* and contains music by young composers of the Chickasaw Nation.

Postmodernism has many facets. The most significant aspect of the movement is a deliberate return to the past. In painting, artists returned to representation and figuration, after many years of abstractionism. In architecture, buildings once again began to display decorative structures and fantasy, after the austere (and, to some, ugly) functionalism of the mid-century. In music, the return to the past was exemplified by a return to the language of tonality, so resoundingly rejected for so many years. It was suggested that the main characteristics of tonal music—a key center, repetition, and return—correspond to basic impulses in the human brain and are therefore fundamental to human nature.

Other facets of Postmodernism are a tendency to quote from earlier historical styles and a deliberate cross-fertilization of the European-American tradition with the arts of other cultures. Quotation is common in Postmodernist painting and architecture as well as in music. Paintings make overt reference to well-known paintings of the past, and buildings copy famous styles of earlier eras. Compositions contain snippets or long extracts from older musical works. These references are juxtaposed in new and startling ways, and the old is embedded in a context of the new, throwing new light upon both. There is also a deliberate attempt to incorporate styles from other parts of the world, as the world becomes a smaller place.

Finally, Postmodernism deliberately reaches out across the traditional barrier between classical and popular music. Classical music of the early twenty-first centuries has moved closer to rock and even rap. The dividing line between operas and musicals (such as those of Andrew Lloyd Webber) is narrowing sharply. And performing groups deliberately mix genres: a string quartet plays arrangements of Jimi Hendrix; chamber groups include electric guitars, amplification, and video in their performances; performance artists play the violin, sing, and paint their bodies onstage.

What is common to these ideas is a deliberate eclecticism (mixing of styles). The late twentieth century and early twenty-first century seem to be a period open to all influences, past and present, local and foreign, popular and refined. Does this mean that this is a period without identity? The first era that has no defining artistic style of its own? Only a style borrowed from other times and places? Or does it mean that the new mixture is the way of the future, in which all barriers will come down, the past will be absorbed into the present, and all art will become one in a global unity of shared experience?

We'll see.

Postmodern Music

One of the ways in which Postmodernism first began to manifest itself in music was by quotation. In one composition entitled *Nach Bach* (*After Bach*, 1967), the American composer George Rochberg suspends little fragments of Bach's harpsichord music in a surrounding context of dissonance and abrupt silences. Luciano Berio's *Sinfonia* (1969) has a movement-length quotation from Mahler's Second Symphony, overlaid with readings of modern poetry, shouts, and tiny fragments of quotations from many *other* composers. And the third movement of Lukas Foss's *Renaissance Concerto* (1986) is based on the music of Orfeo's lament from Monteverdi's *Orfeo*.

The return to tonality was another striking feature of Postmodern music. David del Tredici (b. 1937) is best known for a series of extended compositions based on the stories *Alice in Wonderland* and *Through the Looking Glass*. The music is wonderfully inventive and captures the tone of Lewis Carroll's quirky prose with a modern aesthetic. *Final Alice* (1976), for example, is a long symphony with a big, rich orchestra, amplified voice, and a small rock group. The harmonies are late nineteenth century, but the context is totally new, and the result is bizarre, beautiful, humorous, and touching by turns.

Tonality is mingled with Modernism in the work of the English composer Oliver Knussen (b. 1952). Knussen's setting of

Maurice Sendak's children's story *Where the Wild Things Are* (1983) can be performed both as an opera and as a concert piece. It is a good way to introduce children to modern music.

Multimedia Postmodernist work is perhaps best represented by the performance artist Laurie Anderson (b. 1947). A trained violinist, Anderson is also an actress, singer, poet, and storyteller. She creates works that use spoken words over rock patterns, high-tech video, and large backdrops, against which she projects her fragile-looking, razor-sharp stage personality.

The incorporation of musical elements from other cultures may be found in the works of Alan Hovhaness (1911–2000), Frederic Rzewski (b. 1938), and David Hykes (b. 1953). Hovhaness wrote an extraordinary number of works, all neo-tonal and many of them influenced by Armenian and Far Eastern music. Rzewski's *The People United Will Never Be Defeated* (1975) is based on a revolutionary ballad from Chile, and his *Four Pieces* for piano (1977) use other Latin American melodies. In the 1970s and 1980s, Hykes became fascinated with the special, "multiphonic" singing of the Tibetan monks, in which the singers produce low tones in their throats and at the same time high, floating harmonics. Hykes taught himself and several other American singers this technique and founded the Harmonic Choir, for which he has written many works. His song "Rainbow Voice" is featured in the vampire movie *Blade III* (2004). Other influences on Postmodern music come from China, Japan, Indonesia, India, and Africa, but also from Native America. An example of the latter is *O-Ke-Wa*, based on the Seneca people's song for the dead, and written in 1974 by the American composer Daniel Lentz (b. 1942).

The meditative, spun-out quality of music from the East has been a major contributor to New Age music, which is also neo-tonal, but with a minimal sense of drive and resolution; it is floating, gentle, calm, and without form. A newer category of New Age music is known as Space Music. Formed mostly on synthesizers and buoyed on a cushion of echo, it evokes the openness, vastness, and formlessness of outer space.

The merging of popular and "serious" music is perhaps the most interesting trend in Postmodern music. Starting in the 1960s, but continuing strongly into the 1970s and

Find the **Quick Listen** on **MySearchLab** "David Hykes 'Rainbow Voice'"

Watch the **Inside the Orchestra** video on **MySearchLab**

Find the **Quick Listen** on **MySearchLab** "Oliver Knussen *Where the Wild Things Are*"

1980s, a new type of music was born, which was labeled **minimalism**. Like many other musical style terms, this one came from the art world. Artists such as Frank Stella, Agnes Martin, and Robert Wilson reduced their paintings to the bare minimum, with flat surfaces, thin lines, simple shapes, and primary colors.

Minimalist music borrows from rock music the idea of harmonic simplicity and repetitive rhythm. It uses very limited materials and remains at an almost constant tempo and dynamic. The result is music that is hypnotizing in its sameness, inducing an almost trancelike state in the listener, and in this perhaps it also was influenced by music from the Far East. It changes the listener's perception of the passage of time. Many examples of minimalist music involve very slow shifts over a period of time; we have seen a similar pattern in African mbira music in the first chapter of this book. Perhaps because of its links to rock, minimalism brought classical music back into favor again and attracted large audiences.

The central principle of minimalist music is that under seeming changelessness there *is* change. And later minimalist compositions concentrate upon this very idea: a very slow and gradual change disguised under a surface of apparent stasis. Steve Reich (b. 1936) explored this idea in his *Piano Phase* (1967). Two pianists play a constant sixteenth-note pattern simultaneously. Very gradually, one of the pianists accelerates, getting "out of phase" with the other, until the notes finally coincide again ("back in phase").

Philip Glass (b. 1937) became a cult figure in the 1970s and 1980s, attracting a large following with his music. He has written an enormous amount of music, including some important modern operas, several symphonies, concertos, chamber music, and film scores, including *The Thin Blue Line* (1988), *The Truman Show* (1998) (in which he also has a cameo appearance), *The Fog of War* (2002) and *Notes on a Scandal* (2006). The video game "Grand Theft Auto IV" features his music on the radio station known as The Journey. His music has moved beyond minimalism to include rock, electronic music, ambient music, and world music, all of which are combined with traditional concert forms, such as opera, symphony, and string quartet.

The most successful minimalist composer of the late twentieth and early twenty-first centuries was John Adams, who favors traditional orchestral and vocal forces. Adams's best-known works are his operas, which are based on contemporary political events. The first was *Nixon in China* (1987), which is set during the historic visit of President Nixon to China in an attempt to forge links between the two countries. The second, *The Death of Klinghoffer* (1991), is based on the terrorist murder of a wheelchair-bound American tourist on a cruise ship in the Mediterranean. *Doctor Atomic* (2005) is about the American physicist Robert Oppenheimer and the creation of the first atomic bomb. The extraordinarily powerful and moving aria at the end of Act I, "Batter My Heart," is set to words from the early-seventeenth-century metaphysical poet John Donne, matched by Adams's expressive music.

Fusion

Perhaps the most important aspect of the Postmodern era is the narrowing of gaps between all types of music. The jazz trumpeter Miles Davis and others created a mixture of jazz and rock that was called fusion. There are many different kinds of fusion today, created by artists as diverse as Keith Jarrett, Malcolm McLaren, Yo-Yo Ma, and Eric Clapton.

One of the most fertile meeting places of the several worlds of music has been the theater. Postmodernism created a strong revival of music theater in the 1980s and 1990s. Among the most successful of these productions were those by Andrew Lloyd Webber. His works combine the style of the Broadway musical with the continuous musical settings and extended scenes of opera; the heavy beat and synthesizer-enhanced sound of rock; the sentimental lyricism of pop; and elaborate, high-tech, Postmodern stage effects.

In the modern era, as one contemporary composer and cultural commentator has written, "Multi-track, multi-layer experience becomes the norm: Ravi Shankar, John Cage, the Beatles, Gregorian chant, electronic music, Renaissance madrigals and motets, Bob Dylan, German *Lieder*, soul, J. S. Bach, jazz, Ives, Balinese gamelan, Boulez, African drumming, Mahler, *gagaku*, Frank Zappa, Tchaikovsky,... all become part of the common shared experience."

We have made a false division of music in our time: there is music only of entertainment, and a music only of profound statement or searching. If we want to be fully human as artists, we have to be able to move freely through the whole range of human experience.
—Composer Ellen Taaffe Zwilich

Find the **Quick Listen** on **MySearchLab** "John Adams 'Batter My Heart'"

Find the **Quick Listen** on **MySearchLab** "Reich *Piano Phase*"

Find the **Quick Listen** on **MySearchLab** "*Notes on a Scandal* Soundtrack / Invitation"

The "Downtown" Scene

"Downtown" music refers to classical music that is contemporary and tries to break down the formality that accompanies the presentation of most classical concerts. I have already mentioned how popular music and classical music have drawn closer together in recent years. One further indication of this can be seen in the rise of new young ensembles that like to perform outside the traditional classical music venues like concert halls. They play in museums, art centers, churches, galleries, coffeehouses, and sometimes on the street or in parks. These ensembles include groups like Bang on a Can, which is made up of instrumentalists playing clarinet, saxophone, electric guitar, cello, keyboards, percussion, and bass. This group holds marathon concerts, sometimes lasting many hours or a whole day, and at which audience members are encouraged to dress in informal clothes and to come and go at will.

The string quartet Ethel plays with amplified instruments and incorporates improvisation into their performances. They have toured with rock musicians and play original music as well as compositions by contemporary composers.

Relâche is a new music group that often presents multimedia performances and has commissioned music from very many young composers. The ensemble is based in Philadelphia but travels around the world and is made up of flute, oboe, clarinet, saxophone, viola, bassoon, keyboards, percussion, and double bass.

We shall listen to a very short but entertaining piece played by Relâche and composed by Guy Klucevsek, who is an accordion player as well as a composer. He has released many recordings. His music is lively and attractive, often infused with a nostalgic glance at traditions from Eastern Europe. "Dance?" is one movement in a dance suite of short movements entitled *Wing/Prayer*, which was commissioned by the ensemble Relâche for the members of the Pennsylvania Ballet. It is great fun, with the feel of a gypsy dance and cleverly changing patterns of duple and triple meter.

LISTENING GUIDE

((•─ Listen on **MySearchLab**

GUY KLUCEVSEK (b. 1947)

"Dance?" from **Wing/Prayer**

Date of composition: 2002
Orchestration: flute, clarinet, strings, piano, bass, percussion
Duration: 1:10

CD III, 11

Time	Listen for
0:00	Just enjoy!

Inclusion

It is a commonplace of historiography (the writing of history) that the present is too close to see with any perspective. Who are the great composers of today? Will their works last? We don't know the answers to these questions.

One thing *is* clear, however. In the last 20 or 30 years, women and minorities and musicians from a far wider world have finally been taking their rightful place in American music making. In every chapter of this book, we have considered the role of women in the history of music. On the whole, with significant exceptions, it has been a history of exclusion or marginalization. One striking element of modern times has been the unraveling of this pattern and the acceptance of women as full partners in the world of music. Although there are one or two orchestras in Europe that (believe it or not) still do not hire women, most European and North American orchestras contain large numbers of female musicians. There is an increasing number of conductors who are women, and some of the foremost composers of our age are women.

Representation of African American musicians in the world of classical music still lags behind. There are a few black players in orchestras, some black conductors, and very few well-known composers.

To try to represent this picture of growing inclusiveness, I have chosen to present you with the work of five contemporary composers—two women (one American, one Finnish) and three men (one African American, one English, and the other Jewish from Argentina). These works do not claim to speak for their composers' gender, race, sexual preference, or ethnicity. They are not typical of any stylistic trends. They simply show that the differences between male and female or black and white or American and foreign in music disappear in the mass of qualities that human beings share. The music of a gay composer or a black composer or a woman or an Arab or a Jew or a Japanese master of the *shakuhachi* speaks to

us because it is the communication of one human being to others. All we have to do is listen.

The first work we shall discuss is *Sound Patterns* by Pauline Oliveros. Born in Houston in 1932, Oliveros has written numerous compositions, served as composer-in-residence at several colleges, and toured the country in performances of contemporary music. In 1992 she won a fellowship from the National Endowment for the Arts. She is the founder of a group of women musicians and has worked frequently with actors, dancers, and filmmakers. She has written four books, is openly lesbian, and teaches in New York and California.

Sound Patterns is written for a mixed chorus (sopranos, altos, tenors, and basses). It involves no text. Rather, the composer calls for a huge range of nonverbal sounds from the singers, including clicking, trilling, hissing, sliding, screeching, whooping, popping, *ow*-ing, and *zz*-ing. The music mixes men's and women's voices—loud and soft, group and separate textures, high and low—all in a kaleidoscope of sound.

LISTENING GUIDE

((•—Listen on **MySearchLab**

PAULINE OLIVEROS (b. 1932)

Sound Patterns

Date of composition: 1964
Mixed Chorus
Duration: 4:02

CD III, 12

Sound Patterns is written for a mixed chorus (sopranos, altos, tenors, and basses). It involves no text. Rather, the composer calls for a wide range of nonverbal sounds from the singers, including clicking, hissing, trilling, sliding, screeching, whooping, popping, *ow*-ing, and *zz*-ing. The piece ends up as a kaleidoscope of sound.

The work is so fascinating in its variety and so continuous that a timed Listening Guide would only be a distraction. Listen and enjoy!

Olly Wilson is an African American composer who was born in St. Louis, Missouri, in 1937. He has degrees in music from Washington University in St. Louis, the University of Illinois, and the University of Iowa, and he is emeritus professor of music at the University of California at Berkeley, where he taught from 1970 to 2002. Wilson has won numerous prizes, grants, and

fellowships, including a Guggenheim Fellowship that allowed him to spend a year studying music in Africa. He has published a book on black music in America. In 1995, Olly Wilson was elected to the American Academy of Arts and Letters. Wilson has specialized in electronic music, much of which was created in the Electronic Music Studio at Berkeley.

Composer Olly Wilson.

LISTENING GUIDE

((•⟶ Listen on MySearchLab

OLLY WILSON (b. 1937)

Sometimes (extract)

Date of composition: 1976
Orchestration: tenor and taped electronic sounds
Duration: 6:02

CD III, 13

Sometimes is based on the spiritual "Sometimes I Feel Like a Motherless Child." It is written for tenor and tape, and it makes extraordinary demands on the singer. The tape uses both electronic sounds and manipulated snippets of the tenor's voice. Throughout the work, which lasts more than 15 minutes in its entirety, the spiritual lends its powerful presence (even when it is absent).

Time	Listen for
0:00	Tape noises.
0:09	Taped whispering: "motherless child."
0:35	More activity; manipulated taped voice and electronic sounds; echoes.
1:00	Tape noises, both screeching and low.
1:10	Sounds like those of a bass guitar.
1:28	Loud bass. Pause.
1:39	Whistle sounds, feedback, clonks, ringing sounds, chimes, blips, etc. Pause.
2:30	Voice and manipulated taped voice; noises. "Sometimes…"; crescendo.
3:23	"I feel…." Tape noises; crescendo.
3:43	"Sometimes…." Tape noises.
4:08	Very high singing, "Sometimes…"; much more activity, crescendo.
4:33	Voice over bass tape noises.
4:38	"I feel like a motherless child."
4:56	"True believer…." Whistles, blips, feedback.
5:17	Voice and distorted taped voice ("Sometimes I feel…").
5:44	Extremely high singing.
5:58	Pause.

Kaija Saariaho is a Finnish composer who was born in 1952. She grew up in Helsinki but now lives in Paris, where she has been active at the Institute for Research in Sound and Music, a progressive and influential institute for experimentation in electrical and acoustic sound and composition. She has been the recipient of many awards and prizes. She was proclaimed "Musician of the Year" for 2008 by *Musical America* and in 2011 she won a Grammy award for Best Opera Recording. Her works are mainly chamber music, but in the last 10 years or so she has also composed for larger forces, including orchestral and choral works and three operas. Her music often combines electronics and live music to create lovely and mysterious sounds. Her second string quartet, named *Terra Memoria* ("Earth and Memory"), of which we shall hear an extract, was played for the first time at Carnegie Hall in New York City in 2007. Her 2010 opera *Émilie* is based on the life and work of the Émilie du Châtelet, who was an eighteenth-century mathematician and physicist and the first woman to establish an international reputation as a scientist.

LISTENING GUIDE

((•—Listen on MySearchLab

KAIJA SAARIAHO (b. 1952)

Terra Memoria for String Quartet (extract)

Date of composition: 2007
Orchestration: two violins, viola, cello
Duration: 3:18

CD III, 14

Terra Memoria means "earth and memory." It is dedicated to "those departed." In her notes on this composition Kaija Saariaho writes,

> Some thoughts about [the dedication]: we continue remembering the people who are no longer with us . . . Those of us who are left behind are constantly reminded of our experiences together: our feelings continue to change about different aspects of their personality, certain memories keep on haunting us in our dreams.

Saariaho has a refined ear for the sound of strings. The instruments combine and overlap in delicate counterpoint, though individual voices sometimes are heard clearly among the web of sound. The overall mood is both resigned and nostalgic. The recording heard here is a live performance by the Emerson String Quartet, who played the premiere of the piece in Carnegie Hall, New York City, in June of 2007. We shall hear the last few minutes of the piece, which in its entirety lasts about 18 minutes. Throughout, the composer takes advantage of special techniques of string playing, including **pizzicato** (plucked), **trill** (a quick alternation between two notes), **sul ponticello** (bowing near the bridge, which produces a glassy sound), **glissando** (sliding between notes), and playing **harmonics** (which involves touching the string very lightly to produce a high ghostly sound). All these are not used gratuitously but always for expressive purposes.

Time	Listen for
0:00	This passage is very slow and marked "very calm, with tenderness." Between very high and very low notes the middle instruments (especially the viola) play mournful phrases.
0:43	Louder expressive counterpoint gives way to a single loud chord, which diminishes in volume. High violin and low cello slide apart to a new chord.
1:10	More motion. Cello and viola play repeated pizzicato figure. High violin and expressive viola play in counterpoint.
1:58	Rhythmic figure alternates with high glassy sounds that combine sul ponticello, harmonics, and trills.
2:15	Regular pizzicato resumes. Viola has mournful phrases again amid ghostly atmosphere. Slow descending cello glissando. The sound gradually moves to the point of nothingness.

[Sir] John Tavener (b. 1944) is an English composer who converted to Orthodox Christianity in his 30s, and his music since that time has focused on liturgical texts. His *Celtic Requiem*, composed in 1969, impressed the Beatles and was first recorded on their Apple label. It is a haunting mixture of Irish laments, English songs, and Latin chants. His *Out of Night (Alleluia)* from 1996 is for voice and viola, although the composer suggests that it be performed by just one person, playing and singing at the same time. In a way it could be seen as a renewed return to the music of medieval chant—the music we studied near the beginning of this book. (Compare this piece with the two-minute plainchant Kyrie that we listened to on p. 57.)

LISTENING GUIDE

((•—Listen on MySearchLab

JOHN TAVENER (b. 1944)

Out of Night (Alleluia)

Date of composition: 1996
Viola and Voice
Duration: 1:42

CD III, 15

Out of Night (Alleluia) was written to be played to greet the dawn in one of the most remarkable places in the Holy Land. St. Catherine's monastery dates back to the first century and is situated on a high hill in the middle of the Sinai desert. As the sun rises to burn the sands from their freezing night temperatures, this piece is played by a viola player who also sings simply the Alleluia—Praise God.

Osvaldo Golijov (last name pronounced Goli*hof*) comes from Argentina, where he was born into a Jewish family in 1960. He grew up surrounded by classical music, Jewish music, and tango. He moved to the United States with his wife in 1986 and studied for his Ph.D. in composition at the University of Pennsylvania. He now teaches at the College of the Holy Cross in Massachusetts. He has received a MacArthur Fellowship and in 2007 two Grammy awards for his opera *Ainadamar: Fountain of Tears*. He has composed chamber music, orchestral music, songs, a Passion (the *Saint Mark Passion*, first performed in the year 2000 to commemorate the 250th anniversary of Bach's death), an opera, and the soundtracks for three movies. His most recent work is *Sidereus*, an orchestral composition based on a book written by Galileo after he saw the moon through a telescope for the first time. He is currently working on a violin concerto and a new string quartet.

Golijov's music shows that although for much of the twentieth century tonality and traditional harmony were regarded as "used up," in fact such is by no means the case. Many composers in the early twenty-first century have discovered an enormous fund of resources by using the old tonal language with a new, modern, and exciting accent.

Golijov's song "Lúa descolorida" exists in three forms: with soprano and piano, with soprano and orchestra in *Three Songs for Soprano and Orchestra*, and as an aria for Peter in the *St. Mark Passion* as the expression of Peter's remorse after his betrayal of Jesus. The first version, which we shall hear, was written in 1999. The desolate text is by the nineteenth-century poet Rosalia de Castro, who lived in Galicia in northwest Spain and wrote in a dialect known as Gallego.

LISTENING GUIDE

((•—Listen on MySearchLab

OSVALDO GOLIJOV (b. 1960)

"Lúa Descolorida"

Date of composition: 1999
Orchestration: soprano and piano
Duration: 5:39

CD III, 16

In this song, the voice spins a slow, pure melody over simple, haunting C-major harmonies in the piano. The song seems to exist in a dream. The harmonies are traditional, perhaps even old-fashioned, but the result is beautiful and new. Golijov himself describes the music as "quietly radiant."

Lúa Descolorida

Lúa descolorida
Como cor de ouro palido,
vesme i eu non quixera
me vises de tan alto.
O espaso que recorres,

Colorless Moon

O Colorless Moon
like the color of pale gold:
you see me, and I don't want you,
up so high, to see me.
In the course of your journey

levame, caladina, nun teu raio.
Astro das almas orfas,
lúa descolorida,
eu ben sei que n'alumas
tristeza cal a mina.
Vai contalo o teu dono,
e dille que me leve adonde habita.

Mais non lle contes nada,
descolorida lúa,
pois nin neste nin noutros
mundos tereis fertuna.
Se sabe onde a morte
ten a morada escura,
dille que corpo e alma xuntamente
me leve adonde non recorden nunca,
nin no mundo en que estou nin nas alturas.

take me, O silent one, in your ray.
Star of orphan souls,
Colorless Moon:
I know that you do not shine light on
sadness as sad as mine.
Go and explain to your Lord,
and tell him to take me to where He lives.

But don't tell him anything,
Colorless Moon,
because nowhere, even in other worlds,
will I have a different fate.
If you know where Death
has her dark abode,
tell her to take my body and my soul together
to a place where nobody will remember me,
not in this world, nor in heaven.

Conclusion

In the early twenty-first century, classical music is in a lively but anxious state. Exciting concerts of new music are still being given, and the fusion of styles, as well as the inclusion of formerly excluded voices, makes the music more interesting and of wider appeal. However a large number of classical-music concerts even today are devoted to music of earlier centuries. Many older people grew up in the 1950s and 1960s, when new classical music was difficult and unappealing. These people turned backward for their musical, emotional, and spiritual satisfaction. In the eighteenth century, almost all the "classical music" people listened to was *new* music. They were interested in the latest Haydn symphony or the newest Mozart opera, not in last year's music, and certainly not in the music of several hundred years earlier.

Today we are fortunate that the music of the past is so easily available to us, and we can find pleasure in older styles and plumb the depth of masterpieces of earlier eras. But new classical music is becoming a rarefied taste. It is not just that older people are afraid of it; young people are more attracted to music that is undemanding and provides quicker gratification. This is a pity, for all worthwhile things take effort. Try listening carefully to the fascinating East/West music of Tan Dun, who won an Oscar in 2001 for the score to the film *Crouching Tiger, Hidden Dragon.* Or take a few minutes and go to your music library (or take a plunge on iTunes) and listen to a luminous new piece by John Corigliano or Jennifer Higdon or John Adams or Kyle Gann or Uri Caine or Rebecca Saunders or Nico Muhly or Augusta Read Thomas or. . . . The names of these people do not appear on Pepsi ads or in neon lights. But they have something very important to say *to you.*

STYLE SUMMARY

The Twentieth Century

Stylistically, the music of the twentieth century can be divided into three periods: early (Modernism), middle (Serialism), and late (Postmodernism). The early (Modernist) period was an age of revolution, in which all the old rules were broken. The greatest representatives of musical Modernism were Debussy, Stravinsky, and Schoenberg. Debussy wrote music that was suggestive, unfocused, impressionistic. His use of the orchestra was highly coloristic, and he managed to evoke cloudy skies, turbulent seas, and rainy gardens both in his orchestral music and in his music for solo piano. Stravinsky was

An unconventional-looking score for a twentieth-century composition.

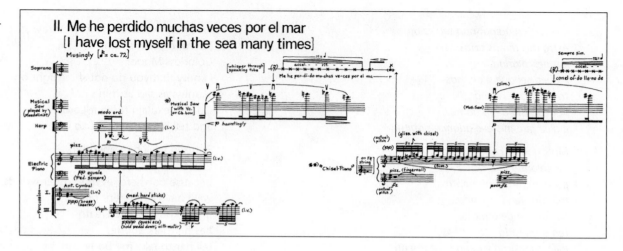

such an original composer he influenced composers for most of the century. He wrote big, powerful orchestral pieces in primitive style; he incorporated jazz sounds and techniques in other works; and he invented a new "neo-classic" style that borrowed from the clarity and transparency of the eighteenth century and yet was enlivened with animated, quirky, off-beat rhythms and pungent dissonances.

Perhaps the biggest revolution of Modernism was that stirred up by Schoenberg. He replaced the centuries-old system of tonality with a new system based on all twelve pitches. This twelve-tone system (or Serialism) became the basis of composition for many composers of the mid-twentieth century. It was rigid and intellectually coherent, but only a few major compositions written in the style have found favor with the general public.

While Schoenberg and his colleagues and followers were pursuing the acerbic, somewhat academic lure of Serialism, other, more popular musical styles were asserting themselves. In America, the sounds of jazz and Broadway infiltrated much classical music, and popular and classical music came closer together.

In the last third of the twentieth century, this merging of styles culminated in the Postmodern movement. This movement drew on an eclectic variety of influences: rock, Baroque, Africa, the Middle East, politics, electronics, film. As the music became more inclusive, so did the musical world. Women finally were fully accepted as composers, performers, and conductors, and African American, Hispanic, Asian, and other musicians became more prominent in the world of classical music.

The most notable trend at the end of the century was a return to melody, consonance, and tonality. The clashing, difficult sounds of Modernism and Serialism were replaced by compositions of great sensuous beauty and a return to a romantic quality of emotional expression. Perhaps it is no wonder that most of the music of the twentieth century was filled with dissonance, angst, violence, and anger, for it had been so in the real world, too. A century of two world wars, Hiroshima, and the Holocaust was not likely to produce music of peace and calm. Music reflects the society that creates it, as I have said all along.

FUNDAMENTALS OF TWENTIETH-CENTURY MUSIC

- ❏ Tonality is replaced by other organizational systems, including "twelve-tone" or serial music
- ❏ Nontraditional scales are used
- ❏ Traditional instruments are deployed in startling new ways
- ❏ New instruments using electricity are invented, culminating in the synthesizer and computer
- ❏ Composers question all aspects of music making, including the length of pieces, the participation of the performers, and even the idea of a concert itself
- ❏ Popular music and the music of other cultures are blended with "classical" styles
- ❏ Music returns to tonality and attractiveness at the end of the century

FOR FURTHER DISCUSSION AND STUDY

1. List the many composers who came to North America from Europe in the twentieth century. Make another list of the twentieth-century American composers who deliberately chose to convey a sense of their own culture in their music.

2. Schoenberg's term "the tyranny of tonality" is interesting in its suggestion that the tonal system exerts an overpowering pressure to conform. Later commentators spoke similarly of music being emancipated from "the tyranny of the barline." Discuss why composers used this language of open rebellion, rather than quietly changing the way they did things.

3. Why were many composers of the first half of the twentieth century attracted to older (pre-Classic) music? Give some specific examples of composers and works influenced by these forms.

4. "Atonality" (no tonality), "polytonality" (many tonalities), and "pantonality" (all tonalities) are all terms that have been used to describe Schoenberg's music. Which do you think is the most accurate? Why?

5. The first performance of *Pierrot Lunaire* required 40 rehearsals—and then the critics hated it. Why would musicians work so hard to compose and then perform music that the general public doesn't like?

6. See how many musical compositions you can find from the twentieth century that are about war.

7. Using traditional musical instruments, experiment with producing new, nontraditional sounds with them. For instance, on a flute you could blow air or click the keys as percussive sounds.

8. Listen again to the mbira music we studied in Chapter 1. What similarities does that music share with minimalist music, or the music of a prepared piano? In what ways are they different?

✓●—Study and Review on MySearchLab

The Twentieth Century
and Beyond, Part II: Jazz,
an American Original

What is jazz? Most of us recognize it when we hear it, but it's not so easy to list the essential ingredients of jazz. First of all is the rhythm. Jazz usually has a steady rhythm that continues from the very beginning of a piece to the end. That rhythm is often underscored by percussion instruments, which play a central role in the performance of jazz. The most characteristic part of jazz rhythm is **syncopation**: accenting the "offbeats." (See p. 24 for a more detailed explanation of syncopation.) The combination of a steady beat and accented offbeats contributes to what is known as "swing." Swing is the *feeling* generated by the music. Swing is what makes you want to move your head or tap your foot. Or both!

Another primary ingredient of jazz is the use of "blue notes." Blue notes are notes that are played or sung low or flatter than the pitches in a conventional Western scale. Common blue notes in jazz are the third, fifth, and seventh notes of a scale. Often, these notes are not exactly a half step lower but rather indeterminate in pitch, and they can be "bent" or "scooped" by many instruments and by singers. These blue notes contribute to the expressive nature of much jazz performance.

Third, jazz often contains special sounds produced by conventional instruments. Trumpets playing "wah-wah," trombones sliding between notes, clarinets squealing in the high register—these are sounds directly associated with jazz but avoided in "straight" concert music. Jazz singers also deliberately make use of unusual sounds. A special kind of singing in which the vocalist improvises with invented syllables ("doo-be-doo dah," etc.) is known as **scat singing**. There are also instruments rarely used in concert music that are central to jazz. Foremost among these is the saxophone, which comes in many sizes, from the small soprano sax to the enormous contrabass. Most common in jazz are the alto and tenor saxophones.

Finally, most people would say that improvisation is a necessary element in jazz. Certainly in many forms of jazz, improvisation plays a central role in the creation of the music, and some of the best jazz performers have been spontaneous and inventive improvisers. There is a difference, however, between genuine improvisation and the performance of a free-sounding melodic line that has been worked out in advance. Some of the most famous jazz performers would repeat their best solos night after night. This does not mean that

The saxophone comes in many different sizes—from sopranino to subcontrabass.

they were not playing jazz. Perhaps the best approach is to say that improvisation is a typical but not an absolutely necessary ingredient of jazz.

Great jazz artists, however, are often great improvisers. This means that they are not just performers but *composers* as well.

The History of Jazz
Origins

Although jazz seems to have developed in several places simultaneously, one of the most important of these was New Orleans. In the late nineteenth century, New Orleans was one of the most culturally diverse and thriving cities in the United States. Its people were of African, French, Spanish, English, and Portuguese origin. There were first-, second-, and third-generation Europeans; African Americans who were former slaves or descendants of former slaves; Haitians; Creoles; and a constant influx of new immigrants from Europe, the Caribbean, and other parts of the United States. As a flourishing port, New Orleans also attracted sailors and visitors from all over the world.

A jazz musician is a juggler who uses harmonies instead of oranges.
—Jazz author Benny Green

Jazz is about the only form of art existing today in which there is freedom of the individual without the loss of group contact.
—Dave Brubeck

JAZZ: FOUR KEY ELEMENTS

1. Syncopated rhythm (accents on the offbeat)
2. Flatted "blue" notes
3. Unusual instrument sounds
4. Improvisation

The city had one of the liveliest musical cultures of any city in America. There was opera and chamber music. European ballroom dances were heard side by side with sailors' songs and hornpipes. Street sellers advertised their products with musical cries. Work songs and "field hollers" (chants sung by workers) mingled with the piano music of elegant salons. The bars, gambling joints, dance halls, and brothels were filled with smoke, liquor, and music.

Band Music

Everywhere in New Orleans were the bands: marching bands, dance bands, concert bands, and society orchestra bands. Bands played at weddings, funerals, parades, and political rallies, or just for the joy of it. Some of the musicians were classically trained; most could not read a note. But almost everybody played. Bands often held competitions among themselves to see which could play the best. And the sound of a band in the street was an excuse for children (and adults) from all the neighborhoods to come and join the fun.

The standard instruments in late nineteenth-century American bands were the trumpet (or cornet—a mellower form of trumpet), clarinet, trombone, banjo, drums, and tuba. This instrumentation provided the proper balance between melody instruments, harmony instruments, bass, and percussion. All these instruments were, of course, portable. Only later, when band music moved indoors, did the instrumentation include piano and string bass, and the stationary drum kit was invented.

Band music was the first of the three major musical influences on early jazz. The other two were ragtime and the blues.

> Ragtime: white music, played black.
>
> —Jazz historian Joachim Berendt

Ragtime

Ragtime was a type of piano music (sometimes also played on other instruments) that became popular in the 1890s. It was originally played mostly by African American pianists in saloons and dance halls in the South and the Midwest. "Ragging" meant taking a popular or classical melody and playing it in characteristic syncopated style. Later the style caught on and developed a form of its own, and ragtime was played by both black and white musicians to audiences all over the country.

Ragtime music is usually in duple meter and has the feel and tempo of a march. The left hand plays a steady, regular beat while the right hand plays a lively melody in syncopated rhythm. A ragtime composition usually consists of a series of related sections with a repetition pattern, most often AA BB A CC DD or something similar.

The most famous composer and performer of ragtime was Scott Joplin, whose father was a slave but who himself received a formal music education and composed classical music as well as a large number of piano rags. Scott Joplin was born in 1868 and eventually got a job as a pianist in the Maple Leaf saloon in Sedalia, Missouri. His most famous piece, "Maple Leaf Rag," was published in 1899 and sold so well that Joplin moved to St. Louis to concentrate on composition. In 1909 he settled in New York and composed a full-length opera, *Treemonisha*, which he attempted (without success) to have professionally produced. Joplin died in 1917, completely unrecognized by the musical establishment.

LISTENING GUIDE

((•⟶[Listen on MySearchLab

SCOTT JOPLIN (1868–1917)

Maple Leaf Rag, *for piano solo*

Date of composition: 1899
Tempo: *Tempo di marcia* ("March tempo")
Meter: $\frac{2}{4}$
Key: A♭ major
Duration: 3:14

CD III, 17

Scott Joplin's "Maple Leaf Rag" was published in 1899 and became immensely popular. Like most music at the time it was published in sheet music form; it became the first instrumental sheet music to sell over a million copies. It is typical of much ragtime music written around the turn of the century. A steady left-hand accompaniment keeps the march beat going throughout the piece while the right hand plays a lively, syncopated melody against this steady beat. The sections are repeated in the usual pattern: AA BB A CC DD. Each section is 16 measures long. The slight changes between sections, the standard but slightly irregular repetition pattern, the contrast between the rock-steady left hand and the dancing right hand—all of these characteristics make for a composition of great attractiveness and help to explain the enormous popularity of ragtime in the early years of the history of jazz. In this recording, we hear a **piano roll** (early mechanical recording) made by Joplin himself in 1916.

Time		Listen for
	A	
0:00		Strong, steady chords in left hand; syncopated rhythm in right hand; short arpeggiated phrases.
	A	
0:21		Repeat.
	B	
0:42		Melody begins higher and moves down; *staccato* articulation.
	B	
1:03		Repeat.
	A	
1:24		Opening section is played only once here.
	C	
1:45		Change of key to D♭ major (IV); rhythmic change in right hand; left-hand leaps.
	C	
2:06		Repeat.
	D	
2:28		Return to original key; strong final cadence.
	D	
2:48		Repeat.

The Blues

The blues is a form, a sound, and a spirit, all at the same time. It began as a type of vocal music that crystallized in the 1890s from many elements. Among these were African American spirituals, work songs, and street cries. The blues began as unaccompanied song but soon came to use banjo or guitar accompaniment. The common themes of early blues are sadness in love, betrayal, abandonment, and sometimes humor.

There is great variety in sung blues, but if there is a "standard" form, it is this: a series of three-line stanzas, in each of which the first two lines are the same:

I followed her to the station, with a suitcase in my hand.

I followed her to the station, with a suitcase in my hand.

Well, it's hard to tell, it's hard to tell, when all your love's in vain.

When the train rolled up to the station, I looked her in the eye.

When the train rolled up to the station, I looked her in the eye.

Well, I was lonesome, I felt so lonesome, and I could not help but cry.

(From Robert Johnson, "Love in Vain")

Find the **Quick Listen** on **MySearchLab**
"Robert Johnson 'Love in Vain'"

Each line is set to four measures, or bars, of music, so this pattern is known as **12-bar blues** (4 bars × 3 lines = 12 bars). The chord progressions in 12-bar blues are very simple, using only tonic (I), subdominant (IV), and dominant (V) chords. The overall pattern of 12-bar blues looks like this:

	MEASURE 1	MEASURE 2	MEASURE 3	MEASURE 4
Line 1	I	I	I	I
Line 2	IV	IV	I	I
Line 3	V	V (or IV)	I	I

> She had this trouble in her, this thing that wouldn't let her rest sometimes, a meanness that came and took her over.
>
> —Jazz saxophonist Sidney Bechet about Bessie Smith

Every stanza of the song follows the same pattern. The singer may accompany him- or herself on a guitar and may occasionally vary the accompaniment a little by introducing other chords or extra beats, but the basic pattern stays the same. Also, the singer has ample opportunity for varying the melodic line according to the expression of the text and his or her own personal feeling. The best blues singers use the rigid structure of blues as a vehicle for the most subtle variations in pitch (blue notes) and rhythm. Slight shadings of the pitch, little ornaments, and especially deliberate "misplacement" and constant manipulation of the rhythm are part and parcel of blues singing. The effect is of a very flexible and very personal vocal style against a square and simple background.

The form of the blues, with its special combination of flexibility and rigidity, began to be widely used by instrumentalists in the 1920s and has strongly influenced other types of popular music and jazz ever since.

Our example of blues singing is by Bessie Smith (1894–1937), known as the "Empress of the Blues." **(See Listening Guide.)** Bessie Smith grew up in Tennessee and from an early age helped support her family by singing on street corners. After false starts as a dancer and a vaudevillian, she devoted herself full time to singing blues.

Smith had a hit in 1923 with her very first recording. Audiences were stunned by the mature, tragic quality of her voice and by her sensitive, personal style—which seemed to speak directly to the listener. On her way to a singing session in 1937, her car crashed into the side of the road, and by the next day, Bessie Smith was dead.

LISTENING GUIDE

((•—Listen on **MySearchLab**

BESSIE SMITH (1894–1937)

"Florida-Bound Blues"

Date of performance: 1925
Duration: 3:14

CD III, 18

Bessie Smith often recorded with a small ensemble, but many of her performances feature piano and voice alone. Some of the great jazz pianists of the day recorded with Smith; and this recording features pianist Clarence Williams, who was also active as a songwriter, music publisher, and record producer.

"Florida-Bound Blues" is a standard 12-bar blues with words and music in an AAB pattern. Listen, though, for subtle changes in the words and melody between the first two lines of each stanza. In the first stanza, for example, "North" and "South" are sung as short notes in the first line but extended in the second line.

Among Smith's many vocal trademarks found in this recording is the addition of a chromatic note before the last note of a line.

The bare-bones melody:

Bessie Smith's version:

Sometimes she makes a quick slide, but sometimes she stretches out the added note.

Another common effect is a sudden pitch drop at the end of a line, producing a more intimate spoken sound. This device was a dependable way of creating a bond with an audience that was often doing plenty of talking on its own.

"Florida-Bound Blues" also shows the broad, world-weary tone that permeates her work and provides glimpses of her offhand sense of humor. Above all, this recording provides a clear picture of her masterful control of pitch, rhythm, and volume.

Time	Listen for	
0:00	Piano introduction	Piano immediately puts listener off balance before settling into a solid key and rhythm.
0:11	*Goodbye North, Hello South.*	Strict rhythm in piano is offset by Bessie's extra beat in the first line.
	Goodbye North, Hello South.	Vocal control: listen to the change of volume on "North" and "South."
	It's so cold up here that the words freeze in your mouth.	Compare the heavily blued note on "words" to the centered pitch on "freeze."
0:46	*I'm goin' to Florida where I can have my fun.*	Piano introduces a smooth, more melodic response to vocal.
	I'm goin' to Florida, where I can have my fun.	Listen for the added chromatic note on "fun."
	Where I can lay out in the green grass and look up at the sun.	Note the piano "roll" filling in the space after "grass."
1:22	*Hey, hey redcap, help me with this load.*	Listen for the deliberate variety and humor in these two lines.
	Redcap porter, help me with this load (step aside).	Each of the repeated notes is approached from below, creating a pulse in the line.
	Oh, that steamboat, Mr. Captain, let me get on board.	
1:58	*I got a letter from my daddy, he bought me a sweet piece of land.*	Heavily blued notes on "from my daddy" ("daddy" means "lover").
	I got a letter from my daddy, he bought me a small piece of ground.	Bessie varies this line by not taking a breath in the middle, making the ending breathless.
	You can't blame me for leavin', Lord, I mean I'm Florida bound.	
2:35	*My papa told me, my mama told me too.*	A new ending for the melody of the first two lines.
	My papa told me, my mama told me too:	
	Don't let them bell-bottom britches make a fool outta you.	Vocal line moves up on "fool," highlighting the punch line at the end.

New Orleans Jazz

New Orleans jazz (sometimes known as Dixieland jazz) flourished in the city of New Orleans, especially in the red-light district called Storyville. Small bands played in the brothels and saloons, and a standard form of "combo" arose: a "front line" of trumpet, clarinet, and trombone, and a "rhythm section" of drums, banjo, piano, and bass. Every instrument in a Dixieland band has a specific function. The main melody is played by the trumpet, while the clarinet weaves a high countermelody around it. The trombone plays a simpler, lower tune. In the rhythm section, the drums keep the beat, the piano and banjo play chords, and the bass plays the bass line (usually pizzicato—plucked).

Louis Armstrong's Hot Five, Chicago, 1925 (from left to right): Armstrong, Johnny St. Cyr, Johnny Dodds, Kid Ory, Lil Hardin.

jazz, a piece usually begins with the whole band playing the first chorus, and then features alternations of (accompanied) solo and collective improvisation. Sometimes everybody stops playing for two or four measures except for a single soloist. This is known as a "break."

Some of the most famous musicians and bandleaders of early jazz were Jelly Roll Morton (piano), Louis Armstrong (trumpet), Joe "King" Oliver (trumpet), Bix Beiderbecke (trumpet), Sidney Bechet (clarinet and soprano saxophone), and Jack Teagarden (trombone).

The most important figure in jazz from the 1920s was Louis Armstrong (1901–1971). After he left New Orleans, Armstrong settled in Chicago, where, with his composer and pianist wife, Lil Hardin, he made a series of groundbreaking recordings. His brilliant trumpet playing and enormously inventive improvisations paved the way for a new focus on solo playing. Armstrong's career spanned more than 50 years in American music, and in later years, when asked to speak about his life, he would simply point to his trumpet and say, "That's my living; that's my life."

In Chicago, Armstrong brought jazz from an era of dense polyphony, with many simultaneous lines, to an era of the astonishing solo performance. The performance we will hear is a Hot Five recording—trumpet, clarinet, and trombone for the musical lines, and piano (Lil Hardin), guitar, and banjo for rhythm and fill-in harmony.

"Hotter than That" is a remarkable performance on many levels. It might be seen as a textbook of early jazz: it contains bits of the earlier polyphonic New Orleans style as well as the flashy solos that became popular in the 1920s, and it displays breaks, stop-time, and call-and-response, all standard parts of the vocabulary of early ensemble jazz. Beyond that, it is one of the first truly great jazz recordings, showing Armstrong at his exuberant best on both trumpet and vocals. (See **Listening Guide**.)

> The recordings of [Louis Armstrong's] Hot Five and the Hot Seven contributed more than any other single group of recordings to making jazz famous and a music to be taken seriously.
> —Jazz historian Gunther Schuller

The sound of Dixieland jazz is of many lines interweaving in a complex but organized way. The effect is of collective improvisation but with every instrument having a carefully defined role. The most common musical forms are 12-bar blues and **32-bar AABA form** (the standard form of thousands of pop songs throughout the twentieth century).

The 32-bar AABA form has four, eight-measure sections:

- A—eight measures
- A—eight measures
- B—eight measures
- A—eight measures

The first statement of the tune takes up the first 32 measures. Then the band plays variants of the tune or improvises on its basic chord progressions, while keeping to the 32-measure format. Each statement of the tune or the variation on it is known as a "chorus." In Dixieland

LISTENING GUIDE

((•⟶ **Listen** on **MySearchLab**

LOUIS ARMSTRONG (1900–1971)

"Hotter Than That"

Date of performance: 1927
Instruments: trumpet, clarinet, trombone, piano, banjo, guitar
Duration: 3:04

CD III, 19

"Hotter Than That" is built around a 32-measure tune written by Lil Hardin. The 32-measure chord pattern is repeated several times, and the performers improvise all their melodic lines over this stable chord structure. The end of each 16-measure section is played as a break: everyone drops out except the soloist, who leads the song into the next half of the chorus or into the next chorus itself. The basic structure of the performance is shown here:

Intro:	full ensemble (8 bars)
Chorus 1:	trumpet solo with rhythm section (32 bars)
Chorus 2:	clarinet solo with rhythm section (32 bars)
Chorus 3:	vocal with guitar (32 bars)
New material:	vocal and guitar duet (16 bars)
Chorus 4:	trombone solo with rhythm section (16 bars) full ensemble (16 bars)
Coda:	trumpet and guitar

In the third chorus, Armstrong puts aside his trumpet and sings, scatting through the entire 32 bars. Pay special attention to the similarity between his trumpet playing and his singing: he uses the same clean attack, the same "shake" at the end of a long note, the same "rips" up to a high note, and the same arpeggiated style of melody. He also builds a string of 24 equal syncopated notes, intensifying the swing in the rhythm.

After the scat chorus, Armstrong and guitarist Lonnie Johnson play a call-and-response chorus, imitating each other's notes, inflections, and rhythms. In this section, as in the whole song, every note drives the song forward, producing a work of great energy and unity.

Time	Listen for
	Intro
0:00	Full ensemble, New Orleans–style polyphony. Listen for the individual instruments.
	Chorus 1
0:08	Trumpet solo. Listen for Armstrong's confident rhythm and occasional "burbles."
0:24	Break: background drops out, Armstrong "rips" to a high note.
0:26	Armstrong improvises on arpeggios. "Shake" on long notes.
0:42	Break: clarinet jumps in on trumpet line, prepares for solo.
	Chorus 2
0:44	Clarinet solo. Same tempo, but not as much rhythmic variety.
1:00	Break: clarinet dives into a long blued note.
1:02	Clarinet solo continues.
1:17	Break: Armstrong jumps in, preparing the scat chorus.
	Chorus 3
1:20	Scat chorus. Listen for variety of sound: jagged lines vs. smooth lines, notes hit perfectly vs. notes slid.
1:35	Break: "rip" to high note.
1:39	Scat in syncopation with guitar.
1:53	Break: whining scat, preparing for:
	New Material
1:55	Scat/guitar dialogue. Call-and-response.
2:08	"Rip" to high note in voice, imitated in guitar.
2:13	Piano transition to:
	Chorus 4
2:17	Trombone solo, ending with chromatic climb to:

2:32	Break: Armstrong on an energetic climbing sequence into:
2:35	New Orleans–style polyphony by full ensemble, Armstrong on top.
2:43	Multiple breaks ("stop-time").
Coda	
2:47	Full group, followed by:
2:49	Guitar/trumpet interchange.

Swing

In the 1930s and early 1940s, the most popular jazz style was **swing**. The Swing Era takes its name from the fact that much of the music of the time was dance music. Because swing was usually played by large bands with as many as 15 or 20 musicians, the Swing Era is also called the Big Band Era. This period also saw the growth of much solo playing, such as that of tenor saxophonists Coleman Hawkins and Lester Young, trumpeter Roy Eldridge, and pianists Fats Waller and Art Tatum.

The most important changes in the evolution from Dixieland jazz to the big bands were the larger number of performers, the use of saxophones in the band, and the use of written (composed or "arranged") music. For the first time, jazz was mostly written out, rather than mostly improvised. Swing music became extraordinarily popular during these years, and huge ballrooms would be filled with enthusiastic crowds dancing to the music. Some of the great swing bands of the time were those of Fletcher Henderson, Count Basie, Duke Ellington, and Benny Goodman.

The instruments of the big bands were divided into three groups: the saxophones, the brass section, and the rhythm section. The saxophone group included alto and tenor saxophones, and saxophone players ("reedmen") could usually also play clarinet. The brass section included both trumpets and trombones. The rhythm section included guitar, piano, bass, and drums. In addition, the bandleader (usually a pianist, a clarinetist, or a trumpeter) would often be featured as a soloist.

PERFORMANCE IN CONTEXT

The "Home of Happy Feet"

Music, dancing couples, and spectators wandered freely in the Savoy Ballroom (1926–1958). This New York City hotspot was equally famous for its quality music, virtuoso dancers, and lack of segregation. White and black patrons mingled on the dance floor: the only hierarchy was one of skill. The ballroom's music featured some of the biggest names of the Big Band Era: musicians Benny Goodman, Cab Calloway, Chick Webb, and Ella Fitzgerald, and dancers Frankie Manning and Norma Miller, to name only a few. The Savoy Ballroom was located in north Harlem. At its peak, an estimated 700,000 patrons a year passed through its door. Dances featured or invented at the ballroom (including the Lindy Hop, the Flying Charleston, and the Jitterbug Jive) frequently grew into nationwide crazes. There has been a major revival of swing dance in recent decades. On May 26, 2002, a commemorative plaque for the Savoy Ballroom was installed on Lenox Ave between 140th and 141st Streets.

Duke Ellington, directing his band from the piano, 1943.

Ellington was the first to make full use of the rich palette of colors available to the jazz orchestra. Similarly, Ellington's harmony was years ahead of that of his contemporaries, using extended chords, deft chromatic motion, and novel combinations of disparate sonorities.

The bandleader who did the most to popularize swing was Benny Goodman (1909–1986). Known as the "King of Swing," clarinetist Goodman led a band that was heard by millions across America on a weekly radio show, and he achieved the unprecedented in 1938 by bringing his band to Carnegie Hall, the traditional home of classical music. Goodman was also the first to break through what was then known as the "color barrier" by hiring black musicians such as pianist Teddy Wilson and vibraphonist Lionel Hampton to play among white musicians. This was an important step in what was still an officially segregated country.

Another influential aspect of Goodman's work was his formation of small groups— sometimes a trio or a quartet, but most often a sextet. Goodman's sextet and his other small groups paved the way for the virtuoso solo playing and small combos of bebop.

We listened to the Duke Ellington band performing "It Don't Mean a Thing (If It Ain't Got That Swing)" in Chapter 3. Here we'll listen to it again, in the context of jazz history and paying attention to the swinging style of the band, the color and variety of the arrangement, and the subtle ways in which Ellington makes the form of the piece interesting, by inserting extra passages into the conventional chorus–chorus–chorus pattern.

Find the **Quick Listen** on **MySearchLab**
"Benny Goodman at Carnegie Hall 1938"

Find the **Quick Listen** on **MySearchLab**
"Duke Ellington 'Take the A Train' in Color"

Visual presentation was an important element of the big bands. Similarly, the sound of the big bands of the Swing Era was smooth and polished. This was partly because of the prominence of the smooth-sounding saxophones, and partly because the music was almost entirely written down. The polyphonic complexity of collective improvisation had given way to an interest in a big homophonic sound, lively presentation, and polish.

One of the most important and influential composers in the history of jazz was Duke Ellington (1899–1974). He is said to have been responsible for as many as 1,000 jazz compositions. Ellington was a man of many talents, being at one and the same time a master songwriter, an innovative composer and arranger, an imaginative and capable pianist, and an extraordinary bandleader.

LISTENING GUIDE

((•— Listen on MySearchLab

DUKE ELLINGTON (1899–1974)

"It Don't Mean a Thing (If It Ain't Got That Swing)"

Date of performance: 1932
Orchestration: voice, three trumpets, two trombones, three saxophones, piano, banjo, bass, drums
Duration: 3:11

PLEASE NOTE: CD I, 6

The soloists in this performance are Ivie Anderson (vocals), Johnny Hodges (alto saxophone), and Joe "Tricky Sam" Nanton (trombone). The contrast in timbre among them is an important feature of the performance, as is the contrast between the composed parts for the band and the improvising by the soloists, and between the growling brass and the sultry saxophones. The whole performance is lively and infectious.

The title of "It Don't Mean a Thing (If It Ain't Got That Swing)" became a motto for an entire era (the date of this recording, 1932, was right at the beginning of the Swing Era) and has survived as a catchphrase in the jazz world up through today.

Time	Listen for
0:00	Introduction with vocalist Ivie Anderson's scat improvisation and driving bass and drum.
0:11	Improvised trombone solo atop the subdued saxophones and trumpets who also respond (blare?) to the phrases of the trombone's solo.
0:46	First chorus of song. Blue note on "ain't." Responses from band.
1:23	Transitional section of contrasting character, including Johnny Hodges's saxophone solo.
2:17	Hodges and the band play variants on the tune.
2:43	Scat improvisation by Anderson.
2:52	Return to first line of lyrics and fadeout by muted trumpets on the music of their response.

Bebop

Jazz is freedom.
Think about that.
You think about that.
—Thelonious Monk

In the early 1940s, a reaction to the glossy, organized sound of some of the big bands set in. Some jazz musicians began to experiment again with smaller combos and with a type of music that was more intellectually demanding, more for listening than for dancing. This style is known as **bop** or **bebop**. The name probably derives from some of the nonsense syllables used in scat singing ("Doo-wah doo-wah, be-bop a loo-wah"). And the most frequent phrase ending in bebop solos is ♩♪, which fits the word "bebop" perfectly. There is also a composition by Dizzy Gillespie that is called "Bebop."

The pioneers of bebop were Charlie Parker, nicknamed "Bird" (alto saxophone), Dizzy Gillespie (trumpet), and Thelonious Monk (piano). In turn, these three players influenced other musicians, including Stan Getz, Miles Davis, Sarah Vaughan, and John Coltrane. In fact, it would be difficult to find a jazz musician who has not been influenced by Parker, Gillespie, and Monk.

Bebop is a very different kind of music from swing. It is harder, irregular, and less predictable. It is played by a small group (for example, saxophone and trumpet with piano, bass, and drums). The tempo is generally faster, and there is far more solo improvisation. The chord progressions and rhythmic patterns are complex and varied. Bop is generally considered the beginning of modern jazz.

With its fast pace and its emphasis on solo improvisation, bebop depended on the inventiveness, quick thinking, virtuosity, and creativity of individual musicians. Charlie Parker, Dizzy Gillespie, and Thelonious Monk worked independently, but had a similar approach to the new music. They also performed together and developed considerable complexity in their playing. Their solo improvisations were quick and unpredictable, full of fiery fast notes, lengthy pauses, and sudden changes of direction. Although bop was still based on popular songs (AABA form) or on the 12-bar blues pattern, the simple harmonies were enriched with new and more dissonant chords, and the accompanying rhythms were more complex. Soloists often deliberately overran the underlying sectional patterns and began and ended phrases at unexpected and unconventional places.

Bebop musicians sometimes wrote new tunes themselves, but more often they improvised around well-known songs of the day. Beboppers avoided improvising on the melody; their solos were built strictly on the chord patterns and often made no reference to the tune. As a result, their music could sound quite different from the original song.

A distinct culture surrounded bebop. It was music of rebellion. Swing had been accepted, and even taken over, by the white establishment, and bebop was, in a sense, a reaction to this. It was designed to be different.

Beboppers in 1948. From left to right: Thelonious Monk, Howard McGhee, Roy Eldridge, Teddy Hill.

Charlie Parker at the peak of his career.

For such controversial music, bebop is based on a remarkably conservative structure. Normally it begins with a 32-bar tune. Often the melody instruments play the tune in unison. Then each instrument improvises over the chords of the tune.

The great genius of bebop was Charlie Parker (1920–1955), a brilliant, self-destructive saxophonist who died at the age of 34 from alcoholism and drug addiction. His improvisations changed the way a generation thought about jazz. His playing was profound, dizzying, subtle, and complex; his phrasing was unconventional and inspired; and his tone was edgy and intense—liquid in one line and sandpaper in the next. Parker absorbed music of all kinds, including Stravinsky and Bartók; he loved painting and dance. And he was both loyal and inspiring: Dizzy Gillespie called him "the other half of my heartbeat."

We shall listen to a remarkable performance by Parker, entitled "Confirmation," which he recorded in 1953. "Confirmation" is in 32-bar AABA form. This format provides a frame for the extraordinary creativity and brilliance of the saxophonist.

> Bird [Parker's nickname] was kind of like the sun, giving off the energy we drew from him. In any musical situation, his ideas just bounded out, and this inspired anyone who was around.
> —Max Roach, jazz composer and drummer

LISTENING GUIDE

(((•—Listen on MySearchLab

THE CHARLIE PARKER QUARTET

"Confirmation"

Date of performance: July 30, 1953
Personnel: Charlie Parker, alto saxophone;
 Al Haig, piano; Percy Heath, bass; Max Roach, drums
Duration: 3:01

CD III, 20

"Confirmation" is one of the most stunning of Parker's many extraordinary performances. The studio tapes show that the piece was recorded straight through, with no splicing, no alternative takes, and no errors. It is important to remember that although the first few measures (the initial A of the AABA form) and the third group of eight measures (the B section) have been worked out beforehand, all the rest of what Parker plays is made up on the spot. All the running notes, the rhythmic figures, the cascades of musical gestures—all of these are created in the very moment of performance. Not only that, but each time Parker plays the A section—every single time—he varies it considerably. It is hard to imagine that anyone could come up with such rich creativity in such an instantaneous way.

Charlie Parker's alto saxophone is accompanied by piano, bass, and drums. These serve to create a harmonic foundation and keep a consistent beat, against which Parker's ingenuity, flexibility, and expressive flights can shine. Toward the end of the piece, each of the other players gets a few measures to improvise on his own: first the pianist, then the bass player, and then the drummer. Parker wraps everything up with everyone playing together again.

The form of the piece is the favorite one of the bebop era: AABA. Just to remind you, each section of this form lasts for 8 measures. So each statement or *chorus* of the whole form lasts for 32 measures. There are three whole choruses with Parker, then the piano plays the A section twice (16 measures), the bass player has 8 measures, the drummer has 8, and then Parker returns to play B and A once more (the final 16 measures). To keep your place, keep counting measures (*1*, 2, 3, 4; *2*, 2, 3, 4; etc.) all the way through (it's easier if you focus on the bass, which plays on the beat all the way through).

Time	Listen for
	Introduction
0:00	There is a brief four-measure introduction by the piano.
	Chorus 1
0:05	The tune is a typical bebop composition: angular, irregular, and offbeat. Yet Parker makes it sound melodic as well as deeply rhythmic. The rhythm section is rock solid, though the drummer manages to be splashy and interesting at the same time. Although the chorus contains three statements of the A section, Parker makes it sound different each time. The B section (0:25–0:34) is not as highly differentiated in this piece as it is in some bebop compositions, though its harmonies are different.
	Chorus 2
0:44	Parker really starts to fly on this chorus (remember his nickname: "Bird"). He also plays in the lower register of the saxophone to give variety to his solo.
	Chorus 3
1:22	The third chorus is unified by rapid, descending chromatic phrases, which in turn are balanced by arch-shaped arpeggios. A triplet turn is a common motive, and Parker plays right across the "seams" of the AABA form to make long, compelling musical statements of his own.
	Piano Solo (AA)
2:00	Al Haig takes 16 measures for his improvisation, which is quite musical for a normal human being, but sounds a bit dull after listening to Charlie Parker!
	Bass Solo (B)
2:16	Percy Heath gets to play some different rhythms with hints of the tune for eight measures.
	Drum Solo (A)
2:28	Amazingly, Max Roach manages to suggest the melody on his eight measures. (Try humming it along with him.)
	Final Half Chorus (BA)
2:35	Parker repeats the B and A sections as a final half chorus, playing with intensity but closer to the original melody. Percy Heath (who was said to be overwhelmed by Parker's playing on this recording date) gets in the last word!

Cool Jazz

Cool jazz was really a subcategory of bop. It continued to use small combos, and the rhythmic and harmonic styles were similar. Cool-jazz pieces also were based on popular tunes or blues patterns. The departures from bop can be noted immediately in the overall sound of the groups and in the improvised solos. The playing is more subdued and less frenetic. Pieces tend to be longer, and they feature a larger variety of instruments, including the baritone saxophone, with its deep, full sound, and even some classical instruments, such as the French horn and the cello, which are characteristically mellow in sound.

The Modern Jazz Quartet.

Some groups specializing in cool jazz became quite popular in the 1950s. Miles Davis formed a group with nine instruments, including French horn and baritone sax; the George Shearing Quintet used piano, guitar, vibraphone, bass, and drums; and perhaps the most popular group of all (certainly one of the longest lasting) was the Modern Jazz Quartet, which featured vibraphone, piano, bass, and drums. The vibraphone (an instrument like a xylophone, with metal bars and an electrically enhanced, sustained, fluctuating tone) is the perfect instrument for projecting the "coolth" of cool jazz.

In the 1950s, the musician who pushed the outer boundaries of jazz was the trumpeter Miles Davis. Davis was influential on many fronts. He formed small, highly creative bebop ensembles; he recorded whole albums in front of big bands in a concerto-like format (*Sketches of Spain, Porgy and Bess*); and he got together a sextet that made the most popular jazz album of all time: the dreamy, introspective *Kind of Blue* (1959). (If you want only one jazz album in your collection or on your playlist, this is the one to buy.) In his success, his attitude, his clothes, and his spare, understated music, he became the emblem of personal cool.

Davis's principal sideman during these years was the tenor saxophonist John Coltrane. Coltrane was the opposite of Davis in his playing: he played streams of notes where Davis played very few. They made a perfect combination. Coltrane left Davis to form his own band in the 1960s and became one of the most intense and expressive players of his time.

Free Jazz

A move away from the preset chord progressions that were the basis of jazz up to that time led to the development in the 1960s and 1970s of what is known as free jazz. This style depended both on original compositions and on creative improvisation. The most influential musician of this period was Ornette Coleman, alto saxophonist, trumpeter, violinist, and composer. Several pieces have been named for him, and an album of his, made in 1960 and entitled *Free Jazz*, gave its name to the whole period.

Free jazz is abstract and can be dense and difficult to follow. Besides abandoning preset chord progressions, it often dispenses with regular rhythmic patterns and melody lines as well. The drumming is energetic, full of color and activity, without a steady and constant pattern of beats. Melodic improvisations are full of extremes: very high notes, squawks and squeals, long-held tones, fragmented phrases, and sudden silences. Many free-jazz groups have experimented with the music of other countries. Idioms borrowed from Turkish, African, and Indian music appear in many free-jazz compositions, and some groups have made use of non-Western instruments, such as sitars, gongs, and bamboo flutes.

Free jazz in its purest form was controversial and less widely accepted than other jazz styles. It could be difficult to listen to and was often raucous and dissonant. Totally free collective improvisation must necessarily have many moments of complete chaos. (Coleman's *Free Jazz* has two bands improvising simultaneously with no predetermined key, rhythm, or melody.) Free-jazz composers responded to this problem by writing compositions that would begin and end with a set theme or melody, allowing room for free improvisation in between. Obviously, in these

Find the **Quick Listen** on **MySearchLab**
"Modern Jazz Quartet Live Blues"

Find the **Quick Listen** on **MySearchLab**
"Coleman *Free Jazz*"

Miles Davis.

JAZZ AND CLASSICAL

Some of the elements of jazz—syncopation, for example—appear in classical music. Some Bach melodies are fascinating in their syncopations and cross-rhythms, Beethoven wrote some variations that sound like ragtime, and Debussy invented many of the chords used later in jazz. But jazz brought to the musical scene an art that was highly original and full of vitality. And many classical composers of the twentieth century turned to the inspiration of jazz in their own work.

Jazz exerted a strong influence on Stravinsky. His first work to incorporate elements of jazz was *L'Histoire du Soldat* (1918); subsequent compositions that employ jazz techniques include *Ragtime* (of the same year), *Piano-Rag-Music* (1919), and the *Ebony* Concerto for clarinet and jazz band (1945).

Ravel, Milhaud, Copland, and Bernstein were four other famous twentieth-century composers influenced by jazz. The Ravel piano concertos each contain jazzlike episodes, and his Violin Sonata has a second movement entitled "Blues." Milhaud's *Création du Monde* incorporates influences from the jazz he heard in Harlem nightclubs in the early 1920s. Copland's music is full of jazzy rhythms and harmonies, as is that of Bernstein, who moved especially freely between the two worlds.

The composer who most successfully brought together elements of jazz and classical music was George Gershwin. His *Rhapsody in Blue* (1924) is a perfect example of a symphonic work permeated by elements of the jazz style.

The pianist Cecil Taylor has played in an improvisatory style that is halfway between jazz and classical music. And so-called nu jazz combines the sounds of electronic classical music and jazz improvisation. In 2000 the French producer Ludovic Navarre, who uses the stage name St. Germain, produced a nu-jazz album called *Tourist*, which became a world-wide hit. And Boxcutter (Barry Lynn) combines nu jazz with dubstep in his album *The Dissolve* (2011).

cases the melody provides a common basis for the intervening improvisations and eliminates the randomness of complete freedom. Also, the influence of Eastern and African music brought to free jazz a common language of drones and new scale patterns.

Fusion

Fusion is the name given to the musical style of the 1970s and 1980s that combined elements of jazz and rock music. Perhaps it was the lack of an audience for free jazz or the overwhelming popularity of rock that encouraged jazz musicians to incorporate elements of rock into their performances and compositions during this period.

Rock and jazz have some origins in common: early blues, gospel music, and popular ballads. But they developed along separate lines. Rock is largely vocal music and is based on simple and accessible forms and harmonies. Jazz is mostly instrumental music, and some forms of jazz are quite complex, ignoring popular appeal.

Fusion was the first jazz style to achieve wide popularity since the mass appeal of swing in the 1930s and 1940s. Its most influential proponent was Miles Davis, who made two records in 1969—*In a Silent Way* and *Bitches Brew*—that established the fusion style for the 1970s and 1980s.

The primary characteristics of fusion are the adoption of electric instruments (electric piano, synthesizer, and electric bass) in place of their traditional ancestors, a large percussion section (including several non-European instruments such as hand drums, bells, gongs, shakers, and scrapers), and simplicity of form and harmony. Fusion is often based on straightforward chord progressions and highly repetitive rhythmic patterns. Over this accessible and almost hypnotic foundation, however, fusion presents a kaleidoscopic variety of sounds.

The most popular fusion group of this era was Weather Report, founded by musicians who had worked with Miles Davis on *In a Silent Way* and *Bitches Brew*. The leading light of the group was Joe Zawinul, composer and pianist, but all the members were expert musicians who worked together brilliantly. The result was a remarkable combination of solo lines merging into a rich group sound. Other important groups were founded by Herbie Hancock and Chick Corea.

Back to the Future

The 1990s witnessed a big jazz revival and the coexistence of many different jazz styles. Dixieland groups, big and medium-sized bands, bebop players, experimenters with

Find the **Quick Listen** on **MySearchLab**

"In a Silent Way"

electronic music, and fusion players (often with only a small proportion of jazz in the mix) all attracted audiences. The main trend was a conservative one. Wynton Marsalis and his groups revived older styles of jazz instead of creating new ones. Many colleges and universities added jazz courses to the curriculum. Women began to be more active than ever in jazz, most of them singers, pianists, or composers. They included composers Toshiko Akiyoshi, Marian McPartland, Carla Bley, and Maria Schneider; singers Diane Schuur, Abbey Lincoln, Cassandra Wilson, and Dianne Reeves; pianists Joanne Brackeen, Eliane Elias, Geri Allen, and Renee Rosnes; singer-pianist Diana Krall; saxophonist Jane Ira Bloom; and drummer Terri Lyne Carrington.

In the twenty-first century jazz has become an international language. It has large audiences and great performers in Japan, as well as in Western Europe (especially Scandinavia), Latin America, the Caribbean, Africa, and Eastern Europe.

In the 1990s, many of the jazz legends passed away, among them Miles Davis (1991), Dizzy Gillespie (1993), and Ella Fitzgerald (1996), but in the new century a new generation of talented younger players established itself on the mainstream jazz scene. Saxophonists Joshua Redman and James Carter; trumpeters Roy Hargrove and Nicholas Payton; pianists Eric Reed and Jacky Terrason; bassist Christian McBride; drummer Leon Parker; and singers Karrin Allyson, Stacey Kent, Madeleine Peyroux, and Kurt Elling all display a deep knowledge of jazz tradition and a remarkable fluency in a variety of styles.

As an alternative to mainstream jazz, various blends of jazz with ethnic, pop, rap, and classical idioms continue to take place, and new musical horizons are being explored by such diverse avant-garde artists as John Zorn and Steve Coleman. A special kind of blend was called "acid jazz." This music is a hybrid of traditional jazz and popular dance rhythms, created by manipulating "samples" of classic jazz records to form a background for new improvised solos, rap vocals, or both. Acid jazz functions primarily as dance music. A bluesy, complex, repetitive but rhythmic style of jazz called "funk" or "groove" music has also become popular. Its best-known exponents include guitarist John Scofield, saxophonist Maceo Parker, and the organ-bass-drums trio Medeski, Martin,

and Wood. And nu jazz combines electronica with jazz solos.

In addition to the highly eclectic mixture of up-to-date jazz styles available today, a movement has manifested itself that might be called a "return to the past." This movement treats recorded jazz as a great musical repertory, as important in its way as written classical music. Performers attempt to "capture" great jazz styles of past eras in clean, modern performances, enhanced by the new virtuoso instrumental techniques of young performers.

The history of jazz is an elusive one, being concerned with compositions that are fleeting—invented in the heat of the moment. We are fortunate that some of the great improvisations of the past have been captured on recordings and even (by some determined individuals) in notation.

The prime exponent of the "neo-conservative" approach has been Wynton Marsalis, a superb trumpeter and a musician with a great respect for the past. His clean, sophisticated, modern technique, allied with his reverence for the jazz greats of earlier eras, made him the most popular jazz artist in modern times. In 1997, Marsalis became the first jazz musician ever to be awarded the Pulitzer Prize, and he has since become the controversial spokesman and leader of Jazz at Lincoln Center. Although he has managed to create greater awareness of the jazz tradition, many feel that he has stifled creativity and stunted the growth of new styles.

Much exciting new jazz is now being made in countries other than the United States. One of the best was the

> A jazz musician who plays fusion is selling out.
> —Wynton Marsalis

Find the **Quick Listen** on **MySearchLab**

"E.S.T. *From Gagarin's Point of View*"

Find the **Quick Listen** on **MySearchLab**

"Empirical *Live at the Southbank*"

Find the **Quick Listen** on **MySearchLab**

"The Bad Plus— 'Smells Like Teen Spirit' (Nirvana cover)"

Wynton Marsalis.

piano-bass-drums trio called E.S.T., based in Sweden. This group made many recordings, and toured regularly in America, before the tragic death of their leader in a scuba diving accident at the age of 44. A quintet of serious and dedicated young players in England is becoming well-known; they call themselves Empirical. And one American trio, the Bad Plus, is forging a hip new style, incorporating pop and rock into their repertoire.

Jazz purists scorn smooth jazz, which they regard as pop music played on a saxophone with lots of echo. But some listeners enjoy the easy-going sounds of a smooth-jazz player such as Kenny G. Whatever your taste, you can find a panoply of jazz styles in cafes, nightclubs, hotel bars, and restaurants near where you live.

STYLE SUMMARY

Jazz

America inherited many of its musical forms and styles from Europe. Jazz, however, is one of the truly original American art forms.

Jazz was forged in New Orleans and other cities from a vigorous amalgam of African American singing and playing styles and European instruments and harmony. Its strongest early influence was band music, and to this day a jazz group is known as a band. From band music, jazz inherited its instruments: drums as the backbone, trumpet, trombone, clarinet, banjo, and tuba. These instruments could be carried while marching and were loud enough to be heard outdoors. When jazz moved indoors and became stationary, banjo and tuba were gradually replaced by piano and string bass, and the drum kit was invented.

Two other early influences were the syncopated rhythms of ragtime (which was also based on march tempo, meter, and form) and the blues. The blues is simultaneously a poetic form, a harmonic template, a flexible, highly inflected sound, and a people's spirit.

Even more than in classical music, in jazz the music is strongly influenced by individual personalities. And no single person had more influence on jazz than Louis Armstrong—trumpeter, bandleader, singer, actor, individualist, collaborator, and cultural ambassador. It is said, with only slight exaggeration, that he single-handedly invented swing—that almost indefinable element of rhythm that gives jazz its life.

The only period in the twentieth century when jazz could genuinely lay claim to being a

Timeline of Key Jazz Styles	
1900–1920s	New Orleans/Dixieland Jazz
1930s–1940s	"Big Band" Jazz/Swing
1950s	Bebop
1950s	Cool Jazz
1960s	Free Jazz
1970s–1990s	Jazz/Rock Fusion
1990s	Neo-Conservatives (Wynton Marsalis and others)
2000s	World Beat/Eclectic Fusions/European Jazz

popular music was the 1930s, variously known as the Swing Era or the Big Band Era. Both white and black audiences, embraced the new music and its exponents and danced to their radios or in dance halls all across America. Swing bands were polished, showy, and put less emphasis on individual accomplishment than on group sound. This did not stop one of the greatest bandleaders, Duke Ellington, from showcasing some of the strongest individual players of the era as members of his band or from using his band to highlight his own remarkably original and sophisticated compositions.

After World War II changed everything, small groups led the way, concentrating on individual expression, instrumental virtuosity, and challenging improvisation in a style known as bop. The voluble genius Charlie Parker on alto saxophone and the taciturn, oblique trumpeter Miles Davis showed how the new, smaller combos could be a framework for complex, profound statements.

In the 1970s and 1980s an amalgam of jazz and rock, known as Fusion, attracted attention. In more recent times, jazz has been blended with a large assortment of other elements, including Latin sounds and rhythms, synthesized mood music, rap, and funk. These blends are heard all over the airwaves, in nightclubs, and on recordings, though in the 1990s a "return to the past" movement—spearheaded by Wynton Marsalis—led to a re-creation of older styles. Most of the excitement and innovation in jazz is now found in the music made by groups outside the United States, but the latest American jazz performers are striving to breathe new life into a musical genre that has flourished for over a hundred years. Jazz today is torn between a movement back to the past and one that insists on pushing the music into the future.

FUNDAMENTALS OF JAZZ

- ❏ The three primary influences were marching bands, ragtime, and the blues
- ❏ The characteristic harmony and melodies of jazz are based on the blues scale, with variable third, seventh, and, occasionally, fifth notes in the scale
- ❏ Characteristic instrumental sounds are those of saxophone, trumpet (often muted), plucked string bass, and drum kit
- ❏ Performing forces usually range from the trio to the small combo (five or so players) to the big band (about 12 to 15 players)
- ❏ Jazz usually includes an element of improvisation
- ❏ Jazz has become a worldwide phenomenon incorporating influences from hip-hop, rock, and pop

FOR FURTHER DISCUSSION AND STUDY

1. Listen to a Louis Armstrong solo several times, and compare it with the notated version (many are available in Gunther Schuller's *Early Jazz*). Discuss the limitations of conventional notation when it comes to jazz performances.

2. Compare Duke Ellington's "It Don't Mean a Thing (If It Ain't Got That Swing)" with a Baroque concerto grosso (perhaps Corelli's Op. 6, No. 2), noting the similarity between the jazz soloists and the Baroque soloists, the rhythm section and the basso continuo, and the full band and the *tutti* sections.

3. Throughout the history of jazz, there have been outcries against new trends. This happened with bebop, free jazz, and other styles. Why do you think this is?

4. How did the cultural and social atmosphere of the 1960s influence the development of free jazz?

5. A fusion of pop music and jazz is called "smooth jazz" (heard in the work, for example, of saxophonist Kenny G). Is this very popular style truly "jazz"? Why or why not?

6. Read some articles about the controversies surrounding Wynton Marsalis and Jazz at Lincoln Center. Discuss the issues involved.

7. What role, if any, does race continue to play in jazz?

8. Who gets to define what is really "jazz"? Why?

✓•[**Study** and **Review** on **MySearchLab**

The Twentieth Century and Beyond, Part III: Popular Music in the United States

Popular music is one of the most widespread phenomena of contemporary culture. Throughout the world, American popular music is regarded as a symbol of modernity and hipness. The music represents Western commercial and popular culture with the same force as such powerful icons as Coca-Cola and Apple.

In addition to its associations with a technological and commercial society, popular music also connotes youth. Young people buy the largest share by far of CDs and downloads, and most popular performers are under 35. The pop phenomenon began in the 1950s and 1960s, when pop and rock music were symbols of youthful rebellion. It coincided with the post–World War II period of prosperity, when young people had more money to spend than ever before. The vast spread and commercial success of popular music are the result of a society with time on its hands and money to spend.

Styles of Popular Music

By definition, popular music is designed to appeal to the widest possible audience. No formal training is required to appreciate it, and it is usually vocal, because everybody can sing (more or less). Its subject matter (often love or sex) is attractive to almost everyone, and the style and structure of the music are frequently simple and repetitive. Often the refrains of popular songs are very catchy.

They have a rhythm that immediately suggests the music, even if you don't know the melody. Once you do know the melody, the music is so accessible, and the rhythm and melody are so molded to the words, that it is impossible to forget them.

The three most important elements in popular music are the words, the rhythm, and the melody. (Because harmony is one of the more complex elements of music, popular music has tended to keep the harmony fairly simple.) Different types of popular music tend to stress one or another of the three factors over the other two. For example, the most notable characteristic of rock music is the driving rhythm. In country music, the words are often foremost, because they generally tell a story. In pop ballads, it is the smooth melody that creates a special atmosphere.

> When writing popular songs, always bear in mind that it is to the untrained musical public that you largely look for support and popularity. Therefore, do not offer them anything which in subject matter or melody does not appeal to their ears. To do so is just so much time thrown away.
> —Charles K. Harris

Timeline of Popular Music Styles

PERIOD	STYLE	REPRESENTATIVE COMPOSER(S)/ PERFORMERS	HOW MUSIC WAS DISTRIBUTED
1850–1880	Minstrel	Stephen Foster	Sheet music for home performance
1880s–1910s	Vaudeville/Tin Pan Alley	Charles K. Harris	Sheet music for home performance; vaudeville & Broadway stages
1920s–1940s	"Classic" American Popular Songs/The American Songbook	Irving Berlin; George Gershwin; Cole Porter	78 rpm records; Broadway theater; radio; film
1950s	Early Rock 'n' Roll	Chuck Berry; Elvis Presley	45 rpm records; radio; television
1960s	Pop/Rock	Beatles; Rolling Stones	45 rpm and LP records; radio; television
1970s–1980s	Heavy metal; punk; disco; dance-pop	Led Zeppelin; Sex Pistols; Donna Summer; Michael Jackson	MTV; Top-Forty radio; cassette tapes; CDs
1990s–2000s	Rap/R&B	2 Live Crew; Ice-T; Kanye West; Jay-Z; Beyoncé	CDs; MTV; downloads

Beginnings: 1850–1950

How did the phenomenon of American popular music begin? Where did it come from?

American popular music has a long history, reaching back to the mid-nineteenth century. The first important popular songwriter was Stephen Foster (1826–1864). Foster's songs were first introduced by performers like George Christie, who led the famous performing troupe, Christie's Minstrels. Minstrel shows—in which white performers wore blackface makeup and imitated African American songs, dances, and humor—were tremendously popular in America from the 1840s through the 1880s. These shows were notorious for the racist content of their routines and their demeaning portrayal of African Americans. But they also spread and popularized songs that rose above these circumstances and that have long since shed their association with the minstrel tradition. During his lifetime, Foster wrote some of the most enduring songs of the American tradition for the minstrel stage, including "Oh! Susanna," "Camptown Races," and "Old Folks at Home."

"Old Folks at Home" is typical of the early popular song in three ways. First, it has a catchy melody. In fact, its first line is so catchy ("Way down upon the Swanee River") that most people think

Stephen Foster.

of it as the song's title. Second, the words are sentimental. And third, the harmony is extremely simple, using only three chords throughout.

| G | | G | C |

Way down upon the Swanee River,

| G | D | | |

Far, far away,

| G | | G | C |

There's where my heart is turnin' ever,

| G | | D | G |

There's where the old folks stay.

| G | | G | C |

All up and down the whole creation

| G | D | | |

Sadly I roam,

| G | | G | C |

Still longing for the old plantation,

| G | | D | G |

And for the old folks at home.

| G | | G | |

All the world is sad and dreary,

| C | | G | D |

Everywhere I roam,

| G | | G | C |

Oh, darkies, how my heart grows weary,

| G | | D | G |

Far from the old folks at home.

With the success achieved by Stephen Foster and other songwriters, music publishers began to realize the commercial potential of popular music. Charles K. Harris (1865–1930), a songwriter who set up his own publishing

COMPOSERS, PATRONS, AND AUDIENCES

Patronage and Commercialization

Throughout the history of music, financial backing has been needed to support the composition and production of musical performances. A person or an institution providing such backing is known as a patron. Patrons can support music in a variety of ways: by buying tickets for concerts, by volunteering their time to help a musical organization, or by donating funds.

As we have seen, in Europe during the Middle Ages, the greatest patron of music (and all the arts) was the Church. In the Renaissance, Baroque, and Classic eras, the foremost patrons were wealthy aristocrats, who employed composers and performers in their courts. In the nineteenth century, the main support for music gradually spread to the middle classes. Public concerts became common, and music was funded by ticket sales and by the sale of printed music for amateurs to perform at home. During the twentieth century, this reliance on wider support has continued to grow, and now the central driving force behind the production of most popular music has become commercial gain. The potential profits are enormous.

As the multinational corporations that produce recordings become more and more powerful, it is worth asking what really shapes the musical tastes of today's music consumers. Are our tastes being formed by our own individual preferences or by the combined forces of millions of dollars of advertising?

company, landed a major hit in 1892 with the publication of his song "After the Ball." Within a few years, the song had sold an unprecedented two million copies. Remember that in the era before records, radio, or television, all home entertainment was "homemade"—provided by a willing voice, a piano, and copies of songs in sheet music.

One of the most productive periods in the history of American popular song came in the 1920s, 1930s, and 1940s. This was the era of great songwriters such as Cole Porter, Irving Berlin, Richard Rodgers, Jerome Kern, and George Gershwin, and of popular singers such as Al Jolson, Bing Crosby, and Frank Sinatra. It was also the era of new technologies that revolutionized popular music. Sound movies, radio, and the phonograph all hit their stride in the 1920s, and all three supported and promoted popular songs.

Cole Porter (1891–1964) was born into a wealthy Episcopalian family in Indiana. He attended both Yale and Harvard before becoming a socialite. However he also spent his time writing music. He composed dozens of musicals with hundreds of songs, whose main feature is their clever lyrics and wonderful melodies. His shows include *Anything Goes*, *Kiss Me Kate*, and *High Society*. Among the more famous songs are "Let's Do It, Let's Fall in Love," "Night and Day," "I Get a Kick out of You," "I've Got You Under My Skin," "You'd Be So Nice to Come Home To," and "Too Darn Hot."

Irving Berlin (1888–1989) was a Russian Jewish immigrant who came from a poor family and had to go to work at the age of 11. He started out selling newspapers and singing on the street. Although he never learned to play the piano or read music beyond an elementary level, by the time of his death he had written over 3,000 songs, including "God Bless America," "Puttin' on the Ritz," "Cheek to Cheek," and "White Christmas." He also composed film scores and musicals, the most famous of which is *Annie Get Your Gun* (1946).

Richard Rodgers (1902–1979) was one of the most successful songwriters of the 1930s and 1940s, writing the music for many of the era's famous shows, including *Oklahoma!*, *Carousel*, and *South Pacific*, as well as many songs not associated with shows. He began his career collaborating with Lorenz Hart and then worked with Oscar Hammerstein II. The list of his song hits is almost endless; it

Scene from the original production of *Porgy and Bess*, 1935–1936.

includes "Oh, What a Beautiful Morning," "Some Enchanted Evening," and "Blue Moon," which was composed in 1934 and which we shall study as an example of an American popular song in its heyday. (**See Listening Guide.**)

In the 1930s, George Gershwin (1898–1937) wrote the music and his brother Ira wrote the lyrics for many songs that have become American classics. They include "'S Wonderful," "I Got Rhythm," and "Love Walked In," as well as the great songs from the opera *Porgy and Bess*, such as the enduringly popular "Summertime" and "It Ain't Necessarily So."

There are hundreds of other composers whose names are largely forgotten but whose music lives on in songs such as "Singin' in the Rain," "Pennies from Heaven," and "Tea for Two." All the song titles I have mentioned so far constitute only a brief list compared with the thousands that once swept the country. Stylistically, most of these songs conform to the model of the sentimental ballad: lyrical melodies, simple harmonies, repetitive rhythm, and a recurring refrain (chorus).

Note: The songs in this chapter are widely available, and they can be easily and cheaply downloaded from legitimate Web sites.

Frank Sinatra is a singer who comes along once in a lifetime. But why did he have to come along in *my* lifetime?

—singer Bing Crosby

LISTENING GUIDE

(((•━Listen on MySearchLab

"BLUE MOON"

Music by Richard Rodgers, words by Lorenz Hart

Date of composition: 1934
Date of recording: 1945
Performer: Frank Sinatra

From very early on, the music industry recognized the advantages of tying a popular song to a particular singer. The success of the song depended to a large extent on the degree of "stardom" of the singer. Early sheet music often had the words "as sung by . . ." printed on the cover, or displayed a photograph of the singer.

One of the most successful singers in the late 1930s and early 1940s was Frank Sinatra (1915–1998). He toured with dance bands, and his romantic appeal and individual singing style endeared him to millions of listeners. At his concerts, teenage girls screamed and fainted in one of the earliest displays of mass adoration of a popular music figure. Sinatra's death in 1998 at the age of 82 caused a resurgence of interest in his life and in his music. A look at Sinatra's version of "Blue Moon" will demonstrate both his special style of singing and the character and structure of the pop song at this stage in its history.

This ballad follows the character of most songs from the 1930s and 1940s in that it is slow, lyrical, and sentimental. Sinatra's singing style beautifully conforms to the character of the song. It is relaxed, casual, and somehow intimate. He sounds very comfortable, almost as if he were talking. The sense of relaxation is conveyed particularly by the way his voice "slides" in and out of phrases.

The structure of the song is simple. It is cast in AABA form, with eight measures for each section. The music for the first section (A) is repeated for the second section (A); then there is a contrast (B) before the return of the A section again. In this song, the pattern is very easy to follow, because all three A sections begin with the words of the title. As with many songs of the era, the B section uses more colorful chords than the A section, which emphasizes the contrast between the two.

Time	Listen for
0:00	[Instrumental introduction]
0:16	**A section** (beginning with words of title)
0:33	**A section** (new words, but still beginning with title)
0:49	**B section** (change of key; change of words)
1:06	**A section** (starting again with words of title)

COPYRIGHT AND ROYALTIES FOR POPULAR MUSIC

For the whole of the nineteenth century and up to 1914, the laws of copyright did not cover the *performance* of a piece of music. The composer and the publisher received royalties only on sales of *printed* music; for all the times a piece of theirs was played or sung, they received nothing at all. This situation was remedied with the formation in 1914 of the American Society of Composers, Authors, and Publishers (ASCAP). Whenever a piece was played or a song was sung in a dance hall, nightclub, hotel, or restaurant, and whenever a record was played over the radio, the composer and the publisher received a royalty payment. By 1940, the major radio networks were paying fees to ASCAP of $4.5 million a year, and most of these fees were distributed to ASCAP members. At this time, a rival organization called Broadcast Music Incorporated (BMI) was formed, also providing copyright protection for the composers and publishers of popular music. Today, almost everyone working in the music industry is covered by one or the other of these organizations. In 2008, ASCAP collected over $933 million in licensing fees and distributed $817 million in royalties to its members. In 2009, BMI collected over $905 million in licensing fees and distributed $788 million in royalties. Nowadays the whole question of copyright is being challenged by the widespread use of illegal downloading and filesharing.

The Fortunate 1950s

The post–World War II period in the United States was a time of unprecedented economic prosperity. Low unemployment and high productivity combined to produce an economic boom, and relief at the ending of the war and a new optimism for the future led to what has been called the "baby boom." Middle-class families had several children, and the birthrate soared. Many Americans also had more leisure time and higher incomes than ever before.

This idyllic life was represented by the new television shows of the 1950s that pictured the perfect family, complete with working father, beautifully groomed mother, two or three kids, and a dog. Insights into the social climate of the time can be obtained by watching reruns of such shows as *Father Knows Best, Leave It to Beaver,* or *The Donna Reed Show.*

By the late 1950s, the babies of the "baby boom" were becoming teenagers, enjoying the fruits of the new prosperity. The average teenager bought two new records a month, but there were many who bought 12 or more.

Some of the Most Successful Popular Songs Before 1950

TITLE	DATE	COMPOSER
Old Folks at Home	1851	Stephen Foster
When Johnny Comes Marching Home Again	1863	Louis Lambert
After the Ball	1892	Charles K. Harris
The Birthday Song	1893	Patty Hill and Mildred Hill
Bill Bailey, Won't You Please Come Home	1902	Hughie Cannon
Oh, You Beautiful Doll	1911	Seymour Brown/Nat D. Ayer
Swanee	1919	George Gershwin/Irving Caesar
Avalon	1920	Al Jolson/Vincent Rose
Tea for Two	1924	Irving Caesar/Vincent Youmans
Sweet Georgia Brown	1925	Ben Bernie/Maceo Pinkard/Kenneth Casey
Ain't Misbehavin'	1929	Fats Waller
I Got Rhythm	1930	George and Ira Gershwin
On the Sunny Side of the Street	1930	Jimmy McHugh/Dorothy Fields
Smoke Gets in Your Eyes	1933	Jerome Kern
Blue Moon	1934	Richard Rodgers/Lorenz Hart
Begin the Beguine	1935	Cole Porter
Summertime	1935	George Gershwin/DuBose Heyward
Over the Rainbow	1939	Harold Arlen
White Christmas	1942	Irving Berlin
Some Enchanted Evening	1949	Richard Rodgers/Oscar Hammerstein
Rudolph, the Red-Nosed Reindeer	1949	Johnny Marks

Technology fueled the teenage buying spree. Long-playing (LP) records swept the country in the 1950s, replacing the old 78s. These new discs contained much more music and were able to reproduce sounds with far greater accuracy. Single songs were also released on small 45 rpm discs. Most teenagers had access to a small record player. And radios, which had been large pieces of furniture in the 1940s, were now equipped with transistors—another scientific breakthrough—which made them much smaller. By the mid-1950s, teenagers could take their transistor radios, running on batteries and weighing little over a pound, to the park, to a picnic, or to the beach. Just as the Walkman™ would do in the 1970s and 1980s and the iPod in the 1990s and 2000s, the transistor radio allowed teens to take their music with them, away from the prying eyes (and ears) of their parents. The dominance of American culture by popular song had begun.

Rock and Roll: The Beginnings

The early influences on rock and roll were many and varied. First and most important was the mixture of slow blues singing with a harder, more rhythmic accompaniment that became known as **rhythm and blues**. Most early R&B artists were black. They included singers such as Muddy Waters, who grew up on a Mississippi plantation and moved to Chicago "with a suitcase and a guitar." Rhythm and blues mixed the rural sound of the blues with the electrified edge and raucous rhythms of the city streets. The personal sound of one man with a guitar was expanded in R&B to include a small group of musicians.

Also vital to the early growth of rock and roll were the hard-driving sounds of Little Richard and Chuck Berry. Little Richard was from the South, and he pounded the piano and screamed his lyrics like a wild man. He

Muddy Waters performing in 1971.

and his group were responsible for some of the early hits of rock and roll, such as "Tutti Frutti," "Long Tall Sally," "Rip It Up" (all 1956), and "Good Golly, Miss Molly" (1958).

Chuck Berry was born Charles Edward Anderson Berry in 1926 in St. Louis, Missouri. He grew up singing in the local Baptist church choir and learned the guitar in high school. In 1955 he went to Chicago, where Muddy Waters introduced him to the independent Chess record label, which was a pioneer in the early recording of rock and roll. He began to tour regularly and had a string of hits between 1955 and 1959. Berry appeared in a number of films aimed at the teen audience, and he seemed poised for a long and successful career. However, in late 1959, he was arrested while driving home from performing in Texas to Chicago; in the car was an underage white girl. At the time, it was against the law to "transport a minor" across state lines (presumably for "immoral" purposes). Berry was tried and imprisoned and not released until 1964. The momentum of his career was shattered, and it never recovered, although now in his mid-80s he continues to perform live.

Chuck Berry played fast songs with an irresistible beat. A list of his songs includes some of the early classics of rock and roll: "Roll over Beethoven," "Rock and Roll Music," and "Johnny B. Goode." These songs and many others of his were immensely influential on 1960s rockers like the Beatles and the Rolling Stones. John Lennon once said, "If you tried to give rock and roll another name, you might call it 'Chuck Berry.'"

Unlike most of the other famous rock stars of the 1950s, Berry wrote all his own music. His guitar playing is inventive, rhythmically interesting, clean, and hard. His voice is laser-accurate, bluesy yet clear. His fancy moves on stage were smooth and hypnotic. His songs spoke directly to teens who were sitting in class but ready to party.

Another early influence on rock and roll was country music. Before the term "rock and roll" was widely used, the early sound of Elvis Presley and others was known as "rockabilly" ("rock" + "hillbilly"). It combined the drive of rhythm and blues with the elements of country and western, a style popular in the rural South for its fiddle playing, guitar picking, and warm vocal harmonies. Rockabilly stars who scored big hits at this time were Jerry Lee Lewis ("Great Balls of Fire" and "Whole Lotta Shakin' Goin' On"), Johnny Cash ("I Walk the Line"), and Carl Perkins ("Blue Suede Shoes"). All these

LISTENING GUIDE

CHUCK BERRY

"Johnny B. Goode" Words and music by Chuck Berry

Date of performance: 1957
Personnel: Chuck Berry, vocals and guitar;
  Lafayette Leake, piano; Willie Dixon, bass;
  Fred Below, drums
Duration: 2:37

CD III, 21

"Johnny B. Goode" is a 12-bar blues at medium-fast tempo, but the pervasive subdivision of the beat (two notes for each beat), both in the instrumental playing and in the lyrics, makes for a more hectic, driven feel. Both the guitar playing and the singing are amazingly accurate, especially for what was surely an unedited take. But the high range of the voice and the almost shouted quality of the singing provide a feeling of raw spontaneity. If you didn't know that Chuck Berry was both singing *and* playing the guitar, you would think that these were two separate people. The guitar playing is clean and clear and very prominent. Berry plays the guitar introduction and several instrumental breaks and choruses, but he also plays short, lively, responsive phrases to his own singing, which add to the excitement of the performance. The drummer plays a strong backbeat (heavy on beats 2 and 4), which is what gives the prominent pulse and tension to rock and roll. The pianist in the background cannot be clearly heard throughout, but when he lets loose in the last few choruses, you can hear him pounding away in double time or running emphatic glissandos (sliding his finger along many keys very quickly). The instrument has a truly honky-tonk sound.

In "Johnny B. Goode," the words come thick and fast. There is no repetition of the first line, and *two* lines of verse are set to each four-measure segment of the music. The story thus hurries along in breathless fashion. Two syllables of each word are sung to each beat, and the rushing words leave no time for air or for fills.

Unlike the standard blues also, this song has a refrain. Each "narrative" chorus is followed by a refrain chorus and a final clinching repeat of the title.

In this performance there are nine choruses, which fall into the following pattern:

Time	Listen for
0:00	1. Intro + Instrumental chorus
0:17	2. **Narrative** chorus
0:34	3. **Refrain** chorus
0:51	4. **Narrative** chorus
1:08	5. **Refrain** chorus
1:26	6. Break + Instrumental chorus
1:43	7. Break + Instrumental chorus
2:00	8. **Narrative** chorus
2:18	9. **Refrain** chorus

Three of these choruses are narrative choruses, and each one is followed by the refrain chorus.

The refrain choruses establish a haunting syncopated rhythm, one that is crucial to the rhythmic profile of the whole song. This rhythm is punctuated by four accents, on the first syllable of each word. The first three accents fall on the beat—on beats 1, 2, and 3 of the four-in-a-bar rhythm. But the last accent arrives *ahead* of the beat. It comes after beat 4 and before beat 1 of the next measure, giving a jump to the rhythm that is exciting and catchy.

artists were white, poor, and from the rural South. Another rockabilly star from this time was the unlikely-looking Buddy Holly, skinny and bespectacled. Buddy Holly was on the threshold of an important career when he died in a plane crash at the age of 22. Buddy Holly ("Peggy Sue" and "That'll Be the Day") was particularly influential. He was a versatile and creative singer, and his band's name (the Crickets) inspired the name of another insect group in the early 1960s . . . the Beatles.

Elvis Presley

Despite strings of hits, none of these singing stars came close to achieving the phenomenal fame of Elvis Presley. Presley came from a poor background in Mississippi. Born in 1935, he moved with his family to Memphis when he was 13. He worked in a factory and drove a truck until he turned to music, singing with a small group. At the age of 18, he went to the local recording studio, where anyone could

> I can't sing very well, but I'd like to try.
>
> —Elvis Presley, on first entering a recording studio.

Elvis Presley at the beginning of his career.

make a record for four dollars, and recorded a song as a present for his mother. Six months and two or three recordings later—promoted by his record company, Sun Records, and its owner, Sam Phillips—his records suddenly began to attract attention on radio stations. Elvis took his group around the South. And on his very first tour, in the summer of 1955, the hysteria started. A country singer described the scene:

> The cat came out in red pants and a green coat and a pink shirt and socks, and he had this sneer on his face and he stood behind the mike for five minutes, I'll bet, before he made a move. Then he hit his guitar a lick, and he broke two strings. So there he was, these two strings dangling, and he hadn't done anything yet, and these high school girls were screaming and fainting and running up to the stage, and then he started to move his hips real slow like he had a thing for his guitar. That was Elvis Presley when he was about nineteen, playing Kilgore, Texas.

By 1957, Elvis mania was sweeping the country. And the new technology fueled the fire. Presley appeared on *The Ed Sullivan Show*, one of the most popular television shows of the day. Within months after his appearance, Elvis had a series of hits at the top of the charts, including "Love Me Tender," "Hound Dog," and "All Shook Up." A new radio format, the Top Forty, aired Presley hits almost constantly. Elvis appeared in the movie *Love Me Tender* in 1956. It was the first of 31 movies he was to make during his career.

After this period, Presley began to retreat from the rockabilly sound to the more mainstream sentimental ballad that had been the staple of popular music for decades. This smoother, more acceptable Elvis appealed to an even wider audience and sold even more records. By the end of his career, Elvis Presley had sold the largest number of records in the history of recorded sound: more than 250 million. The commercial success of Elvis the singer led to the creation of an entire industry. In the late 1950s, fans could choose from a range of "Elvis products," including bobby socks, blouses, skirts, shoes, and lipstick ("Hound Dog" Orange, for example). There were also Elvis pajamas, an Elvis pillow, and a glow-in-the-dark Elvis poster. By the end of 1957, the Elvis business had grossed $55 million.

This poor-boy-made-good couldn't spend money fast enough. He bought a mansion in Memphis, called Graceland, for himself and his parents. He also bought a fleet of Cadillacs, an airplane, and hundreds of television sets. And yet his very fame eventually made his life miserable.

Elvis became depressed and sometimes violent. He retreated into drugs and alcohol. Gradually the charismatic teenage sex idol turned into an overweight, drugged parody of himself, singing ballads in Las Vegas hotels, squeezed into a sequined costume. He died in 1977 at the age of 42, a victim of the commercial world of popular music.

Rebellion

In his early years, Elvis Presley symbolized something very important for American youth. He was the symbol of freedom, of rebellion. His unconventional clothes, the messages of his music, and especially his raw sexuality appealed to the new and growing group of American teenagers. The spirit of rebellion was in the air. James Dean projected restlessness and moody defiance in his films *East of Eden* (1953) and *Rebel without a Cause* (1955). The young Marlon Brando appeared as a member of a motorcycle gang in *The Wild One* (1953) and as a troubled dockworker in *On the Waterfront* (1954). And J. D. Salinger's novel *Catcher in the Rye* (1951), about a disaffected teenager, was extremely popular with high school students throughout the 1950s and 1960s.

This wild and rebellious spirit was captured by a song that did more to popularize the term "rock and roll" than any other. The song was "Rock Around the Clock," and it was sung by Bill Haley and the Comets. "Rock Around the Clock" first came out in 1954, but it was re-released in 1955 and became a major hit when it was used in the opening and closing sequences of *Blackboard Jungle*, a movie of teenage violence and rejection. Bill Haley later described his own view of how rock and roll was born: "We started out as a country and western group, then we added a touch of

> I was very lucky. The people were looking for something different, and I came along just in time.
>
> —Elvis Presley

The gates of the Presley mansion Graceland.

LISTENING GUIDE

((•—Listen on MySearchLab

ELVIS PRESLEY

"Blue Suede Shoes" Words and music by Carl Perkins

Date of live recorded performance: 1956

Like a number of Presley's early hits, "Blue Suede Shoes" was written and first recorded by another artist—in this case, Carl Perkins. But Presley's recordings of these songs were often the principal catalyst for their immense popularity, and they became immediately associated with his name. His studio recording of "Blue Suede Shoes" didn't match the phenomenal success of some of his early No. 1 hits ("Heartbreak Hotel," "Hound Dog," "Don't Be Cruel"), but it did make it to No. 20 on the pop charts in 1956. There is also a recording of a mid-1950s live performance which captures the atmosphere and intensity of the early Elvis phenomenon. The performance is swinging, rough, and exciting.

The song is essentially a basic 12-bar blues progression with a rockabilly backbeat. The 12-bar blues is an extremely common chord progression in jazz, pop, and rock music. As we have seen, it consists of three lines of four measures ("bars") each, in the following pattern:

I	I	I	I
IV	IV	I	I
V	IV	I	I
	(or V)		

"Blue Suede Shoes" is in the key of B♭, so the song uses these chords throughout: B♭ (I), E♭ (IV), and F (V).

Time	Listen for
0:00	[Brief guitar riff as an introduction]
0:02	**B♭[I]**
0:06	**E♭[IV] - B♭[I]**
0:10	**F[V] - E♭[IV] - B♭[I]**

This pattern is repeated for all subsequent verses

The live performance omits the third verse, which Presley included on his studio recording:

You can burn my house, steal my car, drink my liquor from an old fruit jar,
Do anything that you wanna do, but uh-uh honey lay off of my shoes.
Now don't you step on my blue suede shoes.
Well, you can do anything, but lay off of my blue suede shoes.

rhythm and blues. We didn't call it that at the time, but we were playing rock and roll."

Rock and roll fed into the dance craze that gripped America's young people in the 1950s. School dances, "sock hops," picnics, and parties were soon filled with rock and roll music, and with teenagers jiving, stomping, and swinging.

Rock and roll represented a dramatic change from the smooth musical style that had dominated popular music for the previous hundred years. It was rough, raucous, loud,

electric, and intense. Most of the early rock and roll songs were fast. And then, of course, there was the beat: a pounding accent on the first beat of every measure. Both the sound and the lyrics were often frankly sexual.

And that's where the problem came in. The 1950s were the start of a phenomenon that has become a central force in the American social psyche: the so-called generation gap.

Adults, used to the smooth and sentimental sound of most popular music, were appalled at the suggestiveness of rock and roll. In 1956,

Time magazine expressed the attitude of the older generation:

> There is no denying that rock 'n' roll evokes a physical response from even its most reluctant listeners, for that giant pulse matches the rhythmical operations of the human body, and the performers are all too willing to specify it.

Local police departments banned rock and roll dances. Radio disc jockeys joined together to keep the music off their shows. Speeches were made in the House of Representatives. Religious leaders sermonized against rock and roll. A distinguished psychiatrist called rock and roll "a communicable disease," and a composer described it as "acoustical pollution." Elvis Presley was the focus of the greatest concern. One minister labeled him "a whirling dervish of sex." And when Presley appeared on *The Ed Sullivan Show*, he was filmed only from the waist up, so that the television audience couldn't see the legendary gyrations of "Elvis the Pelvis." But young people knew what rock and roll did for them. A fan wrote later, "Elvis Presley turned our uptight young awakened bodies around. Hard animal rock energy/beat surged hot through us, the driving rhythm arousing repressed passions."

Early Rock and Roll: Structure and Style

Many early rock and roll songs are based on the 12-bar blues pattern. As you saw with Presley's "Blue Suede Shoes," this pattern consists of three phrases of four measures each, with the following chord sequence:

Text:	A	A	B
Chords:	I–I–I–I	IV–IV–I–I	V–IV (or V) I–I

The lyrics to 12-bar blues often follow the pattern AAB—that is, the first line of text is repeated and then followed by another line, which usually rhymes with the first.

As a result of this limited number of chords, the harmonies are extremely repetitive—insistent rather than complex. This puts more focus on the rhythm, which is also insistent, with a strong accent on the first beat of every measure and secondary accents on the second and fourth beats. Both the harmonic pattern and the beat continue unchanged from the beginning to the end of the song.

Early rock and roll bands usually featured a limited number of instruments: piano, bass, and drums, with an electric guitar and occasionally a saxophone. Some included a string section to accompany slow songs, but heavy orchestration was largely reserved for recordings directed at older audiences. Almost all songs from this time lasted two and a half minutes because they were designed to fit on one side of a 7-inch 45 rpm record.

The lyrics of early rock and roll concentrated on a few subjects guaranteed to appeal to teenagers: love, sex, and dancing. As rock and roll transformed the landscape of American popular music, some room was still left for the 32-measure, AABA-form slow ballad that was popular in the first half of the century. Sentimental songs always have an audience. There was a brief rash of sentimental songs that displayed a morbid fascination with death. "Teen Angel" (Mark Dinning, 1959) and "Tell Laura I Love Her" (Roy Peterson, 1960) both describe tragic deaths of young people, one by a train and the other in a car crash. But the main subject of slow songs was romance. And teenagers were quite happy to have a few ballads played at their parties for slow dancing.

Early Rock and Roll: Black and White

An important social element of rock and roll was the racial integration that it helped to accomplish. The Supreme Court ruled in 1954 that equal access must be granted to all students in the nation's public schools. Rock and roll was itself a melding of black and white music: the blues plus country and western. Audiences at concerts began to be more mixed, and teenagers from different ethnic backgrounds bought many of the same records and listened to the same radio shows. And yet these manifestations of equality did not occur without serious setbacks. White racist organizations in the South attacked rock and roll in the press as a "plot to mongrelize America." And in 1956, the black jazz singer and pianist Nat King Cole was beaten at one of his concerts in Birmingham, Alabama. Some black singers were even banned from radio and television shows.

To prevent the racism in American society from cutting into their profits, record companies often hired white singers to "cover"—that is, copy—popular hits by black singers. Pat Boone covered many hits in the 1950s, toning down the originals both in their lyrics and in their style. The covers were smoother, less raucous, with lusher instrumental accompaniment. Boone was one of a number of clean-cut, white, middle-class young people—such as

Frankie Avalon, Paul Anka, Brenda Lee, and Bobby Darin—who helped make rock and roll more widely acceptable to the American mainstream. But as a result, black singers were often denied the success that was their due. Bo Diddley later complained, "With me there had to be a copy. They wouldn't buy me, but they would buy a white copy of me.... I don't even like to talk about it."

The Turbulent 1960s

The 1960s were a decade of profound social upheaval. The period began with optimism and excitement, as the young and charismatic John F. Kennedy was elected president of the United States. Idealistic civil rights workers, both black and white, sought to increase registration of black voters in the South and end housing discrimination in the North. The Rev. Dr. Martin Luther King attracted nationwide attention as he fought with unprecedented success (and immense dignity) to end segregation and racism in America without the use of violence.

Soon, however, the idealism and optimism were shattered. President Kennedy was assassinated in 1963. The passage of the Civil Rights Act in 1965 was regarded by many new militant black groups as "too little, too late." Riots broke out in many cities in the summers of 1965–1968. And in 1968, both Martin Luther King and Robert Kennedy, the president's brother, were gunned down. But the most divisive force in American society in the 1960s was the Vietnam War.

The American presence in Vietnam began in the 1950s. And by the time the war ended with a Communist victory in 1975, countries counted their dead: more than 600,000 North Vietnamese, more than 200,000 South Vietnamese; 57,000 American dead and 155,000 wounded.

The Vietnam War was one of the focal points for student uprisings throughout the 1960s and early 1970s. Young people did not want to be drafted to face the possibility of dying thousands of miles from home in a war that many of them did not believe in. But the alienation of young people in the 1960s had other causes, too. Partly, it was a continuation of the generation gap of the 1950s; partly, college students began to regard their courses as irrelevant. Many young people "dropped out" of society, living in communes, wearing deliberately outrageous clothes, and taking drugs. Large numbers of young people, known as "hippies," wore beads, dressed in flowery clothes, and experimented with mind-altering or "psychedelic" substances, including LSD, which was legal until 1966.

The alienation of almost an entire generation of young people, the baby boomers, was strengthened by the events of the early 1970s. In 1973, the vice president of the United States, Spiro Agnew, resigned his office amid charges of corruption and bribery. In 1974, as a result of a scandalous abuse of power, President Richard Nixon resigned in disgrace.

Throughout this era, it was popular music that bound members of the younger generation together. The main performers of the 1960s were regarded as emblems of an entire social

JOHN F. KENNEDY'S INAUGURAL ADDRESS (EXTRACTS)

In his inaugural address, John Kennedy invoked an idealism and displayed a quality of leadership more inspiring than Americans had seen, or would see, for many, many years:

"Let the word go forth from this time and place, to friend and foe alike, that the torch has been passed to a new generation of Americans, born in this century, tempered by war, disciplined by a hard and bitter peace, proud of our ancient heritage, and unwilling to witness or permit the slow undoing of those human rights to which this nation has always been committed....

"Let every nation know, whether it wishes us well or ill, that we shall pay any price, bear any burden, meet any hardship, support any friend, oppose any foe to assure the survival and the success of liberty....

"And so, my fellow Americans, ask not what your country can do for you; ask what you can do for your country. My fellow citizens of the world, ask not what America will do for you, but what together we can do for the freedom of man."

movement. They also created worldwide sensations and had an incalculable influence on pop and rock music from that time until today. Foremost among them were the Beatles, Bob Dylan, and Jimi Hendrix.

The Beatles

The Beatles represented the first wave in what has been called the "British Invasion" of America. During the 1960s, England became a world center of pop and rock music. Rock music in England was the expression of working-class frustrations. There were severe economic hardships in a country that had spearheaded the defense of Western Europe during World War II. Food rationing continued until nearly 10 years after the war. There were few jobs, and with the end of the draft, young people were leaving school with no expectations and little to do. "Music was a way out," explained the Beatles' drummer, Ringo Starr. "Back then, every street had a band. We all picked up guitars and drums and filled our time with music."

All four members of the Beatles came from modest backgrounds in Liverpool, an industrial city in the north of England. The group was founded in 1959. By 1962, they had conquered England and much of the rest of Europe. They

The Beatles in the early 1960s.

played before the queen and scored major hits with two singles: "She Loves You" and "I Want to Hold Your Hand." Their first album, *Please Please Me*, stayed at the top of the British charts for six months. Two years later, they embarked on their first tour of the United States. In 1964,

PERFORMANCE IN CONTEXT

From the Concert Hall to the Stadium

The Beatles' first tour of the United States, in 1964, set records for concert attendance. With Beatlemania raging, even the Washington Coliseum—a converted hockey arena three times the size of Carnegie Hall—had quickly sold out. As a result, the Beatles began their 1965 U.S. tour at the largest possible venue: Shea Stadium, the home of the New York Mets baseball team. This historic concert pushed technology to its limits and jumpstarted a new era for rock and roll. Filling a 55,000-seat, open-air stadium with music was no easy task. VOX, the company that made the Beatles' guitar amplifiers, designed a new sound system for the concert. Tens of thousands of screaming fans quickly drowned this out, but the concert was still a success. Technology soon improved, and rival bands such as the Rolling Stones also held stadium concerts. The same sound amplification technology also allowed the creation of large, outdoor music festivals. The most famous of these, 1969's Woodstock Festival, took place outdoors on a 600-acre country farm, with half a million people in the audience.

The Beatles at Shea Stadium in New York City, August 15, 1965.

We're more popular than Jesus Christ right now.
—John Lennon, 1966

in the course of one week, the Beatles appeared on *The Ed Sullivan Show*, played two concerts at Carnegie Hall, appeared before 8,000 fans at the Washington Coliseum, and pushed "I Want to Hold Your Hand" to the top of the American charts. In 1965, they toured the United States again, including a concert at New York's Shea Stadium before 55,000 screaming teenagers. The nationwide tour grossed more than $56 million.

The most important musical influences on the Beatles were rhythm and blues and American rockabilly. They covered some Chuck Berry songs, such as "Roll over Beethoven," but their main model in the early years was Elvis Presley. "Nothing really affected me until Elvis," said John Lennon. "Elvis changed my life," said Ringo Starr. "He totally blew me away, I loved him so."

With the advent of the Beatles in the early 1960s, the character of popular music changed in fundamental ways:

1. Rock music became an international activity, no longer the exclusive province of the United States.
2. Every rock group developed its own identifiable sound, and its own specific look. In the early days, for example, the Beatles all wore the same clothes and had matching haircuts.
3. Rock groups became self-contained, identifiable entities, with specific personnel, each of whom was assigned a particular role. In the case of the Beatles, George Harrison was the lead guitarist, John Lennon played rhythm guitar, Paul McCartney played bass guitar, and Ringo Starr was the drummer; Lennon and McCartney sang most of the vocals. Each member of the group stood at the same place on the stage each time they performed. Each earned his own following and had his own fan club.

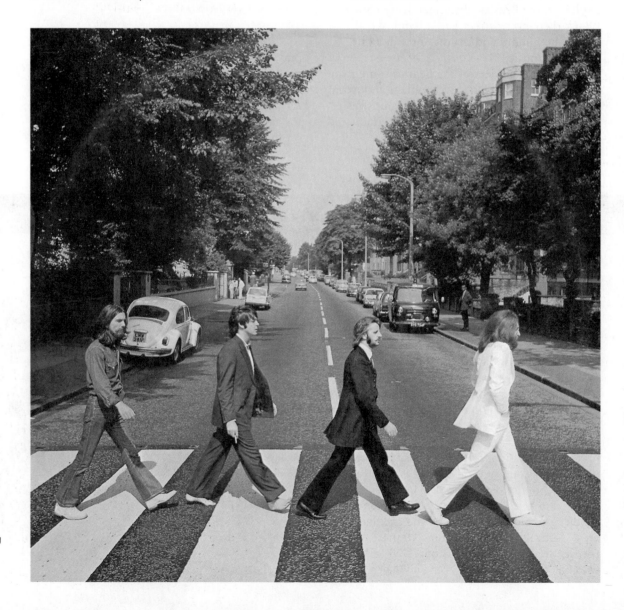

The Beatles walking from their studio in Abbey Road, London, 1969.

Many other rock groups surfaced in the 1960s, the most famous of which was the five-member group the Rolling Stones. Their manager described them as "the opposite of those nice little chaps, the Beatles." The song that captured the aggressive spirit of the 1960s generation more than any other was the scathing, snarling "(I Can't Get No) Satisfaction." Since that time, the Rolling Stones have become one of the most long-lived and best-known rock groups in the world.

The Beatles' career as a group may be divided into two periods: the public and the private. The public period is represented by the first half of the 1960s when they toured, played live, and made records of songs they could sing on stage. The private period—the second half of the decade—was devoted exclusively to recording, using the technology of the studio in novel ways that could not be reproduced in a live performance. During this latter period, they made several technologically advanced records—singles and albums—that had an enormous influence on recording techniques for the whole of the later history of rock music.

We will examine two Beatles songs from the 1960s. The first one, "It Won't Be Long," comes from what I have called the public period in the Beatles' career. The second, "Strawberry Fields Forever," is from their private (studio) period. (**See Listening Guides.**)

With the release of their album *Sgt. Pepper's Lonely Hearts Club Band* (also a studio production from 1967), the Beatles truly revolutionized the making of popular music records. Henceforth, the record album took on a new dimension in artistic production. Rather than bringing together a collection of previously released hits and perhaps a few new songs, the new "concept album" was a completely integrated entity, with all new songs that were connected, either literally or thematically. Every aspect of *Sgt. Pepper* received special attention, including elaborate jacket and sleeve design with printed lyrics. The music is enormously varied and inventive, but the record is unified as a kaleidoscopic reflection of the various facets of contemporary life, including loneliness, alienation, affection, friendship, and the new drug culture.

The Beatles were no longer constrained by many of the conventions surrounding popular music. Dancing was no more a central focus of their audience. People could sit and listen to their songs (and analyze and discuss them), and that began to inspire more intellectual participation on the part of their listeners. The creativity of the Beatles found many outlets, including books (John Lennon's *In His Own Write*), solo performances ("Yesterday," "Blackbird," "Imagine"), films (*Help!*, *A Hard Day's Night*, *Magical Mystery Tour*, *Yellow Submarine*), social and political activity, and exploration of the philosophy and music of the East, especially India. Perhaps the most controversial aspect of their constant curiosity was their widely publicized experimentation with drugs.

As a group, the Beatles lasted until 1970, when they broke up with some bitterness and acrimony. All four then began individual careers, with varying degrees of success. But

LISTENING GUIDE

((•─ Listen on **MySearchLab**

THE BEATLES

"It Won't Be Long" Words and music by John Lennon and Paul McCartney

Date of recording: 1963

An example of the Beatles' early, public sound is "It Won't Be Long," from their second album *With the Beatles* (released November 1963). Notice here the prominence of the electric bass and the background vocals. It is also typical of the early Beatles' sound in the sense of urgency and the way they packed every second of every song with musical action. The song is driving and full of surprises: a rocking verse, a doo-wop bridge, and many changes of mood and dynamics. Other features that are trademarks of the Beatles' early style are the answering "yeah" exclamations and the constant interchange between lead (Lennon, double-tracked) and background (McCartney and Harrison) vocals.

But the principal element that made the music of the Beatles more interesting than that of any other group of the time was its harmonic interest. They tended to use more interesting chord progressions and more complex harmonies than was found in most pop music. In "It Won't Be Long," the chorus (the repeated words) is in the minor, whereas the verses (the changing words) are in the major. We can also hear an unusual chord progression—tonic to lowered submediant and back again (I–♭VI–I)—on the words of the two-line verses. Colorful harmonies like this give added richness and depth to this song.

Notice, too, some other wonderful musical touches: (1) how the repeated guitar riff is derived from the beginning of the vocal melody of each verse, and (2) the mournful chromatic descending background vocals behind the main melody on the bridge.

LISTENING GUIDE

((•◻Listen on MySearchLab

THE BEATLES

"Strawberry Fields Forever" Words and music
by John Lennon and Paul McCartney

Date of recording: 1967

The Beatles' private, or studio, period can be represented by "Strawberry Fields Forever," a song that originally appeared in February of 1967 on a double-A-sided single with "Penny Lane" on the other side. In this song, notice the instrumental innovations (including orchestral instruments, flute sounds, and an Indian harp), the backward taping of cymbals, and the rather daring chord progression (I – minor V – major VI – IV – major VI – IV – I). Notice also the somewhat mysterious and elusive nature of the words and how they are matched by mysterious and elusive music. By now the Beatles had moved far away from the conventional lyrics of the standard pop song.

The release of this record was followed almost immediately by a promotional video, a very new idea in the 1960s. The electronically produced studio sound makes this song a production rather than a performance. Even today, with the enormous advances in technology that have occurred since 1967, it would be difficult to render a live performance of it.

the individual achievements of the four men never matched the extraordinary synergy they experienced as a group. Among all the world-wide successes the Beatles gained, the millions of dollars they made, and the controversies they caused, one achievement stands out: from 1963 to 1970, the Beatles released 22 singles and 11 albums, with music ranging from the early, energetic, tight-harmony *Please Please Me* to the strange and questing *Rubber Soul* to the amazingly varied *Sgt. Pepper* and, finally, *Abbey Road*. In only seven years, they changed the entire course of popular music.

> I heard Woody Guthrie. And when I heard Woody Guthrie, that was it, it was all over.... Woody was my god.
> —Bob Dylan

Bob Dylan as a young man.

Bob Dylan

Apart from the many, many groups that sprang up in the 1960s, there were two individuals who had a powerful influence on pop and rock music during that turbulent decade. They were Bob Dylan and Jimi Hendrix.

Bob Dylan's brand of folk-inspired, intensely committed **protest song** caught the imagination and fired the spirits of millions of young people in the rebellious, activist 1960s. Dylan sang about the threat of nuclear war, civil rights and racism, and the power of the military-industrial complex. "There's other things in this world besides love and sex that're important," Dylan said.

The protest song was not new. American slaves used to sing songs of protest under the guise of ballads or lullabies. And from the 1930s to the 1950s, the tradition of the protest song was continued by Woody Guthrie (1912–1967) and Pete Seeger (b. 1919), who composed, sang, and accompanied their own songs on the guitar. Guthrie and Seeger are responsible for some of the best-known songs in the American tradition, and were at the forefront of the fight for decent working conditions, the struggle for Civil Rights, the peace and antiwar movements, and environmental consciousness for decades. Woody Guthrie was the composer of "Grand Coulee Dam," "Reuben James," and the wonderful "This Land Is Your Land," which lays claim to being a more appropriate national anthem than the one we have now. Pete Seeger wrote "Where Have All the Flowers Gone?," "If I Had a Hammer" (with fellow folksinger Lee Hays), and "Turn! Turn! Turn!" (with lyrics from the Bible).

During the 1960s, Bob Dylan captivated the popular music world with his intensity and commitment. He seemed to personify a generation constantly in search of answers to new and profound questions. The protest songs—especially those with an antiwar sentiment, such as "Masters of War" and "Blowin' in the Wind" (1963)—strongly caught the 1960s mood of bitterness and alienation. Dylan's snarling, nasal delivery and his rough guitar and harmonica playing gave bite and impetus to the music. Like that of the early black rockers, Dylan's music was too raw for most listeners and sold best when covered in versions by Peter, Paul, and Mary ("Blowin' in the Wind," "The Times They Are a-Changin'"); Joan Baez ("Don't Think Twice, It's All Right," "It's All Over Now, Baby Blue"); and the Byrds ("Mr. Tambourine Man"). Dylan is a restless and creative spirit, and no sooner had he made a major hit in one style than he was exploring something new and different. He was always ahead of his fans, shifting from folk ballads to protest songs to electrified rock to country.

Bob Dylan has changed his focus many times since those early days, and each time his followers have complained. Since the 1960s, he has sung Christian anthems, Jewish ballads, raucous rock, and deeply moving love songs. Many of his songs, both from the 1960s and later, are so original they defy classification. One of these is the brilliant, bitter, mournful "Sad-eyed Lady of the Lowlands" (1966). Other examples include the exquisite "Sara" (1975), a testament of love for his (then) wife, and the intense, expressive "Love Sick" (1997). Bob Dylan continues to compose, perform, protest, release records, and experiment with expressing his mind and heart in music. His 1997 album *Time Out of Mind*, with its mature and searching reflections on the human condition, may well be the best thing he has ever done, while *Modern Times* (2006) explores the themes and country roots of American popular music. In 2009 came the relaxed and laid-back *Together through Life*. In 2010 the latest in a series of "official bootleg" albums was released, which includes many rare and unreleased items.

Jimi Hendrix

In the 1960s, Jimi Hendrix was a unique figure. He was part black and part American Indian, and he was a genius at the electric guitar, which he played left-handed and upside down. Accompanied only by bass and drums, Hendrix sang and played high-intensity versions

Jimi Hendrix playing his "Strat" upside down.

of other people's songs (including his own protest: a wildly distorted, lamenting, dragged-out "Star-Spangled Banner"). But he also sang and played many highly original songs of his own, including "Purple Haze" (1967), "Foxy Lady" (1967), and the remarkable "Voodoo Chile [child]" (1968).

The guitar playing of Jimi Hendrix was loud, sometimes angry, and always brilliantly inventive. He used electronic devices such as the wah-wah pedal and the fuzz box as well as effects such as feedback to create a dizzying array of sounds, and his virtuosity on his instrument was unparalleled. He played the Fender Stratocaster, the choice of many early rockers. The "Strat" featured a vibrato bar, and Hendrix's modifications of this device and his use of other special techniques allowed him to create "jet-engine" and "dive-bomb" effects. Hendrix's playing was an inspiration for the sounds later explored by many heavy-metal guitar soloists, though very few guitarists can match his brilliance even today. He used his guitar to express musical ideas of startling originality, intensity, and complexity. He died tragically in 1970 at the age of 27.

Other Trends in the 1960s

The amount and variety of popular music during the 1960s could take up a book by itself; here we must be content with just a few notes on some of the other musical trends of

THE STRATOCASTER

The Stratocaster is a specific model of electric guitar that was developed by Leo Fender in 1954. It was popularized some 12 years later by Jimi Hendrix, who explored the instrument's every aspect. The Stratocaster was soon adopted by Eric Clapton (who still considers it his top choice and has a model of it bearing his own name). These endorsements have inspired other manufacturers to copy the instrument as much as legally possible. The shape of the body is probably the most recognizable in all of today's popular music, because the Strat is used by players from country to rock to jazz. Modern versions retail for about $2,000, and vintage guitars for tens of thousands of dollars, but in 1954 the guitar originally sold for $229. For an additional $20, one could purchase the instrument with the patented "synchronized tremolo," which enabled the player to incorporate vibrato effects by moving a lever.

The Supremes.

The Motown sound was distinctive—polished, smooth, heavily orchestrated, with a danceable beat, and the echoey, call-and-response quality of gospel singing. The biggest hits of the Motown groups were "Stop! In the Name of Love" and "You Keep Me Hangin' On" (the Supremes); "Standing in the Shadows of Love" and "I Can't Help Myself" (the Four Tops); "My Girl" (the Temptations); and "A-B-C," "The Love You Save," and "I'll Be There" (Jackson 5).

Motown was responsible for launching the solo careers of Diana Ross, Stevie Wonder, and Michael Jackson. But the most important aspect of the Motown legacy was the establishment of a vital place for black entrepreneurs in the commercial world of popular music and a new and highly attractive sound to add to the many sounds of the 1960s.

Surfing Songs   Another element in the sounds of the 1960s was the music of the surfer groups. Surfing became a California craze in the early 1960s, partly as a result of the movie *Gidget* (1959), which depicted a beach romance. By the summer of 1963, 100,000 teenagers were addicted to the new sport, which had connotations of sun, sand, brawn, and bikinis. "If you're a good surfer," said one California boy, "you're always in. All you've got to do is walk up and down the beach with a board and you've got girls."

Surfing songs featured a high, bright sound with close harmonies and bouncy rhythms. Formed in 1961, the kings of the surfing song were the Beach Boys, who carried their tanned, clean-cut image and distinctive multivoiced harmony around the nation with such hits as "Surfer Girl," "California Girls," "Fun, Fun, Fun," and the national anthem of the surfing craze, "Surfin' U.S.A."

the era. Each of these was a significant force at the time and also had important consequences for the later development of popular music.

Motown   Motown was the creation of Berry Gordy, a producer and songwriter who built one of America's most successful music empires. Named after the great city of the automotive industry ("Motortown" = Detroit), the company created an assembly line of successful black groups, including the Supremes, the Temptations, the Miracles, the Four Tops, and the Jackson 5.

Folk The history of folk song goes back to the early seventeenth century in America, and of course much further back than that in Europe. The subject matter touches on the fundamental themes of rural human existence: love, death, nature, parting, work. Folk songs often tell a story. The melodies are simple, often modal, without large skips or awkward intervals. They are attractive, singable, and memorable.

In the 1960s, folk music experienced an enormous upsurge of interest among young people. The Kingston Trio had scored a major hit with their recording of the traditional folk ballad "Tom Dooley" in 1958. For the next few years, the Kingston Trio remained one of the favorite groups in America. They sang folk songs in smooth harmonies accompanied by acoustic guitars. Other successful folk groups included the Limeliters and the perennially popular Peter, Paul, and Mary, who combined traditional songs with twentieth-century American classics (Pete Seeger's "If I Had a Hammer"), as well as new songs written by group members (the wonderfully evocative "Puff, the Magic Dragon").

Country Country music dates back to the 1920s, when a brand of folk music—featuring steel guitar, violin ("fiddle"), and quick rhythms—began to take on its own style. This style became known as country and western when, in the 1940s, songs became popular that featured the American West ("Riders in the Sky," "Don't Fence Me In"). This coincided with the growing appeal of radio shows, movies, and, slightly later, TV shows that were based on cowboy legends.

Country music gained widespread appeal in the 1940s and 1950s with such singing stars as Hank Williams and Eddy Arnold. The topics were rural, sentimental, or religious, and they spoke of love gone wrong and life in the country. The songs were delivered in a nasal twang, with an occasional sob or "catch" in the voice and accompanied by a relaxed beat. Country music is a narrative form: the songs tell a story.

Country music caught on in a big way in the 1960s. Both Buddy Holly and Elvis Presley began their careers in country bands. Bob Dylan recorded a country album (*Nashville Skyline*) that included a duet with country-music star Johnny Cash.

It was during this period that country music began to cross over into the pop charts. One of the biggest country hits of the period was Tammy Wynette's "Stand by Your Man" (1967). Other successful country singers of the 1960s were Buck Owens, Jim Reeves, and Merle Haggard.

Country music is accessible and easy to understand. Its domain includes western swing, cowboy songs, bluegrass (with its fancy banjo and fiddle work), and sentimental ballads. Many of its stories contain old-fashioned moralistic points of view or religious convictions rooted in rural society. The songs often have repeated sections or refrains, and the words are clear and prominent. Accompanying instruments include steel guitar (sometimes a pedal steel

> I'm proud to say I know it: Here is a hell of a poet. And lots of other things. And lots of other things.
> —Johnny Cash on the LP jacket of *Nashville Skyline*

As a hobby, I collect country music titles. Some of my favorites include the following:

"Dropkick Me, Jesus, Through the Goalposts of Life"
"Did I Shave My Legs for This?"
"All My Ex's Live in Texas"
"Messed Up in Mexico, Livin' on Refried Dreams"
"You Done Stomped on My Heart and You Mashed That Sucker Flat"
"Get Your Tongue Outta My Mouth 'Cause I'm Kissing You Goodbye"
"Get Your Biscuits in the Oven, and Your Buns in the Bed"
"I Cain't Get Over You 'Til You Get Out From Under Him"
"All the Guys That Turn Me On Turn Me Down"
"I Wanna Be a Blue Light Special in the K-Mart of Your Heart"
"I Would Have Wrote You a Letter, But I Couldn't Spell Yuck!"
"I've Been Roped and Thrown by Jesus in the Holy Ghost Corral"
"We Used To Kiss on the Lips, but It's All Over Now"
"If I Can't Be Number One in Your Life, Then Number Two on You"

Got any good ones to send me for the next edition of *Understanding Music*?

J. Y.

guitar that the player can use to *slide* between notes), fiddle, banjo, and "honky-tonk" piano. A typical country bass line bounces from the tonic to the dominant and back again.

The British Blues Revival At the height of the Beatles' popularity, an additional musical current was evident in England. This was the British blues revival. British groups such as the Yardbirds attempted to revive old blues styles and translate them into the rock idiom. Eric Clapton was the first of a trio of brilliant guitarists who were associated with the Yardbirds, followed by Jeff Beck and Jimmy Page; this trio had a lasting impact not only on the new interpretation of the blues but also on guitar virtuosity.

One group that lasted for only a short time during the 1960s was known as Cream and featured Eric Clapton on guitar, Jack Bruce on bass, and Ginger Baker on drums. These players were regarded as the very best in the profession, or the "cream of the crop." As a group, they lasted only from 1966 to 1968, but what they brought to rock music had important implications.

Clapton's guitar-playing abilities and his musicianship caused him to be respected and imitated in all branches of popular music. His work contributed to the extremely high profile of the electric guitar, which became a universal symbol of rock music. But his proficiency as an instrumentalist also encouraged mastery by players of other instruments. Eric Clapton continues to be a driving force in rock and popular music.

The 1970s and 1980s: Variety, Legacy, and Change

The story of popular music in the 1970s and 1980s is one of great diversity. Many of the musical currents that had contributed to the ferment of the 1960s remained strong. The imaginative and prolific work of the Beatles, the spread of folk and country music, the revival of the blues, the use of new recording techniques—all these paved the way for a new variety in the tempo and texture of pop and rock music. Bob Dylan's restless shifts between musical styles (and his continuing presence on the scene) added to the openness and flexibility of the music. And the legend of Jimi Hendrix, as well as the more controlled virtuosity of the members of Cream, expanded the horizons of instrumental performance throughout the field of rock music. The power of the 1960s legacy

can be measured by the fact that recordings by these performers are almost as popular today as they were in their own time.

During the 1970s and 1980s, the baby boomers grew older. The members of the rebellious generation, whose rallying cry used to be "Never trust anyone over thirty," were now in their 40s. The 1970s brought a concentration on individual accomplishment rather than on social goals. The 1970s were known as the "Me Decade," in which people seemed to turn their backs on the social causes of the 1960s. In the 1980s, corporate interests were buoyed up, real estate boomed, and many members of the upper class got very rich indeed. But while some individuals and businesses flourished, unemployment doubled, the standard of living dropped, and public spending was drastically cut.

During this time, popular music spread into the mainstream. Rock music became the staple sound of radio stations all over the country. It could be heard in bus stations, supermarkets, and elevators. Nostalgia for the 1960s and even for the 1950s grew as the 1980s progressed. Many radio stations began to play exclusively "golden oldies." "Oldies for the oldies" is what these programs might be called. Movies were made that chronicled the life stories of pop stars from the 1950s and 1960s. Indeed, many of the artists from the 1960s were still performing, a little grayer perhaps, but still active and still pursuing that elusive perfect song: Paul McCartney, George Harrison, Ringo Starr, Bob Dylan, Joan Baez, Joni Mitchell, the Stones, the Grateful Dead, Paul Simon, Eric Clapton. And many new groups and performers played classic hits from the 1960s. In many ways, therefore, the sounds and style of pop and rock music had not changed radically.

One of the great legacies of the 1960s was diversity, and diversity was the hallmark of pop and rock in the 1970s and 1980s. *Acid rock* was an outgrowth of the drug culture, "acid" being a term for the drug LSD. The most successful acid-rock groups were the Grateful Dead, the Doors, and Jefferson Airplane, later renamed Jefferson Starship. Acid rock was extremely loud; Jerry Garcia of the Grateful Dead termed it "sensory overload." It also featured songs of considerable length, with extended guitar solos, and a deliberately outspoken approach to sex. Marty Balin of Jefferson Starship said, "The stage is our bed and the audience is our broad."

Acid rock evolved into *heavy metal*—a loud, thickly textured rock style with a deeply pounding beat, based primarily on the sounds of guitars and drums, and often heavily distorted and employing "power chords." Power chords use the lowest, open strings of the guitar; they are based on the root and the fifth of the chord, usually omitting the third. Chords in this position introduce the fewest dissonances, and sound most powerful when punched at tremendous volume. Heavy-metal bands included Led Zeppelin, Black Sabbath, and Metallica.

Fusion was the result of a mixture of rock and jazz. The leader of this new musical trend was the great jazz trumpeter Miles Davis, who blended the freer improvisatory sounds of jazz with the electric edge and heavy beat of rock. Other fusion bands included Weather Report; Blood, Sweat and Tears; Steely Dan; and Pink Floyd. Each of these groups scored successes with carefully produced albums, featuring the latest advances in electronic sound.

The 1970s brought a resurgence of interest in solo performers: Carole King, Joni Mitchell, Roberta Flack, Judy Collins, Carly Simon, and Linda Ronstadt were the most prominent female singers; James Taylor, Stevie Wonder, Paul Simon, and Elton John became the most popular male singers. Often their sound was in deliberate contrast to the high decibels of acid rock, with more relaxed, introspective singing that was accompanied by acoustic guitars, background strings, or sometimes just a single piano.

Country music suddenly became a part of the popular mainstream in the 1970s. Singers such as Johnny Cash and Willie Nelson crossed over from country into pop. Many songs in this era successfully blended the traditional country style—storytelling, acoustic accompaniment, and twangy accents—with rock elements to produce the blend known as country rock. One of the biggest stars of country rock was Willie Nelson, who produced an extraordinary string of hits starting in the mid-1970s and continuing throughout the 1980s and into the 1990s. Nelson is an inventive and original songwriter, and his particular blend of country themes with the harder edge of rock found millions of responsive listeners throughout the country. He spoke of his music as appealing to "both rednecks and hippies."

A new fad of the 1970s, discos, originating in Europe, ushered in a special musical style and brought back the popularity of dancing. The disco sound was light, crisp, and very intense, with fast drumming, high vocals, and a solid, thumping bass. With their flashing strobes, walls of mirrors, recorded sound, and emphasis on the audience, discos reflected the narcissism of the "Me Decade."

The so-called Queen of Disco was Donna Summer, whose "Love to Love You Baby" sold millions of copies. And a disco movie, *Saturday Night Fever*, simultaneously established disco as a national phenomenon and catapulted an Australian group to international stardom. The Bee Gees, who had been around since the 1960s, sold more than 30 million copies worldwide of the double-LP soundtrack to *Saturday Night Fever*.

Some 1970s phenomena seemed to suggest that the originality and interest had gone out of pop music. Gigantic, and in some cases grotesque, stage shows accompanied rock tours. This focus on the visual element set the stage for the music videos of the 1980s.

In the 1970s, more rock stars made more money than ever before. By about the middle of that decade, it was estimated that at least 50 rock musicians were each earning more than $2 million per year. But if the musicians were making money, it was nothing compared with the profits of the record industry. In 1950, total record sales in the United States amounted to $189 million; by the late 1970s, that total had increased to $4 billion. Companies created, promoted, and sold rock groups. Music was no longer the province of the counterculture. It was the product of corporate America.

In the 1980s, an antiestablishment trend once more reasserted itself. It had begun a few years earlier with the rise of a deliberately shocking style of rock known as *punk*, which continued into the 1980s. Punk rock featured performers with outrageous costumes and

Elaborate costumes and makeup of the rock group Kiss.

nasty names. Leading groups were the Sex Pistols and the Ramones. Lyrics were offensive and often violent. The titles of some songs from this time include "Slip It In," "Killing an Arab," and "Suicide Madness." Punk rock was a short-lived phenomenon, though it left its mark on later rock styles.

A technological phenomenon of the 1980s revolutionized the way young people experienced popular music. Music Television (or MTV), a cable channel broadcasting nonstop music videos, was launched in 1981. Technology also influenced the sound of rock groups themselves. Synthesizers allowed the realistic duplication of sounds, which could be combined, modified, and manipulated in the most sophisticated ways.

MTV helped to create the extraordinary rebirth of Michael Jackson (although the channel had been on the air for nearly two years before it came around to featuring a black artist!). Jackson had a long history as a singer. He appeared in the late 1960s at the age of 10 with his brothers in a group known as the Jackson 5 (later the Jacksons). Jackson's biggest success came during the 1980s when his solo album *Thriller* (1982) sold more than 40 million copies worldwide, which was helped by a slick video. (**See Listening Guide.**) He was described as "the biggest thing since the Beatles" and as "the hottest single phenomenon since Elvis Presley." Unfortunately, like Presley, Jackson also died young—in 2009, at the age of 50.

Michael Jackson.

Question: "Do you think Michael Jackson has a Messiah complex?" Noel Gallagher of the group Oasis: "Who does he think he is? Me?"

Other singers whose careers were buoyed up on the MTV wave include Whitney Houston and Madonna. Both singers traded heavily on visual appeal. Houston was a fashion model as well as a singer, and her videos (and later her movies) pushed her albums to instant success. Madonna (Madonna Louise Ciccone) adopted a Marilyn Monroe image, and her dance training, combined with an overt sexuality, made her videos widely popular. Madonna's "Material Girl" seemed to catch the spirit of the money-making 1980s. (**See Listening Guide.**) She later traded even more heavily on her body by releasing simultaneously a CD entitled *Erotica* and a book, *Sex*, displaying herself in various nude poses.

I am my own experiment. I am my own work of art. —Madonna

"World music" came to the fore in the 1980s, bringing into the American popular scene the sounds of many other cultures. Perhaps the most popular of these was *reggae*, which leapt out of Jamaica in the 1970s and spread like wildfire. Reggae has a light, infectious sound, characterized by cross-accents played by the rhythm guitar on the offbeats.

Madonna.

LISTENING GUIDE

((•—Listen on **MySearchLab**

MICHAEL JACKSON

"Billie Jean" Words and music by Michael Jackson

Date of recording: 1982

Michael Jackson's album *Thriller* contains ten songs, nine of which reached the Top Ten as singles! Perhaps the most typical of Jackson's style is "Billie Jean." The music is fast and glossy, with a high, artificial, synthesized sound and a persistent disco beat. Jackson's voice is high, slick, and breathless. Toward the end, a little variety is introduced by means of some funky guitar tracks. The "funk" sound is produced by plucking the strings on an electric bass guitar a little harder than normal so that they slap against the fretboard.

CENSORSHIP IN POPULAR MUSIC

The idea of controlling music in society has been around for a long time. About 2,400 years ago, the Greek philosopher Plato said that the types of music people listened to should be controlled by the state. During the Middle Ages and the Renaissance, it was the Church that specified how music should be composed and performed. And in later centuries, secular rulers held a virtual monopoly over the music that was allowed in their realm. Often, composers had to submit a work to a committee before it was allowed to be published or performed.

The question of censorship is still very much alive in the twenty-first century, particularly in reference to popular music. In the 1950s, when rock and roll started, there were many people calling for it to be banned. In the 1980s, an organization named the Parents Music Resource Center was formed, which fought successfully for the appearance of advisory stickers on certain records.

At a government hearing in 2007 industry executives defended their "freedom of expression," while Faye Williams of the National Congress of Black Women said that "greedy corporate executives...lead many of our young people to believe that it is okay to entertain themselves by destroying the culture of our people." And gangsta rapper Master P testified that he had cleaned up his act since realizing that he didn't want his own children listening to his music.

No subject is taboo: there have been songs about oral sex, incest, and masturbation, as well as songs about murder, rape, and violence against women.

Should there be some controls on this kind of music? Should anybody be free to listen to these songs, including young children? If not, at what age do you draw the line? The Federal Communications Commission already legislates the appropriateness of certain words and subject matter on radio and television. So far, the controls on records have been voluntary; the sticker system is administered by the recording industry itself. Singers sometimes release two versions of a record, one with a sticker and one without. Under intense pressure, the rapper Ice-T removed the song "Cop Killer" (a song that reveled in the idea of murdering a policeman) from his album *Body Count*, so that while earlier copies of the album contained the song, later copies did not.

In the 1990s several radio stations from Los Angeles to New York adopted a policy that barred all songs promoting violence or drugs or containing degrading comments about women. And in 1993 the minister of the Abyssinian Baptist Church in Harlem held a rally at which he ran a steamroller over tapes and CDs he considered offensive.

Censorship pressures can come from both sides of the political spectrum. Paul Simon, attempting to build bridges by using black musicians from South Africa on one of his records, got into trouble with liberals in America because he was accused of violating a cultural boycott against that country. And pressure from feminists persuaded the country singer Holly Dunn to have her song "Maybe I Mean Yes" banned from radio stations. (The last line of the chorus suggests that when she says "no," she might mean "maybe.") Is that censorship? Or is it only censorship when it comes from conservative groups?

LISTENING GUIDE

MADONNA
"Material Girl" Words and music by Peter Brown and Robert Rans

Date of recording: 1984

"Material Girl" was one of the principal hit singles from Madonna's phenomenally successful album *Like a Virgin*. The video to the song introduced one of Madonna's many well-known images: a Marilyn Monroe–like blonde bombshell, fawned over by a large chorus of male suitors (who form a robotic chorus later in the song). The song is a fairly straightforward dance-club pop number. It is based on several recurrent melodic lines or riffs and has a persistent rhythmic beat and catchy lyrics.

The wonderfully inventive musical tradition of Africa was also discovered by musicians in the 1980s and strongly influenced singing styles and instrumental techniques in pop and rock music.

One final technological innovation of the 1980s that had an enormous impact on the spread (and the profits) of popular music was the invention of the compact disc. It was introduced in 1983 and quickly gained popularity. Gradually, CDs and the newly popular cassettes began to replace vinyl LPs. Many consumers not only bought new recordings as they came out on CD but also bought CDs to replace all their favorite old albums. It was a bonanza for the record industry. A CD cost less than a dollar to manufacture and sold for between $12 and $20. The profits were enormous. In 1987, CBS made more than $200 million in profits. In 1989, Time Warner announced profits of nearly $500 million.

The 1990s and Beyond

In the 1990s, the world became aware that the end of the decade would bring not only the end of a century but also the turning of a millennium. On the international scene, there was staggering change. The monolithic Union of Soviet Socialist Republics splintered into many of its formerly separate components, as the largest Communist system in the world collapsed. Many other countries of Eastern Europe tentatively embraced democracy. South Africa struggled toward greater equality; Europe struggled toward economic unity; countries in the Middle East struggled toward peace.

In America, there was both hope and despair. In the spring of 1992, riots broke out in Los Angeles, causing death and destruction over many city blocks. Large numbers of Americans had not benefited from the economic surge of the 1980s. Indeed, America as a whole was fast becoming aware of its limitations. The standard of living in the United States fell below that of several other nations. The illiteracy rate was soaring and, perhaps most scandalous of all, the health rate of the richest nation in the world stood at 12th among Western nations.

Divisions between segments of society widened rather than narrowed. Prejudice erupted in new and overt instances of anti-Semitism. Public schools and colleges became less tolerant of freedom of thought and began to enforce a new conformity of ideas known as "political correctness." Many African Americans, impatient at their lack of progress toward equality, returned to militancy and rage.

In the new century new terrors erupted. The World Trade Center towers in New York City were destroyed by terrorists flying commercial jets, another airplane was flown into the Pentagon, and another crashed in a field in Pennsylvania; 3,000 people were killed. In response the United States invaded Afghanistan and Iraq, although most of the hijackers had come from Saudia Arabia. The U.S. government traded on public fear of terrorism to amass unprecedented power, engage in torture, and begin spying on its own citizens. In 2008 there erupted the most severe economic crisis since the Great Depression, and America rapidly lost its position as the preeminent financial power in the world. The first black president in American history was elected in a popular landslide. But by 2011 the country was politically divided as never before. Money rules elections and sets the political agenda; most of the members of Congress are millionaires; and there are individual American corporations (Apple, ExxonMobil) that are worth more than the entire Treasury of the United States.

GENRES IN POPULAR MUSIC TODAY

In the last couple of decades the number of musical genres in popular music has exploded, perhaps reflecting a societal fragmentation. Many of these categories are not clearly defined, but adherents of one or another are passionate about their favorites. Nowadays the genres include, in no particular order: twee, youth crew, crust, indie, hyphy, hardcore, nerdcore, grindcore, deathcore, alternative, trance, ambient, electronica, funk, punk, post-punk, grunge, grabber, sludge, beat, house, salsa, reggae, rap, timba, cajun, industrial, goth, shock rock, techno, emo, screamo, black metal, new rock, R&B, surf pop, teen pop, adult contemporary, Afropop, brit pop, synth pop, bastard pop, bubblegum pop, country pop, dance pop, dream pop, electropop, technopop, Eurobeat, house pop, indie pop, jangle pop, Latin pop, swamp pop, noise pop, pop punk, pop rap, pop rock, power pop, sophisti-pop, sunshine pop, new romantic, nu metal, blues rock, garage rock, glam rock, heavy metal, classic rock, hard rock, extreme metal, black metal, doom metal, death metal, thrash, progressive, new wave, psychobilly, southern rock, doo wop, funk, new jack swing, soul, neo soul, drum and bass, two-tone, dancehall, dub, ska, new age, folk rock, folktronica, progressive folk, neofolk, G-funk, grime, Miami bass, pornocore, crunk, breakbeat, big beat, psychedelic, Euro dance, gabba, hi-NRG, rave, trip hop, glitch, lo-fi, alternative country, country blues, urban cowboy, honky tonk, blue grass, singer/songwriter, easy listening, thrash metal, and furniture music. And of course you can multiply all of the above by their national and ethnic varieties: Australian jangle pop, Chicano heavy metal, etc.

Please let me know if I have missed any. . . .

Around the world massive environmental damage continues, and in the United States wealth continues to accrue to the wealthy, while concern for health care, education, children, and the elderly has deteriorated in an atmosphere of political extremism. Many studies have shown that it is wealth *disparity* (the gap between the rich and the rest) that causes civilizations to decay. In the United States the top 10 percent of the population now owns 80 percent of the entire wealth of the country; *16 percent* of Americans are on food stamps, and nearly 20 percent of young people under 25 cannot find work.

The principal new musical phenomenon of the last two decades has been **rap**. Rap is half-spoken, rather than sung, with a strong and complex rhythm, backed by bass, synthesizer, and percussion. These sounds are often created and mixed in the studio rather than being played by live musicians. Rap began by trading on ideas of violence, aggression, and resentment. Urban street life provided the backdrop of guns, murder, and drugs, and the messages were heavy-handed, direct, and to the point. Lyrics spoke of drug dealers, violence in the streets, legal injustice, and loveless sex. In reaction, a few other rappers began talking about more positive messages, such as political involvement, female empowerment, and criticism of the violent strain in the music.

Some rap records in the 90s provoked serious controversy. The song "Cop Killer" by the rap artist Ice-T flaunted a murderous joy: it spoke of the delights of slitting a policeman's throat and watching his family mourn. Police organizations around the country called for a boycott of Time Warner, Ice-T's record company, and the vice president of the United States publicly joined the call. The result: the record surged strongly in the charts.

There are some ugly elements in rap music. Some rap songs displayed overt racism against Asians; some were offensively homophobic. But a common trait was prejudice against women. Many rap songs referred to women as "bitches" or "ho's" (whores), and some even advocated deliberate violence and brutality against women.

The public militancy of rap was partly a reflection of a divided society, but it was also partly boosted by commercial considerations. Record companies soon discovered that aggression and a militant image sold a lot of records. Bill Stephney, a rap businessman and one of the founders of the group Public Enemy, said that he had deliberately polished the group's militant image: "In many respects, that was done on purpose...to curry favor with a white audience by showing rebellion."

Many black leaders denounced the most vicious aspects of rap. Others saw a real danger in the militant pose of much rap music, with its stereotype of the "drug-dealin', Uzi-totin', gangsta of today." They found the stereotyping similar to that of nineteenth-century minstrelsy.

In all the writing and hand-wringing over rap, almost nothing was said about the music. It featured a repetitive, heavy bass (often produced electronically) with a hard, high drumbeat (made on a drum machine). Rapid splicing, overdubbing, and heavy engineering produced a glossy, hypnotizing sound. And against this hypnotic, percussive layer, the spoken rhythmic lyrics streamed, sometimes cleverly rhymed, sometimes cringefully awkward.

As rap settled into the mainstream, it tended to fall into two categories. The first, "gangsta rap," continued the angry image, with heavy rhythm and little or no melody or harmony. The second—sometimes called pop rap—spoke more of unity than of violence, often featured female singers, and tended to incorporate more melodic interest. Creative blends of rap with rock, rap with reggae, and rap with jazz showed that the musical ferment caused by the worldwide spread of popular culture was far from over. Rap even became the medium for gospel and Christian music.

The songs of actress and rapper Queen Latifah, written from the woman's point of view, often seemed to be a response to the macho world of hard-core rap. Queen Latifah spoke of respect and of community. Her song "Unity" appeared in 1993 on her album *Black Reign* and won a Grammy in 1995.

After the turn of the millennium, the commercial element of all popular music was its most prominent feature. Record companies became more sophisticated than ever at marketing their products, using programs on MTV—such as *Total Request Live*, as well as magazines and music outlets—to give the maximum exposure to a star or a group at just the right time. Successful debut albums

SCRATCHING, SAMPLING, LOOPING, AND AUTO-TUNE

In the 1990s one of the elements of rap music shifted toward the DJs or *turntablists*, who created sounds by manipulating the turntables playing LPs. The most commonly used technique involves moving the record rapidly back and forth while it is being played. DJs battle each other in displays of virtuosity. They work with two turntables simultaneously, combining and manipulating the sounds through a mixer. Recently, computer techniques have evolved to simulate the sound of scratching without physical manipulation of actual LPs. An enormous variety of sounds can be produced by a skilled *scratcher*.

Sampling involves the use of a short extract of a previous recording as a musical element in a new recording. The most commonly used samples are those of a recognizable riff or a catchy instrumental introduction from a song. Sung or spoken extracts can also be sampled. The ultimate in sampling is a *mashup*, in which a composition is created by overlaying the vocal track(s) of one song onto the instrumental tracks of another. In Europe this genre is known as *bastard pop*.

Looping is another technique common to rap and other popular music. It is the frequent repetition of a short fragment of sound (so called since it was originally produced by actually creating a short loop of magnetic tape and playing it on a tape machine). The sound can be a sample from an earlier recording, or it can be a fragment from the new song itself.

It is also common today to see laptops providing loops, samples, noises or prerecorded tracks at live shows. Acts using laptops combined with live playing or singing include Battles, Björk, Radiohead, and Erykah Badu. Girl Talk (Gregg Gillis) appears on stage with nothing but a laptop, playing loops and samples. His album *Feed the Animals* is made up of samples from over three hundred different songs.

Proprietary software known as Auto-Tune was designed to correct small intonation flaws in the studio. But it can also produce a special effect on the human voice, making it warble or flutter in fake emotion, or sound clipped, inhuman, and robotic.

All of these techniques, taking advantage of new technology, add to the hip, urban, electric edge of modern popular music.

were followed by singles that whetted fans' appetites for the next inevitable blockbuster. This format of the debut album, followed by massive exposure, followed by a single, followed by a huge hit, was utilized in the year 2000 by the companies promoting three popular-music phenomena. Britney Spears sold 1.3 million copies of her new album, the white rapper Eminem 1.7 million copies, and the pop group 'N Sync an amazing 2.4 million copies—all in the first *week* of sales. Before that year, the Backstreet Boys had held the record with 1.1 million. Figures for first-week sales have now become part of the hype.

'N Sync and Britney Spears recorded for the same company and depended upon the same upbeat pop sound, pretty looks, and smooth moves for their appeal. In fact, the pop world in the early years of the twenty-first century seemed to be full of "boy bands" and "teen queens." The rapper Eminem, however, was a different proposition: he was ironic, clever, parodistic, and often vicious.

Nowadays publicity is much more diversified, coming from computer videos, television programs, social networking sites, individual Web sites, and online music stores. The principle aim is to create an image for the artist, and the image involves a manufactured public persona, clothing, looks, dance moves, business interests, and (of course) sex appeal. It almost seems as though the music is secondary. All these sources also allow noncommercial ("indie") music to be promoted and become popular. Sometimes artists release tracks on the Web for free to stimulate interest in the entire album. But popular music is still a highly lucrative venture. In 2010 the online music store iTunes announced that it had already sold *ten billion* songs. Teenagers in the United States now number over 40 million, and they have massive buying power. In the year 2007, before the economic crash, American teenagers were able to spend over $160 billion.

English performers were popular, with the alternative bands Coldplay and Radiohead (whose albums *Viva La Vida* and *In Rainbows,* respectively, were among the year's best sellers) and the soul-leaning teenagers Duffy and Adele all hailing from the United Kingdom. An American teenager also caused a sensation with her own songs, which hovered between pop and country. This was Taylor Swift, who became successful at the age of 18. Radiohead also shook the record industry, which was already starting to suffer significantly from the

Queen Latifah.

popularity of both legal and illegal downloads, by celebrating the end of their contract with EMI by releasing *In Rainbows* in a pay-as-much-as-you-want scheme on their own Web site before a traditional later release. Radiohead is so unlike the normal pop or rock group that it is almost inaccurate to call them a band. They use electronic music and unusual orchestral instruments on their recordings, and their multi-instrumentalist lead guitarist Jonny Greenwood is a classical-music composer, composer in residence at the BBC, and a film-score composer. He wrote the remarkable score for the 2007 movie *There Will Be Blood.*

Today rappers continue to dominate the pop charts. Many of the most successful downloads are rap songs. The themes have broadened: they continue to include violence and sex, but now money and politics have become common. Rappers flaunted "bling" and luxurious accessories and rapped about money, Lamborghinis, and success: for example, "All about the Benjamins" (P. Diddy), "I Get Money" (50 Cent), "Money Maker" (Ludacris), "Still 'n Luv Wit' My Money" (Paul Wall & Chamillionaire). Many producers and record executives are well-known in their own right, both for their brilliance in the studio and for their entrepreneurial activities and public personas (Dr. Dre, Grandmaster Flash, Timbaland, and Diddy [aka Puff Daddy, P. Diddy, Puff, and Puffy]). In politics the candidacy and election of Barack Obama inspired dozens of rap songs, including Jay-Z & Mary J. Blige's "You're All Welcome," Jin's "Open Letter to Obama," Nas's "Black President," and Young Jeezy's "My President" from his third album *The Recession* (2008). In 2011 newly popular rappers were Nicki Minaj, Lupe Fiasco, and Wiz Khalifa. Just at the point financial markets around the world took a historic plunge, a full-length collaboration between Jay-Z and Kanye West continued the theme of "luxury rap." On *Watch the Throne*, an album that looked as though it were plated in gold, the two rappers talk about their indulgences in expensive fine art, fancy clothes, and top-end appliances.

In the 2011 Grammy awards, Eminem won best solo performance for "Not Afraid" and best album for *Recovery*. Best rap song and best collaboration went to Jay-Z and Alicia Keys for "Empire State of Mind." A country-music trio, Lady Antebellum, won record of the year and song of the year for "Need You Now." But the Grammy for album of the year was

Beyoncé.

won for the first time by a Canadian indie group: the multi-instrumentalist band Arcade Fire, which features seven performers who play guitar, bass guitar, keyboard, drums, piano, violin, viola, cello, double bass, xylophone, glockenspiel, French horn, accordion, harp, mandolin, and hurdy-gurdy.

The glam-rock icon Lady Gaga (Stefani Germanotta) became phenomenally successful in 2010 and 2011. Her stage shows were more about her appearance than about her music. She says, "When I'm writing music, I'm thinking about the clothes I want to wear on stage." Her 2011 album *Born This Way* (2011) hit the top of the charts almost immediately, and the single "Born This Way" became a worldwide hit and the fastest-selling single in the history of iTunes, selling a million downloads in only five days. However a real singer like Adele makes an important distinction: "I am not making music for the eyes," she says. "I am making music for the ears."

Many other popular-music genres, such as dance-pop, funk, pop, soul, and contemporary R&B continue to find enormous popularity. A singer who has made her mark in all of these genres is Beyoncé Knowles, who came to popular notice as the lead singer of the all-female group Destiny's Child and then started a solo career in 2003. Her third solo album *I Am... Sasha Fierce* was released in 2008 and included the phenomenally successful "Single Ladies (Put a Ring on It)," accompanied by a sexy video. In February 2010, the song "Telephone," featuring both Beyoncé and Lady Gaga, reached number one on the U.S. pop songs chart, thus becoming the sixth number-one single on the chart for both singers. In 2011, Knowles released her fourth studio album *4*, which became her fourth consecutive number-one album.

She was given a Billboard Millennium Award at the 2011 *Billboard* Music Awards and has a total of 16 Grammy Awards—three as a member of Destiny's Child and 13 as a solo artist. She is the composer or cowriter of many of the songs she sings, and, like some other highly successful music artists, has branched out into other fields. She gained a Golden Globe nomination for her acting role in the movie *Dreamgirls* in 2006, has acted in several other films, and has launched her own fashion and perfume companies. She has made commercials for soft drinks, designers, cosmetics, and video games. She will star in a remake of the film *A Star is Born*, to be directed by Clint Eastwood and is married to the rapper

RAP SHEET

Some rappers like to foster a criminal reputation, which they believe gives them "street cred." Sometimes the facts are deliberately exaggerated. 50 Cent, for example, has boasted at times about doing a stint of "seven to nine," but fails to disclose that the sentence was months, not years, and was at a correctional boot camp rather than in prison. Akon's music company is called Konvict and his breakthrough album was named *Konvicted*, but he too has been accused of exaggerating his criminal reputation, though he did serve some time in jail for car theft.

Here are some of the genuine charges filed against people in the rap world, whether deliberately sought for publicity purposes or not:

T.I. (gun and drug possession), Snoop Dogg (gun and drug possession), 50 Cent (gun and drug possession), DMX (gun and drug possession), Ja Rule (gun and drug possession), Rick Ross (gun and drug possession), Lil Wayne (drug possession), Method Man (drug possession), Fabolous (gun possession), Eminem (gun possession, assault), Suge Knight (assault), Sean "Diddy" Combs (assault), Shyne (assault), ODB (assault), Busta Rhymes (assault, weapons possession), Jay-Z (stabbing), Mystikal (sexual battery, extortion), Lil' Kim (conspiracy, perjury), Slick Rick (attempted murder), C-Murder (murder).

And the violence surrounding the rap world was all too real for the following:

Stage Name	Real Name	Age	Circumstances of Death
2Pac	Tupac Shakur	25	Shot and killed in 1996 while riding in a limousine in Las Vegas
The Notorious B.I.G. (aka Biggie Smalls)	Christopher Wallace	24	Shot and killed in 1997 after a party for Soul Train Music Awards in Los Angeles
Big L	Lamont Coleman	24	Shot and killed in 1999 by a childhood friend in Harlem
Jam-Master Jay	Jason Mizell	37	Shot and killed in 2002 in a recording studio in Queens, NY
ODB	Russell Tyrone Jones	35	Died in 2004 of a drug overdose in Wu-Tang Clan recording studio in New York City
Mac Dre	Andrew Hicks	34	Shot and killed in 2004 while riding in a car in Kansas City, MO (In retaliation Anthony "Fat Tone" Watkins was murdered.)
Proof	DeShaun Holton	32	Shot and killed in 2006 in Detroit, MI by a security guard after allegedly killing a man over a game of pool in a club
Pimp C	Chad Butler	33	Died in 2007 in Los Angeles of a drug overdose
Eyedea	Micheal Larsen	28	Died in 2010 in St. Paul, MN of a drug overdose

Jay-Z. Together the two performers earn well over $100 million a year.

The traditional model of artists becoming successful through sales of their albums is rapidly giving way to a new model. As online music takes over, and songs are widely transmitted (often illegally) via the Web, recordings have become a method of advertising other profitable ventures.

For an art form that in the 1960s reveled in authenticity and not "selling out," there is very little integrity left to sell. Commerce has bought up most popular music. Corporations sponsor tours, videos, and even albums. The punk icon Iggy Pop sells car insurance, Led Zeppelin supports Cadillacs, and the once fiercely-independent Bob Dylan is now being paid to promote women's underwear.

As popular music spreads around the globe, serious questions arise. Will the enormous profitability and accessibility of pop and rap swamp more complex and demanding types of music, like classical music and jazz? Will young people grow up appreciating the diversity, complexity, and richness of other musical traditions? And, around the world, will the multiplicity of world musical cultures survive the overwhelming popularity and commercial pressures of Western pop? In 20 years or so, we'll know the answers to these questions.

STYLE SUMMARY

Popular Music

The most important requirement of popular music is that it must appeal to a large number of people. This obviously affects musical style: popular music must have catchy rhythms or an attractive melody or interesting words or some combination of all three.

By far the largest proportion of popular music is vocal. Most of us seem to like listening to singing because it makes the music more personal to us. From the mid-nineteenth century to the present, popular music has mostly been synonymous with song. From Stephen Foster, who composed many songs that became staples of American popular culture, through to the pop singers and rappers of today, it is the sound of singing (or rapping) that has the widest appeal. Perhaps that is because we can (more or less) reproduce the sound ourselves without any special training.

Popular songs usually have simple harmonies and repetitive rhythms. However, the great songs of the 1950s, 1930s, and 1940s have wonderful melodies and clever, literate lyrics. At that time, jazz and popular music became strong mutual influences. Popular singers like Frank Sinatra and Bing Crosby sang with jazzy inflection, and jazz bands and small combos based their music and improvisations on popular songs.

In the 1950s, a new popular music swept through England and North America. Variously known as rock and roll, rhythm and blues, and (with a country influence) rockabilly, it employed electric guitars, hard rhythms, more raucous singing, and more intense sexuality to become (with its offshoots) the most widespread form of popular music ever.

One of the reasons for the popularity of rock and roll was commercial. The spread of radio, television, movies, phonographs, and recordings had made popular music available in millions of homes. Commercial interests were not slow to capitalize on this.

In the 1960s, popular music became the music of the "counterculture." Rock bands with a standard format of three electric guitars and drums were wildly popular, though some individuals with prodigious talent, such as the poet-singer-songwriter Bob Dylan and the virtuoso electric guitarist and singer Jimi Hendrix, stood out. The blues were the structural basis of many of the rock and pop songs of the day. Sentimental songs, not much different from those at the turn of the century but with an updated accompanying sound, became great popular hits.

Throughout the remainder of the twentieth century, those two formats—the small group of singers and guitarists on the one hand and the individual singer (sometimes also playing guitar) with pop or rock accompaniment on the other—remained constant. The form and content of the songs, whose subject matter can often be summarized in one word—love (or sex)—also stayed fairly fixed, though their length increased.

The only really new musical style was rap. With its heavily synthesized, multitrack background, it depended a great deal on modern technology. Rap and all popular music also depend on a massive machinery of corporate interests, which spends millions of dollars in advertising and generates billions of dollars in profits.

FUNDAMENTALS OF POPULAR MUSIC

- ❏ Popular music is usually less demanding than classical music
- ❏ Popular music has attractive melodies, simple harmonies, and catchy rhythm
- ❏ Popular music is mostly vocal
- ❏ The subject matter is often love (sex)
- ❏ Rock turned popular music rougher, sometimes raucous
- ❏ Rap began angry and alienated, though it was soon assimilated into the mainstream
- ❏ By now popular music has become an enormous, highly manipulated, international business

FOR FURTHER DISCUSSION AND STUDY

1. Discuss the major popular music styles of the twentieth century and the related changes in technology that influenced their growth.

2. Listen to Little Richard's version of "Tutti Frutti" and compare it with Pat Boone's cover. Describe the major differences that you hear. Which version is "better"? Why?

3. Discuss today's young rebellious stars and compare them to those of the 1950s and 1960s.

4. Look up articles in *Time*, *Newsweek*, *Life*, and other magazines from 1964 and summarize how the American press viewed the arrival of the Beatles.

5. Compare the photos of the Beatles, the Supremes, and Kiss, noticing how clean-cut the first two groups look in comparison with Kiss's flashy costumes and makeup. Are there any modern groups that survive simply by playing their music, or is it necessary to have a public image of some sort?

6. Compare the promotional video for "Strawberry Fields Forever" with a video from today's MTV.

7. Interview people who lived through Beatlemania to find out what effect it had on them. Could any performer create the same kind of mass hysteria today?

8. Michael Jackson's career after *Thriller* was anything but smooth. Discuss some of the controversies surrounding the singer and how these have affected his popularity. Should a singer's personal life influence how people view his or her recordings?

9. Madonna achieved considerable notoriety for her *Erotica* book, which was sold in a sealed silver bag. It was both condemned as exploitative and praised for extolling the new sexual freedom of the modern woman. Discuss, with reference to the overtly sexual marketing strategies of other recording artists.

10. Discuss the benefits and problems associated with musical censorship. Should music be censored? If so, which music? Who should do the censoring? How should the rules be implemented and enforced?

✓●─[**Study** and **Review** on **MySearchLab**

(Fuller discussions of these terms may be found on the pages indicated.)

ABA form Tripartite form, found in opera arias and some slow movements of instrumental works, featuring an opening A section, a contrasting B section, and a return to the A section, which is often sung with embellishments. (See p. 94.)

Absolute music Music that is complete in itself with no reference to an outside concept such as a narrative, a painting, or a state of nature. (See p. 165.)

Alberti bass Accompaniment in which the chords are broken up into individual short notes played in a repeated rhythm. (See p. 119.)

Arch form Five-part form in which part one corresponds to five, part two corresponds to four, and part three is the apex. (See p. 235.)

Aria Lyrical section of opera for solo singer and orchestra, usually in ABA form. (See p. 94.)

Ascending contour Melodic line that rises. (See p. 179.)

Atonality The lack of a key system or tonal center in music. (See p. 215.) (Musical example: Arnold Schoenberg, *Madonna* from *Pierrot Lunaire*, p. 227.)

Bar lines Lines in a musical score that designate short units of equal length. (See p. 24.)

32-bar AABA form Format involving four eight-measure phrases, the first two and the last being the same. This form is very common in popular songs and jazz. (See pp. 31, 266.)

12-bar blues The form and chord progression associated with playing or singing the blues. (See pp. 31, 264.)

Baroque The period in European music from about 1600 to 1750. (See p. 87.)

Basso continuo Single instrument or small group of instruments, usually including a harpsichord, playing the bass line in Baroque music. (See p. 91.)

Bebop or bop Form of jazz that developed in the 1940s for small combos, with harder, more improvisatory music. (See p. 270.) (Musical example: Charlie Parker, *Confirmation*, p. 271.)

Binary form A form with two sections, each of which is repeated, as in the pattern AABB. (See p. 50.) (Musical examples: Wolfgang Amadeus Mozart, Minuet and Trio from Symphony No. 18 in F Major, K. 130, p. 50, and Franz Joseph Haydn, Minuet and Trio from Symphony No. 45 in F-sharp Minor, p. 127.)

Bitonality Two different keys sounding simultaneously. (See p. 220.) (Musical example: Charles Ives, "Putnam's Camp" from *Three Places in New England*, p. 238.)

Blue note Flattened or "bent" note played or sung in jazz. (See p. 261.) (Musical examples: Bessie Smith, *Florida-Bound Blues*, p. 264, and Duke Ellington, *It Don't Mean a Thing (If It Ain't Got That Swing)*, p. 269.)

Bunraku Traditional Japanese puppet theater. (See p. 12.)

Caccia Medieval Italian secular song in which two voices sing in a round. (See p. 66.)

Cantata *Chamber* cantatas were unstaged dramatic works for a single singer or a small group of singers and accompanying instruments. *Church* cantatas involved solo singers, choir, and instruments and focused on the liturgical theme of a particular day. (See p. 90.)

Canzona Renaissance instrumental work, often involving counterpoint. (See p. 82.) (Musical example: Giovanni Gabrieli, *Canzona Duodecimi Toni*, p. 82.)

Castrato Male singer castrated before puberty to retain high voice. Castratos were common in the eighteenth century. (See p. 109.)

Chamber music Music written to be played in a small space, usually involving a small number of instruments. (See pp. 33, 121, 166.)

Character piece Short programmatic piece usually for solo piano. (See p. 179.) (Musical example: Robert Schumann, *Träumerei (Dreaming)* from *Kinderszenen*, Op. 15, p. 179.)

Chorale A Protestant hymn sung in unison by the entire congregation in even rhythm. Often harmonized for use by church choir. (See p. 90.) (Musical example: Johann Sebastian Bach, *St. Matthew Passion*, p. 105.)

Chromatic Moving by half step. (See p. 96.)

Classic The period in European music from about 1730 to 1800. (See p. 115.)

Comic opera (Italian: *opera buffa*; French: *opéra comique*; German: *Singspiel*.) Light opera, with amusing plots, down-to-earth characters, simpler music, and spoken dialogue. (See p. 120.)

Concerto Instrumental work, usually in three movements, highlighting contrast. Baroque concertos were usually written in the pattern fast-slow-fast, featuring ritornello form. A *concerto grosso* featured a small group of instruments contrasted with the whole group. A *solo concerto* featured a single instrument contrasted with the whole group. (See p. 97.) (Musical example: Antonio Vivaldi, *La Primavera* ("*Spring*") from *The Four Seasons*, p. 100.) Classic and Romantic concertos tended to be solo concertos, retaining the fast-slow-fast pattern, and combining ritornello form with Classic forms, such as sonata form or aria form. (See pp. 122, 123.)

Concerto form Three movements, in the pattern fast-slow-fast. (See p. 99.)

Consonant Sounding smooth together. (See p. 21.)

Continuo See **basso continuo**.

Courtly love Stylized convention of poetry and code of behavior developed in the medieval courts of southern France. (See p. 59.) (Musical example: Beatriz de Dia, *A chantar*, p. 60.)

Da capo From the beginning. (See p. 108.)

Dance suite A group of varied instrumental dances in the same key. (See p. 90.)

Development   The section in a piece of music toward the middle, in which there is rapid key change and the manipulation of thematic material that had appeared earlier. (See p. 122.)

Didjeridoo   Wooden wind instrument in use among the Australian aborigines. (See p. 10.)

Dissonant   Sounding rough together. (See p. 21.)

Divertimento   A chamber work meant as a "diversion"; generally lighter in style and with five, six, or more movements. (See p. 118.)

Double-stopping   Playing more than one string at a time on a stringed instrument.

Enlightenment   Eighteenth-century philosophy that favored a rational and scientific view of the world. (See p. 115.)

Ensemble   Usually used to refer to opera scenes in which several individuals sing together.

Episodes   Passages of music occurring between the reiterated sections in a rondo or ritornello. (See p. 123.)

Étude   Solo instrumental piece focusing on a particular aspect of technique. (See p. 176.)

Exposition   The opening section of a piece of music in which the principal keys and thematic material are introduced. (See p. 122.)

Expressionism   Artistic and musical movement focusing on extreme emotions, such as fear or anguish. (See p. 224.) (Musical example: Alban Berg, *Wozzeck*, Act III, Scenes 4 and 5, p. 231.)

Fanfare   A stirring phrase or a complete short work that is written primarily or entirely for brass instruments. (Musical example: Aaron Copland, *Fanfare for the Common Man*, pp. 48, 240.)

Form   The organization of a work of art, literature, or music. (See p. 19.)

Fugue   Highly organized contrapuntal work featuring a theme or "subject" that occurs in all the musical lines in turn until all the lines are sounding at once. (See p. 104.)

Fusion   Music combining elements of both jazz and rock. (See p. 298.)

Fuzz box   Device that adds distortion to the sound of an electric guitar. (See p. 295.)

Gagaku   Ancient Japanese orchestral music. (See p. 12.)

Gamelan   Indonesian musical ensemble involving mostly metal percussion. (See p. 12.)

German song   A work for voice and piano set to a German text. (Musical example: Franz Schubert, *Die Forelle Gretchen am Spinnrade*, p. 169.)

Grand opera   Spectacular type of nineteenth-century French opera, with elaborate stage sets, ballet, and crowd scenes. (See p. 183.)

Gregorian chant   See **plainchant**.

Ground bass   A phrase in the bass that is repeated over and over again. (See p. 94.) (Musical example: Henry Purcell, Dido's Lament from *Dido and Aeneas*, p. 95.)

Hardingfele   Norwegian folk violin. (See p. 9.)

Harmony   Notes sounding together. (See p. 28.)

Impressionism   Movement in painting of the late nineteenth and early twentieth centuries in which the outlines are vague and the pictures dreamy and suggestive. Also refers to a parallel movement in music. (See p. 218.)

Impromptu   Instrumental piece, usually for piano, that gives the impression of being improvised. (See p. 176.)

Jali   Official singer and historian of the Mandinka tribe of West Africa. (See p. 4.)

Kabuki   Japanese style of traditional musical theater, involving an all-male cast. (See p. 10.)

Koto   Japanese instrument plucked like a zither. (See p. 12.)

Leitmotiv   Musical phrase or fragment with associations to a character, object, or idea. (See p. 195.)

Libretto   The text for an opera. (See p. 189.)

Liturgical music   Music for a religious ceremony. (See p. 56.)

Lute   A plucked instrument with a rounded back, short neck, and frets. (See p. 66.) (Musical example: Guillaume de Machaut, *Doulz Viaire Gracieus*, p. 65.)

Lyric opera   Type of French opera midway between grand opéra and opéra comique, usually featuring plots of tragic love. (See p. 184.)

Madrigal   Secular vocal work, often in Italian, for a small group of singers. (See p. 78.)

Magnus Liber Organi   "Great Book of Polyphony." Late twelfth-century collection of polyphonic compositions designed for the Cathedral of Notre Dame in Paris. (See p. 62.) (Musical example: Perotinus, *Viderunt Omnes*, p. 63.)

Main theme   The melody that is introduced at the outset of a piece of music. (See p. 123.)

Manuals   The keyboards on an organ.

Mazurka   A Polish dance in lively triple meter with an accent on the second or third beat. (See p. 176.)

Mbira   African instrument made of a small wooden box or gourd with thin metal strips attached. (See pp. 9, 14–15.) (Musical example: *Chemetengure/Mudendero*, p. 15.)

Melismatic   Musical setting of text with a large number of notes to a single syllable. (See p. 56.)

Melody   An organized musical line. (See p. 18.)

Meter   A regular rhythm. (See pp. 24, 65.)

Middle Ages   The period in European music from about 400 to 1400. (See p. 55.)

Minimalism   Musical style of the 1960s to the 1990s involving very limited materials, constant repetition, and very gradual change. (See p. 251.)

Minuet (and trio)   An instrumental work in the tempo (moderate) and meter (triple) of a favorite seventeenth- and eighteenth-century dance, in binary form. The trio is in form and structure like another minuet, but it usually has a contrast of texture, instrumentation, and sometimes key. (See p. 50.) (Musical examples: Wolfgang Amadeus Mozart, Minuet and Trio from Symphony No. 18 in F Major, K. 130, p. 50, and Franz Joseph Haydn, Minuet and Trio from Symphony No. 45 in F-sharp Minor, p. 127.)

Minuet-and-trio form   Often used for third movements of Classic instrumental works. Both minuet and trio are in two parts, each of which is repeated. The minuet is played twice, once before and once after the trio. (See p. 122.) (Musical examples: Wolfgang Amadeus Mozart, Minuet and Trio from Symphony No. 18 in F Major, K. 130, p. 50, and Franz Joseph Haydn, Minuet and Trio from Symphony No. 45 in F-sharp Minor, p. 127.)

Modernism   The cultural movement, stressing innovation, that dominated the first sixty to seventy years of the twentieth century. (See p. 213.)

Modes   System of melodic organization used in music of the Middle Ages and early Renaissance. There are four main medieval modes, designating pieces ending on D, E, F, and G, respectively. (See p. 57.) (Musical example: Kyrie, p. 57.)

Modulation   The process of moving from one key to another. (See p. 164.)

Monody   Type of early Baroque music for solo voice and **basso continuo** with vocal line imitating the rhythms of speech. (See p. 91.) (Musical example: Claudio Monteverdi, extracts from *Orfeo*, p. 92.)

Motet   (Renaissance) A vocal setting of a Latin text, usually sacred. (See p. 78.) (Musical example: Giovanni Pierluigi da Palestrina, *Exsultate Deo*, p. 78.)

Movement   Large, separate section of a musical work. (See p. 31.)

Music drama   Term coined by Wagner to refer to his operas, which involve ancient myth, resonant poetry, and rich, dramatic music. (See p. 193.)

Nationalism   A nineteenth-century movement that stressed national identity. In music, this led to the creation of works in native languages, using national myths and legends, and incorporating local rhythms, themes, and melodies. (See p. 159.)

Neo-Classicism   A stylistic movement in which the features of a Classic period are reintroduced in later times; in music the stylistic period of the 1920s. (See p. 223.)

Neumatic   Musical setting of text with varying numbers of notes per syllable. (See p. 56.)

Nocturne   Moody, introspective piece, usually for solo piano. (See p. 176.)

Noh   Ancient Japanese theatrical genre, with highly stylized acting. (See p. 12.)

Octatonic scale   Scale with eight notes within the octave, separated by a series of alternating whole and half steps. (See p. 215.)

Octave   The nearest distance between two notes of the same name. (See p. 21.)

Opera   A staged musical work involving a narrative, singing characters, and instruments. (See pp. 89, 166.)

Opéra comique   Small-scale French nineteenth-century opera, with humorous or romantic plots. (See p. 184.)

Opera seria   ("Serious opera") Italian Baroque form of opera in three acts, with conventional plots, and alternating recitatives and arias. (See p. 99.)

Oral tradition   The practice of passing music (or other aspects of culture) orally from one generation to another. (See pp. 2, 6.)

Oratorio   An unstaged dramatic sacred work, featuring solo singers (including a narrator), choir, and orchestra, and usually based on a biblical story. (See p. 90.)

Orchestral song cycle   Song cycle in which the voice is accompanied by an orchestra instead of a piano. (See p. 208.)

Orchestration   The apportioning of musical material among the instruments of an orchestra. (See p. 162.)

Ordinary of the Mass   The collective name for those five sections of the Catholic Mass (Kyrie, Gloria, Credo, Sanctus, Agnus Dei) that occur in every Mass. (See p. 73.)

Ostinato   Constantly repeated musical phrase. (See p. 220.) (Musical example: Igor Stravinsky, *Le Sacre du Printemps* (*The Rite of Spring*), p. 221.)

Overture   The music that is played before the start of an opera; the first movement of a Baroque dance suite. (See p. 120.)

Pantonality   Term referring to the simultaneous existence of all keys in music. (See p. 259.)

Passion   Similar to the oratorio. An unstaged dramatic sacred work, featuring solo singers (including a narrator), choir, and orchestra, and based on one of the Gospel accounts of the last days of Jesus. (See p. 90.) (Musical example: Johann Sebastian Bach, *St. Matthew Passion*, p. 105.)

Pentatonic scale   A scale with five notes; the most common form has the following intervals: whole step, whole step, minor third, whole step. (See p. 215.)

Piano roll   Perforated roll of paper used in the early twentieth century to reproduce music on a special mechanical piano. (See p. 263.)

Plainchant   Monophonic liturgical vocal music of the Middle Ages. (See p. 56.) (Musical example: Kyrie, p. 57.)

Point of imitation   Section of music presenting a short phrase imitated among the voices. (See p. 74.) (Musical example: Josquin Desprez, Kyrie from the *Pange Lingua* Mass, p. 75.)

Polonaise   A Polish dance in slow triple meter with a marchlike rhythm. (See p. 176.)

Polyphony   Music with more than one line sounding at the same time. (See p. 30.) (Musical example: Perotinus, *Viderunt Omnes*, p. 63.)

Polyrhythms   Different meters sounding simultaneously. (See p. 220.)

Polytonality   The existence in music of two or more keys at the same time. (See p. 216.)

Postmodernism   A cultural movement of the last part of the twentieth century, involving a juxtaposition of past and present, popular and refined, Western and non-Western styles. (See p. 248.)

Prelude (toccata)   Free, improvisatory work or movement, usually for organ. (See p. 103.)

Primitivism   Artistic movement of the early twentieth century concentrating on nonurban cultures and untamed nature. (See p. 217.)

Program music   Instrumental music that tells a story or describes a picture or a scene. (See pp. 100, 165.) (Musical example: Antonio Vivaldi, *La Primavera* (*"Spring"*) from *The Four Seasons*, p. 100.)

Programmatic symphony   A symphony that has reference to an outside concept such as a narrative, a painting, or scenes from nature. (See p. 184.)

Protest song   A song devoted to a social cause, such as the fight against injustice, antiwar sentiment, etc. (See p. 294.)

Quartal chords   Chords based on fourths rather than thirds. (See p. 216.)

Quarter tones   Pitches separated by a quarter of a step rather than a half or a whole step. (See p. 217.)

Ragtime   Early jazz in which the melody is highly syncopated, usually in duple meter and march tempo. (See p. 262.) (Musical example: Scott Joplin, *Maple Leaf Rag*, p. 262.)

Rap   Popular music style of the 1980s and 1990s with fast, spoken lyrics and a strong and often complex beat. (See p. 303.)

Recapitulation   The reintroduction of music that had occurred earlier, but is played now in the tonic key. (See p. 122.)

Recitative   Music for solo voice and simple accompaniment, designed to reflect the irregularity and naturalness of speech. (See p. 91.) (Musical example: Claudio Monteverdi, extracts from *Orfeo*, p. 92.)

Recitative accompagnato   Dramatic recitative accompanied by the orchestra.

Reggae   Popular music style from Jamaica, with a light, catchy sound, characterized by offbeats played on the rhythm guitar. (See p. 300.)

Renaissance   The period in European music from about 1400 to 1600. (See p. 70.)

Requiem Mass   Mass for the dead. (See p. 166.)

Rhythm   The organization of stressed beats. (See p. 23.)

Rhythm and blues   Blues music played with a heavy beat and electric instruments; often associated with African American performers. (See p. 284.)

Riff   A short, repeated, melodic phrase often found in popular music. (Musical example: The Beatles, *It Won't Be Long*, p. 293.)

Ritornello   An orchestral passage in a concerto that returns several times, in the same or in different keys. (See p. 93.) (Musical example: Antonio Vivaldi, *La Primavera* (*"Spring"*) from *The Four Seasons*, p. 100.)

Rondeau   A fixed form of poetry or music in the pattern: ABaAabAB. (See p. 65.)

Rondo form   Often used for last movements of Classic instrumental works. A theme constantly returns, alternating with contrasting passages (episodes). (See p. 123.) (Musical example: Franz Joseph Haydn, String Quartet, Op. 33, No. 2, in E-flat Major, p. 129.)

Rubato   The loosening of strict and regular time for a passage of music in performance. (See p. 176.)

Scat singing   Singing syllables that are not associated with words. (See p. 261.)

Scat   To sing with made-up syllables. (See p. 261.) (Musical example: Louis Armstrong, *Hotter Than That*, p. 266.)

Secular music   Music that is nonreligious. (See p. 66.)

Serialism   The organization of musical elements (usually pitches) so that they occur in a fixed order repeatedly throughout the piece. (See p. 243.)

Shakuhachi   Japanese end-blown bamboo flute. (See pp. 7, 11–12.) (Musical example: *Koku-Reibo*, p. 13.)

Shamisen   Japanese plucked instrument with three strings and a long neck. (See p. 12.)

Sinfonia   Three-movement instrumental introduction to eighteenth-century Italian opera. (See p. 120.)

Sitar   A long-necked, resonant, plucked stringed instrument from India. (See p. 7.)

Sonata   Baroque: A work for a small group of instruments. Sonatas include solo sonatas (one instrument and basso continuo) and trio sonatas (two instruments and basso continuo). Also divided by style into *sonata da camera* ("chamber sonata"), whose movements were based on dance rhythms, and *sonata da chiesa* ("church sonata"), whose movements were more serious in character. (See p. 90.) Classic and Romantic: Work for solo piano or piano and another instrument in three or four movements. (See p. 121.)

Sonata form   Organizing structure for a musical work or movement. It has three main parts: an *exposition*, in which the main themes are presented and the primary key moves from tonic to dominant; a *development* in which many keys are explored and the themes are often presented in fragments; and a *recapitulation*, in which the music of the exposition returns, usually staying in the tonic key throughout. (See p. 122.) (Musical examples: Wolfgang Amadeus Mozart, Symphony No. 40 in G Minor, K. 550, p. 134, and Ludwig van Beethoven, Symphony No. 5 in C Minor, p. 146.)

Song cycle   Series of songs linked together. (See p. 167.)

Sprechstimme ("speech-song")   Technique of singing, halfway between speech and song. (See p. 227.) (Musical example: Arnold Schoenberg, *Madonna* from *Pierrot Lunaire*, p. 227.)

Stops   Buttons or levers on an organ that direct the air into different sets of pipes.

String quartet   Work, usually in four movements, for two violins, viola, and cello. (See pp. 33, 121.) (Musical examples: Franz Joseph Haydn, String Quartet, Op. 33, No. 2, in E-flat Major, p. 129.)

Strophic song   Song in which all stanzas are sung to the same music. (See p. 167.) (Musical examples: Beatriz de Dia, *A chantar*, p. 60, and Franz Schubert, *Die Forelle Gretchen am Spinnrade*, p. 169.)

Suite   A series of short pieces, usually based on various Baroque dance forms. (See p. 90.)

Swing (1) The feeling generated by the regular rhythm and the syncopated accents of jazz. (See p. 48.) (2) Dance music played by jazz bands in the 1930s and early 1940s. (See p. 48.) (Musical example: Duke Ellington, *It Don't Mean a Thing (If It Ain't Got That Swing)*, pp. 49, 269.)

Syllabic Musical setting of text with one note per syllable. (See p. 56.)

Symbolism Literary movement of the late nineteenth and early twentieth centuries concentrating on suggestion rather than description. (See p. 219.)

Symphonic poem Programmatic orchestral work in one movement. (See p. 166.)

Symphony Orchestral work, usually in four movements, the first being moderate in tempo, the second slow, the third a minuet or a scherzo, and the fourth fast. (See p. 166.) (Musical example: Ludwig van Beethoven, Symphony No. 5 in C Minor, p. 146.)

Syncopation The stressing of a note that comes before the expected beat. (See p. 26.)

Telharmonium An early electronic keyboard instrument. (See p. 218.)

Thematic transformation Technique of changing or varying a theme in its different appearances throughout a work. (See p. 186.)

Theme and variations Form of a work or a movement in which successive statements of a melody are altered or embellished each time. (See p. 31.) (Musical examples: Ludwig van Beethoven, *Six Easy Variations on a Swiss Tune*, p. 144, and Franz Schubert, Quintet in A Major (*The Trout*), p. 169.)

Theremin An early electronic instrument named after its inventor that creates sounds from the motion (in the air) of the player's hands. (See p. 218.)

Through-composed song Song in which the music is continually evolving. (See p. 167.) (Musical example: Arnold Schoenberg, *Madonna* from *Pierrot Lunaire*, p. 227.)

Tone color The distinctive sound of an instrument or voice. (See p. 33.)

Total serialism Strict organization of all musical elements (dynamics, rhythm, pitch, etc.) of a musical composition by arranging them into series. (See p. 243.) (Musical example: Pierre Boulez, *Structures I* for two pianos, p. 244.)

Transcription The act or result of modifying a piece of music so that it can be played by instruments other than those originally designated. (See p. 186.)

Troubadour Poet-musician of medieval southern France. (See p. 59.) (Musical example: Beatriz de Dia, *A chantar*, p. 60.)

Trouvère Poet-musician of medieval northern France. (See p. 59.)

Twelve-tone system Twentieth-century compositional technique in which the composer treats all twelve pitches as equal and uses them in a highly organized way. (See p. 224.) (Musical example: Arnold Schoenberg, Theme and Sixth Variation from *Variations for Orchestra*, Op. 31, p. 228.)

Verismo Literary and operatic style featuring down-to-earth plots and characters. (See p. 184.)

Virtuoso A performing musician (usually instrumentalist) who is outstandingly gifted. (See p. 97.)

Wagner tuba Brass instrument with a range between French horn and trombone. (See p. 195.)

Wah-wah pedal Device for electric guitar that changes frequencies on the same note. (See p. 295.)

Waltz A European dance of moderate triple meter with a heavy accent on the first beat. (See p. 176.)

Whole-tone scale A scale with six notes, each separated from the next by a whole step. (See p. 215.)

Word-painting The technique of depicting the *meaning* of words through music. (See p. 57.) (Musical example: Thomas Morley, *Sweet Nymph Come to Thy Lover* and *Fire and Lightning*, p. 81.)

TEXT CREDITS

142 Handwritten Score, "Symphony No. 6" ("Pastoral") by Beethoven. Copyright © 2000 by Verlag Beethoven-Haus Bonn.

227 "Pierrot Lunaire" and "Madonna" by Arnold Schoenberg. Used by permission of Belmont Music Publishers, Pacific Palisades, CA 90272.

228 "Theme & Sixth Variation from Variations for Orchestra" by Arnold Schoenberg. Used by permission of Belmont Publishers.

245 A "Radical Sixties" Musical Score. From Polonius Platitudes by Edwin London. Copyright © 1971 by Edwin London (ASCAP). Reprinted by permission of composer.

258 "Me he perdido muchas veces por el mar" by George Crumb. Ancient Voices of Children. Copyright © 1970 by C.F. Peters Corporation. Used with permission. All rights reserved.

242 Lyric excerpts from West Side Story written by Leonard Bernstein. Reprinted by permission of Boosey & Hawkes.

263 "Love in Vain Blues" words and music by Robert Johnson. Copyright © 1978, 1990, 1991 by King of Spades Music. All rights reserved. Used by permission.

264–265 "Florida Bound Blues" by Clarence Williams. Copyright Universal-MCA Music Publishing, a division of Universal Studios, Inc. All rights reserved. Used by permission.

295 Johnny Cash quote from the LP jacket of Bob Dylan's "Nashville Skyline" album Johnny Cash quote from the LP jacket of Bob Dylan's "Nashville Skyline" album. Used courtesy of Sony Music Entertainment.

289 Excerpt from "Music: Rock 'n' Roll" Time magazine, 7/23/56. Copyright © 1956 Time Inc. Used with permission.

PHOTO CREDITS

CHAPTER 1

1 Steve Cole/Photodisc/Getty Images
2 The Pierpont Morgan Library/Art Resource, NY
2 Tim Gidal/Prentice Hall, Inc.
3 Pearson Learning, Inc.
3 Pearson Learning, Inc.
4 Merrill Education
5 Dorling Kindersley, Ltd.
7 Pictorial Press Ltd/Alamy
8 Jeremy Yudkin
8 Somatuscan/Dreamstime
9 Dorling Kindersley, Ltd.
9 Mrallen/Dreamstime
10 Colin Sinclair/Dorling Kindersley, Ltd.
10 Bondsza/Dreamstime
11 Philip Dowell/Dorling Kindersley, Ltd.
11 Eagleflyin/Dreamstime
11 francosperoni/Fotolia LLC
12 Jack Vartoogian/FrontRowPhotos.com
14 Ankevanwyk/Dreamstime
15 Shanachie Entertainment

CHAPTER 2

17 gnohz/Shutterstock
33 Martin Richardson/DK Images
33 Eugene Gordon/Prentice Hall, Inc.
34 Linda Whitwam/Dorling Kindersley, Ltd.
34 Volkman Kurt Wentzel/National Geographic Stock
36 Library of Congress Prints and Photographs Division [LC-DIG-ggbain-23448]

36 Library of Congress Prints and Photographs Division
37 Jfeinstein/Dreamstime
37 Laima Druskis/Prentice Hall, Inc.
37 Michael Newman/PhotoEdit
37 Alenavlad/Shutterstock
38 John Bacchus/Silver Burdett Ginn
38 Laimute E. Druskis/Prentice Hall, Inc.
39 Dorling Kindersley, Ltd.
40 Max Alexander/Dorling Kindersley, Ltd.
40 Dorling Kindersley, Ltd.
41 William P. Gottlieb/www.jazzphotos.com/Library of Congress Prints and Photographs Division Prints and Photographs Division [LC-GLB23-0070]
42 Vicki Valerio KRT/Newscom
43 ITAR-TASS Photo Agency/Alamy
43 Everett Collection Inc/Alamy

CHAPTER 3

46 Comstock Images
49 Scala/Art Resource, NY

CHAPTER 4

54 Lebrecht Music and Arts Photo Library/Alamy
56 Lebrecht Music and Arts Photo Library/Alamy
59 The Pierpont Morgan Library/Art Resource, NY
60 Fitzwilliam Museum
62 Library of Congress Prints and Photographs Division
62 Superstock
64 James McConnachie/Rough Guides/DK Images
64 Library of Congress Prints and Photographs Division [LC-DIG-pga-01016]
67 MauMar70/Shutterstock

CHAPTER 5

69 Lebrecht Music & Arts Photo Library
70 Library of Congress Prints and Photographs Division
70 Anilah/Shutterstock
71 Scala/Art Resource, NY
73 World History Archive/Alamy
75 Josquin Desprez/Bildarchiv der Osterreichische Nationalbibliothek
80 Library of Congress Prints and Photographs Division
82 Iofoto/Dreamstime
85 The Pierpont Morgan Library/Art Resource, NY

CHAPTER 6

86 Alenavlad/Shutterstock
87 Réunion des Musées Nationaux/Daniel Arnaudet/Hervé Lewandowski/Art Resource, NY
88 Réunion des Musées Nationaux/Hervé Lewandowski/Art Resource, NY
88 Rembrandt Harmensz van Rijn (1606–1669). Self-Portrait at Old Age, 1669. Oil on canvas. 86 × 70.5 cm. National Gallery, London, Great Britian. Erich Lessing/Art Resource, NY.
97 Library of Congress Prints and Photographs Division
98 akg-images/Newscom
99 Lebrecht Music and Arts Photo Library/Alamy
102 Mary Evans Picture Library/Alamy
102 E. G. Haussmann, Johann Sebastian Bach, 1746/Stadtgeschichtliches Museum Leipzig
107 Library of Congress Prints and Photographs Division [LC-USZ62-85005]
108 Angelo Hornak/Alamy

CHAPTER 7

114 Steve Gorton/Dorling Kindersley, Ltd.
115 Library of Congress Prints and Photographs Division
115 Library of Congress Prints and Photographs Division
116 Library of Congress Prints and Photographs Division [3c24552]
117 Sergio Pitamitz/DanitaDelimont.com/Newscom
121 String Quartet. Color engraving, 18th century, Austrian. Mozart Museum, Prague, Czech Republic. Bridgeman-Giraudon/Art Resource, NY.
125 Library of Congress Prints and Photographs Division
126 Hamman, Edouard Jean Conrad (1819–1888). Portrait of Franz Joseph Haydn printed by Ed Hamman. Bibliotheque Nationale, Paris, France. Bridgeman-Giraudon/Art Resource, NY.
126 Maran Garai/Shutterstock
130 Library of Congress Prints and Photographs Division
132 Erich Lessing/Art Resource, NY
133 INTERFOTO/Alamy
133 Album/Newscom

CHAPTER 8

138 Blazej Lyjak/Shutterstock
139 Library of Congress Prints and Photographs Division [LC-USZ62-29499]
142 INTERFOTO/Alamy
144 Erich Lessing/Art Resource, NY

CHAPTER 9

158 Michael Woodruff/Shutterstock
160 Bildarchiv Preussischer Kulturbesitz/Art Resource, NY
161 Peter Buckley/Prentice Hall, Inc.
161 U.S. Department of Agriculture
162 Library of Congress Prints and Photographs Division
163 Lebrecht Music and Arts Photo Library/Alamy
166 Library of Congress Prints and Photographs Division [LC-USZ62-43353]
168 Library of Congress Prints and Photographs Division [LC-USZ62-43355]
170 Library of Congress Prints and Photographs Division [LC-USZ62-30885]
171 akg-images/Newscom
172 Felix Mendelssohn-Bartholdy (1809–1847). German composer. Watercolor, 1829. Musikabteilung, Mendelssohn-Archiv./ Ruth Schacht/Art Resource, NY
174 INTERFOTO/Alamy
176 Library of Congress Prints and Photographs Division [LC-USZ62-103898]
178 Hervé Lewandowski/Réunion des Musées Nationaux/Art Resource, NY

CHAPTER 10

183 Dorling Kindersley, Ltd.
186 Library of Congress Prints and Photographs Division
189 Library of Congress Prints and Photographs Division
194 akg-images
196 Library of Congress Prints and Photographs Division
198 Library of Congress Prints and Photographs Division
200 Library of Congress Prints and Photographs Division
205 Library of Congress Prints and Photographs Division

CHAPTER 11

212 Pictorial Press Ltd/Alamy
214 Library of Congress Prints and Photographs Division [LC-USZ62-96633]
214 Library of Congress Prints and Photographs Division
215 National Archives and Records Administration
219 Claude Monet (1840–1926), "The Cathedral of Rouen, Facade," circa 1892/94. Oil on canvas, 100.6 × 66 cm. Juliana Cheney Edwards Collection, Museum of Fine Arts, Boston/ Archiv fur Kunst und Geschichte, Berlin/akg-images
219 Marcel Baschet (1862–1941) (C) ARS, NY. Claude Debussy in Rome in 1884. Chateaux de Versailles, France. Bridgeman-Giraudon/Art Resource, NY
220 National Archives and Records Administration
222 akg-images/Joseph Martin/Newscom
225 Library of Congress Prints and Photographs Division [LC-USZ62-131639]
229 DIZ Muenchen GmbH, Sueddeutsche Zeitung Photo/Alamy
233 National Archives and Records Administration
234 akg-images/Newscom
236 CSU Archives/Everett Collection
236 National Archives and Records Administration
237 Library of Congress Prints and Photographs Division
239 Everett Collection Inc/Alamy
241 William P. Gottlieb/www.jazzphotos.com/Library of Congress Prints and Photographs Division Prints and Photographs Division [LC-GLB23-0070]
243 Richard H Smith/Lebrecht Music & Arts/Alamy
245 From the "Polonius Platitudes," copyright 1971 by Edwin London
248 Dorling Kindersley, Ltd.
249 AP Photo/Jan Bauer
253 Eliot Khuner

CHAPTER 12

260 Laima Druskis/Prentice Hall, Inc.
261 Jeff Morgan 08/Alamy
263 Pictorial Press Ltd/Alamy
264 Library of Congress Prints and Photographs Division [LC-USZ62-100863]
266 JazzSign/Lebrecht Music and Arts Photo Library/Alamy
268 Archive Photos/Getty Images
269 Library of Congress Prints and Photographs Division [LC-USW3-023947-C]
271 William P. Gottlieb/www.jazzphotos.com/Library of Congress Prints and Photographs Division Prints and Photographs Division [LC-GLB23-0620]
271 Library of Congress Prints and Photographs Division [LC-USZ62-120470]
273 Pictorial Press Ltd/Alamy
273 Pictorial Press Ltd/Alamy
275 JazzSign/Lebrecht Music and Arts Photo Library/Alamy
276 Martin Thompson/Lebrecht Music and Arts Photo Library/Alamy

CHAPTER 13

278 Photos 12/Alamy
280 akg-images/Newscom
281 Library of Congress Prints and Photographs Division [LC-USW33-054917-C]
284 Ric Carter/Alamy
286 Everett Collection Inc/Alamy
287 Library of Congress Prints and Photographs Division [LC-DIG-highsm-04470]
291 MARKA/Alamy
291 STARSTOCK/Photoshot
292 Pictorial Press Ltd/Alamy
294 Everett Collection
295 AF archive/Alamy
296 Pictorial Press Ltd/Alamy
299 GUSTAVO FIDANZA/DIARIO POPULAR/Newscom
300 a.berti/MARKA /Alamy
300 Pictorial Press Ltd/Alamy
305 Everett Collection Inc/Alamy
306 Trinity Mirror/Mirrorpix/Alamy

COVER

Maugli/Shutterstock
Pavel K/Shutterstock